From Red Terror to Terrorist State

RUSSIA'S INTELLIGENCE SERVICES AND
THEIR FIGHT FOR WORLD DOMINATION

FROM FELIX DZERZHINSKY
TO VLADIMIR PUTIN

1917–202?

Yuri Felshtinsky
&
Vladimir Popov

GIBSON SQUARE

This edition first published by Gibson Square in London, 2023

rights@gibsonsquare.com

www.gibsonsquare.com

CONTENTS

'Stalin was a genius political criminal whose crimes were legitimized by the state itself. It is from the amalgamation of criminality and politics that the unique phenomenon, Stalinism, was born.'
Abdurakhman Avtorkhanov
Proiskhozhdeniye Partokratii (the origins of partocracy), 1973

'A group of the FSB operatives sent by you on business for working undercover in the government is fulfilling its tasks at the initial stage.'
Vladimir Putin, Prime Minister of Russia, speech to FSB personnel, Moscow, December 20, 1999, Anniversary of the Cheka

'We did not reject our past. We said without dissimulation: "The history of the .Lubyanka in the twentieth century is our history".'
Nikolai Patrushev, Director of the FSB, Komsomolskaya Pravda December 20, 2000, Anniversary of the Cheka

'The Duma of Russia adopted the third and final reading of a bill that allows President Vladimir Putin to run twice more in the Presidential Elections after the Constitutional Amendments were adopted. This means that he will be able to remain in power until 2036.'
Ekho Moskvy (echo of Moscow), March 24, 2021

List of Abbreviations

AFB — Federal Security Agency

APN — Soviet Press Agency Novosti

APS — Apparatus for Seconded Personnel (*see also ARO*), 1998-

ARCCF — American-Russian Cultural Cooperation Foundation

ARO — Active Reserve Officers, 1955 (*see also APS*), 1953-1998

ASEM — Asia-Europe Meeting

AU — American University

BIS — Security Information Service—national intelligence agency of the Czech Republic

CC — Central Committee

CEC — Committee for External Communications

CNI — Center for the National Interest

CPG — Communist Party of Germany

CPR — Center for Public Relations of the KGB/FSB

CPSU — Communist Party of the Soviet Union, 1912-1991

DECR — Department of External Church Relations of the Russian Orthodox Church

DoJ — US Department of Justice

ETIRC — European Technology and Investment Research Centers

FARA — Foreign Agent Registration Act

FSB — Federal Security Service of the Russian Federation, 1995-

FSK — Federal Counterintelligence Service of the Russian Federation, 1993-1995

GDR — German Democratic Republic (East Germany), 1949-1990

GITIS — State Institute of Theater Arts

GKU — Main Control Directorate

GPU — State Political Directorate, 1922-1923

GRU — Main Intelligence Directorate of the General Staff of the Soviet Army, 1918-1992

GUGB — Chief Directorate of State Security, 1934-1941

GULAG — Administration of the Soviet Forced-Labor Camps

JAC — Jewish Anti-Fascist Committee

JV — Joint venture

IMEMO — Institute of Global Economics and International Relations

INO — Foreign Department of the OGPU

IRC — Initiative for Russian Culture

ISAA — Institute of Strategic Assessment and Analysis

KGB — Committee of State Security

KMO — Soviet Committee of Youth Organizations

Komsomol — The All-Union Leninist Young Communist League

KRO — Congress of Russian Communities

LG — *Literaturnaya Gazeta* (literary gazette), leading weekly

MB — Ministry of Security

MBVD — Ministry of Security and Internal Affairs of the RSFSR

MCD — Main Control Department

MFA — Ministry of Foreign Affairs

MGB — Ministry of State Security

MISI — Moscow Institute of Civil Engineering

MOC — International Olympic Committee

MPLA — People's Movement for the Liberation of Angola

MSB — Inter-Republican Security Service

MSIIR — Moscow State Institute of

	International Relations	RNE	Russian National Unity
MSU	Moscow State University	ROCA	Russian Orthodox Church Abroad
MUR	Moscow Criminal Investigations Department	RSFSR	Russian Soviet Federative Socialist Republic, 1917-1991
MVD	Ministry of Internal Affairs	RSKhD	Russian Student Christian Movement
NDR	Our Home is Russia, 1995-2006	RUBOP	Regional Department for Combating Organized Crime
NFA	People's Front of Azerbaijan		
NGO	Non-governmental organization	RT	Russia Today TV Channel
NKGB	People's Commissariat of State Security	SALTT	Strategy & Leadership in Transformational Times
NKVD	People's Commissariat of Internal Affairs	SBP	Presidential Security Service, 1993-
NRA	National Rifle Association	SCSE	State Committee on the State of Emergency (also *GKChP*), August 1991
NTS	National Alliance of Russian Solidarists		
NTV	Independent TV Channel (Moscow)	SMERSH	Military counterintelligence service *Smert' shpionam* ('death to spies')
OECD	Organization for Economic Cooperation and Development	SNK	Council of People's Commissars, the government, 1917-1946
OGPU	Joint State Political Directorate, 1923-1934	SR	Socialist-Revolutionaries
		SS	Schutzstaffel, a major paramilitary organization under Adolf Hitler and the Nazi Party in Nazi Germany
OPA	Office of the Presidential Affairs		
ODP	Office of Domestic Policy		
ORT	Public Russian Television, 1995-2002	SS	Secret Service
		SVR	Foreign Intelligence Service, 1991-
OTRK	Ostankino TV and Radio Complex (Moscow)	TASS	Telegraph Agency of the Soviet Union
OVR	Political Party Fatherland—All Russia, 1998-2002	UES	Unified Energy System of Russia
		UFSB	Regional FSB
PDPA	People's Democratic Party of Afghanistan	USSR	Union of Soviet Socialist Republics
PFU	Patrice Lumumba Peoples' Friendship University	VAAP	All-Union Copyright Agency
		VChK	All-Russian Extraordinary Commission for Combating Counter-Revolution
PMR	Pridnestrovian [Transnistrian] Moldavian Republic		
PR	Public Relations	VDV	Airborne, air-assault, and amphibious troops
PGU	First Chief Directorate of the KGB, 1920-1991	VGU	Second Chief Directorate
		VOOPIik	Protection of Monuments of History and Culture Society
RAU	Russian-American University		
RISR	Russian Institute for Strategic Research	VTP	All-Union Chamber of Commerce (also known as TTP)
RFPF	Russian Federal Property Fund	VX	Nerve agent

What's in a Name? Cheka to FSB

It is easy to find yourself confused by the various incarnations and political hierarchies of the Intelligence Services described below. Trust us: it is just as confusing in Russian as it is in English. One can only surmise that this was done, in part, to make it virtually impossible to trace the beginnings and endings of the embodiments of what can be loosely described as the Intelligence Services of the USSR/Russia over the past century.

In December 1917, Lenin's Bolshevik government first created the organization to seize power. Thereafter, throughout the lifespan USSR it was continually reformed and renamed in the hope that this would bring about a change in its power-hungry DNA. But its nature remained unchanged despite the reorganizations and renaming. Today it is called the FSB—the Federal Security Service of the Russian Federation.

One thing always stayed the same. From 1918, after the capital of Soviet Russia was transferred from Petrograd to Moscow, the Intelligence Services were always housed in one building on Lubyanka Street—in the heart of Moscow. This is how the building got called the 'Lubyanka' and the term became an alternative term for the 'Cheka'. In the book, 'Lubyanka' will be used as a shorthand for clarity to refer to whatever name the Intelligence Services had at the time.

In terms of importance, 'the' Lubyanka always seemed second after the Kremlin as it was Lenin's brain child. This book argues—with the benefit of over a century of Russian sources and the personal operational files of co-author Vladimir Popov, a former KGB Colonel (1972-1991)—that 'seemed' is the operative word. From its inception, the Cheka was always the challenger behind the scenes—beginning with its first head Felix Dzerzhinsky's successful neutralization of Vladimir Lenin as set out below.

VChK

Signed by Lenin, on December 20, 1917, the SNK (Council of People's Commissars) of the Russian Republic passed a resolution that established the VChK, colloquially referred to as 'Cheka' after initials 'ChK' (the All-Russian Extraordinary Commission for Combating Counter-Revolution and Sabotage). In August 1918, the VChK changed its name to All-Russian Extraordinary

Commission for Combating Counter-Revolution, Profiteering and Corruption, still with the same abbreviation VChK. The first head of the VChK was Felix Dzerzhinsky, who led the organization until its dissolution in 1922. It is important to note that the VChK was formed by the SNK (the Soviet government) and was a government organ under its Chair Vladimir Lenin.

GPU

On February 6, 1922, the All-Russian Central Executive Committee of Soviet Russia abolished the VChK and reestablished it as the State Political Directorate (GPU) falling under the People's Commissariat of Internal Affairs (NKVD). At the same time, part of the function of VChK was transferred to the People's Commissariat of Justice. This change signaled ostensibly a demotion. The VChK was previously directly subordinate to the SNK, but now fell under the People's Commissar of Internal Affairs. Still, Dzerzhinsky remained both the head of the State Political Directorate (GPU) and the head of NKVD. One could say, therefore, that while the VChK-GPU was being demoted, Soviet Intelligence chief Dzerzhinsky himself was promoted and even given his own seat on the SNK as a People's Commissar (Soviet minister).

OGPU

On November 15, 1923, following the formation of the USSR (Union of Soviet Socialist Republics) in December of 1922, the Presidium of the USSR's Central Executive Committee established its own Joint State Political Directorate (OGPU) as part of the USSR's Council of People's Commissars. The USSR went back to the arrangement as it had been in Russia. OGPU, like the VChK before it, was again made directly subordinate to the SNK of the USSR. Thus the organization itself was promoted once more in an attempt to keep the OGPU on a short leash. Dzerzhinsky served as the head of OGPU until July 20, 1926, but was not made a member of the SNK of the USSR. He was succeeded by Vyacheslav Menzhinsky, who served until his death on May 10, 1934.

NKVD

On July 10, 1934, the Central Executive Committee of the USSR eliminated OGPU and subsumed it under a new institution: the People's Commissariat of Internal Affairs of the USSR. It was given the old abbreviation NKVD as the Chief Directorate of State Security (GUGB). No one was appointed to replace Menzhinsky, now deceased, and his post was eliminated. Genrikh Yagoda was named People's Commissar of Internal Affairs of the USSR.

NKVD/NKGB/MGB/MVD

On February 3, 1941, the NKVD was split up into two independent branches: the

NKVD and the People's Commissariat of State Security (NKGB). But in July of the same year, the NKGB and the NKVD were merged once again into a single People's Commissariat of Internal Affairs, again called the NKVD. Then, in April of 1943, the 'NKGB' was created anew but as an addition to the amalgamated NKVD and NKGB. On March 15, 1946, the NGKB was transformed into the Ministry of State Security of the USSR (MGB). Also, at the same time, all People's Commissariats started being referred to as ministries. Thus, the People's Commissariat of Internal Affairs (NKVD) became the Ministry for Internal Affairs (MVD).

MVD

On March 7, 1953, two days after Stalin's death, the MVD and MGB were merged into a single body renamed collectively the MVD of the USSR. This reorganization recreated the structure that had existed in July of 1941.

KGB

On March 13, 1954, a year following Stalin's death, the Committee for State Security (KGB) was established as part of the Council of Ministers of the USSR. The KGB's subordination to the Council was highly important: the Intelligence Service, in its various incarnations during the Stalin period, had managed to alarm all Soviet and Communist Party elites. And so, it was forced once again to lose its status as an independent ministry that it had so far enjoyed from time to time. In 1978, the reference to the 'Council of Ministers' was eliminated from the agency's title. From then on, it was known simply as 'KGB of the USSR', which signaled increased status of the KGB and that it was no longer subordinate to the Council of Ministers of the USSR. In the year of the dissolution of the USSR, on May 6, 1991, the Head of the Supreme Council of the Russian Soviet Federative Socialist Republic (RSFSR), Boris Yeltsin, and the head of the KGB of the USSR, Vladimir Kryuchkov, approved the formation of a Committee for State Security of the RSFSR (the KGB of the RSFSR), with the status of a federal committee.

MSB/SVR

On November 26, 1991, the President of the USSR, Mikhail Gorbachev, signed a decree 'On the Establishment of Temporary Provisions for the Inter-Soviet Security Service (MSB) of the USSR.' Two days later, on November 28, Gorbachev signed a decree 'On the Establishment of the Transitional Provision on Inter-Soviet Security Service of the USSR (MSB).' A few more days passed, and on December 3, 1991, Gorbachev signed a decree 'On the Reorganization of the Organs of State Security,' which abolished the KGB and replaced it with two new agencies: The Inter-Soviet Security Service (MSB) and the Central Foreign Intelligence Service of the USSR (SVR) which specifically replaced the First Chief

Directorate (PGU) of the KGB. In other words, the old PGU became the 'new' SVR.

MBVD

On December 19, 1991, before the dissolution of the USSR, (from December 8-21, 1991), Boris Yeltsin, as the first elected President of the RSFSR, established the Ministry of Security and Internal Affairs of the RSFSR (MBVD). With the creation of the MBVD, the USSR's MSB was effectively abolished. However, on January 14, 1992, the Constitutional Court of the newly-minted Russian Federation (today's Russia)[1] ruled that Yeltsin's decree was unconstitutional and annulled the decree that created the MBVD.

MB/FSK/FSB

Between 1992–1993, Russia's Intelligence Services fell under the Russian Ministry of Security (MB). On December 21, 1993, Yeltsin abolished the MB and established the Federal Counterintelligence Service of Russia (FSK) in its place. This organization was headed by Nikolai Golushko who was later succeeded by Sergei Stepashin. On April 3, 1995, Yeltsin signed yet another law: 'On the Organs of the Federal Security Service in the Russian Federation,' under which the FSB became the legal successor to the FSK.

Part One:

The Cheka and the Soviet Union

From Red Terror to Terrorist State

Russia in the twentieth century had one long-ruling leader: Joseph Stalin. Stalin headed the Soviet Union for 30 years (1923-1953). Remarkably, in the twenty-first century, Vladimir Putin had already surpassed the twentieth-century USSR leaders Vladimir Lenin, Nikita Khrushchev, and Leonid Brezhnev in longevity by 2023. After being President for eight years (2000-2008), he was Prime Minister for four years (2008-2012) under his own protégé Dmitry Medvedev as President. As Russian law stands today, Putin will be able to continue as President of the Russian Federation until 2036 and will be surpassing Stalin in 2030.

These leadership statistics, however, mask a more complex story that this book seeks to describe fully. Vladimir Putin's rise to power was not just chance but was the evolutionary high point of a battle that started at the foundation of the USSR and carried on without cessation thereafter: the attempts of Soviet (later Russian) Intelligence Services to wrest state power from their political counterparts. For the most part, the Communist Party of the Soviet Union (CPSU) dominated the state institutions and prevailed in the endless battles for power with the Chekists (the name by which members of the Russian intelligence services are often referred). But after the collapse of the USSR in 1991, when it finally, and practically voluntarily, relinquished power, there followed a decade of transition in which politicians gradually yielded power to the FSB (previously known as KGB). In a rocky, cascading series of anti-constitutional, back-stage coups the Intelligence Services were finally able to raise one of their own, former FSB chief, Lieutenant Colonel Putin, to the Russian Presidency.

For Putin himself this was not a career change. There was no Damascene moment where he decided to reinvent himself as a politician. He had served in the KGB his entire life in various capacities. The Russian Presidency was simply a new appointment, an indivisible part of his career in the Intelligence Services. From 1985 to 1990, he served in the German Democratic Republic (GDR) and worked in Dresden undercover as the director of the Dresden House of Friendship between the USSR and the GDR. Upon returning to Leningrad, he continued his service in the KGB as the assistant to the Dean of International Affairs at Leningrad State University and then as advisor and First Deputy to Leningrad's mayor, Anatoly Sobchak. In August 1996, he was appointed as Deputy Manager of the Affairs of the President of Russia in Moscow and in July 1998, he was appointed as Director of the

FSB. Then, on 9 August 1999, Yeltsin appointed him as Acting Prime Minister and an announcement was made on the same day that he would run for president in 2000. And, finally, on December 31, 1999, Yeltsin resigned and appointed Putin as Acting President.

In this book, we try to explain how the Soviet-Russian Intelligence Services came to power, the history of their fight for power with the CPSU, and discuss why the new state that replaced the nascent Russian Federation in 2000 in all but name is made up of the Chekist cohort among the Russian population, relying on long-existing structures and institutional points of view. Operating beyond state law and guided by its own internal rules, this organism, which initially seized Russia by snatching just a single post—the post of President of Russia—swept like an unleashed virus over the country from 2000. Usurping first its massive riches, it always also sought expansion by annexing neighboring land—a desire present from the moment it was first conceived in 1917 and perpetuated throughout its century-long existence.

After more than two decades under Putin, Russia has become a rogue state that does not conform to any known form of government and whose actions and motives are hard to predict. Unlike the old USSR, it is not driven by any particular ideology. Only by studying the history of the birth and formation of this unique Chekist state can we make sense of it and understand what exactly is going on in Russia today, who are its decision makers and how and what to expect from the junta housed in the Kremlin. What purpose is served by its behavior in Ukraine, Belarus, Moldova, Georgia? It took seven decades for the USSR to implode. To what extent is the current Cheka regime sustainable and what are the other risks it poses to the rest of the world? Inevitably the question must be addressed under what conditions and when it might collapse, or face the need to choose a new leader, and whether that will make a difference.

Even in 1996, under President Boris Yeltsin, a non-democratic system guaranteeing the victory of the Kremlin's chosen candidate was being assembled. At the time, that candidate was Yeltsin (a democrat), running to be reelected as President for a second term against Gennady Zyuganov (a communist). Back then, large-scale election fraud was deemed permissible to save the embryonic democratic state. Millions were given to Yeltsin's Presidential campaign by Russia's budding oligarchs. Everything was being done for the good of Russia, for the sake of freedom and democracy. After all, taking votes from Zyuganov in favor of Yeltsin was seen as an honorable move. It is hard to say how many votes were stolen, but Yeltsin, who entered the 1996 race with a 3% approval rating, came out as a winner (if one believes the 1996 election results). Democracy in Russia survived another day. And as a reward for their successful campaigning, Yeltsin's sponsors —that is, the Russian oligarchs— received control over prize Russian assets until the next election.

But it was during those four crucial years from 1996 that democracy slipped away from Russia. The oligarchs, who had in unison supported Yeltsin during the 1996 Presidential campaign, began fighting with each other over the profits spouting from

Russian companies. As they squabbled, they used every modern PR technique available and maligned each other before the whole country to increase their shareholdings. They also deprecated democratic government, democratic institutions, democratic principles, ideas, and even freedom of speech to grab a larger slice of the economy.

When the 1999/2000 election year started the Kremlin's presidential campaign managers did not plan to win fairly. The constitution prevented Yeltsin from being elected for a third term, but that didn't stop them from selecting a new candidate. Their mission was, as in 1996, to win at all costs and to maintain control of the Kremlin. In 1999, once again the communist party and their candidate Zyuganov were neck-and-neck with the party supported by the Kremlin.

Victory was won again by using Intelligence Services techniques alongside conventional methods. Fake terror attacks on Moscow apartment buildings in September 1999 created a false flag that became the signal for troops to invade Chechnya (an autonomous Russian republic within the federation), starting the Second Chechen War. Different people were assigned various functions in the clandestine operation to ferry Putin, the Kremlin candidate and former FSB director anointed by Yeltsin as his successor, to power. Boris Berezovsky handled public relations on Channel One, the main Russian TV channel. Roman Abramovich handled financing. The Intelligence Services handled terror attacks and wars…

The playbook was always for Yeltsin to resign three months before the end of his term, on December 31, 1999, and for him to appoint the Prime Minister as 'Acting President' to take his place for the remaining months of his office. The Kremlin candidate would thus defend his candidacy for the Presidential Election of 2000 as 'Acting President' from inside the Kremlin and, 'winning the election', would become the official President, ostensibly with the legitimate approval of Russian voters.

By 1999, the Kremlin's presidential candidates were stacked in such a way that the outgoing President Yeltsin could choose to replace himself with any candidate as long as it was one of three names only. Curiously, all three choices before Yeltsin were Intelligence Services' officers. Candidate number 1 was Evgeny Primakov, the former director of the Foreign Intelligence Service (SVR), who served as Prime Minister of Russia since September 1998. But Primakov disappointed Yeltsin. He colluded with the State Duma and the communists, and was dismissive of Yeltsin, considering him a lame duck. The word 'impeachment' was heard more and more frequently in the Duma, whose chair was a Communist. Yeltsin understood that to mean that, as President Primakov would not guarantee him and his family full immunity after his resignation, and that they could end up in prison for political and economic crimes. Thus, in May 1999, Yeltsin ousted Primakov and appointed as Prime Minister candidate number 2, Sergei Stepashin, former Director of the FSK (the name before 'FSB' was adopted) and the architect and initiator of the First Chechen War.

Stepashin did not please Yeltsin either, as he, too, was willing to compromise with his competitors and enemies. In August 1999, Yeltsin dismissed Stepashin and appointed candidate number 3—the last card in the deck, FSB Director Vladimir Putin. Then, as planned, on December 31, 1999, Yeltsin resigned and Putin became 'Acting President'. On the outside, it still looked as if a real election was taking place but Putin becoming the official president was now a formality and on May 7, 2000, he was inaugurated as the second President of the Russian Federation.

Putin came to power not as a representative of the oligarch clan or 'family', at least not merely as their plant, but as a representative of the very system he had worked for his entire life. The post of President became another 'job' for him. Now he just had to parachute his Chekist colleagues, former and current, in the highest echelons of power under appropriate covers and give them control of the country—its politics, economy and finances, and its people.

With the help of Yeltsin's oligarchs, who were only interested in money in the end, he subjugated the press, television, the electoral machine, the courts, free press and once-independent broadcasters, anchors and bloggers. By 2004, the year of his reelection, Putin held all the Government's strings in his hand, including the once-proud Russian Parliament that had dared to threaten the previous President with impeachment.

Putin's second term as President was devoted to two issues: consolidating the Intelligence Services' power over the country as well as the election of the next President since, under the Constitution, Putin would have to relinquish power like Yeltsin at the end of his second term. Several other Chekist strongmen were eyeing his office and Putin did not yet have the audacity, or Chekist consensus at any rate, to redraft the Constitution so that he could be re-elected for more terms. As Putin was about to demote himself to Prime Minister, there was a list of two acceptable candidates who could become President: Dmitry Medvedev, who was fully controlled by Putin himself, and Putin's long-standing friend, KGB/FSB General Sergei Ivanov, an Intelligence Services careerist like Putin.

Having the deciding vote on this critical matter, Putin settled on Medvedev, realizing that he could easily demote Medvedev in four years as he had never been part of the Intelligence Services. But Putin would not be able to remove the more senior Ivanov after he had been President for four years. From the Chekists' point of view, it made no difference which officer ran the country. If he were to become President for two terms, General Ivanov simply assume Putin's role as the Chekists' leader and likely strip Putin of the wealth he had secretly accrued in tandem with oligarch Abramovich, as well as whatever power Putin had left.

As a result, Medvedev became President in 2008. Throughout his term no one inside Russia or abroad took him seriously as an independent leader, despite the Russian invasion of Georgia (which had been an independent country since the collapse of the USSR in 1991) under his watch. The invasion took place three months after he took office in May 2008 while Putin and he were at the opening of the Beijing Olympics, illustrating their client relationship. In 2012, as planned four years earlier, Medvedev relinquished the Presidential throne and Putin 'won' his third election.

It soon also became clear what program Putin was pursuing after the consolidation of his power over three terms. In March 2014, Russia invaded Crimea and claimed the peninsula as Russian territory. After the annexation of Crimea, the world was divided into optimists and pessimists. The former thought Putin would stop at Crimea. The latter that Crimea was only the beginning, the first stage in a long journey planned for Russia by Putin to create 'Novorossiya', New Russia, connecting Russia with Moldova via Ukraine.

The Crimean Peninsula surrendered without a fight. At the time, everyone could live with it—the West and the rest of the world, and Ukraine more or less—since the takeover was bloodless. European and American leaders reckoned: if Crimea is as far as he will go, we'll ignore it and continue as before. But they also ignored what he said.

Putin repeated what he had stated before that the time had come to correct the 'historical errors' of 1991 that led to the fall of the Soviet Union and that the collapse of the USSR was the greatest personal tragedy of his life. Instead of a return to communism, however, he now advocated its ideological opposite. He rebranded himself as a Russian nationalist and claimed that there is a special 'Russian gene' that sets Russians apart from the rest of the global population and that there is a 'Russian World', an amalgamation of peoples who speak Russian. Since the interests of this 'Russian World' scattered across the globe must be protected, Russia will defend them, no matter where these Russians are and whether or not they want Russia to protect them. And yes, ideally, that this 'Russian World' should be united under the auspices of one state. It was not very different from Hitler's championing of 'Germans' wherever they were.

One of the major problems for Russia is Putin's numerous complexes—his insistence that everyone should treat Russia like they do the United States. It is very difficult to explain and articulate what is precisely wrong with this idea. True, Russia is a big country and the richest in the world in terms of mineral resources, and it has enough nuclear weapons to cause irreparable damage to the entire planet; but Russia has little else. By entering Crimea in March 2014, Putin signed the death sentence to the new Russia formed in 1991 on the ruins of the Soviet Union—the modern Russia he never embraced and always hated. After two Chechen wars, the war with Georgia, and now Crimea, the Russia of 1991, content with its borders, was forever gone.

The successful annexation of Crimea created euphoria in Russia and preparations began to capture the whole of Ukraine in 2014. Several components of these preparations were obvious: creating a powerful military foothold in Crimea; conducting a whole series of military training in regions bordering Ukraine, in the Kaliningrad Region, and in the Baltics; the constant probing of air borders and violations of foreign airspace, near and far, by Russian military aircraft, the unprecedented anti-Ukrainian and anti-Western propaganda campaign deployed on all Russian television channels and in the Russian press, the concentration of Russian troops along the Russian-Ukrainian border, the calling up of Russian reservists, sending wrecking groups to Ukraine to start a 'civil war' in the Eastern regions of the country, and the subsequent justification of the invasion of Ukraine by the Russian Army.

Russia's designs on Ukraine were very different from her parallel move to dominate the former USSR republic Belarus through economic and political coercion. For the first time since 1945, post-war Europe was faced with a European state determined to seize another by violence. Putin's plan threatened Europe's general balance of power, stability, status quo, and peace itself. Europe in the 1990s had witnessed the collapse of an empire, the reunification of Germany, and even the interference of world powers in the conflict between former Yugoslavian states. But not a single great European state after 1945 had tried to subdue a neighbor. Russia had tried it in Georgia in 2008, and now it was having a second go in Ukraine.

European states, including Russia, had been partners who shared a belief in free markets. Now, Russia became a strategic enemy of the European Union and NATO. This was a fundamentally different, expansionist Russia, with which other countries and coalitions had to try to coexist rather than cooperate. It was an entirely different world.

After being hit with Western sanctions as formal punishment for its invasion of Ukraine and the annexation of Crimea, Russia encountered the economic consequences of its actions: the value of the Russian Ruble was halved, inflation and price growth increased in the country, real estate prices fell, and Russians started traveling overseas less often as such trips became too expensive with the falling Ruble. But there was no noticeable protest movement in Russia itself, and Putin continued with what he had started in March 2014. Changes to that track in response to sanctions and the West's reaction did not come. As Putin said in a speech on Red Square to mark the first anniversary of the annexation of Crimea on March 18, 2015: 'We shall overcome the hardships that we so easily created for ourselves in recent times.'

Russia became the single source of instability in Europe. The Kremlin's new mission was to capture all neighboring countries that used to be part of the USSR by using the 'Ukraine Scheme'. That is, start a war to annex territory and insist that Russia is not involved in the war.

Thus, Russia began agitating against Moldova. After the occupation of Crimea, the Kremlin accused the country of violating the rights of Russians in Transnistria, Moldova's independent breakaway region bordering Ukraine. On a 2014 visit, Dmitry Rogozin, the minister responsible for Russia's military industry attempted to collect a 'petition' of citizens of Transnistria to join Russia as an enclave. When the Moldovan Government prevented Rogozin from taking the documents to Moscow, he stated that next time he would be flying to Moldova in a bomber.

In early July 2015, Rogozin introduced a simplified procedure for granting Russian nationality to young residents of Transnistria. Its purpose was very simple. During future military actions in Moldova it would not be possible to distinguish between Russian troops and Transnistrian 'separatists' and 'militias'. Out of 500,000 people that Russia identified as 'citizens of Transnistria', 220,000 received Russian passports.

The same scheme had first been used in 2008 in the Georgian republics of Abkhazia and South Ossetia, where anyone who wanted was issued a Russian passport, after which the Russian Army invaded under the pretext of protecting 'Russian citizens' from 'harassment by Georgian authorities'. Plans to issue Russian passports were also discussed about Russian speakers living in Baltic countries Latvia, Estonia and Lithuania, all three NATO members.

However, one should not overstate the willingness of the Russian-speaking population of former Soviet Republics to align themselves with Putin's imperial ambitions. In Ukraine, for example, the pro-Russians who had clamored for 'referendums' on the status of this or that region of Ukraine in March May 2014, were chastened after Russian troops entered Luhansk and Donetsk regions and their lands were ravaged by Russian tanks. The price of war was too steep even for the most fiercely pro-Russian residents of Eastern Ukraine.

None of the twentieth-century major wars started with the realization that they would one day be called 'world wars.' Even Hitler did not know that World War II was starting when he attacked Poland. He counted on the fact that, with the German-Soviet non-aggression pact in place, Great Britain and France would not dare declare war on Germany over the invasion of Poland. In 2014, similar questions were asked in the Kremlin. Were Western Democracies willing to surrender Ukraine like Czechoslovakia in 1938-1939? Would NATO allow the Baltic countries to be attacked like Poland was in 1939? Was Putin ready to escalate Russian aggression and go to war for the 'Russian World' and rebirth the Russian empire?

Soon, the answers became clear even to the Kremlin. Snapping out of the initial shock—which Putin had taken as a sign that Europe and the US were ready to give Russia all the territory it wanted—the West started organizing its resistance. None of the major world leaders recognized the annexation of Crimea or the assertion of Crimea as an 'original Russian land.' Sanctions were imposed until Crimea was returned to Ukraine. The French lost out on orders but refused to sell warships to Russia. President Barack Obama added Russia to the list of the US's primary enemies (even if he had previously laughed at his opponent, Mitt Romney, in a Presidential debate, for claiming that Russia was America's main strategic enemy). The Pentagon conducted tests of a new atomic bomb. NATO, still during the Obama Administration, deployed rapid response forces in Europe. The Baltic countries insisted that NATO troops be stationed in their territory. Neutral Finland recruited new reservists and increased its military budget. The Danes were willing to place NATO nuclear warheads on their ships. Sweden monitored Russian submarines. Moldova conducted military exercises with Poland, Georgia, Romania, and the US. And all of them together intercepted Russian military aircraft came close to neighboring borders hundreds of times from 2014-2015. No one gave in and Putin realized that an outright invasion was not on the cards and retreated from war on Ukraine.

But neither Putin nor the Chekists in the Kremlin retreated from their desire to create a new, greater Russia. From an opportunistic plan to exploit Ukraine's civil turmoil in 2014-2015—utilizing it to grab the East if not the whole country with minimal military resources—it now evolved into a better organized full-blown military operation. Over the six-year planning cycle of the Russian military, the Kremlin started methodically preparing to have a second go capture Ukraine as it had Crimea: this time with over 200,000 troops ready to roll in as part of the new playbook. With troops intended to be in place in a matter of days, followed by a 'referendum' expressing that a 'majority' of Ukrainians wanted to join the Russian Federation, the annexation of Ukraine would be a fait accompli to the world like Crimea. It was only the Covid pandemic that stayed execution until 2022.

Over these eight years, as Russian tourists crowded to Crimean beaches to enjoy the Black Sea sunshine, Kremlin hawks witnessed with interest that Ukraine was mobilizing a considerable standing army to defend itself after it had let Crimea, Luhansk and Donetsk be occupied without putting up a fight. This was welcomed with glee at the Kremlin. Once Ukraine was annexed, a joint Ukrainian-Russian army would double Russia's European capability and make steamrolling over Moldova and the Baltic states by the same process of 'protecting' 'Russian-speakers' that much easier. NATO might have a lot missiles, but in 2022 it still had few boots on the ground in the former USSR republics.

And so, the Ukraine invasion of February 2022 was meant to be over in a few weeks after the capture of Kyiv and President Volodymyr Zelensky. However, Russia failed spectacularly to capture either Ukraine's president or pivotal regions in what was meant to be a blitzkrieg. Ukraine's army successfully halted the Russian invasion on land although it had to relinquish most of its coastline in the absence of a navy. Supported by massive NATO aid, it was even able to push the new Russian border back here and there over the course of 2022.

The key question for our time is whether the failure of Russia's February 2022 plan dented the Kremlin's expansionism? In part, the answer will depend on whether one considers Vladimir Putin to be both a dictator and the origin of the new Russian Federation that came into being from 2000 and whether Russia's hunger for empire is driven by Putin only. As Stalin famously said, 'When there's no person, there's no problem'. In other words, will removing him would bring back stability?

This is not the view of the authors of this book. This book is intended to set out that the state headed by Putin—based on the omnipotence of the Intelligence Services and personal loyalty—has no analogies in world history and is a result of the Chekists' struggle for power since 1918. No other country in the world has ever been led by their Intelligence Services and utilizes a mafia-style relationship between the State and the business world. Putin is without doubt the primus inter pares, but he is not the source of the Kremlin's ideas and attitudes. The wellspring of those in power, no matter what you call them—Chekists, mafia, clan, junta, organized crime(?)—are the Russian Intelligence Services, located next to the Kremlin in the FSB building known as Lubyanka. To understand Russia's future we need to understand the Cheka's past.

1: Formation of the Soviet Government

Before we begin our narrative of events that unfolded over the last century, a comment on Soviet historiography is in order. None of the books on Soviet history published in the USSR until about 1989—millions upon millions of copies—contain a single word of truth. Their sole purpose was to falsify 20th-century Russian history and present it to the reader in a false light, with layers upon layers of falsehood: Stalin-era, Khrushchev-era, Brezhnev-era, etc. In other words, Soviet historians' accounts bore no relation to reality. As the Soviet joke goes, the future is certain—it is the past you have to worry about.

In 1989, the situation began to change, and with time Russia saw the publication of many serious historical works. However, even they often failed—quantitatively and psychologically—to cleanse the minds of millions of Russians of decades of multi-layered lies and to turn things around. What's more, the prevailing mood in Russia quickly changed from 'we want to know everything', to information fatigue and the conviction that 'we already know everything.' That is why much of what the reader will find in this book will be new and surprising.

The VChK (All-Union Extraordinary Commission) formed by Felix Dzerzhinsky, a member of the Secretariat of Russia's Bolshevik Party, at Lenin's insistence on December 20, 1917 was the world's first known intelligence service in the modern sense of the term. That is the reason the Dzerzhinsky monument stood for so many years in the heart of downtown Soviet Moscow, across from the VChK/NKVD/KGB headquarters on Lubyanka Square. For the same reason, mass-produced Dzerzhinsky portraits and busts have decorated, and still decorate, the office of every employee of Russian (Soviet) Intelligence Services. Even Russia's current president, Vladimir Putin, has a small bust of Dzerzhinsky on his desk. However, this is not because Dzerzhinsky was the first Chair of the VChK. It's mainly because Dzerzhinsky was the first to realize the potency and importance of the Intelligence Services as an instrument for seizing power. Instead of genuflecting before Lenin and the SNK (Council of People's Commissars), Dzerzhinsky launched a ferocious battle against them—which he won eventually, but everything in good order.

The Soviet leadership needed the VChK because it did not mean to compete with political opponents but to exterminate them. Moreover, it was not counterrevolutionaries that Lenin saw as the greatest danger but his own recently acquired comrades-in-arms and allies in the revolutionary movement. It was mainly for the purpose of crushing fellow revolutionaries—Constitutional Democrats (Kadets), Social-Democrats (Mensheviks), Socialist-Revolutionaries (SRs), Left Socialist Revolutionaries (Left SRs), anarchists—that Lenin tasked Dzerzhinsky's special agency. It was no accident, either, that the man Lenin chose to run it was Dzerzhinsky, a far-left extremist even by Bolshevik standards. He knew that Dzerzhinsky, who later acquired the permanent nickname 'Iron Felix,' would kill without compunction. Only Intelligence Service agents themselves saw this moniker as flattering.

It should be remembered that in the vast ocean of the Russian revolutionary movements, the Bolsheviks were but a tiny extremist group organized very similarly to the Italian mafia and founded entirely on personal loyalty to the chief (Lenin) and family ties, with entire clans involved in the life of the Party. A small outfit—it could not possibly hope to successfully seize power in Russia. That is, if you believe in the theories of Karl Marx and play by the rules accepted in the revolutionary movement and in revolutionary circles. Russia had practically no proletariat and was a peasant country. But what if one were to forget about Marxist theory and discard its rules? How about seizing power by splitting a formerly monolithic enemy and pitting the fragments against each other?

Even so, one cannot act alone. During the key days of revolution, the unprincipled Lenin found himself an extremely important ally in Lev Trotsky. Because he had not been a Bolshevik from the start of revolution in the spring of 1917, Trotsky suffered from a crippling inferiority, if not impostor, complex. So, when Bolshevik Lenin proposed to Trotsky, the Chair of the Petrograd Soviet, that they form a political bloc and head a future government together, Trotsky immediately agreed. Allied by a deeply personal pact, it was two of them against all the others.

The USSR myth that Lenin's authority among the Bolsheviks was absolute is one of many apocryphal ones. The Bolsheviks' own Central Committee (CC) ignored Lenin's directives. The Petrograd Soviet, headed by Leon Trotsky, was balanced between the Bolsheviks and the Mensheviks.[2] Convened in October 1917 in Petrograd, the Second All-Russian Congress of Soviets was a body of several socialist parties, of which the Bolsheviks were neither the largest nor the main revolutionary party. None of these entities, therefore, saw Lenin as their absolute leader and none of these constituent parts of the October armed uprising in Petrograd had any intention of submitting to his will. Lenin always imposed himself and was always viewed with suspicion.

Nor did Lenin and the Bolsheviks have many options during the first year of the Russian revolution. They could either cede power to the bloc of socialist parties or they could radically destroy these parties, establishing a one-party dictatorship. The Bolsheviks chose the latter path. The question whether the Bolsheviks made this choice freely or were forced to is largely academic. Lenin's relentless desire to preserve power for himself in order to implement his political program drove them forward.

Since the Bolshevik Party was the only one willing to acknowledge Lenin's sway—sometimes with caveats—he had to embark on a path of brutal repression from the first hour of the Revolution. Repression was enforced by Dzerzhinsky's VChK. Results materialized. By late 1917, Dzerzhinsky's Bolshevik Secretariat colleague, Yakov Sverdlov, became the head of the Soviet parliament.[3] The Bolshevik Secretariat thus controlled both parliament (via Sverdlov) and the intelligence services (via Dzerzhinsky). Lenin's Council of People's Commissars (SNK) of Russia was the only body still beyond Bolshevik control. It was against the SNK, then, that Dzerzhinsky and Sverdlov began their own battle.

Up until 1917, Germany appeared to be the leader of the revolutionary movement. Its Social Democratic Party was the most powerful in the world. If there was going to be a world revolution, a revolution in Germany seemed a prerequisite. The revolution did not necessarily have to begin there, but its victory in Germany seemed to all revolutionaries to be an essential steppingstone to international success. The Social Democratic tropes of the time did not admit any alternative road to world revolution of the masses. Prior to March 1917, Lenin himself saw no greater role for himself than that of the leader of the extremist wing of Russia's Social Democratic movement. It was unquestionably secondary to the Communist movement in Germany.

After November 1917, however, these long-held assumptions had to be re-examined in view of events in Russia. What was more important: to preserve Soviet rule in Russia at any cost—where the revolution had already taken place—or to try to organize a revolution in Germany, even at the price of losing Soviet rule in Russia?

In 1918, the answer to this question was not as obvious as it might seem today. The consensus among Europe's socialist leaders was that Russia was backward and that it would be impossible not only to build socialism, but also to hold on to power for any extended period without support from other European socialist revolutions, if only because of (as the Communists believed) Russia's 'capitalist encirclement'—its hostile neighbors would consider it imperative to overturn Russia's socialist regime. Many revolutionaries continued to believe that only a revolution in Germany would guarantee that the Soviet government could remain in power in Russia.

Lenin thought otherwise. In November 1917, returning from Switzerland and seizing power in Russia with lightning speed, he showed his many opponents how much they underestimated him and his small extremist Bolshevik sect. For Lenin, the German revolution took second place to the already victorious revolution in Russia. Even more than that: the revolution in Germany must not happen too quickly, since when it did, the center of gravity of the Communist world would shift to the industrialized West and Lenin would be left behind as nothing more than the head of the government of an 'underdeveloped,' 'backward,' and 'uncultured' country, of no interest to anyone after Communism's victory in Germany.

That was the backdrop against which Lenin insisted on signing the March 3, 1918 Brest-Litovsk Peace Treaty on extreme terms. In exchange for Ukraine, most of

Belarus, Lithuania, Estonia and Latvia, Germany agreed to end its invasion of Russia. Lenin got his way, defying the will of the entire Bolshevik party. To achieve this, he was willing to allow a formal split in the party into two for the first and only time. He permitted the creation of a Left Socialist Revolutionary bloc which advocated the dissolution of the peace treaty with Germany and an immediate revolutionary war against European imperialism. Dzerzhinsky was one of the leaders of the Left Communists.

Under pressure from Lenin, the Bolshevik Central Committee even agreed to exchange ambassadors with 'imperialist Germany'. Today, this step does not appear as something extraordinary. But in April 1918, when the German revolution could have erupted at any moment, official recognition of the 'Hohenzollerns' by the Soviet government was not needed to preserve Lenin's 'breathing-space' from the German invasion. It was not simply an error of judgement from the point of view of those desiring world and, therefore, a German revolution. The recognition of Germany betrayed the accepted dogma of world socialism.

The Germans appointed Count Wilhelm von Mirbach as ambassador to Russia. He had already spent several weeks in Petrograd, the capital of imperial Russia, and was thus familiar with the general outlines of the Russian revolution. Mirbach arrived in Moscow on April 23. The German embassy occupied a two-story townhouse that belonged to the widow of the sugar manufacturer and collegiate counselor von Berg. The ambassador's arrival coincided in time with the *coup d'état* in Ukraine,[4] the occupation of Finland by German troops, and the Germans' gradual but systematic advance eastward, beyond the line demarcated by the Brest-Litovsk agreement.

Naturally, the Soviet government expressed its displeasure to Mirbach as soon as the opportunity arose—when his letters of credence were presented on April 26. The ceremony took place in a cold and perfunctory manner. After it ended, Sverdlov did not invite anyone to sit down or engage in private conversation.

On May 16, in a meeting with the German ambassador at the Kremlin, Lenin admitted to Mirbach that the number of his opponents was growing and that the situation in the country was more serious than it had been a month earlier. He likewise indicated that the character of his opponents had recently changed. Previously, they had been made up of representatives of right-wing parties; now, however, he had opponents within his own camp, in which a left wing had formed.

The main bone of contention of this opposition, Lenin went on, was that the Brest-Litovsk treaty was a mistake. More and more Russian territories were ending up under German occupation; the peace treaties with Finland and Ukraine had still not been ratified; famine was spreading. A series of recent developments had confirmed the correctness of the arguments put forward by the left-wing opposition. While he was still deeply committed to the treaty, a genuine peace, he noted, was still very far away. Mirbach paid particular attention to the fact that Lenin did not threaten him starkly with a possible reorientation of Soviet policies. He simply stressed the fact that his own position within the party and the government was extremely shaky. In speaking with Mirbach, Lenin set specific goals for himself. Apparently, he hoped to persuade the German ambassador that it was necessary to agree to certain concessions, letting him know that otherwise, with or without Lenin, the Soviet government would be forced to abandon its German policy due to pressure from the left.

Mirbach's report on his conversation with Lenin is the only known document attesting to Lenin's admission of the failure of his Brest-Litovsk policy. The treaty did not bring about either the coveted peace or the 'breathing-space' Lenin had promised. From the German point of view, the agreement was no more than part of a military strategy and served as a means of propping up the Western front. If so, Germany's worsening situation in the West increased its Russian appetites in the East. Military action on the Eastern front did not cease even for a day. Germany continued to present new ultimatums and occupied entire districts and cities. The worst fears of most of the Party's membership were coming true.

From the moment the Brest-Litovsk Treaty was signed, Sverdlov began his very noticeable ascent. Taking advantage of Lenin's mistake, he began wresting the leadership of the Bolshevik Party and government away from Lenin. Due to the resignation of all the Left SRs and some Left Communists, the Soviet government (the SNK) examined 'the general ministerial crisis' on March 18—the day after the Fourth Congress of Soviets wrapped up its work. Sverdlov had delivered this message even though he was not formally a member of the SNK. It showed how Sverdlov was gradually edging out Lenin, not only within the party, but also within the Soviet government.

In March and April, Sverdlov was mostly busy coordinating the cooperation of various political factions. In May/June, he took charge of all of the Party's work and took on the role of 'General Secretary'. He was often appointed as Lenin's co-speaker, that is, was attached to Lenin as a commissar; he was the Bolshevik's Central Committee's (CC) speaker at the Moscow Municipal Party Conference and presented the 'Theses of the Central Committee on the Present Political Situation', drafted by Lenin and ratified by the CC on May 13. In the transcript of a CC meeting on May 18, Sverdlov's name is at the top of a list of those present. The CC meeting on the next day, May 19, was a complete triumph for Sverdlov. In minutes of the CC published for the first time in April 1989, absolute control of the Bolshevik Party was assigned to him.

It is not possible to trace the further waxing of Sverdlov's power (and the decline of Lenin's authority) in the CC because transcripts and minutes from May 19 to September 16, 1918, have not been located. One possibility why they did not survive is because of the cult of personality created around Lenin by the Soviet government after his death. Any evidence of Lenin's position and influence appearing in an extremely unfavorable light would be unwelcome.

In defiance of Lenin's wishes an intensive campaign of anti-German subversion was mounted in Ukraine. It started in May, 1918, under the oversight of the Secretariat of the Bolshevik CC, that is of Sverdlov. On May 3, in order to undermine Germany's military might and prepare a Communist coup in Ukraine, the CC passed two resolutions to form a Ukrainian communist party. The texts of these two resolutions do not appear in the transcript of the CC's meeting. This was no accident.

One of the resolutions—on the Ukrainian Communist Party's break-off from the Russian Communist Party as an independent party—was intended to be publicized. By proclaiming the independence of the Ukrainian Communist party, the CC absolved itself of any responsibility for the subversion the Bolshevik Party were organizing in German-occupied Ukraine. Anti-German agitation could now be carried out effectively in the open without the risk of complicating poor Soviet-German or Soviet-Ukrainian relations. Germany's complaints were dismissed by foreign minister Georgy Chicherin[5] on the grounds that the Bolsheviks of Russia had no connection to the Bolsheviks of Ukraine. The second resolution that day stated that the Ukrainian Communist Party remained part of the Russian Communist Party. Meant to stay secret, it reminded Ukrainian Bolsheviks that they were subordinate to the unified CC of the Russian Communist Party and were not an independent party.

In the summer of 1918—after the collapse of the large-scale German offensive on the Western front and after the arrival of American troops in France—the inevitability of Germany's defeat in the world war became clear. Lenin's own predicament, however, was no less dire. On June 25, in a letter to foreign minister Richard von Kühlmann, who had led the Brest-Litovsk delegation, Mirbach summed up the Bolshevik hightide in Moscow, noting that 'after two months of careful observation' he could no longer 'give Bolshevism a favorable diagnosis. We are, without question, standing by the bedside of a dangerously ill person, whose condition might now and again improve, but who is doomed,' Mirbach wrote. Mirbach proposed that Germany would fill the 'newly formed vacuum' in Moscow with new 'government organs, which we will keep ready, and which will be wholly and entirely at our service.'

These goings-on in the German embassy did not remain unnoticed by the Soviet Intelligence Services. In the days when Mirbach wrote to Berlin about the need for changes in Germany's Eastern policy, the VChK, headed by the Left-Communist Dzerzhinsky, set up a section for 'monitoring the embassy's guard and possible criminal activity by the embassy.'

It is worth noting that the staff of the German embassy had been nervously anticipating unpleasant events for a long time. On June 3, Kurt Riezler, an advisor at the German mission in Moscow, described the future in the darkest of terms in a remarkably emotional missive to Berlin:

In the last two weeks, the situation has very rapidly come to a head. Famine is on the way and is being choked off with terror. The pressure exerted by the Bolsheviks' mailed fist is enormous. People are being quietly shot by the hundred. All this is not so bad, but there can no longer be any doubt that the physical means by which the Bolsheviks maintain their power are running out. Supplies of petrol for motor vehicles are coming to an end, and even Latvian soldiers sitting in their vehicles are no longer reliable—not to mention the peasants and the workers. The Bolsheviks are extremely nervous and can feel their end approaching, and all the rats are therefore beginning to leave the sinking ship…. [foreign minister] Karahan[6] has put the original of the treaty of Brest ready in his desk. He intends to take the document with him to America and to sell it, with the emperor's signature on it, to the highest bidder….

Nobody can tell how they will face their end, and their dying agony may last several more weeks. Perhaps they will try to flee to the city of Nizhny Novgorod or to Yekaterinburg. Perhaps they intend to fall in their own blood, like desperate men, or perhaps to invite us to leave in order to be rid of the treaty of Brest— 'the breathing space,' as they call it—and with it their compromise with typical imperialism, thus saving their revolutionary consciences in their dying moments. These people are completely incalculable, especially in their despair. In addition, they once again believe that the more and more undisguised 'military dictatorship' in Germany is encountering enormous opposition, especially because of the further advance in the East, and that it is bound to lead to the revolution… Please forgive this personal effusion about a state of chaos which, even viewed from here, is all too impenetrable.[7]

Driven into a dead end by Lenin, brought to a state of crisis, split up and losing power, the Bolshevik Party could now do nothing but grasp at the straw that in March 1918 had been offered to it by Trotsky: 'No matter how much we equivocate, no matter what kind of strategy we invent, we can be saved in the full sense of this word only by a European revolution.'[8]

Perhaps to start war in the summer of 1918 was no less risky than to have continued it in March, but by June the Bolsheviks had no options left. Lenin's 'breathing-space' policy had yielded no positive outcome. It was irrelevant whether or not Lenin had been correct in March. During three months of breathing-space, the Revolution had lost its dynamic force. The despair of the Bolshevik regime was reaching its peak and can be pinpointed to an exact date: July 6, 1918. On that day two Soviet Intelligence Service agents—Yakov Blumkin and Nikolai Andreyev—arrived at the German embassy with a mandate from Dzerzhinsky and his deputy Ivan Ksenofontov. Bypassing Lenin and the CC, they demanded a meeting with Ambassador Mirbach on an 'urgent' matter. It was to save the Bolshevik government and along with it—more ironically—the breathing space Lenin had wanted the Brest-Litovsk Treaty to create.

2: Felix Dzerzhinsky's Conspiracy

The 6-7 July conspiracy of 1918 was probably one of the most multilayered conspiracies of that era. Or one could put it differently: a couple of conspiracies unfolded at once. Here they are in order of importance.

First of all, there was Dzerzhinsky's conspiracy against Lenin. On 6 July, VChK agents Blumkin and Andreyev assassinated the German ambassador, Count Mirbach, with the intent of provoking the Germans into formally dissolving the Brest-Litovsk peace treaty. This in turn was to force the hand of the Bolshevik Soviet government into declaring a revolutionary war against Germany and Austro-Hungary, as well as the dismissal of Lenin from the post of SNK Chair since he was the originator of a policy that lay in tatters.[9]

The second conspiracy was the Bolsheviks' arrest of the Left SR Party leadership, including those who were members of the Left SR faction at the Fifth Congress of Soviets, which held during that time at the Bolshoi Theater in Moscow. As a result of this operation, a *de facto* one-party dictatorship was established in Soviet Russia as of July 7, 1918.

To make it easier to sort out the tangled web of the detective story of July 6-7, it is useful to note a pattern. Every time two Soviet or Russian Intelligence Services agents carry out an assignment given to them by their direct superiors, the Kremlin launches a massive damage-control operation. It will include feeding the news media a dizzying number of false theories that have no relation to reality and to what happened. Piling one false theory on another makes it easier to confuse the public and may make it impossible to unearth the true facts. And so it did after the murder of Count Mirbach by two intelligence agents in Moscow on July 6, 1918. In this respect, nothing has changed over a century. It happened, for example, after the poisoning of Alexander Litvinenko by two agents of Russian special services in London on November 1, 2006. It also happened after the attempted poisoning of Sergei Skripal by two agents of Russian special services in Salisbury on March 4, 1918. Again, it happened after the poisoning of Alexei Navalny on August 20, 2020. Likely, the assassination of fascist Aleksandr Dugin's daughter Darya (August 2022) with a car bomb and military blogger Vladlen Tatarsky (April 2023) with a bomb masquerading as a bust, were similar operations.

There is not much merit in detailing the many false versions fed to the press from July 6, 1918, onward in the form of articles, statements, eyewitness testimonies, trial transcripts and books, beyond describing the facts. VChK Chair Dzerzhinsky had reached the conclusion that Lenin was leading the Revolution into a dead end. To save both the Russian Revolution and world revolution, he undertook steps, as chief of the Soviet Intelligence Services and a member of the CC of the Bolshevik Party, to change the course of the Soviet government's foreign policy. The coup began well in advance of the assassination. At Dzerzhinsky's direction (which is very important), VChK assassin Blumkin opened a file against 'the German ambassador's nephew', Robert Mirbach, in early June 1918. In other words, in early June, Dzerzhinsky was already plotting to have the German ambassador assassinated in order to sink the Brest-Litovsk Treaty and prompt a revolutionary war against Germany. It is relevant that Dzerzhinsky was by background a Polish revolutionary and that his family lived abroad. Revolution in Germany and Poland was of far greater personal interest to him than revolution in Russia, a country to which he had emigrated. Even so, after Mirbach's murder, Dzerzhinsky denied any knowledge of the planned assassination, just as Putin today denies any involvement in Russia's Intelligence Services.

In June, one of Mirbach's two assassins, Yakov Blumkin, who was then just 19 or 20 years old and a member of the new Left SR Party, was given a job with the VChK as head of the counterintelligence department responsible for 'monitoring the embassy's guards and possible criminal activity by the embassy' of Germany. As Martin Latsis, future head of the Ukraine VChK, later testified, 'Blumkin exhibited a strong urge to expand the department' with militant espionage and 'more than once submitted projects to the VChK.' However, the only assignment that Blumkin really ever worked on was 'the case of the Austrian Mirbach'; indeed, Blumkin 'devoted himself entirely to this case' and spent 'whole nights interrogating witnesses.'[10]

Mirbach's nephew was an opportunity for the young Chekist to show what he was capable of. According to the information gathered, Robert Mirbach had served in the 37th infantry regiment of the Austrian army, was taken prisoner, wound up in a camp, but was released after the ratification of the Treaty of Brest-Litovsk. While waiting to go back to Austria, he had rented a room in a hotel in Moscow where he lived until the beginning of June, when the Swedish actress Landström suddenly committed suicide in the same hotel. Whether this suicide was really a Chekist assassination is difficult to assess at this distance in time. What is certain, however, is that the VChK claimed that Landström had committed suicide in connection with counter-revolutionary activities. It also arrested all the hotel's residents. Among them was the 'nephew of the German ambassador,' Robert Mirbach, supposedly.

The Chekists' subsequent moves—Blumkin's above all—were undeniably inventive. The VChK immediately notified the Danish consulate, which represented Austria-Hungary's interests in Russia, of Robert Mirbach's arrest. On June 15, the Danish consulate entered negotiations with the VChK concerning 'the case of the arrested officer of the Austrian army, Count Mirbach.' During these negotiations, the Chekists suggested to the consulate's representative that Robert Mirbach might be related to the German ambassador. On June 17, a day after the negotiations began, the Danish consulate gave the Chekists a document which the Chekists were not expecting:

> The Royal Danish Consulate General hereby informs the All-Russian Extraordinary Commission that the arrested officer of the Austro-Hungarian army, Count Robert Mirbach, according to the written report of the German diplomatic representation in Moscow addressed to the Danish Consulate General, is indeed a member of a family that is related to the German ambassador Count Mirbach, residing in Austria.[11]

Since the first document of the Danish consulate is dated June 15 and the second June 17, one must assume that the written response of the German embassy to the Danish consulate's query was given on June 16, immediately after the Danish consulate's query was received, and that it was humane in intent. That is to say, it was decided by the German embassy that describing the unknown Count Robert Mirbach as a relative of the German ambassador might help the unfortunate Austrian officer's predicament and, indeed, that he might be released immediately, especially since the charges against him seemed frivolous to the Ambassador's aide Kurt Riezler. The German ambassador's own involvement in the case of the 'nephew' was apparently limited to his permission to describe Robert Mirbach as a relation. Ambassador Mirbach did not know his namesake and had never met him.

The 'case of the ambassador's nephew' now became the foundation for the case against the German embassy and the ambassador personally.[12] The main piece of evidence in Blumkin's possession was a document ostensibly signed by Robert Mirbach, but was really a not very good forgery. Handwritten in Russian, it pledged to share information about the German embassy.[13] The 'pledge' itself was written by one person, the addendum and signature in Russian and German by someone else.[14] When this 'proof' was first published in 1920,[15] there was further falsification: 'Hungarian citizen' was deliberately changed to 'German citizen' to underscore Robert Mirbach's (non-existent) connection to the German ambassador.

Nervous, the German ambassador now denied any relation to Robert Mirbach and regarded the 'Robert Mirbach affair' as provocation. In mid-June, the embassy officially notified the foreign minister—and thus Dzerzhinsky—that it possessed information on a planned attempt on the lives of German embassy staff members.[16] On June 28, the embassy gave the foreign ministry new materials on the matter.[17] The Chair of the VChK told the Germans that if he did not know who their informers were, he could not assist the embassy in preventing the assassination attempts.[18]

On the morning of July 6, shortly before Mirbach was murdered, Riezler, the ambassador's aide, once again went to the Soviet foreign ministry[19] to complain that the embassy was getting information about an imminent attempt on the ambassador's life from all over the place. He was told everything would be reported to Dzerzhinsky at the VChK. Not much later, assassins Blumkin and Andreyev visited the embassy at 2.15pm with them they had a mandate to discuss the matter signed by Dzerzhinsky and stamped with the VChK seal.[20] At a large marble table in the embassy's reception hall, Blumkin told Riezler that Dzerzhinsky had given him strict instructions to speak to the Count in person. Not without hesitation, Mirbach came out to see the visitors.

As they were discussing the matter,[21] Blumkin, pulled out a revolver and fired it across the table first at Mirbach, who jumped up and ran out to the room that adjoined the reception hall, but was at that moment struck down by a bullet fired by Andreyev.[22] Then there was an explosion, after which the VChK terrorists jumped out the window and rode off in the car that was waiting for them. Mirbach was dead and two or three steps from the ambassador was a large hole in the floor. A second bomb hadn't gone off.

Mirbach's assassination became the first planned major operation of the Soviet Intelligence Services.[23] He was dead, but in the confusion, the assassins had forgotten the briefcase that contained the 'Robert Mirbach file' and their mandate signed by Dzerzhinsky.[24] Moreover, two highly damaging witnesses to the crime—Riezler and a translator, whom Blumkin had repeatedly tried to shoot—remained alive. One can only guess to what the events of July 6 would have led to if the operation didn't have Dzerzhinsky's fingerprints all over it.[25]

Lenin, who had no idea that Chekists were involved in the murder, telephoned Dzerzhinsky to inform him of what had happened. After that he summoned Sverdlov to his office. Together, Lenin, Sverdlov and the Soviet foreign minister,[26] decided to go to the German embassy to express our condolences.[27] Dzerzhinsky, however, stole a march on them and arrived at the embassy first, anxious to remove the incriminating evidence. He was shown Blumkin's and Andreyev's mandate with his signature and was met with a rebuke: 'What do you say now?' Collecting the documents, he quickly left the embassy and no one ever saw the 'Robert Mirbach file' again.[28]

The main danger to Lenin was that, if Mirbach's assassination became public knowledge, the Fifth Congress of Soviets, a body of 1164 delegates then in session at the Bolshoi Theater (4-10 July), would applaud the attack and vote to dissolve the treaty. Or, even more disastrously, decide to form a new government made up of Bolsheviks and Left SRs as, for the most part, the Left SRs, like the Left Communists, had opposed the Brest-Litovsk Peace Treaty. Lenin and Sverdlov, therefore, suspected that the Left SR was behind the plot. Lenin decided not to announce the ambassador's death until after the entire core of Left SR activists at the Bolshoi Theater, some 450 people, had been arrested. The operation to arrest the Left SR faction at the Congress was overseen by Sverdlov in his capacity as Committee Chair.

Following a report by Sverdlov on 10 July,[29] the Soviet government's obliging politeness toward Germany disappeared. They refused to be present at the service held at the church where the coffin of the murdered ambassador lay in state. Only foreign minister Chicherin attended the farewell ceremony when Mirbach's body was sent back to Germany. He arrived an hour late, forcing the entire procession to wait for him.

On July 14 matters escalated. That day, Riezler handed Chicherin an ultimatum from Berlin. It demanded that an entire battalion—over a thousand German troops—be allowed to enter Moscow to provide security for the German embassy. One might have expected that a Soviet refusal would have led to the end of the 'breathing space'. But events unfolded contrary to such logic as World War I drew to a close. On July 15, Chicherin categorically rejected the entrance of German troops into Moscow. Confronted with such a rigid position, Germany decided to vacate the embassy. On August 9, the German mission, with 178 members, arrived in Petrograd from Moscow, and soon departed for the city of Pskov, then (still) occupied by the Germans. On August 22, the UK, France and Russia demanded as a precondition for starting peace negotiations that Germany first annul the concessions received under the Brest-Litovsk Treaty: Lenin's 'breathing space' had succeeded.

The events of June 1918 were the first conspiracy of the Soviet Intelligence Services against a leader of the Soviet state—Lenin. But in terms of the conspirators' goals, it ended in total failure. Mirbach was murdered as planned, the Germans presented Lenin's government with an ultimatum as expected, and this ultimatum was categorically rejected by the Soviet government; the conspirators had counted on that as well. But the Germans did not respond by dissolving the Brest-Litovsk Peace Treaty. Nor did the SNK and the Party CC declare a revolutionary war against Germany, because Lenin managed both to outplay the Left Communists and use the murder of the German ambassador to crush the Left SR opposition party.

However, Lenin could clearly see afterwards that Dzerzhinsky had been driving the conspiracy. His response was swift. The VChK was disbanded on July 7, the day after the assassination, and Dzerzhinsky was removed from his post, pending investigation. This issue was addressed at a special meeting of the CC on the same day. Moreover, Dzerzhinsky's removal was made very conspicuously and not only printed in the newspapers but posted all over the city. Dzerzhinsky's deputy Yakov Peters was made temporary Chair of the VChK. The VChK collegium, the executive body elected internally by the VChK itself, was dissolved and earmarked be reorganized in days. Anyone who was 'directly or indirectly complicitous' in Blumkin's 'activities as a provocateur and double agent' was to be 'removed' *Izvestiya* said.[30]

With regard to Dzerzhinsky, the Soviet government reached a conclusion in a little over a month. He was reinstated in his post on August 18, 1918, and the VChK resumed its work under his leadership. The informers of the German embassy[31] were 'removed'. They were arrested and disappeared without a trace right after the Mirbach assassination. Mirbach assassin Andreyev vanished from Moscow and later died somewhere on the front lines of the Civil War—the Soviet government made no effort to find and arrest him. As for Blumkin, he also successfully evaded capture. He turned himself in to the Kyiv VChK on April 17, 1919, and made a full confession. In his own words, he 'served the Revolution to the best of [his] ability' ever since. On May 16, 1919, he was officially pardoned, released, and sent back to work for the VChK, where he served in high-level posts for the remainder of his life. On November 3, 1929, he was executed by firing squad for unsanctioned contacts in Constantinople on April 16 with Trotsky and his son Sergei Sedov who had been recently expelled from the USSR.

The result was that by the end of July, Dzerzhinsky, the conspirator and Left Communist, was temporarily sidelined and under a cloud of suspicion from Lenin. Lenin himself wasn't toppled, but his authority as head of the government was nonetheless weakened by insubordination of agents from the government's own Intelligence Services. The power vacuum was temporarily filled by Sverdlov. A quiet and obscure Party apparatchik known only in narrow Party circles, he rose over the course of these months to Executive Committee Chair of the All-Russian Congress, and Bolshevik Party Central Committee member, and CC Secretary.

Gradually, he asserted dominion over all Bolshevik Party business. His signature could now be spotted on various documents far more often than anyone else's. Starting in July 1918, he signed documents using his titles: CC Secretary, or even simply 'Secretary.' Some were even signed 'for the Secretary' by his wife. As early as August 1918, Party documents were being sent out to the field in the name of 'the Secretariat of the CC' (not just 'the CC,' as had been customary before).[32] In other words, in these months Sverdlov carved out a role that would be given to yet another grey workhorse of the Revolution. A few years later, Joseph Stalin—Sverdlov's friend and fellow exile from the far Siberian Turukhan Region—would be appointed as General Secretary of the Communist Party of Soviet Russia/USSR.

3: The First Attempt to Assassinate Lenin

Reinstated in his post on August 18, 1918, Dzerzhinsky immediately got to work. Then again, had he ever left? His deputy and temporary replacement Peters recalled six years later that Dzerzhinsky 'controlled the VChK' even after being stripped of that position on July 7. He also said that the new VChK 'collegium was formed with his direct input.'[33] Dzerzhinsky intended to finish what he had started as head of Soviet Intelligence. Having failed to sabotage the Litovsk-Brest peace treaty, Dzerzhinsky doubled down on the 'foul' peace by removing the chief architect of that policy: Vladimir Lenin, the head of the government.

The people around Lenin were not unaware of what was happening. 'The summer of 1918 was exceptionally hard,' Lenin's wife Nadezhda Krupskaya later reminisced. Lenin 'was no longer writing anything; he couldn't sleep at night. There's a picture of him taken in late August, shortly before he was wounded: he's standing lost in thought. The way he looks in that picture, it's as if he has just survived a grave illness.'[34] Lenin was already down; all that remained to be done, it seemed, was to finish him off.

In Soviet history, this affair—yet another conspiracy by the Intelligence Services against the head of the government—is known as the 'Kaplan assassination attempt' of August 30, 1918. But, like the assassination of the German ambassador in July, the attempted assassination of Lenin was planned by Soviet intelligence agents and the product of a broader anti-Lenin plot in the Bolshevik Party's upper echelons. So broad was it that even Sverdlov was aware of the conspirators' plans and actively tried to remove Lenin. After recovering, Lenin figured out Sverdlov's involvement in the August plot and paid him back in kind—only 'he didn't miss'. On March 16, 1919, Sverdlov was to die at the age of 33.

Their internecine struggle took place at the height of the mortal struggle against 'international imperialism'. How could Sverdlov have planned to eliminate Lenin at such a moment and how Lenin could have permitted himself to settle scores with Sverdlov?[35] In the case of Lenin, it was because he considered internal enemies were far worse than external ones. On the fifth anniversary of his death, a government minister approvingly quoted these words by Lenin:

Imagine that a commander is fighting a war against an enemy and that he has an enemy in his own camp. Before he goes to the front to fight the enemy, he must first clean out his own camp and free it of enemies.[36]

It accurately takes the temperature among Bolshevik leaders. From 1918-1919, Lenin was cleaning out enemies in his own camp. And Sverdlov did his own cleaning, just not as successfully. Then, it was Stalin who 'cleaned' for thirty years. Then, Lavrenty Beria....

August 30, 1918 is generally seen as the date that marked the beginning of the Red Terror in response to the assassination attempt against Lenin. The accepted view has been that the attack was organized by the leaders of the Socialist Revolutionaries' (SR) combat group, a rival to the Bolsheviks. Fanny Kaplan was an SR who was arrested and confessed to everything. She was then either shot or, according to another account, secretly pardoned. But is this correct?

Dzerzhinsky himself was not in Moscow when the attempt on Lenin's life took place. In a remarkable historical coincidence, on the morning of the assassination attempt, the head of the Petrograd VChK, Moisei Uritsky, was murdered by a student.[37] Dzerzhinsky immediately set out for Petrograd to investigate the murder of his friend and VChK colleague. Though he was not in Moscow when Lenin was shot, several years later, in 1922, at a public trial against the SR, the Soviet government conceded an unusual fact that linked (the physically absent) Dzerzhinsky to Lenin's assassination. In a remarkable symmetry with the successful murder of the German ambassador, the government admitted that the assassination attempt on Lenin had been planned by two VChK operatives[38] who had infiltrated the SR Party on VChK orders.

What we know as a matter of historiographic facts becomes an important question:

Lenin was shot at and wounded.

The shots were fired from two handguns.

One of those involved in the attempt may have been a woman.

The two people charged in the attempted assassination of Lenin in 1922 were Soviet State Security agents.[39]

They were not convicted of the assassination attempt.

The people who carried out the attempted assassination were not arrested either on the scene or shortly afterwards.

What don't we know:

There is no proof that Kaplan was the shooter.

There is no proof that Kaplan was the woman executed for attempting to kill Lenin.

There is no proof that any woman who shot at Lenin was executed at all.

The name of the person who ordered the assassination attempt is unknown.

The reality is that we know very little about this attempted assassination other than that it happened. Who, then, were the two agents? They were called Grigory Semenov and Lidiya Konopleva[40] and from early 1918, both served in the VChK.[41] In fact, they infiltrated the SR Party as Dzerzhinsky's agents soon after the Soviet State Security agency, the VChK, was created. Thanks to their undercover work, all of the SRs' combat activities, controlled, directed, and organized by two Chekists, came to nothing more than a trap set to collect evidence. The two agents were part of preparations for Soviet Russia's first-ever public political trial—the trial of 1922 against the despised SR Party. Everything else surrounding the work of these agents—their stories about being arrested by the Bolsheviks, about resisting these arrests, about planned escapes, and about their repentance—can only be Chekist fabrications, aimed at spreading disinformation to international audiences, above all foreign social democrats. Later, many more public trials were held, all using the same blueprint. In every case, officers or agents of the VChK[42] were used during the trial after infiltrating the soon-to-be-condemned group at the direction of the Intelligence Services at Lubyanka. Semenov and Konopleva were preparing to assassinate Lenin while at the same time putting the heads of the SR Party leadership on the executioner's block. Obviously both orders could only have come from Dzerzhinsky.

We are already familiar with Blumkin, the VChK agent and participant in the assassination of Mirbach. Blumkin was soon pardoned. Received back into the ranks of the Bolshevik Party, he spent the remainder of his life working for Soviet counterintelligence, principally abroad. Semenov and Konopleva had similar careers therefore. Similarly, a century later, the assassins of Alexander Litvinenko and Sergei Skripal simply continued their careers in Russia.

The preparations for the trial of the SRs took a certain amount of time. The party of Socialist-Revolutionaries was the oldest revolutionary party in Russia and was held in high esteem by the leaders of the international socialist movement. To condemn a party of pre-revolutionary terrorists for terrorism against the Soviet government was a stretch. As expected, the social democratic parties of Europe and the Second International rose to the defense of their friends in the SR. Semenov and Konopleva, Lenin's would-be assassins, were the prosecution's biggest trump card in defusing the foreign show of solidarity.

All that remained was to make the SR conspiracy of August 30, 1918 sound plausible. This was not easy. Dzerzhinsky had started preparing the attack on Lenin with Semenov and Konopleva's involvement shortly after the signing of the Brest-Litovsk Peace Treaty and the creation of the Left SR fraction. The first step was to get the SR Party to greenlight the operation to remove Lenin. But the CC of the SR Party refused to participate in the Soviet leader's assassination. 'Give up not only the work you are doing, but give up all work, go to your family, and take a rest,'[43] was the response of Abram Gots, a member of the CC of the SR Party, when Konopleva proposed to assassinate Lenin. After that, she never raised the matter again.

There were also the events on the day itself. The Commandant of the Kremlin[44] recalled: 'August 30, 1918, got off to a lousy start. Grim news was received from Petrograd [Uritsky had been killed]'. Dzerzhinsky 'immediately took off for Petrograd, in order to oversee the investigation in person.' Lenin 'was supposed to speak on that day at the Mikhelson Factory. People close to him, learning about Uritsky's death, tried to stop Lenin, to talk him out of going to the meeting. To calm them, [Lenin] said at lunch that maybe he would not go, but then he himself called for a car and drove off.'[45]. He drove off without bodyguards. Moreover, at the factory there were no bodyguards for Lenin either.

It is extremely important to determine the time at which the shooting took place. This seemingly elementary topic turned out to be incredibly convoluted. Lenin's driver Stepan Gil testified on the night of August 30, that is, immediately following the shooting, that he had 'arrived with Lenin around 10pm at the Mikhelson Factory... After the end of V.I. Lenin's speech, which lasted about an hour, a crowd of about 50 people rushed from the building in which the meeting was held toward the car and surrounded him.'[46]

It is hard to believe that Gil was mistaken and did not remember the time at which he had let Lenin off at the factory gates. If what he says is accurate, then Lenin's speech ended around 11 pm. On that day, however, Soviet 'decree time' was shifted back one hour. Therefore, Lenin arrived at the factory at approximately 10pm according to the old decree time or at 9pm according to the new decree time, and spoke for about an hour. It is impossible to establish the time of the attack on Lenin any more precisely.

Even so, it is the exact time of the attack that contains the answer to another puzzle about the shooting. It is obvious that at least some time must have passed between the shots fired at Lenin and the report that was delivered to Sverdlov about these shots. Sverdlov signed the announcement at 10.40pm. This is entirely plausible if one assumes that between 10pm and 10.40pm, Sverdlov got a telephone call informing him that an attempt had just been made on Lenin's life. Thereupon, without tarrying a single minute he immediately composed the phonogram with his signature on this dramatic news. However, there is one striking detail that militates against this interpretation. Its first sentence reads: 'Several hours ago a villainous assassination attempt was carried out against Comrade Lenin.... We have no doubt that here, too, we will find the tracks of the SRs.' After identifying the culprits and the enemies of the Revolution—the SRs—with pinpoint accuracy and, after specifying to the minute, the time at which the announcement was written—10:40pm— Sverdlov was exceptionally vague about the most important part of the bulletin—the time of the attack itself—by 'several hours'. When had Sverdlov prepared his announcement?

The descriptions of the attack itself were numerous but contradictory. Lenin's driver, Gil, did not see the assassin. Kaplan had been arrested far from the scene of the shooting and following a chase, carrying a briefcase and an umbrella, because someone in the crowd had recognized her (late at night, in the dark) as 'the person who shot at Lenin.' Moreover, as it later turned out, none of the questioned witnesses who had been present at the scene of the shooting had seen the person face-to-face who shot Lenin. None of them were able to identify Kaplan as the would-be assassin.

Kaplan's first interrogation was dated August 30, 11:30pm. According to the 'verbatim' transcript, which Kaplan refused to sign, she admitted that she was guilty of attempting to assassinate Lenin: 'On this day, I shot Lenin. I shot him of my own volition.'[47] It was a very peculiar transcript. It seemed to suffer from the same vagueness that plagued Kaplan. Considering that no more than 30 or 40 minutes had passed since the assassination attempt and the interview, 'on this day' seemed more like a prepared statement than a verbatim admission on the spot. To give the investigators credit, they did ask Kaplan to provide proof that she had really done the shooting. But she could not give any details about the assassination: 'How many shots I fired—I don't remember.' 'I won't tell you what gun I used; I don't want to talk about details.'

Another woman was detained on the evening of August 30, after the attack on Lenin: M.G. Popova. She had approached Lenin near his car after the meeting to ask him questions and was wounded by one of the bullets. She was taken to the Military Commissariat (where Kaplan was also brought); and from there, to the VChK jail in Lubyanka Square, together with Kaplan, in separate cars. Over a period of four days—from August 30 until September 2—over 40 witnesses were questioned. The last interrogation of Kaplan that is known to us was dated August 31, however.

The Kaplan interrogations at the VChK were very formal. All six interrogations were conducted during the twenty-four hours of Kaplan's arrest and were very short. She was interrogated by different people who asked the same questions. Apparently, there were no doubts that Kaplan had carried out the shooting. But Kaplan had to provide all of the evidence against her herself. The investigators had no other evidence against her. No one could identify her. No weapon had been found on her. Nothing suspicious was found.[48]

Kaplan agreed to sign the transcripts of only two of the interrogations. She possessed no information that was of interest to the VChK and could not say anything of substance about the attack on Lenin. Who had guided her actions, who had helped her track Lenin's movements, who had supplied her with the pistol? She did not provide any information on this. And it certainly wasn't because the Chekists were unable to get that evidence out of her. We need not use our imagination to wonder just how the VChK could have tortured a terrorist who had just taken a shot at the 'leader of the world revolution' if they needed to get evidence and learn the names of her accomplices. Clearly, for whatever reason, no one was genuinely interested in what Kaplan had to say.

Popova was treated differently. On the morning of August 31, Popova's husband and two daughters were also arrested and put in the VChK jail as hostages.[49] They were released by the beginning of September, and at the beginning of October

Popova herself was let go, her case being terminated for lack of evidence. Thus, the suspect Popova was held in jail and questioned for over a month, while Kaplan—who was supposedly involved in the assassination attempt and who confessed to carrying out the terrorist attack—was interrogated for one day![50]

The VChK case file on the assassination attempt against Lenin on August 30, 1918, has several pages missing: pages 11, 84, 87, 90, and 94.[51] They were removed from the file and hidden from the eyes of future investigators because they contained the testimony of witnesses who claimed that Lenin had been shot by a man. Lenin himself, who was never questioned about the incident, had also seen that the person who fired the gun was a man. At least, when Lenin regained consciousness, he asked, 'Did they catch him or not?'[52]

On September 1, on Sverdlov's orders, Kaplan was transferred from the VChK jail to a cell in the Kremlin, located under Sverdlov's office. We know about the details of Kaplan's transfer to the Kremlin from the memoirs of the Commandant of the Kremlin:

> One or two days [after the assassination attempt] I was summoned by Varlam Avanesov [A member of the VChK collegium chaired by Dzerzhinsky].
>
> 'Go to the VChK at once and get Kaplan. You will put her here, in the Kremlin, under reliable guard.'
>
> I called for a car and drove to the Lubyanka. Taking Kaplan, I brought her to the Kremlin, to a semi-basement room underneath the children's half of the Bolshoi Palace. The room was spacious, with high ceilings ... Another day or two passed and Avanesov again summoned me and showed me a VChK resolution: Kaplan was to be executed, the sentence was to be carried out by the Commandant of the Kremlin, [Pavel] Mal'kov....
>
> 'When?' I asked Avanesov quickly....
>
> 'Today. At once.'[53]

A page later the commander claims that he shot Kaplan at 3pm on September 3. Setting aside for a moment what happened with Kaplan, Sverdlov's behavior was once again inexplicable. A woman in the vicinity of the crime scene was arrested, subjected to several brief and generic interrogations by various people, taken to the Kremlin on orders from Sverdlov between August 31 and 3 September. In the Kremlin, she may or may not have been subjected to better questioning, and on September 3 she may or may not have been shot. Furthermore, since Sverdlov gave orders to 'destroy the remains without a trace,'[54] we have no material proof of Kaplan's execution apart from one author's assertion that Kaplan's corpse was doused with gasoline and burned in an iron barrel in Aleksandrovsky Garden.[55]

Ostensibly, the woman referred to as 'Kaplan' was brought to the Kremlin for the sole purpose of having her shot. It was done in a great hurry, since they shot her right there in the Kremlin, and in broad daylight. Also, after September 3, it was no longer possible to determine anything: whether the woman at the Kremlin was the detained woman with the umbrella and briefcase; whether the detained woman was the same woman who had been talking to Gil before the start of the meeting, before the attack; whether Kaplan was the assailant, that is the woman who had fired at Lenin; whether the woman shot in the Kremlin was Kaplan; or whether the woman shot in the Kremlin was the same woman who had been detained on August 31.... Who was executed in the Kremlin on September 3, 1918? The list of primary questions of evidence that could only be answered if the woman was alive is endless. Yet it was none other than Sverdlov who closed the 'case' against Kaplan by destroying the most important piece of evidence—the prisoner herself. A proper investigation was clearly the last thing he was interested in.

Since then another pivotal question has emerged about the 'Kaplan' case. Was only one woman involved in the ambush on Lenin's life? Lenin was shot four times. However, the shots were fired from two guns of different caliber—apparently a revolver and a Browning. Today, we know this because Russia's Prosecutor General twice commenced posthumous investigations into the circumstances surrounding the assassination attempt against Lenin. On June 19, 1992, the old criminal case was reopened 'due to newly uncovered circumstances'. In truth, the only new circumstance was the fall of the Soviet regime in the USSR. The investigation focused on the arraignment, sentencing, and execution of Kaplan on September 3, 1918, under an illegal resolution passed by the presidium of the VChK.

As a result, by the summer of 1996, six investigators worked on the investigation. They did not work in tandem, however, but replaced one another over the four years—each one having to start afresh with familiarizing themselves with the case. The Lubyanka (then called the 'Ministry of Security', today the 'FSB') conducted a comprehensive forensic examination of the Browning (No 150489) and the empty shells retrieved from the scene, as well as the four bullets that had hit Lenin. Its experts' examination was inconclusive. They determined that, of the two Browning bullets, one had probably been fired from this gun, but it was impossible to establish whether the second bullet had been fired from it as well. While conducting a reenactment of the crime in 1996, the Browning jammed and no longer worked. When comparing the two bullets that had been removed from Lenin's body during his operation in 1922 and the two that were removed from his corpse when it was embalmed in 1924, it was discovered that they were different. This finding cast a dramatic new light on Lenin's assassination. A second person had taken part in the shooting.

This is just the right time to return to Semenov and Konopleva. Both were Chekists planted as counterintelligence agents in the SR Party to gain information on the SR for the Soviet VChK. The SRs regarded both agents as 'one of ours', but, in fact, Semenov and Konopleva were only loyal to Dzerzhinsky's agency. Their real role at the SR was to serve as Soviet spies. This became relevant when, in 1921, the Soviet (Bolshevist) leadership decided to conduct the first show trial in Soviet history—that of the SR party. This was not without its problems. The SR was Russia's largest socialist party, and one that had an impeccable history of revolutionary combat. Its leaders included the legendary commando Boris Savinkov. Furthermore, by 1921, few trusted the Bolshevik government's 'objectivity' when it came to telling the truth. Around the world, numerous socialist parties belonging to the Second International would be following a trial of SRs closely. The prosecution could not be allowed to fail. SRs charged had to be convicted, no matter what. It was here that Semenov and Konopleva were given key roles in this case. They had to present themselves as disillusioned SR Party members and testify at the trial against the Party leadership arrested by the Chekists.

Thus, it was decided very early in 1921 that Semenov and Konopleva would join the Bolshevik Party, which had by then changed its name to Russian Communist Party (Bolsheviks). At the time, Chekists were not always members of the Bolshevik Party—that 'tradition' arose later. In the case of Semenov and Konopleva, the CC did not want any surprise moves by Dzerzhinsky agents who did not come under the Party whip. Furthermore, the two joined the Party in secret. Semenov formally joined the Party in January 1921 with recommendations from prominent Bolsheviks and secretaries of the CC.[56] Konopleva joined the Bolsheviks in February 1921. Her recommendations also came from well-known people—only Stalin was higher up in the Party.[57]

Subsequently, after the decision was taken at the end of 1921 to stage a show trial of the SR Party leadership, Konopleva and Semenov were tasked with preparing the dossier that incriminated the SR Party. On December 3, 1921, Semenov finished writing his diary exposing the SR leadership's subversive activities. The manuscript of the diary, which is stored in the archives of the SR trial, bears a handwritten note by Stalin. He liked it:

I've read this. J. Stalin.
(I think that the question of printing this document, the ways in which it might be used, and the (future) fate of the diary's author should be discussed by the Politburo.)
J. Stalin.[58]

And in fact, after the Bolsheviks successfully ended the trial, both Semenov and Konopleva were promoted to higher posts and ranks by Stalin and the Politburo of the Communist (Bolshevik) Party.

On December 5, 1921—two days after completing the document that was reviewed by Stalin personally—Semenov submitted his 'report' to the Communist (Bolshevik) CC about the anti-Soviet and subversive activities of the SR.[59] Today, it reads like flimsy provocation, badly put together and crudely scripted. However, on January 21, 1922, the Party's Politburo issued instructions to Russia's Foreign Intelligence to ensure that Semenov's dossier would appear in print abroad within two weeks. Other proactive measures by the Intelligence Services followed.

On March 2, 1922, the Berlin-based Russian émigré newspaper *Rul'* (*Steering Wheel*) made its first mention of Semenov's report. It had just been 'published' in Berlin by German publisher G. Hermann. *Rul'* was regularly used by Soviet Intelligence to plant information that needed to be 'propagated' in the foreign press. Of course, no one would have noticed the booklet otherwise. Immediately after this, it was 'reissued' in Soviet Russia. Its Russian edition guilelessly stated that the 20,000 copies had been printed by the printing office at Lubyanka, 18 (then called 'GPU').

Konopleva, in turn, put together a paper trail that backed up her own image as an SR-turncoat: an SR-whistleblower, who had repented and gone over to support the Soviet government against traitors. For the Chekists, it was important to have materials in the archives that showed that Konopleva (like Semenov) was not only a VChK operative but had also genuinely been an SR supporter. On January 15-16, Konopleva produced the goods. On January 15, 1922, she wrote a letter to the CC of the SR in which she alerted them very publicly of her intention to 'inform the CC of the Russian Communist Party about the military, combat, and terrorist activities of the SRs from the end of 1917 until the end of 1918 in St. Petersburg and Moscow.' On the same day, Konopleva testified 'officially' that the CC of the SR had prepared terrorist attacks against four Bolshevik leaders[60] in addition to Lenin. In other words, she provided the evidence required for the death sentence of the leadership of the SR Party. The letter's final words—'former member of the SR Party, member of the Russian Communist Party'—were meant to say it all.

During 1922-1924, Konopleva served in Military Intelligence (later called the GRU), gave lectures on planting explosives to Lubyanka (then called 'GPU') intelligence operatives, and then worked for the Moscow department of public education at publishing companies. Her past came back to haunt her, though. Under Stalin's Great Purge she was arrested in Moscow on April 30, 1937, 'for possession of the SR Party archives' (that is, the materials from the 1922 trials which she herself had helped prepare to execute the defendants), accused of having ties to Semenov—who by then had also been arrested—and shot on July 13, 1937. In another reversal of fortunes, of her reputation at any rate, she was rehabilitated 'for lack of a chargeable offense' on August 20, 1960, under Khrushchev.

Semenov, too, worked in Military Intelligence at the Soviet defense ministry headed by Trotsky. His major assignments in 1922 included organizing terrorist attacks against White Army military leaders.[61] In 1927, Semenov was sent to China as a resident agent for Soviet intelligence. On February 11, 1937, he was arrested and charged with participating in an anti-Soviet right-wing organization since 1928. As with Konopleva, it was claimed he had ties to former Stalin ally, Nikolai Bukharin, and under Bukharin's orders was the leader of a 'right-wing combat and terrorist organization,' for 'organizing former militant SRs into a number of terrorist groups', and of 'using these groups to prepare terrorist attacks against' the Soviet government. On October 8, 1937, the Supreme Court's military tribunal sentenced him to death and executed him on the same day. On August 22, 1961, two days after Konopleva,

Semenov's reputation was also rehabilitated. A military tribunal vacated his case because the charges against him could not be proven.[62]

Claims that Nikolai Bukharin[63] had a connection to the assassination attack on Lenin in 1918 were first entertained in 1938, during his trial. From being typecast as Bolshevik heroes in 1922, Konopleva and Semenov were now portrayed as terrorist assassins. This made Bukharin's position precarious because he had vouched for Konopleva when she joined the party in 1921 and also because, in 1922, he had acted as counsel for Semenov when the counterintelligence agent gave his evidence for the prosecution during the SRs' trial. Bukharin had done neither on his own, but had merely acted on formal resolutions passed by the CC of the Bolshevik Party. Little surprise that, on February 20, 1937, Bukharin tried to clear himself in an outraged letter to the CC in which he extolled former VChK agent Semenov:

> I cannot pass by the monstrous charge against me that I allegedly gave Semenov terrorist directives…. No mention is made here of the fact that Semenov was a Communist, a party member…. I defended Semenov in accordance with a resolution by the CC of the Party. Our party believed that Semenov had done it a great service and accepted him into its ranks…. Semenov effectively revealed all the SRs' combat groups to the Soviet government and the party. All the SRs who remained SRs considered him a 'Bolshevik provocateur.' He appeared in the role of an informer at the trial against the SRs also. The SRs hated him and avoided him like the plague.[64]

To little avail. Stalin had very little interest in the truth and Bukharin's revealing of exonerating facts changed nothing. At the trial of the 'anti-Soviet bloc of rightists and Trotskyites' in 1938, government prosecutor Andrei Vyshinsky simply continued to claim that Semenov had received terrorist directives from Bukharin personally (strictly speaking true, if the word 'terrorist' were replaced with 'Party'). Somewhat later, the *Great Soviet Encyclopedia*, published under Stalin, added the finishing touches to the rewrite of the attempt on Lenin's life:

> By now it has been incontrovertibly proven that heinous Trotskyite-Bukharinite traitors were also involved in preparing the killing of the great Lenin. Moreover, the loathsome scoundrel Bukharin was an active organizer of the villainous assassination attempt against Lenin, which had been prepared by the Right SRs and took place on August 30, 1918. On that day, Lenin spoke at a workers' meeting in the Mikhelson Factory. On leaving the factory, he was gravely wounded by Kaplan, a White-SR terrorist.[65]

In 1938, however, the great surprise was that Bukharin did not deny the most serious accusation against him—trying to murder Soviet leader Vladimir Lenin. And here is why: the Lubyanka (then called the 'NKVD') had approached its preparation of the Bukharin trial with utter dedication. During the trial, the NKVD was ready to introduce two important new witnesses. One of them was… Fanny Kaplan. After Sverdlov's demise, she had apparently come back from the dead to haunt the living.

The other one was a Vasily Novikov, a former member of the SR. On December 15, 1937, NKVD investigators had questioned Novikov, who had been arrested long before. According to Semenov's testimony at the 1922 trial, Novikov had been one of the main participants in the attack on Lenin four years prior. Dressed as a sailor, he had made two appearances on the scene: he had caused congestion near the exit when Lenin was leaving the building; and after Lenin had been shot and was lying on the ground, he ran toward him with a revolver to finish him off (but did not reach him and did not finish him off). After the shooting, Novikov had allegedly escaped in a cab that was waiting for him. Back in 1918, however, after being arrested he should clearly have shared Kaplan's 'fate' for taking part in the terrorist attack—but instead was released. Although in 1922 described as a 'perpetrator', he had somehow managed not to get shot in 1918.

As a former SR, Novikov ultimately ended up in prison and in 1937, before the Bukharin trial, the NKVD remembered his existence and questioned him. In preparation for the trial they interrogated him in prison. He 'delighted' investigators by providing the miraculous evidence that Kaplan (whom the Commandant of the Kremlin said he had killed on Sverdlov's orders), was alive and well:

Excerpt from the transcript of the interrogation of the convict Vasily Novikov, born 1883, from December 15, 1937.

Question: Have you named all the former members of the SR terrorist brigade with whom you met in subsequent years?
Answer: I omitted to mention the participant of the assassination attempt against V.I. Lenin, F. Kaplan, whom I met in the Sverdlovsk prison in 1932.
Question: Describe in detail the circumstances in which this meeting occurred.
Answer: In July 1932, in a transit prison in Sverdlovsk, during a walk in the prison yard, I met Fanny Kaplan accompanied by a guard. Even though she had greatly changed since our last meeting in Moscow in 1918, I nonetheless instantly recognized her. I did not have a chance to talk to her during this meeting. I don't know whether she recognized me—when we met, she gave no indication….
I have read this transcript and confirm its accuracy.
Novikov's signature.[66]

In the end, the NKVD decided against producing the two 'witnesses' at the Bukharin trial.[67]

4: Lenin's Resurgence

In 1918, Lenin's attitude toward the official account of Kaplan's shooting was skeptical. According to Sverdlov, by September 1, Lenin was 'cross-examining the doctors in jest.' Of course, Lenin had no time for jokes. He was cross-examining the doctors quite seriously, trying to understand what had happened and what was happening.[68]

Taken to the Kremlin after the shooting, surrounded by doctors, Lenin thought he was going to die. Vladimir Bonch-Bruevich, Lenin's executive secretary and the Secretary of the SNK—a man who was devoted to Lenin personally—was the first to come to Lenin's side, along with Bonch-Bruevich's wife, Vera Velichkina, who had medical training. Only in her presence were doctors permitted to give Lenin morphine, an overdose of which could kill a sick person. The first injection of morphine was made by Velichkina herself.

According to Bonch-Bruevich's memoirs, Lenin tried to ascertain whether he was badly hurt: "'What about the heart? It is far from the heart... The heart cannot be hurt?" Lenin asked. And then he said something very strange, as if he thought that he was being killed by his own people: "Why torture me? Why not just kill me at once?" he said quietly and fell silent, as if falling asleep.'[69]

It turned out, however, that even in a wounded state, Lenin could make things difficult for Sverdlov if he remained in the Kremlin. Let us refer to the commandant's memoirs: '[Lenin] started getting up from his bed. On September 16, for the first time after his illness, he took part in a meeting of the CC of the Russian Communist Party, and on the same evening he chaired a meeting of the SNK. Ilyich had returned to work!'[70] Good news.

Sverdlov didn't think so. His central objective was to demonstrate to party workers that the Soviet government could function perfectly well without Lenin. All of September and the first half of October, Sverdlov and another[71] took turns presiding over SNK meetings. All other top leadership posts were already Sverdlov's.[72] 'We're surviving without Vladimir Ilyich,' Sverdlov once said to Bonch-Bruevich. Can there be any doubt that Bonch-Bruevich reported this conversation to Lenin? In any case, he remembered that comment and wrote it down for our benefit.[73]

Sverdlov soon found a way of removing Lenin from the Kremlin. The Commandant of the Kremlin recalled: 'I was summoned by Yakov Sverdlov. The head of the Moscow provincial executive committee was also in his office; Yakov Sverdlov instructed the two of us to find a decent house outside the city where Ilyich could be temporarily moved, so that he might rest and recover all his strength. "Keep in mind", Yakov Sverdlov instructed us, "that no one must know about this assignment. Don't tell anyone anything. Do everything by yourselves and keep me informed".'

This was how Lenin's famous Gorki Estate entered history. It wasn't Lenin's until then but had once belonged to the former city governor of Moscow.[74] Around September 24-25 Lenin was dispatched from the Kremlin to Gorki. 'Dzerzhinsky assigned ten Chekists to provide security at Gorki, subordinating them to me. I drove them to the location… and on the following day I drove Vladimir Ilyich and Nadezhda Konstantinovna [Krupskaya, Lenin's wife] to Gorki', the Commandant recalled. There were but few visitors who made it to Gorki: Sverdlov, Stalin, Dzerzhinsky, and Bonch-Bruevich. As would repeatedly happen again in 1922-1923, Lenin was impatient to return to the Kremlin, but he was prevented from doing so. To keep Lenin in Gorki for longer, major repairs were begun in his apartment in the Kremlin.

However, it wasn't just Lenin who was 'away' in October 1918. It was Dzerzhinsky, too. In the first days of October 1918, the VChK Chair went away to Switzerland where his wife and son had been living that entire time. He was joined by a member of the VChK collegium[75] who had also featured large during the saga with the attempted assassination of Lenin and the killing of Kaplan. They traveled under assumed names and Dzerzhinsky's pseudonym was 'Domansky'. They also drastically changed their appearance: Dzerzhinsky had shaved off his beard, mustache, and hair. The trip was Sverdlov's idea. It looked, more than anything else, like an attempt by Sverdlov to protect Dzerzhinsky by sending him abroad while the recuperating Lenin and his secretary Bonch-Bruevich were investigating the circumstances of the assassination attempt.

Dzerzhinsky also seems to have been on Soviet business. His wife Sofia—whom he otherwise hadn't seen in nearly eight years—lived in Bern and worked as a secretary at the Soviet diplomatic mission which had just opened in Switzerland in September 1918. Dzerzhinsky's seven-year-old son Jan only knew his father from photos. Dzerzhinsky had not given his family advance notice of his arrival. From Bern, all three of them went to Lugano. But after only a week, Dzerzhinsky went to Berlin, leaving his family once again behind. Yet, it was not until late October that he returned to Moscow. By then, the revolution in Germany had unleashed—the very revolution that both minister of defense Trotsky[76] and the Left SR led by Dzerzhinsky had been predicting.

Events unfolded rapidly in Germany. On October 4, a new government announced that it was ready to sign a peace treaty under the terms and conditions outlined in the 'Fourteen Points' formulated by US president Woodrow Wilson.[77] On October 5, it annulled the Brest-Litovsk Treaty. On November 4, revolution began in Austria-Hungary. The next day, November 5, Austria-Hungary signed an armistice. Allied troops occupied Constantinople. A republic was proclaimed in Bulgaria. There were rumors that Kaiser Wilhelm II would abdicate. And, in fact, on November 8, a republic was proclaimed in Germany with Social Democrats coming to power. On November 11, the government of the newly proclaimed German Republic signed a ceasefire agreement in Compiegne. On November 13, at an Executive Committee meeting Sverdlov read out a resolution annulling the Brest-Litovsk agreement and on the same day the Red Army crossed into German-occupied regions formerly part of the Romanov Empire.

Thus began one of the Red Army's decisive offensives, whose aim was the establishment of a Communist regime in Europe. On November 25, the Germans were forced to leave the town of Pskov, and on November 28, the town of Narva. On the same day, the Riga Soviet of Workers' Deputies proclaimed itself to be the only legitimate government in Latvia. On November 29, a Soviet government was formed in Estonia, and on December 14, in Latvia. Meanwhile, on December 30, a Communist Party (the CPG), co-led by Rosa Luxemburg,[78] was formally created in Germany.[79]

During these days, Lenin was effectively marginalized. All key decisions regarding revolution in Germany were made by the CC of the Bolshevik Party without him. Even the decree terminating the Treaty of Brest-Litovsk was published as a decree of the Soviet parliament, signed by its Secretary Yakov Sverdlov—and not as a decision of the government—the SNK, which Lenin still headed from Gorki Estate. The revolution in Germany was young and Lenin was losing his power. The initiative at this time lay with the Party and not with the Soviet government. With Luxemburg and Trotsky in charge of the ideological side of the Communist World Revolution, and with Sverdlov and Luxemburg's co-leader Karl Liebknecht in charge of the practical side, Lenin was ceasing to be pre-eminent. It may have been precisely for this reason that, while Liebknecht and Luxemburg were still alive, he waited with founding the Third International ('Comintern') to organize Communist civil war across borders.

But once again, Lenin got lucky. The defeat of the Communist revolutions in Germany and later in Hungary stemmed Lenin's loss of power in Soviet Russia. On January 15, 1919, his rivals for the crown of the international Communist movement, Luxemburg and Liebknecht, were murdered and the Communist revolution in Germany was crushed. As it turned out, the wave of revolutions of 1917-1919 fell apart along with it as well. Russia remained World Communism's only triumph.

Having fully recovered from his injury, Lenin set out to settle scores with his foes within the Party and to regain the authority that had nearly slipped away from him. Because of the 'Kaplan' case, Lenin of course suspected Sverdlov of being behind the plot to assassinate him. When Sverdlov returned to Moscow from a trip to the provinces on March 8, 1919, it was reported the next that the 33-year-old Sverdlov had fallen 'gravely ill', having caught the Spanish 'flu. Eight days later he died. However, Sverdlov's niece Ida Averbach[80] was known to say that 'Uncle Yakov did not die a natural death.' Did he die of natural causes, or not? It is certainly true that his untimely death was the first instance of a particularly deadly affliction that started to grip those vying to lead Russia—much like 'suicide' seems to be a common cause of death among those who challenge Vladimir Putin's Kremlin.

The coded language of the memoirs left by leading members of the Bolshevik old guard who managed to survive Stalin's purges is not always easy to understand. Lenin's executive secretary Bonch-Bruevich, who died in 1955, was one of them. He had constantly been at Lenin's side and was no ordinary secretary. From the first days of the revolution, he had headed an informal group created even before the VChK that acted as Lenin's personal Intelligence Service or, rather, internal counterintelligence. There was little that he wasn't aware of. Many things must be read between the lines, a very common phenomenon in the Soviet era. Bonch-Bruevich's recollections contain the following lines on Lenin's visit to Sverdlov, before the latter's death on March 16, at 4:55am:

Fall of 1918… In the Kremlin, over the course of two days, three women died of the Spanish flu. Vladimir Ilyich was in the country, recovering from his serious wounds. After receiving news of the deaths of the women, he expressed the most heartfelt condolences to their families and gave instructions for providing them with assistance. Not a month went by before Yakov Sverdlov came down with the same Spanish flu…. One had to see how concerned Vladimir Ilyich was…. By this time, he was already living in the Kremlin… Despite doctors' warnings about the fact that the Spanish flu was highly contagious, Vladimir Ilyich came to the bedside of the dying [Sverdlov]… and looked right into Yakov Sverdlov's eyes. Yakov Sverdlov grew silent, became thoughtful, and whispered: 'I am dying…. Farewell.'[81]

From Bonch-Bruevich's memoirs, it follows that Sverdlov was still alive when Lenin came to see him, but dying when he left.

This melodramatic passage from Bonch-Bruevich's memoirs, makes little sense however. First, the detailed anecdote is framed by the fact that three women in the Kremlin died of Spanish 'flu in two days—making the point exactly how virulent the lethal disease was—a month prior to Sverdlov's death. It emphasizes the question, how many people would have piously gone to sit at Sverdlov's 'bedside' if the latter had indeed been contagiously ill with the lethal Spanish 'flu? Lenin himself was always very careful and, in any case, busy organizing the Communist Third International.

Did Bonch-Bruevich really expect the reader to believe that after the hand of man had narrowly failed to strike him down in August, Lenin would have challenged the hand of god in March for man trying to oust him? Oddly, nor does Bonch-Bruevich tell the reader that one of the three women who died in the 'fall of 1918' was very close to him: his wife Velichkina, a doctor of the same age as Lenin. She died on September 30, five or six days after Lenin's departure for Gorki—something Bonch-Bruevich more than anyone would have known. Thus, for those who knew all the facts, six months rather than 'not a month' separated the two events he grouped together in his carefully crafted but unbelievable vignette. However, all these conflicting clues make perfect sense if the well-informed arch-survivor Bonch-Bruevich really logged the vicious assassinations decimating the Bolshevik top rather than the crocodile tears caused by a virus. And why—having lost his wife—he continued to severely control access at Gorki Estate to the recuperating Lenin from September 1918.

Assassinations were plentiful in the spring of 1919. Only in March 1919, two months after the leaders of the German Communist Party and Lenin's rivals for leadership in the Communist International were murdered, and immediately following the mysterious death of Sverdlov—Lenin's rival for leadership in the Bolshevik Party—did Lenin convene the first Comintern congress, initiating the practice of breaking up Western Communist parties and handpicking delegates to suit Soviet ends. As head of the Communist International, he appointed a Bolshevik who had not written a single theoretical article, but who was a skillful party operator.[82] And since the German revolution had suffered an obvious defeat, Soviet Russia became officially the center of the world Communist movement.[83]

Despite Sverdlov's failed attempt to isolate and oust Lenin, the head of Soviet Intelligence, Dzerzhinsky, retained his post upon his return to Russia from a trip abroad. He even got promoted. On March 30, 1919, fourteen days after Sverdlov's death, he was appointed as Soviet interior minister. Dzerzhinsky was not only 'Iron Felix,' he turned out to be 'Unsinkable Felix' as well. His new ally in continued battle with Lenin was Sverdlov's successor at the secretariat of the Communist (Bolshevik) Party CC—Joseph Stalin. At the time, Stalin did not yet call himself 'General Secretary' as the post did not yet exist.

With Sverdlov dead and the Communism revolution scythed in Germany, Lenin seemed once again all-powerful by 1922. He had ended military conflicts at home and abroad, formed the Union of Soviet Socialist Republics (by the end of 1922), negotiated peace treaties with virtually all neighboring countries, established control over the Third International, now called Comintern, and won full recognition as the ideological and de facto leader of the international Communist movement. Although he had lost the shine of invincibility in the intervening years, the star of the 53-year-old Lenin seemed once again in the ascendant.

5: Dzerzhinsky's Elimination of Lenin

It was at that very moment that 52-year-old Lenin suddenly fell 'gravely ill'—like Communist Party secretary Sverdlov three years prior. He suffered a stroke in May, 1922, that was both to end his political career and terminate the supremacy of the Soviet government, as Russia's pre-eminent seat of power. For historians, the subject of Lenin's illness and death has long been shrouded in mystery. Yet it would be fitting to call it the point of departure for all Soviet history. The accepted view has been that Stalin as Party Secretary may have had a hand in accelerating Lenin's death. At least, he has been seen as virtually the only Soviet leader who had no interest in seeing the leader of the Soviet SNK regain his health.

But this ignores the fact that it was Dzerzhinsky, the chair of the VChK, who led the conspiracy to end Lenin's rule. He and his people were responsible for Lenin's physical decline. In this context it is worth noting in particular that in 1921, under an initiative handled by Dzerzhinsky's deputy Genrikh Yagoda—'the pharmacist Yagoda' as Trotsky called him—a special toxicological laboratory was created by the Lubyanka. It subsequently became known as 'the special office' or 'Laboratory No 12.' Through his seat on the SNK and the Cheka, of course, Dzerzhinsky was aware that Lenin's health continued to be affected by the 1918 attempt to murder him. But since Lubyanka has not exactly been generous to historians in releasing its internal historical documents, it's more difficult to say what exactly was happening in Dzerzhinsky's agency in relation to Lenin as opposed to the impeccable records of the Communist Party of which Stalin was the secretary.

In Dzerzhinsky's plot to remove Lenin from power, Stalin looked after the political side of things. As the Communist (Bolsheviks) were the only political party left in Russia, its significance, and therefore Stalin as inheritor of the powerful role Sverdlov had created, was in the ascendant. Stalin's formal appointment as General Secretary of the Party in April 1922 was not the beginning of his rise to power but an acknowledgement of the fact that he had already concentrated sizeable power in his own hands. Two factors had made Stalin's ascent possible at the very beginning of the 1920s: Stalin's personal qualities combined with Lenin's continuing weak health due to the wounds inflicted by the failed assassination, which prevented this subtle psychologist of internecine strife from noticing the rise of his nemesis.

Lenin's demands—political and personal—were being sabotaged by the Party secretariat, where Stalin oversaw everything. By mid-1921 the Party's Politburo had placed him in charge of organizational work of the CC. His job included preparations for CC plenary meetings, executive committee sessions, and so forth, which meant that he was in essence carrying out all the tasks of a General Secretary, even though this post was not created for him until a year later.

In mid-1922, against his wishes, Lenin was removed as SNK chair as a result of a conspiracy involving a large number of Bolshevik Party chiefs. To be exact, it involved the entire Party leadership except Trotsky and members of Lenin's family. Battling on Lenin's side, they too were involved in the dramatic events of those days. However, since they were in a minority, they were unable to prevent his demotion.

The next stage followed shortly after Lenin's removal. On May 23, Lenin left for Gorki to get some rest, and it was here, while away, that he had his first serious stroke on May 25-27. It left his right arm and leg partially paralyzed and his speech impaired. A letter written on June 10, 1922 by a member of the Party secretariat alludes to Lenin's predicament and reveals that Dzerzhinsky was openly thought of as Lenin's most-likely successor:[84]

> Things are so bad with Ilyich that we cannot even gain access to him. Dzerzhinsky and [Pyotr] Smidovich protect him, like two bulldogs, from all outsiders and permit no one in to see him or even to enter [Gorki Estate] that he occupies. I believe this tactic to be senseless since it leads only to the dissemination of fabrications and the most incredible rumors.... At the present time no one can stand forth openly except Dzerzhinsky, and Trotsky's much-vaunted popularity is simply a myth....[85]

As early as June 10, then, there was talk that Dzerzhinsky had isolated Lenin and was the only party leader who could publicly aspire to his position—and that it was desirable to create a 'directorate' as a counterweight to Lenin on the one hand, and to Dzerzhinsky's pretensions on the other. There was talk as well of Stalin being the only man in the Party who understood what the power play was behind the scenes.

Things moved fast. *Rul'* in Berlin reported on June 15 that Stalin had formed a 'troika' with two other members of the Party's Politburo who would informally take over Lenin's role as Party leader—without making a public announcement:

> In view of Lenin's departure from government, a 'troika' has been formed ... Trotsky is not a part of this 'troika'... The Bolsheviks want to get everything done on the quiet. The purpose of the troika will not be officially announced; there is only an unofficial Communist Party resolution.

On June 18, *Rul'* published yet another important document which brought up Lenin's poisoning and referred to him as the 'former' Chair of Russia's SNK:

> Official communique of Lenin's illness: the Soviet government's communique of

Lenin's illness states that

Vladimir Ilyich Lenin, former chair of the SNK, is suffering from severe exhaustion whose effects have been complicated by poisoning. To regain his strength, Comrade Lenin must for an extended period, and at least until the fall, remove himself from all matters of government and refrain from any activity. He is considered likely to return to political work after a period of prolonged rest, since in the opinion of the medical authorities a restoration of his strength is possible.

A White émigré anti-revolutionary newspaper, *Rul'* was not, and could not, be the best-informed source on Soviet Russia. However, this article replicates an official communique. Presumably, as before, a leading party functionary deliberately leaked this sensational document about Lenin's retirement, which was disclosed nowhere else.

On June 30, in an article entitled 'Lenin's Illness,' *Rul'* quoted Professor Georg Klemperer (a renowned internist and cousin of the famous conductor) who had just returned from one of his visits to Moscow where he had been invited to treat Lenin. He reported that Lenin was not suffering from 'progressive paralysis' but from 'stomach poisoning'. This was the second report in June to mention Lenin's poisoning, or to be more precise, the poisoning of his food:

First, Lenin's present condition is in no way related to his wounds. Furthermore, rumors about Lenin's progressive paralysis have no basis in fact. We have performed a Wasserman test and have obtained negative results. Cerebral fluid was tested and showed no signs of syphilis and in general a diagnosis of progressive paralysis may be ruled out. Lenin is suffering from extreme exhaustion.... Stomach poisoning has further exacerbated the state of his health.

Next, on July 19, *Rul'* reported that one of the Party troika, Alexei Rykov, had taken over Lenin's role as head of the government: 'Rykov's name in the list of government officials present was followed by his new title of Chair of the SNK, from which it became clear that Rykov had replaced Lenin in the post of SNK Chair.'

Who, then, was poisoning Lenin during this entire period with such dedication? And, if a medical expert was convinced Lenin was suffering from poisoning, why was it not being investigated by either Dzerzhinsky's agency or the Politburo?

Years later, Lenin's defense minister Trotsky provided answers to these questions. In October 1939, the former SNK member wrote a sensational article in which he disclosed, for the first time, the possible poisoning of Lenin by Stalin. This was after Trotsky's comrades-in-arms and friends as well as members of his family had been eliminated one by one; after the show trial of Party and government leaders in Moscow and the executions of senior military officers; and after Stalin had signed his non-aggression pact with Hitler. Dzerzhinsky was, of course, also long dead at this point.

The article may have been Trotsky's first attempt to make public what he knew. If his revelations, which bordered on Soviet treason, had been received with interest in the West, perhaps Trotsky might have become more talkative. But the free world remained silent. No one was interested in Trotsky's exposé at the time. The Soviet Union's leftist sympathizers did not want to endanger Stalin and the Socialist order he represented, while the anti-Soviet right suspected Trotsky of being as much a liar as any other Communist. No one yet understood the scope of Stalin's murderousness. Trotsky's article, written for US weekly *Life* magazine and submitted by him on Friday, October 13, 1939, however, was never published by them.

Having wasted ten months on it, Trotsky gave up waiting and published an abridged version of the article in US weekly *Liberty*—he received top billing on the cover but shared it with the picture of an ice skater and headline 'Clark Gable's Secret Wish'—on 27 January 1940. In the article, he revealed that Stalin had in February, 1923, told members of the Politburo, after the secretaries left, that Lenin had asked for poison to be able to commit suicide in case his illness progressed to an unbearable state.

Did [Lenin's] student [Stalin] take any measures to accelerate his teacher's death? I, more than anyone, understand the monstrosity of such an allegation... Two years ago, I first wrote down facts that were once (1923-1924) known to not more than seven or eight persons, and only in part. The only ones among them who are still alive, apart from myself, are Stalin and Molotov.... During Lenin's second illness, probably in February 1923,[86] at a meeting of the Politburo, after the secretary left, Stalin informed the members of the Politburo (Grigory Zinoviev, Lev Kamenev, and me) that [Lenin] had unexpectedly summoned him and demanded that poison be brought to him....

He then describes Stalin's shifty demeanor as he shared this information with his Politburo colleagues.

I remember how unusual, mysterious, and strange Stalin's face looked. The request that he had told us about was a tragic one; but his face was frozen in a half-smile, like a mask. I had observed a similar incongruity between his words and his facial expression on earlier occasions. This time, it was completely unbearable. The horror was further augmented by the fact that Stalin did not express any opinion about Lenin's request, apparently waiting to see what the others would say: did he want to get a sense of the others' reactions without committing himself? Or did he have some other idea in the back of his mind?... There was no vote, the discussion was not a formal one, but we parted with the self-evident conclusion that delivering poison was out of the question.... But I now ask myself another, more far-reaching question: Did Lenin really ask Stalin for poison? What if Stalin made up this whole story to prepare his own alibi? He didn't have the slightest reason to fear that we would check up on him: none of us would have asked the ailing Lenin if he had really asked Stalin for poison....[87]

As if that wasn't sensational enough, Trotsky then accused Stalin outright of murdering Lenin one way or another.

More than ten years before the famous Moscow trials, on a summer evening, on a veranda at a dacha [summer house], over a bottle of wine, Stalin confessed to his allies at the time, Kamenev [the third member of the Politburo troika], and Dzerzhinsky, that the greatest pleasure in life was to clearly identify the enemy, to prepare everything thoroughly, to take one's revenge mercilessly, and then to go to bed.... Whether Stalin delivered poison to Lenin, with a hint that the doctors had given up all hope of recovery, or whether he resorted to more direct measures, I don't know. But I know for certain that Stalin could not just sit around and wait passively while his fate was hanging by a thread and he could resolve things simply by moving his hand.[88]

Not long after, Trotsky himself was assassinated shortly after he arrived in Mexico in exile on 21 August, 1940. He was murdered by Ramon Mercader, a Lubyanka ('NKVD') operative who had infiltrated Trotsky's inner circle much earlier.

In 1983, forty years later but a decade before the fall the USSR, the topic of Lenin's death was also addressed by Abdurakhman Avtorkhanov, an elite Soviet historian of Chechen origin who escaped from the Soviet Union during World War II and became a founder of Radio Free Europe. His article addressed the possibility that Stalin poisoned Lenin and was entitled, 'Did Stalin Kill Lenin?'[89]

Among the Georgian party elite... there were persistent rumors that Lenin did not die of natural causes but was killed by swallowing poison that had been given to him by Stalin. This story appeared in several different versions—Stalin was either supposed to have given this poison to Lenin at the latter's insistence, to save him from horrible torment, or else he was supposed to have poisoned Lenin through an agent-doctor ... (who even had a name). According to another version, Stalin found a Georgian folk healer for Lenin... who did not heal Lenin but medicated him to death with poisonous herbs. It is interesting that poison invariably figures in all versions of the story, as if Stalin really did bring Lenin a little vial of poison.[90]

There seems good evidence that poison induced Lenin's first stroke of May 25-27, 1922. Here, a trial statement about plans to murder Lenin by Semenov, Lubyanka's counterintelligence agent working undercover at the SR, corroborates that this was the case. Semenov testified during the trial (June 8 to August 7, 1922) that the SRs, 'believed it was possible to poison Lenin by slipping something like that in his meals, or to plant a doctor who would infect him with a dangerous disease'.[91] These assassination plans attributed to the SRs were being falsified precisely during the months when someone was feeding Lenin poison. Later, not surprising given the success with Lenin, Stalin's *modus operandi* when disposing of his enemies during the thirty years of his reign would be 'slipping poison into meals' or 'planting a doctor'.

Still, is it possible that Lenin himself might indeed have wanted to commit suicide and asked Stalin to provide poison and assist with euthanasia? Let us trace the chronology of Lenin's conflict with Stalin from 25 May 1922 to his death on 21 January 1924. On September 11, 1923, a council of physicians that had convened in Gorki gave Lenin the all clear. For the first time since the May stroke, he was ready to return to work at the beginning of October.

On the following day, September 12, Lenin was visited at Gorki by Stalin who spoke with him for over two hours. It stands to reason that the conversation touched on the draft resolution to improve federal relations between Soviet Russia and the other Soviet republics which were due to form the USSR at the end of the year. This was called the 'nationalities issue'.

On September 22, Lenin asked Stalin to acquaint himself with a new draft and other documents pertaining to the issue. A committee meeting had been scheduled for September 23 to approve a resolution negotiated by Stalin that Ukraine, Belorussia, Georgia, Armenia, and Azerbaijan would enter the USSR as autonomous republics. However, only the CCs of Armenia and Azerbaijan supported his proposal. The CC of Georgia (Stalin's home state) was one to insist on the preservation of 'all attributes of independence' in the republics. On September 26, Stalin visited Lenin in Gorki to discuss the impasse—referred to as the 'Georgian question'. After a lengthy conversation that lasted two hours and forty minutes, Stalin agreed with some of Lenin's amendments. On October 2, Lenin returned to his office in the Kremlin where he carried on working without health interruptions for another 74 more days.

December 12 was a day like any other. In the morning, Lenin arrived in Moscow from Gorki and at 11.15am he entered his office in the Kremlin. He then went to his apartment. At noon, he returned to the Kremlin and spoke with his SNK deputies until 2pm.[92] At 5:30pm, Lenin came back to his office and spoke on the phone. From 6:00 until 6:45pm, he talked to Dzerzhinsky, who had returned from Tiflis, Georgia, about an 'incident' involving the Georgian CC.[93] A faction of Georgian Bolsheviks wanted to remain an autonomous state within the USSR rather than be subsumed under a Russian Federation. The rest of the evening he devoted to the question of the Russian state's monopoly on foreign trade, and at 8.15pm he went home.

However, December 12, 1922 was anything but a day like any other. It turned out to be the last day of Lenin's work in his Kremlin office. What happened?

'On the eve of my illness, Dzerzhinsky told me about the work of the [CC] and about the "incident", and this had a very bad effect on me.' Lenin's private secretary[94] recorded as his words. But Dzerzhinsky could not have told Lenin anything new about that. He had already known about the 'incident' for some time. The conversation with Dzerzhinsky must have been about something else altogether.

On December 13, citing his deteriorating health, Lenin dramatically issued a public announcement that he was resigning. In reality, he was healthy and fit for work rather than affected by the 'incident' in Georgia. At any rate, there had been little evidence of deteriorating health for the previous 74 days. If Dzerzhinsky's visit on 12 December had a 'bad effect' it must have been because he was told that a decision had been reached to remove him from the Kremlin. On December 12, Dzerzhinsky succeeded in doing this and he gave him three days to wrap up his affairs.

Lenin spent all three days that followed—December 13, 14, and 15—working as hard as before. He knew his working days in the Kremlin had come to an end. But he was down but not out. Significantly, on December 13, he dictated to one of his personal secretaries a letter to Trotsky proposing an alliance against Stalin (she promptly informed Stalin). He continued to discuss matters of state over the phone and with people who came to see him.

On the morning of December 16, Lenin dictated another letter to his wife Krupskaya. But at 11am, two doctors[95] turned up at the Kremlin and demanded that Lenin return to Gorki to be placed under guard of Dzerzhinsky's 'bulldogs'. That was, evidently, the agreement Dzerzhinsky and Lenin had reached on December 12.

Lenin tried to outwit Dzerzhinsky once more. He categorically refused to go. Offering to compromise, he asked that Stalin be informed that he was willing not to speak at the Congress of the Soviets, where the first item on the agenda would be the 'nationalities issue'—which of the republics would remain autonomous. But since Lenin had publicly resigned, his concessions had ceased to matter. The two doctors, on Stalin's orders, instead forbade Lenin to work—that is, blocked him from exercising what power he had left.

On December 18, a postponed plenary meeting of the Russian Communist (Bolshevik) Party CC took place, with Stalin presenting his draft for a treaty of union among the Soviet republics. Lenin was excluded (Stalin's 'doctors' did not allow Lenin to take part in it). Wary of Lenin's endless attempts to cling on to power, Stalin also put to the CC a resolution that gave him the 'responsibility to ensure compliance with the treatment that doctors have established for Lenin.'[96] In other words, the CC's plenary meeting didn't agree to remove Lenin from power. Rather, it was even worse. They made Lenin Stalin's ward and removed from him the freedom to decide whether he followed doctors' orders or not.

Not that it probably mattered to the CC, but the medical case for enforced rest was dubious. On 20 December, Lenin was visited by Dr Otfried Foerster—a famous German neuropathologist who was a consultant to Lenin's physician. Foerster said, 'His continued complete isolation from any form of activity would not have been able to retard the progress of his illness. For [Lenin] work was life, and inactivity signaled death.'[97] The enforced 'treatment' overseen by Stalin equaled house arrest in anything but name in the absence of a medical reason. The CC plenum's resolution left very little wriggle room. Everything Lenin was allowed to do was subject to Stalin's agreement: 'Comrade Stalin shall be personally responsible for ensuring Vladimir Ilyich's rest, in terms of both his personal contacts with colleagues and his correspondence.'[98]

Evidently, the events of December 12-18 had less to do with Lenin's health than with putting the revolutionary leader under Stalin's supervision. And so, banished from the Kremlin, with Stalin appointed (or more precisely, appointing himself) as Lenin's jailer, Lenin was forgotten about for a while. At least, that's what Dzerzhinsky and Stalin were hoping for.

On December 21, however, Lenin's wife Krupskaya took a letter to Trotsky dictated by him. Technically this did not violate the Party's resolution. The CC had made Stalin personally responsible for Lenin adhering to doctor's orders. If a doctor gave Lenin permission to write a letter and his wife was the conduit, no one was at fault—not even Stalin, as doctor's orders were being strictly observed.

Lev Davidovich,
Dr Foerster has permitted Vladimir Ilyich to dictate a letter today, and he has dictated the following letter to you.

Comrade Trotsky,
It's as if you managed to take win simply without firing a single shot. I urge you not to stop but to continue the offensive, and, to this end, put through a motion to raise at the Party Congress the question of strengthening the foreign trade monopoly and improving its implementation. This should be announced to the group of the Congress of Soviets. I hope you will not disagree and will not refuse to report to the group.
Lenin.

V.I. also asks that he be telephoned with [Trotsky's] reply.
N.K. Ulyanova [Krupskaya].[99]

Taken at face value, this cryptic letter suggests that Lenin had lost his mind. He had just been removed from office and forbidden to work, forbidden to meet with people, and forbidden to correspond with people. Yet here he was reaching out on Soviet 'foreign trade policy'. It begs the question whether Lenin realized that Stalin had been officially appointed as his minder. He had not attended the CC meeting of 18 December and had been cut off from contact with the outside world two days prior. However, Lenin was not naïve about Stalin. It was not by accident that he had Krupskaya take down this letter, rather than his personal secretary. He was trying to reach out to Trotsky in secret. However, Trotsky, who did know about the CC's resolution, also knew that he couldn't respond. A phone call to Lenin required Stalin's 'agreement' lest it would jeopardize Lenin's 'recovery'.

Lenin's letter to Trotsky did not remain a secret for long. On the very next day, December 22, Stalin called Krupskaya to scold her, threatening her with punishment for disobeying the Party with a CC sanction. Insulting her, he also told her that if this ever happened again, he would announce to the world that an early Bolshevik recruit, Alexandra Artyukhina, was Lenin's real wife.

The accepted view is that Krupskaya did not tell Lenin about Stalin's call to her for more than two months—until March 5, 1923—since that was the day on which Lenin wrote Stalin an emotional letter, threatening to break off relations with him. It is clear, however, that Krupskaya did tell Lenin about everything on the same day (as indeed Stalin would have expected her to do). On the night of December 22, Lenin's health rapidly deteriorated. According to Lenin's sister,[100] the next night Lenin's illness 'spread, his right arm and his right leg became paralyzed. From then on, Vladimir Ilyich could no longer write on his own.' Had someone been 'planted' to give a helping medical hand? Stalin could behave like a boor to Krupskaya on 22 December because he was risking nothing. A cunning politician, Stalin would not have wanted to upset Lenin unless he considered him entirely harmless. Stalin knew he held all the cards by now. And what else did he tell her? His real intentions to terminate Lenin? Krupskaya's own response was extreme. Lenin's sister recounts, 'She was not herself at all: she sobbed, rolled on the floor, etc.'[101]

The most important proof of the fact that Lenin knew about Stalin's phone call to his wife came from Lenin himself. The next day, he began his 'Last Testament.' On 23 December, he realized that not only his days as titular leader were numbered, but also his life. He had to dispense as many instructions as possible in whatever time remained to him. At the same time, he had no intention of passively waiting for assassination as can be judged from the number of articles, letters, and notes he produced after December 22. As he began dictating these documents, he pursued two avenues: on the one hand, to compile a testament; and, on the other, to assemble a dossier against Stalin that would undermine his authority in the party.

Neither of these were to have any effect. Lenin failed to see what he ought to have seen: all of his personal secretaries were betraying him to Stalin. The conspiracy woven around Lenin had become so broad and so irreversible that Stalin could operate almost out in the open. The articles and letters that Lenin wrote against him were immediately deposited by Lenin's secretaries with Stalin himself in accordance with the CC instruction regarding Lenin's health. Stalin then, of course, could decide what to do with them. When Lenin's 'Last Testament' was brought to Stalin, he—in the presence of several party leaders—ordered that it be burned.[102]

Stalin struck back by hemming Lenin in further. By the morning of December 24, Lenin's doctors practically forbade him to do any work. Lenin retaliated and issued an ultimatum. If he was not permitted to dictate his 'diaries', at least for a short period of time a day, then he would 'completely refuse to undergo treatment.'[103] It was the equivalent of declaring a hunger strike. This threat worked. This was because, since the CC had made Stalin responsible for Lenin's recovery, it could be argued Stalin was failing in his task if Lenin refused to be treated. Or it worked because Stalin knew that if Lenin refused to undergo treatment, his health might improve as he would no longer receive the poison that was killing him.

Lenin's ultimatum on treatment was discussed, not by his doctors—who had little say in the matter—but by Stalin's faction in the Party's Politburo.[104] It made the following decisions:

Vladimir Ilyich Lenin is to be accorded the right to dictate for five to ten minutes a day, but he is not to write letters and not to expect a reply to his notes. Visits are forbidden.

Neither friends nor domestics are to convey to Vladimir Ilyich any information about politics, so as not to provide thereby occasion for reflection and agitation.[105]

In other words, Lenin was allowed to do some writing but was not allowed to touch pen and paper himself. Only his secretaries could do any writing (and thus Stalin could promptly be brought up to date on what had been written). Lenin was restricted to five minutes of dictation and forbidden to give instructions to his secretary and stenographer. These were really, of course, meant as orders to the staff around Lenin to disregard Lenin if he tried to overrule the CC restrictions.

By now, Lenin perceived his condition as nothing less than a prison: 'If I were free (initially misspeaking himself, then repeating it with a laugh: if I were free), I could easily do all this myself,' he told his secretary on February 1, 1923.[106] Instead, Lenin lay in bed and said with disappointment: 'You won't be able to stop me from thinking! I'm lying and thinking all the same!'[107] Krupskaya recalled: 'That was a terrible thing during the time of his illness. When the doctors told him he couldn't read or work at all. I think that was wrong. Ilyich often said to me: "They can't … stop me from thinking".'

Krupskaya also alluded to incarceration and wrote about this time: 'During the illness, there was a time when I told him, in the presence of a nurse, that, you know, you're recovering your speech, just slowly. Look at it as a temporary imprisonment'.[108]

When on December 24, Lenin finished dictating the second half of the letter to one of his secretaries,[109] he was so concerned by the possibility of leaks that he repeatedly emphasized to her the need to maintain confidentiality:

'What was dictated yesterday, December 23, and today, December 24, is highly classified'… the diary is… 'highly classified. No one should know about it yet. Up to and including the members of the CC'… He emphasized this on more than one occasion. He demanded that everything he dictated be kept in a special place, with strict accountability, and considered absolutely secret.

All these demands of Lenin's were carefully recorded in the *Journal of Lenin's Secretaries* she kept for Stalin and immediately relayed to him.

'Afraid of upsetting Lenin, I did not tell him that Stalin was already familiar with the first excerpt of his letter to the Congress,' she recalled, downplaying the situation. What she should perhaps have said was 'afraid of killing Lenin' or 'afraid of striking Lenin down on the spot'. It is not difficult to imagine how Lenin would have reacted had he been told by her that Stalin was getting word of everything that was happening and that, pursuant to a Politburo decision, every part of his life was under minute surveillance.

Lenin dictated at a steady pace from December 23 through January 23, that is, for exactly a month, after which there was another unexpected intermission. On January 24 he ordered a secretary[110] 'to ask Dzerzhinsky or Stalin for materials from the commission on the Georgian [autonomy] question' and met head-on with strong opposition from both of them. Dzerzhinsky sent his secretary to Stalin, who declined citing the Politburo resolution. Lenin now began to suspect his secretary of double-dealing: 'First of all, about our "secret" business: I know that you are being dishonest with me.' To her assurances to the contrary, he replied: 'I have my own opinion about that.' On January 25, a Thursday, Lenin asked if the materials had arrived. She replied that Dzerzhinsky would have them on Saturday. When Dzerzhinsky visited on Saturday, he said that Stalin had the materials.

On February 1, a Monday, the issue somehow reached the Politburo which gave permission for the materials to be released to Lenin, but only on the condition that Lenin's secretary would retain them for study (which is all that Lenin apparently wanted) and that she would not brief Lenin on them without Politburo permission. In other words, the Politburo had handed over the materials but would not allow Lenin access to them, leaving them in the possession of his secretary, Stalin's spy.

While Lenin was once again on the war path, Stalin was not sitting still either. On Saturday January 27, a few days before the CC's tragicomedy regarding the Georgian autonomy documents, Stalin distributed to the provincial committees of the Russian Communist Party a confidential letter on Lenin's most recent articles. It was issued in the name of the Politburo.[111] The gist of their letter was that Lenin was ill and could no longer be held responsible for his own statements.

On 12 February, a new round of measures to increase Lenin's isolation followed. At the same time, he had another heart attack. The entry in the *Journal of Lenin's Secretaries* for Stalin read:

[Lenin] is worse. A bad headache. He called me in for a few minutes. [Lenin's sister][112] said that the doctors had upset him so much that his lips were trembling. The previous day, Foerster had said that he was categorically forbidden to have newspapers, to meet with anyone, or to receive any political information.... [Lenin] has developed the impression that it is not the doctors who are giving instructions to the CC, but the CC that has given its instructions to the doctors.

Lenin finally understood that something was going on. Increasingly suspicious, he was more and more often 'categorically refusing to take his medications' and demanding that 'he be relieved of the doctors' presence.' The patient realized that it was the people hired by Dzerzhinsky and Stalin who were shortening his life.

Did it make any difference? Testimony has come down to us that it did not. There is the testimony of Boris Nicolaevsky, a well-known and well-respected historian who collected a vast archive on the Russian Revolution, now stored at the Hoover Institution at Stanford University. While awaiting trial, one of his contacts heard one of Lenin's cooks, who was also being detained, admit to mixing drugs with Lenin's food.

[I] was acquainted with an émigré of the war years…. In the Chelyabinsk pretrial detention facility, she had met an old convict who in 1922-1924 had worked as a cook in Gorki, where the ailing Lenin was living at the time. This old man confessed to my acquaintance that he had added drugs to Lenin's food that made his condition worse. He did this on the instructions of people whom he considered to be Stalin's representatives…. If we consider this story to be true, then Stalin's announcement to the Politburo—the one related by Trotsky—has a definite meaning: Stalin was creating an alibi for himself in case people should find out about the work of the poisoner-cook.[113]

But our story has another interesting aspect. According to reminiscences of Vladimir Putin in 2000, his grandfather Spiridon Putin worked as a cook his entire life: first in the kitchens at the Gorki Estate, 'where Lenin and the entire Ulyanov family lived. Then, after Lenin died, Grandpa was transferred to one of Stalin's dachas.'[114] Unlike Lenin's cook in Nicolaevsky's testimony, however, Spiridon was never arrested and seemed to have thrived following Lenin's death, dying of natural causes. Putin agreed this was unusual. In his words, 'Few people who spent much time around Stalin came through unscathed, but my grandfather was one of them. He outlived Stalin.' Thus, it is entirely possible that Putin's grandfather was one of Dzerzhinsky's agents who poisoned Lenin and that he continued to serve the Cheka and Stalin faithfully after Lenin's death with other tasks related to the Lenin family and in-laws as further described below. Putin's father had also worked for the NKVD (like Spiridon, he enjoyed being in the kitchen and 'was the one who usually cooked at home… [in a cramped kitchen that was no more than 'a dark square hallway, without windows']… Nobody could make aspic like he did').

Stalin died a few months after Putin was born, and Spiridon himself died when his grandson was a teenager. In his 'retirement years he was a cook at the Moscow City Party Committee sanitorium in Ilinskoye where his grandson 'used to come for visits… [and] when relatives came to visit there would be long chats around the table, and I would catch some snatches, some fragments of the conversation'.

6: Lenin's Premature Death (Felix Dzerzhinsky)

On 14 February (two weeks after the Politburo 'released' the documents on the Georgian question), the entry in Lenin's secretaries' journal read:

> [Lenin] called me in at 1pm. He has no headache. He said that he is completely healthy. That his is a nervous illness and is such that he is sometimes completely healthy—that is, his head is completely clear—and sometimes he is worse. So, we should make haste to carry out his instructions, since he most certainly wants to have something ready for congress and hopes to be able to do that. But if we drag it out and thereby ruin it all, then he will be ever so cross… He spoke again about his three points, and in particular about the one thing that bothers him most of all, that is, Georgian [autonomy]. He requested urgency. He gave some instructions.[115]

His instructions were also connected with the Georgian question.[116] No doubt all this was passed on to Stalin before the day was out. Lenin was evidently well enough to work between February 15 and March 5. But on March 5 at around noon, he called his secretary in and asked her to take down two letters.[117] The first letter written on March 5 was another coded message to Trotsky:

> I would greatly urge you to take up the defense of the Georgian question in the CC. This case is currently being 'championed' by Stalin and Dzerzhinsky, and I cannot count on their impartiality. Quite the contrary. If you were to agree to take up the defense, then I could rest easy. If for some reason you do not agree, then return the entire case file to me. I will take that as a sign of your refusal.[118]

This letter to Trotsky was accompanied by a note from Lenin's secretary:[119]

> To Comrade Trotsky. In addition to the letter communicated to you by telephone, Vladimir Ilyich has asked [me] to inform you that Comrade Kamenev is going to Georgia on Wednesday and Vladimir Ilyich asks you to let him know if you want to send anything there from yourself personally.[120]

Lenin passed all the relevant documents to Trotsky; and Trotsky did not return them, thereby conveying to Lenin that he would lend his support.

Having secured Trotsky's support Lenin decided to declare war against Stalin and played his trump card on the same day: Stalin's shouting match with Krupskaya of 22 December. On 5 March, Lenin issued to Stalin his ultimatum: either you apologize to her, and thus acknowledge defeat, or you become my enemy in public. Lenin did not tell Trotsky about this letter, although it was precisely on Trotsky's help that he intended to rely in his fight with Stalin. Lenin thought he once again had the upper hand but was ready to accept Stalin's capitulation in private without humiliating him in front of his party colleagues. He was still seeking to keep open the door to future cooperation:

Dear Comrade Stalin!
You were rude enough to call my wife to the telephone and berate her. Even though she let you know that she was amenable to forgetting what had been said, Zinoviev and Kamenev [members of the Politburo and, unbeknownst to Lenin, allies of Stalin] were apprised of it through her. I have no intention of forgetting so easily what has been done to me, and it need hardly be said that what is done to my wife I consider having been done to me. Therefore, I ask you to consider whether you are amenable to taking back what was said and apologizing or whether you prefer to break off relations between us.
Respectfully, Lenin[121].

On the same day, Lenin dictated 'a letter to the [Polikarp] Mdivani faction' of Georgian Bolshevik Communists (with copies to Trotsky and Kamenev), also directed against Stalin and constituting the last piece of officially acknowledged *Leniniana*:

I am following your case with all my heart. I am outraged by [Sergo] Ordzhonikidze's rudeness and the connivance of Stalin and Dzerzhinsky. I am preparing notes and a speech for you.[122]

It is evident that Stalin was aware of this new alliance with Trotsky and quickly took whatever actions he needed to take. Although this can hardly have been the last of his dictations, none of Lenin's notes and speeches on the Georgian question have survived.

Though the 'letter to the Mdivani faction' was sent, the letter to Stalin stayed where it was on March 6.[123] His secretary's considered the letter harsh and either Krupskaya or they themselves fretted about giving it to Stalin. On March 7 the letter was finally handed to Stalin. Lenin's secretary recalled that Stalin consented to apologize:[124]

I delivered the letter by hand. I asked Stalin to write back to [Lenin], since he was waiting for a reply and was worried. Stalin read the letter right then, while I was still there. His face remained calm. He was silent for a while, thought a little, and said— slowly, articulating every word clearly, and making pauses between them, 'This is not Lenin speaking. It is his illness speaking.' And he continued, 'I am not a doctor, I am a politician. I am Stalin. If my wife, a party member, had acted incorrectly and been punished, I would not have considered myself entitled to interfere. And Krupskaya is a party member. But, since [Lenin] insists, I am prepared to apologize to Krupskaya for being rude.

Having delivered Lenin's letter to Stalin, Lenin's secretary 'took down Stalin's brief reply to [Lenin] and was so anxious' that her handwriting was almost illegible. She did not immediately take Stalin's reply to Lenin but, concerned about upsetting him, asked her friends what to do. They told her to clear the letter with Kamenev who thought it was fine.[125] 'After visiting Kamenev, I returned to my office. But I didn't give him the letter, because it was already too late: [Lenin] was unwell', Lenin's secretary wrote.[126]

'Unwell' was somewhat of a euphemism. 'It had been officially announced,' Lenin's secretary recalled, 'that as of March 6 or even the day before, Vladimir Ilyich was no longer in any condition to read or work or have any visitors or do anything. There could be no longer be any contact with him.'

'What happened to [Krupskaya] was not known either,' Lenin's secretary and it seems that Lenin's wife was also taken into custody as part of Lenin's insubordination.

Lenin's sister,[127] evidently also under arrest, was permitted to make a telephone call to Stalin. What was said in that conversation is not known, but from the yelling heard on the other end of the line it was clear that she was demanding to be released immediately and threatening that otherwise she would appeal to the workers of Moscow for help, on Lenin's behalf.[128]

Stalin, it appears, remained unfazed by her threat. On the night of March 9, 1923, Lenin's health took yet another timely turn for the worse and this time he lost the power of speech. At least, that is what was officially stated about Lenin's health that day. In an exquisite case of revenge best being served cold, Stalin, citing Krupskaya herself as his source, reported to the Politburo that she and Lenin had passionately asked for cyanide on 17 March so Lenin could kill himself when the time came, that he had agreed to calm them down, but that in truth he Stalin lacked the will power to grant such a request. It was also a watertight alibi in case it was decided to poison Lenin. It would merely mean that the crafty Lenins had found a way to set Lenin 'free' with a method that Stalin had avowed went against his scruples:

On Saturday, March 17, [Krupskaya] informed me, under the utmost secrecy, of '[Lenin]'s request to Stalin'—that I, Stalin, should assume the responsibility of obtaining and delivering to [Lenin] a dose of cyanide. [Krupskaya] has told me, among other things, that '[Lenin] is suffering unbelievably,' that 'it is unthinkable to go on living like this'; she was most inflexibly insistent that I 'not refuse [Lenin]'s request.' In view of [Krupskaya]'s particular insistence and in view of the fact that [Lenin] was demanding that, I agreed... I did not consider it possible to reply with a refusal, so I declared, 'I ask [Lenin] to calm himself and to rest assured that when the need arises, I will unwaveringly fulfill his request.' [Lenin] did indeed calm down. I must, however, declare that I lack the strength to fulfill [Lenin]'s request and must refuse this mission, no matter how humane and necessary it may be, whereof I hereby inform the Politburo of the CC.[129]

From March 7, 1923 until January 21, 1924, Lenin remained alive—though, according to Stalin at any rate, the 53-year-old desperately wanted to commit suicide—unable to function as a political figure. Lenin's wife and sister, meanwhile, tried to prevent Lenin's health from worsening as he was held at Gorki. As the Cheka's Semenov put it at the SR trial: 'Plant a doctor who will infect him with a dangerous disease.' After Lenin's death, Krupskaya feared for her own life, too. She did not need constant medical attention, but Stalin ordered that Lenin's kitchen staff continued to cook for her and her sister.

Knowing that Trotsky had sided with Lenin, she no doubt feared for his safety. But it was only after Lenin's death, on January 29, 1924, that she mustered the courage to send Trotsky a note, which turned out to be a farewell:

Dear Lev Davydovich [Trotsky]... The attitude that Vladimir Ilyich developed toward you when you came from Siberia to visit us in London did not change up to his very death. I wish you strength and health, Lev Davydovich, and I send you a firm embrace.[130]

Trotsky's position as SNK minister and in Bolshevik party was based on the personal alliance between him and Lenin. Even before Lenin died, Dzerzhinsky and Stalin tried to get rid of Trotsky, ostensibly at the same time as Lenin.

Trotsky wrote: 'In the latter half of January 1924, I traveled to the Caucasus, to Sukhumi [Georgia] to rid myself of a mysterious infection that had been hounding me, whose nature the doctors have not divined to this day. The news of Lenin's death came while I was en route.'[131] Just before his departure from Moscow, on January 18, Trotsky had been twice visited by a Dr Fedor Getye. Having nonetheless recovered from his mystery illness in Georgia, of all places, the forty-three-year-old Trotsky never again went to the Kremlin pharmacy to have his prescriptions filled.[132] Not surprisingly, back in Moscow with his health restored, his political weight while Lenin was alive never recovered.

The responsibility for operation Lenin apparently fell to people from Dzerzhinsky's agency, among them Dzerzhinsky's deputy Yagoda, the 'pharmacist'. Stalin's secretary recorded in detail how the Chekist first visited Stalin that day, with two of Lenin's doctors in tow, and thereafter Lenin himself. When Krupskaya was called away on the telephone, Lenin suddenly died and several empty vials were found next to him.

Kanner [Stalin's secretary] saw Yagoda enter Stalin's office accompanied by two doctors, who had treated Lenin.... Stalin said to one of these doctors: 'You must immediately go to Gorki and urgently examine [Lenin]. [Yagoda] will accompany you.'

That same evening—it was January 20, 1924—Kanner, who was in and out of the room, overheard a few snatches of a conversation between Stalin and Yagoda: 'There will soon be another attack. The symptoms are there….'

On January 21, 1924, the fatal attack occurred. It was terrible, but it did not last long. Krupskaya left the room for a moment to make a telephone call. When she returned Lenin was dead. On his bedtable were several small empty bottles. At a quarter-past seven the telephone rang in Stalin's office. Yagoda reported that Lenin was dead.[133]

Kanner's recollections echo those of a story handed down by Elizabeth Lermolo, an inmate of the Stalinist camp system.[134] Once released, she found her way to the West after World War II and in 1955 published her memoirs after Stalin's death. She recounts the experiences of Gavriil Volkov, Lenin's personal cook who was in the same camp as her in 1935. A Lenin sympathizer who previously worked at the Kremlin, he was hand-picked by Krupskaya to come to Gorki on account of his loyalty to Lenin. He noticed how in January 1923 Lenin's health would plummet whenever Krupskaya was called away from Gorki to the Kremlin and couldn't oversee Lenin's care. The last time was just before Lenin died and Stalin prevented everyone in Gorki from retrieving her. Volkov said the last thing Lenin did was give him a note that said 'I've been poisoned'.

For several days I walked around the prison yard completely alone. One day a man was added to my exercise shift. He was an old-time prisoner, Gavriil Volkov, a Communist. Heretofore he had been allowed to take his walks only in solitude…. There were rumors that he was being held in 'strictest isolation' on direct orders from the Kremlin. And no one knew what he was charged with and why he was in prison…. We had a lengthy conversation. Until 1923 he was employed in the Kremlin as the manager of a dining room that was maintained there for the highly placed party functionaries. Later he became chef at the Kremlin sanatorium in Gorki…. Volkov had been arrested and brought here to the prison … in 1932. The third anniversary of his stay in solitary confinement had just passed…. He didn't know the term of his sentence; as for the reason for his imprisonment, he could only guess. He had never stood trial….

'Not only was I never interrogated but no official was even permitted to discuss my case with me'….

'For a period of eleven years I have kept a frightful secret buried deep within my soul, which I had not shared with anyone….

When Lenin became ill in 1923,' Volkov went on to say, 'the decision was made to hospitalize him in the Kremlin sanatorium at Gorki.'

Volkov was sent there to serve as Lenin's personal chef. Lenin's wife, Nadezhda Krupskaya, approved of Volkov's selection for she had known him in the Kremlin as a trusted and thoroughly dependable person.

He had to work a lot. He had to cook and serve Lenin, his wife, and his doctors, all by himself. He worked for almost a year without a single day off, since he knew that it was his duty to do everything possible to accelerate the recovery of his party's leader. Lenin and his wife clearly valued Volkov's loyalty.

Although Lenin did not feel very well, the doctors promised to get him back up on his feet quickly. Occasionally, he would indeed begin to feel better, and he would come out on the terrace to sit in the sun. From time to time, he had visitors. Stalin came to see him several times. But for the most part Lenin remained alone, apart from the presence of Nadezhda Krupskaya.

Initially, all went well. Lenin's condition, it seemed, gave no cause for alarm. Then, toward the end of the year, shortly before New Year's—the winter was bitter cold,' Volkov recalled, 'Nadezhda Krupskaya was unexpectedly summoned to Moscow on some kind of urgent business. She was detained there for two days, and during her absence Lenin's health took a drastic turn for the worse.

When Krupskaya returned and saw Lenin, she gasped. That's how bad he looked. Naturally, special treatments were prescribed and soon he improved. Everyone felt relieved, life returned to normal.

About ten days later Nadezhda Krupskaya was called back to the Kremlin on some party matter. This time she stayed longer, and Lenin again took a turn for the worse. When Volkov was bringing him his tea one morning, Lenin seemed very upset. He couldn't speak. He made signs to Volkov but Volkov couldn't figure out what he wanted. There was no one in the room except the two of them. Volkov asked him, 'Shall I call the doctor?' Lenin shook his head categorically and contin-ued to gesticulate. Only after long questioning did Volkov finally gather what Lenin wanted. He was asking Volkov to get through somehow to the Kremlin, to tell Krupskaya that he was feeling worse and to ask her to drop everything and return to Gorki. Lenin warned Volkov not to telephone Krupskaya, but to see her in person.

'Needless to say,' Volkov continued, 'I made every effort to do as he asked, but I couldn't get out of Gorki. For one thing, a severe snowstorm made all the roads impassable, by foot or car. And, more importantly, Stalin phoned from the Kremlin and ordered all physicians as well as the entire staff at Gorki to remain at their posts until the health of 'our dearly beloved Comrade Lenin' had improved. In short, Nadezhda Krupskaya did not return from the Kremlin, and Lenin's condition grew worse and worse until he was no longer able to get out of bed.'

And then on January 21, 1924 … at eleven in the morning, as usual, Volkov took Lenin his second breakfast. There was no one in the room. As soon as Volkov appeared, Lenin made an effort to rise, and extended both his hands, uttering unin-telligible sounds. Volkov rushed over to him and Lenin slipped a note into his hand.

As Volkov turned, having hidden the note, Dr Yelistratov, Lenin's personal physician, ran into the room, apparently having been attracted by the commotion. The two of them got Lenin back to bed and gave him an injection to calm him. Lenin quieted down; his eyes half-closed. He never opened them again.

The note, scratched in a nervous scrawl, read: 'Gavriil, I've been poisoned … Go fetch Nadya at once. Tell Trotsky. Tell anyone you can….'

When our walk ended that morning, Volkov took me to the door of my cell. And I never saw him again.[135]

On January 22, at 11am—in other words, 16 hours after Lenin's death—an autopsy was performed. It ended at 4pm in the afternoon. No fewer than nine doctors were present. Despite the empty bottles, the medical report stated that Lenin had died of 'disseminated sclerosis'—a chronic disease ostensibly first diagnosed after the patient had died.

The nine doctors studiously avoided discussing those organs in which traces of poisoning might have been detected. In addition, they mysteriously failed to do a blood analysis. A week later, Dr Boris Vaysbrod, one of the nine doctors present at the autopsy, wrote in *Pravda* however, that the clinicians were not yet able to assemble all details of Lenin's illness into a single clinical picture. Evidently, Dr Vaysbrod was not entirely satisfied by the medical conclusions. Indeed, the report did not include a toxicological analysis and did not describe the contents of Lenin's stomach. Curiously it did indicate that his stomach had been empty and that the walls of the stomach had contracted—although it was known that Lenin had eaten two meals on the day of his death. The report also referred to irregularities in the spleen and liver but did not go into details.

Just before his death, Lenin had asked Krupskaya to read him Jack London's story 'The Love of Life.' Two travelers are crossing an ice-cold river. One twists his leg and can go no further. The other does not turn around and carries on. The man who is hurt goes as far as he can, then collapses from weakness and exhaustion. In order not to die of hunger, he eats raw fish. He fights a wolf that attacks him and tears apart its throat with his teeth. Finally, fishermen notice the dying man on the shore, rescue him, and bring him back to life. Right up to the very end of his life, Lenin hoped that he would survive, that he would be able to overcome the enemy that had attacked him, that he would be rescued by his comrades. Would such a man have committed suicide? Would he have asked Stalin for poison indeed? Trotsky didn't think so and quizzed the autopsy doctors. They, however, understood that their sole purpose was to rubber stamp political statements.

When I questioned doctors in Moscow about the immediate cause of Lenin's death, which had come unexpectedly for them, they were at a loss for an answer. The autopsy, naturally, was performed with every formality: as general secretary, Stalin had seen to this before anything else. But the doctors did not look for poison, even if the more penetrating among them admitted the possibility of a suicide. They probably did not suspect anything else. In any case, they couldn't have had any inclination to go into the matter too deeply. They understood that politics superseded medicine.

Even Trotsky treated Lenin's death as the elephant in the room from 1923. He never probed Krupskaya or Kamenev. Only Bukharin, whose connection to counterintelligence agent Semonov's assassination plans would be publicized at his show trial in 1938, made oblique references at times:

I did not bother [Krupskaya] with questions about the matter. I renewed personal relations with Zinoviev and Kamenev only after two years, when they broke with Stalin. They clearly avoided talking about the circumstances of Lenin's death, giving one-word replies to my questions, and looking away. Did they know something or did they only suspect? In any case, they had been too closely connected with Stalin during the preceding three years and couldn't not be apprehensive that the shadow of suspicion would fall on them too. It was as if a leaden cloud was enveloping the story of Lenin's death. Everyone avoided talking about it, as if they were afraid of listening too closely to their own fear. Only the expansive and talkative Bukharin would privately sometimes make unexpected and strange insinuations. 'Oh, you don't know Koba,' [Stalin] he would say, with his frightened smile. 'Koba is capable of anything.'

Trotsky speculates that Stalin was deeply worried about the fact he had told the Politburo that Lenin and Krupskaya had asked him for poison to end Lenin's life.

[He] might have feared that I would connect Lenin's death with the previous year's conversation about poison, that I would ask doctors to determine whether poisoning had taken place, that I would demand a special investigation. For all these reasons, therefore, it was safer to keep me far away until his body was embalmed, his inner organs cremated, and no professional investigation would any longer be possible.[136]

It did not save Trotsky. The Bolshevik mafia expelled him from its ranks soon after Lenin's death, then banished him to distant regions of the country in January 1928, exiled him from the USSR in January 1929, and finally murdered him in August 1940 after he publicized that Lenin had been assassinated. Ultimately, he could not escape Lenin's fate.

There is one further episode connected to Lenin's death. In October 1932, Lenin's sister[137] decided out of the blue to write her memoirs. These were no run-of-the-mill memoirs, but her detailed recollections of how Lenin fell ill and died. She was known for being an obedient and efficient Party worker rather than as a daring activist like Lenin and yet she was somehow able to use secret archival Party documents for her project. She was given privileged access to these papers on her brother's last moments yet did not insist that they be published. One can only infer that in 1932 she was acting on someone else's orders, someone who could both open them to her and at the same ensure that she would not dare disclose something undesirable—Stalin.

In these death memoirs, she produced an extraordinary posthumous document signed by one of Lenin's secretaries.[138] The document repeated Stalin's claim that Lenin wanted to receive cyanide to kill himself. This time, however, it was not Krupskaya who did the begging but it was Lenin himself he wanted to have it in case he could no longer speak. Despite its importance, Lenin's secretary had apparently 'forgotten' to put it on paper in 1922.

> On 22 December [Lenin] called for me at 6pm and dictated the following: 'Do not forget to take all measures to acquire and … deliver cyanide in the event that the paralysis affects my speech, as a humane measure and in emulation of [Karl Marx's son-in-law, Paul] Lafargue'.[139]

Every word must have been fabrication. It did fit the official version that Lenin could only communicate by speech towards the end of his life and that, if that last bastion was taken away, any reason to live on was lost for him. But there is sufficient testimony that, despite Stalin's diktat against writing 'on doctor's orders', Lenin continued to be able to do so until the very end. Significant, too, is the date—22 December, the day Stalin had the shouting match with Krupskaya, when Lenin finally realized the Stalin was sabotaging him, and he started his Last Testament.[140]

What prompted the memoir to be written in 1932? It was also the year when the two cooks who worked at Gorki for Lenin (but not Spiridon Putin) were detained without charges, nine years after Lenin's death. It's possible that it was related to an incident that Ivan Gronsky, a journalist, editor, and Party functionary, described. Gronsky was one of the very few people who had the right to enter Stalin's office without being announced. In 1932-1933, Gronsky was the head of the Soviet Writers' Union steering committee; in 1928-1934, he served as managing editor of the newspaper *Izvestiya*, and during the years 1932-1937, he was the Editor-in-Chief of the magazine *Novy Mir*. In addition, Gronsky was something like the minister of literature under Stalin. Among his other duties, he was entrusted with the very delicate task of carrying out surveillance over the writer Maxim Gorky who had been nominated several times over for the Nobel Prize in Literature.[141]

It didn't prevent Gronsky from being arrested in 1937 and spending 16 years in prisons and labor camps. After he was released and rehabilitated in 1953, he met a fellow ex-prisoner, Lidiya Shatunovskaya, at Porechye Sanatorium, Belarus. She had been sentenced to twenty years 'for wanting to emigrate to Israel,' and had spent seven years in solitary in the Vladimir Prison. Soon after Stalin's death, she had been released. Shatunovskaya recalled: 'During one of our walks Gronsky, a very smart man and a very careful man, shared with me, a woman and not a party member, his suspicions about Lenin's death and about the mysterious role played by Stalin in the acceleration of this death.'[142]

In 1932, during a meeting with Soviet writers at which Stalin, along with everyone else, had had a fair amount to drink, Stalin 'to Gronsky's horror began to talk to those present about Lenin and about the circumstances of his death.... He mumbled something to the effect that he alone knew how and why Lenin died'. Unfortunately, the month and day of this meeting with writers is unknown. But as we will see below, these events happened prior to October 19, 1932. Shatunovskaya continues:

Gronsky ... carried the drunken Stalin to a neighboring room and laid him on the sofa, where he promptly fell asleep ... On waking, he spent a long and agonizing time remembering what had happened the night before; when he did remember, he leapt up in horror and fury and pounced on Gronsky. He shook him by the shoulder and yelled frantically, 'Ivan! Tell me the truth. What did I say about Lenin's death yesterday? Tell me the truth, Ivan!' Gronsky tried to calm him, saying, '... You didn't say anything yesterday. I simply saw that you were not feeling well, so I brought you into the study and put you to bed. Besides, all the writers were so drunk that no one could either hear or understand a thing.'

Stalin was gradually beginning to calm down when another thought entered his head: 'Ivan!' he yelled. 'You weren't drunk, though. What did you hear?'...

Gronsky, of course, tried in every possible way to assure Stalin that nothing had been said about Lenin's death and that he, Gronsky, had heard nothing and had taken Stalin away only because everyone present had drunk far too much.... From that day on, Stalin's attitude to Gronsky changed completely, and in 1937 Gronsky was arrested.[143]

It was precisely Gronsky's act of removing Stalin that had been his act of self-incrimination (if Stalin's reminiscences had been uncontroversial why remove him?). Despite Gronsky's assurances that Stalin had never said anything about Lenin's poisoning in his drunken state, the distrustful Stalin decided to take extra precautions. On October 19, 1932, at a meeting with Communist writers hosted by Gorky, he 'repeated' his story about Lenin and poison, but in a version that flattered Stalin and could be circulated without provoking gossip.[144] As the literary critic Korneli Zelinsky recalled:

Stalin spoke wonderfully that time. He told us about rare, intimate details of Lenin's life that no one knows. 'Lenin knew he was dying,' Stalin said, 'and one day when we were alone, he asked me to bring him cyanide. 'You are the cruelest man in the Party,' Lenin said, 'you'll be able to do it.' I promised him at first, but then I just couldn't bring myself to do it. How could I give Ilyich poison? I felt sorry for the man, and besides, who could know which way the illness would go. So, I never did give it to him. Then one day we went to visit Ilyich, and he says, pointing at me, 'He lied to me, he's getting wobbly.' No one could understand what he meant at that point. Everyone was taken aback. Only I knew what he was hinting it. It was at that time that I reported Lenin's request to the Politburo. Of course, everyone rejected this request. Gronsky over there, he knows about this.'[145]

Lenin's Funeral

Lenin's funeral on 27 January, 1924, was the beginning of a lasting Soviet tradition. The committee that organized the funeral of a deceased Soviet leader would always be headed by the main pretender to the power of the deceased. And the person appointed to head the committee to organize Lenin's funeral was Dzerzhinsky—who was also the first among Lenin's pallbearers, as photographs show—not Stalin. Nor, indeed, Lenin's friend Trotsky, who did not attend the funeral. Since he was the powerful Soviet minister of defense it was an odd omission and the first sign of his rapidly fading star.[146]

Lenin's funeral was the subject of the March and April issues of the Soviet government's English-language photo-journal *Soviet Russia Pictorial*. Beneath one of the photographs were listed the men who carried Lenin's coffin—Lenin's successors in order of importance.[147] But where was Trotsky? The answer to this question was provided to readers in the June issue, which contained a photograph of Trotsky alongside his physician, Dr Getye. They were in Sukhumi, on the Black Sea: Trotsky was vacationing at the beach.[148]

Dzerzhinsky had consolidated vast power within the government and SNK.[149] Starting March 30, 1919, Dzerzhinsky was interior minister of the RSFSR[150] From April 1921 onward, Dzerzhinsky was also minister of railways, first of Russia (the RSFSR) and then of the USSR. From November 1923, he was Chair of the OGPU (based at Lubyanka) of the USSR of the USSR SNK.[151] On February 2, 1924—soon after Lenin's death—he also became Chair of the Supreme Council on the economy. It was the body through which Dzerzhinsky planned to take over the functions of the SNK, left weakened after Lenin's death, and thus become the head of state.[152]

Trotsky's 'vacation' was, therefore not very peaceful. On March 25, 1924, two months after Lenin's death, Ephraim Sklyansky—Trotsky's deputy in military affairs—was removed from his post at the powerful ministry. He had been the *de facto* chief of the Red Army's campaign during the civil war and the Deputy Head of the Revolutionary Military Council. It was obvious that Sklyansky's transfer to a new position—chair of the *Mossukno* state textile trust—was a prelude to Trotsky's own removal. By way of consolation, Sklyansky was allowed to take a vacation in the United States. The thirty-three-year old saw the USSR again, however. He was another Soviet leader to die young. On August 27, 1925, he drowned in a lake.

Right away, rumors began to circulate in Moscow that Sklyansky—the first agent to be targeted in the US—had been drowned by Dzerzhinsky's GPU agents. It was, in fact, the continuation of a conspiracy between Intelligence Services (Dzerzhinsky) and the Party secretariat (Stalin) to remove rival claimants to power. By a Party CC resolution of April 1925, Trotsky was indeed forced to resign as Soviet defense minister. The SNK was eliminated as an influential government body once Lenin was dead. The ministry of defense was weakened politically after Trotsky and Sklyansky were dismissed from their posts.

They were replaced by thirty-nine-year-old Mikhail Frunze, whose star, it seemed, had just started rising. But on October 31, 1925, Frunze became the latest leader to perish young as he died in Moscow under a surgeon's knife. 'Maybe this is the best thing—for old comrades to go down into the grave so easily and simply,' Stalin observed stoically in his speech at Frunze's funeral on November 3. Immediately after Frunze's death, rumors that Frunze had been killed on Stalin's orders began to circulate. But it appears this directive came from Dzerzhinsky, not Stalin. Here is what Trotsky wrote about the matter in his drafts for an unfinished biography of Stalin:

> He was not destined to remain long at his post as head of the armed forces: in November 1925, he died under the surgeon's knife. But during these few months, Frunze showed too much independence by protecting the army from the GPU … Frunze aimed to free the command staff from the GPU and in a relatively short time he abolished the commissariat corps.

Even so, Stalin replaced Frunze with his own protégé, Kliment Voroshilov. He was one Communist apparatchik who survived all the purges unscathed, dying in Moscow in 1969 at the age of eighty eight.

Stalin had no intention to wait for Dzerzhinsky to poison him. On July 20, 1926, the forty-eight-year-old Dzerzhinsky suddenly died of that affliction that mowed down Kremlin leaders prematurely—of a heart attack, according to the official version. The rumors that he, too, died of unnatural causes—poison—have swirled ever since. At the time of his death, he was resisting Stalin's attempts to move Lubyanka ('GPU') under his control at the Party CC. Here is what Nicolaevsky wrote on September 1, 1954 to Nikolai Valentinov-Volsky (1878-1964), a well-known Russian revolutionary and the author of several books about Lenin, who emigrated from the USSR in 1930:

> Stalin's favorite technique for a long time was to use doctors to poison people … I first refused to believe that Dzerzhinsky had been poisoned … but later I heard the same story … from a man who was the head of one of the groups that worked for Georgy Malenkov, [the Secretary of the Party's CC]. Now, reading [Communist defector] Reiss's notes[153] I came across [NKVD head] Nikolai Yezhov's words that Dzerzhinsky was unreliable. Under such circumstances, I am no longer as categorical in my rejection of the possibility of poisoning.... I know that Dzerzhinsky opposed putting the GPU under Stalin's control.... I know, furthermore, that Stalin's apparatus began to carry out major operations in the fall of 1926 [that is, after Dzerzhinsky's death] that Stalin brought the apparatus in other countries under his control in 1927-1928. And that Stalin undoubtedly made use of Dzerzhinsky's death; Dzerzhinsky's death was useful to him.[154]

As with Lenin's poisoning, the strongest clues supporting the hypothesis that Dzerzhinsky was murdered are provided by Stalin himself. On June 2, 1937, Stalin delivered a long speech about the discovery of a military-political conspiracy[155] at an extended session of the Soviet ministry of defense's military council. At that session, he labelled Dzerzhinsky—his dominant ally when toppling and hounding Trotsky from the Kremlin in 1924—a 'Trotskyist'—placing him among the worst category of USSR enemies—a Soviet traitor. Bizarrely, on the face of it, he also claimed that Dzerzhinsky was seeking to put Lubyanka at traitor Trotsky's disposal. Dzerzhinsky had to be neutralized:

> It is often said that in 1922 some people voted for Trotsky…. Dzerzhinsky also voted for Trotsky, and not just voted for him, but openly supported Trotsky, under Lenin and against Lenin. Did you know this? He was not a man who could remain passive in anything. He was a very active Trotskyite and he wanted to bring the entire GPU to Trotsky's defense. He was unable to do this.[156]

Can there be any doubt that 'he was unable to do this' was a boast by Stalin that he had dealt with Dzerzhinsky after his refusal to bring the GPU under Party control?

It was a blatant replacement of historical facts with fiction. We should clarify that Dzerzhinsky never 'voted for Trotsky'; that as *de facto* Bolshevik leader he headed the commission pursuing 'the Georgian question' with loss of autonomy to Russia,[157] opposing Lenin and Trotsky after the latter had agreed to support Lenin in 1923. Stalin disclosed yet another 'state secret' eleven years after Dzerzhinsky's death without any tangible need for it. If Dzerzhinsky had died of natural causes why would Stalin have needed to make up a story about Dzerzhinsky and how his 'betrayal' was nipped in the bud?

Stalin did, in fact, have a grudge against Dzerzhinsky and the Lubyanka he stood for. It is no surprise that when the Chair of the OGPU (successor of the GPU based at Lubyanka), Viacheslav Menzhinsky, presented the Party's Politburo on November 14, 1932, with a draft resolution on establishing an Order of Felix Dzerzhinsky, Stalin vetoed it.[158] And so, the Intelligence Services remained without a Soviet order of honor of its own.

Dzerzhinsky's death concluded the first period of the battle between Russia's Intelligence Services and government for domination. The outcome of this bloodbath was to destroy what was left of the SNK's authority as Soviet Russia's paramount institution under Lenin. Battered by blows from Dzerzhinsky on one side and Stalin on the other, the institution became a powerless appendage. Having cut down the SNK as a rival structure, the two usurpers, Dzerzhinsky, and Stalin, continued the power struggle—now against each other. This confrontation of 1924-26, short and inconspicuous, was won by Stalin, who had pushed Dzerzhinsky and the OGPU far from the Soviet center of power, restricting the Intelligence Services to the bureaucratic task of being the covert, armed wing of the Party, unquestioningly executing Politburo orders. Over the next seventy five years, Dzerzhinsky's successors would seek to reverse what Stalin had achieved with all the crafty viciousness of the early Bolsheviks when given the chance.

7: Control over the Lubyanka

Dzerzhinsky's removal marked the end of a nearly ten-year period during which the Lubyanka, led by Dzerzhinsky, waged an ambitious struggle for political influence in Russia. He had joined Lenin's Bolsheviks as late as 1917, when they created the Cheka, and he was therefore never an obedient follower of Lenin's style of Marxism. With him out of the way, however, Stalin sought to eradicate any political thinking or aspirations of the Lubyanka. Under Stalin's thirty-year rule, he brutally sought to turn Dzerzhinsky's OGPU into no more than a bureaucratic tool whose deployment was subject to Party decisions only—or, to be exact, to the Secretariat of the Party's Central Committee. Or, to be even more exact—to Stalin himself. Ironically, its relative distance from the core of Soviet ideology meant that it would on the one hand prove the only Soviet structure capable of withstanding the implosion of the USSR in 1991 while on the other it was close enough for it to have an institutional desire to control the country's levers of power.

Stalin's subjection of the Lubyanka started subtle enough. Dzerzhinsky's successor as OGPU Chair, Menzhinsky, was a Bolshevik revolutionary with Polish background like his predecessor. He had joined the staff of the VChK as early as December 8[159] 1917—the day after it was formed. Subsequently, he acted as Soviet consul in Berlin and Dzerzhinsky had visited him on his way back to Moscow in October 1918 from his long, peripatetic journey following the (his) failed assassination attempt on Lenin of August 30, 1918.[160] In September 1919, on his return to Moscow, Menzhinsky was once again employed by Dzerzhinsky's agency, becoming Dzerzhinsky's first deputy at the OGPU in 1923.[161] After Dzerzhinsky's sudden death, as he struggled to dominate Stalin, Menzhinsky himself was to die in 1934. Dead at the age of 59, he lived only ten years longer than Dzerzhinsky.

Was he, too, felled by the Kremlin reaper who targeted so many of his powerful predecessors prematurely? It didn't look like it in his case. He was known to be a chronic sufferer from chest pain and there was little to indicate an unnatural death. From the standpoint of the Soviet state, one could but lament the fact that such a gifted, obedient, and modest government official had suddenly passed away in his prime. It is also worth noting that Menzhinsky, who did not leave his mark on Soviet history with any memorable deeds,[162] remained in the post of Intelligence chief for a fairly long time—eight years. His main qualification for the top job seemed to be that he was healthy enough to continue living but ill enough not to do anything unexpected and lurch for power during his reign over the Lubyanka.

Then, all of a sudden, three years after Menzhinsky's death, came the 1938 show trial of Menzhinsky's deputy Genrikh Yagoda—the Cheka's 'Pharmacist' who had set up Laboratory 12 at the Lubyanka. In 1934, he replaced his boss officially as chief of Intelligence Services of the USSR and was also given the newly-created post of minister of internal affairs.[163] But someone had clearly been impatiently waiting for Menzhinsky's death. On the very day that Menzhinsky died, the post of OGPU Chair was abolished and the OGPU was replaced by the newly created NKVD of the USSR, to which Yagoda was appointed. Practically, it made little difference, as Yagoda was *de facto* leader given that Menzhinsky's poor health required him to lead his department from a couch as best he could.

At his 1938 show trial, Yagoda shocked the public by admitting that, despite appearances of a natural death, he had organized his boss's assassination with the assistance of two Kremlin doctors. Trotsky covered Yagoda's words on the matter in his unfinished biography of Stalin—a biography which he never got to finish because its subject had his biographer murdered with an ice pick:

Doctor Ignatii Kazakov has given his testimony: As a result of my conversation with Yagoda, [Doctor] Lev Levin and I developed a method for curing Menzhinsky that in reality sapped his remaining strength and accelerated his death. In this way, Levin and I killed Menzhinsky. I gave Levin a mixture of *lysates*, which, in combination with *alkaloids*, produced the desired result, that is, Menzhinsky's death.

On May 10, 1934, Menzhinsky was murdered on Yagoda's orders. On the following day, Gorky's thirty-seven-year-old son Maxim Peshkov also suddenly died. His wife Nadezhda (nicknamed 'Timosha') was having an affair with Yagoda. Trotsky—who did not know that Yagoda was sleeping with Peshkov's wife—summarized the testimony at the trial which claimed that Peshkov knew too many undesirable people, and thought that was this was the cause of Yagoda's hit:

Yagoda did not like Gorky's son's way of life. He felt that he was a harmful influence on his father and surrounded his father with 'undesirable people.' This made him decide to eliminate the son and he invited Doctor Levin to assist him in liquidating Gorky's son.

The bout of 1935 premature deaths didn't end there. It was presumably Yagoda—acting with the help of doctors who were subordinate to him and had free access to the Kremlin—who poisoned two further prominent Soviet figures. One was forty-six-year-old Valerian Kuibyshev, member of the CC and chief of the Soviet Planning Agency, who died prematurely on January 25, 1935. The other was Maxim Gorky himself, who died on June 18, 1936, a month after his son.

Here, too, we can turn to a vivid scene in Trotsky's *Life* draft that wasn't published in the short version that appeared in *Liberty* magazine. Trotsky foreshadows the increasingly sophisticated poisons Lubyanka would deploy in the decades ahead, down to Litvinenko, Skripal, Navalny and others in the 21st century:

> Yagoda had a special cabinet with poisons. When he needed to, he took out precious vials from this cabinet and gave them to his agents along with corresponding instructions. The head of the GPU—a former pharmacist, by the way—always displayed an exceptional interest in poisons. He had several toxicologists at his command, for whom he had created a special laboratory, funding for which was supplied in unlimited amounts and without monitoring. It cannot be supposed for a moment, naturally, that Yagoda constructed such an enterprise for his own personal needs... Next to Yagoda on the defendants' bench sat four Kremlin doctors who were accused of killing Maxim Gorky and two Soviet ministers: 'I plead guilty,' testified the venerable Doctor Levin, who was once my own doctor, 'to applying medical treatments that were counter indicated for the illness.' In this way, 'I caused the premature deaths of Maxim Gorky and Kuibyshev.'

The official story in 1935 was that Kuibyshev died of a heart attack, though Kuibyshev's son Vladimir always claimed that his father had been in rude health: 'A medical consultation was held by a board of specifically selected doctors and an autopsy was performed. They concluded that the cause of death was a heart attack. This conclusion leaves room for doubt, and even perplexity, since father had a healthy heart. Two days before he died, on January 23, father, laughing, told his sister Yelena as he saw her out the door: "The healthiest part of my body is my heart!"' Vladimir believed that Kuibyshev's attending physician, Doctor Levin, had killed his father by administering 'carefully rationed doses of specially selected "medicinal-poisons".'

It is possible that Yagoda was framed, but the theory that Kuibyshev, too, really died of a 'premature death' gains further credibility from the fact that, three years later, in 1938, Valerian Kuibyshev's brother Nikolai was executed. Nikolai Kuibyshev was a military leader, corps commander, and Russian Civil War hero, who had been decorated with four Orders of the Red Banner and thrice wounded in battle. At the time of his arrest, he was the commander of the Transcaucasian Military District. He was summoned from Tbilisi to Moscow and arrested on the train back, at night. On August 1, 1938, while he was being interrogated inside Butyrka prison, Nikolai Kuibyshev was shot personally by Beria, the new head of the NKVD.[164]

When Yagoda became the head of the Lubyanka after Menzhinsky's death—on the same day, the post of interior minister was created especially for him[165]. And additionally, as a separate ministry, the Chief Directorate of Intelligence Services (GUGB), also headed by Yagoda. In 1935, Yagoda became the first person to acquire the title of 'General Commissar of State Security'. It didn't last long. On September 26, 1936, Yagoda was removed from his posts and demoted to communications minister[166]. In January 1937 he was removed from that new post as well and expelled from the Party into the bargain. Given his long impeccable service as Menzhinsky right-hand man, his decline was as precipitous as his promotion to the top of the government as Intelligence chief had been stellar. Was this planned all along?

Although the formal announcement of Yagoda's removal from the post was only made on April 4, 1937, Yagoda had been arrested on March 28. On March 15, 1938, after appearing as one of the main defendants in the third show trial, he was executed by shooting at the Kommunarka shooting ground, previously his own country residence. His final hours contained a moral lesson. Yagoda was killed last, after being forced to watch the executions of his condemned co-defendants. Before Yagoda was shot, he was beaten by the head of the 1st Department of the GUGB, Israil Dagin, on the orders of the new chief of the NKVD, Yagoda's successor Yezhov.

Yagoda's wife Ida Averbach, who had worked for the state prosecutor's office, was fired from her job after her husband's arrest and was herself arrested on June 9, 1937. Together with her mother and seven-year-old son, she was exiled to Orenburg, Kazakhstan, for five years. But Stalinism's mafia-style laws required—though not always—the elimination of the entire family. After a review of her case, Ida Averbach was executed after all in the same year as her husband.

Yagoda's family did not escape either. On June 20, 1937, Yagoda's parents and sisters were exiled to Astrakhan, Russia, for five years; on May 8, 1938, they were sentenced to eight years in labor camps. Yagoda's father died in a camp in Vorkuta; his mother, in the Northeastern Correctional Labor Camp. Esfir Yagoda-Znamenskaya (born 1896) was shot on June 16, 1938. Lilia Yagoda (born 1902) was shot on June 16, 1938. His sisters, Rosalia Shokhor-Yagoda (born in 1890, died in Simbirsk in 1950) spent another five years in exile in Kolyma after having served her term; curiously, Frida Friedland-Yagoda (born 1899) was released in 1949 but then given another 10-year sentence in the camps and vanished; Taisiya Yagoda-Mordvinkina (1895-1988) was released on October 29, 1949 and then exiled to the Krasnoyarsk region. No Sicilian mafia could have dreamed up such a cruel vendetta against innocent bystanders.

On September 26, 1936, Nikolai Yezhov replaced Yagoda as minister of internal affairs, approaching his own premature death. What were his compelling qualities? Yezhov was the Chair of the Party Control Commission, a member of the CC's Organizational Bureau and a secretary of the Party's CC. In other words, what commended him most was that he was not a former State Security officer like Menzhinsky or Yagoda but a Communist Party functionary serving directly under General Secretary Stalin.

This was the first departure from a 'tradition' of the first deputy succeeding his boss as chief of the Intelligence Service. Prior to formally taking over, Menzhinsky and Yagoda were *de facto* chiefs of Intelligence. Menzhinsky had carried out Dzerzhinsky's day-to-day responsibilities because the latter was very busy plotting to become Russia's leader; Yagoda had taken over from Menzhinsky because the latter was often ill.

Having become the minister of internal affairs, Yezhov did not leave a single one of his Party posts. In other words, he combined service in Intelligence with Party work. While Menzhinsky had done little in the post, Yezhov became the organizer of the Soviet 'Great Terror' of 1937-1938—the largest-scale purge of Soviet *nomenklatura*, the Party's appointees, as supposed followers of Trotsky.

The Intelligence Services themselves were a major objective. Yezhov started by purging Yagoda's associates and supporters from the Lubyanka's staff. On March 2, 1937, he spoke at the plenum of the Communist Party and harshly criticized his own staff (that is, the appointees of the soon-to-be-arrested Yagoda), pointing out their many failures as investigators and agents. All this corresponded to the tasks set out for Yezhov by Stalin, who had indicated in a code cable he sent—as early as September 25, 1936—to Politburo members while on vacation that 'Yagoda clearly did not do a great job of exposing the Trotskyite-Zinovievite bloc in the OGPU, he tackled this problem four years late.' It was the day after this telegram from Stalin that Yagoda was removed from the post of minister of internal affairs and replaced by Yezhov.

At the February/March 1937 plenum of the Party's Central Committee, the Yezhov moved in on two demoted Party members who long displeased Stalin, Bukharin and Rykov:

The case of Comrades N.I. Bukharin and A.I. Rykov (presenter, N.I. Yezhov)
Lessons learned from wrecking, sabotage, and espionage by Japanese-German-Trotskyite agents (presenters, V.I. Molotov, L.M. Kaganovich, and N.I. Yezhov)
On shortcomings in Party work and measures to liquidate Trotskyite and other double dealers (presenter, I.V. Stalin)

It proved to be just the beginning. 73 speakers addressed the February/March plenum of the Party CC. By 1940, 56 of them had been executed by shooting and two had committed 'suicide'.

In 1937, in his report on Bukharin, new NKVD chief Yezhov used the statements of twenty-six previously arrested Party officials—fabricated or coerced by torture— to accuse Bukharin and Rykov of having 'embarked on the path of direct betrayal of the Motherland, of terror against the leaders of the Party and of the Soviet government, and of wrecking and sabotage of the economy.' The plenum expelled them both from the ranks of candidate (non-voting) members of the CC—their last official titles—and from the Communist Party itself. Both were arrested on the same day.

SNK Chair Molotov presented a report on 'Lessons learned from wrecking, sabotage, and espionage by Japanese-German-Trotskyite agents, with the USSR [minister for heavy industries].' Originally, that report was supposed to be presented by Ordzhonikidze, the minister for heavy industries in question. But he was no longer available. He had already shot himself on February 18, 1937, five days before the plenum of the CC (the official version was that he had died of a heart attack).

The second to speak on this issue was the minister of railways, Lazar Kaganovich, who believed that a large-scale eradication of 'enemies of the people' was necessary. 'Crying about how innocent people could get arrested can only cause harm'.

Stalin himself presented a report 'on shortcomings in Party work and measures to liquidate Trotskyite and other double dealers.' 'Today's wreckers and saboteurs, the Trotskyites,' he said, 'are mostly Party people, with Party cards in their pockets.... What makes them strong is that the Party card makes them politically trustworthy and opens the door into all of our institutions and organizations. What gives them an advantage is that, while carrying Party cards and pretending to be friends of Soviet power, they deceived our people politically, abused trust, and did damage on the sly.'

The plenum of March 1937 approved the report by Yezhov and tasked him with cleaning up Yagoda's NKVD. Between October 1, 1936 and August 15, 1938, no fewer than 2,273 Lubyanka agents were arrested. Of them, 1,862 were charged with 'counter-revolutionary crimes.' On July 17, 1937, Yezhov was rewarded with the Order of Lenin for 'outstanding achievements in leadership at the NKVD and carrying out tasks assigned by the government.'

While Yezhov began with purges inside the NKVD, he did not stop there. NKVD Order No 00447, 'On repressive measures against former *kulaks*, criminals and other anti-Soviet elements,' was signed on July 30, 1937. Extrajudicial agencies—'The Commission of the NKVD' and 'The *troikas* of the NVKD' (three-person panels made up of NKVD officers, prosecutors, and Party officials)—were used to speed up the purge operations. In 1937-1938, Yezhov visited Stalin 290 times and spent a total of more than 850 hours with him (Molotov was the only person with whom Stalin met more frequently and for a longer time). It was under Yezhov that Stalin wiped out the so-called 'Leninist Guard'. The Second Moscow Trial (January 1937), the Military Trial (June 1937), and the Third Moscow Trial (March 1938), at which Yagoda was sentenced to death, also happened on Yezhov's watch. It helped that Yezhov was a sadist who personally participated in torture. He kept the bullets used to shoot Zinoviev, Kamenev and other Bolshevik leaders as souvenirs in his work desk.

Carrying out the decisions of the February/March 1937 plenum of the Party, Yezhov's NKVD arrested 1,580,000 people in 1937 and 1938; of them, 682,000 were sentenced to death by shooting. In addition, the *troikas*—issued false sentences mandating lengthy prison terms with the classification 'ten years with no right to correspondence': false because, in practice, it meant a death sentence and immediate execution.

At an NKVD leadership meeting on May 21, 1937, Stalin declared that 'the intelligence directorate and its entire staff has been infiltrated by the Germans. The intelligence network needs to be dissolved, preferably all of it.' This set off a new purge inside the Intelligence Service: 22,000 of its agents and other employees were arrested.

Between 1937 and 1939, four top intelligence officers were executed: Yan Berzin and Semyen Uritsky in 1937; Semen Gendin in 1938; Alexander G. Orlov in 1939. Virtually all their deputies and directorate department chiefs were also shot.

Soviet intelligence agents working abroad were mostly recalled home in the late 1930s and then executed. From the most important Soviet Foreign Intelligence *rezidenturas* (secret embassy departments)—in Berlin and in Paris—practically everyone was recalled. The work of the *rezidenturas* was paralyzed. On May 25, 1940, Ivan Proskurov, the head of the Main Intelligence Directorate (GRU) of the General Staff of Red Army—reported to the Party CC that more than half of the intelligence cadres had been arrested. Shortly after that, he too was arrested and shot.

As a result of Stalin's purges, the military did not escape either. Two commanders of the Soviet Navy and four Soviet Air Force commanders were executed. Three of the Red Army's five marshals were shot. The two who survived were the least talented but the most loyal: Semen Budyonny and Kliment Voroshilov. Nine of Voroshilov's deputies were shot, however. His military council had 85 members of which 68 were shot and two committed suicides before they could be arrested. All the commanders of the Red Army's military districts were executed. Three of the five first-rank Army commanders and all ten second-rank Army commanders were shot. Fifty of the 57 corps commanders were shot. Of the 186 division commanders, 154 were either shot or imprisoned. Of 26 corps commissars, 25 were subjected to repressions, as were 58 of 64 division commissars. Of 456 Red Army regiment commanders, 401 were subjected to repressions. All this happened while Hitler was building up the German military and preparing for the Anschluss with Austria.

On April 8, 1938, ominously, Yezhov was appointed waterways minister[167] while continuing to serve as head of the NKVD. Given that Yezhov's predecessor, Yagoda, had been appointed minister of railways prior to his arrest (albeit as a transfer, not a second post), this appointment did not look like a promotion. On August 22, 1938, Beria became Yezhov's first deputy at the NKVD and gradually took over leadership at the agency.

In a futile attempt to survive, knowing that a premature Kremlin death awaited anyway, Yezhov wrote a resignation letter to Stalin on November 23, 1938, confessing to numerous errors and transgressions. Mindful of the fate of Yagoda's relatives, he begged Stalin to 'leave my 70-year-old mother in peace.' The next day, Yezhov was removed as head of the NKVD; for the time being, however, he kept his positions as Secretary of the Party CC, Chair of the Party Oversight Commission, minister of waterways. A fellow Georgian of Stalin's, Lavrenty Beria, however, was appointed to succeed Yezhov at the NKVD.

On April 9, 1939, Yezhov was stripped of the post of minister of waterways (the ministry itself was divided into river and sea fleets); the next day, he was arrested in future Stalin deputy Georgy Malenkov's office, with Beria present and participating in the arrest. Beria himself took charge of the Yezhov case.

Yezhov was kept in the Sukhanovo Prison, a special-regime NKVD facility. The indictment against him mentioned not only 'counterrevolutionary activity,' but also homosexual relations. During the interrogations and at the trial, Yezhov rejected all the accusations against him and pathetically admitted to only one error: doing too little to purge 'enemies of the people' from the Intelligence agencies:

> During the pretrial investigation I said that I was not a spy or a terrorist, but they didn't believe me and subjected me to severe beatings. I spent twenty-five years of my life in the Party honorably fighting against our enemies and destroying them. I have in fact committed some crimes for which I may deserve to be shot, and I will talk about them later, but as for the crimes attributed to me in the indictment, I never committed them and am innocent of them all... I do not deny my heavy drinking, but I worked like an ox... Had I wanted to commit a terrorist act against any member of the government, I would not have needed to recruit anyone for that purpose; I could have done this vile deed myself at any moment, using the technology at my disposal.... I purged 14,000 Chekists, but my worst offense is that I didn't purge enough.

On April 24 Yezhov wrote a statement confessing to homosexual relations, with a list of his male lovers and partners. They were all arrested and shot—among them Filipp Goloshchekin, one of the organizers and participants in the execution of the Tsar's family, and Leningrad division commissar Vladimir Konstantinov. On February 3, 1940, Yezhov was sentenced to death. He was shot the next day in the building of the Military Collegium of the USSR Supreme Court. His body was cremated. On January 24, 1941, almost a year after his death, Yezhov was stripped of all his state awards and his so-called special rank.

As with Sicilian mafia, so in Stalinist Russia. After Yezhov's arrest on April 10, 1939, it was his relatives' turn. His brother Ivan Yezhov was arrested two weeks later and shot in 1940. His nephews Anatoly Babulin and Viktor Babulin were shot the same year; a third nephew, Sergei Babulin, was somehow spared. He suffered in the camps and in internal exile until late May 1953 (Stalin died on March 5 of that year), then was freed under a general amnesty. The nephews' mother, Yezhov's sister Yevdokia ('Babulina') was left alone; having two sons shot and the third imprisoned was apparently deemed sufficient. Yezhov's 'old mother' was also left in peace as Yezhov had begged.

In 1988, the Military Collegium of the USSR Supreme Court refused to exonerate Yezhov on the grounds that the crimes he had committed included repression of more than a million and a half Soviet citizens, of whom 'about half were shot' and the murder of his second wife Yevgenia (until 1988, the official version was that she had killed herself).

Beria's rise ran parallel to Yezhov's decline. On September 11, 1938, Beria was promoted to First-Rank Intelligence Service Commissar. On September 29, he was made Head of the Chief Directorate of Intelligence Services (GUGB), which had been restored within the NKVD (and was the predecessor of the NKGB). On November 25, 1938, he was also given the post of minister of internal affairs (like Dzerzhinsky before him),[168] while Beria's position as head of the GUGB was given to Vsevolod Merkulov, who had been promoted a day before to first deputy Minister of Internal Affairs.

Beria's appointment to the Lubyanka marked the end of Chekism's long rout under Stalin, however. Under Beria, the Lubyanka was ultimately to regain some of its old luster. Unlike the Party apparatchik Yezhov, Beria had combined Party work and Intelligence—first in the Transcaucasian region from where he and Stalin hailed and then in Soviet agencies. Beria was, in a way, a hybrid of Yagoda and Yezhov. Following Lenin's precept to leave no enemies alive before an offensive, Beria made sweeping arrests of 'Yezhov's men' in the NKVD, the chief prosecutor's office and the courts between September 1938 and January 1939. Of course, Yezhov himself had earlier conducted a similar purge of 'Yagoda's men' in the NKVD and, in his own words, had had 14,000 Intelligence officers shot. This had been part of Stalin's attack on the Lubyanka. The precise number of 'counterrevolutionaries' executed by Beria is unknown. According to some estimates, approximately 4,200 death sentences were issued in 1939-1940, not all of them to 'Yezhov's men' in the NKVD. But obviously, thousands—perhaps as many as 20,000 or 30,000—Intelligence employees were arrested in the Beria years, and many were shot.

Listing Beria's victims or analyzing the work of the repression, law enforcement, and intelligence agencies he headed is beyond the scope of this book. However, one unfinished case Beria inherited from his Intelligence predecessors is worth noting. There was one leftover of Lenin's era: his widow, Nadezhda Krupskaya. She died on February 27, 1939 (a little over a year after her sister Maria Ulyanova) during the last year of purges of the old Bolshevik cadre who were Stalin's peers and knew Lenin first-hand rather than through the myths surrounding him.[169] After Lenin's death in 1924, the two women who were the last of his closest relatives and had been with him the day he died at Gorki, on Stalin's orders, continued to be looked after by one of Lenin's chefs. This was Spiridon, Vladimir Putin's grandfather. Given Krupskaya's suspicions about Dzerzhinsky's and Stalin's connection to Lenin's premature death, the two women must have understood the continuation of Spiridon's service—the only cook not to have ever been arrested—in their kitchen as, in reality, the assignment of their jailer and potential executioner. Putin recalled that Spiridon was always reluctant to speak about his career in general and long service to the Lenins in particular. Though the connection was illustrious in the Marxist-Leninist Soviet Union, reticence would suit a Cheka agent appointed to the surviving members of the Lenin household. Krupskaya was reported to have died after eating a slice of the birthday cake presented to her with Stalin's compliments. It might be prudent for any Chekist not to detail their close connection to the dark period of Stalin's purges to avoid facing unanswerable questions: for example, who was involved with making the cake for Krupskaya's 70th birthday?

There is no need to enumerate the posts and positions Beria occupied from November 25, 1938, when he became minister of internal affairs.[170] Fairly soon, Beria was second only to Stalin in the Soviet balance of power. Obviously, he always supported Stalin in everything and did everything to Stalin's satisfaction; otherwise, he would soon have shared Yagoda's and Yezhov's fate of a slow decline followed by a swift execution. However, when the moment did come that Stalin was no longer satisfied with him and Beria sensed a change in 'the boss's' attitude, he was able to find a way out of his hairy predicament (we will return to Beria below).

It is difficult to separate Beria the Soviet statesman from Beria the head of the Intelligence Services. As part of this analysis, it is important to note that by March 5, 1953, when Stalin died, Beria was the only pretender left to the post of the next Soviet leader—whatever his exact title. Stalin, the General Secretary of the Party— who had ceased to be the General Secretary even before he died—was not officially the leader of the Soviet state. As General Secretary of the Communist Party of the USSR, which legally had nothing to do with the government, he had *de facto* ruled the country since 1923 once Lenin had been removed and the SNK stripped of its clout.

Abdurakhman Avtorkhanov wrote a monograph on the question of Stalin's removal, *The Enigma of Stalin's Death* (1986). But there was no enigma really. In the context of everything we know (or suspect) about the deaths of nearly all Soviet leaders, very few were lucky enough to die a natural death in their own beds. Avtorkhanov's well-argued theory that Beria, Khrushchev, Malenkov and Nikolai Bulganin (defense minister, 1953-1955) conspired to remove Stalin no longer seems sensational, the way it sounded in 1981 when Avtorkhanov published his book. One might even say that Stalin's unnatural death seems absolutely natural in the context of Soviet Russia.

The fluid nature of the Soviet hierarchy meant that after Stalin had eliminated the threat posed by the Lubyanka, peril could come from other parts of the Kremlin. In fact, the entire Kremlin *nomenklatura* had to keep a close eye on the different agendas of their bosses.

Beria's deputy, Merkulov, was appointed to the newly recreated ministry of intelligence services on February 3, 1941. On May 7, 1946, he was replaced in this post by Viktor Abakumov.[171] Thus, starting in 1946, Merkulov and Abakumov were Soviet ministers of intelligence services. Both were ill-fated and would be disgraced, however. Abakumov fell victim to three Soviet leaders who were pursuing different goals. Stalin was planning the dismissal and execution of Beria; Beria and Malenkov, the removal of Stalin. As it turned out, someone was also simultaneously planning to remove Beria. For Abakumov it all came together on a fateful date: July 11, 1951.

The pretext for Abakumov's dismissal was the 'Leningrad Affair'. What exactly it entailed didn't really matter. Like all the Intelligence trials of that period, it was fabricated from start to finish and its fabrication was engineered by Abakumov—as instructed.

The catalyst was the prominent Leningrad Party official Andrei Zhdanov, who had become a Secretary of the CC[172] and headed the Leningrad regional and city Party committee and was considered one of many potential successors to Stalin. Fifty-two-year-old Zhdanov's premature death in August 1948 had a tragic outcome.

Those condemned in the Leningrad Affair included CC secretary Kuznetzov; Petr Popkov, First Secretary of the Leningrad Regional and City Party Committee; Yakov Kapustin, Second Secretary of the Party's City Committee; Leningrad City Executive Committee Chair Petr Lazutin; and USSR State Planning Board Chair Voznesensky. They were accused of treason and of separatist designs with regard to the Communist Party and the nation. But Zhdanov's fate also affected his Kremlin protégés, two in particular.

During the Great Patriotic War (World War II), Stalin had brought several young Party recruits into his inner circle. One of them was Nikolai Voznesensky. He held the post of First Deputy Chair of the SNK and was a member of the State Defense Committee and the Committee on rebuilding the economy in areas liberated form German occupation. A member of the CC (1939-1949), the USSR Academy of Sciences (1943) and the Politburo (1947-1949), a Stalin Prize laureate (1947), and the head of the State Planning Board for eleven years, Voznesensky was in Stalin's words, the future Soviet leader. Stalin also elevated Alexei Kuznetzov, a member of the CC from 1939, the First Secretary of the Leningrad Regional and City Party Committee in 1945-1946, and Secretary of the CC from March 18, 1946 until January 28, 1949. Stalin was grooming him (or so he said) as his successor in the post of General Secretary of the Party. Both had been recommended by Zhdanov.

All the defendants in the 'Affair' were sentenced to death on September 30, 1950. Voznesensky was put to death on September 30, Kuznetzov on October 1, 1950. These executions themselves became a prologue to a wave of repressions against all high-ranking officials in the regional, city and district Party structures in Leningrad. What's more, officials with a Leningrad Party background who had advanced to leadership posts in various Party, government, and public organizations around the country were also eliminated. Altogether, over 2,000 people in various parts of the Soviet Union were arrested in relation to the Leningrad Affair.

Meanwhile a second 'Affair' was also in the works. This was the investigation of 'a Zionist conspiracy inside MGB [ministry of the intelligence services] of the USSR.' This one was based on skillful opportunism.

A Lieutenant Colonel Mikhail Ryumin served at the MGB[173] as a senior investigator in the Investigative Division on high-priority cases. Born in 1913, he had dropped out of school after eighth grade but had completed a short course in accounting. Before the start of the Great Patriotic War, he had headed the planning and finance section in the administration of the Moscow-Volga Canal construction project (that is, part of the Soviet penal system). During the war, Ryumin worked as an investigator for SMERSH, the military counterintelligence service *Smert' Shpionam* ('death to spies') then headed by Abakumov, the future minister of the intelligence services. When the war was over, Ryumin was transferred to the central staff of the

MGB.

According to one version of the events, Ryumin had lost some secret documents and was facing severe censure. In an attempt to seize the initiative from his boss and make a preemptive strike, Ryumin wrote to Stalin and accused MGB minister Abakumov of the assassination of Professor Yakov Ettinger, a prominent cardiologist who had been under investigation on charges of anti-Soviet activity. Ettinger had supposedly confessed that he had intentionally botched Party apparatchik Aleksandr Shcherbakov's medical treatment, in order to kill him.[174] Shcherbakov, aged 43, had died of a massive heart attack on May 10, 1945, the day after the victory over Nazi Germany. (On this rare occasion, it was likely a premature death from genuinely natural causes—even post Stalin none of the Soviet leaders thought his death had engineered.)

In his libel against intelligence minister Abakumov, Ryumin described his boss as a 'danger to the state,' claiming more broadly that Abakumov had sabotaged the investigation into the subversive activities of 'Kremlin' doctors. He also alleged that a Zionist plot existed inside Abakumov's MGB.

That affair was the beginning of the 'Doctor's Plot'. The statement by Ryumin, senior investigator in the Investigative Department of the MGB, underwent some revisions at the office of Malenkov, Soviet Prime Minister, with input from his deputy Dmitry Sukhanov. It was only after Malenkov had approved the final text that the statement was given the green light. Malenkov—who knew Stalin quite well by then—emphasized parts of Ryumin's report in a way that ensured it would not fail to capture Stalin's phobia of the Lubyanka. Stalin, thereupon, decided to use Ryumin's statement as a pretext to start a new wave of purges in the ranks of Intelligence Services, which Beria had been running for over a decade, while simultaneously unleashing a nationwide anti-Semitic campaign.

Both the 'Affair' and the 'Plot' were cleverly instigated by Stalin's deputies Malenkov and Beria. Skillfully playing on the aging leader's paranoid suspicions and frightening him with imaginary plots by his numerous enemies, they worked to clear the space around Stalin while planting their own people in the ministries of the intelligence services and internal affairs.

The situation unfolded quickly. On July 2, 1951, Ryumin's petition 'Regarding the Dismal Condition of the Ministry of the State Security of the USSR' was submitted to the CC of the Party, and a decree was issued 9 days later. Abakumov, was removed from his post on July 12, 1951 and arrested on 14 July. Even so, he remained a member of the presidium of the Party CC until March 5, 1953—Stalin's death—and he also kept the post of CC Secretary until April 5, 1953. Lieutenant Colonel Ryumin, who replaced Abakumov, was first promoted to minister of the intelligence services with a simultaneous promotion in rank to Major General.

Merkulov was the first to get executed—after Stalin and Beria had died—on December 23, 1953. General Ryumin was executed on July 22, 1954. On December 19, 1954, Abakumov followed suit and was shot.

8: The Doctor's Plot and the Jewish Question

The real reason for the removal (and subsequent execution) of Abakumov was the cover up of crimes committed under Stalin in connection with the premature deaths of the Jewish Anti-Fascist Committee (JAC). Related were the preparations made for a significant new policy in dealing with the Soviet Jews, most of which involved their planned deportation. It is important to remember that, under Stalin, rolling deportation policies applied to numerous groups within the Soviet Union, resulting in families being uprooted, and causing chaos and deep tragedy for millions of Soviet citizens. In this case, Stalin's new policy towards Soviet Jews was just another project that impacted on an ethnic group that was not even among the most populous in the Soviet Union. It all started in December of 1947, when, following orders, intelligence minister Abakumov started fabricating capital indictments regarding the 'Anti-Soviet nationalist activities' of the JAC.

The JAC was a Soviet body that came about soon after Hitler's invasion of the USSR on June 22, 1941. Stalin needed money to fight Germany and it was one of the ways of raising money. Shortly after the invasion, on August 24, 1941, a radio broadcast by 'representatives of the Jewish people' was held. The event was initiated by Stalin himself, but the speedy organization of that event was spearheaded by Beria.[175] The speeches raised the alarm. They called for Jews around the world to take part in a sacred fight against fascist murderers who filled the streets of Europe with blood.

On the following day, the newspaper *Pravda* published a comprehensive account of the event, including the following details:

Among those who gave speeches at the event were People's Artist of the USSR Solomon Mikhoels; Jewish poet Peretz Markish; Red Army officer instrumental in the battles against the German fascists Eronim Kuznetsov; Jewish writer David Bergelson; a Russian academic who is a member of the Soviet Academy of Sciences, a member of the British Royal Society and a Laureate of the Stalin Prize Professor Pyotr Kapitsa; Honored Artist and famed movie director Sergei Eisenstein; an Academic of Architecture and a Laureate of the Stalin Prize Boris Iofan; German writer Theodor Plievier; writer Samuil Marshak; writer Ilya Erenburg; and a Jewish-American press officer Shakne Epshtein.

Over the course of the meeting, a worldwide appeal was made for donations:

Jewish brethren around the world! Our call to you is brought together with the voices of millions of innocent Jews whose blood was spilled needlessly. Our word is meant to be a signal, calling for resistance and revenge. Let every day bring you closer to reckoning with the enemy! Let every hour intensify a sacred fire and yearning for revenge in your hearts. Let your every minute be filled with preparedness for action. Civilization must be freed from fascism and it is your responsibility to eradicate it! May you play your part in this sacred war!

Both the radio-meeting itself and the call by its participants to the Jews worldwide met with widespread response from around the world. The heads of the global Zionist movement reacted with fulsome support for Moscow. Jewish organizations started being formed in many countries to raise funds in support of the Soviet Union.

Following Stalin's orders, the Soviet Ambassador to Great Britain Ivan Maisky met with the President of the World Zionist Organization Chaim Weizmann at the beginning of September of 1942 and secured his support for the Soviet Union. In October of 1941, Maisky met with David Ben-Gurion, the Head of the Jewish Agency for Israel and, later, the first President after independence, who told Maisky: 'We desire deeply to do everything in our power to ensure our victory. We wish to clarify how we can best assist the Soviet Union.... We believe we can contribute beyond the confines of Palestine as well.' On Stalin's orders, Maisky replied: 'You can provide significant assistance by convincing the Americans of the urgency of the crisis and of our need for their help. We require tanks, cannons, planes—as many as possible and, most importantly, as soon as possible.'

The JAC was formed as a permanent Soviet body that could be used as a covert front for the actions of Stalin and the NKVD to have a systematic impact on the actions of Jews worldwide for the benefit of the Soviets. Stalin tasked the Intelligence Service headed by Beria with managing the formalities in organizing the JAC. The radio broadcast of September 24, 1941, had confirmed the project was in a pair of capable hands with Beria.

He moved quickly. Three days after the broadcast, Beria pardoned two Polish Jews, Heinrich Erlich and Viktor Alter, who had been sentenced to death by the Soviet Union on fabricated charges of espionage for Poland and for criticizing the collaboration between the Soviet Union and Nazi Germany between August of 1939 and June 22, 1941; instead of a death sentence, they were now to spend 10 years in prison. They were Polish-Russian members of the General Jewish Labor Bund (the 'Bund'), a secular Jewish socialist party activists. Selected by Beria, they were chosen to further his goals of fostering ties with the Jewish community. They were Socialists rather than Communists. But after their recruitment, NKVD secret agents Erlich and Alter were released from prison and started working on the formation of the JAC under the watchful eye of Beria. Their credentials were impeccable.

Heinrich Erlich was born in Lublin in 1882, studied at the Warsaw University School of Law in the early 1900s and became a member of the Party. During the February 1917 Revolution in Russia, he was a member of the Executive committee of the Petrograd Council of Workers' and Soldiers' Deputies. In October of 1918, he returned to Warsaw. In Poland, Erlich was a visible figure in the Bund as a member of its Central Committee and edited the daily Party newspaper *Volkszeitung*. Upon the start of World War II and of the German occupation of Western Poland, he fled to Soviet-controlled territory. In October of 1939, he was arrested by the NKVD in Brest and sentenced to death on espionage charges and due to his connection to the Bund which was now forced underground.

Viktor Alter was born in 1890 in the Polish city of Mlawa, which was then a part of the Russian Empire. In 1912, he became an active Bund member, resulting in him being exiled to Siberia. After the October Revolution, Alter returned to Poland, heading up the Bund from 1919 until 1939. As was the case with Erlich, after the start of World War II, he fled to the Soviet-controlled Eastern Poland. At the end of September of 1939, he was arrested by the NKVD in Kovel, and also accused of espionage and of acting as a leader of the Bund's underground activities.

Unfortunately for them, they failed to impress Stalin and thus were arrested again in December of 1941. This time, they were accused of having ties with the German intelligence. They soon met premature deaths. According to the official sources, Erlich committed suicide in prison on May 14, 1942, while Alter was executed on February 17, 1943.

Nonetheless, the JAC project continued, now as a Soviet Information Bureau initiative, with the approval by the CC of the Party. To oversee the activities of the JAC, Stalin appointed the Deputy Minister of Foreign Affairs, Solomon Lozovsky, a former Secretary General of the Profintern (1921-1937). As a Deputy Minister of Foreign Affairs, Lozovsky first acted as a Deputy, and then as the Head of the Soviet Information Bureau, a propaganda agency formed after the German invasion of the USSR.

For the work on behalf of JAC, Lozovsky recruited Soviet Jews who were famous both in the USSR and abroad. Actor Solomon Mikhoels became the Head of JAC, and its members included writers Itzik Feffer, Leyb Kvitko, Peretz Markish, David Bergelson, Samuel Galkin; artistic director of the Moscow State Jewish theater (GOSET) Benjamin Zuskin; Chief Physician of the Central Clinical Hospital (The Botkin Hospital) Boris Shimeliovich; Academician of the Academy of Sciences of the USSR and Director of the Academy of Medical Sciences' Institute of Physiology Lina Stern.

On April 7, 1942, Soviet newspapers announced the formation of JAC and published its appeal to 'Jews Around the World.' The appeal was signed by 47 prominent Soviet Jews. JAC started publishing a newspaper called *Einikait* (unity), which was distributed all over the world and called for not just fighting Nazis, but also for helping the Soviet Jews.

Stalin saw raising money from wealthy American Jews as the main goal of JAC. To that end, he sent on a trip to the United States the Head of JAC Solomon Mikhoels and a member of its leadership committee, poet Itzik Feffer. Their pre-trip debriefing was overseen by Beria personally. The two men spent over three months raising money in the United States, meeting with various leading global and American luminaries of science and culture, including Albert Einstein, Charlie Chaplin, Marc Chagall, Thomas Mann, Lion Feuchtwanger, Theodore Dreiser and Sholem Asch. They also had meetings with The World Zionist Organization leader Chaim Weitzmann, the World Jewish Congress leader Nahum Goldmann, and famous American rabbis Stephen Samuel Wise and Moshe Yechiel Epstein.

Former head of the 4th Directorate of NKVD-NKGB (Sabotage and Intelligence) Lieutenant-General Pavel Sudoplatov later recalled the following details of the trip:

> Back in 1943, an actor and Director of the Moscow State Jewish Theater Mikhoels, together with Jewish poet and our trusted agent Feffer, undertook a long trip to the United States as leaders of the Jewish Anti-Fascist Committee. The operational logistics of Mikhoels's trip and the development of his operational links with Jewish groups were led by Kheifets.

Grigory Kheifets was a Soviet Intelligence resident in California, working there under the cover of the Vice Consul of the Consulate General of the USSR.

During their overseas tour, Stalin's fundraisers were able to gather for the benefit of the Red Army an amount of money that was enormous by those days' standards: according to estimates, between $30 and $50 million.

Serendipitously, the JAC's War fundraising was to segue into another NKVD's intelligence in the US. At the end of World War II, Kheifets and Vasily Zarubin, the Soviet Intelligence resident in Washington DC, who was operating under the cover of the embassy's Secretary of the Soviet General Council Office, were focused on a different—nuclear—project, which was led by Beria. They channeled false information to Robert Oppenheimer and Albert Einstein, the American academics who were closely involved in the Manhattan Project (the US program on the development of nuclear weapons). This information claimed Stalin had post-war plans to establish a Jewish Autonomous Republic in Crimea—an invented story that was merely part of the Soviet intelligence-gathering operation. General Sudoplatov writes that it had a dual role of misleading the British and raising further money for Russian post-War restoration:

> In 1945, the Soviet Leadership spread rumors about the pending creation of the Jewish Autonomous Republic in Crimea, where Jews from all over the world, and especially those from Europe who suffered from fascism, would be able to gather. Stalin's bluff had several objectives. First, he wished to placate the British allies who feared the creation of a Jewish state in Palestine, which was under the British Mandate Government. Second, Stalin wanted to raise capital for rebuilding the Soviet national economy destroyed by World War II. Beria gave me an order to 'gauge' the Americans on the issue during my conversations with Harriman, the US Ambassador in Moscow (back in 1945, I met with him under the name of Matveyev).

On Stalin's orders, the false narrative about the creation of the Jewish Autonomous Republic in Crimea was 'fed' not just to Oppenheimer and Einstein, but also to Martin Kamen, another prominent American scientist and a close associate of Oppenheimer, with whom the Soviet Intelligence officer Kheifets became friendly. Kheifets's mistress, Louise Rosenberg-Bransten, was the one who introduced him to Oppenheimer. Another Soviet Intelligence resident officer in the US, Vasily Zarubin, acted through Earl Browder, the General Secretary of the Communist Party of the United States, since Oppenheimer was more of a behind-the-scenes, Party sympathizer. Given that during that period, a major effort was underway in the United States to develop atomic weapons, and Einstein and Oppenheimer were at the helm of this effort, proximity to them provided the Soviet Intelligence operatives with access to these scientists the opportunities to recruit valuable agents privy to classified information. (Indeed, they were not the only Soviet agents who infiltrated Einstein's and Oppenheimer's inner circles, as will be discussed later.)

When World War II ended in 1945, however, Stalin's need for JAC and its US and global network diminished. In 1945, the JAC's 'controller' Lozovsky was fired from the Soviet Ministry of Foreign Affairs. In the summer of 1946, the Foreign Policy Department of the CC of the Party launched an investigation into JAC, and based on the results of the investigation, Alexander Panyushkin, Committee's Deputy Head, informed both leaders of JAC, Mikhoels and Feffer, that the JAC would be shut down. This was a bad sign. But, for the time being, the JAC was just transferred from the auspices of the Soviet Information Bureau to the Foreign Policy Department. Optically, it looked like a demotion rather than the beginning of the JAC's extermination.

Of course, JAC leaders Mikhoels and Feffer were not aware that on October 12, 1946, the Ministry of the Intelligence Services had sent a letter to the CC and to the Council of Ministers highlighting the 'nationalistic leanings of several members of the Jewish Antifascist Committee'—essentially a death warrant. However, Stalin slow-walked the process as he worried about eliminating famous Jewish leaders in view of Mikhoels' recent trip to the United States. Only at the end of 1947 did he give the order to Abakumov to 'eliminate' Mikhoels but to make the premature death of the theater man look like an accident to avoid raising a debate about his death.

To carry out the task, Abakumov formed a special team, which included Sergei Ogoltsov, the Deputy Minister of State Security; Lavrenty Tsanava, Minister of Belarussian Intelligence Services; and Fyodor Shubnyakov, the Head of the 2nd and 3rd Departments of the Second Chief Directorate (Counterintelligence). On the evening of January 12, 1948, Mikhoels was assassinated in Minsk along with Vladimir (Wolf) Golubov, a writer who was with him at that time and who was a recruited Cheka agent. The assassins received medals for their work. It did look like a tragic accident—a truck ran over the victims.

By March 26, 1948, Abakumov had compiled fabricated cases against the JAC, using precisely the facts of their foreign intelligence missions as the reason for their execution.

He sent a report to Stalin informing him that the 'leaders of the Jewish Anti-Fascist Committee, being active nationalists and harboring pro-American views, were actively carrying out anti-Soviet activities.'

On November 20, 1948, JAC was officially disbanded and shut down on account of being a 'Center of Anti-Soviet propaganda.' On the same day, the Politburo ordered that the 'Ministry of Intelligence Services should immediately dissolve the 'Jewish Anti-Fascist Committee, as the facts show that this committee is a hub for Anti-Soviet propaganda and regularly promotes Anti-Soviet information to foreign intelligence services. Accordingly, all newspapers related to the Committee should be shut down and the Committee affairs be reassigned. In the meantime, nobody is to be arrested.'

Arrests began within a month. In December of 1948, both Izik Feffer, the new leader of the JAC, and Benjamin Zuskin, the Director of the Moscow State Jewish Theater, were arrested. The arrests of dozens of other members of JAC, including all of its leaders, followed at the beginning of 1949. All those arrested were accused of 'ties with Jewish Nationalist organizations in America.'

On January 18, 1949, Solomon Lozovsky, who had been earlier removed as head of the Soviet Information Bureau and expelled from the CC and from the Party itself, was arrested. Effectively, he was indicted for organizing JAC, not as a result of orders given in support of communism, but for the purpose of the exact opposite—providing nationalist counterintelligence access to Russia:

Former Head of the Soviet Information Bureau is accused of espionage and of being one of the leaders of the Jewish Nationalist underground operating in the USSR. He was pivotal in transforming JAC into a center of nationalism and anti-Soviet espionage. After securing permission in 1943 to send his accomplices Mikhoels and Feffer to America, he tasked them with establishing connections to the reactionary circles in order to secure their support in the fight against the Soviet Government. He supplied them with sensitive information describing the current conditions of the Soviet economy, industries and culture. Acting on the Americans' orders, he sought to force the transfer of Crimea to the Jews and organized the gathering and handoff of critical sensitive information on the Soviet Union to the Americans. He had a personal relationship with B.Z. Goldberg, the American spy who visited the USSR.

At the beginning of 1949, on Stalin's orders, a comprehensive 'anti-cosmopolitanism' campaign was also initiated. The campaign included mass layoffs of Jews across the country and large-scale criminal investigations into their activities. As a result, USSR's scientific and cultural elite was arrested. The list included 217 Jewish writers and poets, 108 actors, 87 artists and 19 musicians. No longer needing the money generated by JAC's international efforts, the accusations included lack of Soviet patriotism on the part Soviet Jews. Markish wrote at the time: 'Hitler sought to ruin us physically while Stalin wishes to accomplish this spiritually.'

The criminal proceedings against JAC were led by the Military Collegium of the USSR Supreme Court chaired by Alexander Cheptsov, Lieutenant General of Justice. Proceedings behind closed doors began on April 30, 1952. On the same day, Abakumov's successor as minister of the intelligence services Semyon Ignatiev described the arrested members of JAC as 'American spies' in a letter to Stalin. The axe came down quickly. On July 18, 1952, all the accused except Lina Stern and Solomon Bregman (Deputy Minister of State Control of the RSFSR) were sentenced to death. Lina Stern was handed a 3.5-year labor camp sentence and a subsequent 5-year exile to Central Asia. Bregman fell into a coma while in prison on June 16, 1952, and died there on January 23, 1953. The death sentence was carried out on August 12, 1952, when thirteen members of JAC were executed by firing squad.

What turned Stalin's mind against JAC? The premature deaths of its staff and Party controller cannot be viewed separately from history of the creation of the State of Israel, ratified by the United Nations General Assembly on May 17, 1948. Stalin had no problem with Israel's independence as such. Mikhail Vetrov, an assistant of Stalin's deputy Molotov, later recalled Stalin's thinking regarding the matter: 'Let's agree to the creation of the State of Israel. This will be a pain in the neck for the Arab nations and will make them turn their back on Britain. As a result, the British influence will dissipate in Egypt, Syria, Turkey and Iraq.' The United Nations General Assembly came to an agreement regarding the creation on the Palestinian British territory of two states—Arab and Jewish. 'Now there will be no peace there,' noted Stalin after hearing of the UN vote results. And indeed, on that same day, Iraq, Egypt, Jordan and Syria declared war on Israel. Through Czechoslovakia and Yugoslavia, Stalin even started providing considerable military resources to Israel, including planes, artillery and various firearms, at the beginning of the war between Israel and its four neighbors. In an irony of history, Soviet assistance consisted mainly of donating German weapons captured by the USSR after the end of World War II.

However, something unexpected happened that triggered Stalin's paranoia. The creation of the State of Israel seemed to 'activate' Soviet Jews, an engagement that culminated with the arrival in the USSR of the Israeli mission headed by Golda Meir on September 11, 1948. The Jews living in Moscow were elated by the Israeli visit, misreading the fact that the USSR had just cast its vote in the UN supporting the creation of the State of Israel as a belief that Soviet Jews had the full support of the Soviet Government.

Following Meir's visit, *Pravda* published a sour article on September 21, 1948, by famous Soviet writer Ilya Ehrenburg. It stated that Jews in the USSR have nothing to gain by going to Israel since they had already assimilated in their own country. After that the dismantling of JAC was inevitable. Mass arrests of its members and of the Jewish Soviet intelligentsia at large followed, as well as the campaign against 'cosmopolitanism' as a threat to Party Communism.

In that same vein, future Soviet leader Khrushchev, as the First Secretary of the Moscow City Committee of the Communist Party, actively participated in 1950 in an investigation into 'Zionists' at the famous automobile manufacturing plant in Moscow named after Stalin, and personally questioned Mikhail Likhachev, the plant director, accusing him of a lack of vigilance, pandering to 'Zionists' and promoting Jews to leadership positions. 'This direction of leadership has resulted in the creation of a Zionist espionage organization at this factory,' stated Khrushchev at the time. Premature deaths followed. During the investigation of the 'Zionist issues' at the factory, 48 people were arrested, of which 9 received death sentences. The list of the arrested included the sister of Nahum Eitingon, a Major-General in the intelligence services.

It was in this febrile atmosphere that Colonel Ryumin attacked his NKVD boss General Abakumov, by creating the myth of 'terrorist Dr Etinger' who not only had had designs on the life of his patient, Colonel General Alexander Shcherbakov, but was also a Jewish nationalist (that is, a pawn of the newly-minted Israel). Abakumov's crime was to have missed this importance of Dr Etinger to Soviet security. Malenkov and Beria thought it was particularly important that he had missed the significance of Etinger in view of Yagoda's Kremlin doctors who had poisoned Maxim Gorki more than fifteen years prior. It 'clearly' indicated that 'a criminal conspiracy exists among some medical doctors, with the ultimate goal of inflicting serious harm to the physical health and well-being of the leaders of the Communist Party and the Soviet Government in the course of medical treatment'.[176]

It became the basis for what is known as the 'Doctors' Plot'. The directive's outline was prepared by the Politburo Commission under Stalin's orders. As noted, the Commission included its chair, deputy chair of the Council of Ministers of the Soviet Union, and second-in-command in the Communist Party, Malenkov, and deputy chair of the Council of Ministers of the USSR, and second-in-command in the government, Beria.[177] Stalin personally supervised the preparation of this document and strengthened its tone in several places, including the sentences discussing Abakumov's criminal activities and the attendant necessity to remove him as Minister of the Intelligence Services. On July 12, 1951, Abakumov (who had already been removed from his post on July 4) was arrested. He was facing a long detainment period, the majority of which he would spend handcuffed and shackled even during nighttime, pursuant to Stalin's orders.

Stalin's fight against 'Global Zionism' was now also waged internationally. At Stalin's instigation, a court case was initiated in Prague in November of 1952 with respect to 14 prominent Czechoslovakian Communist Party members. They were accused of treason, subversive activities and plotting assassinations of the 'nation's leadership'. The list of the accused included, for example, Rudolf Slánský (Saltzman), Secretary General of the Czech Communist party. The court sentenced 11 people, including Slánský, to death; 3 people were sentenced to life in prison. The process was clearly anti-Semitic in nature, as 11 of the 14 accused were Jewish. Stalin himself closely controlled the proceedings through Soviet intelligence operatives who served as advisors in the various government and Communist Party departments in Czechoslovakia.

On January 13, 1953, Telegraph Agency of the Soviet Union (TASS) published a report about the uncovering of a Zionist conspiracy to eliminate Soviet leadership. On the same day, the newspaper *Pravda* published an unsigned article titled 'Vicious Spies and Assassins Masked as Medical Professors', which contained, among other things, the following statements:

> The majority of participants in the terrorist group—Miron Vovsi, Boris Kogan, Alexander Feldman, Alexander Grinstein, Yakov Etinger and others—were 'bought' by American Intelligence. They were recruited by 'Joint' [American Jewish Joint Distribution Committee]—an international Jewish bourgeois-nationalistic organization, a branch of US intelligence. The criminal nature of this Zionist spy organization, covering up its undercover activities as a charity, has been fully exposed.

On February 9, 1953, a grenade of an unknown origin had exploded on the territory of the Soviet Embassy in Tel Aviv. There were no casualties. Still, on February 12, the Soviet Union announced that it was severing its diplomatic relations with Israel while commencing a full-scale cooperation with the Arab nations, including deliveries of weaponry, training of their military personnel in Soviet military academies and participating by Soviet military in Arab countries' campaigns against Israel.

As we saw, Stalin's death did not save Abakumov. He knew too much and no longer mattered. The new Communist Party leadership proceeded to execute him 'just in case'. As usual, following Abakumov's arrest, his deputies Sergey Ogoltsov and Yevgeny Pitovranov, as well as a large group of leaders within the various central departments of the Ministry of State Security, were also arrested. Another one who fell from grace was Grigory Mairanovsky, a particularly unsavory biochemist who worked on poisons for the NKVD, tested them on political prisoners, and took part in assassinations. On December 13, 1951, he was arrested and accused of espionage for Japan, illegal possession and misappropriation of poisonous substances, and abuse of authority. While in prison, Mairanovsky desperately fought for his life and wrote many letters to Beria.[178] Perhaps these letters helped him avoid execution, or he just knew too little: he was sentenced to 10 years in prison.

After Stalin's death, on November 22, 1955, the Military Collegium of the USSR Supreme Court vacated the sentence of the executed members of JAC due to a lack of evidence. Mairanovsky, after his release at the beginning of 1962, died at home from natural causes in 1964 despite his objectionable scientific career. He was banned from living in Moscow, Leningrad, as well as the capitals of all Soviet Republics. During the last years of his life, he worked in one of the research institutes of the city of Makhachkala, Dagestan. On December 29, 1988, the Commission of the Politburo of the CC reviewed materials underlying the legal and party rehabilitation of the individuals in relation to 'matters of the Jewish Antifascist Committee' and concluded that they were fabricated, noting that the individuals conducting relevant investigations from 1952-1954 were convicted of using falsified court documents.

9: Stalin's Premature Death (Lavrenty Beria)

Unequivocally all of the leaders of the Lubyanka were executed by the Communist Party and the Soviet Government, assuming that Dzerzhinsky and Menzhinsky's premature deaths were intentional, too. Let us allow this point to sink in. The intelligence chiefs were eliminated not by enemies, not by counterrevolutionaries, not by interventionists, not by Nazis, not by nationalists-terrorists, not by anti-Soviet-minded public figures, but by the Communist Party and by the Soviet Government. This is precisely how Chekist officers viewed the widespread Soviet-era terror towards their colleagues—even as the world at large considered them to be the covert enforcement branch of the Communist Party of the Soviet Union and the bloody executioners of the era. If the population at large despised the Communists and Chekists, then equally the Chekists despised the Communists who were the reason for all of the arrests, executions and other premature deaths that cut through their organization.

By the standards of the Nuremberg trials (1945-1946), all Chekist agents of the Stalin era can be viewed as criminals who deserved punishment and even the death sentence. In a sense, perhaps, does it matter who carried out their execution and when—whether it was Stalin himself or his successors? While the Lubyanka may have been a criminal organization under Nuremberg rules—a criminal fig leaf for government assassinations and repression—its individual members together made it a mafia. The mafia did not force its members to become criminals. Throughout Soviet history, clearly, the bloody pendulum of Red Terror, swung in different directions. Its scythe spared few. From one moment to the next, even 'insiders' became the 'outsiders' at different times. Very often very little distinguished one group from the other.

The reality is, however, that the Communist Party, on the one hand, feared the monster it created—the Lubyanka—but on the other hand, needed it desperately since only the Intelligence Services could protect the Party from the enemy—namely, the rest of the world. At the same time, the Soviet Intelligence Services feared by everyone else was afraid only of the Communist Party. This is because they knew only too well that the Communist Party top would from time to time grab the initiative and let the Lubyanka loose on itself to carry out yet another purge and assassinate tens of thousands of Chekists.

Take Lev Shvartsman, Deputy Chief of the MGB Investigation Department of the USSR of Special Importance. He was responsible for the 'case files' of writer Isaak Babel, the writer-journalist Mikhail Kol'tsov and theater director Vsevolod Meyerhold.

Yet he was arrested in October of 1951, together with a number of other Jewish Intelligence officers, for 'nationalistic Jewish conspiracy' under the leadership of the Abakumov fall-out. Shvartsman's death sentence by firing squad on August 26, 1951, was rubber-stamped by the Military Collegium of the USSR Supreme Court. He was an accomplished assassin and in his pre-execution note, Shvartsman offered detailed instructions on the number and type of bullets he should get to shorten his suffering:

> I only ask that if the verdict is not vacated, please use five explosive bullets and a firearm in carrying out the death sentence since I would not die after one, or even two or three explosive bullets—let alone the ordinary ones, but would instead continue to live and suffer while my physical condition is so terrible that I can no longer endure any pain and suffering.

A new swing of the pendulum followed in 1953, after Stalin's death. After a short period of confusion—during which it quickly disposed of Beria at the NKVD as Stalin had of Dzerzhinsky in 1926—the Party assumed absolute control once again. It did not let go of it until Yuri Andropov, the former Head of the KGB[179], came to power in 1982 and became Soviet leader—that is Secretary General of the Communist Party.

We can only guess as to why by the beginning of March of 1953 a group of conspirators decided that the time for Stalin's premature death at 74 had come. Stalin was habituated to eliminating anyone who could pose even a mere theoretical threat to his power. Like a criminal, he never trusted anyone. Even during World War II, he ordered that the apartments of all Soviet Army Marshals were fitted with listening devices so that he knew for certain what his Army leaders were saying about him. A year after the June of 1946 Victory Parade led by the victorious Marshal Georgy Zhukov, Stalin assigned Zhukov to the Odessa Military District, both demoting and exiling him.

At the end of World War II, there were three major players, among others in the Soviet military, who held a Chief Marshal rank based on their military branch: Chief Marshal of Artillery, Nikolai Voronov; and Chief Marshals of Aviation, Alexander Novikov and Alexander Golovanov. They, too, were demoted by Stalin after the war. Marshal Novikov, in addition of being stripped of his rank, was imprisoned on trumped-up charges. On Stalin's orders, Nikolai Kuznetsov, an Admiral and Commander-in-Chief of the Soviet Navy, was also removed from his post in 1947. He was put on trial and demoted to Vice-Admiral.

Having spilled rivers of blood, Stalin was naturally growing more and more suspicious of retaliation. He publicly accused his loyal deputies Molotov and Voroshilov of espionage. At Beria's insistence, he removed from the Kremlin his long-term assistant Alexander Poskrebyshev, who had remained loyal to Stalin despite the execution of his own wife. At the October 1952 plenum of the CC, Stalin directed blistering criticism at former comrades-in-arms whom he hadn't yet had shot. Stalin's purpose was obvious. It was a compelling demonstration to his surviving inner circle that yet another big purge lay ahead. In fact, the new minister of the intelligence services (Semyon Ignatiev), had already received explicit orders from 'the boss' to go after the 'Big Mingrel'. Ignatiev was already busily putting together a 'case file'. Who was the 'Big Mingrel'? Beria, whose father had been a landowner from the Mingrel region of Georgia.

On February 20, 1953, Stalin summoned Ignatiev and Soviet intelligence chief Sudoplatov and assigned to them the task of removing Yugoslav leader Josip Broz Tito. During this conversation, Stalin made a seemingly casual reference to Beria: 'I don't like Beria. He's bad at cadre selection and keeps trying to place his own people everywhere.'

Ignatiev, who was Malenkov's plant, promptly relayed the conversation to Malenkov, who in turn warned Beria. Beria realized that this was no time to lose and that the 'Mingrel case file' was about to be closed with a host of bloody executions. 'He's going to shoot us all,' Beria said to Malenkov.

There was a general sense of looming danger. 'Had [Stalin] lived a year or two longer, I would not have survived, either,' Stalin's loyal deputy Molotov later recalled. Khrushchev, too, wrote in his memoirs, 'If Stalin had not died, I don't know how things would have turned out... [our] lives would have ended tragically.'

At that point, Malenkov and Beria had succeeded in scheming against Stalin's old entourage and replacing them with a new one handpicked by them. Abakumov had been their prime target. He was regarded as personally devoted to Stalin. When he was replaced with Malenkov's protégé, Ignatiev, the job of Ignatiev's deputy was given— with Stalin's unwitting consent—to Beria's man, Sergei Goglidze.

Next, in May 1952, General Nikolai Vlasik was removed as chief of Stalin's personal guard and sent to the city of Asbest, in the Urals, as Deputy Chief of the Bazhenov correctional labor camp. The new chief of Stalin's personal guard was Colonel Nikolai Novik. Just a few months later, in early December 1952, Vlasik was arrested in con- nection with the 'Doctors' Plot' that Beria and Malenkov had conjured up out of thin air. This was only natural since Vlasik had been 'in charge of medical care for members of the government and responsible for their background vetting.' Nor was it surprising that on June 17, 1953, the Military Collegium of the Soviet Supreme Court found him guilty of abusing his official position with especially aggravating circumstances. His case file added up to a sentence of ten years of exile, including removal of his general's rank and state allowances. Vlasik underwent almost daily interrogations, which stopped after Stalin died. Under the March 27, 1953 amnesty, his sentence was reduced to five years, and he was exiled to Krasnoyarsk. By the December 15, 1956 resolution of the Presidium of the Supreme Soviet, Vlasik was pardoned and his conviction was quashed. Even so, Stalin's former loyalist's rank and awards were not restored.

In 1952, most of the guards and other staff at Stalin's so-called 'nearer dacha' in Kuntzevo were also replaced with people beholden to Beria, of Georgian background. This could not have failed to make Stalin feel uncomfortable. 'Toward the end of his life Stalin started locking the doors... he felt some kind of growing fear,' Pavel Yegorov, an officer who was one of the twenty-four so-called 'traveling guards' or 'attached guards,' recalled later.[180]

There are many accounts confirming that Stalin's guard and staff were begging for medical assistance to Stalin while he was dying, and that his closest allies in the Party sabotaged such assistance—and that Stalin died. There are plenty of versions of his demise. One thing is clear: an outwardly healthy, not very old man spent an evening in the company of Malenkov, Beria, Khrushchev and Politburo member Nikolai Bulganin, drank with them into the early morning hours of March 1, 1953, as he often did, and never again saw the light of day. He lay unconscious on the floor in a pool of his own urine.

The leading participants in Stalin's removal were Beria, Malenkov and Khrushchev. Others involved in the conspiracy were Ignatiev, who was also the head of the so-called 'attached' officers in Stalin's personal guard—senior officers on duty that night Ivan Khrustalev and Mikhail Starostin, and deputy superintendent of Stalin's 'nearer dacha', Pyotr Lozgachev.

'All of a sudden there was a call from Malenkov,' wrote Khrushchev in his memoirs. 'He said, 'The guys from Stalin's dacha just called (he gave their last names)—Chekists. They sounded very worried and said that something might have happened to Stalin. We need to go out there immediately. I'm calling you and I've already alerted Beria and Bulganin. Go over there right away.' I quickly called my car, which was at my dacha. Got dressed in a hurry and went over there; it all took about 15 minutes. We had agreed that we were not going to go into Stalin's room but to see the men on duty.'

Khrushchev doesn't mention with whom he agreed, or with whom he went to Stalin's dacha. Somehow, no one thought of calling the doctors, or doing something to help Stalin, apart from going to see the guards.

Earlier in the morning of March 2, 1953, Colonel Starostin, who had taken over the watch from the senior officer on the shift, Colonel Khrustalev, called Ignatiev to report an unusual change in Stalin's schedule. Under Kremlin protocol, he was supposed to do exactly that: report to Ignatiev. Having received such news, the minister was supposed to get to the dacha himself as expeditiously as possible in order to gauge the situation and give the necessary instructions. Instead, for an unidentified reason, Ignatiev ordered Starostin to make phone calls and locate Beria.

It was an exceptional deviation. Beria had nothing to do with Stalin's personal security. The information that Stalin had overslept should not have been something that Ignatiev would have thought worthy of the time and attention of the second most important man in the state. But it did make sense if we assume that Ignatiev did not want to be drawn into a conspiracy as one of the active participants and refrained from making any criminal decisions whatsoever. He gave orders to notify Beria since he knew Beria was involved.

For the entire duration of Stalin's 'illness', Ignatiev did not make even one appearance at Stalin's dacha—even though it was his direct responsibility to go there at once. Malenkov, too, could have ordered 'his man' Ignatiev to Stalin's dacha. Instead, he decided to find out about the situation (and about the progress of the operation to remove Stalin) from someone else—Khrushchev, the Moscow Party chief. Khrushchev went over and learned that Stalin was still alive. Stalin's guards were neither concerned nor suspicious about the fate of the man they were protecting. Ostensibly, no one was worried. The tyrant had been successfully poisoned, his hours were numbered, the guard was doing nothing.

In his reminiscences about this major historical event, Khrushchev avoids specifying where and with whom he went and to which members of the guard they then spoke. With this information, Khrushchev departed from the dacha. To make sure that the news of Stalin's condition did not spread beyond the dacha and the guards did not start calling in doctors to see Stalin, the officers of the guard received a strict warning from Beria not to disclose information about 'the boss's' illness.

Again, this was odd. Officers of the leader's personal guard were to take orders only from the head of state or the chief of the guard—and no one else. These requirements were always extremely strict. For obvious reasons, no exceptions were allowed by Stalin in order to prevent attempted conspiracies within the head of state's inner circle to execute a coup.

The situation was truly paradoxical. Ignatief took no interest in the 'illness' of the man who had the highest level of protection in the country, for which he was personally responsible. In accordance with service regulations, he should have instructed every officer of the guard and every member of the dacha's service staff who was on duty on the night to submit a detailed report on what they had witnessed and what actions they had taken in the crisis as it unfolded. The premises of the dacha, including the kitchen, should have been sealed and carefully examined. Stalin's unfinished bottle of mineral water, for instance, should have been immediately submitted for testing. Nor was Stalin taken to the Kremlin hospital where doctors could have started giving the patient appropriate treatment; instead, he was dying at the dacha without receiving essential medical aid.

Meanwhile, there were many visits from various outsiders, people who had no medical training and who seemed instead to be waiting for the news that Stalin had finally died. Eyewitnesses—including Stalin's daughter Svetlana—noted that Beria was already acting like a boss and freely entering Stalin's personal rooms, which were strictly off-limits to outsiders while Stalin was still alive.

As a result, for three days no one was able to establish until March 5 what was happening to Stalin and what 'illness' was afflicting him. The fact of the Soviet leader's deliberate poisoning was only uncovered on March 5 after the results of tests conducted with a delay of several days came in. The autopsy later confirmed that poisoning had caused hemorrhaging in the brain, stomach and intestines, leading, in turn, to a paralysis of the right limbs and loss of speech. All of this bore some remarkable similarities to Lenin's death. The name Stalin was never mentioned to the doctors who performed the tests. They were told only that the test results would be picked up by Khrustalev, a Cheka colonel and the chief of Stalin's traveling guard. He was the first to learn that Stalin had been poisoned. Khrustalev did not live long after that. There is no solid information on his death, but his life ended prematurely in the same year as Stalin. One version is that he killed himself.

On March 15, 1953—ten days after Stalin's death—Ignatiev, who was not very actively involved in the conspiracy, was relieved of his post. Nonetheless, Ignatiev marked a milestone in the history of the Lubyanka. He was the first chief of that agency who was not shot after losing his job. He continued to serve in various Party and government posts, retired in 1960, lived in Moscow, and died peacefully on November 27, 1983 at the age of seventy nine. While nearly all of his predecessors were interred in unmarked or mass graves, Ignatiev was buried in Moscow's prestigious Novodevichy Cemetery.

Stalin's funeral took place on March 9, 1953. Standing on the Mausoleum, Beria pointed to the coffin with the 'boss's' body and said to Molotov, who stood next to him, 'I'm the one who got rid of him, I saved you all.' The next day, Malenkov declared during the meeting of the Presidium of the Party's CC, 'We believe it is essential to put an end to the policy of personality cult.' Thus, it appeared that the idea of imploding the Stalin personality cult did not come from Khrushchev but from Malenkov. As for Khrushchev, at that point he was mostly afraid to fall victim to yet another purge, this one conducted by Beria. 'As soon as Stalin collapsed, Beria started to spew venom against him. He cursed him, he mocked him. I just couldn't stand to listen to him!' Khrushchev recalled much later in his memoirs on the subject of Beria's behavior toward Stalin during his 'illness'.

There is considerable evidence that Beria was taken hostage by government officials without formal charges or a mandate from the prosecutor's office and killed. Beria's son Sergo and his widow Nina Gegechkori were also held at government dachas near Moscow for several months. Their house arrest was followed by solitary detention in the Lefortovo prison and then the Butyrka prison. At that time, Beria's death had not yet been officially disclosed, and none of his relatives ever saw his body. Much later, it was reported that after Beria was taken (on June 26) he was shot in his government cell on December 23, 1953, by Soviet Marshal Pavel Batitsky.

Just like in the 'good old days,' after the premature death of Beria and the dismissal of Ignatiev, the Party set about eliminating the closest Chekist associates of the fallen chiefs. Among others, all of Beria's deputies and his other close associates were shot: Merkulov, Vladimir Dekanozov, Goglidze, and the brothers Amayak and Bogdan Kobulov. It was the start a major new purge inside the Intelligence Services—this time, it was agents loyal to Stalin and Beria who were being purged.

There was no escape. Soviet Prosecutor General Andrei Vyshinsky, the chief coordinator of Stalin-era trials who had personally rubber-stamped death sentences and been in charge of carrying out Stalin's purges of the intelligence services, Party, government and military in the 1930s, was by then the Soviet representative at the United Nations in New York. In late October 1954, he was summoned to Moscow 'to deliver a report'. Realizing that he was facing arrest and execution for his 1930s crimes in Moscow, Vyshinsky delayed his departure. Then, on November 19, 1954, a special intelligence agent arrived from Moscow to New York on a diplomatic passport. The visit had an immediate effect. On November 22, at 9:15am, the Soviet delegation officially reported that the 70-year-old Vyshinsky had suddenly died of a heart attack while having breakfast at the Soviet mission to the UN.

Vyshinsky's body was never released from the premises of the Soviet mission, and no outsiders—diplomats, journalists, or police—were admitted into the building. Vyshinsky's death certificate was signed by 'Doctor Alexei Kassov,' the official physician of the Soviet embassy in Washington, DC and of the Soviet UN delegation in New York. This caused a conflict between the American authorities which did not want to accept the certificate made out by Dr Kassov, who lacked a license to practice medicine in the state of New York, and the Soviet delegation. Nonetheless, on the morning of November 23, Vyshinsky's body was taken back to Moscow on a specially chartered flight. The agent with a diplomatic passport who had arrived from Moscow four days earlier was also on the flight; so was Dr Kassov, the embassy doctor who never returned to America.

However, nothing reveals the Party's combat with the Intelligence Services—and vice versa—more eloquently than the stories of 'second-tier' Chekists who had worked under Beria and were arrested but did not end up being executed. We will tell several such stories but stress that there were thousands of them. They were loyal to the Communist Party, to which they belonged, and to the Intelligence Services where they worked and which they served with dedication and to the full extent of their abilities. Now, they found, the Party wanted nothing more than to find a pretext to arrest them, humiliate them, torture them and imprison them for the rest of their lives—in the same way as they previously did themselves to others. At times, cadre fortunes changed backwards and forwards with dizzying speed.

Yakov Serebryansky

In November 1923, Yakov Serebryansky received an offer from Yakov Blumkin (the assassin of German ambassador Mirbach during the Brest-Litovsk Treaty), appointed by the OGPU's Foreign Department as resident of covert Soviet intelligence in Palestine, to become his deputy. In December 1923, Serebryansky was made special plenipotentiary of the Foreign Department and left for Yafa with Blumkin. They were to collect information on Great Britain and France's plans in the Middle East and on local revolutionary movements. In 1924 Blumkin was recalled to Moscow, and Serebryansky began to work on his own. He was able to infiltrate the underground Zionist movement and to induce a large group of Russian émigrés to collaborate. They made up the core of a combat squad later known as 'Yasha's group.' In 1924, they were also joined by Serebryansky's wife Polina Belenkaya, also a Soviet intelligence agent.

In 1925-1926, Serebryansky became the undercover resident of the OGPU's Foreign Department in Belgium. In February 1927, he returned to Moscow, where he was admitted to the Communist Party. From Moscow, he went to Paris on another assignment as undercover resident and served there until March 1929, then returned to Moscow and was appointed chief of the First Department of the OGPU's Foreign Department, while simultaneously continuing to lead 'Yasha's group' whose purpose

102

was the deep infiltration of military-strategic targets in the event of a war and for sabotage and terrorist operations in peacetime. This group took its orders directly from OGPU Chair Menzhinsky. Serebryansky recruited more than 200 Soviet agents abroad.

In 1931, Serebryansky was arrested in Rumania, but was soon freed and continued his undercover work. In 1932, he traveled to the US; in 1934, to Paris. In 1935-1936, he was assigned to China and Japan. After the start of the civil war in Spain, he bought and delivered weapons for the republicans. He was also involved in the assassination of Trotsky's son Lev Sedov in Paris in February 1938, together with Chekist agent Mark Zborovsky (codename 'Tulip'), who had infiltrated Sedov's circle of friends.

In the fall of 1938, Serebryansky was recalled from France. On November 10, he and his wife were arrested in Moscow as they disembarked, under a warrant signed by Beria. Until February 1939, they were detained without charges. During the investigation, conducted by future minister Abakumov and later by the investigators Solomon Milshtein and Pyotr Gudimovich, Serebryansky was subjected to what were termed 'thorough methods of interrogation.' The transcript of one interrogation had a note from Beria: 'To Comrade Abakumov: Interrogate thoroughly!'

In the end, on July 7, 1941, the Military Collegium of the Soviet Supreme Court convicted Serebryansky of spying for Great Britain and France, having ties to NKVD 'conspirators' under Yagoda, and plotting terrorist acts against Soviet leaders. He was sentenced to execution by firing squad. His wife got 10 years in a labor camp for 'failure to report her husband's hostile activities.'

Serebryansky's fortunes changed yet again a month later. Following the German invasion, he received amnesty and was reinstated in his NKVD job and as a Party member in August 1941. He now oversaw intelligence-gathering, diversionary and sabotage operations in Western and Eastern Europe. In May 1946, he retired for health reasons. In May 1953, NKVD-General Sudoplatov offered him a post on the central staff of the Ministry of Internal Affairs (MVD), formerly the NKVD, where Sudoplatov was hiring his friends from intelligence who had survived the purges. This proved less lucky for Serebryansky. In July 1953, he was fired from the MVD; on October 8, 1953, he was arrested and sentenced to 25 years of imprisonment. On March 30, 1956, he died at the Butyrskaya prison during yet another interrogation.

Meanwhile, those executing Serebryansky's fall from grace, didn't fare much better. Chekist Gudimovich, who had 'thoroughly' interrogated Chekist Serebryansky on Beria's orders, was dismissed in 1953. Chekist General Milshtein, who had interrogated Chekist Serebryansky in 1938-1939, was himself arrested in July 1953 and shot in January 1955.

Naum Eitingon

Naum Eitingon's career had its own hazardous moments but it didn't end with his premature death. Like Serebryansky's boss Blumkin, he was a member of the Left SR party until it collapsed in 1917-1918. He became a Chekist in the VChK from 1920: he joined the Bolshevik Party; after graduating from the military academy of the Workers' and

Peasants' Red Army with a degree in oriental studies and started a glittering career in the Intelligence Services abroad. He worked at the Foreign Department of the OGPU, at first in China (1925). He was a vice consul of the General Consulate of the USSR in Harbin, Heilongjiang, from 1927-1929. In 1929, he was sent to Turkey, where the exiled Trotsky was living at the time. From 1930-1932, he served as an assistant to Serebryansky at the Directorate for Special Operations, then as chief of the Extrajudicial Operations Section of the Foreign Department of the OGPU. In 1936-1938, he served as deputy to the Soviet intelligence resident in Spain, Alexander M. Orlov.

Apart from the assassination of Trotsky in Mexico, Eitingon's job included organizing intelligence and sabotage operations abroad, including the assassination of Zhang Zuolin, the dictator of Northern China and Manchuria; the abduction of prominent White Army generals Alexander Kutepov and Evgeny Miller in France; the assassination of 'triple agent' Nikolai Skoblin in Spain; the transport of the Spanish gold reserve to the USSR.[181]

In July 1941, Eitingon became Deputy Chief of the 4th NKVD Directorate and Chief of Sudoplatov's Special Group under Beria. At the time, the 4th Directorate of the NKVD and the Special Group were mostly focused on intelligence, terror, and sabotage operations behind enemy lines. In 1945, Eitington branched out in a different direction and became Deputy Chief of the NKVD's (later NKGB's) 'Department S,' focused on the collection and analysis of intelligence related to the development of nuclear weapons. In the post-war years, Eitingon headed operations to eliminate anti-Soviet guerrillas conducted by the government in Lithuania and Western Belarus and organized assassinations of Ukrainian 'nationalist' leaders.

Being Jewish, in October 1951, he was arrested in connection with the non-existent 'Zionist conspiracy inside the MGB.' After Stalin's death, he was released at his former subordinate General Sudoplatov's request and, like Serebryansky, served in the MVD. In May 1953, he became Deputy Chief of the 9th Department of the MVD. In August 1953, he was arrested again. But this time as a member of 'Beria's gang' and sentenced to 12 years of imprisonment. Freed in 1964, he went on to work as a senior editor at the International Books publishing house and died in 1981.

General Pavel Sudoplatov was also a survivor, though he incurred more collateral damage. From October 1933, Sudoplatov worked at the Foreign Department of the OGPU. Apart from Russian, he was fluent only in Ukrainian and thus began to specialize in Ukrainian nationalists. In 1935, Sudoplatov succeeded in infiltrating the inner circle of the Organization of Ukrainian Nationalists in Berlin. On May 23, 1938, carrying out a direct order from Stalin, he managed to assassinate Ukrainian nationalist leader Evgeny Konovalets by handing him a bomb, disguised as a box of chocolates, in the restaurant of the Atlanta Hotel in Rotterdam, the Netherlands.

After returning to the USSR, Sudoplatov served as acting chief of the NKVD's Foreign Department from November 6 to December 2, 1938; then, he was demoted to chief of the Spanish department. In late December 1938, he was suspended from his job and expelled from the Party for 'connections to enemies of the people,' then reinstated in January 1939. He was the organizer of the operation codenamed 'Canard'—the assassination of Trotsky. During World War II, he headed the department that analyzed information on the development of the nuclear bomb in the United States. He was also involved in the operation targeting Solomon Mikhoels, who was assassinated in Minsk in January 1948.

In April 1953, Sudoplatov was appointed Deputy Chief of the First Chief Directorate (counterintelligence) of the MVD. In May, he became Chief of the 9th Department of the MVD (intelligence and diversion). After Beria's arrest and the dissolution of the 9th Department, on July 31, 1953, he was transferred to the Second Chief Directorate of the MVD as Department's Chief. Then, on August 21, 1953, Sudoplatov was arrested in his Lubyanka office as 'Beria's accomplice' and charged with conspiracy. He feigned insanity and remained at the Leningrad Special Psychiatric Hospital until 1958.

On September 12, 1958, the Military Collegium of the USSR Supreme Court found Sudoplatov guilty under Article 58-1 ('counterrevolution'), Part B, and sentenced him to 15 years of imprisonment for 'active complicity with the traitor Beria in preparing a coup d'état, involvement in experiments on human beings, abductions and numerous murders.' He never admitted his guilt. He served his sentence in the Vladimir prison, where he suffered three heart attacks, became blind in one eye. After serving his sentence, he was released on August 21, 1968, and returned to Moscow. Sudoplatov was later exonerated by a decree of the Chief Military Prosecutor's Office of Russia on January 10, 1992, and died not much later on September 24, 1996.

Multiply these stories by thousands or even tens of thousands, and you will get a collective biography of the staff of Soviet intelligence services. Like the Party, the Lubyanka's agents were deeply involved in Communism's perpetual war under Lenin and Stalin. But they were also its blunt instrument. When Khrushchev replaced the Kremlin's perpetual war with international coexistence—which, in effect, meant that nuclear weapons were removed from the offensive arsenal of USSR's international coercion—the Lubyanka was both deprived of its primary role in this perpetual war as well as access to the USSR's most powerful weapon of provocation. In this sense, Khrushchev's 1957 purge of Lubyanka agents was a necessary means to cut out this part of the Cheka's institutional role in the Soviet Union.

Not all of them died in prison, disappeared into political oblivion, or lived on in their contemporaries' memory in the books they wrote. Chief among the survivors— one of the unsinkable men, a man who became the *éminence grise* of the Cheka in Soviet and new Russian history—was none other than one of the suspects arrested in 1951 as part of the 'Zionist conspiracy' inside the walls of the Lubyanka: General Evgeny Pitovranov. We will discuss him in the next chapter. Saved by Stalin from execution, he was secretly to perpetuate the Cheka's Leninist-Stalinist role and create a direct line to the next generation of agents, including Putin.

10: Yevgeny Pitovranov, the Phoenix Rises

The execution of Beria in 1953, and the arrests and execution of tens of thousands of Beria 'supporters' that followed, dealt the Lubyanka a blow, from which the Cheka never fully recovered. But that did not mean that it had any plans to stop its fight to dominate the Soviet Union. It simply meant that the fight, as well as the nature of the Intelligence Services' relationship with the Party, required a different approach. From Beria's execution, the Lubyanka changed direction. From subjugating the enemy at the Kremlin, it instead began to infiltrate the Party's ranks as well as its social fabric, to become an integral component, and to broaden Chekist recruitment to include a vast number of people living throughout the enormous Soviet Union. Thousands upon thousands of Chekists who could 'put two and two together' were enlisted to create a widespread web of influence beyond the department itself. From this period, the Intelligence Services became a cancerous tumor that filled every space in the USSR down to the smallest cracks. Its mafia structure became an all-encompassing alternative career path through which it promoted its own people up the social ladder in secret.

For decades, the most important Chekist at the top was arch survivor General Yevgeny Pitovranov. Pitovranov, who was to become Abakumov's deputy, was born in 1915. In 1938, he graduated from the Moscow Institute of Transport Engineers and also from the Higher Party School run by the Party CC. In the same year, he joined the Chekists. He rose rapidly through the ranks in secondary regions. Pitovranov's first position was deputy head of the NKVD Office for the Gorky Region (now Nizhny Novgorod). Just four years later, he was promoted to head and was soon transferred to an equivalent position in the Kirov Region and became a general at the age of 28. In 1944, Pitovranov was sent to the Kuibyshev region—named in honor of the Revolution hero (whom Beria personally shot in 1938). In 1945, he received a new post as the minister of State Security of Uzbekistan.

Finally, in June 1946, after the Great Patriotic War, he was transferred to Moscow—initially to the post of deputy, becoming chief a few months later, in September, of the Second Chief Directorate of the intelligence services ministry. Under his leadership, the Directorate's agents 'caught' a large number of spies as the Directorate expanded its operations to track down foreign intelligence agents in the USSR who were recruited before the war. While Pitovranov served in leadership positions at the Lubyanka from 1948 to 1950 more than 200 thousand people were arrested.

In 1948, one of the officers under his command—Lieutenant Colonel Fyodor

Shubnyakov—participated in the murder of Solomon Mikhoels, the theatre director and Chair of the Jewish Anti-Fascist Committee (JAC). Pitovranov's agents, while 'fighting cosmopolitanism', were also tasked with monitoring the activities of poet Boris Pasternak, who became a Nobel laureate in 1958. His lover Olga Ivinskaya was arrested in 1949 and charged with 'anti-Soviet agitation' and 'proximity to persons suspected of espionage', and sentenced to five years in prison. During the preliminary investigation, she was held in the prison morgue to intimidate her. She was pregnant with Pasternak's child and suffered a miscarriage. She would only return to Moscow in April 1953, after Stalin's death.[182]

On January 29, 1949, on Stalin's instructions, the Council of Ministers passed a secret resolution to deport 'certain categories' of residents from the Baltic countries with the goal of 'destroying the *kulaks* [small but prosperous farmers] as a class' and suppressing 'armed resistance' to Soviet authority. Pursuant to this decision, the MGB leadership issued an order in February 1949 to conduct an operation with the code-name Priboy (No 0068), creating a procedure for deportations from Latvia, Lithuania, and Estonia. 30,620 families (97,799 people) were deported, 73% of them were women and children of 16 years of age or younger. Starting on March 25, 1949, over several days, more than 20 thousand people were deported from Estonia, over 42 thousand from Latvia, and around 32 thousand from Lithuania. This was not the first Soviet mass deportation, but it is possible that the expulsions from the Baltic states in 1949 were considered by Stalin to be a dress rehearsal for the planned, but never completed, expulsion of Jews to remote areas of the Soviet Union. At this time, the campaign against 'cosmopolitanism' catalyzed by the independence of Israel had just begun.

In 1950, Pitovranov moved up to deputy minister, replacing Abakumov who became minister. Pitovranov was 35 years old at this time. In the words of Sudoplatov, 'Pitovranov stood out sharply among the MGB leadership for his intellect and outlook.' However, after Beria and Malenkov managed to have Abakumov removed and arrested, the newly promoted Lieutenant General Pitovranov was also arrested—in October 1951.

In August 1951, Stalin remarked: 'There are only two paths for Chekists: promotion or prison.' He said this to Ignatiev, his new minister of intelligence services after putting Abakumov in prison. In respect of Pitovranov, Stalin was mistaken—Pitovranov got promoted right out of prison. After spending several months being 'investigated' as to the non-existent Zionist conspiracy in the MGB, the ever-resourceful Pitovranov sent a personal letter to Stalin on April 23, 1952. It read like a brilliant job application—in which Pitovranov set out how to better catch all 'Zionist conspirators' in the entire USSR rather than just Moscow. Ignatiev, as the new minister, did not know what to do with the letter when he received it. After consultation with Malenkov, an experienced party operator and his own mentor, he gave the letter to Stalin. Pitovranov wrote:

Everything being done in the battle against Jewish nationalists, who present now no less danger, if not more, than the German colony in the USSR before the war with Germany, has been reduced to sporadic efforts against individuals and local groups.

In order to make this battle successful, the MGB of the USSR would have to boldly implement the method you mentioned when you received us, MGB officers, in the summer of 1951, specifically: to create in Moscow, Leningrad, the Ukraine (especially in Odessa, Lviv, and Chernivtsi), in Belarus, Uzbekistan (Samarkand, Tashkent), Moldova, Khabarovsk Region (including Republic of Birobidzhan), Lithuania, and Latvia nationalist groups made up of Chekist agents, fabricating connections in certain cases between these groups and foreign espionage circles.... These groups could be used to solidly identify Jewish nationalists and strike them when the moment is right.

Pitovranov also questioned the competence of Soviet intelligence's past leaders, subtly thereby impugning the current holder Ignatiev for not treating the imaginary Zionist conspiracy with the full force of the Cheka's capabilities:

There have not been good intelligence leaders for many years. Under Comrade Merkulov there was the talentless [Pavel] Fitin, and under Comrade Abakumov there was [Petr] Kubatkin the crook, and then we had, although he was smart, the not very prompt or sharp [Petr] Fedotov. I am convinced that Comrade [Sergei] Savchenko is also not the man who should lead intelligence if it is to meet the demands of the CC.... If you deem it necessary, I could report my ideas and relevant suggestions on this issue to Comrade Ignatiev. Knowing how strict, but also generous, you are, I ask you like my own father, Comrade Stalin, to give me the chance to make amends.

That letter to Stalin saved Pitovranov's life. At his next meeting with Ignatiev, Stalin remembered Pitovranov: 'Should he really be in prison?' he said. 'Let's let him out after some time ... we'll get him working at the Intelligence Services again.' And so, on Stalin's personal orders, Pitovranov was released from prison in November 1952. His own fictious 'case file' was terminated so that he could be tasked to create many more everywhere in the Soviet Union to kill Beria and Malenkov's paper tiger.

The reversal was complete. On December 15, Stalin received the Lubyanka leadership—Ignatiev and his three deputies, Generals Ogoltsov (also released from prison), Goglidze, as well as Pitovranov. While discussing reorganization of Soviet intelligence to beef up intelligence on countries at the Soviet borders, Stalin said:

Our primary enemy is America. But our focus should not be only on America. Covert espionage residencies must be created first and foremost in border states. The first base where we should have our people is West Germany.

And since Ignatiev noticed Stalin's respectful treatment of Pitovranov when discussing problems related to reorganizing the MGB, Pitovranov became Ignatiev's direct advisor (although that did not last long). On January 5, 1953, General Pitovranov became the head of Soviet foreign intelligence. After Stalin's death, Pitovranov received a new assignment removing him from Moscow. He became MVD commissioner in the German Democratic Republic, where he doubled Stasi's (Germany's Cheka) staff from around four thousand people to roughly nine thousand.

The day after the mourning for Stalin ended, on March 13, 1954, the Lubyanka was reorganized. The KGB (Committee for State Security) was formed.[183] It reported directly to the Council of Ministers and its first head Ivan Serov, a Chekist, was also appointed as First Deputy Minister of Internal Affairs. This separation of the Lubyanka from the internal affairs ministry (MVD) had already been passed by the Presidium of the CC on February 8, 1954, before Stalin's death. But an ominous mission statement was added regarding the new minister of internal affairs, Beria: 'To terminate the consequences of Beria's repressive activities of the organs of the Intelligence Services as soon as possible and to transform them into a sharp weapon of our party directed against the real enemies of our socialist state, not against honest people.'

How many 'honest people' exactly was a question that interested Khrushchev. In February 1954, while preparing to expose the Stalin regime that he himself loyally served, Khrushchev requested information about the number of individuals in the country who had been charged with anti-Soviet agitation. The data was signed off by the general prosecutor, the minister of internal affairs, and the minister of justice of the USSR. According to their data, from 1921 to 1953, 3,777,380 people were tried for counter-revolutionary crimes, out of which 642,980 people were sentenced to capital punishment, 2,369,220 people were sentenced to detention in camps and prisons, and 765,180 people were exiled. This information was not published until Soviet times ended in 1991.

At the January 1955 plenum of the Party CC, one more member of the conspiracy to unseat Stalin and Beria was removed from his post—Malenkov, the head of the government. He was faulted for his 'bureaucratic' leadership. A short while later, Khrushchev dealt with his remaining colleagues from the Stalin era of party and state leadership. At the June 1957 plenum of the CC, the following individuals were accused of anti-party activities: Molotov, Malenkov, Kaganovich, Voroshilov, Nikolai Bulganin, Mikhail Pervukhin, Maxim Saburov, and Dmitry Shepilov. Marshal Zhukov—who in 1953 had taken part in the assassination of Beria—opened the plenum. Members of the 'anti-Party' group were first dismissed from the CC and then removed from the Party. Having given Khrushchev his full support, in October 1957, Marshal Zhukov was himself dismissed from both the Presidium of the CC and the CC itself and removed as Minister of Defense. However, no further reprisals followed.

Nevertheless, Stalin's poisoning, Beria's murder, and the subsequent shooting of Beria's inner circle—at the ministries of internal affairs (MVD) and intelligence services (MGB)—turned over a new leaf in Soviet history. The Kremlin and the Lubyanka stopped killing each other. The era of murders and shootings was left behind. The Party stopped exterminating Intelligence officers, and the Intelligence Services stopped purging, arresting, and punishing Party and Soviet *nomenklatura*. With the accession of Khrushchev, a measure of peace was restored not seen since 1917. Apart from outward conflicts (for example, the anti-Soviet uprising in Hungary in 1956), Red Terror ceased to be a specter haunting life in the Soviet Union.

It did not however mark an end to grandiose personnel purges. In June 1957, at a plenary meeting of the CC, KGB Chief Serov briefed the plenum on the removal of 18 thousand people from the Intelligence Services. Forty senior agency generals were stripped of their ranks. Practically all leadership personnel in the KGB's central apparatus were replaced. Sixty people taken from Party and Soviet government positions were parachuted into a range of the vacant KGB positions. But no shootings, prison, torture or other violent reprisals attended this purge. Anticipating retaliation, especially against party *nomenklatura*, the Party placed the Lubyanka's key positions under the strictest party control by deputizing its own cadre into the KGB leadership.

Having been mostly abroad in the GDR, Pitovranov managed to escape being included in the 1957 purge. On March 15, 1957, he had been appointed head of the 4th Directorate of the KGB, which handled the fight against the anti-Soviet underground, nationalist groups, and hostile elements. The purge notwithstanding, General Pitovranov soon also became a member of the KGB Collegium, the body of 18 prominent members elected by KGB members. By the next year, Serov, a Chekist himself, lost his job as KGB Chief when, on December 10, 1958, he was appointed head of the GRU, the Intelligence Services branch in the military. This obvious demotion away from the center of power was made to look like a promotion.

Even in 1958, the Party still did not trust the KGB and feared bloody reprisals from the Lubyanka. In Serov's place, Alexander Shelepin was appointed as the new KGB Chair on December 25, 1958. He was previously the head of the Department of Party Offices of the CC. In other words, Shelepin was a Party employee through and through.

As if reassuring the Party leadership, upon taking his post Shelepin said that he wanted to 'reorient the KGB by its roots toward international affairs. Internal affairs should go on the back burner.' But Shelepin, the newly appointed party officer, was not at all confident of his powers. He was wary of having 'Berians' like Pitovranov close to him and hurried to get rid of Pitovranov at the first opportunity, sending him to be the KGB representative in China, where he dutifully served from 1960 to 1962, surviving, however, another major purge carried out by Khrushchev and Shelepin. 'You, [Khrushchev], were completely correct in your speech … when you talked about the need to further shrink the State Security organs,' Shelepin wrote to the CC on April 7, 1959.

At a speech at the 22nd Congress of the Communist Party in October 1961, Shelepin drew several conclusions about the successful subjugation of the newly-created KGB:

The Intelligence Services have been reorganized, shrunk significantly, relieved of inappropriate functions, and purged of careerist elements. All the activities of KGB officers now happen under the unflagging control of the party and government.... The Intelligence organs are no longer the scarecrow that the enemy Beria and his henchman tried to make them in the recent past, but are genuine popular political bodies of our party.

Khrushchev appreciated what Shelepin had achieved and thought it best to promote him elsewhere. On October 31, 1961, at the plenum of the CC, the first after the congress, Shelepin was moved across as Secretary of the CC.

Vladimir Semichastny took his place in the KGB on November 13, being relieved of the post of 2nd Secretary of the CC of the Communist Party of Azerbaijan to take the new position. Just like Shelepin, he was transferred to the KGB from the Party *nomenklatura*. Semichastny later recalled how Shelepin briefed him: 'He didn't lecture me. He described people in shorthand—who to keep close, who to keep a distance, who to get rid of, who to rely on.' The dubious Chekist Pitovranov was classified as a person to 'get rid of', just in case.

And just like Shelepin, Semichastny did not trust Pitovranov's return to the KGB's Lubyanka headquarters in Moscow. When Pitovranov came back from China, he offered him an administrative post: head of the *Vysshaya Shkola* (advanced school) *KGB*. Pitovranov accepted the offer. He didn't have a choice. It was not meant to last for long in any case. In 1965, Pitovranov was let go of. 'I suddenly got a call from the personnel department,' Pitovranov recalled in an interview. 'You must complete a full medical examination.... I saw every doctor on Varsonovyevsky Lane [where the KGB's central clinic was located]'. 'They tell me: "Unfortunately, you're completely healthy". After the medical, Semichastny invited me to see him: "[Pitovranov],' he says, 'congratulations on your fiftieth birthday. Thank you, you have worked hard, but it's time to let others work. It's time to rest and relax."' Fifty years old and full of strength and energy, Pitovranov found himself outside the organization he had devoted so many years of his life to. How he must have hated the Party.

But by now, Khrushchev himself had lost power. The plenary meeting of the CC of October 14, 1964 Leonid Brezhnev as chair, had an agenda item that stated: 'The aberrant situation in the Presidium of the CC in relation to the wrongful actions of the 1st Secretary of the CC of the CPSU, Comrade N.S. Khrushchev.' Khrushchev's time was up—the last surviving member of the conspiracy against Stalin and Beria who had not yet been fired or killed.

The resignation of Khrushchev and the rise of Brezhnev as Soviet leader (1964-1982) did not change the balance of power between the Kremlin and the Lubyanka in the latter's favor. The Soviet state remained firmly in Party hands, and the Intelligence Services were merely auxiliary functions of the USSR. However, as became known later, instead of another short-term KGB head like Ignatiev, Serov, Shelepin, and Semichastny—who, taken together, held the post for a total of 14 years—on May 18, 1967, a new head of the KGB was appointed: Yuri

Andropov, who had held the post of Secretary of the Party CC.

As soon as Brezhnev was established in his new position as leader of the CC, he hurried to rid himself of former Lubyanka heads Shelepin and Semichastny, who had become a burden for him. It was no accident that he was called 'Iron Shurik [Shelepin]' among Chekists and his own circle. It was a reference to 'Iron Felix' Dzerzhinsky and the epithet expressed the hope that this KGB leader would be able to concentrate all power of the Soviet state in his hands.

The 'Iron Felix' analogy was not fanciful. Shelepin was a devout Stalinist, a supporter of the hardline approach in domestic and foreign politics. It was this quality that alarmed Brezhnev and other Politburo members, who feared new purges with the next change in leadership. Thus, Shelepin was sent to lead the All-Union Central Council of Professional Unions. For Shelepin, this assignment spelled the terminus of his glittering career. Professional unions in the USSR were organizations in name only. They had no real significance in the Soviet Union. The same happened to Semichastny. He was made 3rd First Deputy Chair of the Council of Ministers of Ukraine, a position created just for him. Semichastny himself equated his position correctly with political exile.

Because he feared the two previous KGB directors as competitors in the battle for power, Brezhnev made Andropov the new Chair of the KGB. Andropov came to Lubyanka, like his predecessors, from the Party apparatus. The party made sure to protect itself from any surprises from those whose duty was to ensure the security of the state by constantly diluting the KGB with party members. Again, many Party *apparatchiks* were transferred to the KGB at the same time as Andropov. As there were no intelligence professionals, special KGB courses were created to train them for their leadership positions.

A month after arriving in his new office, KGB Chair Andropov's political status was even elevated. He was confirmed as candidate (non-voting) member of the Politburo. Only Chekist leaders Dzerzhinsky, Yezhov, and Beria had simultaneously been members of the Politburo.[184]

In order to be successful, Andropov, who had no Intelligence experience, himself needed experienced advisors who knew what they were doing. Previous KGB directors—Serov, Shelepin, and Semichastny—were in disgrace, which made them unfit as advisors. Following Lubyanka tradition, Andropov saw KGB senior staff who had worked with Semichastny and stayed with the agency after his removal as potential allies of the exiled former chief. Brezhnev appointees would not qualify either because of their close ties with Brezhnev—it made them potential contenders to lead the KGB. He needed a knowledgeable person who was also, at that moment, an outsider. Enter the 50-year-old, retired Lieutenant General Pitovranov, recently fired by KGB Chair Semichastny. Pitovranov himself remembered the following about his first meeting with Andropov:

After Andropov was named Chair of the Committee for State Security (KGB), a few days later I was called and asked to appear at the CC…. [Andropov] had a long talk with me. It covered many subjects: the agency's work in the field, in the Center, how the Center manages local entities, how intelligence and counterintelligence work is coordinated—it was basically an overview about how and why the Committee for State Security lives.

'You understand, I've had little connection with these affairs,' Andropov said. 'You were recommended to me as an experienced and intelligent man, so I decided to speak with you.'

Pitovranov claims that during this first meeting Andropov mooted a new, additional, investigative organization for double-checking information received from the KGB and GRU (military intelligence). According to Pitovranov, Andropov said:

I know that Comrade Stalin had the idea firmly in his mind that we should not limit ourselves to the intelligence work we do today. There must be options for rechecking the information received from the KGB and GRU. We need some kind of supplement to the work they do. It needs to be both secret and useful to the state. Think about what kind of structure, existing in parallel to existing Intelligence agencies, we could propose. But first we need to weigh everything, think it over, and decide for sure whether it is worth doing.

It is hard to believe that, having just taken command of the massive Lubyanka apparatus, Andropov immediately reached the conclusion he wanted to create a parallel structure. Any change to the politically sensitive intelligence organs of the USSR was the exclusive prerogative of the Party CC or the government's Council of Ministers. Any discussion between Andropov and Pitovranov on the subject would obviously be well beyond their brief and, considering the mass shootings for treason of 1954-1956 by a twitchy government, fatally risky.

Pitovranov often repeated a phrase: 'never admit to anything'—never tell the truth. Stalin, who was suspicious and revealed his plans to no one, would not likely have shared cherished thoughts about creating a secret 'parallel' body in the Intelligence Services with anyone either, least of all with the ex-convict Pitovranov. What may well have happened at a later stage is that Pitovranov attributed his own ideas to Stalin when speaking to Andropov, who could not fact-check the story. Andropov need not have believed Pitovranov. It was better to borrow an idea from Stalin, rather than from underling Pitovranov.

As a befitted a KGB Chair, Andropov held Beria and Stalin in appropriate esteem. Then Chief of the KGB's PGU[185] Vladimir Kryuchkov recalled Andropov's mild views of his ruthless predecessors:

Khrushchev, when he began exposing Stalin, was already so bloody himself that he should not have opened his mouth. And about Beria ... [Khrushchev] said a lot of things that were not true. That is why ... someday an objective view of Beria will be restored.... About Stalin, Andropov held the firm opinion that the day will come when Stalin's name is worthily celebrated by all nations.... Unlike Khrushchev, he [Andropov] never called Stalin a criminal.

Pitovranov did convince Andropov of the expediency of using Soviet foreign trade agencies as parallel organizations. 'My new task,' Pitovranov said, 'consisted of finding a couple dozen people we could rely on. I found them. I did not take these people from their jobs in foreign trade. I just plugged them into my orbit and pointed them to some additional questions. They began switching from specific commercial transactions to serious and promising operational [Intelligence] cases.'

Foreign trade organizations traditionally had a good number of KGB agents on their staff. Every foreigner was seen as a potential enemy spy, so anyone who had professional contacts with foreigners was recruited without exception. Those who did not want to become KGB agents did not last long in their jobs as they were treated as people who were not loyal Communists. As undercover agents, trade staff kept their jobs and continued to perform their usual functions supplemented with additional tasks assigned by the Intelligence Services—or, as Pitovranov described it, 'plugging' such people into his 'orbit'.

Pitovranov conducted the first foreign political operations through the Franco-Soviet Chamber of Commerce. It was created in Paris in 1967, the year Andropov became KGB director, under an agreement at the highest level between France and the USSR. A branch of the chamber was opened in Moscow. The special Soviet foreign intelligence espionage *rezidentura* began its work, created by personal order of Andropov. It fell under the KGB's First Directorate (PGU) and Andropov appointed Pitovranov as the first head of this deeply covert intelligence subgroup.

Andropov personally oversaw the main operative issues. He made sure that 'Department P' (as the *rezidentura* led by Pitovranov was initially called) had its own budget and communications channels with overseas representatives that were independent from the Lubyanka KGB. Pitovranov seemed to have taken his inspiration from Serebryansky. 'Department S' was later transformed into an entire Directorate S. Department P got its name from the first letter of Pitovranov's last name, just like Department S was created by the NKVD by giving it the first letter of its first head, Serebryansky. He was one of the many purged Chekists, but he was also the founder of the 'Yasha' combat group in Palestine—precisely the type of special operations group Pitovranov's Department P intended to propagate abroad.

Department P was given the informal and harmless title of the 'Firm'. In the mid-1970s, Pitovranov's 'Firm' gained the status of an independent Special Operations department and started to be called Department 'F[irm]' of Directorate S' headed by Pitovranov, whose official title was 'Senior Advisor.' He recalled:

In the first years of the 'Firm's' existence, [Andropov] participated in planning many of our operations, and to a certain extent our department was a training polygon for him. I came to him with a ready operation plan and explained why it had to be done this way. He listened. I think this work helped him master the specifics of Chekist business more quickly.

His first 'polygon' was France: 'Major achievements have been made in France,' Pitovranov remembered. 'A man very familiar with the country and the nature of the French soul was sent to manage the 'Firm's' branch there' (Pitovranov deliberately did not mention the last name of this Soviet covert agent familiar with 'the French soul'). However, as a result, the 'Firm's' list of friends, in Pitovranov's words, included 'numerous politicians and businessmen, and their relatives, wives, and lovers.'

Soviet leader Brezhnev, when traveling to Paris, certainly knew what the French would ask for in talks and to what extent they were willing to negotiate. And all of that was thanks to Pitovranov's *rezidentura*. Pitovranov himself completed 184 overseas trips under Andropov on operational assignments.

By the time Andropov was appointed as Chair of the KGB, Pitovranov was already part of the leadership of a Soviet foreign trade body. It was harmlessly called the USSR Chamber of Commerce (VTP). The idea of placing Pitovranov in the VTP came to his most talented disciple—Filipp Bobkov. He was Deputy Head of the Second Chief Directorate (VGU)[186] of the KGB and a future First Deputy Chair of the KGB with the rank of general. He was the one who, after Pitovranov's dismissal from the KGB, advised him to serve in the inconspicuous VTP. 'It has good opportunities in the foreign economic line and perhaps in other directions as well,' Bobkov said.

Pitovranov understood what was meant by 'other directions:' 'I told him how, when I worked in the GDR, I always accompanied Patolichev on his trips around the country.' Nikolai Patolichev was the Soviet Union's minister of foreign trade. Pitovranov was basically talking about currency transactions and foreign trade operations. A few days after his conversation with Bobkov, Pitovranov was assigned to the post of Deputy Chair of the VTP—which few people in the USSR knew existed. However, Pitovranov reformed it into a significant body of USSR-wide and international significance, the like of which the USSR had never seen—a state within a state.

With his coming to the VTP, Pitovranov recruited the former head of one of the departments of the Higher School of the KGB, Nikolai Knyazev, instructing him to manage the chamber's personnel. In Pitovranov's words, Knyazev held the post of deputy director in the *rezidentura* and oversaw counterintelligence. Another assistant to Pitovranov was his former advisor on a trip to the GDR, Khachik Oganesyan. Pitovranov instructed him to handle intelligence issues.

Pitovranov's foreign-intelligence group included First Deputy Director of the PGU General Boris Ivanov, who unsuccessfully tried to recruit his boss, Alexander Sakharovsky, for Pitovranov. Ivanov suggested on multiple occasions that Sakharovsky meet personally with Pitovranov, but the careful and experienced Sakharovsky, who led the PGU for 15 years until 1971, refused, knowing that not all the affairs of Pitovranov's *rezidentura* were quite 'above board'. He deliberately avoided having to get involved in its activities and did not want to be close to Pitovranov.

In August 1971, Pitovranov got lucky: Oleg Lyalin, a senior engineer with the Soviet trade office, disappeared in London. He was an agent of Sakharovsky's PGU at the Lubyanka.[187] Lyalin defected to the UK, with whose MI6, it later turned out, he had been cooperating for several years. Taking advantage of Lyalin's betrayal[188], Andropov made an important personnel rearrangement on Pitovranov's recommendation. Sakharovsky, who never recovered from Lyalin's defection[189], was replaced with Fyodor Mortin, who remained in this new position until 1974. He was replaced with Vladimir Kryuchkov, who remained in charge of the PGU until 1988.

The special status Andropov assigned to Pitovranov's group meant that the heads of the PGU were not kept abreast of its foreign activities, neither Sakharovsky, nor Mortin, and not even Kryuchkov—even though he was one of Andropov's most trusted aides for many years. Pitovranov continued to report directly to Andropov. Unsurprisingly, Pitovranov and Kryuchkov's relationship was forever strained.

> Our relationship was ruined because he was very jealous of my work with [Andropov],' Pitovranov recalled about Kryuchkov. He 'was never fully informed about it—that made him very nervous. He is the head of intelligence and does not know exactly what we are reporting to the KGB Chair. Does our information match his reports or not? Are we reporting that his residencies missed their marks?

Andropov's regular meetings with Pitovranov took place in a safe house on Sretenka Street: 'We spoke face to face. There wasn't even security there. Everything was checked in advance and isolated from prying ears,' Pitovranov recalled. Andropov sat down at the table, drank a glass of his favorite Rhenish wine, snacked on tiny finger-food, puff pies with cabbage and asked: 'Well, tell me what you have.' He listened very attentively, occasionally making notes on a piece of paper. If several options were provided and a decision had to be made, Andropov considered them for a long time.

Department F[irm]'s work brought Pitovranov closer to Andropov. The atmosphere of their meetings was 'not just comradely, but sincerely respectful, even deeply heartfelt', Colonel Alexander Kiselev, a member of Pitovranov's group and the head of Department V (within Directorate S), recalled about his bosses. Department V was the office of Special Operations and secret financing of foreign pro-Soviet rebel bodies and movements.[190] It was this department that covered Pitovranov's activities where they fell within the purview of the PGU (the KGB's prestigious 1st Directorate). Kiselev only reported to Pitovranov. Pitovranov's strict instructions to Kiselev were that matters of substance should in turn only be discussed with Andropov himself and that Andropov's assistants were not cleared to receive information other than staffing and other HR questions:

> Let's ... focus on those issues that will unavoidably come up during the discussion of our plans with the Chair [Andropov]. Remember, only one person is aware of

our problems—his assistant Yevgeny Kalgin, you will resolve all organizational issues with him alone. Let me emphasize—organizational issues only. Operational, informational, and other critically important issues we will report only personally to [Andropov]. That is a strict order.[191]

As Pitovranov gathered more information, his political ambitions became greater and greater each year. Using his espionage trade *rezidenturas*, he collected compromising material about anyone who might interfere with his goals. Brezhnev's son Yuri was constantly on his radar. Yuri was First Deputy Minister of Foreign Trade. He was known to be an alcoholic, but because his father was the Party's General Secretary that did not stop him from holding on to such a senior post and remaining a candidate member of the CC. Pitovranov received information from his agents about how Yuri was seriously abusing his official position by taking large bribes from foreign partners and entering into contracts that benefited those foreign partners and him, but not the USSR. One such bribe was a hundred-piece antique style furniture set inlaid with semi-precious stones.

Pitovranov's main target was, of course, General Secretary Brezhnev, not his son. The son's compromising activities cast a shadow on his father. As always in such situations, Pitovranov reported the information to Andropov personally, bypassing the intelligence hierarchy. But Andropov was ill and accidentally gave Pitovranov's message about the furniture-set bribe to one of his assistants. Accidentally or deliberately it was given it to the Deputy Chair of the KGB, Georgiy Tsinev, a trusted friend of Leonid Brezhnev.

It lit the blue touch paper at the Lubyanka. Tsinev was outraged. KGB personnel were categorically forbidden from collecting information about senior Soviet and Party leaders further to the post-Stalin truce between the Kremlin and the Lubyanka. If such material was found, it was to be immediately destroyed. Bypassing this rule could ruin your career. In this case, an agency order was violated in relation to a candidate for membership in the CC and the son of the General Secretary of the CC.

It was PGU Chief Kryuchkov who—he said, was not aware of this information—had to explain himself to Tsinev. In accordance with agency protocol, he demanded that Kiselev's dossier on Yuri Brezhnev be destroyed immediately. And yet, Pitovranov's subordinate, Colonel Kiselev, did not do so:

Why I had to destroy such an informative agent report was not clear to me. Even though I violated official discipline, I'm still convinced that I acted correctly. I was even praised by [Pitovranov].... At my own fear and risk, I decided to wait for one of my direct bosses.[192]

It is worth spelling this out. Kiselev, a Chekist officer who had been found out to have grossly violated regulations (during Andropov's sickness) by KGB Deputy Chair Tsinev and PGU Chief Kryuchkov, was proud of the praise he received from the formally retired 'senior advisor' of Department F, General Pitovranov. He knew that Pitovranov would protect him because Pitovranov was protected by KGB Chief Andropov.

'For nearly thirty years I was a frequent guest of that family,' Kiselev writes, emphasizing his close relationship with Pitovranov,[193] who truly never abandoned 'his people.' When Alexander Khlystov, the deputy head of a PGU department with connections to Pitovranov's firm, was fired from the KGB with immediate effect on his boss Kryuchkov's orders because of his unflattering review of Leonid Brezhnev, Pitovranov did not abandon Khlystov. He simply appointed him instead to lead a VTP department.[194]

Pitovranov also had access to Brezhnev himself, through Tsinev, who, in fact, was his long-time subordinate and next-door neighbor. Tsinev once invited Pitovranov to play a game of dominoes as he needed a fourth player. The third player was Tsinev's son-in-law, and the second was Brezhnev. Scoring 'goats' with Brezhnev, Pitovranov became keenly aware of the ineptitude of the leader of the Party and the government and his very low intellectual level. The country needed a new leader who could raise it out of deadlock. To Pitovranov, and Kiselev after him, that person was Andropov.

'Foreign intelligence is made up of living people…. That is the part of that community, known as the Soviet nation, experiencing ideological degradation and economic catastrophe under the wise leadership of the CPSU,' Kiselev wrote 'wise' with irony, anger, and annoyance, and explaining why the KGB was against the Party and why the last hope of the Cheka was Yuri Andropov, who was being pushed by Pitovranov to seize power.

The famous orthodox communist author and editor of the *Zavtra* (tomorrow) newspaper Alexander Prokhanov echoed him:

> One of the most mysterious, under-studied, and elusive figures in Russian history is the true theorist and father of *perestroika* [restructuring]—KGB Chief, and then General Secretary of the CPSU, Yuri Andropov. Andropov is a great, strange, demonic figure of the twentieth century. Andropov, the almighty head of the [KGB], moderated from the shadows for a long time, influencing processes inside the party, and then, after winning a gigantic official victory, became the leader of the country. With the rise of Andropov, the KGB began controlling the Soviets, the party, the economy, and the culture. This triumph of intelligence instantly changed the internal structure of power.[195]

When he became the head of the KGB, Andropov experienced a measure of professional stress as he was not given a team of his own to rely on.

The cautious Brezhnev, who came to power as the result of the coup against Khrushchev, surrounded the newly appointed KGB chief with his own trusted people. Andropov's deputy was Semyon Tsvigun, who had been Chair of the KGB of the Moldovan Soviet Republic when Brezhnev was the First Secretary of the CC of the

Communist Party of Moldova. Another one of Brezhnev's trusted lieutenants in the KGB was Tsinev, a long-time colleague from Dnipropetrovsk, Ukraine, who headed military counterintelligence. Tsinev was married to the sister of Brezhnev's wife. When Andropov was appointed as KGB Chair, Tsinev made a member of the powerful KGB Collegium at the same time. As an extra precaution, Brezhnev appointed yet another fellow Ukrainian from Dnipropetrovsk as head of KGB Personnel—Viktor Chebrikov. A year later, he was also appointed as one of Andropov's deputies. Additionally, the Party continued diluting State Security with its own appointments. 'The CC sent the KGB lots of "civilians",' Chebrikov said. 'In a very short time, high-quality people came to the KGB.... They all later became deputy chairs, department and directorate heads.' Andropov understood very well that Tsinev and Tsvigun were there to watch his every step. They would appear in his office on the third floor of Lubyanka without an invitation.

At the KGB, Andropov acted with great secrecy. You would reach the office by passing through the main entrance marked with a number '1'. Few knew that you could also reach the office of the KGB Chair via the inner courtyard of the Lubyanka. You could reach the inner courtyard by taking a car through double, successive gates, after which a narrow passage led to the far-right corner of the building, where a door to the KGB Chair's office opened onto the courtyard. A designated elevator led to the office, which could only be used by the head of the agency himself with a special key, or those close to him who were given the key. All the other elevators in Lubyanka were operated normally. Andropov's special key-access elevator reached the so-called special zone, on the third floor of the KGB's main building where the agency chief's office was situated. Naturally, the entire third floor fell into this special zone. Even the employees of the KGB's central apparatus could only access it with special passes.

Under Andropov as KGB Chair, there was always a black Volga car parked practically right up against the exit from the special zone with carefully curtained side and rear-view windows. The car only looked like a Volga on the outside. It was a specially modified Chaika or ZIL make, designed for transporting party and state elites, with a powerful 315-horsepower engine, a three-speed automatic transmission, and bullet-proof tires. The driver of this vehicle was invariably Andropov's assistant Yevgeny Kalgin who had followed his boss all these years to whatever appointment. Andropov mainly used this car to travel to covert meetings. Before leaving in it, Andropov would always wear a disguise and change his outfit. He did not want to be recognized when visiting those buildings where the KGB's safe houses were located.

To maintain secrecy when Andropov traveled in this vehicle, staff from the Lubyanka's Commandant's office who handled the building's security did not let anyone into the inner courtyard before the car left it or before a passenger arriving in the inner courtyard of the KGB building stepped out of the vehicle. They could only guess who might be inside the car. For official trips, Andropov used a completely different vehicle—a ZIL-115. These cars were reserved exclusively for members and candidates of the Politburo. The security guards and drivers of these vehicles were officers of the

9th Directorate of the KGB. General Secretary Brezhnev's driver, for instance, was a lieutenant colonel.

Andropov, not having any friends, fell in love with the secret double life at his agency. In the years he led the KGB he took no holidays. Perhaps he was forced to work weekends to avoid being monitored by Brezhnev's spies, Tsvigun and Tsinev, or to get away from his strained family relations. For Andropov his secret meetings were a form of recreation, although his companions, as a rule, considered these meetings strictly businesslike.

Agents and resident spies, safe houses and secret apartments, visual and auditory monitoring of individuals, and the surveillance service were integral parts of that life. 'Andropov never invited guests over, and never went to see anyone himself. Even for birthdays. Sure, sometimes he went with other Politburo members to celebrate New Year with Brezhnev. That's about it…. So, it would seem he literally did not have any friends,' Kryuchkov said about Andropov.

Kryuchkov's predecessor, Chebrikov, who worked under Andropov for many years, said that no one, even those closest to him, fully knew Andropov. They attributed that to events in Hungary in 1956, when Andropov served as the Soviet ambassador in Budapest during an uprising against Soviet power. To terrify Soviet embassy employees, the bodies of executed Hungarian party functionaries and employees of the Hungarian special services were hung upside down from streetlamps and trees across from the Soviet embassy. Legend has it that Andropov's son Igor was kidnapped by rebels. He was freed by Soviet special operations soldiers led by the future head of the KGB in Azerbaijan, who later became the leader of the Republic of Azerbaijan, Geydar Aliyev. Andropov became his patron after the Hungarian uprising. The revolution had a deep impact on Andropov and his family. Andropov's wife became addicted to drugs, while his son Igor fell for hard liquor.[196]

Andropov suffered from chronic illness, too: he was kept on an artificial kidney for years. Academician Yevgeny Chazov became the director of the 4th Chief Directorate under the Ministry of Health in 1967 and deputy minister by 1968. Chazov monitored the treatment of all the senior members of the party and government, and knew about all their ailments and family secrets. He directly oversaw the treatment of Soviet leaders Brezhnev's, Andropov's, and Chernenko's illnesses.

But everything Chazov knew was also no secret to another Chekist—General Bobkov, Pitovranov's disciple. Bobkov was head of the 5th Directorate[197] and Chazov was his agent. From the moment the 5th Directorate was created, it supervised the Ministry of Health among other operational support units, which the 4th Chief Directorate under the Ministry of Health fell under. Thus, the group of generals led by Pitovranov, including his best students—Boris Ivanov and Bobkov—possessed the most accurate information on the health of the country's top leadership. Brezhnev was in the worst shape of all for a long time.

By the end of December 1974, Andropov introduced Deputy Chief of the PGU (the KGB's 1st Directorate) Vladimir Kryuchkov to Brezhnev to be confirmed as the

PGU chief. Kryuchkov recalled:

> Before the meeting, [Andropov] warned me not to be too surprised if the General Secretary seems out of it. It is important, he said, to talk louder and don't ask again if you have trouble understanding him. So, I was prepared for this when I arrived at the Kremlin, but what I saw exceeded all my expectations. An extremely sick man sat at the table. He struggled to get up to greet me and could not catch his breath for a long time after collapsing back into his chair. Pitovranov persistently pushed Andropov to remove Brezhnev:
>
> — [Andropov], you must see that the country and the party do not have a leader.
> — Well, what do we do about it?
> — We need to think about getting a leader.
> — What a task you have given me!

Andropov demurred because in the opinion of various leaders of socialist countries it was necessary to keep Brezhnev in power for the sake of the stability of the Eastern bloc.[198] To his entourage—PGU officers—Pitovranov did not hide his negative opinion of Brezhnev: 'All that's left for them is writing some books … such idiocy,' he once said, referring to Brezhnev and the General Secretary of the Bulgarian Communist Party, Todor Zhivkov.[199]

Behind the scenes Pitovranov tried to scheme and create a Politburo leadership *troika* in which absolute power would belong to 'president' Andropov. Alexei Kosygin would remain Prime Minister, and the leader of the Party would be First Secretary of the CC of the Belarus Soviet Republic, Pyotr Masherov. He had probing discussions with Kosygin and Masherov. But these meetings did not go unnoticed by Brezhnev's circle. For a short while, premature deaths once again haunted the Kremlin. On October 4th, 1980, 61-year-old Masherov suddenly died in a car accident. Kosygin was removed from the Politburo that same October and forced to resign as Prime Minister. The 74-year-old died two months later on December 18, 1980. It was only reported three days after the fact.

And two years later, on November 10, 1982, Brezhnev himself died. Andropov, as Pitovranov planned, became the Soviet leader. He was not at first president, but became General Secretary like all those before him. He became 'president' a year later when he also accepted the post of Chair of the Presidium of the Supreme Soviet (as did Brezhnev in his time). But by then he had let the Cheka in through the back door by creating Pitovranov's secret agency. While it may have fallen under his own personal control, the net result was that Chekist agents had multiplied once again beyond the Party's control. Indirectly Brezhnev was to blame. By installing two KGB deputies who reported informally to him rather than their boss Andropov, he had hemmed him in. Ironically, Andropov, the man who was tasked to keep the Lubyanka under Party control, was now in charge of both the Party and the Soviet Union as a result of Chekist scheming that had finally come to fruition for the first time since Dzerzhinsky.

11: The KGB and Soviet Intellectuals

One cannot tell the full story of the Soviet Intelligence Services—or of modern Russia—without describing the career of General Bobkov, one of Pitovranov's closest disciples and allies. In the previous chapter, we described how Pitovranov manipulated Andropov to create a foreign-trade intelligence department that was in part unsupervised by the Party, to have a second source of information. Together with Bobkov, Pitovranov intended to create a similar body within the Soviet Union itself. Bobkov's main task in those years was to build a foundation for challenging the Party's political and ideological control over the Intelligence Services. In order to free itself from such control by the Politburo and Party CC, the KGB had to tap a force within the USSR that the Party didn't yet control itself. The way Pitovranov and Bobkov saw it, the force with the most potential were the Russian arts—literary, visual, or musical. The arts provided powerful organizing points for a Soviet society thoroughly sick and tired of the ravages inflicted on it by Communist utopianism. The radical-nationalist organizations whose origin go back to Soviet days—be it Alexander Barkashov's Russian National Unity or Dmitry Vasiliev's *Pamyat* (memory) movement—all had the KGB behind it. No such group or organization in the Soviet Union could slip by without being noticed or, indeed, supervised, directed and developed by the KGB.

Andropov was the driving force in liberating this part of Pitovranov's Cheka from Party control. On July 3, 1967, a few months after Party bureaucrat Andropov was appointed to the KGB, he took charge. After repeated consultations with Pitovranov, Andropov sent a memorandum to the Party CC (1631A, the letter at the end of the number referred to the signer of the document, in this case Andropov). Among other things, his memo focused proposed defending Communism from 'alien ideology' inside the USSR by utilizing 'about 50 nationalist groups' that might otherwise fall into the hands of US 'ruling circles' determined to start 'psychological warfare':

Materials in the possession of the Committee of State Security indicate that reactionary forces in the imperialist camp, headed by the ruling circles of the USA, are constantly stepping up their efforts with regards to intensifying subversive actions against the Soviet Union. As part of this effort, they regard psychological warfare a key element in the general fight against communism…. Our adversary endeavors to move ideological operations inside the USSR itself, with the intent of not only causing the degradation of ideas in Soviet society but also creating favorable conditions for acquiring sources of political information in our country.

In 1965-1966, State Security agencies uncovered about 50 nationalist groups in several republics, with a total membership of over 500 people. In Moscow, Leningrad and some other locations, anti-Soviet groups have been uncovered, whose members proclaimed ideas of political restoration in their so-called program documents....

Under the influence of alien ideology, some politically immature Soviet citizens, especially among the intelligentsia and young people, are forming apolitical and nihilistic views, which can be utilized not only by hardcore anti-Soviet elements but also by political chatterers and demagogues who may push such persons to commit politically harmful actions.

Andropov proposed creating an independent unit within the Lubyanka that would catalogue, address and prevent ideological sabotage of Soviet culture not only from 'imperialists' but also from Soviet 'political chatterers and demagogues':

To organize work on identifying and studying that could be utilized by the adversary with the intent of carrying out ideological sabotage;

To uncover and neutralize hostile activity by anti-Soviet, nationalist and religious-sectarian elements, as well as the prevention, in cooperation with the Ministry of Protection of Public Order, of mass disturbances;

To monitor the adversary's ideological bases and anti-Soviet émigré and nationalist organizations abroad, working together with intelligence agencies;

To organize counterintelligence work among foreign students attending universities in the USSR, as well as among members of foreign delegations and collectives visiting the USSR under the auspices of the Ministry of Culture and of artistic and cultural organizations.

The Politburo discussed Andropov's memorandum at its July 17, 1967 meeting and passed his proposal. Next, the Council of Ministers approved a resolution once again to grow the staff of the KGB and increase its budget with a view to creating a 5th Directorate. Order No 0096 (double zero orders were top secret), issued on July 27, 1967, confirmed the staffing and budget of the 5th Directorate.

Pitovranov's Trojan Horse was inside the gates. The 5th Directorate, too, was a creation of his. He had previously run the Lubyanka's 4th Directorate—which had a role analogous to this new 5th Directorate—from 1957 to 1960, when it fell under the ministry of intelligence services (MGB). Clearly, the new directorate should therefore have been numbered as 4. But precisely because this new directorate was actually the reconstituted old 4th MGB/KGB Directorate, Pitovranov insisted that the new unit should be given the number five, to avoid association with the 4th Directorate, which had been a minor department.[200]

Its first Chief was Alexander Kadashev, a Party *apparatchik*, previously the Secretary of the Party in Stavropol. On Pitovranov's sly recommendation, Kadashev made his Cheka protégé Bobkov as First Deputy. Soon the inexperienced civilian Kadashev was dismissed from his post on the grounds of unsatisfactory performance and in December 1968 career Chekist Bobkov took over and became its chief.

Bobkov was born on December 1, 1925 in Ukraine. His childhood and school years were spent in the Donbas Region. In 1941, the Donbass was occupied by German troops, and Bobkov moved to the Kuzbas Region, where he took a job at a factory and then worked as a Komsomol (the Soviet Leninist Young Communist League) activist. In 1942, he went to the Russian front as a volunteer. He spent his 18th birthday in a field hospital recovering after being wounded a second time. By the end of the war, he had received the Order of Glory and two medals 'For Valor.'

After the end of the war, Bobkov was assigned to work in the Cheka. In July 1945, he arrived in Leningrad and enrolled in the SMERSH counterintelligence school. After graduating, he worked in Intelligence agencies, first in Leningrad, then in Moscow. On Pitovranov's recommendation, he was given the post of Party Secretary for the entire 4th Directorate of the KGB. In yet another reshuffle of the Lubyanka by the Party, on February 5, 1960, the Council of Ministers of the USSR approved Resolution No 134-46.[201] On February 11, the 4th, 5th, and 6th Directorates were abolished by KGB top secret order No 0026, and their staff were transferred to what was now called the VGU. Bobkov became head of the 10th Department of the VGU, which became in practice the replacement of the old 4th Directorate. Apart from whom reported to whom at the top, everything remained the same—including Bobkov's career prospect. The next year, Bobkov rose to Deputy Chief of the VGU. In 1983, he even became the First Deputy of the KGB, traditionally the top KGB officer who *de facto* runs the agency and its daily operations.[202]

Bobkov was without doubt a remarkable man. The writer and historian Nikolai Yakovlev, who had ties with the KGB and who authored the once-sensational book, *August 1, 1914* (1974) had this to say about Bobkov in a supplement to a new edition published in the early 1990s, describing Bobkov as a brilliant man as well as an intellectual who 'never quite fully trusted himself either':

> I began to make occasional visits to the Lubyanka, where I had intellectual discussions—first, somewhat tense ones with Andropov, and then absolutely fascinating ones with Bobkov, who was rising fast on the career ladder. Between the late 1960s and the early 1980s, I watched him rise to Army general and First Deputy Chair of the KGB. I read somewhere that for a number of years, he was the real chief of that agency. I don't know if that was true, but I can certainly believe it. Comparing the two of them, for all of Y.V. Andropov's intellectual polish, I would unquestionably give higher marks to F.D. Bobkov, who was vastly superior to his nominal boss and, above all, was much better prepared. It's difficult to judge purely professional matters, since [Bobkov] never brought them up in our conversations; but, judging by his subordinates' worshipful attitude toward him, they found him more than ade-

quate. I am talking about something else: the entire package of issues contained in the capacious concept of ideology. I have never met anyone better informed, anyone with such vast knowledge and such an unbelievable, almost supernatural memory. One could never take him by surprise; any question in this area was followed by a clear and exhaustive answer.... Like any other person who worked with him, I gradually began to feel profound respect for the General.... He never trusted me, though I cannot shake off the playful thought that I found myself in good company: I think Filip Bobkov never quite fully trusted himself, either.

In the mid-1970s, Marshall Nikolai Yakovlev co-authored *The CIA against the USSR* with Bobkov. For obvious reasons, General Bobkov—who was then part of the KGB top, unlike the retired Yakovlev—was not listed as its co-author. It was only much later, after the collapse of the Soviet Union, that he published his first book under his own name—*The KGB and Power*. The book was published in Bulgaria, then in South Korea, and finally, in 1995, in Russia. In Russia its cover was marked, 'for official use only' and was not available for sale to the general public.

Bobkov's *The KGB and Power* was an attempt to separate the KGB from the Communist Party and show that the 'power' (the Party) had been issuing *diktats* to the KGB for all those Soviet years, while the KGB, merely an obedient instrument in the hands of 'power' (that is, 'the' Communists), had been forced to obey the destructive orders issued by the Party. It was his version of the Nazi apology, '*befehl ist befehl*' (orders are orders).

In a later book, *The Last Twenty Years: Memoirs of a Chief of Political Counterintelligence* (2006, available to the public), Bobkov also tried to profile himself as an ordinary government official who worked for his country and was no different from any other law enforcement officer. 'Intelligence Services are an instrument of the state, along with the army, the police, prosecutors' offices, courts, and other institutions of law enforcement and justice'; 'Intelligence Services serve their states, they pursue their government's policies by their specific operative means,' wrote Bobkov.

Bobkov's authority and respect among subordinates was absolute. But in addition to respect, he also instilled deep fear in his deputies and department and section chiefs. Even though Bobkov never displayed any physical brutality in his supervisory work, the hallways and offices of the 5th Directorate seemed never far removed from such excesses. No one dared contradict General Bobkov; no one dared give him nicknames.

This ability to inspire terror was a necessary qualification for a leader of the KGB's ideology directorate. But, in Bobkov's case, his additional ability to charm outsiders with a pleasing appearance and blue-eyed face turned out to be no less important a professional qualification. That was because the recruitment of countless Soviet citizens and (much more rarely) of citizens and subjects of other countries as Intelligence agents became one of Bobkov's, and the 5th Directorate's, most vital tasks. The 5th Directorate paid attention to the 'creative intelligentsia', in particular. They were extensively recruited and then handled through KGB residents—abroad, but mainly in the USSR.

We are used to thinking of KGB residents as serving only abroad and curating Soviet agents in foreign countries. And, in fact, practically every country had Soviet Foreign Intelligence *rezidentura* and residents who ran them. However, far more residents served within the Soviet Union at a wide range of 'targets,' starting with those of the greatest strategic importance. Television, radio and modern print media were technologies dating from the same era as the USSR and were formidable means of propaganda and of shaping the public mind in the Soviet Union. For that very reason, they were from the beginning constantly and watchfully monitored by the Intelligence Services. It's no surprise, then, that 5th Directorate staffers under Bobkov's leadership were focused on recruiting agents from the ranks of writers and journalists—or that they found their principal ideological opponents in the same milieu and fought them using every weapon at their disposal.

There were numerous early examples of creative intellectuals being recruited by the Cheka. Let us examine several such cases, since these recruitments—very ordinary for the Soviet era—had their consequences both for the USSR and for post-*perestroika* Russia in the 1990s. It is vitally important to understand that the involvement of Soviet (later Russian Federation) citizens in the work of the Intelligence Services existed on such a massive scale that it was everywhere. Many people judged on their cultural achievements during the Soviet Union as well as after its collapse had secret lives that were often far more dramatic than the tiny tip of the iceberg that was visible. The entanglement of these celebrities often started with the need for the USSR for foreign intelligence and the fact that the arts offered often easy access to well-connected and very well informed elites abroad.

Wooing Albert Einstein

Let us start with the distant past and the Mikhalkov-Konchalovsky set. The writer Sergei Mikhalkov (1913-2009) was born and died in Moscow. On his father's side, he was a descendant of the aristocratic Mikhalkov family. Probably for that reason, the family moved to Pyatigorsk after the Revolution. In 1928, Sergei Mikhalkov published one of his first poems, 'The Road', in the magazine *Na Pod'yeme* (on the rise), based in Rostov-on-the-Don. In 1933, Sergei Mikhalkov returned to Moscow.

He spent some time working in a textile factory and on a geological prospecting expedition. At the same time, he began to do freelance work for the letters section of the official Soviet newspaper *Izvestia*, whose Editor-in-Chief at the time was Nikolai Bukharin. The enterprising young journalist caught the eye of the NKVD and agreed to cooperate with the agency. This gave him ample opportunities for publication in the national press. His poems, redolent with Soviet patriotism (his aristocratic family background was forgotten for the time being) appeared in the magazines and in major Soviet newspapers.

In 2000, the twilight of his days, Mikhalkov said mildly of Stalin that 'he made many mistakes' but was a 'brilliant statesman', 'exceptional', 'fascinating':

I was raised in a different country. The one that no longer exists. A man who has lived through the Soviet era from start to finish should be held accountable under the laws of that time…. The most interesting conversations I had were with Stalin. Even with everything we now know about him, everything that has been written and said, he was still an exceptional statesman…. Stalin was an exceptional personality. Of course, he made many mistakes, many innocent people suffered, but he was a fascinating man.[203]

In 1936, at the age of 23, Mikhalkov got married. His bride, Natalya Konchalovsky, was ten years older and had already been married once. She came from a famous family. The father of Mikhalkov's wife was the well-known artist Petr Konchalovsky; her grandfather was the artist Vasily Surikov. Before her marriage to Mikhalkov, Konchalovsky had a daughter, Ekaterina, with her first husband (whom she had married in her early twenties).

Her first husband was Alexei Bogdanov, a Chekist. His brother, Petr Bogdanov, was a prominent Soviet functionary who headed the USSR foreign trade organization, 'Amtorg'. Amtorg was founded in 1924 in New York by a Soviet double-agent, Armand Hammer, an American. His company was created with the help of Soviet capital and acted as an intermediary in import/export between American companies and Soviet foreign-trade organizations. Amtorg's Soviet branch, 'Sovtorg', had its offices in Moscow. From the moment Amtorg was created, the organization became an important base for the Soviet foreign intelligence agencies of that era—The Foreign Department (INO) of the OGPU and Red Army military intelligence. Amtorg was staffed exclusively by Soviet citizens who worked for Soviet foreign and military intelligence and used Amtorg as their cover to steal US technology and organize deliveries to the USSR of American goods barred from export to the Soviet Union.

It was under the cover of his brother's Amtorg organization that both Bogdanov and Konchalovsky, Mikhalkov's future wife, traveled to the United States, where they also got married—Bogdanov divorced his previous wife by letter. The Bogdanovs were assigned to Seattle, Washington. The official purpose of the trip was to prepare a contract for the construction of whaling boats for the USSR. The actual purpose was to organize a Soviet intelligence network in Seattle, the location of a major Pacific base of the US Navy, of large shipyards where naval ships were built, and of the Boeing airplane factory.

Apart from writers, artists also acted as cover for Chekist intelligence. Konchalovsky's godfather was the famous Soviet sculptor Sergei Konenkov. By the 1920s, he had gained recognition as an undisputed master. His works were widely known not only in the USSR but also abroad, where he was hailed as the 'Russian Rodin.' In 1922, he also remarried. His new bride was Margarita Vorontzova, a woman of aristocratic background. Konenkov wrote in his diary, 'Margarita was so lovely that I thought I was looking at the creation of some ineffable artist.'

When in 1923, a Russian and Soviet art exhibition was held in New York.

Konenkov and his new wife traveled to the United States, ostensibly to participate in the exhibition. In fact, they had also been dispatched to the US for the purpose of creating an intelligence network of Soviet agents. The US did not formally recognize the USSR until 1933, and there were no Soviet diplomatic missions in the US that could have been used as cover for Soviet Foreign Intelligence *rezidentura*, as they were in other countries.

By an extraordinary coincidence—or not—Konchalovsky had arrived in the US with her then husband, the Chekist at Amtorg, practically at the same time as her godfather, the sculptor Konenkov, and his wife Margarita—whose Soviet intelligence codename was 'Lucas'.

In New York, the Konenkovs got to work and began to host a bohemian salon enthusiastically attended by members of the American elite. Konenkov played the accordion and generously poured drinks for the guests at a carved wooden bar that he had built himself. His young and beautiful wife Margarita was a charming and welcoming hostess who mesmerized their guests. A similar salon was hosted by Konenkov's goddaughter Konchalovsky and her spy husband Bogdanov on the other coast of the United States, in Seattle. They too were charming to their numerous guests, whom the husband entertained by playing the piano.

Konchalovsky's marriage to Bogdanov was dissolved when she filed for divorce. It was not a good time for the Bogdanovs. In 1937, Petr Bogdanov was arrested and executed during the purges. His brother Andrei Bogdanov was also arrested and shot shortly afterwards. But by then, Konchalovsky was already married to poet Mikhalkov.

Sergei Mikhalkov had courted his bride for a very long time and very persistently. He started by asking her daughter Katya about her mother's other suitors. One of them, Pavel Vasiliev, was a remarkably talented man. He was also a poet. His work had first appeared in the newspapers in Vladivostok where he had been living and studying. Pasternak wrote about him with great warmth in 1956 of 'the creative expressiveness and power of his talent':

In the early 1930s, Pavel Vasiliev made roughly the same kind of impression on me as Yesenin and Mayakovsky had earlier, when I had first met them. He was comparable to them—especially to Yesenin—in the creative expressiveness and power of his talent.... He had the kind of vivid, dynamic and joyful imagination without which there can be no great poetry and which I never again encountered to such an extent in anyone else in all the years that have elapsed since his death.

In 1928, Vasiliev moved to Moscow. He got published in Moscow magazines and held poetry readings; soon, he became one of the capital's most popular poets. At the same time, however, he acquired a reputation as a rowdy drunk, based both on his behavior and on numerous reports to various authorities including Intelligence agencies. In 1935, Vasiliev was expelled from the Writers' Union and sentenced to eighteen months of imprisonment for beating up the poet Jack Altausen, who had maligned

Vasiliev's lover Konchalovsky.

It was at this point that Pitovranov's 4th Directorate got involved. The prosecutor's report on Vasiliev stated that he planned a 'terrorist attack against Comrade Stalin' after having on previous occasions, his 'case file' claimed, launched into verbal attacks on Communism:

The 4th Department of the GUGB received information that the writer and poet Pavel Vasiliev, had been recruited to carry out a terrorist attack against Comrade Stalin. The investigation found that the accused had expressed counter-revolutionary fascist views for a number of years prior to his arrest. Earlier, in 1932, the accused, Vasiliev Pavel, had received a suspended sentence of three years of imprisonment for membership in a counterrevolutionary group in literary circles. In 1935, he was sentenced to eighteen months in a correctional labor camp for beating the poet and Komsomol member Jack Altausen. Under questioning, the accused, Pavel Vasiliev, fully admitted his guilt.

Vasiliev apparently confessed to his crimes which made it an open and shut case and he was sentenced to death on July 15, 1937, and shot on July 16. Before Vasiliev's premature death, in 1936, the first year of Stalin's Great Purge, Konchalovsky had already married Sergei Mikhalkov. There was a certain distance between her and her former lover Vasiliev. Mikhalkov later reminisced how Konchalovsky finally gave in:

To tell the truth, Natasha was reluctant to marry me—she was, of course, a bit nonplussed by the age difference. ... I insisted on formalizing our relationship, fearing that I would lose the smart and charming woman I loved, and in the end, Natasha gave in.

And so, in 1937, at the age of 24, Sergei Mikhalkov became a member of the Writers' Union of the USSR. Remarkably, two years later, the 26-year-old author—hardly the most popular or even less so the most gifted of Soviet poets, and not even a Party member at that—received the highest of state honors—The Order of Lenin. The statute on the Order of Lenin described it as follows:

The order of Lenin is the USSR's highest decoration: awarded for especially outstanding merit in the revolutionary movement, in one's field of work, in the defense of the socialist Motherland, in fostering friendship and cooperation between peoples, in the cause of strengthening peace, and for other especially outstanding achievements in the service of the Soviet state and society.

How did the relatively unknown Mikhalkov get the Lenin order, the Soviet equivalent of the Nobel Prize? When the question of awarding the Order of Lenin to the far better-known Soviet poet and Party functionary Demyan Bedny came up in

1934—after the founding congress of the Writers' Union of the USSR—Stalin opposed it. Stalin's favorite poet and writer Konstantin Simonov, who was the same age as Mikhalkov and had graduated from the Literary College with a diploma of excellence, was admitted to the Writers' Union in 1938 but did not get the Order of Lenin either until 1965—well after Stalin's death.

Another far worthier recipient of the order would have been Mikhail Koltsov, a correspondent for *Pravda*, the official paper of the Party, and for a number of other major publications. The best-known Soviet journalist, he founded the magazine *Ogonyok* (the spark) and became its Editor-in-Chief; he was also the editor of the magazine *Za Rubezhom* (abroad), a member of the *Pravda* editorial board, a founder of the satirical magazine *Krokodil* (crocodile) and the humor magazine *Chudak* (the maverick). After the Soviet Writers' Union was created, furthermore, he headed its Foreign Department. He was a delegate to the international congress for the defense of culture in Paris in 1935 and the head of the Soviet delegation to a similar congress in Barcelona in 1937. In 1936, he went to Spain in the midst of its civil war as a *Pravda* correspondent and where he simultaneously carried out tasks for Soviet intelligence. His reward for all these loyal achievements was not the Order of Lenin but arrest in December 1938 and execution in February 1940.

It seems, Sergei Mikhalkov's merits were in the category of 'other especially outstanding achievements in the service of the Soviet state and society' connected to his wife's involvement with the Intelligence Services rather than with literature as such.

Mikhalkov's godfather and his wife, the Konenkovs, were to spend 22 years in the United States. During this time, Margarita ('Lucas') managed to win over the affection of the great physicist Albert Einstein and to get him to introduce her to Robert Oppenheimer, the head of the Manhattan Project which developed America's nuclear bomb, and his wife Catherine. Beria's subordinate Sudoplatov boasts about them in his autobiography *Special Tasks: The Memoirs of an Unwanted Witness: A Soviet Spymaster* (1994):

> Acting under the supervision of Liza Zarubina, the sculptor Konenkov's wife, our tried and trusted agent, got close to the top physicists Oppenheimer and Einstein in Princeton. She managed to charm Oppenheimer's circle of friends…. Under the direction of Liza Zarubina and our New York resident [Pavel] Pastelnyak, ['Lucas'] exerted a constant influence on Oppenheimer; earlier, she had already persuaded him to hire specialists known for their left-wing convictions, whom our illegals and agents were already prepared to cultivate.

They were rewarded unlike others. Upon his return to Moscow in 1945, Konenkov received a large studio and an apartment in a prestigious house on Gorky Street, Moscow's main street (since renamed). For the remainder of their lives, the Konenkovs stayed in close contact with Sergei Mikhalkov and his wife, who both continued to work for Soviet intelligence. Together they were deeply involved in the recruitment of the French ambassador to the USSR, Maurice Dejean. The ambassador had close ties to and influence over the President of France, General de Gaulle. Besides the tried and trusted agents Konchalovsky and Mikhalkov, another agent, the actress Larisa Kronberg-Sobolevsky, was also involved in cultivating and recruiting Ambassador Dejean.

Yulian Semyonov's Thriller

Yulian Semyonov (1931-1991) was the creator of a new literary genre: the political thriller glorifying the Chekists as people with 'clean hands, a fiery heart and a cool head.' The streets of Soviet cities would be deserted during broadcasts of *Seventeen Moments of Spring* (1972), a serial based on Semyonov's novel with the same title. Its hero Max Otto von Stierlitz, a Soviet spy embedded deep in the Third Reich, became a true if fictional Soviet national hero. Among Semyonov's readers and fans was KGB Chief Yuri Andropov. Not surprisingly, Yulian Semyonov's work was of vital importance in creating a positive image of the KGB. They were so close that fellow writers jealously referred to Semyonov as 'Andropov's pet'.

Again, the Konchalovsky-Mikhalkov set was involved. Ekaterina, Konchalovsky's daughter with her first husband (Sergei Mikhalkov's stepdaughter) was married to the thriller writer, Yulia Semyonov. His real surname was Lyandres, which did not have the same currency. His father, Semyon Lyandres (1907-1968), once worked in the Soviet government at the Supreme Council on the People's Economy and the People's Commissariat of Heavy Industry since 1930; at one time, he had been an aide to the minister of heavy industry, Ordzhonikidze. In the mid-1930s, Lyandres was offered the job of Deputy Editor-in-Chief and managing editor of official government newspaper *Izvestia*. In 1942, however, he was arrested and detained for several months; in 1952, he was again arrested and this time sentenced to eight years in the camps.

His son Yulian worked tirelessly (and fearlessly) to get his father released. But Semyon was only released in 1954, after Stalin's death, and returned from camp an invalid. In the late 1950s, he worked as deputy director of *Goslitizdat* and in the 1960s, as Deputy Editor-in-Chief of the magazine *Voprosy Literatury* (literary issues).

Yulian Lyandres studied at the Moscow Institute of Oriental Studies in 1948. But because of his efforts on behalf of his father, he was expelled from the Institute in his fifth year and his membership of Komsomol (the young Communist organization) was cancelled. It was only after Stalin's death that he was able to complete his education and study history at the Moscow State University (MSU) while also teaching Pashto (spoken in Afghanistan) there.

It was not an auspicious start for a successful author. But, suddenly, in 1955, the works of the hitherto unknown author Yulian Semyonov began to be plugged in various publications and Semyonov's writings appeared in prestigious Soviet print media. How did this remarkable reversal come about given the many blots on his past?

The MSU where Yulian taught Pashto had many foreign students. For that reason alone, they were closely monitored by the Lubyanka, just like the faculty and the Soviet students. A young, energetic, erudite and gregarious man—one, moreover, who taught the rare Pashto and whose father had been a victim of repression—was naturally of interest to those in the Intelligence Services such as Pitovranov/Bobkov. And since Yulian was an adventurous man who was eager to see and travel around the world, he was receptive to the offer to become an agent and go to Afghanistan for a prestigious 'business trip' abroad. He first set foot on Afghan soil in 1959.

Yulian's work for Soviet intelligence took him to many places and involved difficult and dangerous missions. Besides Afghanistan, he worked in Spain under the rule of General Franco; in Chile under the presidency of the socialist Salvador Allende; in Paraguay under the dictatorship of General Stroessner; then it was on to Vietnam and Laos, where he was an eyewitness of its guerrilla warfare. He wrote engaging and riveting accounts of the things he saw, but only a small portion of what he wrote saw the light of day; the rest remained in the archives of Soviet special services.

In Soviet times, this connection between writers recruited as agents and their Chekist handlers was used by both for maximum mutual benefit. If he couldn't use his real patronym, at least Yulian could use his beloved father's first name as his *nom de plume*. Above all, Yulian represented the interests of the Pitovranov/Bobkov group within the KGB. A Jew, the son of a former political prisoner, and a multilingual one at that—one could find no better agent to infiltrate 'Zionist centers'. The Intelligence generals genuinely believed (or at any rate pretended to) in the existence of an international Jewish conspiracy and waged war against this phantom as best they could.

The Cheka's Undercover Foreign Correspondents

Another journalist whose career rocketed after being recruited by the 5th Directorate was journalist and editor Vitaly Syrokomsky, who worked in Party organizations and in Soviet journalism (he spent years toiling as the *de facto* Editor-in-Chief of *Literaturnaya Gazeta* (literary gazette) or 'LG' while its nominal Editor-in-Chief, CC member Alexander Chakovsky, was forever working on his novel *The Blockade*). He told the story of how journalist-agents helped the KGB solve the problem of creating foreign correspondent bureaus where Soviet spies would work under cover as journalists. The writers wanted these bureaus because they offered opportunities for foreign travel. The Chekists wanted them for the same reason.

Syrokomsky claims that the correspondent bureaus were his idea. He boasted in 2001 that everything about it was resolved in a 10-minute chat between Andropov and Andrei Gromyko, Soviet foreign minister (1957-1985), that he made his boss have with them:

> LG did not have its own foreign correspondents…. I suggested creating correspondent bureaus, jointly with the KGB, in the USA, England, West Germany, and France. Under this scheme, the KGB would get four more 'covers,' and we would get dispatches from four major Western countries. I asked that 'Chak' [Chakovsky] call Andropov.

Andropov sized up the situation right away. We heard Andropov (the membranes of government phones carry sound very well) say to someone on another telephone, 'Andrei! Chakovsky just called with what I think is an interesting idea.'

And then he explained the gist of it to Andrei Gromyko. The foreign minister agreed with his Party comrade at once. Thus, everything was resolved in 10 minutes.[204]

However, Andropov certainly could not have sorted out a complicated bureaucratic matter in 10 minutes, let alone figured out how to 'get' the foreign ministry to pay for this project (that was the only purpose of the call to Gromyko). Just to give an idea of the number of steps involved in the proposal, Syrokomsky was in regular contact with leaders of the 5th Directorate, Bobkov and his deputy Ivan Abramov. Syrokomsky had operational meetings with the latter and the two of them discussed the correspondent bureau project. Abramov directed the Chief of the 1st Department, Colonel Pass Smolin, to study the matter further. Smolin passed on these instructions to the Chief of the 2nd Section of the 1st Department, Lieutenant Colonel Vladimir Strunin, and Strunin's subordinates prepared a 'memo to the Committee' (that is, to KGB leadership) on opening LG foreign-correspondent bureaus abroad. The leadership of the 5th Directorate submitted this document for approval to the First Chief Directorate, after which it finally ended up on Andropov's desk.

Chakovsky's call to Andropov was most likely part of a show scripted in advance. Andropov was 'for it,' but did not want to be the first to propose this project, since it would require considerable funds in foreign currency to pay for maintaining the bureaus, paying the correspondents, and paying their families' living expenses. That was why Andropov suggested that Syrokomsky should 'take the initiative' and set up Chakovsky's phone call to the KGB. Knowing from his Chekist contacts that the project had already been greenlit, the 'brave' Syrokomsky 'asked' that his boss, the Editor-in-Chief of *Literaturnaya Gazeta*, dial the KGB Chair for his thoughts on the matter.

Here's more of Syrokomsky's narrative on how complex the operation was to make sure that the cover of the foreign-correspondent bureaus as Cheka launchpads was not blown by ham-fisted Intelligence agents:

The next day, a 'summit' was held at a KGB safehouse in downtown Moscow: the head of the First Chief Directorate of the KGB … Kryuchkov, his first deputy Ivanov, Chakovsky, and I. Basically, everything was discussed, and the comrades from foreign intelligence agreed with my framing of the question: LG needed special, professional-quality materials, otherwise the Chekists [attached to the correspondent bureaus disguised as journalists] were going to have their cover blown right away.

The reason why Andropov supported Pitovranov's specialist outfit was because he knew that if he wanted an Intelligence branch that was separate from the KGB, 'the right people' had to be selected as correspondents in order not give away the real Intelligence operation they were hiding. It's, therefore, no surprise that Yulian Semyonov ended up being one of LG's literary 'foreign correspondents'. Syrokomsky recalls that 'Andropov's pet' Yulian merely had to put in a call to the KGB chair on his direct line to get the job:

I remember how Yulian Semyonov—well-known writer, my old friend, and Andropov's pet—'pushed his way' into a correspondent's post. He came to see me at the office and declared that he wanted to spend two or three years working in Central Europe, mostly in the Federal Republic of Germany, working as a *LG* correspondent. I replied that I could not make such a decision on my own. 'What needs to be done, then?' I motioned with my eyes to show that a call needed to be made on a special line and stroked my shoulders [to indicate shoulder stripes]. He got it at once and picked up the phone. '[Andropov], this is Yulian. Sorry to bother you, but here's the thing…' The conversation continued for about ten minutes. Then, Yulian said, beaming, 'It's settled, old man. I'm going! Send a memo to the CC.' I sent [the memo] and, just in case, called Kryuchkov's first deputy…. He had no objections.[205]

The story of how Syrokomsky himself was recruited also deserves a mention. Syrokomsky was Jewish. Yet in 1946, when the anti-Semitic campaign against 'cosmopolitanism' was warming up, he was able to get into the Moscow State Institute of International Relations (MSIIR), the most prestigious Soviet institute of higher education. Here is how Syrokomsky himself described MSIIR in his little-known autobiographical essay, *The Enigma of the Patriarch*:

MSIIR was a forge for producing 'elite' cadres: diplomats and intelligence agents, Party workers and government officials. Here, everything was taught 'with complete perfection': foreign languages, at the level of Moscow's famous Foreign Languages Institute; Marxism-Leninism, at the level of the Higher Party School under the CC; history as one would learn it in Moscow State University's history department; law as one would learn it in law school… But after all this, the graduate was fit for work in any field.

During the Soviet period, the MSIIR was controlled by the 7th Department of the VGU. The same Department was in charge of counterintelligence surveillance of the foreign ministry. As a Jew, the only way Syrokomsky could have remained a student was by agreeing to join the Lubyanka as an agent. All the more so since, as a student, Syrokomsky came up with the idea of publishing a student magazine. This was a golden opportunity from the Cheka's point of view, as this gave him the opportunity to influence and interact widely with many fellow students and use these contacts for the benefit of Soviet special services. The Lubyanka's backing certainly helped secure permission from the MSIIR administration to allow the student magazine to appear in the first place.

All this was a story he couldn't tell truthfully, even many years later after the fall of the Soviet Union. The way Syrokomsky tells it in 2001 is that a talent-spotting KGB general came across his brilliant articles and called him in merely to offer him the editorship of a German-language newspaper the Soviet union happened to have in East-Berlin—as if Syrokomsky's talents as a journalist swayed the KGB to appoint him to the job:

In early April 1961, I was suddenly summoned to the KGB to see some important general. He was very friendly, told me that he had been reading my articles for a long time, and made a suggestion.

'You're an experienced newspaperman,' he said, 'you've been working for the press for ten years, you know German. We have a German-language newspaper that comes out in Berlin, *Tägliche Rundschau* (daily review). Why don't you go there for a few years? You'll be appointed managing editor, which means that you will be essentially running the office. The publisher—Soviet military headquarters in Germany—will give you a free hand. You'll regain complete fluency in German, too. Go on, do it...'

I agreed at once. After all, my diploma from the Institute defined my professional field as 'historian and foreign affairs expert with a focus on Germany.'

Being invited to the KGB at the Lubyanka was no sinecure. The pass required for admission to the building for people who were not a part of the KGB's central staff had to state the name of the officer who had issued the invitation. Moreover, the KGB agent had to introduce himself in person to those he invited to his office: to state his position, rank, and full name.

Syrokomsky vaguely calls the officer 'some' general, but it was none other than Pitovranov. Syrokomsky knew Pitovranov very well. In the early 1960s, Syrokomsky worked for two years as an assistant to the Party's First Secretary of the Moscow City Committee, Pyotr Demichev, and thereafter to Nikolai Yegorychev. The latter was a constant in the orbit of the KGB's Pitovranov group. When Yegorychev, who had fallen from favor in the 1970s, returned to Moscow after 14 years of 'exile' as ambassador to Denmark, Pitovranov appointed him as his First Deputy Chair of the presidium of the Soviet Chamber of Commerce and Industry, a body which he himself headed. In 1988, on the eve of the collapse of the Soviet Union, Pitovranov, KGB First Deputy Chair Bobkov, and Intelligence General Ivanov, made sure Yegorychev became the Soviet ambassador to Afghanistan. Why? Soviet troops were then being pulled out of the country and an entire army was leaving. This opened up vast opportunities for enterprising people to make money.

It was, therefore, no accident that Pitovranov invited Syrokomsky for a talk in 1961. Appointments to editorial positions were, in any case, not decided by the Intelligence Services. Traditionally, the Party CC had the prerogative. However, Pitovranov could place its trusted agents in high-level positions in the media by recommending them to Party officials. By inviting Syrokomsky for a talk, Pitovranov was signaling that the KGB trusted him and held his services to the agency in high regard. Given that the Party thought it had absolute control over the Lubyanka officials of the CC would understand it to mean that Syrokomsky was going to be a safe pair of hands.

And when the Soviet Union's first 'proper' (16-page) newspaper was launched in 1967 as a publication of the Federation of Soviet Writers' Associations (later the Writers' Union of the USSR), with a somewhat lighter tone than the orthodox rest of the Soviet press, it was Syrokomsky, the tried and trusted KGB agent, who was appointed to be its Deputy Editor-in-Chief.

His pact with the devil was a golden gift to the journalist as well. Not many senior editors in the central press had direct contacts with the upper echelon of the 5th Directorate. 'I had a monopoly on interviews with major politicians: presidents, prime ministers, ministers of foreign affairs,' boasted Syrokomsky. During these interviews with the amiable and knowledgeable journalist, talk of course ranged widely. And even though foreign-policy issues did not fall under the purview of the 5th Directorate, his reports with exhaustive details obtained during interviews—reports that were always intended to capture nuances that were not publicly said—were invariably submitted to his Intelligence chiefs.

Syrokomsky was also deployed in straightforward KGB operations. He described how he used KGB *kompromat* to try and get the West German ambassador to pull a Soviet spy exposé on West-German TV:

> Late at night, I was asked to have an urgent meeting with the West German ambassador and tell him that the sensational report on spies among Soviet diplomats made by Western German television must not go on their air…. Otherwise, the press in Moscow was going to publish exposés on the conduct of certain diplomats from West Germany in the USSR…. Some Western Kremlinologists claimed more than once that LG was a KGB tool.

LG's literary correspondent bureaus in New York, Tokyo, London and Paris were called 'joint correspondent bureaus' for a reason. They were places where officers of Soviet foreign intelligence worked under the guise of journalists. For instance, Syrokomsky recalled that in New York, 'one of our excellent workers was the well-known writer, playwright and essayist Genrikh Borovik, who could be accused of many things but certainly not of working for the KGB.' However, while Borovik did not work for the KGB in the sense that he was a staff member or an officer, he was nonetheless an undercover agent of the 1st Department of the KGB's PGU (1st

Directorate).

LG itself fell under the 2nd Section of the 1st Department of the 5th Directorate. Every single scrap of information entered 'Special File No 1110' as part of the section's caseload. It assembled a wealth of compromising material on the Writers' Union of the USSR, the newspaper *LG*, and Syrokomsky himself. 'Compromising', meant, according to Lubyanka terms.

Inevitably, given his lenient leash Syrokomsky became the subject of a draft memorandum to the CC himself. It was prepared by the 5th Directorate's 2nd Department Chief Strunin and his staffers, senior operative Captain Evgeny Auzhbikovich and operative Captain Nikolai Nikandrov. It did not bode well for him. If he had been an ordinary KGB asset. However, the draft never went further than Bobkov's deputy, General Ivan Abramov, for the simple reason that Syrokomsky was Abramov's regular undercover contact. When some of the paper's staffers urged the unsuspecting Syrokomsky to be a little bit more cautious in his comments on political issues, the latter, completely unaware of the looming danger, would smugly reply that he had no cause to fear because General Abramov was a friend of his.

When Syrokomsky was so emboldened that he thought he could act with no regard for the KGB, his 'friend' Abramov finally allowed the compromising materials about him to go forward, reminding the 'journalist' who was in charge. Syrokomsky was removed from the post he had occupied for years by the Party CC and replaced, on the KGB's recommendation, by the more respectful Yuri Izyumov.

Syrokomsky's unique talent was still considered useful and he was offered a choice of two jobs: one at the Progress Publishing House, which employed more than 100 foreigners, and the other one at the Soviet Copyright Agency (VAAP). Both organizations were under strict counterintelligence surveillance by staffers of the same 2nd Section of the 1st Departments of the 5th Directorate.

Syrokomsky chose the VAAP, where KGB Colonel Gennady Zareev served as Deputy Chief director and former foreign intelligence officer Colonel Vasily Sitnikov was Deputy Chair of the board. KGB Lieutenant Colonel Plakhuta also worked at the agency. Syrokomsky was on a constant close KGB watch. He later recalled that time as his worst years:

> The two years in VAAP were the most painful part of my life. Forced to do bureaucratic work for which I was unsuited, I developed a serious illness: artery spasms. I was barely able to make it out alive.

Obviously, KGB men were never 'friends' to anyone, least of all Syrokomsky. Like Andropov, they had no 'friends' either—just agents and targets.

The Cheka's International Poet
The popular Soviet poet Yevgeny Yevtushenko also collaborated with the KGB on the quiet for many years, working as an agent for the 5th Directorate. This collaboration

began when Pitovranov was still in charge; then, Bobkov took over and worked directly with Yevtushenko.[206] As a souvenir of this recruitment, Pitovranov kept a collection of Yevtushenko's poems with a gift inscription that also touched on the theme of friendship:

> Worse yet than to mistake a foe for friend
> Is to mistake a friend for foe in haste.
> To Pitovranov from Yevtushenko

The Cheka have always had—and still has—a rigid rule: never expose an agent, not even as punishment or revenge. As Colonel Sergei Vasiliev, Chief of the KGB 1st Department of the KGB Press Bureau, in 2005 told the writer Stanislav Kunyayev, another agent recruited in the 1970s: 'No matter what they might do, no matter what turn history might take, our agency has a basic law: our informers, our secret agents are not to be ratted out or unmasked—not ever, not for anything.'[207]

For this reason, many KGB officers have side-stepped or simply denied the fact that Yevtushenko was an Intelligence collaborator in their memoirs. The memoirs of General Sudoplatov—arrested as part of Beria's fall and released in 1968—are typical in this regard. He described a festival in Finland during which 'absolutely no attempts to recruit him as an informer' were made by the KGB, after which Yevtushenko somehow became a spontaneous supporter of Khruschev's 'new' Communism:

> The KGB's ideological directorate took an interest in my wife's [NKVD officer Emma Kaganova] experience working with the creative intelligentsia in the 1930s. Former students at the NKVD school whom she had trained in the basics of recruiting agents consulted her, as did Colonel Ryabov, on how to use Yevtushenko's popularity, contacts and connections for operational purposes and for propaganda for foreign consumption. My wife suggested developing a friendly confidential relationship with him and making absolutely no attempts to recruit him as an informer, but instead sending him, accompanied by Ryabov, to the International Festival of Youth and Students in Finland. After the trip, Yevtushenko became an active supporter of the 'new Communist ideas' that were being advanced by Khrushchev.

That same 1962 trip to Finland was, however, described in a rather different way—one that came close to blowing Yevtushenko's cover as an agent—by Bobkov in an obscure 2008 interview. He described Yevtushenko as the man of the moment who doused the festival's major anti-Communist trouble incited by anti-Soviet ideologues and US intelligence. Instead of sitting on the fence during the festival, Yevtushenko made sure the provocateurs were discredited:

> The festival in Helsinki unfolded in a complicated atmosphere. The American

Intelligence services, working together with anti-Soviet organizations in the West such as the NTS—the National Alliance of Russian Solidarists, an anticommunist White émigré organization (NTS), did everything they could to sabotage the festival, caused unrest in the city and blame it on the festival organizers and on international youth unions that worked closely with the Komsomol. The poet Yevgeny Yevtushenko, a member of the Soviet youth delegation, helped a great deal in discrediting the provocateurs.[208]

Yevtushenko was a keen helper. Like any agent recruited by State Security—one who, moreover, had direct access to 5th Directorate chief Bobkov—Yevtushenko carried out numerous KGB assignments both inside and outside the Soviet Union.

In May 1975 at the Metropol Hotel, in a room reserved for such meetings, the KGB held a 'precautionary conversation' with the writer Vladimir Voinovich and attempted to recruit him. He himself, however, believed that during this meeting, an attempt was made to poison him. The news of this attempted poisoning spread quickly around the world, and it was quite an uncomfortable situation for the KGB. Voinovich recalled that it was Yevtushenko who used his reputation to deflect KGB criticism and warned people he would report them:

> I don't know if the poet Yevgeny Yevtushenko acted on someone's instructions or on his own, but during those days he would passionately argue to everyone he came across that no one had tried to poison me... while imprudently bragging about how well-informed he was: 'Believe me, if anybody knows for sure, I do.'... You have to wonder: just how did he know this?... His role as a messenger from 'the agency' to [Joseph] Brodsky and [Vasily] Aksyonov is a well-known fact. Even as a young man, Yevtushenko would publicly say that anyone permitted himself any anti-Soviet comments at one of his events, he would personally shop the offender to the KGB. In my 'dissident' years, Yevtushenko did his utmost to tarnish my reputation and make my already difficult and dangerous predicament even worse—for instance, by telling foreigners who asked what was happening to me that I was a bad writer and a bad man, that I was doing just fine and didn't deserve their concern.[209]

Nobel Prize laureate and US Poet Laureate Joseph Brodsky wrote in his memoirs that fellow poet Yevtushenko somehow found out that his parents were trying to get their papers to join him in the United States and volunteered to help. Moreover, Yevtushenko stressed that he had a reliable friend inside the KGB whom he had known since the 1962 youth festival in Finland and that all he needed to do was call this friend, and the issue would be settled. However, he categorically refused to give the friend's name. It's not hard to hazard a guess that Yevtushenko's 'reliable' KGB friend was General Bobkov—who must have seen some benefit in letting Yevtushenko help Brodsky.

12: Russian Nationalism, the New Hymn

The entire 'creative intelligentsia' within the Soviet Union was a member of the Soviet 'creative unions'. The purpose of the 5th Directorate created by Andropov-Pitovranov was to start monitoring this group in particular through a very fine grain in order to direct the 'about 50 nationalist groups' Andropov had identified in his 1967 Politburo memo, as well as other cultural currents in the Soviet union. In charge of this key task was the 2nd Section of the 1st Department led by Vladimir Strunin, whom we have met already several times in the previous chapter. His KGB officers were known as 'the literary group' inside the department. The KGB of each republic of the Soviet Union had its own 'literary group'. At local and regional directorates, such functions were carried out by an operative of the Directorate's 5th Department. Though Strunin's Section evidently existed in plain sight of the Party, the Kremlin took very little interest in it. Nationalism seemed no more than a collection of local and therefore peripheral threats to its absolute dominion over the Soviet Union if not, more precisely, the Lubyanka.

The central 'literary group' in Moscow at the Lubyanka was fairly small. In the early 1970s, it consisted of senior operative Zareyev (then still a captain), senior operative Captain Auzhbikovich, senior operative Major Viktor Fedotov, senior operative Captain Nikandrov, and junior operative junior lieutenant Vladimir Popov. His Deputy was Lieutenant Colonel Valentin Beteyev, who had the odd quirk of insisting that he was called 'Vladimir Ilyich' (like Lenin), not, evidently, a 'literary' nickname.

Each officer handled specific organizations. Zareyev was in charge of the Soviet Council of Ministers' Committee on Publishing, Printing and Bookselling, including the Progress Publishing House. In addition, jointly with Nikandrov, Zareyev handled the tricky Writers' Unions of the USSR and the Russian Federation, as well as the Maxim Gorky Institute of World Literature. Fedotov was the operative in charge of the Gorky Institute, its advanced-level literary and screenwriting programs at that college, as well as the editorial offices of the *Literaturnaya Gazeta* (literary gazette) and *Literaturnaya Rossiya* (Russian literature), and the 'Soviet Writer' publishing company. Auzhbikovich was tasked with coordinating the work of the 5th Directorate with corresponding departments in other socialist countries. In the early 1980s, Auzhbikovich died prematurely in a car crash.

The massive amount of information collated and processed by security agencies, reflecting every aspect of life in the vast Soviet world, was delivered to the Center, that is, to KGB headquarters at the Lubyanka, Moscow. The other divisions of the central KGB *apparat* also obtained large amounts of information in the course of their work in the areas to which they were assigned. The analysis of information coming in from the field and from the capital was used to develop the KGB's strategies and tactics in preventing activities hostile to the Soviet system. The same information, received and analyzed, became the basis for briefings to the 'Authority' (that is the Party CC) as well as to local Party structures and State Security Departments. Thus, the appropriate departments of the Intelligence Services were kept amply informed of developments within the literary and artistic organizations of the USSR.

The 'literary group' collected information that reflected the atmosphere in all literary circles around the enormous USSR. Thus, from the moment the 5th Directorate was created in 1967 by Andropov, the 'literary group' began to amass a tremendous amount of material, consisting mostly of KGB agents' reports. All these reports were fed into 'Special File No 1110' already mentioned. It eventually grew to more than 100 volumes at 300 pages each. The size of these volumes was limited by the size of the boxes for archive storage, and thus could not exceed certain dimensions. Considering that all the documents were printed double-sided on every page, one can only imagine the colossal—by the standards of that time—amount of information contained in these volumes.

It was Captain Nikandrov who maintained operative contacts with the prominent novelists of Russian nationalism, or Slavophiles. Strictly speaking, this movement was antithetical to the idea of Communism, but Andropov and Pitovranov were keen to mine its potential force as purist Communist ideology had fallen out of favor after Stalin's death. Hailing from Novosibirsk, Siberia, Nikandrov remained a provincial at heart and showed an undiluted enthusiasm for 'village' writers, that is novelists who wrote critical stories about rural Russia under Stalin bathed in bucolic nostalgia for what had been lost rather than to plug utopian ideas. As a result, shortly after being transferred to the 'literary group,' he established working relations with literary critic and scholar Vadim Kozhinov, poet Valentin Sorokin, and literary critic Yevgeny Sidorov, whom he recruited as a KGB agent.

In 1970, after additional interviews of Sorokin at the Lubyanka headquarters, Nikandrov recommended the 34-year-old for the post of Editor-in-Chief of the newly created *Sovremennik* (contemporary) Publishing House, which fell under the RSFSR (Russian) Writers' Union and the RSFSR Council of Ministers' State Committee on Publishing, Printing and Bookselling—both also monitored by Nikandrov. In 1974, the now 38-year-old Sorokin went on to collect the prestigious Lenin Komsomol Prize. From 1983 onward, he was the head of Soviet Higher Literary Courses and, in 1986, the RSFSR State Prize was added to the laurels of the Slavophile poet. It was at Sovremennik, under Sorokin's leadership, that most of the books of the 'village writers' for whom Nikandrov had so much sympathy were published.

The scholar Kozhinov supplied Nikandrov with confidential inside information.

So did Valentin Rasputin, a young writer from Irkutsk and a rising star. Rasputin and Nikandrov were introduced to each other by Rasputin's former classmate at the university who had become an officer in the KGB's First Chief Directorate (PGU). Rasputin's school friend submitted detailed reports on all their meetings to the 'literary group' and so, when Rasputin visited Moscow, Nikandrov met with the prodigy personally to vet him.

Nikandrov's operative contacts also included the poet and literary critic Stanislav Kunyayev, who, partly thanks to support from the Chekists, became Secretary of the Moscow Writers' Organization in 1976 and then Editor-in-Chief of *Nash Sovremennik* (our contemporary) magazine in 1989. Of course, the unfortunate Kunyayev had no idea that the Soviet Union would collapse and that his collaboration with the KGB under codename 'Rodin' would become public:

From the monthly report of the KGB 5th Directorate, May 1989:
Via the agent 'Rodin,' the magazine *Nash Sovremennik* has published material on the émigré writer L[ev] Kopelev (codename 'Swine'), exposing his ties to anti-Soviet centers in the West.

But it did. 'Rodin' was the codename agent Kunyayev picked when he signed the document agreeing to cooperate with the KGB.

In the mid-1970s, Nikandrov acquired an agent from the camp that rejected the 'Russianist' literary movement. This was the well-known satirical poet Alexander Ivanov, who chose the codename 'Tugar.' With the help of 'Tugar', the 'literary group' of the 5th Directorate was among the first 'confidential readers' who received 'hot' typewritten copies of Vasily Aksyonov's novel *The Burn* (1975) and the uncensored *Metropol* (1979) for a few hours, to be quickly returned to 'Tugar' after KGB copies were made. With Nikandrov's help, 'Tugar' became the host of the popular TV show 'Around Laughter.' But his double life was eating at him from inside. He drank heavily and went on binges, which caused his premature death from alcohol poisoning.

The most troublesome target for operative surveillance for the 5th Directorate and the KGB directorate for Moscow and the Moscow region was the Soviet Writers' Union (a.k.a. the Soviet Writers' Union) and its Moscow chapter. The Writers' Union stood out among other creative associations—not in a good way—because its widely discussed clashes of ideas often turned into widely discussed scandals and controversies. The union was under constant and vigilant watch by the Party CC and the KGB. Consequently, all events organized by the Writers' Union, its Moscow chapter, or the Central Writers' House were monitored by never-sleeping Intelligence agents and by the handler Nikandrov, who always had close at hand a monthly calendar of the Central Writers' House events on which Bobkov's Deputy, General Abramov, demanded regular reports.

At the time, Nikandrov was thinking of recruiting Felix Kuznetsov, a critic and the First Secretary of the Moscow Writers' Organization (the Moscow chapter of the Soviet Writers' Union). However, he worried about trouble from the Party's Moscow city committee in case of failure. It was a rather delicate situation Nikandrov had to navigate.

Felix Kuznetsov was born in 1931. He had graduated from Moscow State University with a degree in philology and completed graduate school, receiving a 'Candidate of Sciences' degree in 1966 and a doctorate in 1970. He worked in a variety of central print media, taught at the Gorky Institute and the Patrice Lumumba Peoples' Friendship University (PFU). He had become head of the Moscow Writers' Organization in 1976.

Kuznetsov was known as a literary critic who wrote from a perspective of strict Party orthodoxy. That was precisely what drew Nikandrov's attention, especially since the Moscow Writers' Organization—the leading writers' association in the Soviet Union in terms of overall membership and number of acclaimed literary masters in its ranks—played a pivotal role in the country's literary and cultural life and was autonomous within what was permitted. At the same time, the Moscow Writers' Organization was a harbor both for liberal writers and for their antagonists, the 'Russianists.'

In order to keep these different dynamics under control, it was important for the Chekists to have their man at the helm, in the post of First Secretary. While Nikandrov was trying to decide how exactly he should go about recruiting Kuznetsov, a young city KGB officer, Captain Vladimir Zubkov, beat him to it. A graduate of the Moscow Aviation Institute and a former Komsomol activist, Zubkov was an operative at the 1st Section of the 5th Department of the Moscow and Moscow Region KGB directorate. He recruited Kuznetsov in the spring of 1977. By then, the RSFSR Writers' Union was led by Bobkov's protégé and veteran agent, the poet Sergei Mikhalkov. So the KGB was fairly well-informed on the situation in the Moscow, RSFSR and Soviet writers' unions.

It was at this point, to keep up with the 'Muscovites' (as the KGB's central staff referred to colleagues in the Moscow and Moscow Region KGB Directorate), that Nikandrov recruited critic Yevgeny Sidorov, who was Gorky Institute pro-rector. Soon events happened. A year later, in 1978, Sidorov replaced Vladimir Pimenov as head of the Institute. It was a post Pimenov had held for years. The Gorky Institute had another valuable agent on its staff: pro-rector Yuri Chirikov, recruited back in 1975 under the codename 'Svetov.'

The 2nd Section of the 1st Department of the 5th Directorate had other staffers besides the 'literary group.' One of them, Major Nikolai Zhavoronkov, was particularly interesting. He was the handler for the Soviet Artists' and Architects' Union. In the early 1970s, he had been transferred from the 5th department of the Moscow and Moscow Region KGB directorate to its 5th Directorate. At that point, he was a senior operative. Over these years of service at the 5th Department of the Moscow and Moscow Region KGB Directorate, Zhavoronkov had become an expert on the art 'underground' and avant-garde artists.

This meant in practice that he already had a fair number of agents among them. With their help, the appropriate State Security departments were able, for example, to be prepared for the unsanctioned exhibition of avant-garde artists on September 15, 1974 in Moscow, which went down in history as 'the bulldozer exhibition.' This moniker came about because the unsanctioned (as they were then called) artists, who had no opportunity to exhibit their work in official salons, organized an open-air exhibition in the new Belyayevo district in southwestern Moscow. Citing emergency construction work, Moscow authorities sent bulldozers to overrun the exposition, methodically destroying the artists' works in the process. The exhibition's artists and visitors were also attacked with street-washing cars. Though brutally crushed, the exhibition still made waves. Thanks to foreign journalists who were present, its suppression was widely covered in the media abroad. Party authorities and the KGB had to compromise and allow an exhibition to be held a couple of weeks later, on September 29, in the attractive Izmailovo Park.

When Major Zhavoronkov was assigned to the 5th Directorate, a whole network of agents from the ranks of artists, prominent art scholars and art collectors was handed over to him. Among these agents was the famous painter Ilya Glazunov, who had done Party portraits of Brezhnev and the like but also of Western movie stars such as Gina Lollobrigida and Anita Ekberg. Glazunov worked directly with Bobkov, the Chief of the 5th Directorate. Their collaboration had begun when Bobkov was still a staffer at Pitovranov's ill-fated 4th Directorate of the KGB and the Second Chief Directorate of the KGB. Because of work overload as chief of the 5th Directorate, Bobkov tasked Zhavoronkov with maintaining regular contact with Glazunov. And, now that Zhavoronkov was given access to Bobkov's own network of agents—known throughout the 5th Directorate—he was soon transferred to a new post, Deputy Chief of the 5th Directorate because of the excellent work he was doing.

Increasingly prominent in Bobkov-Zhavoronkov's network of agents were Russian nationalists. Like all movements, they were closely monitored by the 5th Directorate, which was well informed of their activities. In particular, they were well aware of Glazunov's monarchist tendencies and of the fact that he hosted a literary salon that nurtured Russian nationalists. At the same time—because Glazunov was a highly experienced undercover agent—he was in essence, an agent provocateur, something that eventually became obvious even to some of his supporters—such as the poet and writer Vladimir Soloukhin and writer Lev Borodin, who was arrested in February 1967. But Glazunov's monarchism appealed to Pitovranov and Bobkov, and nationalists like him were increasingly valuable in the eyes of the KGB.

Glazunov was born in Leningrad in 1930, after the revolution. During the city's wartime siege by the Germans, he lost his parents, who died of starvation. He was evacuated, which saved his life. Upon returning to Leningrad, he studied at the Repin Art and Architecture Institute from 1951 to 1957. The first exhibition of his works was held in 1957 in Moscow at the Central House of Art Workers and was a big success.

In 1965-1966, the official Komsomol magazine *Molodaya Gvardiya* (young guard) serialized Glazunov's book *The Road to You*, in which he set out to comprehend Russia's history and culture through the lens of its Russian Orthodox spirituality. Also in the 1960s, he created the patriotic 'Motherland' club, ostensibly for the protection of monuments of history and culture. The club's other founder was the architect and restorer Pyotr Baranovsky, a passionate champion of Russia's old churches and monasteries in danger of destruction. He had been imprisoned for his advocacy in 1933. 'One of the club's most important tasks,' Glazunov wrote many years later, 'was to propagandize our country's cultural and historical heritage and draw as many people as possible to defend it against a final Bolshevist onslaught.... These people became the principal strike force of our patriotic movement, a new thing in those years.'

In 1968, the Soviet government, frightened by the events in Czechoslovakia, banned the activities of Glazunov's Motherland club, which were becoming overtly Russian nationalist. Other more powerful nationalist organizations—above all, the Soviet Society for the Protection of Monuments of History and Culture (VOOPIik), founded in 1965 as a republic-wide civil association—were ready to take up the baton. They were even more radical. They were, however, under direct control of Pitovranov.

The initiative to found VOOPIik was taken by Vyacheslav Kochemasov, the former Secretary of the Komsomol CC and the Deputy Chair of the Russian Soviet Council of Ministers. Pitovranov had gotten to know him during his work in East Germany where Kochamasov had served as an advisor at the Soviet embassy from 1955 to 1960.[210] In 1961-1962, Kochemasov was Deputy Chair of State Committee on cultural relations with foreign countries of the USSR Council of Ministers. This body was a front used by Soviet Intelligence to seek out potential agents among émigrés and their descendants. Having founded VOOPIik, Kochemasov became its First Chair. Inflated by Pitovranov, it was an immense success. By 1980, according to official data, VOOPIik had 1,936 district and city chapters and 92,400 grass-roots organizations across the Russian Soviet. At its peak in the 1970s and 1980s, VOOPIik society was one of the largest associations in the Soviet Union, with a membership of over 10 million.

Within the VOOPIik, a 'Russian Club'—a semi-unlawful association of nationalist-minded Russian intelligentsia—functioned from 1968-1969 for the comprehensive study of Russian history and culture. The club was headed by the writers Konstantin Semanov and Dmitry Zhukov. The former was an agent of the 5th Directorate; the latter, a career officer at the GRU, or military intelligence, which collaborated with the 5th Directorate on driving VOOPIik forward.

Thus, VOOPIik, under the leadership of Pitovranov's old friend Kochemasov—whose closest aides included Soviet military intelligence officer D.A. Zhukov—was intentionally cultivating Russian nationalism. No wonder Zhukov was also entrusted with a new KGB project: an anti-Semitic documentary called *Secret and Clear* (1973). Documentary filmmaker Boris Karpov, the founder of the *Othechstvo* (Fatherland) film studio and of the movement that later came to be known as 'Russian Orthodox cinema' was assigned to direct it. He was also an agent of the 4th Department of the 5th Directorate.

Glazunov, too, was actively involved in the creation of VOOPIik. 'I am a monarchist not only because the idea of monarchy is a holy and eternal tradition in human history but also because everything I love in Russian history has to do with monarchy. Russia is a country that had no colonies... Tsarist Russia was the freest, the wealthiest, the most spiritual country in the world. Its contribution to humanity's culture is known to everyone,' Glazunov wrote in a cherry-picking sketch of Russia.

Mysteriously, even before Andropov became KGB chief, the eccentric Glazunov was allowed to travel freely to Italy in 1963 at the invitation of the actress Gina Lollobrigida and the film director Federico Fellini in order to paint their portraits. Others who posed for Glazunov in Italy included the country's president, Alessandro Petrini, and Pope Paul VI. This was highly unusual. In 1961, ballet dancer Rudolf Nureyev had defected to the West in a sensitive blow to the USSR's international prestige.

One can only imagine on what level, and by whom precisely, the visit to Italy by 'simple Russian artist Glazunov' was prepared, authorized, and coordinated at the time. In 1963, every Soviet citizen seeking approval for foreign travel had to undergo special vetting by the Intelligence Services. Requests and all personal data were forwarded after submission to the Departments of Visas and Registrations of the MVD subdivisions or to the appropriate offices that referred specialists for work assignments abroad. Anyone seeking permission for travel to a capitalist country, or to socialist countries subject to the same strict rules for approval (Yugoslavia, North Vietnam, the People's Republic of China), was required to supply the names of the parents of the person who would be receiving travel papers—and of all the parents' siblings.

In the case of Glazunov, information in the KGB's possession indicated that Glazunov's uncle (his father's brother) had collaborated with German occupiers and had been sentenced to 10 years of labor camps for collaboration. The uncle's wife and children lived in the United States and Canada. Yet none of these obvious blemishes in Glazunov's biography did, for some reason, become an obstacle to his travel outside the Soviet Union.

It was the same when Andropov became head of the KGB. In 1968, Glazunov traveled to France at the invitation of Count Sergei Tolstoy (the head of the French Doctors' Association), of the actors Yves Montagne and Simone Signoret, and of the ballerina Yvette Chauviré. General Charles de Gaulle also agreed to pose for a portrait. Again, one can imagine at what kind of national level Glazunov's trip to France had to be coordinated and approved when it was going to include a meeting with

President De Gaulle.

During his stay in France in 1968, Glazunov got acquainted with Nikolai Rutchenko, who was active in the only or at least the leading anti-Soviet organization of that time: The National Alliance of Russian Solidarists (NTS). According to Glazunov, a member of the Soviet Foreign Intelligence *rezidentura* working in Paris under the cover of the Soviet embassy warned him off in no uncertain terms that such contacts were unacceptable. Curiously, Glazunov treated the caution with insouciance. Glazunov even met the son of Pyotr Stolypin, the onetime Tsarist Prime Minister and Minister of Internal Affairs, Arkady Stolypin. He, too, was an active NTS member and for many years, the Chair of the NTS honor court. In 1969, Arkady Stolypin became a member of the editorial board of the Germany-based NTS journal, *Posev* (sowing). Clearly, Glazunov had long been recruited by Soviet intelligence, as all those meetings that would have resulted in a heavy 'case file' for anyone else, caused him no trouble at all. In all likelihood, they were part of a carefully choreographed Intelligence plan.

Here's what Glazunov himself says about his trip in his memoirs: 'I had a lifelong friendship with Tomas Kolesnichenko, a smart, charismatic, talented man with a deep sense of humor. He allowed me to use his apartment…. His university friends Yevgeny Primakov and Stepan Sitaryan would stop by…. His father was then deputy minister.'[211] Let us decode this passage. Tomas Kolesnichenko was an important Soviet foreign intelligence career officer (in the prestigious First Chief Directorate of the KGB), who worked in Italy as the official *Pravda* correspondent. He established a good relationship with the leadership of the Italian Communist Party and with the country's business elites. The president of the Italian Fiat Group, Gianni Agnelli, was friendly with Italian Communist Party leader Palmiro Togliatti and helped his party financially. All this greased the wheels and the Soviet Union got a contract on advantageous terms for the construction of an auto plant to produce Zhiguli (Lada) automobiles.

Yevgeny Primakov, whom Glazunov met at Kolesnichenko's place, too, was a high-level KGB agent and a future director of the Lubyanka (then called 'SVR'). Together with Vladimir Putin, he would also be one of the three potential successors Boris Yeltsin could choose from in 1999. Stepan Sitaryan was the son of Stepan Sitaryan, a prominent economist, an academician, and at one point the Deputy Chair of the USSR Council of Ministers. At the time, foreign intelligence—the PGU of the KGB—was one of the most attractive areas of employment—where the children of the Soviet elites could channel their energies. It is entirely possible that Stepan Sitaryan, the young man mentioned in Glazunov's account, was working there as well. Hence the friendship with other people involved in intelligence work—for instance, with Primakov.

Glazunov's lucky career never ceased to flourish during the Soviet Union. From 1978, Glazunov taught at the V.S. Surikov Moscow State Academic Institute. In 1981, he became the head of the Soviet Museum of Decorative, Applied and Folk Art in

Moscow, which he created. In 1987, he became rector of the All-Russian Academy of Painting, Sculpture and Architecture. Where did it all start? Glazunov gave the answer himself in 2010. For many years, Moscow had two eminent salons of Slavophiles and Glazunov's was not the first one. Sergei Mikhalkov, the Chekist poet, transformed the painter's impoverished circumstances in 1957 and Mikhalkov's stepson, the Soviet and Hollywood filmmaker Andrei Konchalovsky, introduced them to each other.

> The cubby [the first home Glazunov and his wife acquired in Moscow in 1957] was two meters long and the same in width. All that could fit was a cot and a table. And that's how we huddled until Sergei Mikhalkov, to whom I owe literally everything, appeared in my life. We were introduced by [his stepson Andrei] Konchalovsky. He liked my paintings; what's more, Andron said that it was my work that inspired his script for Andrei Rublev.[212]

Zhavoronkov was Bobkov's assistant but he himself had not been made part of Bobkov's undercover operations. As a result, he merely treated Glazunov as a KGB asset whose extensive connections could provide access to high-level foreigners. Bobkov, on the other hand, used Glazunov as an agent provocateur embedded in the Slavophile movement.

The Russian nationalist Yuri Lunkov, a staffer in the Propaganda Department of the Moscow City Committee of the Komsomol (1962-1965) and then at the Soviet Committee of Youth Organizations (KMO) in 1965-1970 who had a close friendship with Glazunov at the time, recalled how his friend got away with outrageous jokes— even one about hanging all Communists from lampposts:

> He had a headquarters where many people would come. He didn't have regular, formal meetings; but he did have visitors around almost every evening. Once we were sitting around the table at his space, we were all Party members, [including Yuri] Torsuyev, Secretary of the Komsomol CC. And then Glazunov says, 'I dream of the days when we hang all Communists from lampposts.' Not many people said such things in the 1960s. And everyone went, 'Hahaha!'

Well-funded by the KGB, Glazunov entertained lavishly to be able to draw everyone into his web. The artistic and literary salon Glazunov hosted at his home was visited by members of the Soviet literary and artistic elites. But also by high-level foreigners—among them the Spanish ambassador to the USSR Juan Antonio Samaranch, who was recruited by an officer of the 3rd Department of the Second Chief Directorate. That department covered the Spanish embassy in Moscow. Not much later, the KGB-recruited Juan Antonio Samaranch became the head of the International Olympic Committee (MOC) with the help of the Soviet leadership.[213] In 1978, Glazunov painted a portrait of Samaranch against the backdrop of Russian icons, and a portrait of his wife against the backdrop of a Moscow monastery. It is likely that Glazunov, the provocateur, was the one who got Samaranch addicted to the Russian antiques which the latter smuggled out of the USSR—setting the stage for his recruitment by State Security.

Karate, KGB Style

Political commentator Alexander Samovarov notes that 'the KGB essentially created a "virtual reality" in the USSR.' Everyone who got involved in 'underground politics joined a contingent that was thoroughly supervised and sometimes even guided…. In the USSR, one could be a monarchist, a nationalist, a supporter of the West, etc. But this 'dark,' behind-the-scenes world was carefully supervised and directed by the KGB, which is why in most cases repressions were unnecessary.'[214] It is a good way of describing how the Andropov's 5th Directorate operated under Pitovranov-Bobkov. Every deviation from mainstream Communism was monitored, assessed and manipulated by connecting KGB agents. The *Pamyat* (memory) group was an ultranationalist, virulently anti-Semitic movement. But *Pamyat* was also yet another project fully controlled by the KGB. It was instigated by the 2nd Department of the 5th Directorate, then headed by Colonel Yuri Balev. Among Glazunov's close and like-minded associates was yet another agent recruited by the Directorate: Dmitry Vasiliev, who went on to head *Pamyat*.

Glazunov's patriotic club *Rodina* (motherland) also reopened under KGB control. Valery Ganichev, Editor-in-Chief of *Komsomolskaya Pravda* (Komsomol truth) later a history PhD and Chair of the Writers' Union of Russia (four years after Sergei Mikhalkov), reminisces:

> Ilya Glazunov helped created that famous Motherland club…. Of course, the club was closely watched by the KGB. Nonetheless, it was where a lot of the younger guys got their training; many believe this club became the foundation of the future *Pamyat*… a real ideological center.[215]

A good example of the exceptionally efficient bureaucratic machine that Pitovranov and Bobkov created was karate, a new Eastern martial arts sport (in the Soviet Union) that became extremely popular. In 1978, an Alexei Shturmin became the head of the All-Union Karate Commission; in 1979, he was chosen Vice President of the USSR Karate Federation. Immediately, the sport attracted close scrutiny from the desk in the 5th Directorate which oversaw the channels of international sports exchanges (the 3rd Section of the 11th Department). A large number of agents' case reports were compiled on Shturmin, alleging not only various financial improprieties at the karate schools run by him and his colleagues, but also the cultivation of teacher worship by students which piqued interest.

To keep tabs on what was going on—and watch Shturmin himself—the KGB recruited one of the USSR's leading karate trainers at Shturmin's school, Tadeusz

Kasyanov. His recruitment was carried out by Colonel Boris Tarasov, the section head, and a senior subordinate Lieutenant Colonel Nikolai Semin. Much as in a pyramid scheme, Kasyanov then 'developed' and recruited Shturmin himself (falling under a different department, the 6th of the VGU as it happened). The recruitment of Kasyanov and Shturmin meant that the KGB was now in control of the USSR karate schools.

Even so, in 1981, after presenting cherry-picked operative materials to the KGB top and to the CC, the 5th Directorate was able to get karate instruction banned in the Soviet Union and to make it punishable as a criminal offense. What probably proved fateful was the fact that Shturmin received an honorary post as cultural attaché at the Dutch embassy in Moscow—the very consulate that served as a liaison to Israel, with which the Soviet Union had no diplomatic relations at the time.

In 1982, the karate file—now closed—was reassigned to the newly created 13th department of the 5th Directorate. This department controlled informal associations, including nationalist/Slavophile ones. It was headed by Lieutenant Colonel Alexander Moroz. It was Moroz's department that was assigned to deal further with Shturmin. His handlers were Major Oleg Nikulich, a senior operative in the 1st Section of the new department, and his colleague, senior operative Major Nikolai Tsaregorodtzev.

It was not good news for Shturmin. Despite being a KGB agent, it did not save him from arrest. His handlers arrested Shturmin under the supervision of Lieutenant Colonel Ernest Belopotapov, Deputy Chief of the 13th Department. Shturmin was accused of trafficking in pornography, since the search of his home yielded a video-tape with intimate content that showed Shturmin himself with one of his female friends. He was sentenced to seven and a half years of imprisonment, of which he served six years. Shturmin's closest karate partner Kasyanov spent a year and a half in detention while he was being investigated. He was not helped by his membership in State Security's agent network, either.

Be that as it may, the 5 Directorate officers went through the files of those active in the karate movement to look for talent they could place elsewhere. Thus, in the early phase of Shturmin's development, the Chekists took notice of the then-obscure karate trainer, Alexander Barkashov, who was soon recruited as an agent. His recruiter was the same Major Nikulich.

Barkashov was the only one among the heads of Shturmin's karate schools who managed to avoid being prosecuted for instruction in this sport. What was so special about him? Alexander Barkashov was born on October 6, 1953 in the Moscow Region. Nothing is known about his education. From 1972 to 1974, he served in the Soviet Army as a conscript. Upon returning from the Army, he worked as an electrical fitter at a power plant. But during that time, Barkashov began to study karate at the Central Karate School, launched in 1969 in affiliation with the 'Labor' weightlifting center, and run by Alexei Shturmin.

In 1985, Barkashov's handlers at the 13th Department ordered him to infiltrate the *Pamyat*, whose *de facto* head from that year was Dmitry Vasiliev. At first, Barkashov became Vasiliev's bodyguard, then his deputy. Dmitry Vasiliev was born on May 30, 1945 in the city of Kirov. In 1963, he graduated from theater school. From 1963 to 1965, he served in the Soviet armed forces as a conscript and was stationed in Hungary. For a period of time after returning from the Army, he worked at the Moscow Theater MKhAT, leaving after a conflict with its head, Oleg Yefremov.

By then the artistic and charismatic Vasiliev had already caught the eye of the Chekists from Pitovranov's 'Firm', who recruited him as an agent.[216] With Bobkov's approval, Vasiliev was embedded in the personal circle Ilya Glazunov, becoming his private secretary and confidant. Among other things, agent Vasiliev was instructed to make a record of everything that happened in the salon of his boss, agent Ilya Glazunov.

In 1990, Barkashov got his own chance when he was allowed to found his own movement, the neo-Nazi *Russkoye Natsionalnoye Yedinstvo* (Russian national unity, RNE) advocating the expulsion (or killing, depending on who one believes) of non-Slavs and restoration of the Russian Orthodox Church. In 2000, Putin's first year as Russian President, the FSB, cancelled Barkashov's movement and he was a leader without followers. Few would have predicted that, while the names of the top-level KGB officers who directed this entire Soviet process (starting with Pitovranov and Bobkov) would remain unknown, the names of their numerous agents would appear on the front pages of newspapers, on the Internet and on television news programs as leading political figures in the new Russia. For one, since 2014, Barkashov's brand of militantism is once again useful to the Lubyanka in the Ukraine, the Russian-speaking Donbas in particular.

13: Pitovranov's Special Operation in Afghanistan

There were no ordinary people in Pitovranov's covert close circle. KGB Colonel Alexander Kiselev was one of them. He was a man of brave deeds and harsh judgements, and he was not afraid to express them out loud. Kiselev was born in 1932 and graduated from the Odessa Maritime School and the Odessa Institute of Naval Engineers. In 1956, he was recruited by military counterintelligence and served in the Soviet Navy. In 1959, he was transferred to the Directorate of Undercover Espionage. From 1959 to 1962, he worked in the Middle East, and from 1963 to 1968 in Great Britain. From 1973 to 1985, Kiselev was head of Special Operations (the 8th Department) of the PGU's Directorate S. He traveled to more than 40 countries on intelligence missions.

But in reality Kiselev worked only for Pitovranov with a direct chain of command to KGB Chair Andropov. Kiselev's specialty was secret financing of pro-Soviet rebel bodies and movements abroad. This fit neatly in Pitovranov's 'Firm' (Department P) at the Lubyanka which administered the Soviet Union's foreign trade bodies and had its own autonomous budget to allocate without wider KGB supervision. From his vantage point Kiselev was to undertake the risky job of chief saboteur to undermine the Party's control over the Soviet state, if not the Soviet Union itself.

What drove him to do so? He answers the question himself by identifying the corruption of Politburo members and their relatives, in particular Brezhnev's 'Holy Family':

> The end of the seventies and beginning of the eighties was a difficult time for the country. The absence of will or action and the old 'games' of the Soviet senior leadership made the insolvency of the current political structure and economic model all too evident. The Service also faced several additional, highly complex, and entirely new tasks. These included exposing the abuses of many leading officials in the state and party apparatus, including the general secretary's 'Holy Family.'

The 'Service' referred to Pitovranov's espionage unit (the 'Firm') at the Lubyanka. Note that the words 'the insolvency of the current political structure and economic model' were not quoted from a dissident. They expressed instead the opinion of one of the national heads of Soviet intelligence, which, like the entire KGB, was 'an armed detachment of the party'. In fact, therefore, they were far worse than if they had been thought up by a dissident. 'Exposing the abuses of many leading officials', meant nothing more than collecting *kompromat* for Andropov on leaders of the Soviet state and party, actions that were entirely illegal and contradicted standing orders of the CC and KGB departmental regulations regarding all activities within the Lubyanka.

Kiselev writes with pride who authorized these acts of subverting the Party—General Pitovranov and his disciple General Boris Ivanov—and the absolute secrecy with which he had to operate to execute his tasks on behalf of Andropov:

> Since these abuses were mostly economic in nature, combating them became the prerogative of the 'Firm,' or, more accurately, a significant portion of its daily cares. Several projects the office handled, both from the Center and overseas, ended with sensational legal proceedings. However, nowhere—neither in court hearings nor in the press—was a single name of any of our personnel mentioned. And it should remain that way—they were not vainglorious. But I will name their supervisors with pride. They were B.S. Ivanov and E.P. Pitovranov. I name them with pride because we must remember the real climate of those years, when the slightest hint of such activities ended the same way—with immediate dismissal, an 'abbreviated' pension, and the stripping of all honors.
>
> To maintain absolute secrecy, I managed all operational dossiers myself, only engaging case officers to execute particular, individual elements of ongoing projects. But what we managed to hide from the most senior state leaders did not always remain a secret to the Second Chief Directorate, counterintelligence. But this is understandable, as we were sometimes forced to 'plow the same field', where they always held implicit advantages.

It is crystal clear from this admission who was engaged in exposing the sensational corruption of party *nomenklatura* during the years Andropov was KGB director, and who so irreversibly shook the foundations of the Soviet system with his case files. In fact, it is difficult to believe that all of this was written by a general of the Soviet (thereafter Russian) Intelligence Services since he candidly confessed to high treason. How else can we interpret the conspiratorial activities of collaborators Pitovranov, Ivanov, and Kiselev, led by KGB Chair Andropov, directed against the party leadership and the country in violation of the formal orders of the KGB and the Party?

In 1982, the year Andropov became Soviet leader, Pitovranov's 'Firm' within the 1st Directorate (the PGU) was no longer needed to counteract economic crimes—including those committed by Soviet and party *nomenklatura*. Or, to be more precise, the work continued but now within a newly formed KGB Directorate of its own—the 6th. It was tasked with 'the defense of the Soviet economy from the subversive activities of the intelligence services of foreign states and organizations'. Any major case fell under the jurisdiction of the 6th Directorate. Like Andropov himself, Pitovranov's 'Firm' had been promoted.

But that still lay ahead when the USSR decided to invade Afghanistan in 1979.

General Ivanov played a major role in this decision. He worked in Kabul posing as the head of the USSR's trade office, controlled by the 'Firm'. Like Kiselev, he was a formidable man and Deputy Chief of the PGU at the time, apart from being part of Pitovranov's proximate orbit. Ivanov had started working for the Intelligence Services before World War II. In 1962, he replaced Vladimir Barkovsky at the KGB's New York *rezidentura* as undercover spy. In March 1964, along with future defector General Oleg Kalugin—who worked in the US posing as a Soviet foreign correspondent—Ivanov planned the murder in Washington of Soviet intelligence officer and deserter Yuri Nosenko. Kalugin, in his book *Farewell, Lubyanka* (*Spymaster* in English, 1994), recalled how Ivanov instructed him to shoot Nosenko himself:

> In March [1964], not long before I was to travel back home, Boris Ivanov invited me to come see him. 'This conversation is highly confidential,' he began. 'Soon there will be a meeting at the State Department between our embassy personnel and Nosenko. It has been proposed that you should attend this meeting.' I shrugged: 'If you need me, what's the problem?' I did not expect the next question: 'Do you remember how to shoot? At the meeting with the traitor can you kill him?'—'Of course, I can,' I answered, not yet fully realizing this was a bit of a gamble. After all, it would mean prison, and a long sentence. I had no diplomatic passport and no protection. As if reading my thoughts, Ivanov offered: 'We'll get you out after. We'll do an exchange for someone, don't worry.'—'I'm not worried,' I said firmly. 'I'm ready.'

Kalugin thought highly of Ivanov. He favorably compared Ivanov's operational skills to General Kryuchkov, who was Andropov's second-in-command for all standard KGB operations (except for the few areas Andropov controlled personally through Pitovranov).

> He [Kryuchkov] was intimidated by the professional erudition... of B. Ivanov, senior deputy and chief of the First Chief Directorate and foreign counterintelligence.... He bore the brunt of operational affairs, and his operational experience was, perhaps, unrivaled.... Kryuchkov must have secretly envied him.... Ivanov, despite his protests, was relieved from supervising foreign counterintelligence on the pretext of 'the need to focus attention on organizing the battle against the primary enemy', and, after some time, was sent to Afghanistan as Andropov's special representative to the Taraki-Amin government.'

Given the role the Afghanistan invasion played in the downfall that doomed the USSR, it is not difficult to divine its origin in the activities of the Andropov-Pitovranov-Ivanov axis.

The instability problem in the USSR's neighbor Afghanistan existed for some time. On April 17, 1978, Mir Akbar Khyber, a prominent figure in the People's Democratic

Party of Afghanistan (PDPA), was shot in Kabul. Two days later, on April 19th, a large protest of more than 20 thousand demonstrators took place in Afghanistan's capital against the country's leader, Mohammed Daoud who had overthrown the Afghan monarchy in 1973. On Daoud's orders, several prominent figures in the PDPA—Nur Muhammed Taraki, Babrak Karmal, and Hafizullah Amin—were arrested. The latter, however, managed to persuade the military to come over to his side, and a *coup d'état* followed that would go down in history as the 'April Revolution' of 1978. Daoud's regime fell (he himself was assassinated, it was discovered years later). It was at this point that Ivanov was sent to Kabul to be Andropov's personal source of information:

Further Afghan upheaval followed. Havana, Cuba, hosted from September 1-9, 1978, the 6th Conference of Heads of State or Government of Non-Aligned Countries. Opposition leader Taraki, now in power, attended the conference on behalf of his country as the new head of Afghanistan. On September 9th, he stopped in Moscow on his way home for a friendly meeting with Soviet leader Brezhnev. Brezhnev was satisfied with how it went. However, upon arriving in Kabul that very same day, September 9, Taraki was suffocated with a pillow by army officers loyal to Amin. Amin had given these orders and he seized power in Afghanistan. The problem was that it came as a surprise to Soviet intelligence and the Politburo. Whatever trust Amin had had, there was now suspicion as to what he might up to next.

In truth, the Soviet Union had less to fear than the 'imperial' USA. Amin was a thoroughly pro-Soviet political figure. Fikryat Tabeev, the USSR's ambassador to Afghanistan from 1979 to 1986, also said that 'Amin is as much an agent of the CIA as Beria is a British spy.' And in the words of Colonel Alexander Morozov, the former deputy spy at Kabul *rezidentura* in the period preceding the deployment of Soviet troops in Afghanistan, 'Amin found quotes for his speeches in 'History of the Communist Party of the Soviet Union,' published during Stalin's time, which he always had on hand. A large portrait of Stalin was hung in Amin's office in his palace. Seeing this portrait, Boris Ivanov disarmed Amin's vigilance by telling him, "Comrade Amin, I'm a Stalinist too!"[217] He was not feigning it. Ivanov really was a Stalinist, as was Amin. Numerous sources and the testimonies of his associates, supporters, and contemporaries talked about this. Abdul Karim Misaki, minister of finance in the government of Afghanistan from 1989 to 1990 recalled that Amin 'was a communist,' and that 'he really loved Stalin and tried to emulate him.'

To his misfortune, however, Amin had twice studied in the US. In 1957, he matriculated at Columbia University, New York, and graduated with a master's degree in education. In 1962, Amin returned to Columbia University to finish his dissertation though he never completed it before his return to Afghanistan in 1965. Amin's studies at Columbia University became the reason to accuse him of having been turned at Columbia and working undercover for the CIA,[218] the latter Ivanov reported from Kabul as a fact to not only Andropov, but directly to Brezhnev as well.

General Lev Gorelov, a military expert and former Chief Military Advisor to the armed forces of Afghanistan wrote in 2009: 'Moscow was suspicious of Amin, and relations became cool. The situation was exacerbated by a telegram to Brezhnev sent by Lieutenant General Ivanov, the KGB's chief representative in Kabul, containing information that Amin, who studied in the US before the Saur [April] Revolution, was allegedly an American agent.'[219]

While Taraki was still alive and Amin was gathering strength to take over, the KGB had previously launched its first attempt on Amin's life in Taraki's residence as the country's leader. Ivanov was involved in the operation as the person who advised Amin to visit his political mentor, who had become Amin's enemy by that time, knowing that Amin would be killed at the meeting. But the attempt failed. Amin survived and moved behind the walls of the Tajbik palace, Kabul, for safety.

Then Ivanov organized another assassination—a 'reconciliation dinner' for Amin and his enemies, at which Amin and his guests were poisoned. This latest assassination attempt was carried out by agent Mikhail Talybov,[220] a Soviet undercover agent who worked in Kabul posing as Amin's chef. But, since Ivanov had coordinated his activities in Afghanistan poorly with other Soviet bodies, the Soviet doctor assigned to Amin by the Soviet Ministry of Health was not aware of the KGB desire to end Amin's life prematurely and saved his life and that of his guests.

Having failed twice failed to assassinate Amin—who had now become Afghanistan's leader—Ivanov argued that more drastic measures were required to rid Afghanistan of its 'CIA spy': a military invasion. The KGB was adamant about Amin's removal—since he had personal access to Amin, General Ivanov even offered to murder Amin by pulling the trigger himself.

Experts in the Soviet military of Ivanov's level disagreed whole-heartedly. Their assessment of the situation in Afghanistan and the Afghan army were on the opposite pole of the spectrum. Even the arrival of Boris Ponomarev, Secretary of the CC for International Affairs in Kabul could not smooth them out. General Vasiliy Zaplatin, an advisor to the head of the Main Political Directorate of the Afghan army, who was sent to Afghanistan in May 1978 was another witness of the tension. One meeting he attended became so heated that the Soviet officers in attendance—representatives of the army and the KGB—'were at each other's throats.' The army was non-committal in its assessments, whereas the KGB was in favor of solving the Afghan problem quickly and radically. In many ways, the events of 1979 foreshadowed what was to be repeated under Lubyanka-President Putin in Ukraine in 2013/14 (successfully with the quick capture of Crimea and the occupation Donbas and Luhansk regions) and 2022 (resembling the doomed invasion of Afghanistan).

In September of 1979, General Gorelov arrived in Moscow for a meeting of the Politburo to discuss the issue of invading Afghanistan. Head of the Army's General Staff Nikolai Ogarkov categorically asserted that 'the deployment of Soviet troops is impossible.' Army General Ivan Pavlovsky, who at the time was inspecting the work of advisors in Afghanistan, and Gorelov were also categorically opposed to the troop deployment.

Minister of Foreign Affairs Andrei Gromyko, Minister of Defense Dmitri Ustinov (1976-1984), and Ponomarev were also present at the meeting with Brezhnev. Brezhnev asked Gorelov to report on the situation in Afghanistan. Gorelov set out the relative weakness of the Afghan Army and the difficulty of mountain warfare. However, he also pointed out the truism that if the USSR attacked, the US would promptly start arming insurgents with superior weapons.

– 'Leonid Ilyich [Brezhnev], I have information, but not as deep as the ambassador. I know the situation in the army in detail.'
– 'Answer me, please, do we need to deploy troops or not?'
– 'No, Leonid Ilyich.'
– 'Why?'
– 'First, the Afghan army today has 10 infantry divisions, three army corps, 350 aircrafts, 1500 artillery batteries, and 900 tanks. It is capable of controlling the status quo in the country and on the border. Numerous successful operations to eliminate Pakistani factions confirm that. Second, if we deploy our troops, the Americans will strengthen their aid to anti-Afghan groups. They will give them technology and arms, send over advisors, and invade Afghanistan. Third, our army is not prepared for a fight in the mountains. It does not know how to do that.'

Minister of Defense Ustinov interrupted Gorelov to disagree with his own expert, but they let the general continue before giving the floor to Ivanov to speak. Ivanov's words carried the Politburo with him:

– 'Don't speak for the army.'
– 'I'm only saying what I know for sure. Fourth, the Soviet Union will suffer huge material and human losses. Our boys will fight in the first echelon, and the Afghans in the second....'
They heard me out and asked me to wait in a separate room. The KGB representative in Kabul, Lieutenant General Boris Ivanov, briefed after me.

When Ogarkov, Pavlovsky, and Gorelov were traveling back, Ogarkov said: 'We lost.' 'I guessed that Brezhnev had chosen the side of the KGB's B.S. Ivanov, who was fervently in favor of deploying troops,' Gorelov remembered.

What might have swayed the Politburo is made clear by General Zaplatin. Ivanov fed the Politburo the idea that Amin was going to allow the US to 'place medium range Pershing rockets on Afghan territory'. Amin had all of a sudden turned Afghanistan into a nuclear threat on the Politburo's doorstep by potentially creating the USSR's own Cuba crisis, or so Ivanov claimed:

From the numerous examples provided above, a relatively convincing picture emerges of what the USSR's reasons were for the fateful decision to deploy Soviet troops to Afghanistan. They were based on deliberately false information about Amin being a US agent, the complete disintegration of the Afghan army, and the intention of US leadership to place medium-range Pershing rockets in Afghan territory. The primary source of this information was the KGB's representative in Afghanistan, Lieutenant General Boris Ivanov.

Of course, the US had no intention of locating nuclear arms in an unstable country with an unreliable leadership like Afghanistan. Only the Kremlin's 'geriatrics' might have believed that—having been fed disinformation by sophisticated provocateurs Pitovranov and Ivanov, sanctioned and piloted through by their boss Andropov as Politburo member.

The first group of KGB special forces, which received the title 'Zenith-1,' under the command of Colonel Grigory Boyarinov, arrived in Afghanistan on July 5th, 1979, several months before the Politburo's deployment of Soviet troops in the country. The Zenith-1 officers carried out reconnaissance of strategically important objects in Kabul, including the Tajbik palace where Amin was hiding out. Their activities were kept secret from the Afghan authorities. The group included 38 officers. They all carried foreign passports with false last names and posed as civilian specialists in various business sectors. The next group—'Zenith-2'—consisted of 18 officers. By December 1979, the number of amalgamated specialist troops had grown to 130.

In the end, the 'mishap' of Soviet doctors who saved Amin from a painful death was corrected by a unit of Soviet special operation forces that stormed the palace and mercilessly slaughtered everyone, including women and children. As participants in the storm later recalled, the Afghan rugs that covered the Tajbig palace floors in abundance oozed, saturated with human blood. Shah Wali, the foreign minister under Amin, recalled that there were many collateral Afghan casualties in the assault. Amin might even have surrendered to the many Soviet functionaries crowded in his palace. But no one gave them the choice to surrender:

When the assault on the palace took place, besides the Afghans, you had medics, translators, and KGB advisors responsible for Amin's safety located in the palace. As far as I know, one doctor was killed. My wife perished. Amin's small sons were killed, and his daughter was wounded. Many others were killed. But all of those people, including Amin and his circle, might have surrendered without a single shot fired.

General Vasiliy Zaplatin, the Soviet army's chief advisor to the Afghan army, was convinced that Ivanov was engaged in deliberate provocation that could only exacerbate the situation.

He recalled that, 'the assault on Amin's palace and subsequent deployment of Soviet troops to Afghanistan pursued the same goal: removing the current head of state, Amin, and placing Karmal in power. The Soviet leadership was somehow convinced that only Karmal could consolidate society, end the civil war, and keep Afghanistan friendly to us. There was absolutely no trust in Amin, especially after his murder of the previous president, Taraki.'

After the invasion, the General Staff of the Soviet army checked for any information about Amin being an American agent, but no compromising information on Amin was found. General Gorelov recalled in 2009: 'We looked into the matter thoroughly, searched for evidence, and conducted an entire investigation, but did not find any confirmation. Amin, although he studied in the US, served his own people and fought for power like other Afghan leaders before and after him.'[221]

Zaplatin went even further and said 'it was all a lie' and that Amin was, in fact, infatuated with the USSR:

Even after the storming of the palace, in which Amin himself and two of his sons perished, his wife, along with his two surviving daughters and youngest son, did not want to go anywhere but the Soviet Union, stating that her husband was a friend to the Soviet Union and that was the only country she would go to. And that is what she did. After the storming of Amin's palace, much was said about him being a CIA agent, but nothing could ever be proven, and it was clear from the beginning that it was all a lie... Amin strove to send the best students in the lyceum he directed, as well as family members, not to the USA or Germany to study, but only to the Soviet Union.

Could it all possibly have been a mistake on Ivanov's part? Yuri Drozdov, Chief of Directorate S—undercover espionage at the KGB—provides an answer to this question. He led the KGB rezidentura in New York from 1975 to 1979. Ivanov, then still Deputy Head of the PGU, flew to meet with him to step up the fight against 'international Zionism.' Much earlier, in 1957 in the GDR, Drozdov reported to General Pitovranov. Then, in 1964, he was a *rezidentura* spy in Beijing, where General Pitovranov worked two years earlier as an advisor on security issues at the Chinese Ministry of Public Safety. Pitovranov, Ivanov, and Drozdov knew each other quite well.

He was deeply involved in the KGB's Kabul operations. 'Boris Ivanov coordinated all the work between our agency and representatives of other bodies,' Yuri Drozdov wrote in his memoirs, *Zapiski Nachal'nika Nelegal'noi Razvedki* (notes of the head of undercover intelligence, 1999, 2016). 'During his tenure, Intelligence bodies were created under the country's new leader—Chair of the Revolutionary Council of the Democratic Republic of Afghanistan Babrak Karmal.' 'Completely absorbed by Afghanistan, he [Ivanov] traveled to Moscow for various reasons, maintained interest in the affairs of the "Firm", and provided key counsel. Pitovranov often visited him in Kabul as well,' Kiselev confirmed in 2003.[222] After the successful operation to eliminate Amin, Ivanov returned to Afghanistan, where he began creating new Afghan Intelligence Services under Afghanistan's new leader, Karmal. He flew to Moscow from time to time, invariably met with Pitovranov, and maintained interest in the affairs of the 'Firm'.

Thus, the entire Soviet concept of the need to invade Afghanistan, which led to the collapse of the Soviet Union several years later, was based on the spurious assumption that Hafizullah Amin, Afghanistan's leader, was cooperating with 'American intelligence' and planned to switch his allegiance to the US. Nothing in these assumptions corresponded to reality. It was an intentional provocation by the KGB (Andropov) of the Party (Brezhnev). Ivanov was interested in one thing only during and after the assault—that Amin would die. None of the Zenith-troops were worried about which Afghans might die in the process. Once Amin was dead, the question whether he was or was not a CIA spy could be mooted *ad infinitum* but had lost all currency.

Four days after the murder of Amin, Andropov debriefed his key KGB agents in Kabul. Present were Kryuchkov, his right-hand man Party matters, Lieutenant-General Kirpichenko, First Deputy Head of the PGU (1979-1991), and Pitovranov's agents Drozdov, Chief of Directorate S, and his subordinate Kiselev. Kirpichenko had directed the special troops who had carried out the bloodbath. Everyone was pleased with the swift execution of Amin. Afterwards, Drozdov spoke to Andropov. No doubt both were also pleased that the KGB team had efficiently expunged the living proof of Ivanov's lie about the CIA and Amin and thereby Andropov's fingerprints on the provocation. Drozdov suggested they should not be in this situation again and create a highly trained team of non-KGB commandos—Vympel.

On December 31st, 1979, I and Vadim Kirpichenko, in the presence of Vladimir Kryuchkov, briefed Yuri Andropov about our role in the Afghan events. When the discussion was over, I mentioned how, after evaluating the experience, we should think about forming a special personnel unit in the KGB system. Yuri Andropov looked at me without saying a word. In the middle of January, we had another meeting. I came with a document describing the idea for creating 'Vympel.'[223] Throughout 1980, after many discussions and arrangements with the government and the Politburo, the KGB leadership agreed on the need to form such a unit.

At a closed joint meeting of the Council of Ministers of the USSR and the Politburo of the CC of the CPSU on August 19th, 1981, the country's senior leadership made the decision to create an entirely secret special operations unit in the Committee for State Security of the USSR to conduct operations outside the USSR within the 'special period.'[224]

And so, on August 19, 1981, months before he became Soviet leader, KGB Chief Andropov signed the order to form a special operations unit in the KGB—the KGB Independent Training Center, better known as the special operations unit 'Vympel' or, more accurately, the KGB's private army—a precursor of the Kremlin's Wagner Group today—and he kept it close under his personal control as it fell under the command of Pitovranov associates Drozdov and Kiselev. Unlike official Soviet agents, Vympelers could establish contacts with both friend and foe—much like the cultural icons recruited by Pitovranov could gather round them both Soviet friends and skeptics:

> Vympelers worked in Afghanistan for many years. They worked in groups of ten, fifteen, or twenty men, with marginal support from the armed forces. They handled the very difficult and important task of reconciling military activities between two opposing forces. This was accomplished with preparedness, knowledge of the situation, effective intelligence gathering, the ability to establish contact with the enemy, the Mujahideen, the authorities, and militia leaders, the ability to build relationships with the leaders of Soviet military divisions, and militia representatives, etc.

Vympelers did not just 'work' in Afghanistan. According to Drozdov, Vympel officers were active in different hotspots around the world—in Cuba, Vietnam, Mozambique, Angola, Nicaragua, Laos, Libya, Egypt, Syria, Jordan, and a range of other countries—much like the Wagner Group today.

In 2009, Lieutenant General Igor Giorgadze, former head of the Georgian Intelligence Services, testified to the training level of the KGB's 'special operations agents': 'They gave us training to make sure a man could complete a mission anywhere on the globe. From disabling launchers for strategic nuclear rockets to kidnapping a VIP and transporting him to the Soviet Union.'[225] They were known to be highly trained agents and saboteurs. And all of them were in fact subordinate to Pitovranov, Ivanov, and Kiselev.

Even as the long-term consequences of the invasion became clear, General Ivanov's Pitovranov work in Kabul was done. His presence in Afghanistan ended in 1982 after a nervous breakdown that led him to be returned home, although his service in the KGB continued as before. Ivanov began working undercover at the Foreign Ministry. In 1983, he joined the Soviet delegation to an international commission of the Organization for Security and Cooperation in Europe in Stockholm.

The Money Trail
Only after the Soviet invasion of Afghanistan did it become clear why Pitovranov and Ivanov—and by extension, Andropov—were interested in eliminating Amin. Apart from anything else, Pitovranov's 'Firm' had access to foreign currency streams beyond the Party's control. Pitovranov had his own high-ranking KGB recruit in Afghanistan, Saleh Daoud, a distant relative of the former Afghan king and a major business figure. 'He was very friendly toward the Soviet Union and hoped to significantly boost commercial activity through the chamber of commerce's mediation,' writes Kiselev. 'Pitovranov promised him commercial collaboration.'[226] The KGB thought that Daoud, who had broad connections in business circles, as well as with the sheiks and chiefs of the most influential tribes in Afghanistan, could be useful to the Soviet espi-

onage *rezidentura* Daoud's numerous relatives, educated people who already held posts in the country's government, would only help to that end. Where they also considering he might become the country's leader instead of Amin, Taraki or Karmal?

In Kabul, Pitovranov and Ivanov began implementing a plan to use Daoud, who had had to flee Afghanistan and move to Italy when Amin came to power. Pitovranov traveled there to meet with Daoud. Kiselev suggested,[227] 'Yevgeny Pitovranov met with him by chance' in Milan. Of course, it was not by chance. Pitovranov arrived in Milan to give instructions to his agent, who agreed to return to Afghanistan, but who also reminded Pitovranov of his promise to get him a job in the Soviet-Afghan chamber of commerce controlled by the 'Firm'. Amin had by now been deposed and replaced with Karmal. In Pitovranov's opinion, Daoud 'could be useful for our Service,' wrote Kiselev. After hearing Pitovranov, Daoud obediently flew to Kabul without delay.

Pitovranov had another meeting with Daoud, this one in Kabul, but not at the embassy or the chamber of commerce. He traveled across the troubled Afghan capital to Daoud's home, thinking their conversation might be recorded at the embassy or chamber of commerce. That would be impossible at Daoud's home, where the KGB did not have surveillance equipment. There they could speak openly to reach their central agreement, and subsequent meetings could be held in official Soviet offices.[228]

One important operational task that Soviet intelligence had to address, jointly with officers from the GRU, the Soviet military Intelligence, was the destruction of caravan routes that were used to carry supplies from Pakistan to Afghanistan's armed opposition. The caravans, which had been a thing of the past, were resurrected in the 1980s during the Soviet occupation of Afghanistan, when they were widely used by insurgents to transport arms and ammunition from the Pakistan border. Afghan gems and narcotics were smuggled in the opposite direction from Afghanistan to Pakistan to fund the supplies needed by the various military groups fighting the Soviets and Afghan government forces.

Interestingly, not all caravans were treated equally. Some disappeared without a trace. Alexei Chikishev, a GRU military intelligence officer who participated in combat operations in Afghanistan and studied the activities of special forces activities in his book *Spetsnaz v Afganistane* (special forces in Afghanistan). There were the caravans that the military could flatten, loot as they wished, or let pass by demanding bribes for 'humanitarian' reasons. But there were also the caravans by nomadic tribes that they were not allowed to touch:

> The struggle with the caravans and closing the borders was an issue that always caused headaches for the Soviet command. Special forces did not just attack caravans delivering weapons, but also transports of food, medical supplies, and various basic necessities meant for the civilian population.... In some units, commanding officers might gather tape recorders, cameras, and watches found in destroyed caravans into a pile and flatten it with an armored car. In others, the commanding

officer turned a blind eye to all looting, collecting his share from his soldiers... The leadership would take helicopters to the combat area to pick out the best loot for themselves.... Consumer attitudes among senior officers, who demanded all sorts of things, from comfortable imported field uniforms to money, became a very widespread phenomenon.... The only caravans to escape the onslaughts of special forces unharmed were those of the nomadic tribes. They were not touched, as there were strict orders and instructions regarding them.[229]

Orders detailing this distinction were coming from Kabul, where, in addition to the Soviet military command, the Soviet *rezidentura* led by Ivanov was stationed. While coordinating the activities of Soviet intelligence units in Afghanistan, Ivanov had the opportunity to organize special forces operations deep behind the lines of Afghan insurgents in such a way that some caravans reached their targets without interference, while others were intercepted and handed over to the chiefs of warring tribes or, in certain cases, destroyed. It was a lucrative time for the KGB's 'Firm'.

Pitovranov and Ivanov disguised the Firm's commercial activities with information provided by Daoud, which was supplemented by information received from the entire network of 482 Afghan agents. This allowed them to present Daoud as the most important agent of Soviet foreign intelligence in Afghanistan since Daoud's knowledge of specific financial transactions turned out to be extremely useful. Chiefs paid with Afghan emeralds or drugs for the safe passage or capture of caravans. If the volume of opium produced in Afghanistan before 1979 fluctuated between 200 and 400 metric tons per year, by the time Soviet troops withdrew in 1989, it had reached 1000-1500 metric tons.

Helpfully Daoud's caravan world operated without a paper trail. A financial system known in the Arab world as *hawala* has been used widely in the Middle East and Asia since the 8th century AD. It has different names in different countries, but the essence of the system remains the same. *Hawala* translates from Arabic as 'promissory note' or 'receipt.' In the Egyptian Arabic dialect, *hawala* refers to bartering or a direct exchange of material goods. This type of mutual settlement was based exclusively on mutual trust. Transactions were not registered with traditional financial or banking institutions. *Hawala* was nothing more than a semi-legal payment system that was not controlled by local authorities—including the Soviet Union. It was outside of currency control and taxation. The annual volume of global transactions using this system was 200 to 500 billion dollars, according to various estimates.

The most traditional methods for mutual settlements were payments in gold and precious stones and other gems. The largest global settlement centers for these transactions were London and Dubai. Precious gems and gold were smuggled in by *hawala* couriers. Colonel Kiselev had a long-time contact in London from the time he had been stationed there on behalf of the Firm—Izya Rubin—whom he could ask for information about these centers. Izya had two older brothers: Abik and Teodore. They were very well informed on these arcane settlements. 'Abik was married to the daughter of a co-owner of the Namibia Diamond Corporation and was a shareholder in a well-known Dutch diamond company. He was a prominent member of London Goldsmiths' Guild,' Kiselev writes.[230] The South African company he referred to was De Beers, named after the Dutch De Beers brothers.

Saleh Daoud directed Pitovranov and Ivanov's treasure first to London, where it was received by one of Kiselev's many London's contacts. They took a percentage and converted it and then forwarded it to an offshore haven. This was the island of Nauru where 450 offshore banks had found a safe haven on the tiny Pacific Island nation with an area of 21 square kilometers.

The circle of people involved in the KGB's undercover espionage's complex and secret financial operations was kept to a minimum. KGB Chair Andropov was partially privy to the operations, but the head of these operations was, without a doubt, Pitovranov. Besides critical operational experience, he possessed extensive experience in foreign trade operations via the chamber of commerce. Ivanov covered Intelligence for him as staff, and Kiselev, as an ordinary operative, was not privy to all the details.

With clandestine operations, it was difficult to deny the actions of the undercover KGB agents' *rezidentura*. Andropov was well aware of the sensitive problems this could create, not least towards with his fellow Politburo members. He created a special KGB protocol for General Drozdov to contact him directly if their safety was 'compromised'. The undercover espionage leadership could now report directly to the Chair of the KGB, bypassing the PGU hierarchy above them:

> Andropov stressed that undercover espionage must live and work according to its own laws and rules and be as autonomous as possible within the foreign intelligence system. He gave us the right to independently inform him and the Authorities in cases where the safety of undercover agents and their stations were compromised.

Meanwhile, as we will see in the next chapter, Afghanistan was not the only country where the KGB's 'Firm' was making money to pay for its Vympel army. It was no accident that Soviet 'special operatives' were active in the very parts of the world where 'conflict' or 'blood' diamonds were mined, which came to the global market from regions with internal armed conflicts, where drug trafficking and illegal arms trafficking flourished. Undercover Soviet intelligence was thrown in to help these 'operatives.' If something went wrong, the operations could always be disowned as not being connected to the Soviet Union.

14: Angola, the KGB's Foreign Cash Cow

One of the unintended byproducts of the Afghanistan occupation (1979-1992) was the creation of a source of foreign income and capital controlled only by the KGB's foreign sections, notably the 'Firm'. The caravan routes' informal financial transaction network presented the KGB's Afghan *rezidentura* with a choice Pitovranov's Firm had never had before in countries with a banking system based on a paper trail—most of the developed or developing world. It could either declare the funds that it handled to the Party handlers of the KGB, and see it disappear in the USSR's foreign reserves to be spent by the Party or line the pockets of the 'Holy family' or be used by other corrupt Politburo relatives. From the files they kept, they knew exactly what happened with regular foreign transactions. Small wonder that the Firm kept their financial dealings in Afghanistan from Party oversight. Over the years it was to make a big difference.

Instead of having to rely on budget allocated by Party rulers in the Kremlin, Pitovranov's Firm was increasingly amassing a budget to make autonomous operational decisions. Even Andropov, who moved across to the Kremlin as Party leader after two years, need not necessarily be involved. He died in any case halfway during the invasion. He was briefly replaced as head of the KGB by a Chekist (the head of the Ukrainian KGB), but Gorbachev as USSR leader (1985-1991) reverted to the practice of appointing a Party official to keep the Cheka under the Kremlin's control—little reason to make him party to the KGB's foreign funds.

As we will see below, as a result of the financial expertise of Pitovranov's Firm, the KGB's foreign agents began to act like a multinational corporation making money off global conflict, alongside—yet in secret independent from—the Soviet Party hierarchy. As we will see in this chapter, it meant that, as the USSR stumbled towards its collapse, piecemeal and in roundabout ways the KGB gained an independent footing over time. Independent from Party vicissitudes, it could withstand anything coming from the Kremlin including, in the end, the collapse of Communism.

'Intelligence friends' of Pitovranov

In order to conduct financial operations overseas, Pitovranov needed individuals who could act as permanent staff executing the Firm's covert and increasingly sophisticated offshore banking transactions. These recruits were not on the official Soviet Intelligence payroll but were engaged as Intelligence agents by him, nonetheless.

Pitovranov, director of the Chamber of Commerce of the USSR and former Deputy Minister of the Intelligence Services, called them 'intelligence friends.' By assisting the special forces to the best of their ability, they fit that description quite well. They were servants of Pitovranov and the group of Chekists he led and its undercover operations from the Kremlin. In simple words, they, too, were Soviet spies albeit privatized ones.

One such 'intelligence friend' was Shabtai Kalmanovich. He was born on December 18, 1947 in Kaunas (Lithuania). His father was the deputy director of a rubber products factory; his mother was the chief accountant at a meat processing plant. Kalmanovich graduated from the Kaunas Polytechnic Institute where he specialized as a chemical production automation engineer. During his studies at the institute, he was recruited to the 5th Department of the Lithuanian KGB to monitor Jewish citizens with 'nationalist leanings'. Kalmanovich's place in the KGB's network allowed him to successfully finish his university education instead of being expelled as a member of a family seeking permanent residence in Israel. For twelve long years, his family had been trying to get permission to emigrate to Israel, but finally received it as a cover for moving Kalmanovich, a KGB agent, overseas.

The mass deployment of Soviet agents to Israel on such a footing was planned and handled by the 8th Department of the 5th Directorate. It was led by Valery Lebedev yet another capable student of Bobkov, Head of the 8th Department. Equally, the KGB focused on further penetration of the primary enemy—the US, as well as countries that were its political and military allies. Oleg Kalugin, in his book *Farewell, Lubyanka*, said that many 'signed an oath of allegiance' (useful as *kompromat*) or even received 'lie-detector test training':

> Because KGB Directorate K controlled practically all operational games with enemy Intelligence services, the issue of checking agents involved in the games became particularly important when a flood of emigrants poured into the West. Hundreds and possibly thousands of 'refuseniks' going to Israel and the US signed an oath of loyalty and promised to help their former homeland going forward. In some cases, agents leaving for the West were given brief special training and were subjected to lie detector tests.

Upon arriving in Israel in 1971, Kalmanovich began working with different political parties as an activist, helping emigrants from the USSR get settled. He particularly focused on organizing events and shows for artists and singers. In an interview, Kalmanovich described how in the beginning of his life in Israel he 'was a student at Jerusalem University,' 'lived on a scholarship' and 'nearly starved'. 'Money had a different value to me then. But I earned $80.000 organizing shows… and I went to Germany with the money,' he said.

Indeed, Kalmanovich was sent to Germany by the KGB 'to buy construction equipment for Africa from a Persian who lived between Munich and Moscow', another KGB agent by the name of Serush Babek—he was to die prematurely under highly mysterious circumstances in 1992. Born in Iran, he lived in Germany, held German citizenship, but ended up in the Soviet Union and married a Russian wife.[231]

In the mid-1970s, Babek worked as a translator with Progress publishing house in Moscow specializing in foreign literature translations. Supervised by the 5th Directorate, the publishing house fell under Major Auzhbikovich, the head of the 2nd Section of the 1st Department. They recruited Babek as a KGB agent in 1976 and he carried out missions on behalf of the 5th Directorate. For instance, he followed the famous Soviet singer-songwriter Vladimir Vysotsky during his overseas tours and tried to stay informed of the plans and intentions of Vysotsky and his wife—the famous French movie star Marina Vlady, a member of the CC of the French Communist Party.

Babek was repurposed as a Pitovranov 'friend' and parachuted into a different line of business—illegal arms dealer—with Kalmanovich as his main business partner in Africa. By the end of the 1980s, he had become a major operator. His arms shipments mainly went to warring military groups in Angola, Mozambique, Namibia and South Africa. By 1989, Babek owned fourteen joint ventures. He actively conducted operations through Germany, where his company International Processing System was organized and operating. It functioned as an illegal supply channel of radio and computer equipment around the embargo to the USSR. At one point, Babek was identified by the German Intelligence as a smuggler of classified technology, and he spent several months under arrest.

Pitovranov developed the Firm's African interest through another writer: Mário Neves. He was a Portuguese writer, journalist and the Portuguese ambassador in Moscow and the director of the Association of Lisbon Fairs. From talks with him in private, Pitovranov began to realize the huge economic potential of Portugal's African colonies, which it had lost in 1974 after the Carnation Revolution. Neves, who was well acquainted with some major Portuguese businessmen active in Africa, gave the appropriate introductions to Pitovranov, who skillfully set about using these contacts in the interests of his Chekist group from his position at the Soviet Chamber of Commerce.

There were twenty Bantustans (homelands) in South-West Africa (now Namibia) at the time. They were reservations for the native Black population. Individual Bantustans received formal independence but were not recognized internationally as sovereign states. One of these unrecognized states was Bophuthatswana, the richest Bantustan in the South Africa in terms of mineral resources. And this is exactly where Kalmanovich was sent to buy 'construction equipment'. Acting at the direction of his KGB masters, with the appropriate introductions from the Portuguese businessmen working with Pitovranov, Kalmanovich was able to penetrate the inner circle of Bophuthatswana's leader, Lucas Manyane Mangope.

Civil wars raged in Angola, Mozambique, and Namibia since 1975. Pitovranov turned his gaze on precisely these countries with their rich mineral resources. South

African troops participated in these wars. The Soviet Union, at the request of Agostinho Neto who was the leader of the People's Movement for the Liberation of Angola (MPLA) provided significant military and financial assistance to this ideological-brother party. Besides the USSR, Fidel Castro's Cuba also gave military support to the MPLA. Pitovranov's interest was not to end suffering, death, and destruction. He saw it as an opportunity akin to Afghanistan to earn a lot of money. And that is exactly what Kalmanovich's handlers tasked him to do. Publicly he got rich by building crocodile farms, stadiums, and homes, but in reality by using the opportunities provided by Soviet Intelligence services to supply arms to warring groups. Though these groups had no money, they could pay with diamonds, platinum and gold.

Thus, from 1984 to 1989, the KGB's Vympel unit often conducted operations in countries where 'conflict diamonds' were extracted. The funds generated from their sale were used to support rebel movements, among other things. According to experts, the annual turnover of 'blood' diamonds amounted to 4% of the global market in diamonds At that time, the annual volume of international diamond trade was approximately $7 billion—in other words, $300 million went illegally to blood diamonds.

In Sierra Leone, Kalmanovich played an active role in the election campaign of the commander of the army, Joseph Momoh as president of the country. The first introduction between the two was made after determined string-pulling by the KGB to insert their agent in Momoh's campaign. After becoming head of state, Momoh rewarded Kalmanovich with a license to exploit Sierra Leone's diamond mines.

One can only guess at the profit generated by Pitovranov's group. But, as the man who was doing the dirty work in Africa for his Chekist masters, Kalmanovich's wealth provided some insight. In the short time he worked in Africa, Kalmanovich made $20 million, a colossal amount in the 1980s. He bought a castle in Cannes, a villa in Tel-Aviv, and his own plane for more convenient travelling. In Tel-Aviv, Kalmanovich built a building that was dubbed by the locals as the 'glass palace'. It was used by the unofficial consulate of Bophuthatswana in Israel. 'No matter how much money I spent in those days, there was still a lot of it,' Kalmanovich remembered.

Kalmanovich's change from the music business to war business was not without its risks. In May 1987, he was arrested in London with his business partner Vladimir Davidson in relation to the attempted sale of 'blood' diamonds. Released on bail, Kalmanovich fled to Israel. It did not help him much. He was arrested on December 23, 1987 and charged with 'having connections with regimes hostile to Israel, conducting espionage for a foreign state, and causing harm to the security of the State of Israel.' Kalmanovich's indictment specified that 'the defendant was in contact with agents of foreign intelligence services and passed to them classified information, thereby inflicting harm on the country's security.' On his lawyer's advice, Kalmanovich settled with the Israeli Prosecutor's Office and agreed to serve a prison sentence of nine years, foregoing trial. He was released five and a half years later.

One of Bobkov's agents, Iosif Kobzon, played an active role in securing

Kalmanovich's early release. Kobzon was a famous Soviet pop singer, born in 1937 in Donetsk Region of Ukraine. He graduated from the prestigious Dnepropetrovsk Mining College in 1956 and from 1956 to 1959, Kobzon served in the Soviet Army. During his service, he was invited to join the Transcaucasian Military District's song and dance ensemble. In 1959, he became a soloist on the All-Union Radio. From 1962 to 1989, he was a soloist at Moskontsert, Soviet Moscow's most prestigious cultural institution.

A popular pop singer with clear leadership qualities and of Jewish descent, Kobzon naturally attracted the attention of officers from the 5th Directorate of the KGB who screened for Jewish nationalists and overseas Zionist centers (the 8th Department). In the early 1970s, Kobzon was recruited as a KGB agent and, proving to be valuable, was soon received personally by the head of the 5th Directorate, Bobkov, who became his personal handler. Kobzon remained in that position until Bobkov's retirement in January 1991. Their personal friendship thereafter continued for the rest of their lives.

Kobzon was deeply indebted to his patron. Bobkov's 5th Directorate supervised the Ministry of Culture and Goskontsert (the Soviet entertainment company), thanks to which, even at the beginning of his stage career as a Moskonsert soloist, Kobzon received the highest rate of payment for his performances. As with all KGB agents, accolades soon came his way. Bobkov also facilitated Kobzon receiving the titles of Honorary Artist of the RSFSR (1973), National Artist of the RSFSR (1980), and National Artist of the USSR (1987). Very few Soviet performers held such high honors.

But what did Kobzon do in return for the KGB to become a 'National Artist?' Stationed in Afghanistan was the 40th Army. In addition, there were many KGB representatives: from the PGU, the VGU, 3rd, 5th, and other relevant KGB Directorates. The 3rd Directorate of the KGB (3rd Department) supervised the Afghan caravans and handled the processing and analysis of the information received from the KGB operatives in the country. Gennady Arshinov was the officer who handled the drugs deliveries to the USSR with the Soviet Army's military transport aircrafts. However, for obvious reasons he could not use KGB officials as mules as this risked exposing the KGB's flagrant corruption. Enter Kobzon. Starting in 1980, Kobzon did nine concert tours in Afghanistan where he performed for Soviet troops carrying the contraband with him on the way back.

Meanwhile, a Major Alexander Yevdokimov who worked in the 5th Directorate's *rezidentura* in Kabul cottoned on to the fact that drugs were being smuggled in the luggage of Kobzon's musical ensemble returning from Afghanistan to Moscow. Not knowing that this cargo was sanctioned by Bobkov, his own 5th Directorate Chief, Yevdokimov duly informed Arshinov at the KGB's Third Chief Directorate, which oversaw military transport aviation and its home base at Chkalovsky Airport located just outside Moscow. As Kobzon was 'a representative of the creative *intelligensia*', the matter was referred to Bobkov, who had to decide what to do with him. Yevdokimov proposed seizing the cargo when Kobzon returned to Moscow. But the Chkalovsky Airport did not have customs checkpoints. In any case, only response to Yevdokimov's numerous coded messages on the need to conduct a customs inspection of Kobzon and his group was: 'Deemed inappropriate.'

Just how exceptional (both in the sense of lucrative and as a break with the Communist past) Pitovranov's covert business operations were, is made clear by the fact that Kobzon became one of the first illegal Soviet millionaires. This was already the case by the early 1980s, after a few years of the Afghan occupation and the Firm's illegal drugs trade. Like Bobkov's other valuable assets, Kobzon's career prospered in direct proportion to his usefulness to the KGB. Starting in 1984, Kobzon directed the Vocals and Pop Music Branch of the Gnessin State Music and Pedagogy Institute and then the Department of Vocalists of the Gnessin Russian Academy of Music. In 1989, he became a lead soloist and creative director of the Moskontsert.

It was not the last use of Kobzon. When Kalmanovich wound up in an Israeli prison arrested as a foreign spy, Bobkov ordered Kobzon to help with the campaign to release him. A cover story was invented that Kobzon was one of Kalmanovich greatest friends (pure fiction) and fed to the media. Laying it on thick, Kalmanovich claimed, 'Our families became friends long before my arrest. There was no pecuniary interest or competition between us, no mutual business. Hence, a true friendship developed'. But neither ever said exactly when their close friendship blossomed, or which 'families' were meant. This was not a question without importance since Kobzon had been married three times, and Kalmanovich as well. In paean to his friend, Kalmanovich recalled that Kobzon would visit him in his Israeli cell with his 'favorite fish in tomato sauce, sprats and gobies, chocolate candies':

Whatever they say about Kobzon, he's an incredible friend. He spent his own money to fly to Israel to visit me. Iosif was a delegate of the Supreme Soviet then, and he was not subject to search when he came to prison. He smuggled in my favorite fish in tomato sauce, sprats and gobies, and chocolate candies....

It didn't stop there. Kobzon apparently pulled out all the stops for his new best friend. The crooner promised Israel that he would help with the resumption of diplomatic relations which had been severed since 1967 (they resumed in 1991). Ostensibly single-handedly, Kobzon also produced an eyewatering line-up of top Party politicians begging Israel for the release of the prisoner who was a fugitive from justice for the tawdry crime of smuggling blood diamonds. He even got Gorbachev to join the chorus and throw his reputation behind the man:

I'll never forget how much he did for me. He got everyone going. People I had never met in my life were calling for my early release at Kobzon's request ... Kobzon brought official letters from [Mikhail] Gorbachev, [Gennady] Yanayev, [Boris] Pugo, and [Alexander] Rutskoy petitioning for my early release. There were several other people serving sentences in Israel for the same crimes, but Gorbachev did not, let's say, ask about them. Kobzon got all those letters together on his own by beating on the doors of Kremlin offices.

The Israeli government was facing an unprecedented barrage of pressure for the release of the louche Kalmanovich. Yet none of it was ostensibly from Moscow. The Russian Ambassador in Israel, Alexander Bovin, described the saga with Kobzon and Kalmanovich colorfully and with a touch of irony: Moscow never instructed him to intervene directly, the push to free Kalmanovich was 'all' Kobzon's doing. Kobzon was even received by Israeli Prime Minister Shamir as Kobzon wheeled out Ilya Glazunov who said he would paint Shamir for 'free' if he would 'Just let Kalmanovich out of jail'.

I never had any instructions from Moscow about Kalmanovich. There was a conversation with Kobzon on the subject roughly a month ago (when he came to see me with Glazunov). But I somehow missed [the conversation]. I should have paid attention.... Kobzon arrived in Israel on a cruise ship with the artist Ilya Glazunov. Prime Minister Shamir received him.... The Prime Minister's assistant asked, 'Can you paint a portrait of Shamir?'—'Of course,' Ilya Glazunov answered. 'How much will that cost?'—'Nothing,' the artist replied. 'Just let Kalmanovich out of jail.'

Such was the nature of the friendship between Glazunov and Kalmanovich that Glazunov had to read the surname off a piece of paper Kobzon had slipped him in advance.

It didn't stop there. Though ostensibly writing a personal appeal, Alexander Rutskoy, the Vice President of Russia, wrote an involved, flattering letter to Shamir about Kalmanovich on March 12, 1992, reminding him that Kalmanovich was supposed to be released on resumption of diplomatic relations with Israel (which happened in October 1991).

Dear Mr Prime Minister,

In August 1991, I sent you a letter, in which I asked that you show a sense of humanity and, for health reasons, free former citizen of the USSR Shabtai Kalmanovich who is serving sentence in Israel. It is the fifth year of his imprisonment now, and the state of his health has sharply declined.

At a meeting with me in September 1991, Mr. Aryeh Levin assured me that Kalmanovich would be released immediately after diplomatic ties are established between our countries. It has been a while but no positive decision on that issue has been made.

In this regard, I am forced to follow up on my original appeal for you to do everything in your power to secure the early release of Kalmanovich for health reasons.

I hope for your understanding and look forward to seeing you soon in the ancient land of Israel.

Ten days later, on March 22, 1992, Ambassador Bovin himself visited Shamir again. Presumably also as a 'personal' rather than 'official' observation, the ambassador said to the Prime Minister that Kalmanovich's imprisonment was a 'thorn' in Russo-Israeli relations—which must have seemed to the puzzled Israelis as somewhat making a mountain out of a molehill given that other things had happened during their 24-year hiatus:

I am very grateful to you, Mr Prime Minister, for successfully facilitating the elimination of 'thorns and traps' from Israeli-Russian relations. However, some thorns remain. One of them is, without a doubt, the Kalmanovich issue.... This issue needs to be resolved. I will not repeat the arguments in favor of his early release. They have been stated many times, and I would add nothing new. I am just asking you to consider this issue once again. Please allow me to leave you a letter about this matter.

A few days later, Bovin also mentioned Kalmanovich in a conversation with the Speaker of the Knesset, Dov Shilansky, who promised to discuss it with the Prime Minister. On June 9, a letter was received from Joseph Ben-Aaron, Director General of the Prime Minister's Office, stating that the Kalmanovich case was 'being studied.' In July 1992, Yitzhak Rabin became Prime Minister, and in early September Bovin sent Rabin a letter training the charm attack on the new Israeli leader to pull the levers of state to set aside the rule of law and let the smuggler off early:

I cannot and do not want to discuss the legal side of the issue... The time when distrust and suspicion dominate relations between our countries is fading into the past. And may the Kalmanovich case, born out of that time, fade away with it. The early release of this man could be another indication that there is no going back, that Russia and Israel are looking to the future.

On November 1, Ambassador Bovin raised the issue of Kalmanovich again in a conversation with Rabin. When informing Moscow of the conversation, he reported that 'the process will take another month-and-a-half to two months.'[232] Finally, in December, Israeli Ambassador Aryeh Levin told Rutskoy that the Israelis had decided to release Kalmanovich 'on condition of his immediate departure from Israel.' On March 10, 1993, the President of Israel personally signed the order for Kalmanovich's early release. On March 13, Kobzon arrived in Israel and suggested to Bovin they celebrate the release. It didn't stop there. 'When we arrived in Moscow,' Kalmanovich recalled, 'Kobzon opened all the doors for me. I am very grateful to him for that.' Of course, Kobzon did not open 'all the doors' for Kalmanovich. The doors were opened by Kalmanovich's handlers from the KGB—Pitovranov, Bobkov, and Ivanov. They had unlimited powers and full control of Moscow through the 5th Directorate's numerous and high-placed agents.

The people who were really celebrating, however, were at the Lubyanka. The real reason driving the persistent charm offensive and pulling out all the stops with regards to the insignificant Kalmanovich was that he had access to all the international accounts of Pitovranov's group, which he had used up to the moment of his arrest in Israel. This was why Pitovranov and his team of KGB Generals had such keen interest in his early release. Together they had agreed that Kalmanovich would be ordered to provide full information on the bank accounts only after he was released from prison. Using their KGB contacts, they orchestrated the efforts in such a way that the entire Soviet apparatus came to their rescue without knowing it.

In Moscow Kobzon and Kalmanovich, through setting up several 'joint-stock companies', proceeded to settle all financial payments as instructed by the KGB owners of Kalmanovich's accounts. With their financial assignments at an end, the apparently inseparable friends who—together with their families—had so longed to be reunited 'had a falling out' and thereafter went their own way, never to look back again. 'Our paths in business parted. Sometimes we cross paths and greet each other politely,' Kalmanovich recalled as to his 'close' friend who ostensibly moved heaven and earth to get him out of jail. Their ventures compensated Kobzon for acting as KGB intermediary in freeing him from Israeli prison.

KGB Diamonds

From the beginning of the Russian Revolution, religion, its leaders, and people of faith in general, were not popular in the Soviet Union given Marx's characterization as '*Opium des Volkes*' (people's analgesic), that is, its presence is an expression of suppression. Thus, the USSR subjected religious groups to various levels of persecution. Hasidic Jews were among the most persecuted groups and often operated contrary to Soviet law, teaching their children in underground Heder schools and facilitating the emigration of their followers from the USSR to overseas. It goes without saying that, throughout the USSR, Hasidic communities and their leaders were under constant scrutiny by the Lubyanka and its Soviet satellite offices. In 1927, for example, OGPU arrested in Leningrad the sixth Lubavitcher Rabbi, Yosef Yitzchak Schneerson, as well as his secretary Chaim Lieberman, and confiscated letters written by 'the philosopher and mystic' Alexander Barchenko.

Like all illegal or semi-legal groups, they were also a good hunting ground for new Cheka recruits—co-operation as a stay of persecution being the carrot—to control and direct their reach. Barchenko had organized an expedition to Tibet in the 1920s to search for Shambhala, the legendary birthplace of a mythical new age. Expedition members included Chekist Yakov Blumkin, Mirbach's assassin (who posed as a Persian merchant named Sultanov), a seller and collector of unique and ancient

Hebrew books. Another was the Russian painter Nicholas Roerich, a Gorky supporter. It was with Blumkin's help that Barchenko ended up working for Dzerzhinsky's OGPU where he served under another high-ranking Chekist, Gleb Bokii. The OGPU stood behind all these activities allocated over RUB 100,000 to Barchenko, an enormous amount. This money was used to recruit agents from among the religious leaders, who, using their supreme moral authority, could influence their followers and society at large for the OGPU's benefit. Barchenko planned to hold a congress of Russian and Eastern religious and mystical societies in Moscow. And through his connections with Hasidim, Ismailis, Muslim Sufi dervishes, Karaites, and Tibetan and Mongolian lamas, Barchenko promoted the ideas of global revolution in various countries.

Barchenko established contact not only with the sixth Lubavitcher Rabbi prior to Schneerson's arrest, but also with his successor. His Chekist infiltration was no secret to Hasidic leaders, and they resorted to strict secrecy in their activities. The seventh Lubavitcher Rabbi, who lived for many years in the US and was in touch with the sect residing in the USSR, followed these requirements to the letter. He signed his missives as a 'Grandfather' and was convinced that agents of Soviet intelligence had even penetrated the office of their Chabad movement in New York.

Enter two Tashkent Hasidic Jews. Lev Levayev (also known as Leviev) was born on July 30, 1956, in Tashkent. His parents were Bukharan Jews and followers of the Lubavitcher Rabbi. His father, Avner, worked as the director of a major department store, which allowed his family to live quite comfortably. Avner Levayev was an active member of the Tashkent society of Lubavitch Hasidim and an underground rabbi. His wife Hana, the mother of their four daughters and one son, Lev, was his trusted assistant. Active figures in the Hasidic community of Tashkent, Lev Levayev's father and grandfather could not help being in the sights of the Soviet Intelligence Services in Tashkent. Their fates couldn't be more different, however. In numerous interviews, Lev Levayev spoke of his father Avner's religious activities and those of his grandfather, and how the latter was sent to Siberia for 25 years for such activities.

In fact, his father Avner managed to not only continue his religious activities undisturbed but to amass into the bargain a serious fortune for Soviet times (estimated by Lev Levayev at $1 million). Even more surprising was the fact that Levayev's father made a million dollars and managed to use these funds to buy diamonds and move them overseas. This was truly a feat akin to finding Shambala. In May 1959, the Supreme Soviet of the USSR ordered the KGB to oversee all currency operations to detect smuggling. The main department controlling these operations was the 16th Department of the VGU. Identikit departments were created in the KGB branches in all other Soviet and Autonomic Soviet Republics in the USSR. One high-profile case in those years concerned three currency dealers. Initially, they were sentenced to 15 years in prison. But their sentence was commuted and they were executed instead. Except for a miracle, it was impossible for Avner Levayev—the son of a Siberian convict and therefore by definition under close scrutiny—to pull off what he managed to do unless he was a Chekist undercover agent recruited to spy for the Lubyanka.

With Avner's fortune in diamonds now parked abroad, Avner and his family managed to emigrate to Israel. Or, more accurately, Avner was ordered to emigrate at a time when the Kremlin was deeply suspicious of the young State of Israel and its influence on Russians of Jewish descent. At the age of 15, Lev Levayev went to Israel with his family and began studying in a Chabad yeshiva of his father and grandfather's sect. After serving in the Israeli army, he got a job as diamond cutter in an Israeli factory. Then, like his father before him, and unlike his grandfather, his fortunes took off fueled by the Soviet fortune made by his father and smuggled to Israel. There is no information about when exactly he started his own business. But in the early 1980s, he acquired shares in Africa-Israel Investments, founded in 1934. That became the impetus for his precipitous ascent to the top of Israel's financial firmament. He would later become an international financier, for example, investing in a New York building acquired in 2017 by Jared Kushner, Donald Trump's son in law.

A very complex individual became Lev Levayev's associate during this time—Arkadi Gaydamak. KGB agent Victor Louis (born Vitaly Levin), a foreign correspondent in the USSR for the *Evening News* and the *Sunday Express* newspapers in Britain from the early 1950s—who acted as an early KGB mouthpiece for disinformation directed at foreign intelligence services and global society at large—said, 'Every good agent is at least a double agent.' Considering Louis's complex life, he knew what he was talking about. Gaydamak's activities fit Louis's expression perfectly.

He was born on April 8, 1952 in Moscow. There is no information about his parents, but he emigrated to Israel in 1972 and then moved to France in 1973. In 1974 (or, according to some sources, in 1976), he launched his own business—a translation agency of technical documents into the Russian language. Not only was it a successful company that managed to be given a lot of business, Gaydamak himself freelanced as 'an interpreter for the Soviet delegations that came to Paris' because he had 'solid information sources on the happenings in the USSR':

> I completed a two-year course in electronics engineering in Paris, and that helped me launch my career as a technical translator. In the early 1980s, I became a medium-sized entrepreneur for those days and built enterprises that did technical documentation and translations. I met Charles Pasqua through this work long [before] he became Minister of the Interior. At the same time, I acquired many influential contacts from the USSR. When Soviet delegations came to France, I often participated in various negotiations, including political ones. By the end of the 1980s, I had solid information sources on the happenings in the USSR.[233] In the 1980s, I was an interpreter for the Soviet delegations that came to Paris. That's when I met Mr Pasqua.[234]

Since he fell under their domain, agents in Pitovranov's 'Firm' made sure to make good use of Gaydamak. His translation agencies in France and Canada collected a massive amount of scientific, technical, and political information for the KGB. In fact, his success was unheard of. 'By the mid-1980s,' Gaydamak recalled, 'I had an extensive, close relationship with representatives of the Soviet administration and ministries, right up to Politburo members.' Which Politburo member might he have been close to? The most likely candidate is Andropov as none of the others would have any reason for contact. But mentioning the name of the KGB's Chief would obviously have raised suspicion in France (whose citizenship he had taken) with potentially disastrous consequences.

Others benefited, too, from Gaydamak's 'technical translations' In 1957, a highly classified Intelligent Service body was created in Israel. It was originally called the Bureau of Special Tasks but was later renamed the Bureau of Scientific Relations, abbreviated as LEKEM (for *ha-Lishka le-Kishrei Mada*). This new security service's primary mission was to maintain the secrecy of Israel's nuclear program. It fell under the Israeli Ministry of Defense and reported directly to the defense minister and the head of state. By the end of the 1970s, LEKEM's functions had expanded significantly, and the organization began collecting scientific and technical data from technologically developed countries. Gaydamak's technical documentation translation agency was a constituent part of LEKEM's all-encompassing activity.

LEKEM was abolished in 1986. It followed the arrest, in 1985, and subsequent sentencing to life in prison of US naval intelligence officer and former LEKEM agent Jonathan Pollard on charges of spying for Israel. In 1986, the Israeli whistleblower Mordechai Vanunu revealed to the world the existence of an Israeli nuclear weapon on which he had worked as a nuclear technician. LEKEM's functions were transferred to the Mossad, Israel's Intelligence Service.

Like show-organizer and KGB 'intelligence friend' Kalmanovich, translator and KGB 'intelligence friend' Gaydamak had been tasked with illegal arms trading as a new line of business to develop. And so, with help from his Cheka handlers, he began supplying arms in Angola's civil war—except, he supplied the other side. As a sign of his gratitude for 420 tanks, 12 helicopters, 6 warships, 150 thousand shells, and 170 thousand assorted explosives which had helped claim victory in the war, Angolan President José Eduardo dos Santos, who was educated in the USSR, appointed Gaydamak as his advisor and issued him with an Angolan diplomatic passport.

The Angolan leader was grateful to Gaydamak for other amazing feats, too. Not only did Gaydamak's efforts allow dos Santos to bypass the UN embargo and equip his army, but also because Gaydamak wizardry was able to help shrink the size of Angola's debt to the USSR (and to the new Russia) from $5.5 billion to $500 million. Only an insignificant portion of that money ended up in the new Russia. Most of it was deposited in the accounts of Gaydamak's Cheka handlers.

An international arrest warrant was issued for Gaydamak in which the French prosecutor's indictment identified him as a Soviet intelligence Colonel. Additionally, a Paris court that tried a group of individuals on charges of illegal weapon sales to Angola sentenced former French Minister of the Interior Charles Pasqua to one year in prison and imposed a suspended sentence of one year on the son of former French President Francois Mitterrand, Jean-Christophe Mitterrand. Gaydamak himself hid from the French court in Israel but was sentenced in absentia to six years in prison. His French partner Falcone received the same sentence.

Later, During Gorbachev's *perestroika* years (late 1980s-1991), Gaydamak and Levayev started doing business in the USSR. Soviet mineral resources were pouring forth from the Soviet Union as the Iron Curtain was becoming less impenetrable. The Pitovranov's-Bobkov's group played an active role in all of it. In 1999, the fortunate Gaydamak was granted the right to create an export company for diamonds by the Angolan government. He invited Lev Levayev, a major player in the diamond trade, as his business partner. This was part of Gaydamak's sprawling legitimate business empire. Besides the diamond business, Levayev had many other businesses related to Russia. As a 'foreigner' Levayev's movements were obviously closely monitored by the Lubyanka, the more so when he started working with Gaydamak.

His association as a 'friend' of the Firm did not end well for Gaydamak. On October 27, 2009, he was found guilty by a French court of organizing arms supplies to Angola in violation of the UN embargo. The indictment stated that Gaydamak and his partner, French entrepreneur Pierre-Joseph Falcone, sold Soviet-made arms and ammunition to Angola of a fair market value of approximately $790 million between 1993 and 1998. Evidently, the Firm had excellent access to the accounts Gaydamak controlled on their behalf as no special effort was made to gain his early release.

15: The Death of Yuri Andropov

As Pitovranov saw it in the 1950s, the threat to the survival of the Soviet Union was the Communist Party. It interfered with order in the USSR through its dysfunctional purges which saw large swathes of the population, and, more importantly, large swathes of professional Chekist agents, who were devoted to maintaining its institutions, perish or get ejected from the Intelligence Service. As Lubyanka's second-in-command under Abakumov, he witnessed first-hand how Beria and Malenkov schemed from the Kremlin to have his boss executed by Stalin on spurious grounds, and, of course, his own miraculous escape from a premature Kremlin death on Stalin's whim after he wrote the draconic Soviet leader a letter from his cell. The solution Pitovranov pursued after the death of Stalin and Beria was the creation of the KGB Active Reserve Officers (ARO) program. KGB personnel were to be planted alongside civil branches of power in the USSR just like the undercover spies planted overseas by the 4th Directorate that he headed. It is this concept that was simplified in the popular imagination with the expression that a 'Chekist never retires', or 'ex-Chekists don't exists'.

Chekist AROs of the KGB (and its sister organization in the military, GRU) served in many governmental departments, ministries, agencies, and state organizations. Their deployment in a specific institution followed a standard bureaucratic procedure in the Soviet Union. The KGB made a recommendation to the Central Committee of the Communist Party on the need for such and such a post in the relevant ministry or agency. The Secretariat of the Party's Central Committee would draft an order approving (or denying) the KGB's recommendation. If it was approved by the Secretariat, it went up to the full Politburo for confirmation. The Politburo, assuming it accepted the Secretariat's approval, would then order the Soviet government to create the ARO 'department' at the relevant body. (We should add that the Main Intelligence Department of the Soviet Army (GRU) founded its own version of the Active Reserve. Thus, everything discussed here should be multiplied by some coefficient, which certainly exceeds 'one', but we do not know by how much.)

In many cases, transferring to ARO status meant a promotion. For instance, on Bobkov's initiative, such an ARO post was created at the Party's CC. Thus, Bobkov's subordinate Evgeniy Ivanov was appointed to the CC. He was sent to the Department of Administrative Bodies, which oversaw the Soviet Union's entire enforcement system: the General Prosecutor's Office, Supreme Court, KGB, and MVD. Ivanov worked there for approximately two years, and then returned as Deputy Head to supervise the staff of the VGU, the KGB's Counterintelligence Division. He was promoted to Major General and soon became head of the 5th Directorate and was made a Lieutenant General. Thus, dispatching a KGB officer to this or that entity as an Active Reserve Officer was treated as a matter of great career advancement.

Over time, ARO posts were introduced everywhere—even the lesser important entities—from agencies, institutes, to enterprises, businesses, television, and in the mass media since every kind of social activity was by definition a state activity under Communism. Cheka officers who were part of the Active Reserve continued to be part of the Lubyanka hierarchy, reporting to the KGB division they were seconded from. In their dual role, they did whatever their civilian role demanded as if they were regular employees. At the same, undercover, their primary task was to monitor and control activities in the interests of the Intelligence Services.

Given the formal subordination of the Lubyanka to the Kremlin, no such dual bureaucratic placement—even if, in secret, a mafia one—of Soviet State employees could be undertaken without Party authorization. The ARO protocol, as a Lubyanka institution, could not have been born without the initial authorization by the Kremlin.

On October 24, 1955, the Presidium of the CC passed its first resolution called 'Regarding Officers of the KGB Working in Other Organizations, Ministries, and Agencies.' Obviously, no one paid attention to this technical and unpublished resolution in the chaotic year of 1955—two years after the deaths of Stalin and Beria and in the year that Khrushchev pushed Malenkov out as the Soviet Prime Minister. Based on this resolution, the ARO began capturing positions for the KGB in absolute secrecy.

Unfortunately for future generations, after the collapse of the USSR the KGB was never keen to provide access to its internal archives regarding the creation of ARO, and we must make do with sporadic crumbs that were made public. On November 10, 1958, KGB approved its 'Instructions on the Dismissal to the Reserve or Retirement of the KGB officers in the Active Reserve'. This was one of the earliest known references to the ARO. On December 24, 1958, the 'Instruction for Activity of the ARO' was adopted by the Soviet government and sent to civil ministries and agencies. At this point, Pitovranov was serving in Moscow as Head of the 4th Directorate of the KGB and was one of the 18 members of the KGB Collegium.

Active Reserve officers gradually came to be deployed in all ministries and agencies throughout the entire Soviet Union. The active reserve captured the entire country, from top to bottom: first from the top by taking the most delicious, gravy-train posts, and moving gradually down to the middle and lower levels, eventually occupying every corner of the Soviet Union. Entire institutes were created to train Cheka officers who went into the Active Reserve and whose numbers were growing. Again, Pitovranov and Bobkov were behind this development.

Everything was set up in plain sight under Party control. On April 2, 1968—soon after Andropov was appointed KGB Chair—the Institute of Specific Social Research at the Academy of Sciences of the USSR was proposed by the top-secret resolution (No St-49/3c) of the Secretariat of the CC. On April 24, by another top-secret resolution (No St-50/263), the creation of the Institute was approved by the Politburo. As a follow-up to these two resolutions, on October 15, another top-secret resolution (No St-60/5c) was passed: 'Regarding the Main Direction of the Institute of Specific Social Research at the Academy of Science of the USSR.' The resolutions were kept secret because the Institute was meant exclusively for the KGB and the CC of the Communist Party. In June 1972, the Institute changed its name to the Institute of Sociological Research at the Academy of Sciences of the USSR. But now KGB officers, rather than Party officials, began to work there.

From time to time, the KGB continued to publish clarifying documents regarding the ARO, indicating that the Active Reserve remained alive and well throughout these years. The operative word in all these resolutions was 'counterintelligence'. Usually applied to foreign nations, here it indicated Soviet bodies. The word 'undercover' will be repeated below by Vladimir Putin when he explained to his KGB/FSB colleagues what his own ARO appointment meant to him.

Thus, in 1972, the 'Provision Regarding Officer Staff of the Committee for the Intelligence Services under the Council of Ministers of the USSR Enlisted in the Active Reserve of the KGB and Deployed in Ministries, Agencies, Institutions, Educational Institutions, Organizations, and Enterprises, for Counterintelligence Work to Ensure the Regime and Protection of Secrecy' was adopted. In 1981, the KGB collegium (the group of top KGB officials) drew its own conclusion concerning the ARO in a lengthy secret document called 'Regarding the Current State and Measures for Further Improving the Work of the Active Reserve in the Counterintelligence Divisions of the Central and Field Departments of the KGB.' In this document, the Collegium consisting of 18 individuals elected in secret by the KGB itself and not accountable or subordinate to anyone except the KGB Chair, stated that power in the country had been seized by the Lubyanka through the ARO and outlined future plans to improve and expand the activities of the ARO, consolidating its power even further. In 1982, the KGB's Collegium issued a further instruction formally streamlining and superseding the 1981 document. It was called the 'Provision on Active Reserve Officers of the KGB Working Undercover in Counterintelligence Divisions in the Ministries, State Committees, and Agencies of the USSR'.

Why did the Kremlin not see what they were giving into? The Party top seems to have been hardly aware of the fact that these very same ARO officers would become the gravediggers of the Kremlin, if not the USSR itself. Not the West, not NATO, not the 'enemy', 'imperialists', 'interventionists', dissidents, but 'loyal Party knights' would bring the Partocracy of the Soviet Union to its knees. Perhaps, it looked attractive to the Party as a compromise in its favor to end the deadly internecine warfare between their two Moscow power centers. Once the Lubyanka's back was broken by inserting non-Chekists as heads at various leadership levels within the Intelligence Services (an arrangement favoring control over professional competence), a parallel monitoring system alongside the usual bureaucratic chain of command may no longer have looked like a threat to Kremlin dominance. As long as all information was shared with the Party—which it would be because heads of department would be Party officials—the parallel ARO system seemed like a gain for the Kremlin. In addition, on paper, this system staffed by the Cheka but administered by the Party gave the Kremlin ever tighter control over the Soviet Union.

Certainly, 1958, the year of the Active Reserve's first incarnation, coincided with the removal of Ivan Serov, a Chekist from the Lubyanka as the first Chair of the newly formed KGB. On December 10, 1958, the Presidium of the Party CC demoted him sideways to the GRU and on December 25, 1958, Alexander Shelepin was appointed as KGB Chair. He was the first-ever Party appointment with no previous Chekist background. Perhaps the Kremlin thought on the one hand that they had regained absolute control and on the other hand worried how the USSR population would continue to follow its lead without Stalin's terror. Propagating the ARO system throughout the Soviet Union may increasingly have seemed like the only option left for Moscow to preserve its absolute central dominion over the vast country. In any case, there was no bloodshed and from hereon, the Kremlin would cease its deadly purges of the Lubyanka. The Lubyanka would be the only institution left that carried out premature deaths in the USSR and abroad (together with the GRU)—either undercover or through 'case files' to be executed through the Soviet legal system—albeit always in a constant dialogue with the Kremlin.

During the last months of Brezhnev's life (1906-1982), a fierce struggle for power at the most senior level ensued inside the elite *nomenklatura* in Moscow. On January 19, 1982, Semyon Tsvigun, the First Deputy Chair (the crown prince) of the KGB shot himself. He was considered to be 'Brezhnev's man'. Tsvigun's death at 64 gave rise to many rumors against Brezhnev. One of the reasons for the rumors was the absence of his signature on Tsvigun's official obituary. Allegedly Tsvigun had been trying to call Brezhnev's attention to the criminal connections of one of the 'Holy' family, his daughter Galina. General Secretary Brezhnev would not want to sign off on suicide, which gave grounds for talk about Tsvigun having been eliminated. In the end, it was all just a speculation. Six days after Tsvigun's 'suicide', on January 25, 1982, Mikhail Suslov (1902-1982), Brezhnev's Number Two in the Party passed away. The optics of two possibly premature deaths posed a problem for Brezhnev. Tsvigun's death weakened his hold over the KGB and Suslov's death weakened Brezhnev's position in the Politburo and the Central Committee. Brezhnev, sensing his own physical decline, was forced to think seriously about making major changes to the country's leadership to survive a challenge to his position and or, given his own age and health, plan his succession and secure the safety of his family from prosecution.

Who did he want to replace him? Ivan Kapitonov, who headed the Department of Organizational and Party Work of the CC for 19 years and who managed Party personnel at the highest level of the Kremlin, recalled a conversation with Brezhnev in October 1982 when the latter said: 'See that chair? That's where [Volodomyr] Shcherbytsky will sit. Make all staffing decisions with that in mind.' Brezhnev pointed to the General Secretary's chair. Shcherbytsky was his protégé, and Ukraine's Party leader (the First Secretary of the Party CC of Ukraine).

Brezhnev certainly did not want to see Andropov succeed him. On May 24, 1982, Andropov was moved away from the post of KGB Chair to the post of Secretary of the Party CC under Brezhnev as the Party's General Secretary. The official story was that Andropov was taking up the vacant seat of the deceased Suslov, Brezhnev's right-hand man. In that sense, it looked like the Politburo wanted to give Andropov a promotion to the job previously occupied by the USSR's second most powerful man for as long as Brezhnev himself. It could be argued that it was a first step before moving Andropov up to General Secretary which, for political reasons, the Politburo didn't not want to do as it would entail the removal of Brezhnev from power.

The more likely explanation is that it was a sideways move meant to downgrade Andropov's chances of succeeding as leader. If Andropov was seen by the Politburo as their leader-in-waiting, it would mean Brezhnev had already lost his leadership position in USSR's customary power structure from May 24—as a lame-duck General Secretary. Instead, it was Andropov who looked slightly abandoned. Changing from Lubyanka Chief to the administrative offices of Secretary of the CC at the Kremlin likely meant a slight loss of prestige. He had already once before been Secretary of the CC (1962-1967), before going to the KGB. In that sense he was treading water (like the first Chief of the KGB Ivan Serov, who moved across to the GRU). Meanwhile, as Andropov gave up the Lubyanka to go back to the CC, his successor at the Cheka was a complete stranger. But, the new appointee Vitaly Fedorchuk strengthened Brezhnev hand with a strong new ally. Fedorchuk was a close ally of Shcherbytsky, the man Brezhnev planned to make his successor as General Secretary. He was appointed as the new KGB Chief on May 26, 1982—on Brezhnev's personal orders. Despite all these potential negatives, it would have been very difficult for Andropov to decline the honor of taking the job vacated by the USSR's number two wen asked by the Politburo chaired by Brezhnev.

Either way, Fedorchuk's ultimately short-lived appointment as KGB Chair became a new, important milestone in the history of the KGB. Unlike Shelepin, Semichastny, and Andropov, new head Fedorchuk was once again a career officer who had first joined the Cheka in 1939. Thus, his appointment broke the existing KGB tradition of recent decades according to which the Lubyanka's head had to be a Party official. On May 26, 1982, that tradition ended for good. This must have pleased the KGB collegium even if they regretted Andropov's death. The Cheka never again let the advantage go. From that day forward, Lubyanka leadership posts were once again held by KGB officers. And although many sources say that Andropov, Pitovranov, and Bobkov were unenthusiastic about Fedorchuk's appointment as KGB Chair, they certainly took advantage of the last whims of a sick and dying Brezhnev whose Politburo sanctioned the new system of succession where only Chekists would run the Agency.

Despite his credentials, Fedorchuk didn't last long. On November 12, 1982, Andropov was elected to be the next General Secretary at a plenary meeting of the CC. Shortly after, on December 17, Fedorchuk was removed as KGB Chair and appointed minister of internal affairs, replacing Nikolai Shchelokov who was disliked by Andropov and Bobkov (and later expelled from the Party on 'case file' of corruption).

In 2006, Fedorchuk admitted to hating Andropov, who apparently 'felt the same way about him.' The main reason for their tense relations, Fedorchuk said, was his personal disapproval of the campaign against dissidents in the country. Fedorchuk said this campaign was driven by the Intelligence Services previously headed by Andropov. But 2006 was the year the assassination of Russian journalist Anna Politkovskaya reverberated around the world (together with the murder of dissident Alexander Litvinenko in the UK) and bragging about persecuting dissidents was no longer in fashion. So, Fedorchuk may have been insincere.

The person whom Fedorchuk referred to as organizer of the anti-dissident campaign was the 5th Directorate chief, Bobkov, who of course had Andropov's full support. The close Bobkov-Andropov connection was a serious threat to Fedorchuk from the very beginning and ultimately resulted in his removal. Fedorchuk's successor was Army General Viktor Chebrikov. He had been one of Andropov's deputy chairs since 1967. Professionally and intellectually, however, he was far inferior to Bobkov, who was appointed as Chebrikov's First Deputy Chair. In effect, Bobkov became the *de facto* KGB Chair under Chebrikov as he ran day-to-day operations.

Andropov, as General Secretary on 12 November, 1982, days after Brezhnev's death, and then on June 16, 1983, 'President' of the Supreme Soviet, was a unique coup for the Lubyanka in its fight for USSR dominion. For the first time since 1917, a Chekist leader had succeeded in becoming the undisputed leader of the Soviet Union. None of his predecessors had succeeded (meeting with a premature death before they could do so) in this goal: not Dzerzhinsky, who participated in the plot to poison Lenin and then marched at the head of his funeral procession, nor Beria, who led the conspiracy to eliminate Stalin and as first pall bearer at Stalin's funeral.

Yet, it was the natural conclusion of the process that Pitovranov had set in motion in 1958 through the creation of the KGB's 'Active Reserve Officers' (ARO). By 1982-3 the program had infiltrated all aspects of the life and activities of the Soviet State, notably the Party and the government. There was only one body that had not yet been subjugated—the Politburo of the Party. Andropov's appointment as leader of the Soviet Union was the crowning moment. It eradicated the last vestiges of the Communist Party's monopoly on Soviet power and it certainly terminated the Party's political stranglehold it once had over the KGB (and GRU—the Cheka's military officers). The complete transfer of USSR political power from the Kremlin to the

Lubyanka was only a matter of time.

But the aftermath of Brezhnev's 18 years as General Secretary proved to be one of many deaths—like the last year of Stalin's 30-year rule. Andropov was a chronic sufferer from diabetes and died of kidney failure on February 9, 1984, at the age of 69. After the deaths of Stalin and Beria, this was the greatest loss for Pitovranov. His figurehead, his hope, and 'his' President had passed away. With Andropov's death, the power captured both personally by Pitovranov and institutionally by the Lubyanka evaporated. Once again, the Party seized the initiative at the Kremlin. Vasily Kuznetsov, a totally unknown figure was appointed to Andropov's position at the Supreme Soviet as Acting Chair of the Presidium, the USSR's 'President'. Earlier, four days after Andropov's death, the most senior member of the Politburo, Konstantin Chernenko, a former Brezhnev protégé, became General Secretary. He consolidated his power two months after with his appointment to one of the other two major Soviet offices—Prime Minister or President. On April 11, 1984, Chernenko, like Andropov and Brezhnev before him, became 'President'—all of the USSR's last General Secretaries were 'drawn' to this post. After the collapse of the Party and the USSR, it remained as the most important office at the Kremlin.

On March 10, 1985, Chernenko died. The next day—with unprecedented speed, to avoid creating a power vacuum and tempting the KGB to take power for a second time after Andropov—Mikhail Gorbachev became General Secretary. He was born on March 2, 1931, and thus was expected to live for a long time still. Pitovranov's group now had a fight on their hands for their 'place in the sun' under new circumstances. Fortunately for Pitovranov, the most serious event was the complete disintegration of all USSR governmental bodies—or, to put it more simply—absolute chaos. The only governmental institution that turned out to be able to withstand this chaos was the Lubyanka. And so, aided by its foreign income, it became the only Soviet body that survived the chaos more or less intact.

16: The Doomsday Scenario

In 2007 writers, Sergei Kugushev and Maxim Kalashnikov, described another branch of Pitovranov's Firm (calling it 'a covert organization of the most loyal people'). Its development began as early as the 1970s. Apart from the infiltration of all cultural, foreign, administrative and economic bodies of the Soviet Union, the Firm saw a need for a new 'reliable financial base for the broken but, in Andropov's view, not defeated Russian and Soviet Nationalist model'. The result was that, while Andropov was still alive in the early 1980s, 'the first entrepreneurial organizations' appeared and promising Western financial investment organizations were studied under the KGB's auspices under 'Operation Net':

> We can only reconstruct this most secret part of Andropov's plan and make guesses about the scale of his operations. We will provide just three facts here. In the late 1970s, Andropov created a covert organization consisting of the most loyal people inside the KGB of the USSR.... He only communicated with just a few selected close associates... The network worked particularly closely with those KGB divisions that were engaged in financial operations with the West. They created a network of firms, companies, and banks that funded and implemented KGB's goals and programs. Simultaneously, Andropov supported the Central Committee of [Komsomol] in creating centers of scientific and technical activity of the youth—the first entrepreneurial organizations in Russia that appeared in the early 1980s....
>
> Another piece of evidence was the planning of 'Operation Net' to deliberately create a financial network in Europe and America, which would not only serve the purposes of Intelligence, but would also expand and capture the fastest developing and most promising financial investment organizations in the Western World. These were all parts of the plan that were supposed to provide a reliable financial base for the broken but, in Andropov's view, not defeated Russian and Soviet Nationalist project. We believe that this part of Andropov's plan was executed only partially. The General Secretary's death put a halt to these efforts. However, certain elements of the program were carried out in the late 1970s.[235]

Andropov's sudden demise dealt a particularly significant body blow to the Firm's plan to reshape the Soviet Union. Without him at the helm, his reforms could not be issued from the top down, as they were in China. It could only be achieved through the weakening of the Communist Party's political and economic monopoly, notably its disastrous centralized planning, and the full collapse of the USSR. Modified to take into account his death, *glasnost*, which diluted the power of the Communist Party, and *perestroika*, the end of the Party's economic dictatorship, described the adapted 'Andropov' plan. Mikhail Gorbachev, the new Soviet leader from 1985 was to adopt both.

Why should we believe these writers when they say this plan dated back to the 1970s? Kalashnikov was a Russian nationalist writer in 2007. But who was Kugushev? In July 2019, an interview on Radio Liberty with Simon Kordonsky cast some light on the man. Kordonsky was a member of the 1980s Moscow-Leningrad *perestroika* group of economists led by Yegor Gaidar and Anatoly Chubais (both *perestroika* architects and future senior ministers under Boris Yeltsin). He was the deputy editor of an influential academic magazine (edited by a KGB ARO) and Kugushev was both his and Gaidar's KGB handler. Kordonsky's was asked to write a provocative academic article on 'how to switch from Socialism to Capitalism' under a *nom de plume*:

> I became Deputy Editor of *The 20th Century and the World* magazine. And you know who was the Editor-in-Chief? Anatoly Belyayev—a Lieutenant General from Intelligence who transferred to the Active Reserve. And Gaidar's and my handler at the time was Kugushev. He was a full-time employee of the KGB's analytical group. He made all this happen…. In 1989, Kugushev asked me to write a piece on how to switch from Socialism to Capitalism. And I wrote it—under the penname 'Altayev'. The piece called 'Scenario X' was later published. It was far from the only article about this ideology. Scenarios for adopting the 'Chinese Module' had already been developed…. But the people who were supposed to make all this happen felt the 'taste of the money'. They wanted to live like the West but keep their status.

Marius Laurinavičius, a Senior Analyst at the Vilnius Institute of Political Analysis, also described Kugushev as the KGB officer who controlled from the mid-1980 rising 'reformists' Yegor Gaidar and Anatoly Chubais.

In February 1991, when the USSR was still intact, Kugushev himself published an article in *Komsomolskaya Pravda* that succinctly captured both the covert Andropov-Pitovranov plan of the 1970s and surprisingly accurately the future of modern Russia under Vladimir Putin. Writing in the official organ of the Komsomol, the KGB officer said that only a 'strict government' consisting of 'businessmen, soldiers and Intelligence officers' would be able to implement 'market reforms'. Neither the Party nor Communism were even mentioned in his quote to the Party's youth members:

> It is a coalition of serious businessmen, military personnel and Intelligence officers, with wide support from the population, that can stop further robbery of the

country and conduct privatization for the sake of the people. If we leave emotions to the side and look at the historical experience in various countries that tried to move from totalitarianism to a market economy, we must recognize that in any case reforms relied on, if not directly then indirectly, a very strict government. Logically, there is another way—market reforms implemented by a strict government.

Regrouping after Andropov's death, Pitovranov's 'Firm' developed new plans in several areas, recruiting new agents to execute them, to continue with what Pitovranov had set in motion since the 1970s. What had started under Andropov in Afghanistan was now put on a firm KGB footing. Three areas seemed the most critical: creating agencies where Intelligence personnel would be hired to work officially; creating Russian and foreign organizations to be controlled for operations, especially overseas; creating a financial base to be controlled by the Pitovranov group for all future activities for years and years ahead. The KGB's 'Classified' Department of the Institute of Sociology of the Academy of Sciences became a platform to study the various happenings in the USSR. Fifteen 5th Directorate officers from the 6th Department (Analytics) were assigned there. They reported directly to Bobkov. Deputy Director of the Institute of Sociology, a KGB agent, was appointed to lead the group. The 'Classified' Department later separated from the Institute of Sociology and became an autonomous organization, with Bobkov as its leader.

Capturing a New Project

A young scholar targeted by the Firm was Alexey Podberezkin (later a candidate in the 2000 Presidential Elections). Podberezkin was born in 1953 in Moscow in a working-class family. He graduated from an Evening Secondary School and served in the Army. After demobilization, he suddenly had a very lucky break. He was able to enroll at the prestigious MSIIR for preparatory courses. MSIIR was highly selective, mainly because many of those referred to as the Soviet 'golden youth'—children of the Soviet and Communist Party elite and famous members of the intelligentsia—studied there. Nothing in Podberezkin humble background would have predicted that MSIIR would become his alma mater.

So, who helped the talented and ambitious Podberezkin? KGB rules prevented the recruitment of 'golden youth' and the same applied to relatives of Intelligence officers. The Lubyanka's VGA, whose 7th Department oversaw the MSIIR, was tasked with identifying unreliable persons and prevent their potential employment in a key job. On the other hand, to the KGB someone like Podberezkin was a highly-prized student. Ordinary folk, former blue-collar workers and ex-soldiers, were rare at MSIIR, but there was a serious demand for them at the Lubyanka. Many agents recruited among university students were from the middle and lower strata of Soviet society. They believed that, by helping the KGB, they could prove their loyalty to the Soviet system, in exchange for which they could count on the Lubyanka's support.

Indeed, the KGB actively promoted their agents anytime an opportunity arose.

Having powerful supporters at the KGB, the talented Podberezkin remained at MSIIR for two years as a research fellow after graduating in 1979 as the KGB needed an 'inside' agent at the institution. In 1981, Podberezkin was transferred to work at the Soviet Committee of Youth Organizations (KMO). Public sources confirm that, in 1982, Podberezkin defended his PhD Dissertation on 'Military Policy Issues'. But nothing more was known, not even the location where his dissertation was held. After that, he led a team of research 'consultants'. Podberezkin now fell under Pitovranov's 5th Directorate, the KGB body controlling the KMO. (A senior operative, Major Evgeny Semenikhin (1st Section of the 1st Department—who began his service at the 7th Directorate), was in charge of KMO's operational surveillance. In this capacity, Semenikhin was succeeded by Captain Alexander Kochetkov, who thereafter directed Podberezkin behind the scenes.)

Dmitry Rogozin, Vladimir Putin's Deputy Prime Minister until 2018 and a well-known nationalist political firebrand before, also worked at KMO. He described the KMO as a 'spy nest' for counterintelligence and foreign intelligence.

The KMO of the USSR was created back in the years of the Great Patriotic War under the name 'The Anti-Fascist Committee of Soviet Youth' and was an organization independent of the Central Committee of Komsomol. We were linked by a common department of affairs and a building in the center of Moscow on Khmelnitsky Street (now, Maroseika Street), in which approximately 100 employees or, rather, 'senior officials,' occupied the second and third floors. In fact, it was a real 'spy nest.' The better half of the employees at the USSR KMO simultaneously worked either in Foreign Intelligence or in Counterintelligence. We called them 'multitaskers.' They were constantly absent from work, giving the excuse of 'needing to get in contact with the Center.'

Having proven himself as a talented 5th Directorate agent, Podberezkin managed to transfer to a significantly more attractive job in 1985. With help from his KGB controllers, he transferred to the Institute of Global Economics and International Relations (IMEMO), overseen by the same Cheka team.

In fact, Podberezkin's promotion to IMEMO was the prompt for the 5th Directorate to move Rogozin across. Rogozin studied at the International Department of the Moscow State University (MSU) where he was head-hunted as an agent by Lieutenant Colonel Vladimir Maslennikov. He had been Dean of the Philology Department at MSU but changed careers to become a KGB officer in Pitovranov's 5th Directorate (where he was head of the 1st Section of the 3rd Department). With Maslennikov's support, Rogozin became an intern on Central Television while still a student at MSU. Having built a solid KGB reputation for himself, it was in turn the 22-year-old Rogozin's promotion to take Podberezkin's place as a KGB plant on the inside of KMO.

Meanwhile, at the distinguished IMEMO, Podberezkin became a Senior Research Fellow and an Instructor at the Diplomatic Academy of the Ministry of Foreign Affairs (MFA). Podberezkin's next dissertation, which earned him a PhD in History in 1990, was called 'The Importance of the Combat Management System in US Military Doctrine,' after which Podberezkin was considered a specialist in the areas of national security and military policy. This second dissertation was also secret and held at the Red Banner Diplomatic Academy of the MFA. It was marked 'For Official Use Only' and its first chapter addressed 'The Marxist-Leninist Basis for Analyzing Military Doctrines and their Development in the Second Half of the 1980s'.

Presumably, he found that there was no such basis because Podberezkin left the ranks of the Communist Party in 1990 immediately after defending his dissertation. Even in 1990, the last year of the Party, it was still an unwise career move, unless one was a dependable Chekist, of course: untouchable and unconcerned that sanctions by USSR's bodies might follow such a dramatic move. It could get you fired, make you a professional pariah, being stripped of civil rights, lead to commitment in an asylum. Instead, it was after leaving the Party that KGB support for Podberezkin's career really began to take off.

In April 1990, the Lubyanka's 5th Directorate created a new institute called the 'Russian-American University' (RAU). Podberezkin was the official founder and the first president. Despite its name, little was 'American' about the Russian-American University. RAU was made up of KGB officers and scholars who specialized in the US, said Rogozin (who was to work there too in Podberezkin's wake) in his 2010 memoirs. In 1992, Podberezkin was directed to create another KGB brainchild out of RAU: the International Non-Governmental Scientific Research Organization, or 'RAU-Corporation' for short.[236] This organization was not academic but published a monthly popular analytical magazine *Obozrevatel'* (observer). A contributor to the magazine's inaugural issue was Leonid Shebarshin, former Head of the PGU and the last (acting) Chair of the KGB. The magazine's Editorial Board included other former subordinates of Bobkov's—Alexey Bolshov, an officer of the 5th Directorate (later, Directorate Z) and Major General Valery Vorotnikov, who led Directorate Z from January 25-September 25, 1991.

Podberezkin's important task at the Firm's RAU-Corporation was to create a new ideological project: developing a coherent national idea and ideology of State patriotism with which the Firm could replace the Party's dogma (1917-1991) as the reason for preserving the Soviet State. RAU and RAU-Corporation positioned themselves as the center of the 'opposition to the Liberal-Democratic, pro-Western direction of the Russian Government,' according to MSIIR's website. MSIIR was intimately connected with both RAU and RAU-Corporation and would not have stated anything Pitovranov's Firm had not sanctioned. It was to be a nostalgic platform 'for consolidating progressive forces across society forming a basis for seeking reasonable compromise among various political forces in the interests of resurrecting Russia as a great world power'. The key words were 'Russia as a great world power'—the most painful loss that the USSR's collapse inflicted on the Firm's generals. Where they once strode as kings, they were now seen as wraiths.

In 1990, to beef up the young KGB talent at RAU-Corporation, the 27-year-old Rogozin was transferred by the Firm to Podberezkin in 1990. During his exemplary years at the KMO, Rogozin administered International Organizations for the 5th Directorate so the Lubyanka could closely monitor youth exchange channels. He traveled abroad several times a month and also organized major international forums. In 1989, he organized a trip for a Soviet youth delegation to France for 'Paris '89', the World Youth Meeting dedicated to the 200th anniversary of the French Revolution. When determining who would be part of the delegation, Rogozin followed instructions from the 5th Directorate and filled it with the Intelligence agents and officers.

At RAU-Corporation, Rogozin became its first Vice-President and stayed in that role until 1994. It was from RAU-Corporation that Rogozin was put on another Chekist assignment: to become a political figure aiming for a seat at the top of the newly-formed Russian Federation. Rogozin founded the *Congress Russkikh Obschin* (congress of Russian communities, KRO), a national-patriotic movement, which he continued to lead until it merged in 2002 in a new political party, *Rodina* (motherland). Taking advantage of 'Russian nationalism' that was growing in popularity from year to year, Rogozin gained political clout, becoming founder, Vice-Chair and leader of political party *Rodina*.

In 2010, when Rogozin published his memoirs, it was not yet fashionable to admit to being a Chekist. Instead, the politician wrote how as a young man he always yearned to become a spy, only to go into great detail how and why he was not approved for intelligence work during his service at the KMO. In order to 'prove' his sincerity, he downplayed his promotion to the RAU-Corporation by calling Podberezkin a 'conman' and saying that the organization was 'involved in everything: opening private schools and beauty salons, reselling of something to someone, even monitoring UFOs'. While flagging up the institute's top Cheka credentials, he himself 'really' only became part of the RAU off-shoot because he had 'no other offers' and they 'paid quite well':

> After the KMO, I went to work at an even stranger institute named the 'Russian-American University' (RAU), which was created and led by someone named Alexey Podberezkin. I met this active con-artist (who had also once worked at the KMO) during an official trip. He invited me several times to come work at RAU, and since I had no other offers, I agreed. They paid quite well those days. The 'Russian-American University' had absolutely nothing to do with America, except for the fact that its leadership consisted of quite a few scholars and veterans of the Intelligence Services who had concentrated their business activity on 'Enemy No 1'. The University was involved in everything: opening private schools and beauty salons, reselling of something to someone, even monitoring UFOs.

KGB General Alexey Sterligov also served at the RAU-Corporation. He was an old-school Chekist. Born in 1943 in a small village in the Tula Region of Russia, he graduated in 1966 from the Moscow Automobile and Road University and was sent to the KGB Higher School after being recruited through Komsomol channels. In 1967, he became an officer at the Moscow Regional KGB Department where he served in counterintelligence (the 2nd Department: later the 2nd Service) and as Party Secretary, which boosted his career.

Vitaly Fedorchuk's downfall in December 1982 proved Sterligov's good fortune. Fedorchuk, having been dismissed as KGB Chair and appointed as the Minister of Internal Affairs in December of 1982, petitioned the Party CC to send a group of experienced Chekists to the Ministry of Internal Affairs to 'bolster' its staff capabilities. As a result, 150 State Security officers from the Moscow KGB swarmed to leadership positions at the Ministry of Internal Affairs. Sterligov was among them. In 1983, after Andropov's death, he became a Colonel and Head of the Department to Combat Embezzlement of Socialist Property for Moscow. Sterligov was later transferred as an ARO to the USSR Council of Ministers and promoted to Major General. From July to October 1990, he served as the Affairs Manager for the Council of Ministers of the RSFSR. Then out of the blue, just like his soon-to-be boss Podberezkin, KGB General Sterligov left the Communist Party in 1990. If leaving the Party was dangerous for Podberezkin, it was tantamount to treason for a KGB General, with premature death beckoning. But, for some reason, faithful Stalinist Sterligov did not suffer any consequences for leaving the Party as he joined the well-paid ranks of 'spy-nest' RAU.

Apart from Rogozin and Podberezkin, Bobkov allowed many other agents to prove their usefulness as covert Chekist politicians in democratic Russian Federation. They had all been the Firm's agents embedded in various Soviet agencies and institutions overseen by the 5th Directorate (renamed Directorate Z 'Defense of the Constitutional Order') in August 1989. Many of them made it quite far.

Yevgeny Primakov, who was Yeltsin's last Prime Minister and one of the alternatives to Putin as successor in 1999, was an agent launched by Pitovranov and closely connected to Ivanov and Bobkov as well. As a young Arabic linguist, Primakov had been hired by the Main Office for Radio Broadcasts to Foreign Countries in 1956. As if by magic, the 26 year old was appointed to lead its Arabic Edition, with no fewer than 70 specialists reporting to him. On Ivanov's instructions, then the PGU's First Deputy Director, Primakov maintained regular contact with Kurdish rebel leader Mustafa Barzani during official trips to the Middle East as a correspondent for *Pravda*. And this was far from the only mission Primakov carried out for the PGU. In 1970, Primakov was appointed Deputy Director of IMEMO, another 'spy-nest' of the Intelligence Services.

One of the Firm's first forward moves of a Lubyanka agent was Oleg Shenin. In August 1991, he would be one of the Politburo members who took part in the failed coup against Soviet leader Gorbachev, a putsch they called 'The State Committee on the State of Emergency'. Shenin was born in 1937 and, after finishing his education in construction at a Soviet technical school, he worked on the construction of a top-secret underground settlement called Krasnoyarsk-26 (its postcode). Renamed as Zheleznogorsk during the Yeltsin years, it was located 64 kilometers north of Krasnoyarsk on the bank of the Yenisei River. In Soviet times, any information about it was 'classified' because part of the construction was a mining and chemical plant (in 2023, owned by Rosatom) that produced weapons-grade plutonium—the key component for manufacturing the USSR's nuclear weapons. Tens of thousands of Soviet GULAG prisoners were involved in building the subterranean town with a tunnel length greater than the Moscow subway system.

Rising meteorically through the ranks, at the age of 27, Shenin became head of construction and built the local Achinskaluminstroy aluminum plant: from 1967-1974, he was one of its top managers. In 1974, Shenin moved into politics and was elected First Secretary of the Achinsk Municipal Party Committee, and he remained faithful to Communism for his entire life, even forming his own Communist party in the Russian Federation after the collapse of the USSR. In fact, this was not the only Krasnoyarsk connection to 21st-century Russia. Sergey Shoygu, Russia's minister of defense since 2012, and one of Putin's inner circle, began his professional career at Shenin's factory. Shoygu's father was a friend of Shenin's and Shenin helped Shoygu to launch his national career.

Pitovranov and Shenin first met in Afghanistan. In 1980, Shenin, then a relatively young Party *apparatchik*, was dispatched to Afghanistan as a zonal advisor in the Afghan provinces of Nangarhar, Laghman, and Kunar. That is where KGB General Ivanov and bureaucrat Oleg Shenin—two committed Stalinists—found the perfect allies in each other. Ivanov introduced Shenin to Pitovranov, who often traveled to Afghanistan during the first years of the Afghan occupation, and so Shenin became connected to the covert Chekists' Firm. Far removed from any particular insight into the Kremlin politics behind the invasion, he wholeheartedly supported the war. Many years later, in 2001, he would say 'Back then [in 1979] we already felt the danger of spreading Islamic fundamentalism and deployed troops at the request of the lawful government of Afghanistan. Frankly, I never considered that to be a mistake. On the contrary, the mistake was the ill-conceived military withdrawal.'[237]

Shenin became an important pawn of the Firm in its financial dealings. Pitovranov and Ivanov needed their own man at the top echelon of the Party in 1990, and Shenin fit the bill. Traditionally, Foreign Intelligence (the KGB's PGU department) had been the organization that implemented undercover operations by the Party to finance foreign Communist parties and create enterprises and confidential overseas financial institutions.

Ivanov (by now First Deputy Head of the PGU) needed the rules changed. And so, in 1990, at the XXVIII Congress of the USSR Communist Party, Shenin, by then the Party's First Secretary of the Krasnoyarsk Region, was elevated to Secretary of the Party CC and made a Politburo Member. In his inaugural speech to the CC on

August 29, Shenin said: 'The situation will become more complicated. We need to prepare ourselves and the Party Committees for the State of Emergency'.[238] Almost immediately after his election to the Politburo, on August 23, 1990, Shenin prepared a detailed, technical memorandum 'Regarding Urgent Measures to Organize the Commercial and Foreign Economic Activities of the Party' for the Politburo's review. The hand of his handlers, Ivanov and Pitovranov, who understood the finer points of this complicated area, was easy to recognize.

The Money Trail

As the USSR stumbled towards the last years of its life, it became self-evident to the Party and KGB leadership that their regime was facing a real internal threat of collapse. Panic gripped the Party. In order to hedge against chaos, the Kremlin began to urgently develop a program to transfer money to accounts where funds were held for when disaster struck. To do so, they needed their own banks, numerous corporate organizations and joint enterprises specializing in money laundering.

The authors of one study estimate that the Party created some 1,500 companies, extracting $5 billion as well as plundering the USSR's gold reserves, leaving no more than 289 tons—less than what Nazi Germany had left after World War II—while loading the country with $144 billion of debt:[239]

> In a short period of time, the Communist Party managed to create roughly 1,500 joint enterprises and other entities, with total combined capital of about 14 billion rubles and 5 billion dollars. Shadow Party economics gained momentum before the collapse of the Soviet Union and provide anonymous shares and funds in the Western companies and banks to secret owners. Inside the country, the Communist Party of the Soviet Union and the Russian Communist Party became co-founders or owners of the controlling stakes in a number of banks…. By the time of the USSR's collapse, they had ruined the country's budget, amassed $144 billion in debt, and smuggled gold out of the country, leaving the democrats a pitiful inheritance of 289 tons.'[240]

While the corpse of the USSR was still breathing, the *nomenklatura* began to eviscerate what it could get away with under Gorbachev's loosening grip on the Soviet enforcement agencies.

It was at this moment of feeding frenzy that the Firm's long preparation and deep experience from Afghanistan and Angola with running accounts through offshore tax havens determined its future dominance. Unlike the Party, Pitovranov's Firm had an established (if informal) command structure in place through ARO, and controlled the USSR's and Party's key administrative levers through which it could embezzle large chunks of assets from the moribund Soviet Union while pretending that they were acting for the good of the State rather than their own salvation.

Their core platform was the International Department of the Party Central

Committee (CC). It was the successor of the Executive Committee of the Comintern which Stalin dissolved in 1943 after accusations by his anti-Hitler allies Roosevelt and Churchill that Comintern had been engaged in subversive activities against the USSR's new allies. The International Department's function was the same. It was the Party's center for international policymaking and strategy regarding financial and material assistance to foreign Communist parties and other ideologically similar political movements and groups in foreign countries. Besides direct financial assistance, provided via the Soviet KGB *rezidentura* (administered through the PGU, which Ivanov was to lead in 1980s), so-called 'friendly firms' were also formed abroad. These firms received special treatment and incentives in transactions with the Soviet Union, allowing them to flourish through covert subsidies—effectively money-laundering for political purposes—accumulate extra profits that were then used to secretly finance pro-Soviet parties, movements and organizations.

Andrey Zhukov was one of the first PGU officers who was sent to work on the Party CC by Deputy KGB Chair Bobkov as an Active Reserve Officer. Zhukov was born in Leningrad in 1948. In 1971, he graduated from the Physics Department at Moscow State University. Upon graduating, the 23-year-old was recruited by the PGU. In 1987, he was already in charge of his own PGU Department, and Bobkov transferred him from there to the International Department of the CC of the Party as an Active Reserve officer—a promotion—where he served there undercover as a consultant.

At the PGU, the Firm controlled the person who monitored AROs like Zukhov. Thus, academic economist and Chekist Alexander Lebedev got entangled with the interests of Pitovranov's 'Firm'. Alexander Lebedev was born in 1959 into a family of Moscow scholars. His father Evgeny was a professor at Bauman Moscow State Technical University; his mother Maria was an English teacher at the Moscow State Institute of International Relations (MSIIR). From 1977-1982, Lebedev studied Economics at MSIIR, focusing on the global monetary and financial system. Two years after receiving his degree, in 1984, the 25-year-old was recruited by the PGU, like the young Zhukov.

Lebedev was officially in charge of 'preventing' the withdrawal of capital from the USSR. In reality, as PGU officer, he registered Soviet entities in London for the PGU. The profits of these entities ended up offshore in the Cayman Islands, where Ivanov, PGU's First Deputy, monitored and controlled the KGB's 'sovereign' stash of money on behalf of Pitovranov's Firm. In post-Soviet times, his KGB connections did not hold him back. He was to become one of Russia's oligarchs. He owned Russia's largest bank before moving to Britain and buying two main newspapers, the *Evening Standard* (London's newspaper) in 2009 and the *Independent* in 2010. In 2017 a former Chancellor of the Exchequer (the UK's treasury) would be appointed editor of the *Evening Standard* and Lebedev's son, Evgeny, would be elevated to the House of Lords in 2020 by Boris Johnson, then Prime Minister and a friend from the time the latter was London's Mayor and received press support.

Another PGU officer who was promoted to the Active Reserve and served under-cover in various places while remaining a member of the Pitovranov-Bobkov Firm, was Colonel Leonid Veselovsky. Pitovranov became close to the PGU Colonel in Portugal during frequent business trips there. Veselovsky was subsidizing the Portuguese Communist Party on behalf of PGU and Pitovranov was overseeing the Firm's illegal arms trade in civil-war-torn Angola—a former Portuguese colony. He, Ivanov and Bobkov gradually integrated Veselovsky into their Firm-related activities.

In November 1990, Veselovsky was recalled from overseas and deployed to the Management Department of the CC as an Active Reserve Officer. Just like his PGU colleague Zhukov, Veselovsky was tasked with facilitating the transfer of enormous sums of money controlled by the Party to organizations controlled by the KGB. The goal of this operation was to create a financial foundation for establishing a State Security-controlled regime in the country and to replace the politically bankrupt system established by the Communist Party.

It was Veselovsky who developed a comprehensive system for getting the Party's money out of the USSR further to the August 23, 1990, Politburo memorandum, 'Regarding Urgent Measures to Organize the Commercial and Foreign Economic Activities of the Party'—the memo introduced by the Firm's agent, Oleg Shenin who was the Politburo's new member from 14 July 1990. Veselovsky gave detailed evidence to the investigation of the August *putsch* a year later of which Shenin had been part. In September-October 1991, he said it was his 'commercial facility' that was the reason for his recall from Portugal to work in the CC's new department that organized the Party's 'Economic Interests'—that is the department that squirreled Party money away in tax havens on orders coming from the CC top while they were still in charge of the Soviet treasury:

In November 1990, by the request of the leaders of the Central Committee of the Communist Party [Ivashko and Kruchina] and by the decision of the KGB leadership [Vladimir Kryuchkov, KGB Chair and *putsch* co-conspirator of Shenin's], I was transferred from the PGU to the Management Department of the CC of the CPSU. By the decision of the Secretariat of the CC of the CPSU, I was appointed Deputy Head of the Sector for Coordination of the Economic Activity of Commercial Facilities. The reason for my transfer to the CC was an urgent need in the Management Department to establish a division capable of coordinating the economic activities of the commercial facility of the Party in the changed environment. I was chosen because of my academic background as an international economist, my work experience overseas; I was also known to most leadership on the CC for my prior work.

... I assume that not the least important consideration in settling on my candidacy was the fact that, being on a long overseas assignment for the Agency in a country with a difficult situation [Portugal], I was tasked with connecting with the [local] Communist Party [of Portugal], which at the time was semi-legal.... I had to brief Bobkov periodically regarding my activities in the Department of Management of the Central Committee of the Communist Party....

Having read the memorandum 'Regarding the Main Principles for Organizing Economic Activities in the Interests of the Communist Party,' I confirm that I wrote it before my appointment as Deputy Head of the Department of Management of the CC of the CPSU. Kruchina, who was then the Head of the Department, requested that I investigate the subject, which I did to the best of my ability.

In 1993, Veselovsky's central memo—'Regarding the Main Principles for Organizing Economic Activities in the Interests of the Communist Party.'—which he wrote for his Party bosses, was published in full in *Zhurnalist* (journalist) magazine. It was a fraud's charter and described in bureaucratic detail how the Communist Party's money was to be transferred and laundered abroad in secret by selecting 'trustworthy individuals' and the 'creation of a separate category of unofficial Party members':

Monetary resources reflected in financial documents may only be openly invested in public, social, or charitable organizations, which will complicate their withdrawal in the future. Funds that come in as income to the Party accounts and reflected in financial documents must be used to acquire anonymous shares, the funds of individual companies, enterprises, and banks, which would both ensure stable income regardless of the Party's position in the future and also enable different future stock exchange investments with the goal to reduce visibility of the Party's participation while retaining control.... Implementation of these measures requires an urgent selection of suitable trustworthy individuals who can be entrusted with implementing separate components of the plan. The creation of a separate category of unofficial Party members who will ensure its viability in any conditions during the emergency period has not been ruled out.[241]

Who belonged to this 'separate category' is not difficult to fathom. Veselovsky directed millions of dollars from Soviet accounts to overseas bank accounts specifically designated and controlled by the Firm. Veselovsky himself was evidently also one of these 'trustworthy individuals'. Two weeks before the 19 August *coup-d'état*, he resigned from his plum job at the Management Department of the CC and went to Switzerland. He would only return to Russia after the *putsch*. He was not the only one who was mysteriously absent before the coup.

At the receiving end of the money transfers, Pitovranov Firm's managed the 'trustworthy' foreigners who acted as trustees abroad. These were the usual suspects, such as 5th Directorate (Angola) agents Kalmanovich and Gaydamak.

There were many other connections. As part of his work as a Soviet official. Leonid Veselovsky was a consultant of a Swiss company called Seabeco. It was founded by Boris Birshtein, who was born on November 11, 1947, in Vilnius,

Lithuania. In 1972, he became the director of a textile factory in his hometown, and, like Kalmanovich, he wanted to emigrate to Israel. However, before being allowed to emigrate—something coveted by many Soviet Jews—he worked for several years as a 5th Department KGB agent in the Lithuanian Socialist Republic. Birshtein's assignments included the usual: identifying Jewish citizens who were spreading 'Zionist propaganda', or who desired to emigrate to Israel, or who were organizing '*ulpans*' (groups) to learn the Hebrew, Israel's national tongue. The Directorate's 8th Department organized and coordinated training and deployment of KGB agents connected with emigration to Israel. Birshtein did well and his handlers at the Lithuanian 8th Department allowed him to emigrate in 1977.

Like Kalmanovich and Gaydamak, Birshtein had to continue his work as a KGB agent while in Israel as it was not the terminus of an agent's KGB obligations. In 1982 Birshtein emigrated to Canada from Israel via Switzerland and became a Canadian citizen—as Gaydamak had become a French citizen. On September 6, 1982, two months before Andropov became the Soviet Union's General Secretary, Birshtein registered a company, Seabeco, in Zurich, Switzerland—using the first letters of his children's names: 'Simona' and 'Alex', his last name (Bershtein, with an 'e') and the word 'company'. Thereafter, Birshtein became one of the most influential businessmen in *perestroika* Russia and, by extension, in the world.

As the company conducted important *perestroika* business, the Head of Birshtein's firm enjoyed the personal protection from Soviet interference from Nikolay Kruchina, Manager of the Affairs of the CC and KGB Chair Kryuchkov, and Bobkov, Kryuchkov's Deputy. In 1990, Seabeco became one of the companies the Management Department of the CC involved in its overseas transactions. Veselovsky found a way of using Seabeco for most of the financial operations he was tasked to execute. Goods with a value anywhere from $50 million to $150 million per year were exported from the USSR at prices 50-60% below market prices. Part of the proceeds from their sale went to bank accounts controlled by the CC and by the KGB.

It seems safe to assume that Veselovsky was not the only PGU officer engaged in channeling Party money to accounts controlled by the Firm. Indeed, within the USSR, the same was happening.

In early 1991, Vladimir Yakunin returned to his native Leningrad from an official assignment in the US. Yakunin was born in 1948 and graduated from the Leningrad Mechanical Institute with a specialization in Aircraft Production in 1972. Upon graduation, he enrolled in 'School No 101', the innocuous name of a training school for Soviet Intelligence personnel to avoid attracting attention. After Andropov's death, the KGB's School No 101 became known as the Andropov Red Banner Institute. The institute has since reverted to a more unassuming name: The Foreign Intelligence Academy.

Upon completing his two-year training, Yakunin was sent to the 1st Department of the Regional KGB Directorate for the Leningrad Region. He worked as an ARO as a Senior Engineer at the State Committee of the Council of Ministers of the USSR in the Foreign Economic Relations Department; then as a Department Head at Moscow Institute of Physics and Technology in the Academy of Sciences of the USSR. Yakunin's service during that period related to the interests of PGU Department T (scientific and technical intelligence). In 1985, Yakunin joined the staff of Central Soviet Intelligence. Under a diplomatic passport, he was sent on a foreign assignment to the USA, where he was appointed a Secretary of the Permanent Representative of the USSR to the UN.

In April 1991, Yakunin formed an entity to attract foreign investment, called the International Center for Business Cooperation, with a group of his friends and associates. He was also appointed to the Board of Directors of Rossiya Bank owned by the brothers Yuri and Boris Kovalchuk. This bank was partially founded with seed money from the Communist Party Committee for the Leningrad Region. In 1991, it moved funds to various organizations not officially affiliated with the Party. Thus 50 million rubles, a quite substantial amount, was moved to this bank.

Another organization set up for Party money-laundering was the *Molodyozhny Kommerchesky Bank* (youth commercial bank), later renamed Finist Bank. Alexander Shcherbakov, Chair of the Board of Governors of Finist Bank from 1989 to 1993, described in 2010 how his bank refused point blank to return Party money placed in business accounts in the autumn of 1991, even when criminal investigators asked for it:

> In the Fall of 1991, investigators from a special unit at General Prosecutor's Office came to us looking for 'Party money.' We did in fact have a deposit from the Communist Party's Management Department of the Central Committee. We replied to our guests: 'Provide us a court order specifying its legal rights' successor, and we will immediately comply....' In the end, several banks did send the money to specified accounts, but we and several other banks would not do that... So, we continued to hold 275 million of those Soviet rubles in a deposit account. And that's where it all remained; a legal rights' successor has not been found to this day.

In fact, the funds held at Finist Bank explain where Podberezkin's and Rogozin's RAU organization got its mafia money from. The main founder of the RAU was Finist Bank, which had previously received the Party money that was never returned but was spent on the RAU and RAU-Corporation. The rapid 'rise' and success of the RAU and RAU-Corporation was simple.

Long-standing collaborator of the Pitovranov Firm, the PGU Active Reserve Andrey Zhukov, was also a founder of the RAU. Like Rogozin, he later became the Vice President of RAU-Corporation. This RAU alumnus, too, had a career as a Russian Federation politician. He was a Duma deputy and a member of its International Affairs Committee. But it was his deep involvement in smuggling money and diamonds that he became most famous for. On April 7, 2006, the

Kommersant newspaper reported the following in the article 'Diamonds 11 Year Sentence':

Moscow City Court has issued a verdict in a sensational case concerning smuggling diamonds worth $25 million to Israel, in which Andrey Zhukov, ex-consultant to the International Department of the CC and current State Duma Deputy from the 'Rodina' Faction, was a suspect. His closest partners in the diamond business, [Zhukov's] CEO Deputies at the Aurum Plus enterprise, Arkady Mirzayev and Tatiana Kuzmina, were sentenced to 11 years in prison. From the court verdict it followed that Mirzayev and Kuzmina were members of an Israeli-Russian criminal organization through which they smuggled to Israel 33,478 carats of diamonds valued at $25 million, and were also involved in the illegal precious gems trading valued at $35 million, as well as the money laundering involving 49 million rubles. During the trial, the organizers of the criminal enterprise were not identified, however... according to the case file, one of them, Andrey Zhukov, was a former foreign intelligence officer who later became a State Duma deputy and a member of its Committee on International Affairs.

Zhukov's business partner in the diamond business was Vladimir Davidson. Born in Poland in 1939, he emigrated to Israel and changed his name to Ben David Zeyev. In Israel, he also had Kalmanovich as one of his business associates.

On May 24, 1989, the Soviet-American joint venture *Most* (bridge) was registered. The founder of the joint enterprise on the Soviet side was a company called Infax, headed by Vladimir Gusinsky. He was a 5th Directorate agent who had tried to recruit US billionaire Ted Turner in 1986.

Gusinsky was born in Moscow on October 6, 1952. After finishing school, he studied at the Gubkin Moscow Institute of Oil and Gas for several years but was expelled because of the poor grades. He served in the Soviet Army from 1973-1975. After demobilization, Gusinsky enrolled at the State Institute of Theater Arts (GITIS), from which he graduated in 1980. However, he did not manage to find employment in Moscow after graduation and had to work elsewhere ('on the periphery'). But Gusinsky really wanted to return to Moscow. Then one of his professors at GITIS advised him to seek help from a 'colleague', the KGB officer Vladimir Tsibizov who was a fellow GITIS graduate.

Gusinsky met Tsibizov through a group of mutual acquaintances and quickly found a common language with him: Tsibizov offered his help and Gusinsky agreed. Thus, a 5th Directorate agent under the codename 'Denis' was recruited in the early 1980s, handled by the 2nd Section of the 1st Department. Quick and creative, 'Denis' was first deployed by the 5th Directorate to organize the opening ceremony for the XII World Festival of Youth and Students sports festival in Moscow in 1985. Then Gusinsky was 'thrown' at organizing the opening ceremony of the Goodwill Games in Moscow in July 1986, during which Gusinsky, at the direction of his Chekist officers, managed to establish close connection with the organizer of the American side of the Games, the billionaire Ted Turner.

Turner had been rapidly developing his business in the US since the 1970s, and by the mid-1980s, he was already the owner of a whole range of leading American TV channels and sports teams. He was the one who suggested the idea of holding international sports competitions that were supposed to be an alternative to the Olympic Games planned for Moscow and boycotted many countries after the Soviet invasion of Afghanistan.

The Soviet Intelligence already had decided on a detailed monitoring of Turner at the initial preparations stage for the Goodwill Games in Moscow. Securing him as an agent was too tempting of an idea to pass up. Recruiting Turner would mean new opportunities for Soviet propaganda and disinformation, which explains Turner being surrounded closely by Intelligence officers and KGB agents during his visit to Moscow in 1986. Among the agents sent to monitor Turner was 'Denis'—aka Gusinsky.

Gusinsky was the main organizer of the cultural program for foreign participants in the Moscow Games. One day, a river cruise was arranged for authorized foreign and Soviet journalists at the games. Turner was the guest of honor. Among the undercover KGB officers accompanying Turner on the cruise was Major Alexander Mikhailov, a senior officer in the 5th Department of the Moscow and Moscow Region, who later became a General and the Director of the Center for Public Relations (CPR) of the FSB.

During the pleasant cruise, extravagantly irrigated with various foreign beverages and overladen with traditional Russian delicacies, 'Denis' managed to win over the American guest. While the actual recruitment of Turner as KGB agent never materialized, Gusinsky would use this important connection when he started to build his *Most* empire.

Infax was registered by Gusinsky back in 1988 with help from the Ministry of Foreign Economic Relations of the USSR, with which Pitovranov had worked closely since 1966 as the leader of the Chamber of Industry and Commerce. It was Pitovranov who 'backed' the Gusinsky organization on behalf of the KGB at the time. The Most group's financial branch, Most-Bank, also headed by Gusinsky, was set up in September 1989—it soon handled the Moscow's finances.

Prominent law firm Arnold and Porter served as the American partners of the *Most* joint venture. Headquartered in the US capital, Washington D.C., the firm was founded soon after World War II by three experienced attorneys: Arnold, Fortas, and Porter. Thurman Arnold had been a law professor at Yale Law School, Assistant to the US Attorney General, and a judge on the US Court of Appeals, before founding the firm. The name of his partner, Abe Fortas, was removed from the firm's moniker after he was appointed to the US Supreme Court. The remaining founder of the firm, Paul Porter, had held leading positions with various prominent US institutions, including having been a Chair of the Federal Communications Commission, in his prior professional life. Arnold and Porter had offices in Brussels, London, New York, San Francisco, Los Angeles, Silicon Valley, and in Washington, D.C. Eight hundred experienced lawyers worked there.

One can only wonder how the newly formed Infax managed to become a business partner of such an internationally prominent and respected American law firm, especially since any legal entity in the USSR in those years engaging in overseas economic relations had to secure a license from the Ministry of Foreign Economic Relations. But the hastily formed Infax had no issues at all with getting a license through Pitovranov's connections at the Ministry. Finding a foreign partner for Infax proved more challenging. But Ivanov, now former First Deputy of PGU, helped Gusinsky. He had twice before led the Soviet Foreign Intelligence *rezidentura* in the US. His official cover at the time was Advisor to the Permanent Representative of the USSR at the United Nations, and member of the UN Commission on Human Rights and the Sub-Commission on Prevention of Discrimination and Protection of Minorities. While working in the US, General Ivanov had established a broad web of connections in the American establishment, and he had no trouble identifying a potential business partner for Infax.

Gusinsky was not the only KGB agent through whom entities and banks were established. Stolichny Bank was founded by Alexander Smolensky, a 5th Directorate agent. Smolensky had been an agent since the time when he had worked at the Union of Sports Supply printing office of the State Committee for Soviet Sports. He was recruited under the pseudonym 'Aunt Shura' and was used mostly to monitor foreign Zionist centers.

Boris Fedorov was the Chair of the Board for National Credit Bank, a 5th Directorate agent and a personal friend of Shamil Tarpischev, a close ally of the Minister for Sports in Yeltsin's cabinet and Yeltsin's private tennis coach. Tarpischev was recruited in 1980 (the year of the Olympics), and was used for counterintelligence support of the international sports exchange channel.

Moscow, the Firm's first Decisive Victory
Moscow was the primary geographic stronghold for Pitovranov-Bobkov's group. The 5th Directorate had everything 'under control' through its expansive network of agents. It was one of them, Gavriil Popov, who proved to be one of the most important and useful of Moscow agents. He was born in Moscow in 1936. In 1959, he graduated from the Economics Department at Moscow State University (MSU), and in 1963 he completed his graduate studies there. He became an Associate Professor at the MSU Economics Department and Faculty Dean.

Given his career success, he decided to build a dacha in Moscow suburbs. A problem arose when the project exceeded the financial means of the Popovs, but they did not want to economize. The inventive Gavriil found a solution by making money from paid consultations to graduate students and other students seeking academic credentials. Despite looking legitimate, the 'consultations' were in fact bribery—cash for degrees.

The MSU Economics Department was monitored by Colonel Yuri Balev (who also handled Glazunov). Balev started methodically collecting compromising evidence on its head Gavriil Popov in a 'case file'. Everything was ready for handing these materials over to Soviet prosecutors to convict Popov for academic bribery. Exploiting Popov's self-evident greed, Bobkov threatened the dacha builder with exposure and made him an offer he couldn't refuse: recruitment as an agent, which would free him from the threat of imprisonment. Recruiting the Dean of one of the most prestigious departments at MSU as an agent was a considerable triumph. Putting Popov in jail would be far less useful as his file would then transfer to a different ministry.

Upon finding himself in an impossible but not insoluble situation, Popov agreed to become an agent, but asked that Balev be replaced with a different officer who was not personally after him. Bobkov agreed. He cared more about having agent Popov as a reliable pair of hands than about an ordinary officer, of which the 5th Directorate had many hundreds. As a reward for his success, Balev was transferred to the 2nd Section of the 1st Department of the 5th Directorate, where he was assigned to monitor cellist Mstislav Rostropovich, who had been stripped of Soviet citizenship for supporting the dissident writer Aleksandr Solzhenitsyn.

The career of Gavriil Popov only changed for the better after his recruitment. In 1988-1991, he was the Editor-in-Chief of the magazine called *Voprosy Economiki* (economic issues). In March 1989, he was elected as a Deputy to the Supreme Soviet of the USSR. A year later, in March 1990, Popov became a Deputy on the Moscow City Council from the Democratic Russia Party. On April 20, 1990, he became the Head of Moscow City Council, and in June 1991, he was elected as mayor of Moscow, effectively handing the keys to the city over to Pitovranov and Bobkov. It was the Firm's first political conquest and bridgehead to what it had mapped out.

Part Two:

The Cheka's Russian World

1: State Committee on the State of Emergency (August, 1991)

The 1991 *coup d'état* attempt, also known as 'the August Coup' or 'August Putsch', was far from spontaneous, as those who led the failed coup tried to portray it afterwards. Everything was planned in advance and in advance. Nor was it the first plot to take place inside the Soviet leadership circle. Soviet history from October 1917 to December 1953 was characterized by conspiracies, with numerous coups, removals, poisonings, dismissals, arrests, and murders. The August Putsch was business as usual: another violent attempt at change in State leadership with the Cheka as the 'enforcer' and the Army on full alert just in case.

On October 1, 1988, Chebrikov, who had been appointed KGB Chair in 1982 as placeholder after Fedorchuk's short reign, was removed and replaced with Andropov's former second-in-command Vladimir Kryuchkov—a career Chekist, the KGB's Deputy Chair, as well as a close friend. Despite cracks appearing in the USSR (The Lithuanian Soviet declared independence a month later), the Lubyanka, with its secret funds abroad, was in good shape—or, at any rate, Pitovranov's Firm was, as their small circle controlled them and knew where and what and how to release funds in secret—to keep functioning without interruption in a crisis. The moment seemed close where the KGB could finally implement the plan previously devised by Andropov.

There was another good reason. Originally, the Party's insertion of members in any existing body of influence in the Soviet Union ensured that it had a stranglehold over the State and had dominion over the population. When challenged by the Lubyanka, the Kremlin had brutally fought off their assault—from Dzerzhinsky's to Beria's. The truce, however, that was expressed in the KGB's 1955 Active Reserve (ARO) protocol had since layered a duplicate control system over the USSR that was undercover and staffed by the Lubyanka's most capable and most reliable officers. While the Lubyanka continued to defer to the Kremlin, in truth, in 1988, the KGB held all the cards. Party control was ready to be severed and separated from the State with seamless transfer of central control over the USSR to the Lubyanka's top behind the scenes—if executed at the right time. Even the new ideas to revitalize the USSR, *glasnost* and *perestroika* (and, in the background, 'patriotism'), had been generated and were controlled by the Lubyanka.

The KGB candidate lined up as the next Soviet leader in a peaceful transition (much like Brezhnev had sidelined Khrushchev in a Politburo coup) was Oleg

Shenin. In 2001, the magazine *Duel* summarized the original KGB plan with Shenin as the next leader in 'two or three more years'—even 'Gorbachev listened to him':

Oleg Shenin was Secretary of the CC of the CPSU and potentially the most interesting person in the Party's final years. A man of strong mind and willpower, he oversaw Party-related activities in the Army and in the KGB under [Mikhail] Gorbachev. From 1990 to 1991, the Chair of the KGB of the USSR V[ladimir] Kryuchkov and Minister of Defense D[mitry] Yazov were *de facto* supervised by him. He oversaw and directed secret financial and foreign economic activities for the Party and forged its strategic course in new historical conditions. Gorbachev listened to him. N[ikolai] Kruchina acted on his orders. He authored a memo about issues related to the Communist Party property, which N. Kruchina handed to M. Gorbachev [in early December 1989]. He needed just two or three more years to become the Party leader, and then the course of history would have been different. Without publicly participating in the August Putsch, Shenin was its behind-the-scenes ideologist and chief.[242]

Already in April, 1991, Shenin repeated the phrase 'State of Emergency' that he had first used officially on August 29, 1990, in his maiden speech as Secretary of the Party CC. In April, he also blamed 'Zionist centers within the Soviet Union' for being behind Boris Yeltsin in an address at the Central Office of the KGB:

If one considers how the Zionist centers within the Soviet Union and abroad strongly support certain categories and certain political forces, if that was possible to show and make public, then many people would start to understand who Boris Yeltsin and those with him really are…. Without implementing a state of emergency, I do not see a way forward; I do not see opportunities for either political or economic stabilization.

In all manner of ways, the Intelligence Services started provoking the Party. In May, 1991, the newspaper *Sovetskaya Rossiya* (Soviet Russia) published 'The Ruins Architect', which sharply criticized *perestroika* and its initiators Gorbachev and Politburo member Alexander Yakovlev (who was considered an undercover CIA agent by the KGB leadership). The article was signed by a Gennady Zyuganov, a then little-known *apparatchik* and leader of the Party in the Russian Soviet. In post-Soviet times, he gained considerably more fame as Shenin's successor as Duma leader of the Union of Communist Parties from 2001. In reality, the article was not written by Zyuganov but authored by personnel from the KGB's Analytics Department on Bobkov's orders.

There were other writers who, as Cheka agents, started provoking the Party to pave the way for Shenin, echoing his warning of a 'State of Emergency'. They were notably Alexander Prokhanov and Alexander Dugin, Communist reactionaries controlled by the Lubyanka. In Putin's Russia, they became fierce nationalists in the 'Slavophile' movement first created, infiltrated, and controlled by Bobkov's 5th Directorate officers around Ilya Glazunov and others. Alexander Dugin would gain world fame when his daughter Darya was assassinated by a car bomb in a Moscow suburb. Darya was a writer for a Russian propaganda website on Ukraine owned by Putin's friend Yevgeny Prigozhin, the founder of the Wagner Group of Russian mercenaries. But Dugin was meant to be in the same car and only escaped from a premature death because he changed his mind at the last moment.

Alexander Prokhanov, a journalist, newspaper editor and later novelist, was born in 1938 in Tbilisi, Georgia. In 1968, he started working at the *Literaturnaya Gazeta* (LG), the newspaper that began sending foreign correspondents around the world as a result of a 'quick phone call' to KGB Chair Andropov and Foreign Minister Gromyko by its editor. At the Kremlin, the newspaper came under direct control of the Agitation and Propaganda Department of the Party CC at the Kremlin, as well as officers of the Lubyanka. When hiring new editorial staff, candidates had to be approved first by the KGB officer handling the LG and then confirmed by the Party's CC. For many years Galina Sukhareva, who had served during World War II in SMERSH, was the KGB's agent at the paper. After her initial review, applications were sent to the 5th Directorate (2nd Section of the 1st Department) where candidates were checked against the operational registries of the KGB and the MVD of the USSR and the Literary part of 'File No 1110', which contained intelligence materials on the members of the Union of Soviet Writers and of the LG. If no compromising material was found for a given candidate, they received verbal approval; otherwise, the candidate was rejected without explanation.

At his own request, a year after joining LG, Prokhanov was sent to work as a correspondent in the Far East. At the time, the Eastern borders of the USSR were on high alert. Anti-Soviet sentiments were getting stronger, agitated by China's territorial claims against the USSR. Embedded with Soviet border troops, Prokhanov was one of the first to report on the heavy fighting between the border troops and Chinese forces on Damansky Island and the daily combat at border outposts. These USSR border troops were a branch of the KGB, with their main office located at 1 Dzerzhinsky Square (on Lubyanka Street). Special permission was required from Border Patrol to visit Soviet border regions. This permission system was strictly enforced. Even those wishing to visit relatives living in border areas had to get the necessary permits. Civilians visiting outposts were subjected to an even more rigorous scrutiny and remained under constant surveillance by border troop Intelligence agents.

As it happened, counterintelligence in the Soviet Union's border troops was handled by the 3rd Chief Directorate of the KGB, which also controlled all the Soviet armed forces. For Prokhanov it was the beginning of a long and profitable close connection to the Cheka. Military counterintelligence (GRU) also liked Prokhanov, a young, pliable, ambitious, patriotic journalist, and he started working with them in close association, too.

It was no coincidence that his overseas trips as LG correspondent were to places with a 'limited presence' of Soviet armed forces—Afghanistan, Nicaragua, Mozambique, Angola, Kampuchea…. In all these countries, except Afghanistan, the Soviet Union acted in secret, hiding its participation in internal conflicts. Prokhanov's espionage opportunities as a journalist acting under direction of Soviet military counterintelligence were hard to overstate. As a journalist, he could gather valuable military and political information on the situation in the region while monitoring the Soviet and foreign military personnel he encountered.

During his trips to Afghanistan, among his other assignments for the GRU and the KGB, Prokhanov was involved in the release of Soviet military personnel, held prisoner by the Mujahideen. According to his later testimony, one of the hostages helped release at the time was the Deputy Commanding Airforce officer of the 40th Army, Alexander Rutskoy, Boris Yeltsin's future Vice President (1991-1993) and a thorn in Yeltsin's side.

During the Nagorno-Karabakh conflict in the South Caucasus at the end of the 1980s—the prologue to the collapse of the USSR—Prokhanov met 'as an agent' (his own words) with the leader of the Armenian separatists Robert Kocharyan, who later became the President of independent Armenia. During that same period, Prokhanov also got to know General Albert Makashov, the Soviet Commandant of Yerevan, its capital. In 1991, during the Presidential elections in Russia, Prokhanov was his confidant as Makashov ran against Yeltsin in the Russian Soviet on an anti-*perestroika* platform leavened with anti-Semitism as a marker of his 'patriotism'/Slavophilism (and lost).

Famous as a journalist by 1972, but still unknown as a novelist, Prokhanov started to gather honors as with any Cheka writer in the USSR and was accepted into the prestigious Union of Soviet Writers, the leadership of which was also kept on a short leash by the 5th Directorate. As Prokhanov's biographer Lev Danilkin put it, 'Prokhanov is, first and foremost, an ardent fighter for the Red Empire,' but 'he is a writer only insofar as he is a fighter for this idea'. By the 1980s, Prokhanov's journalism was essential propaganda for the Soviet army as it was humiliated in Afghanistan and fought more successfully in other hot spots around the globe.

In December of 1990, as the Lubyanka's designs on the Kremlin tightened, Prokhanov got a new role. He became the Editor-in-Chief of an Orthodox Communist newspaper of his 'own' creation called *Den'* (day). It was sharply critical of Gorbachev's *perestroika*. Rutskoy, then ostensibly still aligned with Yeltsin, who called Prokhanov his friend, took part in hiring editorial staff, even if the weekly's agenda was sharply opposed to Yeltsin and his own economic and social policies. It was also at 'his' weekly that Prokhanov began his association with the (then) youngish ultra-radical nationalist, anti-Semitic and pro-Communist journalist Alexander Dugin, who became one of the newspaper's main contributing writers and editors.

Dugin was born in 1962 in Moscow. Before Dugin became a public and political figure, he was a Doctor of Political Science, and even a professor at MSU. Yet his start in life had seemed inauspicious. In 1979, he enrolled in the Moscow Aviation Institute but was expelled in his second year. As a result, when defending his dissertation, he submitted to the Academic Council of the Russian State University a diploma from the distance-learning department of the Novocherkassk Engineering Reclamation Institute. At 18, Dugin also joined the 'Black Order of the SS,' which was founded and led by Yevgeny Golovin as its *Reichsfuhrer*. Golovin was one of the first Russian members of the 'New Right' and was considered a mentor by Dugin. In 1988, Dugin joined *Pamyat* (memory), Dmitry Vasiliev's National Patriotic Front controlled by the KGB. He was later expelled from the organization—officially, for having 'maintained and maintaining contact with representatives of emigrant dissident circles of occultist-satanic persuasion'.

Remarkably, Dugin nonetheless visited France a year later in 1989. To the generation of Russians that grew up after the Soviet Union disappeared from the political map of the world, the fact that he went to France would appear nothing out of the ordinary (though that changed after the 2022 Ukraine invasion). But in 1989, traveling abroad was still impossible without permission from Party authorities. It was a stringent procedure. The application process involved submission of a document from an organization sending the applicant on the trip with a description of the specific reasons for the journey. When traveling abroad further to a private invitation, Party authorities still had to give approval, and the KGB always had a say as to whether issuing a travel permit was allowed. Only after these hurdles were passed, a passport for overseas travel could be issued.

Given Dugin's background, the KGB would only have given him permission to travel to France if there was a good reason for them to let Dugin cross the border. Any contacts made in France would lead to highly unpleasant consequences under normal circumstances. But, since that did not happen, it was doubtless the Intelligence Services themselves who were primarily interested in Dugin making those contacts. This was especially the case, given that Dugin was part of the 'golden youth'. His father was Geliy Dugin (1935-1998), a Lieutenant General in the GRU. While it precluded Dugin from becoming an officer based at Lubyanka, it did not prevent him being one of their agents in the field serving under a KGB officer.

Many articles by Dugin a year later (1990-1992) suggest that he had access to KGB archives. In fact, Dugin may have been given extracts prepared by the KGB officers he worked with. Based on these KGB documents, Dugin wrote newspaper and magazine articles, books, and television broadcasts for *Tainy Veka* (secrets of the century) on Channel One. Only a loyal outsider—such as a KGB agent—would ever be granted access to classified archives and to the TV programs based on those materials.

Dugin became famous after the publication of his book *Foundations of Geopolitics: Russia's Geopolitical Future* (1997), with a preface by Lieutenant General Nikolai Klokotov, the Chair of the Strategy Department at the Academy of the General Staff.

'My first textbook on geopolitics, called *Foundations of Geopolitics*, I wrote secretly while working at the Academy of the General Staff. It was compiled from documents handed over to the country's leadership and various political figures', Dugin recalled. It is a telling comment. Documents of this type could only be accessed through the GRU, SVR, MFA or other official organizations, and were always labeled 'secret' or 'top secret' or, less frequently, 'for internal use only'. The circle of individuals with access to such information was highly restricted. More importantly, its external distribution was considered disclosure of state secrets and subject to harsh criminal liability. These documents could, of course, have been given to Dugin by his Intelligence handlers as they had assigned to Dugin the task of popularizing the ideas hatched among Chekist 'patriots'.

Prokhanov's newspaper *Den'*, where Dugin worked, was initially funded by the Union of Soviet Writers. But before being closed, it received regular financial assistance from the Ministry of Defense to stay open. Marshal Dmitry Yazov, the Minister of Defense, gave the magazine three Kamaz trucks during his tenure (1987-1991, until 10 days after the August coup). The trucks were sold, and the profits went to the paper's editorial office, which was located on military land owned by the Ministry of Defense in military building: 18 Frunze, Skaya Embankment, Building 6.

In 1991, everything was going according to the Lubyanka's plan for Shenin's succession of Gorbachev. Then, a Party challenger stole a march on the Lubyanka. On July 20, 1991, Boris Yeltsin, the President of the Russian Soviet abolished the Party's presence in organizations and enterprises located in the RSFSR. A Party politician, he had caught the mood of the Russian population. For the Cheka, Yeltsin's move came as an urgent call to action. Not because the KGB cared about the Party, but because Yeltsin was tearing up a layer of the USSR that the Lubyanka had wanted to preserve for when it wrested power away from the Kremlin behind the scenes. The KGB needed to regain the initiative at all costs, so that the KGB, and not Yeltsin, would slip into the power vacuum their provocation was creating.

Even if the Lubyanka had been caught out by Yeltsin's order, it merely accelerated the existing plan to install Shenin at the head of the USSR. On July 23, 1991, *Sovetskaya Rossiya* published a seminal article called 'A Word to the People.' It began with the words, 'Our Motherland, our country, that great state given into our keeping by history, nature, and our glorious ancestors will perish, break apart, plunge into darkness and oblivion'. Twelve names were listed as authors, including: writers Alexander Prokhanov, Yuri Bondarev and Valentin Rasputin, army generals Valentin Varennikov, Boris Gromov, Albert Makashov, and the Chair of the Farmers Union, Vasily Starodubtsev, the Head of the Association of State Enterprises, Alexander Tizyakov, and Gennady Zyuganov, the Party politician. The article was a call to 'unite and prevent the chain reaction of collapse—the state, the economy, and the individual personality'. It also called for a People's Patriotic Movement to be formed.

The *Sovetskaya Rossiya* article was later referenced as the ideological basis of the August *putsch*, with the putschists calling themselves the State Committee on the State of Emergency (SCSE). Three of the men who signed the publication (Varennikov, Tizyakov, and Starodubtsev) were prosecuted for their activities in connection with the coup. Bobkov was the article's mastermind, although his name was not part of the article and he remained in the background as usual. The words of article were most likely written by *Den*'s Editor-in-Chief Prokhanov. Years later, Prokhanov recalled: 'During the Gorbachev period I was a radical supporter of the SCSE. Alexander Yakovlev said the SCSE was born in *Den*'—in my newspaper. As for being an SCSE agent—I won't deny that.'[243]

Finally, on August 18, 1991, the moment had arrived for the Committee to launch their *coup d'état*. Gorbachev was to be ousted and replaced by Shenin while Yeltsin was to be arrested. Oleg Shenin, General Valentin Varennikov, Oleg Baklanov, First Deputy Chair of the Defense Council of the USSR, Valery Boldin, Chief of Staff of the Office of the President of the USSR, and Yuri Plekhanov, the Head of the 9th Directorate of the KGB, flew to Gorbachev in Foros, Crimea, where he was vacationing with his family. They instructed him that, as the President of the USSR, he must implement a State of Emergency.

On KGB Chief Kryuchkov's initiative, a set of political orders for a State Committee of the State of Emergency (SCSE) had been drawn up and approved before the flight to Foros. Given the fact that neither the KGB nor Kryuchkov had political authority, his orders would previously have been considered treasonable and punishable by death. They included a 'Statement of the Soviet Leadership', 'Address to the Soviet People', 'Resolution No 1 of the SCSE', and 'Notifications to Heads of State and Government, and to the Secretary General of the United Nations'. The preparation of these KGB documents was overseen by Alexei Yegorov, Assistant to the First Deputy Chair of the KGB, and Vladimir Zhizhin, the Deputy Head of the PGU. General Nikolai Leonov, the Head of the Analytics Department[244] of the VGU, was also engaged in preparing the 'Address to the Soviet People'.

Afterwards, the leader (chair) of the SCSE was Gennady Yanayev, Gorbachev's Vice President of the USSR. He was long embedded in the 5th Directorate. In 1968, Yanayev, the First Secretary of the Gorky Regional Committee of the Communist Youth Union, was appointed Chair of 'spy nest' KMO, where Podberezkin and Rogozin would later be insert as 5th Directorate agents on the first steps of their Chekist careers. Under the procedure established by the Lubyanka, issues that required review by the leaders of related Soviet agencies were to be forwarded to the Central office. As a result, Bobkov, Head of the 5th Directorate, and Yanayev, Chair of the KMO, established a close professional contact from the beginning of their respective leadership tenures.[245] While the coup was taking place, Bobkov's son Sergey was one of Yanayev's aides. He was his father's eyes and ears inside in the Kremlin and acted as the link between Bobkov and Yanayev during that time.

Again, Yeltsin defeated the KGB. He thwarted the coup, forcing it to end after 3 days. As President of the Russian Soviet, Yeltsin promptly fired Kryuchkov and appointed a new KGB Chair—Lieutenant General Vadim Bakatin. His first instruction was to conduct an internal investigation to determine the degree to which specific KGB personnel were involved in the organization and implementation of August 18-22. He did not demand, however, that the activities of the Lubyanka as whole were to be investigated, nor did anyone claim that the KGB was suspected of wrongdoing, nor did the investigators find anything that implicated the KGB as an institution. Of course, it was KGB career officers who were investigating those involved in the putsch, most of whom were career officers of the KGB themselves anyway.

Even so, the investigation report ran over multiple pages and pointed to the vast scale of the operation planned by Kryuchkov. Yet no one was executed based on the allegations of high treason even though throughout the Soviet Union's bloody history, after this or that group unsuccessfully attempted a coup, its members and leaders were usually arrested and shot. At any rate, this is how it was until 1956, and what the arrested conspirators should have feared.

But the year 1956 ushered in less bloodthirsty times for the Soviet leadership and. The real leaders and ideologists of the SCSE remained unnamed, unknown, and, so, unpunished, while the participants in the putsch and their aides received purely symbolic punishments despite the gravity of their wrongdoing, even though they violated Article 64 of the Criminal Code of the Russian Federation—high treason—which carried a prison sentence of 10 to 15 years with confiscation of property or the death penalty with confiscation of property. In 1994, all SCSE participants were granted amnesty.

As Yeltsin's action had punctured the Party's aura of invincibility, the Cheka no longer had any use for it. The day after the SCSE coup failed, the Party ceased to exist shortly after 2pm.

Colonel Yevgeny Savostyanov, the Head of the Moscow Office of the KGB recalled the moment in 2015 when the orders were given to terminate the Party. 'I can pinpoint exactly the timing of the high point of my life,' Savostyanov said. 'It was 2:15pm on August 23, 1991. That was the minute I pressed the button in the control room of the civil defense radio transmission system in the building of the CC of the Communist Party of the Soviet Union and announced that the CC is closed and that I would allow 45 minutes for personnel to vacate the building, after which I would arrest anyone remaining. And the entire CC scattered! In the course of 45 minutes.'[246]

During the exact same hour, on the same, Moscow's Mayor Popov, agent of the 5th Directorate, gave the order to seal the Communist Party buildings in Moscow. By 3 pm. KGB operatives had cordoned and sealed the facilities of the Party CC, the Party CC of the of the RSFSR, the Central Control Commission of the Party and the Moscow City Committee of the Party. Popov himself compared the seizure of the Party's buildings with the capture of the Winter Palace in October of 1917 by Bolsheviks:

It is done. I knew it was a blow. The Communist Party will not survive expulsion from its own buildings. Just like the capture of the Winter Palace in 1917, the capture of the CC of the Communist Party was bloodless. But, unlike 1917, there were no gunfire and no shots fired…. In those minutes I realized: the deed is done. The greatest event of the late XX century has happened. The experiment with State Totalitarian Socialism has ended. Whatever happens next, no matter how many years the process takes, no matter how contradictory development is— the countdown to a new era has begun.[247]

KGB Colonel Savostyanov and the KGB agent Popov, who together dispatched the Party on August 23, 1991, truly did start the countdown to a new era—an era that generations upon generations of Intelligence officers had dreamed of since 1917. Memorial plaques and commemorative busts were made of its founding fathers: Dzerzhinsky and Andropov. Yet Popov and Savostyanov had every right to claim to have their own role in the saga.

Had Yeltsin intercepted Pitovranov's and Bobkov's quest to seize power? Not really. It merely meant that the battle must continue. Yeltsin himself was entirely alone. He was surrounded from all sides by ARO officers and agents of the KGB. He never had a chance to escape the trap he fell into even before he became President of Russia. To Pitovranov and Bobkov, Yeltsin was just another provincial and mediocre Party functionary. He was nothing compared to the opponents they had already defeated by the Fall of 1991. That long list now included the scalp of the Communist Party of the Soviet Union.

2: Yeltsin's Impeachment (September, 1993)

The 1991 August Putsch was the first open attempt by the KGB to seize power in the country. And, despite the State Committee on the State of Emergency's (SCSE) failure, the Intelligence Services of the former USSR and modern Russia managed to achieve the desired outcome. Placed under strict Party control after Beria's removal, Chekists cherished the hope of being free of it again. Those dreams came true in August 1991, in part. The Communist Party was gone. Control over the Lubyanka went with it. However, the primary goal remained unrealized. The Kremlin was still not in the hands of the KGB as Yeltsin, an alien to Lubyanka, with an inner circle of liberal-leaning politicians, became the leader of Russia. Even so, already by August of 1991 all contingencies had already been successfully covered. KGB Active Reserve officers deployed in the civil sector—remarkably, on both sides: in the 'Communist camp' and in the 'Democratic camp'—held all the cards for the KGB. The pieces had been arranged in advance on the chess board, with all strategic positions captured. Regardless of how events played out, the Cheka had made sure it would capture the prize at last.

On August 19, 1991, the first day of the SCSE's 'spontaneous revolution', as Yeltsin made his world-famous fiery speech to the people while standing on an armored personnel carrier, his future gravedigger, Alexander Korzhakov, was already there, standing behind him. Completely unknown at the time, Korzhakov was an officer of the KGB's 9th Directorate (personal protection) and was once served as KGB Chief's Andropov's personal bodyguard. Another unknown KGB figure who became part of Yeltsin's inner circle in August of 1991 was Korzhakov's colleague, Viktor Zolotov. He was already a friend of Putin's. From 2016, he would be the chief of the National Guard, troops which fall directly under Putin as Russia's President— a delicate command given only to his most inner circle.[248]

Behind Democrat No 2, Anatoly Sobchak, who gave speech in Leningrad on the same day, stood another yet unknown figure—Vladimir Putin. And the protection of Yegor Gaidar, the first Democratic Prime Minister of Russia, was assigned to a subordinate and protégé of Korzhakov's. His name would also become famous. It was Andrey Lugovoy, another undercover officer of the 9th Directorate of the KGB. He would have remained unknown, but for his world fame as one of the men sent by Vladimir Putin to assassinate his former KGB officer Lieutenant Colonel Alexander Litvinenko in London by pouring into a teacup rare isotope Polonium 210 produced in the successor of Dzerzhinsky's poison Laboratory 12.

Allowing Yeltsin to deflect the SCSE coup in 1991 meant that a few Chekists had to be sacrificed and removed from the board, but victory in the historical chess match was still secure. Behind Yeltsin stood Korzhakov and behind him stood Valentin Yumashev. The complex Soviet history of these three people operating at completely different levels in the same orbit illustrated just how far in advance the KGB insulated noteworthy people. Through officers of the 9th Directorate, Yumashev was yet another KGB figure who became part of Yeltsin's inner circle.

Little is known of Yumashev. And yet we are talking here about a person who was at Yeltsin's side even before August 1991. He later became Yeltsin's Chief of Staff. More remarkably, he served until 2022 as an advisor to President Putin. In other words, he was in power for longer than Yeltsin and Putin combined. How did Yumashev manage to have such a spectacular career spanning both Russia's democratic and an autocratic phase and yet be almost unknown?

Yumashev grew up in 1970s Peredelkino, a highly secure KGB district for dachas in Moscow, in modest circumstances. He shoveled snow around the dacha of the famous Soviet writer Korney Chukovsky, whose daughter Lidiya now lived there (the writer himself passed away in 1969). Novelist Alexander Solzhenitsyn (who was exiled in 1974) lived and worked at Chukovsky's dacha as they were friends. Yumashev was also highly visible to Peredelkino Intelligence personnel as he made money as a guide touring foreign visitors along the dachas of famous Russians in the area.

When Valentin [Yumashev] turned sixteen,' one author writes, 'his family moved from Perm to the outskirts of Moscow. His mother found work not far from their home cleaning writers' dachas in the village of Peredelkino. Valentin was helping her and realized quickly how to make money on his own—for a small fee, he showed foreign tourists the dachas of famous residents at the writers' colony.[249]

Chukovsky's dacha was constantly monitored by Pitovranov's 5th Directorate in connection with Lidiya's human rights activism and frequent political gatherings of people at the dacha (falling under its 9th Department responsible for Soviet dissident activities). Secretaries or other types of helpers of 'non-conformist' writers were often recruited by 9th Department officers, and Yumashev as the janitor who worked there until 1976, when he finished school and joined the Army, would have been highly useful for monitoring the frequent comings and goings of guests at the hospitable home of the Chukovskys.

In the Army, Yumashev served with long-range aviation forces as 'a specialist in communications security equipment' and started writing for Soviet publications while still fulfilling his military duty. Another point in Yumashev's biography illuminated his station. Ten years later, he worked for *Komsomolskaya Pravda*, the official newspaper of the Party's youth branch, Komsomol. No journalist could work there without 5th

Directorate clearance. Anyone 'exposed' to contamination such as at the Chukovsky's dacha would be denied, unless they had full KGB support to work at 'ideological organizations' (such as *Komsomolskaya Pravda*), after having been 'exposed'.

From this publication Yumashev started working in 1987 at the illustrated *Ogonyok* (spark) magazine. So, what was *Ogonyok* like? Its Editor-in-Chief was Vitaly Korotich, who was appointed when the magazine still fell directly under the Party CC and was himself a KGB agent. On the back of *glasnost*, *Ogonyok* started writing about facts and documents instead of utopian Party ideals and was one of *glasnost*'s main 'engines'. Three years later, in 1990, it detached itself from the Party and attached itself to Vladimir Vigilyansky (Chair of the Board of its 'Labor Collective'). Vigilyansky, who will be discussed in detail below, was a journalist who worked at various Russian publications. He was also a KGB agent who had been recruited in 1975 by 5th Directorate Major Vladimir Gusev (a 9th Department senior operative in the 1st Section).

In 2013, former Editor-in-Chief Korotich would himself expose Yumashev (then Putin's advisor) as an agent, glossing over his own KGB antecedents. *Glasnost* initiator at the Politburo and Gorbachev ally Yakovlev had told to watch out for two agents at *Ogonyok*, one of them his Deputy-Editor, Lev Gushchin, the other Yumashev:

> Answer: '… It was at that stage that those guys (he gestures to his shoulders [implying military/KGB uniform]) started invading the magazine with more and more authority, and then came Valya Yumashev. He was responsible for *Aly Parus* ['red sail' celebrations] at *Komsomolskaya Pravda*, but we put him in charge of the Correspondence department, and he organized it beautifully. By early 1990, *Ogonyok* was already 'their' magazine.'
>
> Question: 'So, Gushchin and Yumashev worked for the KGB?'
>
> Answer: '[Alexander] Yakovlev named several names clearly to me: 'Be careful with these people, because they are informing [their superiors] about everything that happens in the editorial office.'[250]

So, the 'engine for *glasnost*', *Ogonyok*, was crammed full of KGB agents. If working for *Komsomolskaya Pravda* without being an agent would have been difficult to work for as someone with Yumashev's background, *Ogonyok* was impossible to get clearance for given its prominent role in the USSR's state of turmoil.

Yet at *Ogonyok* Yumashev was, in his own words in 2019, 'one of the highest paid people in the country.'[251] But Yumashev did not work at *Ogonyok* as a journalist. He was instead in charge of its letters department. The letters pages of Soviet publications were, as a rule, overseen by KGB personnel because it was a way to gather information about the true level of discontent in the country, the true state of affairs, especially in a stormy transition period such as *perestroika*. What kind of journalist (even with a degree from a part-time three-year university, rather than a regular university) would want to transfer from a proper writing job to head a Cheka-sensitive desk in charge of letters to readers instead? Presumably, it is the kind of journalist who follows the orders of his KGB handler to throw themselves at a type of reporting of an entirely different nature.

It was Deputy-Editor Gushchin who hired Yumashev following one phone call after army service and who brought Yumashev from *Komsomolskaya pravda* to lead *Ogonyok*'s Correspondence Office in 1987. Five years later, Yumashev replaced the same Gushchin and was promoted from his ostensibly humble but very well-paid job as head of the Readers Correspondence to Deputy Editor-in-Chief of the (former) *glasnost* magazine.

It was not the only time the Lubyanka directed which agent did what where. Korzhakov was the first to be moved into Yeltsin's orbit. From 1986, when Yeltsin was elected a Candidate Member of the Politburo at the Kremlin, he was assigned a Secret Service detail by the 9th Directorate of the KGB. This was standard procedure for anyone at this elevated level in the Party. From that moment Korzhakov was always near Yeltsin and got to know him well as one of his personal bodyguards. It was one of the easiest ways of the Lubyanka to keep tabs on the members of the Kremlin.

Then, on March 26, 1989, Yeltsin was elected as USSR Deputy for the City of Moscow and received a staggering 91.53% of Muscovite votes with a voter turnout of almost 90%. It was at this point that it was suggested to Yeltsin that he write his first book, *Ispoved' Na Zadannuyu Temu* (confessions on a given topic), to be published in 1990 by... *Ogonyok*. Yeltsin didn't write the book himself. Instead, a ghost writer for the project was proposed. Enter Yumashev, the head of the *Ogonyok* letters pages who became Yeltsin's ghost and, as a result, got very close to him. As choreographed by their KGB superiors, clearly, Korzhakov and Yumashev were now also in direct touch with each other as Yumashev needed to get past Korzhakov to work on the book project with their boss Yeltsin. The book project was entirely in line with the KGB's plans to put pressure on Gorbachev's leadership and replace him as General Secretary and Soviet leader with 'agent' Shenin at the first opportunity.

From Yeltsin's fall from grace, when he removed the Party's representatives in 1991 as President of the Russian Soviet, Korzhakov's duties included not only physically protecting the future President but also vigilantly monitoring his contacts. Obviously, Korzhakov could have terminated Yumashev's contact with Yeltsin at any time. Instead Yumashev's access to Yeltsin continued unabated, not surprising given their allegiance to the same camp, the Lubyanka.

August 19, 1991, the putsch, changed everything further. Given the tense atmosphere, Korzhakov was responsible for access to Yeltsin as the head of his security detail and controlled, whom Yeltsin would and would not receive. Starting August 1991, it was Korzhakov who became Yumashev's handler. He was to help him advance his stellar career under President Yeltsin as the latter's Chief of Staff. With time, Yumashev would eclipse his handler—a frequent occurrence among Cheka agents and officers during those years.

Yeltsin's meteoric rise transformed Korzhakov's fate as well. A radical restructuring of the KGB system followed after the coup and the resignation of Mikhail Gorbachev. The massive organization of the KGB was broken up into various small agencies that were made independent from one another. From the 9th and 15th KGB Directorates (responsible for security of top government officials, Party members and their families, as well as the protection of the vital government facilities), two separate entities were created: the Secret Service of the President (SBP) and the *Glavnoe Upravlenie Okhrany* (Main Security Department, or MSD). From Yeltsin's personal bodyguard—the terminology of the 9th Directorate of the KGB, he was 'attached'—Khorzakov now headed the SBP. Furthermore, in June 1992, Korzhakov got to appoint his friend, General Mikhail Barsukov, to lead the MSD. In 1991, his friend was already Deputy Commandant of the Kremlin and he became Commandant of the Kremlin in December 1991.

Traditionally 'Number 9', that is members of the 9th Directorate, kept to themselves in KGB times, since their divisions were primarily located at the Kremlin. The leadership and personnel of 'Number Nine' were rarely in contact with officers from other KGB divisions based at the Lubyanka. Despite the importance of physically protecting senior state officials and vital state locations, it was considered an auxiliary department. The Directorate had inferior operational skills compared to the highly trained intelligence and counterintelligence officers at the Cheka. As a career 'Niner,' Korzhakov understood that the President's security detail, even when dealing with a President as 'high maintenance' as Yeltsin, was not at the top of the list of priorities.

Korzhakov used the August coup's aftermath to upgrade the status of the President's Secret Service (SBP) to that of a federal body capable of taking charge of the Intelligence Services. In 2008, he said in an interview 'It is customary to think it was Yeltsin's idea, but that is not true. I had the idea of creating the Service as a separate federal structure. Yeltsin merely supported it and made it legal by decree.'[252] Doubtless, he was right. Yeltsin had no interest in the matter and would have never come up with that idea.

The Kremlin's SBP gradually expanded. A counterintelligence office was formed—'Department K'. 'Department P' was also formed, the mandate Korzhakov described as: 'to control the Ministers and other civil servants.' But to retain his position, Korzhakov needed to control everyone, most of all Yeltsin. More than $50 million was spent on acquiring high-quality listening equipment abroad, a significant portion of which was wired into the Kremlin itself as Korzhakov's and Barsukov's subordinates bugged and monitored all Kremlin offices. The *Komsomolskaya Pravda* wrote the following:

> We discovered discover that the Kremlin offices were full of Barsukov's and Korzhakov's super-sophisticated German 'bugs.' The senior officials occupying these offices essentially knew about that but could do little to resist total surveil-

lance by the people perceived as 'Yeltsin's favorites'. For example, Chief of the Presidential Administration Sergei Filatov constantly complained to journalists about being forced to communicate with visitors in his office by way of writing notes back and forth, as well as to hold the most important meetings in the hallway.

In addition, the apartments and dachas of the country's highest officials were also monitored. If necessary, the 'measures were activated'. When Yeltsin's Vice-President Rutskoy got too big for his boots—in Korzhakov's opinion—the SBP destroyed the opulent dacha he was building next to Yeltsin's to send a message:

> My staff reported to me that a massive mansion was being built in Barvikha [outside Moscow] within close proximity of Yeltsin's official dacha, thereby violating our security requirements. I asked: 'Who is doing it?' 'Rutskoy,' was the response. We started inquiring into the details—why, who is sponsoring it. Notably, Yeltsin had provided to Rutskoy a wonderful residence with excellent furniture and every luxury. But Rutskoy was already eyeing the President's seat by that time and was becoming quite clear in his ambitions—practically placing himself among the opposition. Clearly, I could not ignore an official of such magnitude, who had essentially declared war against the current Head of State. Our operatives secretly went to his 'site,' surveyed and considered everything…. One night, the future cottage collapsed into a pile of bricks like a house of cards. This operation was executed so expertly and quietly that no one noticed a thing. But Rutskoy got the message.[253]

Korzhakov's team of course had no authority to investigate the 'sponsors' who financed the Vice President's dacha; this was the domain of the Prosecutor's Office. What's more, destroying someone's private property with an explosion that threatened the lives of others was a criminal act like a mafioso's shot across the bow. But Korzhakov feared neither committing the crime itself nor admitting it many years later, knowing that no one would bring criminal charges against him. As the 'mafia Godfather' of the Secret Service, Korzhakov was always untouchable, even if he destroyed the property of Vice-President Rutskoy, the deputy of President Yeltsin, the 'guarantor of the Constitution'.

While Korzhakov was expanding his Cheka empire from the KGB after August 1991, Pitovranov's Firm redoubled its efforts to capture the Kremlin. The plan was now the removal of Yeltsin as President of the Russian Federation. Shenin and anyone associated with the coup was compromised, but Vice President Rutskoy had clean hands as he was Yeltsin's running mate in the June 1991 Presidential Elections. If Yeltsin resigned, Rutskoy would legitimately become the next Russian President. Whereas the legitimacy of the State Committee of the State of Emergency had relied on Gorbachev's 'voluntary' resignation within the USSR monolith, Rutskoy could

218

claim to have been co-elected by the Russian electorate—important now that the Party was no more. Just as Korzhakov cocooned Yeltsin, RAU's Podberezkin had been inserted at Vice President Rutskoy's end (in the event he would win). He was Rutskoy's advisor and led a group of consultants. Another Chekist, the Stalinist KGB General Sterligov who had left the Party in 1990 to go to RAU, was Rutskoy's Chief of Staff and Economic consultant.

Even before 1988, Bobkov had been involved in organized provocation with irritant *Pamyat*, the movement that had sprouted from KGB agent Glazunov's Slavophile 'Motherland'. In 1987, members of the 'informal' *Pamyat* (memory) movement held a mass demonstration on Manege Square in Moscow in support of *perestroika*, and its leadership was received by Yeltsin, the Party's First Secretary of the Moscow City Committee. Eponymous nationalist organizations were soon formed in several Russian cities.

These were also of course operating under the auspices and control of Bobkov's 5th Directorate. The KGB leadership and the country's central Party organs were regularly informed of *Pamyat*'s activities. Gorbachev's close Politburo ally Alexander Yakovlev recalled a conversation with KGB Chair Chebrikov (1982-1988) on the topic: 'Although Viktor Chebrikov did not name names, I understood from his logic that many KGB agents infiltrated the democratic movement. The only specific data point that I learned was the history of the creation of the 'Memory' Society and its mission.'

From 1988, KGB agent Dmitry Vasiliev headed *Pamyat* and Bobkov instructed his KGB handlers (in the 2nd Department of the 5th Directorate) to change the movement's focus on to ethnic issues—antisemitism in the case of *Pamyat*. Ethnic issues were flaring up everywhere in the USSR and 'managed' provocation was the 5th Directorate's way of dealing with it.

This was a tried and tested method. Major Balov (the KGB officer who ensnared Popov, Moscow's future Mayor) led the 2nd Department of the 5th Directorate from the mid-1980s. After a name change to 'Directorate Z' in August of 1989—little changed, not even the department numbers or heads—his department was given 'ethnic' issues in the USSR to resolve. During the years of *perestroika* the forces threatening the USSR's integrity were intensifying. Bobkov, his superior, had extensive experience suppressing popular demonstrations in his previous years of service in Eastern Europe. Balov's 2nd Department (now of Directorate Z) organized Bobkov's KGB operations in Azerbaijan for example.

Tragic events caused by ethnic hostilities in the Azerbaijani city of Sumqayit in February of 1988 led to massive numbers of casualties. The Armenian genocide took place that was partially provoked by ethnic clashes between Armenians and Azerbaijanis residing in the territory of Armenia. Part of the Azerbaijani in Armenia had begun relocating primarily to Sumqayit and Baku. The Armenian population of Sumqayit, fleeing pogroms and genocide, fled to the territory of Nagorno-Karabakh, which Armenia's nationalist leaders claimed as part of Armenia. All of this served as a catalyst for a deep political crisis in Soviet Azerbaijan, where power practically landed in the lap of the People's Front of Azerbaijan (NFA).

The Armenian pogroms in Baku were provoked by the KGB at the instigation of Bobkov to initiate a state of emergency in Baku and force the subsequent arrest of the NFA leaders. Vagif Guseinov was the Chair of the KGB of the Azerbaijan from August of 1989 to September 13, 1991. It was specifically under the Guseinov that on January 13-19, 1990, Armenian pogroms took place in Baku. These pogroms were the reason for deploying Soviet troops and KGB special forces to the Azerbaijani capital (Baku) on January 19-20, 1990.

In Soviet times, KGB Special Forces' Group A (Alpha Group) was directly subordinate to the KGB Chair and to his First Deputy (that is, Bobkov). Bobkov decided to use Alpha Group in Baku to suppress the unrest. Measures to 'restore order' were directed by Guseinov and Bobkov—who arrived in Baku a week before troops were deployed in the city. As admitted later by then-Defense Minister Marshal Dmitry Yazov, the goal of deploying troops was 'to destroy NFA structures and not allow the opposition to win.'

The outcome was horrific and an investigation by the Supreme Soviet of Azerbaijan found that Soviet troops were guilty of 'cruel and inhumane actions', bystanders were crushed underneath passing tanks, and that wounded people and medics were shot:

> On the night of January 19 to January 20, 1990, in the city of Baku, a criminal act of terrible cruelty was committed, resulting in the mass killing of the peaceful population.... The operation involved major formations of the land, naval, air, and airborne military forces of the USSR, as well as special-purpose KGB and MVD forces. The deployment of these military units in Baku was accompanied by cruel and inhumane actions by the service members, who took the life of anyone who happened to be nearby. Residential buildings and medical institutions were shelled, ambulances and cars passing by and standing on the side of the road were crushed by tanks, the wounded were killed, and medical workers were shot while providing emergency care on the ground. According to preliminary data, as of today 168 people were killed and 715 peaceful civilians were injured. The fates of more than 400 people are unknown. They include women, the elderly, and children.... Many of them died in their apartments, building lobbies, buses, and workplaces. As of today, information keeps coming in about new victims and those who succumbed to their wounds. 28 soldiers died and more than 80 were wounded, many of whom died at the hands of their comrades as a result of the uncoordinated actions of the military command.

Parliamentary elections were set to take place in March of 1990 in the Azerbaijan, and the KGB ploy meant victory was assured for the NFA People's Front. After the collapse of the USSR and the rise to power in Azerbaijan of the People's Front,

Guseinov would be arrested and placed under investigation on charges of organizing an explosion at a Baku TV station in February of 1991. For a while, he was held in a pre-trial detention center. In 1993 he was released, and in February of 1994 he left Azerbaijan and settled in Moscow where he built a successful career as part of Bobkov's team.

Previously, in April of 1988, Soviet troops and KGB Special Forces had similarly been deployed in suppressing protests in Tbilisi, the capital of the Soviet Georgia. In other words, the unrest in Armenia and Azerbaijan was hardly an isolated event. Lithuania was next. During the night of January 12, 1991, Alpha Group was deployed on Bobkov's orders to storm a TV tower held by Lithuanian rebels in Vilnius. 15 people died as a result of the operation. The failed operations in Vilnius and Baku meant that General Bobkov had blood on his hands. On February 20, 1991, he sent in his resignation as KGB First Deputy (and joined the Active Reserve program). On February 29, 1991, Gorbachev signed off on the 'resignation' of the KGB's *de facto* head (whose KGB nickname was 'the brain').

It was unlikely remorse over the two bloodbaths. In 1998, he said he was moved by the impending doom of the USSR as the Soviet Union lost cohesion (which the Lubyanka had been testing under his guidance for so long): 'At the end of 1989, I met with the KGB operational staff in the Baltics. I was supposed to inspire confidence. But I could not lie. And everyone understood that I had nothing to say. The system had started to collapse. That is, it continued to work, but it was no longer a 'collective whole.'[254] But this was unlikely the reason for becoming an ARO. Bobkov left for the *Most* group, which he created for himself well in advance through Vladimir Gusinsky (the agent who had tried to woo Ted Turner in 1986) the year before.

The business success of *Most* (bridge) increased by leaps and bounds as Bobkov recruited the best KGB personnel as Active Reserve officers. He formed its own financial branch—*Most* Bank, and his own Secret Service—the *Most* Secret Service or *Most* SS, also known as *Most*-Bank SS, which quickly became the largest one in the country. *Most* SS gathered information on a wide array of current issues in Russia— from the grouping and hierarchy of political forces in the country to building 'case files' on prominent politicians, businessmen, bankers, and on various state and commercial structures. It reincarnated the 'old' KGB as a privatized entity funded by the Firm's foreign assets while drawing on human, technical, and financial resources from the former agency and hastily transferring tens of thousands of their own staff to Active Reserve status for subsequent placement in civilian organizations or new enforcement bodies. Colonel Balev, who had directed the pogroms in Azerbaijan and the Nagorno-Karabakh tragedy, became one of the employees of the *Most* Company, as did General Guseinov after he was released by the Azerbaijan government in 1994.

It meant that KGB opposition to oust Yeltsin from the early months and years of his rule (August 1991 to October 1993) came from two directions—one from his inner circle, the SBP led by Korzhakov, the other one from the *Most* SS. Neither *Most* SS nor Korzhakov's SBP ever declared their ultimate objective. But, like Bobkov,

Korzhakov raced to increase the SBP's scope of operations while placing ARO officers where he could, using whatever tax allocations he was able to get Yeltsin to agree to.

In 1991, Bobkov led the charge from *Most* SS. The August putsch had been resisted by two people. Viktor Barannikov and Andrey Dunayev. During the SCSE clashes, they organized protection of the White House (the House of Soviets) with loyal police units and police school cadets, led the operation to return President Gorbachev from Foros, and participated in the arrests of KGB Chair Kryuchkov and Minister of Defense Yazov. Seemingly loyal to Yeltsin, they had been elevated to high office following the August events and become, respectively, Minister of the Intelligence Services and Minister of Internal Affairs. These powerful ministers had to be removed by driving a wedge between them and the man who could remove them by decree, Yeltsin. The operation was elaborate, devious and multi-staged.

In order to get rid of Barannikov and Dunayev, the Chekists planned to compromise their straight-shooting reputation vis-à-vis Yeltsin. It involved a number of different 5 Directorate agents and officers: Dmitry Yakubovsky, his controller Major Mikhail Scherbakov and Andrey Makarov, whom Bobkov controlled himself. The set-up for *kompromat* itself was simple. A trip to Switzerland was arranged for the wives of Barannikov and Dunayev. The trip itself, as well as the numerous purchases worth hundreds of thousands of dollars that were sent home in twenty-one suitcases, were ostensibly 'sponsored' by Birshtein's Seabeco. The logistics of the trip and the chaperoning of the two women were handled however by Birshtein's business partner—the 29-year-old KGB agent Dmitry Yakubovsky.

Yakubovsky was born in 1963 in Bolshevo, a city outside Moscow. After completing his military duty, he worked as a supplier in the State Suppliers System and at a construction company in Moscow. He simultaneously studied long-distance at the All-Union Correspondence Institute of Law—Soviet Construction Department. In 1984, he was hired as an assistant to Konstantin Apraksin, the Chair of the Moscow City Bar Association. In 1989, 25-year-old Yakubovsky was hired as a Secretary of the USSR Union of Lawyers.

This is where he appeared on the radar of the 5th Directorate as the Union of Lawyers was managed by the 5th Directorate (1st Section of the 11th Department). Its main oversight was assigned to senior officer Major Mikhail Scherbakov (a former 'Niner'). The energetic Secretary of the Union of Lawyers, Yakubovsky was soon noticed by Scherbakov and recruited as an agent of the 11th Department.

The 25-year-old Yakubovsky was soon hired as the Chief Executive Officer of joint-venture Agrokhim-Seabeco. In December of 1991, Seabeco Trade and Finance AG and Agrokhim (a Russian parent company of Agrokhim-Seabeco) signed a contract for the supply of baby food worth $13.5 million. After the deal was approved by the Moscow city officials (Gavriil Popov, Bobkov's agent, was Moscow's Mayor), the money was transferred to the Seabeco's account at Banque Indosuez in Switzerland. But the terms of the contract between the two companies were never honored and the money never made it back to Moscow.

The 'certificates, receipts, and the whole pile of other papers' documenting the trip and its $300,000 price tag made a lasting impression on Yeltsin. Yeltsin understood that, even if his ministers were innocent themselves, the *kompromat* had made them susceptible to be 'manipulated and just as easily blackmailed'.

From the certificates, receipts, and the whole pile of other papers presented to me, it has become absolutely clear that Viktor Barannikov, the Minister of State Security of Russia, the Army General, and one of my closest and most trusted people, whom I have always liked, has been crudely and distastefully 'bought'. At first, I decided not to jump to conclusions since the documents could have been falsified. That is quite likely, after all. The Minister of the Intelligence Services is a sufficiently serious figure for someone to have an incentive to try to compromise him.

I did not want to believe the bad news. But I had to…. Boris Birshtein's company Seabeco invited the wife of Viktor Barannikov and the wife of First Deputy Minister of Internal Affairs of Russia Dunayev to Switzerland for three days.[255] And there they bought up by the kilo, by the sack, perfume, fur coats, watches, et cetera, et cetera. All for a total of more than 300 thousand dollars…. What could I do? How should I tell Viktor Barannikov about all this? My first thought was: the man became a victim of some intricate plot. He sent his wife for a three-day vacation, and there she got caught in a downpour of dollars, and it broke her. It is clear, in any case, that I have to remove him now. Now Barannikov could be easily manipulated and just as easily blackmailed.[256]

How Yeltsin received the 'case file' was another delicate Bobkov move. This was directed through another long-time agent of the 5th Directorate—Andrey Makarov (codename 'Tanya'). He had attracted the attention of Bobkov during a chess match between Viktor Korchnoi and Anatoly Karpov, and later between Karpov and Garry Kasparov in the late 1970s. Karpov himself was a young recruit of the 5th Department at the Leningrad and Leningrad Region. When he moved to Moscow, he became an agent controlled directly by the Kremlin's 5th Directorate (11th Department). Makarov was at the match because monitored famous chess player Boris Gulko, who had been trying for years to receive permission to emigrate to Israel.

Makarov had an impeccable pedigree. During 1990-1992, Makarov worked at the George Soros Foundation on Bobkov's instruction and was even a Head of the Foundation for some time. In 1993, Makarov became the head of the Interagency Commission of the Security Council of Russia to combat corruption and crime. Thus, Bobkov was always informed through Makarov about the activities of law enforcement agencies with regards to organized crime and corruption at federal level.

It was through Makarov that Yeltsin received the compromising materials on

Barannikov and Dunayev from Birshtein and Yakubovsky's Swiss companies. At the right moment, Yeltsin was presented with the receipts, paid for by Birshtein through Dmitry Yakubovsky's brother's company Distal AG, for the trip and purchases made by the wives of Barannikov and Dunayev.

On July 27, 1993, Yeltsin signed the order to remove Barannikov from office. Dunayev had been removed several days earlier. After being taken out by a deft Chekist maneuver, Bobkov's protégé and former subordinate Lieutenant General Nikolai Golushko became the Acting Minister of the Intelligence Services and was later confirmed by Yeltsin in that position.

The stage was now set for the next coup and Bobkov's means were on the one hand, the Supreme Soviet, a legitimate state body unlike the SCSE, and a paramilitary organization called *Russkoye Natsionalnoye Yedinstvo* (Russian national unity, RNE), on the other. Bobkov had ordered the movement to be founded in October of 1990, by Barkashov, the one-time bodyguard of *Pamyat* leader Dmitry Vasiliev. Barkashov's ultranationalist movement was altogether much nastier and, together with a number of members of *Pamyat*, unified a group of Slavist militants calling for the restoration of Russian orthodoxy and the like, violently rejecting all other religions. The RNE's ideology at its core was fascist, and 'Barkashov's guards' had to pledge an allegiance to their 'Fuhrer.'

Barkashov had been part of the August 1991 choreography when, as one of the first people to underwrite the SCSE's actions, he sent a telegram of support to Vice President Yanayev, one of the chief conspirators. In 1993, a few months before the armed storming of the White House by government forces, Barkashov announced his political support for the members of the Supreme Soviet of Russia rebelling against Yeltsin, stating that the RNE would provide military support to the Supreme Soviet as necessary. In Bobkov's plan, the RNE was the fist behind the Supreme Soviet's legitimacy.

Even before Russia's 'free' elections, the KGB had formed a special task force to organize and manage the election process and populate the Supreme Soviet with its own members. The KGB officers that were chosen for an electoral role received special training to prepare them for the elections, which included detailed descriptions of the problems, needs and desires of the voters in specific districts. As a result, 2,756 KGB officers ran in national, regional, and local elections; 56% of KGB candidates won in the first round.

In 1993, the clash between the two highest institutions of state power in Russia intensified: the executive branch (represented by the President of Russia and his office) and the legislative branch (represented by the Supreme Soviet's leadership, crammed full of communists on the one hand, and KGB officers and agents on the other). During the Eighth (extraordinary) Congress of People's Deputies, which took place March 10-13, 1993, attempts were made to pass a series of Constitutional Reforms that limited Yeltsin's Presidential power. The Referendum Vote of Trust in the President scheduled for April of 1993 was cancelled. In response, on March 20,

Yeltsin signed the order 'On a Special Order of Rule', which rescheduled the Referendum for April 25, 1993, and suspended all activities of the Supreme Soviet of Russia until that date.

At the emergency meeting of the Ninth (extraordinary) Congress of People's Deputies, held from March 26-29, Yeltsin's decree was debated and marked as a *coup d'état* by Yeltsin against the Congress in a vitriolic charge led by Yeltsin's own Vice-President Rutskoy. Thus, the procedure was set in motion to impeach Yeltsin and remove him from power through due process. However, the deputies who supported Rutskoy failed to garner the requisite number of votes (two-thirds) in the Congress: 617 deputies, no more than 60%, voted in favor of impeachment.

In an attempt to seize the initiative and enlist popular support, Yeltsin announced a speech to the Russian people to legitimize his standoff with the obstructive legislative branch. Instead, the March crisis ended with a compromise. Yeltsin did not give his speech, and Congress agreed on March 29 with Yeltsin's proposal to organize a Referendum Vote of Trust in the President on April 25, 1993, during which the Russian population would give its support to one of the branches of government— the President or the Congress. The resolution of March 29 was called 'On the Russian National Referendum of April 25, 1993, the Procedure for Tabulating Its Outcome, and the Mechanism for Implementing It.' On April 21, 1993, the Constitutional Court of Russia approved the procedure for counting the votes in the Referendum. The Referendum of April 25 ended up supporting Yeltsin's program. With the outcome in his favor, Yeltsin removed Vice President Rutskoy.

In addition, he began preparing a new Constitution. On September 21, Yeltsin gave a television address. He stated that the Supreme Soviet had ceased to be a body representing the power of the people and had become a stronghold of opposition to the State itself. He disbanded the representative bodies of power in the country with Order No 1400 'On Gradual Constitutional Reform in the Russian Federation'. Elections for the State Duma were set for December 11-12, 1993.

On the same day, September 21, the Constitutional Court of Russia decided the President's actions were unconstitutional and in direct violation of nine articles of the Constitution. On the next day, September 22, the Supreme Soviet terminated Yeltsin's Presidency from the date of Order No 1400 and transferred Presidential powers to Vice President Rutskoy. At the same time, the Supreme Soviet decided to hold an emergency meeting of the Ninth Congress of People's Deputies which approved the Supreme Soviet's resolution of September 24 to terminate Yeltsin's Presidential powers and the transfer power to Rutskoy. The stage was set, Rutskoy was now Russia's official leader by order of Russia's Constitutional Court. Barricades were erected around the White House, where the defiant members of the Supreme Soviet were housed. Their supporters began to flock to the White House.

During the confrontation between President Yeltsin and the Supreme Soviet in 1993, Bobkov was in his usual scheming mode behind the scenes. He pushed into action both Vice President Rutskoy (who had Podberezkin and Sterligov as advisors) and the Chair of the Supreme Soviet Ruslan Khasbulatov: he deluded them by making them believe they had broad electoral support from Russian voters around the country. In addition, around 200 RNE fighters led by Barkashov showed up to defend the White House on October 3. About 15 of them were able to occupy the Mayor's office near the White House as well. Bobkov's *Most* occupied a few floors there. Barkashov had a detailed floor plan of the building and its communications system, including its underground access. His men had no trouble taking over from the two divisions of Dzerzhinsky Special Operations Forces scattered throughout the massive skyscraper. It was particularly helpful that the latter never received the order to fight back.

Outside the White House and Mayor's office, it was a different matter. On October 3, Yeltsin declared a state of emergency in Moscow. Troops and tanks were called to the capital to confront the opposition. It became clear to Bobkov that the White House defenders had zero chance in a military confrontation. Bobkov didn't really care about the deputies in the Supreme Soviet, but he did not want to lose his RNE fighters, who could still be very useful. Thus, Bobkov made a deal with his protégé General Golushko, now Yeltsin's Minister of the Intelligence Services, for the safe passage of Barkashov's men through the cordon of troops blocking off the White House. The KGB's Alpha Group, which reported directly to Golushko, was given orders to stand down, and the RNE fighters led by Barkashov, unbeknownst to the other White House defenders, left the building a few hours before it was stormed by troops loyal to President Yeltsin.

By the evening of October 4, the Supreme Soviet opposition was broken. The leaders of the White House's defenders (Rutskoy, Khasbulatov, and others) were arrested. Yeltsin assumed direct Presidential rule over the country until elections in the Federal Assembly and a Constitutional Referendum could be held, which were set for December 12, 1993.

Having lost another round to Yeltsin in a big political chess game, Pitovranov's group had still managed to win. Yeltsin had merely won a Pyrrhic victory. It was true that the Firm did not manage to oust Yeltsin in October 1993. However, as the democratic leader of the new Russia, he was already dead in the water. Yeltsin, the shrewd Party operator; General Rutskoy, the straight-talking hero of the Afghan War; and Khasbulatov, the proud and unyielding political figure—they were all victims of classic Chekist provocation. Yeltsin won his fight against Rutskoy and Khasbulatov, men who until recently had been his allies and sympathizers but from whom the Bobkov had easily separated him. Yeltsin himself, too, was doomed after October 3, 1993. He had no more allies and from now on, he could only rely on law enforcement agencies to lead the country. Or, at least, that is what Bobkov and Pitovranov had plotted for.

For Rutskoy and Khasbulatov, KGB provocation ended in 1993 with their arrest and the defeat of the Supreme Soviet. Not a single Bobkov agent, despite the military clash and subsequent political fallout, suffered any repercussions or was punished. All of them emerged unscathed, just as Bobkov and Pitovranov did. Ever cautious, Bobkov did not plan to throw himself under the bus for the Cheka and risk his head as his less capable colleague Kryuchkov did—who became the sixth director of State Security to be arrested (following in the footsteps of Yagoda, Yezhov, Abakumov, Beria, and Merkulov, though he was the only one who was not executed).

It must have offered the Chekists some comfort that the collapse of the USSR in 1991, had not meant a return to the days of sentencing to death former senior officials for treason. Meanwhile, Korzhakov, as head of the SBP, planned to expand it to the scale of the former KGB, while remaining in charge of the agency, and to usurp the state's power through that organization. Having two different people with different approaches—Bobkov and Korzhakov, who were in competition with each other to an extent, was helping, rather than hindering, the Cheka's chances for victory since one of the two was bound to win. From the Chekist perspective, it did not matter who got to the finish line first. It was the result that mattered.

3: Presidential Elections (March, 1996)

There were no winners in the October battle of 1993. The SCSE declared a state of emergency in 1991 and Yeltsin declared Presidential Rule in 1993—a state of emergency of sorts. After shelling the White House, Yeltsin's legitimacy had been tainted, questioned by his political enemies but also his allies. For Yeltsin, this situation could only be remedied by winning the popular vote in the 1996 Presidential Election. As Yeltsin had no desire to rule as a new Stalinist dictator but wanted an electoral mandate to continue as Russia's president, it was naturally the countdown for the next attempt to overthrow him.

Pitovranov and Bobkov, however, emerged unscathed and even managed to strengthen their position during the 1991-1993 crisis. They had successfully created both their own international financial platform, *Most*-Bank, and their own security service *Most* SS. They had legions of loyalists comprised of former KGB officers and analysts, a foothold in Moscow through Mayor Popov, and their own agent network inside the Lubyanka with numerous agents Directorate Z still at the Lubyanka (previously the 5th Directorate).

The director of *Most* SS was Dmitry Gorbachuk, the former head of one of the Police Department Criminal Investigation Divisions of Moscow. However, Gorbachuk was merely the figure head—there were more senior KGB officers serving at *Most* SS. The actual director of *Most* SS although he was formally listed as a 'consultant' (just as Pitovranov was listed as a 'senior consultant' in his 'Firm') was Bobkov.

General Ivanov, former Deputy Chair of the KGB and overseer of the 5th Directorate (Directorate Z), led the *Most* Analytical Department. Also serving there was Colonel Balev who had been Bobkov's right-hand man in the KGB bloody provocations in the Soviet republics. Colonel Maslennikov, the 5th Directorate/Directorate Z recruiter of Podberezkin and philology scholar also worked at *Most*. Before transferring to the Lubyanka's communications team (CPR), Maslennikov headed the 6th Department of Directorate Z. A group of three officers was formed in that department to organize counterpropaganda initiatives through journalists working at various media outlets. KGB personnel from the 6th Department were analysts and not authorized to recruit agents themselves. But exceptions were made for the three officers in the counterpropaganda group. One of the more famous agents recruited by this trio was Alexander Khinshtein, then a young novice journalist from the *Moskovskiy Komsomolets* (Moscow Komsomol) newspaper. Senior KGB operative Major Oleg Mikarenkov recruited him.

In 1992, Major General Valentin Vorotnikov started working as Deputy Director of *Most* SS. After the August 1991 putsch, Vorotnikov was being investigated but managed to get away with just being let go, becoming an ARO and a businessman. In September of 1991 joined the Board of Directors at the *Izumrudny* (emerald) Bank. At the end of 1991, he created the National Security Defense Partnership called Fatherland, which was later renamed the *Vzor* (gaze) Agency for Economic Security and was its General Director. His partner was the Igor Perfiliev, former Deputy Head of Directorate Z, who shared Vorotniko's fate of having been dismissed from the KGB (and becoming an ARO) for participating in the coup. *Vzor* primarily carried out missions for *Most* SS and was *de facto* one of its divisions. It was none other than Perfiliev who recruited and organized for Bobkov surveillance for *Most* SS with former personnel of the 7th Directorate of the KGB.

Vorotnikov left *Vzor* in 1992, finally transferring to join Bobkov, whereas Perfiliev stayed with *Vzor* and served as the main link between *Most* SS and *Vzor*. In the course of his tenure with *Vzor*, Perfiliev personally recruited colleagues from both the 5th Directorate and its successor, Directorate Z, who had stayed on at the Lubyanka. These people were essentially committing malfeasance by using state agency resources for side gigs at *Vzor* and *Most* SS, for which they received financial compensation.

However, it was not feasible for Bobkov to resist Korzhakov's SBP by sheer force alone. It was necessary also to win the battle for public opinion, for influence over voters, and for influence over the electoral system. One had to possess the means of destroying the enemy without firing a single shot—merely with the pen, the microphone, and the camera.

To that end, a company, the *Most* Group Holding, was formed in 1992. The Holding consisted of 42 enterprises in various industries. In June of 1993, TV journalists Igor Malashenko, Oleg Dobrodeyev, and Yevgeny Kiselev created a TV company called *Itogi* (conclusions). A month later, in July of the same year, the *Itogi* founders received an offer they could not refuse: their TV company joined the banks *Most*-Bank SS, *Stolichny* Bank, and *Natsionalny Kredit* Bank to set up an LLP called NTV Television Company. Soon thereafter, Bobkov's *Most*-Bank was the only founder remaining; all others had left.

Simultaneously with NTV, the same three banks founded the daily newspaper *Segodnya* (today). Just like with NTV, only *Most*-Bank remained as its founder several months later; *Most*-Bank also became a sponsor of Moscow radio station The Echo. Bobkov's agents Smolensky (from *Stolichny* Bank) and Fedorov (from *Natsionalny Kredit* Bank) participated in this project in order to mislead the public and avoid the impression that everything was being bought up by *Most*-Bank, which was becoming more and more associated with Gusinsky's name. Based on his experience with the sharp end of Stalinism, Bobkov preferred to remain in the shadows.

When the philologically inclined Colonel Maslennikov came to *Most* SS from the CPR, he stood out in comparison to many of his fellow Chekists for his masterful ability to write. That skill became his specialty at *Most* SS. At Maslennikov's suggestion, Gusinsky founded an undercover group headed by Major Valery Shiryayev, a former 5th Directorate officer of the 3rd Department:

> Its [the group's] tasks included the following: promoting in printed and electronic media materials of diverse nature in the interests of *Most* SS but in the name or under the flag of completely different organizations; determining the origin of materials in printed and electronic media directed against *Most* SS or intended to betray its interests or the interests of organizations and people close to Gusinsky; forewarning of, or preventing, the appearance of such materials in the media by any means possible, as well as compromising the journalists who worked on those materials; assembling dossiers on journalists and media directors, forging informal relationships with them, and determining their weaknesses for subsequent exploitation.[257]

Alexander Svechnikov also worked in Shiryayev's department. In 1973, he graduated from the Geography Department at MSU, and then served in the 5th Directorate 3rd Department. In 1987, he obtained a PhD in Philosophy. In the late 1980s, he became an aide to the Head of the 5th Directorate. After the collapse of the USSR, he continued to work for the FSB for a short while. In 1995, he joined Shiryayev's department under the leadership of his former boss General Ivanov.

In March 1994, *Most*-Bank became the official bank of Moscow, administering the primary assets of Moscow's city government and its current accounts were. It became one of the largest banks in Russia by volume of funds, which included municipal budgetary accounts, accounts of a series of various local governmental institutions, and accounts of several extrabudgetary organizations and funds. Moreover, with the money received from foreign banks via Kalmanovich's connections (from the Firm's Angola operations), with the Communist Party money and thanks to the efforts of Leonid Veselovsky, *Most*-Bank was No 19 on of Russia's top hundred banks (by assets) in 1994, from nowhere the previous year. That is when Bobkov's agent Gusinsky became a Chair of the Council of Representatives of Authorized Banks and a Vice President of the Association of Russian Banks.

After opening offshore bank accounts for Pitovranov and Bobkov, and funding these accounts with substantial sums, Kalmanovich, despite not having 'the right connections' among Moscow elites, was surprisingly easily awarded a reconstruction project related to the famous Tishinskiy Market in Moscow—a kickback, no doubt. He was awarded the construction of another market, as well as other delicious 'bits' of Moscow real estate, all in prime neighborhoods of Moscow. Within a very short time, with Bobkov's help, Kalmanovich became a major businessman and public figure: a producer for the pop-singer Zemfira; the owner of several basketball clubs in Russia and Lithuania, including women's basketball team Spartak; and one of the leaders in Russia's pharmaceutical market.

Bobkov now started grooming Yuri Luzhkov as a potential challenger to Yeltsin. Luzhkov was the First Deputy Chair of the Moscow City Agro-Industrial Committee in 1987, apparently appointed on the initiative of Yeltsin, who was then the First Secretary of the Moscow City Committee. At the same time, Luzhkov was also a Chair of the Moscow City Agro-Industrial Committee and the Head of the City Commission on Cooperative and Individual Labor Activities. In July of 1991, upon the suggestion of Gavriil Popov, Moscow's Mayor, Luzhkov was elected Vice-Mayor of Moscow.

A year later he became Mayor. It is important to understand that Gavriil Popov's resignation as Mayor of Moscow and the rise of Yuri Luzhkov to replace him in June 1992 were all agreed with Pitovranov and Bobkov, with whom Luzhkov enjoyed an excellent relationship. Popov would never have left his post if Bobkov or Pitovranov had objected to it, or if the parties involved had not already agreed with the new Mayor on all issues of importance to them.

Even at the beginning of his career as a Mayor of Moscow, Yuri Luzhkov was already a very well-informed person. Luzhkov's sympathies did not involve President Yeltsin and the democrats around him. He instead believed in the power and political future of, first and foremost, *Most* Group Holding consultant Bobkov and those he represented. Showing loyalty to these forces, Luzhkov clashed in public with all of Yeltsin's appointees—Yegor Gaydar, Boris Nemtsov, and Anatoly Chubais. It was deeply personal. Even in January of 2010, after the sudden death of Gaydar, Luzhkov could not help himself and co-wrote an article together with Gavriil Popov denigrating the former reformist and Russian Prime Minister.[258]

Tatyana Dyachenko, Yeltsin's daughter, wrote in 2010 that the relationship between Luzhkov and Yeltsin began to deteriorate in the Fall of 1994. At the time, Korzhakov was trying hard to persuade Yeltsin that Luzhkov harbored plans to take over as President. This view was not without merit but with one significant *caveat* that it was Bobkov and Pitovranov, not Luzhkov himself, who hatched the plan to install Luzhkov in the Kremlin. And that is exactly why they swapped the wobbly democrat Popov with the self-assured Luzhkov.

Korzhakov's Counter Move

In December of 1994, bolstered by his conversations with Yeltsin, Korzhakov decided to demonstrate to Bobkov that the Secret Service of the President was in charge of the country, and not *Most* SS. Unlike Bobkov, Korzhakov had an unlimited budget. Korzhakov also had the authority associated with being the director of the 'official' Intelligence Services at the Lubyanka. A former Navy Seal diver (frogman) Viktor Portnov, who served in the Special Operations Center established by Korzhakov as part of the SBP, recalled that they were to provoke *Most* to flush out their supporters in the Cheka:

Everyone probably remembers well the banking 'turmoil' at the end of 1994, in which *Most*-Bank was involved. Vladimir Gusinsky claimed then that they could install as President whomever they wanted. To which Alexander Korzhakov responded: 'You don't get to decide who will be the President.' Thus, our unit was tasked with provoking Gusinsky into taking action and finding out whose support he had in power structures that enabled him to make such claims.[259]

'Operation Nose in the Snow' is how journalists described the clash between *Most*'s Gusinsky (Bobkov) and Korzhakov's SBP. On the morning of December 2, 1994, an armored Mercedes and a Jeep with Gusinsky's security detail were driving from Gusinsky's dacha to Moscow and got on the Rublyovsko-Uspensky Highway. At one of the turns, a Volvo carrying Special Operations Center personnel wedged itself between the Jeep and Gusinsky's Mercedes. And like that, tail to tail, at a speed of 100-120 kilometers per hour, they got to Kutuzovsky Avenue in Moscow, and then stopped between the Moscow Mayor's office (where Gusinsky's office was located) and the White House.

Meanwhile, Gusinsky had called Colonel Yevgeny Savostyanov, the Head of the FSB office for Moscow and the Moscow Region (the KGB officer who had given the Central Committee of the Party 45 minutes to vacate their offices on 23 August, 1991, at 2.15pm). Gusinsky also called the head of Moscow's Central Internal Affairs Department to report the attack. It was not clear exactly who was following Gusinsky; it could have easily been some criminals. Savostyanov sent in SFB unit from Counter-Terrorism Department; the Head of the Central Internal Affairs Department sent in a SWAT unit as well. A shoot-out began in which, however, no one was injured, as they quickly realized the attackers were from Korzhakov's SBP. *Most* SS officers had to stand down. Korzhakov's people pulled Gusinsky's personnel from the cars and had them lie face-down in the dirty snow, keeping them there for some two hours.

Korzhakov's operation achieved a major goal. It revealed at least one political ally of Bobkov—General Savostyanov, Director of the FSB for Moscow and Moscow Region. On the same day, based on Korzhakov's order, he was dismissed from his post by Yeltsin. The position was filled with Korzhakov's man—Lieutenant General Anatoly Trofimov, who had monitored dissidents during the Soviet years.[260]

In July of 1995, based on his close relationship with the President, Korzhakov managed to move his friend General Barsukov, a man personally loyal to him but with no operational experience, across from the MSD to the FSB as director of the renamed Intelligence Service. He then managed to reorganize the MSD's 10,000 personnel, who previously reported to Barsukov, to report to him going forward. The MSD thus became an organizational part of the SBP. Accordingly, Korzhakov in reality assumed control over the entire layer of 'protected' officials in Russia, in addition to already being in charge of the physical protection of the top officials. By 1995,

Korzhakov's Secret Service of the President consisted of more than 40,000 people. By comparison, in August of 1991, the National Guard, the KGB's border troops which guarded the vast state borders, consisted of 220,000 people.

Having executed his plan to create an independent Secret Service of the President and to fill leadership positions with people loyal to him, Korzhakov was now Russia's No 2 without anyone, not even Yeltsin, noticing. Naturally, in November 1992, after the removal of Yeltsin's loyalist Gennady Burbulis, who was the State Secretary and the First Deputy Chair of the Government of Russia, Korzhakov began to advance his own Chekist candidate to succeed Yeltsin.

Korzhakov's candidate was Oleg Soskovets, former director of the Karaganda Metallurgical Plant. True to his principle to promote and recruit only the people who were already compromised, Korzhakov chose Soskovets because he already possessed a case file with *kompromat*. Korzhakov knew that a criminal case had been brought against the latter in Karaganda in relation to large-scale embezzlement at his plant.

On April 30, 1993, Soskovets was appointed First Deputy Chair of the Council of Ministers of Russia. On July 16 of the same year, he became the Head of the government's Industrial Policy Council. In these roles, he ran 14 major ministries (including the ministries of fuel and energy, transportation, communications, railways, medical industry and healthcare, and atomic energy). He also chaired more than 20 governmental commissions, including the Commission on Operational Questions, the Interagency Commission on Military and Technological Cooperation of Russia with Foreign Countries, the Anti-Monopoly Commission, the Commission to Improve the System for Payments and Settlements, and several others.

Korzhakov was playing a long game. Having achieved power at a relatively young age (and, as he thought, forever), Korzhakov never considered the possibility he might lose it—a thought that constantly bedeviled Pitovranov and Bobkov from bitter experience in their careers. He was ready to fight for that power by any means, and he deliberately encouraged the man he protected, President Yeltsin, to drink more to render him incapacitated in a longstanding Cheka tradition of slow poisoning.

With Soskovets as Yeltsin's successor, Korzhakov saw himself becoming the *de facto* leader of the country. 'What do you reckon, why couldn't I run a state like Russia?' was a rhetorical question posed by Korzhakov and jotted down by someone from Korzhakov's circle. In the scenario plotted by Korzhakov, he would remain in charge of the SBP, and his associate Barsukov would continue as Director of the FSB. The next presidential elections would simply be cancelled by declaring a state of emergency—over threats of a Communist revenge or whatever. Yeltsin, remaining in his post as the President, would rule with the support of Korzhakov (as the SBP director) and Barsukov (as the FSB director) during the first phase; during the second phase, he would retire for health reasons (since his health was shattered by long-term alcoholism, about which Korzhakov constantly spread rumors), or (who knew?)

maybe he would die of *delirium tremens*. As Korzhakov recalled in one of the interviews,

> After February 1, 1996, Yeltsin was a walking corpse. Period. He could not be elected. I had only two hours at work. I arrived at nine, and by eleven Yeltsin would call: 'Alexander [Korzhakov], shall we have lunch?' That was it, the day was over! They said I was No 2 in the country then. I would correct that now: Don't insult me, I was really No 1 at times. When Yeltsin was completely 'out of it,' who else had their finger on the buttons?[261]

After Yeltsin resigned, Soskovets would take his place as Acting President of Russia. Then 'proper' presidential elections would be held, and Soskovets would win and become a legitimate President. There was even a date for Korzhakov's planned coup: no later than the date already established by law—June 16, 1996. It was no accident that, as Korzhakov stated in his interview, Yeltsin 'could not be elected,' and had become a 'walking corpse,' 'after February 1'—that is, right before the presidential elections.

Korzhakov's plans were clearly known to analysts from Bobkov's *Most* Secret Service. Its top Intelligence officers monitored every step by Korzhakov and his SBP team. Using 'friendly' media and its 'own' journalists, the *Most* Group Holding, which already managed to build its own media empire under Gusinsky, started regularly attacking Korzhakov and his man Soskovets. *Komsomolskaya Pravda*, for example, made Korzhakov's blueprint a matter of public record, as well as the Soskevet's skeleton in the cupboard, and how Korzhakov was controlling Russia's arms trade:

> Not only in the interest of preserving the balance, but also to strengthen his influence, Korzhakov regularly hatched plans to declare a State of Emergency in the country. At the same time, he intended to consolidate control into a single 'fist' over enforcement structures and their budgets, over the military-industrial complex, and over the arms trade; to remove Chernomyrdin; to turn the State Duma into a fictional body; to cancel the Presidential Election in 1996, while naming Soskovets as political successor....
>
> Much has been said and written about the level of corruption of Mr Soskovets, who would not lift a finger for anyone unless he saw personal benefit in it. Advancing Soskovets up the career ladder, Korzhakov knew full well about the criminal case brought against Soskovets by the KGB back when he was the director of the Karaganda Metallurgical Plant. The case was about the embezzlement of a million US dollars.

Today, Soskovet's million dollars does not sound that impressive in modern Russia. Back then, it would be a fatal blow to the candidacy of a potential head of state.

The point about arms trade was not made by accident. In Soviet times, arms sales overseas were handled by the Main Engineering Department of the Ministry of Foreign Economic Relations. The Main Engineering Department personnel were mainly staff officers of the GRU. After the August Revolution of 1991, the SBP Director decided to assume control over the revenues from arms sales. On November 18, 1993, Yeltsin signed Order No 1932-s (secret), forming the state-owned company called *Rosvooruzheniye* (Russian armament) in order to 'streamline' management of complicated business of arms sales. That company would represent the interests of Russia's military-industrial complex *vis-à-vis* foreign arms purchasers. This order gave control over state-owned *Rosvooryzheniye* to the SBP—that is, to Korzhakov. Department V(*ooruzheniye*, armament) was formed at his SBP. Its primary task was to monitor the activities of the *Rosvooruzheniye* company, as well as major state enterprises in charge of the precious metals trade.

Korzhakov appointed Alexander Kotyolkin to lead Department V. He was born in 1954, graduated from the Kiev Military Technical School and served in the air force for number of years. He later joined the GRU and was sent to study at the Diplomatic Academy of the MFA. In the late 1980s, Kotyolkin served as a military intelligence officer under diplomatic cover, at the Soviet permanent mission to the United Nations in New York.

In the US, Kotyolkin caught the attention of the FBI due to his numerous romantic relations with the wives of Soviet diplomats who were UN employees, and because of his relationships with colleagues in the GRU. Kotyolkin was also close with Sergei Glazyev, first the deputy minister, and later, Minister of Foreign Economic Relations in Gaydar's government. With Glazyev's help, Kotyolkin was assigned to the Ministry of Foreign Economic Relations as the Head of the Main Office of Military and Technical Cooperation (the Main Engineering Department's successor). In November of 1994, Kotyolkin became the CEO of *Rosvooruzheniye*, and Korzhakov gained access to the company's revenue stream of hundreds of millions of dollars.

Control over the Ostankino

But Korzhakov needed more than the SBP's enforcement actions and *Rosvooryzheniye*'s funds to neutralize his Cheka competitors at *Most* group. He needed his own TV channel, like Gusinsky at *Most*. TV studio Ostankino and TV Channel One, with its 80% share of the country's television audience (that is, roughly 180 million people) was the easiest target, on the one hand, and the most attractive one, on the other. It not only gave access to Russian public opinion, but also the potential to earn serious 'free-flowing' money via the new opportunities offered by television—commercial advertising.

Indeed, television had endless potential in terms of advertising. Many television broadcasters, in competition with each other, were in a hurry to offer their advertising services on Russia's central broadcasting. A significant portion of the money that was brought in by advertising was paid in American dollars and ended up in the pockets of executive producers and their subordinates working directly with advertisers.

Fourteen brand-new advertising agencies operated on Russia's central broadcasting during this period. They signed contracts with TV producers to sell them airtime. After purchasing airtime, an advertising agency would divide and subdivided it as it pleased and sell it to advertisers. Airtime purchased wholesale was purchased in blocks ranging from ten minutes to several hours a day, and for several days or months per year; it was then sold by the second or minute at much higher prices. The profit from these deals was colossal and the money never made it to the accounts of state television. It was split among a group of people who managed to bypass the state and share the massive television advertising market amongst themselves.

Korzhakov had one legacy problem in establishing dominance over *Most*. Historically, the KGB—Bobkov's 5th Directorate—always had very strong ARO representation in television, as that is where Active Reserve officers often wanted to go—requests were limitless. The plethora of Active Reserve officers in broadcasting provided the KGB with *de facto* control over TV organizations. In charge of Ostankino was a long-time 5th Directorate agent (the 1st Department oversaw television in the 1970s) of the 3rd Section, Valentin Lazutkin. He was officially the deputy to several Ostankino chairmen—Leonid Kravchenko, Yegor Yakovlev, Vyacheslav Bragin, and, finally, Alexander Yakovlev. The name and organization of the TV center was constantly changing, but its location and name 'Ostankino' remained the same.

In the mid-1970s, the 5th Directorate's Yevgeny Ivanov headed the 3rd Section of the 1st Department. Ivanov mainly commanded officers younger than forty. His deputy was Georgiy Kalachev, tasked with overseeing Gosteleradio (state-owned television and radio). Vladimir Skomorokhov and Alexander Prokhorov were the controllers of Goskino (state-owned movie studio). Yuri Novikov oversaw Ostankino, and his colleague, a senior 5th Directorate operative Major Vladimir Toropyni (3rd Section of the 1st Department) oversaw Ostankino's foreign broadcasting. Colonel Valentin Malygin served as the resident Intelligence officer at central television in Moscow. He was previously the Head of the Secretariat of the 5th Directorate. With respect to television, he combined the duties of a resident spy with those of the Chief of the 1st Department at Ostankino. Malygin had a network of approximately ten agents. Mikhail Kravtsov, a KGB district officer for Moscow and Moscow Region, was also transferred to Ostankino. He became the second State Security resident there and directed KGB agents in television. In the end, at least two resident KGB officers and approximately thirty KGB agents worked in the various Ostankino offices. In the early 1980s, the 14th Department of the 5th Directorate was established; it was tasked with overseeing the State Committee for Radio Broadcasting and Television, and the Ostankino TV Center. Lieutenant Colonel Nikandrov was appointed to lead the 14th Department. The head of the Ostankino operations was a senior security officer—Major Tsibizov—who came from the 1st Department of the 5th Directorate.

Malygin, Tsibizov and Nikandrov were very well informed about the happenings in each specific creative office and other departments of Ostankino. The various companies, organizations, and banks striving to establish business relations with the OTRK (as the Ostankino TV and Radio Complex was now abbreviated) were also of interest to them. Among the organizations interested in working with Ostankino, the most promising and preferred (from the 5th Directorate's perspective) were selected; those received the most preferential treatment in television programming.

Malygin was also knowledgeable about future advertising projects that began appearing during *perestroika,* since correspondence between agencies and organizations on all serious matters went through the 1st Department. But most importantly, Malygin could directly influence the manner in which advertising proposals were reviewed and the decisions that were made. Some documents were intentionally disappeared; others bore a written note that State Intelligence did not deem 'appropriate' any contact with a given commercial organization.

The OTRK was a controlled zone. Entrance to the Ostankino TV Center was granted by special permits (that is, permanent passes for employees or temporary passes for visitors). As the Head of Security, Tsibizov was well familiar with the circle of individuals who visited the OTRK. He had discretion to deny a pass to any visitor. On his orders, any employee and their personal belongings could be searched when they entered the building. But, since Tsibizov was drinking heavily by that time and did not care about what was happening, all strings controlling the Ostankino were in the hands of Malygin and the head of the 2nd Section of the 14th Department of the 5th Directorate, Lieutenant Colonel Alexander Komelkov, who also had a drinking problem and for this had the nickname 'eggplant' because of his blue color face.

He and Malygin scheduled television airtime and rented out OTRK facilities to businesses, while clearly not forgetting to line their pockets with rental proceeds. In 1989, however, after numerous scandals and abuses, Komelkov was fired from the service 'for actions detrimental to the reputation of a Soviet officer.'

Now a civilian, Komelkov used the money he extracted from Ostankino businesses to open a new brewery/restaurant on Kutuzovsky Avenue near the *Triumfalnaya Arka* (triumphal arch) monument, which was frequented by members of the Solntsevskaya organized crime group. Since Kutuzovsky Avenue was a government road controlled by the SPB responsible for the security of top officials in the country, the SBP became aware of Komelkov's restaurant. Korzhakov had found his man.

And so, the all-powerful SBP chief trusted by Yeltsin reinstated Komelkov as an Intelligence Services officer, made him a colonel, and appointed him to lead the department overseeing the OTRK. Komelkov was just the right man for Korzhakov in television. It was important that Komelkov had been fired, which meant he was angry with his colleagues, and most of all, with his former chief Bobkov. Finally,

Korzhakov, using Komelkov, could get information on the happenings inside *Most* SS as many of Komelkov's colleagues from the 5th Directorate (Directorate Z) worked there.

Komelkov, for his part, intended to gain insight into Bobkov's plans through his colleague Balev. That plan, however, failed. As a Bobkov appointee, Balev was loyal to him. He did not refuse Komelkov's invitations to 'sit down and chat,' but the conversation never went further than reminiscing about 'the old days' and talking about mutual acquaintances. Tired of pointless conversations, Komelkov told Balev straight that he had been sent by Korzhakov. But Balev categorically refused to become Komelkov's informant. Several days later, Moscow papers reported that Balev (they printed his name Bolev), a top analyst from the *Most* SS, had been severely beaten by unknown assailants near his home.

With Korzhakov's support, Komelkov was quickly able to become quite an influential person on television. The majority of human resource decisions now only took place with his approval. Komelkov also solved Korzhakov's problem of penetrating *Most* SS. Money opened all doors, and Korzhakov's *moles* soon began to penetrate *Most* SS. It was they who were responsible for leaking analytical reports of *Most* SS with detailed information about leading Russian politicians and businessmen which at one point were released to the public.

It was thus becoming public knowledge that Bobkov's and Gusinsky's private commercial organization *Most* Group Holding was collecting compromising material on the President's people. The press was full of transcripts of telephone conversations of well-known people in the country. This underscored the urgency of Korzhakov gaining access to Channel One, the primary channel on Russian Television, as well as gaining control over Ostankino. To make that happen, it was necessary to place 'their guy' in charge of Ostankino.

Vladislav Listev was chosen for that role. Listev came to television at the end of 1987. In a few years, he became one of the top television journalists. However, the story of Listev's uneasy and complicated life, which ended tragically, became a sad illustration of the relationships that the Cheka built with its agents.

Having grown up in a simple family and losing his father at a young age, Listev was able to enroll at the Journalism Department in MSU and transferred to the International Journalism Department after a few years. There were many foreign students at MSU who came to study in the USSR from Third-World countries and even from 'Capitalist' countries. They were all objects of constant surveillance by State Security. MSU and PFU were overseen by the 3rd Department of the 5th Directorate.

Recruiting foreign students for the KGB's agent network required Soviet agents with established popularity and authority among foreign student groups. The outgoing and athletic Listev from MSU's Journalism Department could not help but catch the eye of officers from the 3rd Department of the 5th Directorate. And Listev's long relationship with this department commenced.

Elena Kozeltseva, a 5th Directorate senior operative in the 3rd Department was a Cheka veteran. She began serving under Pitovranov's leadership and ended her career under the command of Bobkov, Pitovranov's protégé. Short in stature and inconspicuous in appearance, Kozeltseva monitored the Moscow State University (MSU) and struck terror in the hearts of the university personnel—professors and administration alike. Ivan Petrovsky, one of the most prominent scholars in the country and the Dean of MSU, would never take a risk of disagreeing with her. Due to her special position and in violation of the KGB's own rules, she lived in an excellent apartment provided by MSU at Leninsky (today, Vorobyovy) Heights, in a building reserved for the university's professorial and teaching staff. One word from Kozeltseva was enough to have a person enrolled in a given department or transferred to another one. Her colleagues in the 5th Directorate were also afraid of her, even though she was just a Major.

On Kozeltseva's recommendation, Listev was among the lucky students to be accepted into the International Journalism Department. Soon he became part of a group of students formed to complete a pre-graduation internship in a foreign country—that is, Cuba or Nicaragua. The paperwork required to travel to those countries was the same as for 'capitalist' countries, which meant that the applicants were subject to a more thorough scrutiny by the KGB.

However, despite the 5th Directorate's interest in sending Listev overseas so he could continue studying targets of operational interest, the trip never took place. He was removed from the traveling student group after information was received that showed him and his close relatives in a negative light. Even the all-powerful Kozeltseva was not in a position to help him. In the end, Listev was hired by Central Soviet Radio.

In 1987, the Agitation and Propaganda Department of the CC initiated the creation of a national series of new television programs meant to influence positively the minds of Soviet people in a time of unprecedented change in the country. In accordance with this directive, a youth program called *Vzglyad* (view) was created. For that program, young, skilled journalists, including Listev, were recruited.

Over time, *Vzglyad* became one of the most popular shows on television. With it, Listev's authority rose correspondingly as the State Security kept promoting him. Korzhakov, a member of the Yeltsin family circle, insisted to Yeltsin and his wife Naina that Listev, as a 'top-quality professional,' held the keys to the future. In 1991, after the failure of the August putsch, Yeltsin appointed Listev as General Producer of OTRK. In September 1994, Listev became Vice-President of the Academy of Russian Television. In January 1995, he was appointed General Director of Public Television of Russia (ORT)—the new, privatized structure of the old OTRK—where Boris Berezovsky was the main shareholder.

It was then that Listev's handlers Korzhakov and Komelkov tasked him with consolidating the entire television advertising market under their personal control. It was agreed that all the money earned from selling advertising time must go to bank accounts controlled by the SBP. In January 1995, right after being appointed General

Director of ORT, Listev made a public announcement, from which it became clear that advertizing on ORT would be handled by a select circle of companies personally controlled by him. On February 20, 1995, Listev announced a temporary moratorium on all types of advertising until ORT developed a new approach. Thus, the war for the redistribution of television advertising time had begun.

Main advertisers' plans and organizations behind them were known to Listev's handler Komelkov and his colleagues Tsibizov and Malygun, Head of the Security department at ORT and Chief of the 1st Department, respectively. Through the names of people who had visited various television broadcasters and who had been issued security passes, Komelkov was able to identify easily the individuals associated with the various organized crime groups in Moscow. He also knew which law enforcement agencies were monitoring these individuals and how advanced the monitoring was.

But Korzhakov was pressuring Listev. They needed funds to generate public opinion in order to support the substitution of the exhausted Yeltsin with the young and active Deputy Prime Minister Soskovets. There was little time as the Presidential Election was nearing and the chances of Yeltsin winning, with his ratings as low as they were, seemed dismal. The amount of support needed was some $50-60 million. This was the sum that ended up spelling Listev's demise as he could not provide Korzhakov with that kind of cash through advertising, and Korzhakov planned his exit.

It is hard to pinpoint the exact timing of when the plan to eliminate Listev took shape. But the operation clearly served multiple purposes. In the first instance, Listev would be taken out. In the second stage, Boris Berezovsky, the main shareholder, and Sergei Lisovsky, the main competitor of Listev in the ORT advertising market, were to be accused of organizing the killing. In the third stage, Berezovsky would be arrested, and Yeltsin, disappointed in Berezovsky and Lisovsky, would give control over ORT to a new group of shareholders proposed by Korzhakov. Meanwhile, Lisovsky would no longer be allowed to continue his activities at ORT as someone under investigation. Therefore, both the ORT and its advertising business would end up in Korzhakov's hands.

In those days, Listev was expecting a meeting with representatives of the Solntsevskaya organized crime group, who were to approach him demanding a payoff of several million dollars given that Listev failed to deliver the project in which they were keenly interested. Given the seriousness of the situation, Listev asked Komelkov to intervene and protect him from financial harassment by the organized criminals. Listev naively thought that the simplest way to protect him would be to deny these people entry to the Ostankino building. The fact that the mobsters were ultimately granted entry passes meant that Komelkov and others at the Intelligence Services had abandoned him.

On March 1, 1995, Listev was murdered in the lobby of his apartment building. It is impossible to imagine that Komelkov would have conducted this operation without Korzhakov sanctioning it. And the best proof that Listev's murder was sanctioned at the highest level of the Intelligence Services is Komelkov's subsequent career growth. After the successful operation to take out Listev, he was appointed as deputy head of Directorate Z. That was a serious promotion.

Just as Korzhakov had planned, the primary ORT shareholder Berezovsky and advertising magnate Lisovsky were the main suspects in Listev's murder. However, the attempt to arrest Berezovsky in his office at 40 Novokuznetskaya Street in Moscow was unsuccessful. Berezovsky managed to contact Prime Minister Viktor Chernomyrdin who prevented the arrest. Materials compromising Korzhakov and Barsukov were promptly planted in media outlets controlled by the *Most* group. Chubais, who was supported by Yeltsin, spoke up for Berezovsky and Gusinsky-*Most*. ORT remained in Berezovsky's hands, and Korzhakov never got the $50-60 million he needed to execute his plan.

Another State of Emergency
In desperation, Korzhakov decided to go down a cheaper route that did not require any television PR, that is to declare a non-existent State of Emergency as in August 1991 and postpone the elections. After the August 1991 putsch and Congress's defeat in 1993, this would be the third State of Emergency in Russia's brief five-year history as an independent nation.

But there had to be a reason for declaring a State of Emergency. The real reason was Yeltsin's impending defeat in the Presidential Election and the impending victory of the new, rising Communist leader Zyuganov. But that was evidently not an acceptable reason for declaring a State of Emergency. Something else was needed—something politically neutral that did not threaten new unrest and accusations of the Kremlin usurping power.

Yeltsin found himself in an unenviable position. After the 1996 Election, no matter how events unfolded, power would wind up in the hands of the FSB, since absolutely everyone involved in the political struggle with any chances of success were Cheka operatives, protegés, or people under Cheka control. Yeltsin's main competitor for power in Russia, the leader of the Communist Party Zyuganov, was completely cocooned in the Lubyanka from the first day of his political career in that among the KGB agents and personnel embedded in his movement were many sincere national communists controlled by the Lubyanka, who were the people who determined the Communist Party's strategy and tactics.

It was not possible for Yeltsin to oppose Zyuganov's well-organized campaign that had support from communist, patriotic, fascist, nationalist, and other not always visible groups relying on Intelligence Services support, with only Korzhakov on his side telling him to cancel the Election. Repeating the October military operation of 1993 by declaring a State of Emergency and shelling Parliament was not possible in 1996 without any provocation from the winning side. But, Yeltsin's victory (with Korzhakov's SBP staying in power), and Zyuganov's victory (with power going to the communists infiltrated by the State Security), were not so different in terms of their result—the Lubyanka taking the Kremlin.

Nevertheless, both options had serious pitfalls. With a Zyuganov victory, the Communist Party could theoretically reclaim power, and everything would revert to where it had been in 1991. Not an attractive option for the Lubyanka. With a Yeltsin win, an illegitimate State of Emergency, which Korzhakov was pushing for, might be ignored and the country's governance could take a democratic turn with governance via elections. These were real risks for the Cheka *en route* to its cherished goal.

To manage that uncertainty, a trap was set for Yeltsin, which made the shelling of parliament in October 1993 look like child's play. Russia was pulled into the fierce and pointless First Chechen War. Back then, of course, no one knew that it would one day be referred to as the 'First'.

Chechnya turned out to be the weakest link in the multi-national Russian mosaic. Considering Dzhokhar Dudayev, General of Strategic Aviation, one of its own, the KGB initially did not oppose his rise to power in the Republic. Dudayev, a member of the Communist Party since 1968, was transferred from Estonia to his native Grozny as if specifically to stand in opposition to the local communists, get elected President of the Chechen Republic, and declare Chechnya's (Ichkeria's) independence in November 1991, seemingly demonstrating to the Russian political elite exactly the extent of damage Yeltsin's democracy would inflict to the country. It was probably no coincidence that another Chechen activist close to the president, Khasbulatov, would also be blamed for having dealt a fatal blow to the young Russian democracy. Khasbulatov, a former activist of the CC of the Komsomol and a member of the Communist Party since 1966, became Chair of the Russian Supreme Soviet in September 1991, the very same body that Yeltsin chased off with tanks in October 1993.

Yeltsin was not inclined to yield to Dudayev in the matter of Chechnya's independence, especially when this potential conflict had one obvious political benefit: it was a real reason to institute a State of Emergency and cancel or postpone the Presidential Election until 'the situation normalizes.' Yeltsin did not have to yield power to Zyuganov simply based on the election; in a country at war, Yeltsin could simply avoid holding the election altogether.

And suddenly the terror attacks began. On November 18, 1994, there was an explosion on a railway bridge over the Yauza River. According to experts, two powerful charges went off with about 1.5kg of TNT each. Twenty meters of railway tracks were destroyed, and the bridge nearly collapsed. However, the bombs went off too early, before the train crossed the bridge. The corpse of the assailant was found blown to pieces at the site of the explosion. The bomber turned out to be the little-known Captain Andrey Shchelenkov, an employee of the also little-known oil company Lanako (more on its owner below). He was killed by his own bomb as he installed it on the bridge. No one was able to turn this event into national news or to blame the Chechens for it. Overall, the operation was a failure.

However, the 18 November, 1994, railway attack was the first known attempt by the Lubyanka to harm Russian citizens—blaming Chechen separatists as a false flag in order to take advantage of angry public opinion and start a military intervention against a 'rebellious' Chechnya. On the day of the Yauza explosion, November 18, 1994, an anonymous phone call to the police reported a truck full of explosives at the Lanako office. A truck—a ZIL-131 containing three MON-50 mines, fifty grenade launcher rounds, fourteen RGD-5 grenades, ten F-1 grenades, and four packs of plastic explosives weighing 6 kilograms in total—was indeed found near the Lanako office, but the regional FSB reported it could not determine who exactly the truck belonged to, even though a Lanako ID was found that very day in the pocket of the deceased Shchelenkov, and the same kind of explosives were used in the Yauza bombing. Since the truck never blew up and the attack failed, too, Chechen separatists could not really be blamed.

Nevertheless, despite the lack of successful terror attacks, a war with the Republic of Chechnya was initiated. A military operational plan was already in place. The Russian State Security were not about to suspend it pending successful terror attacks at home.

On November 23, nine Russian helicopters of the North-Caucuses Military District aviation, presumably MI-8s, carried out missile strikes on the city of Shali, roughly 40 kilometers from Grozny, attempting to destroy the armored vehicles of the tank regiment located there. The Chechens suffered casualties and claimed that they had video footage of helicopters with Russian identification markings carrying out the attack.

On November 25, seven Russian helicopters from a military base in Stavropol Region carried out several rockets strikes on the airport in Grozny and nearby residential buildings, damaging the runway and the civilian aircraft on it. Six people died and roughly 25 were injured.

On November 26, the forces of the Temporary Council of Chechnya (that is, the Chechen anti-Dudayev opposition formed by the Russian Intelligence), with support from Russian helicopters and armor, attacked Grozny from four sides. More than 1,200 troops, 50 tanks, 80 armored personnel carriers (BTR) and 6 SU-27 aircraft took part in the operation. Nevertheless, the operation failed. The attackers lost approximately 500 people and more than 20 tanks; 20 more tanks were captured and approximately 200 troops were taken prisoner.

The combat operation to attack Grozny was organized by Sergei Stepashin, Director of Federal Counterintelligence (FSK) and Colonel Savostyanov (later Chief of the Moscow Regional Intelligence after the KGB had ceased to exist as a name). However, those who described the actions of the Russian military in attacking the city with an armored column as doomed for destruction, did not understand the subtle political calculations of the provocateurs. Those in favor of war needed the Chechens to effectively destroy the column. That was the only way to provoke Yeltsin to initiate full-scale military operations. And indeed, after the column's defeat in Grozny,

President Yeltsin made a threatening speech to the Chechens involved in the clash, and the Kremlin began to condition the public opinion for the great slaughter.

The Chechen side considered Yeltsin's speech an 'ultimatum' and a 'declaration of war.' The statement of the Chechen government asserted that this speech, and any attempts to implement its themes, 'violated the norms of international rights' and gave the Chechen government 'the right to take adequate measures to defend the sovereignty and territorial integrity of the state.' Yeltsin's threat to institute a State of Emergency in Chechen territory was considered by the Chechen government to be 'an undisguised desire to continue military actions and interfere in the internal affairs of another state.'

From the standpoint of Russian domestic politics, the key words in Yeltsin's speech were about declaring the State of Emergency, which Korzhakov had insisted on and which were meant to lead to the next obvious step: instituting 'direct presidential rule' and postponing the 1996 Presidential Election.

On November 30, Grozny was subjected to air strikes by the Russian Air Force. On December 11, the Russian military crossed the demarcation zone of the Chechen Republic. A major war broke out. On December 14, the Russian government reported that, after not even three full days of fighting, 'casualties on both sides numbered in the hundreds.' The next day, it became known that there were also two consolidated regiments from the North Caucuses Military District and two amphibious assault brigades moving in the direction of Grozny, along with regiments from the MVD. Consolidated regiments of Pskov, Vitebsk, and Tula airborne-amphibious troops (VDV), each comprising 600 to 800 people, entered Chechen territory. Consolidated regiments of Ulyanovsk and Kostroma VDV troops began deploying near the town of Mozdok. The troops were preparing to storm Grozny. On the Chechen side, there were more than 13,000 armed individuals concentrated in and around Grozny.

On December 17, the MVD made a statement that at midnight on December 18 regiments of the MVD would be forced to take decisive action and use all available means to restore constitutional law and order in the territory of Chechnya. That same day, Soskovets informed the world that President Dudayev had been summoned to Mozdok to meet with a delegation of the Russian government led by Nikolai Yegorov and FSK Director Stepashin. Soskovets noted that if Dudayev did not agree to come to Mozdok, the military would proceed to liquidate any 'illegal' military units. Four hours before the ultimatum's deadline, at 8 PM on December 17, Dudayev sent a telegram to the Russian leadership offering his agreement 'to start negotiations without preliminary terms at the appropriate level and to personally lead the government's delegation.'

Dudayev never received a response. On December 18 at 9am, Russian forces blockading Grozny began the assault on the city. Front-line aviation and armed helicopters carried out 'precision strikes on Dudayev's command post in Khankala near Grozny, on bridges over the Terek leading north, and on maneuvering groups of armor.' Once the armor was destroyed, as reported by the Temporary Informational Center of the Russian Command, it was anticipated that the troops blockading Grozny would advance in order to carry out their mission of eliminating Chechen military units. The authorized representative of President Yeltsin in the Chechen Republic announced that Dudayev now only had one option left—to surrender.

On December 18, Soskovets, who had received yet another post—Director of the Operational Staff of the Government of Russia regarding Coordination of Activities of Law Enforcement—claimed to the press that Grozny was 'exploring options' for terror attacks on military and civilian targets in central Russia and the Urals, as well as for hijacking a passenger plane.

On December 22, the Press Service of the Russian Government reported that Chechens were blowing themselves up in order to blame the explosions on the Russian army. This report was initiated by Soskovets. On the next day, December 23, 1994, there was an explosion between Kozhukhovo and Kanatchikovo stations on the Moscow District Railway. There were no casualties, and the terrorists were never found.

The way that the event was described by the Russian government's press service is noteworthy:

> There are reports that three experienced soldiers, including a woman, were sent [from Chechnya] to Moscow and tasked with leading a previously deployed terrorist group. A group of foreign citizens seeking contact with the fighters from Grozny has been detained. A batch of radio-controlled explosive devices, 20 kilos of TNT, and 16 radio-controlled anti-personnel and anti-tank mines were confiscated from them. On the night of December 23, the rails at one section of the Moscow District Railway were blown up. Another mine was disarmed. Measures are being taken to track down the diversionary groups active in the Moscow Region.

The report seemed to suggest that the rails were blown up by numerous Chechen terrorists: 'two men and a woman, plus a detained group of foreign citizens who were trying to make contact with fighters from Grozny who had already penetrated the Moscow Region… And another group that may have been responsible for blowing up the rails….' But, besides the fact that the rails in a section of the Moscow District Railway were blown up on December 23, everything else in the report was false. That is, while the Chechens had nothing to do with any of it, Russian Intelligence had the most direct connection to what happened.[262]

On December 27, 1994, at 9pm, there was another terror attack: a terrorist placed a bomb on a remote detonator on a bus at the last stop of route 33 in Moscow. The bomb blew up when the bus was empty. The only casualty was the 23-year-old driver Dmitry Trapezov, who suffered serious bruising and contusion. In addition, people standing near the bus when it blew up received shrapnel injuries.

The organizer of these explosions was native of Grozny, Maxim Lazovsky, a particularly valuable agent of the FSB Department for the Moscow Region (UFSB). He was the owner and director of the Lanako oil firm, which was named after the first two letters of his last name, connected to all these attacks initially labelled as Chechen terrorism. All Lanako employees were either staff or contracted personnel of the counterintelligence apparatus of Russia—in other words, Active Reserve officers. In the Foreign Service, Pyotr Suslov was Lazovsky's handler, while in the FSB, it was Colonel Eduard Abovyan from the Department for Counteracting Illegal Gangs. The explosion on bus 33 route was carried out by Lazovsky's subordinate—Lieutenant Colonel Vladimir Vorobyev.

From February to August 1996, Lazovsky's group was completely liquidated after a successful operation conducted by officers of the 12th Division of the Moscow Criminal Investigations Department (MUR) led by detective Vladimir Tskhay. On January 31, 1997, Lazovksy stood before a judge. The trial lasted just three days. Lazovsky was sentenced to two years in prison. On April 12, 1997, at the age of 39, Tskhaiy suddenly met with a premature death. He succumbed to cirrhosis of the liver, although he neither drank nor smoked. He was most likely poisoned.[263] In February 1998, Lazovsky was released with the time of detention counting as part of his sentence.

The case against Lieutenant Colonel Vorobyev lasted longer. He was arrested by Tskhay on the morning of August 28, 1996, on his way to meet with FSB officers. He was brought to Moscow MUR at 38 Petrovka Street, where he revealed everything, including his status an FSB contractor, to the detectives. He would later deny these confessions. Either way, he was sentenced to five years in a penal colony. The trial proceedings were conducted in closed format. Even the defendant's relatives were not allowed into the courtroom. The FSB described their agent Vorobyev favorably, and that characterization was part of his case file. In his closing statement, Vorobyev stated that the case against him was fabricated by those who wanted to attack both the FSB and him, as its *de facto* agent. The sentence itself he called a 'mockery of the State Intelligence.' Later, the Supreme Court of Russia reduced Vorobyev's sentence to three years (which Vorobyev had already served by that time). In August 1999, immediately before the September 1999 'terror' attacks in Moscow, Vorobyev was released.

The Elections

The date of the 1996 Presidential Election was approved on November 15, 1995. The Election date was set for June 16, 1996. Yeltsin's ratings fluctuated between 3% and 9%, which did not give him or his supporters any serious hope of winning. With such a low rating, Zyuganov's victory and the Communist Party's return to power seemed like a foregone conclusion. At the same time, a defeat for Yeltsin also meant arrest and prison time, as Zyuganov planned to bring charges against Yeltsin related to the shelling of Parliament in October 1993.

On March 15, the Duma, dominated by the Communist Left, passed a resolution not to recognize the clauses of the Belovezha Accords formalizing the termination of the USSR. Yeltsin justifiably considered that action an attempted Communist revanche and proposed dissolving the Duma in response. On Korzhakov's advice, an order to ban the Communist Party and postpone the Presidential Election until 1998 was also prepared. A State of Emergency would be declared throughout Russian territory and the military placed on high alert to prevent any unrest that could be provoked by the Communists. The order was ready, prepared and signed, but not yet promulgated.

In a closed meeting on March 18, 1996, attended by Chernomyrdin, Soskovets, Yegorov and other members of Yeltsin's campaign staff, the majority led by Soskovets called to cancel the Election. However, another person attended Yeltsin's meeting on March 18, Tatyana Dyachenko—Yeltsin's daughter. She had not long before become a member of the Russian Government on Chubais's initiative as 'an advisor to the President on social issues.' Through her, Chubais had access to information on what was happening inside the Kremlin and, more importantly, on Yeltsin himself.

It was Dyachenko who convinced Yeltsin on March 18 before the order was published to hear the opinions of two people: Anatoly Kulikov who was the Minister of Internal Affairs and Chubais. Kulikov's position was that the MVD could not guarantee support to the President in suppressing unrest. Chubais argued that the new Russia was not interested in the return of the Communists and that, instead of tanks, funds controlled by private businesses, mass media and PR experts, including foreign ones, should be used to organize PR campaigns in connection with the election. After an hour-long discussion with Kulikov and Chubais, Yeltsin agreed to hold the election on time and revoked his order.

Was Chubais free from Cheka control? Not quite. Yeltsin's former Chief of Staff, Chubais served at that moment as the chair of the Federal Agency for State Property Management, a state agency that was implementing privatization in Russia, and as First Deputy Prime Minister. Another state agency—the Russian Federal Property Fund (RFPF)—was directly responsible for handling sale transactions involving privatized state property, including all of the details—e.g., identifying property for sale, determining its fair market value, selecting the purchasers. Between 1992 and 2008, Igor Korneyev, an Active Reserve officer from the PGU, worked as an Advisor to the Chair of the RFPF, the Deputy Head of the RFPF, and the Head of the Department for Economic Security of the RFPF. In the 1990s and 2000s, he was frequently assigned as a representative of the RFPF to the boards of directors of many privatized enterprises and was directly involved in making decisions on privatization. As soon as a company had been privatized, Korneyev moved on to be the RFPF representative on the board of directors for the next company. That is how he ensured that enterprises were privatized in accordance with the Lubyanka's wishes as to who should be their new owners. In a 1994 memo drafted by Korzhakov for Yeltsin, Korneyev was referenced as 'Chubais's representative.' In fact, Korneyev was the representative of the Intelligence Services at RFPF, and he continued working there even after Chubais left. The Chairmen and Deputy Chairmen of the Federal Agency for State Property Management kept changing but Korneyev remained. This was the mechanism through which the Lubyanka was able to monitor and guide the economic side of Chubais's activities.

Chubais had another minder. Lieutenant General Gennady Yevstafyev was the head of one of the departments of the Foreign Intelligence Service of Russia. He was related to Arkady Yevstafyev, who graduated in 1986 from the Higher School of the KGB. After that, Yevstafyev, originally from Saratov, worked in the KGB Directorate for the Saratov Region. In 1990, he graduated from the Diplomatic Academy of the MFA and served in the MFA's Department of Information, holding the post of second secretary (and since he spoke English, French, and Danish, he supervised journalists from Great Britain, Denmark, and the Scandinavian countries). Later, he became an Active Reserve officer and in 1991 served in the government's Press Office. In 1992, Yevstafyev was assigned as an Advisor and Press Secretary to Chubais, the promising democrat and First Deputy Chair of the Government; he remained in that role until 1995. In 1993, he also served as a coordinator of the advertising campaign 'For privatization,' which was a PR action to promote the benefits of the privatization program initiated by Chubais and Korneyev. From April 1995 to March 1996, Yevstafyev worked as Deputy General Director of ORT, Director of the Informational Television Agency, and headed the Directorate of Informational Programming. He was relieved of those posts after Chubais retired as First Deputy Prime Minister. That is when Yeltsin's Presidential re-election campaign began.

Barsukov and Soskovets (favored by Korzhakov as Yeltsin's successor), who clearly had no interest in securing Yeltsin's victory, initially managed his campaign. On March 23, Soskovets was removed from his post and was replaced with Chubais, who mustered the group that would later become known as 'the oligarchs' to support Yeltsin's re-election campaign financially, and provide managers and mass media controlled by the private sector for the campaign. Yevstafyev was also included in Yeltsin's campaign staff since the Lubyanka wanted to monitor Chubais's activities.

Bobkov-Gusinsky's *Most* Group also sided with Yeltsin and Chubais, in opposition to their old rivals—Korzhakov, Barsukov, and Soskovets. Gusinsky in those fiery days sat side-by-side with Berezovsky in his headquarters at 40 Novokuznetskaya Street and directed NTV in its coverage of the Presidential Campaign. ORT, controlled by Berezovsky and the Kremlin, also supported Yeltsin unconditionally. As a result, Russian television was completely in the hands of Chubais and his campaign staff. Yeltsin had by now come to realize that the Chechen War was a flagrant provocation by the FSB. He declared the deployment of troops to Chechnya a mistake and signed an armistice with the Chechen leadership in Moscow. And on May 28, during an unexpected and previously unannounced (for security reasons) visit to Grozny, he signed another cease-fire order terminating all military activities from the back of an armored personnel carrier.

It should come as no surprise that, just two weeks after the termination of military activities and five days before the election, on June 11, 1996, at ten o'clock in the evening on the Serpukhovskaya Line of the Moscow Metro, Tulskaya Station, a bomb went off in a half-empty train car. Four people were killed, and twelve wounded. Apparently, the option of using force was never wholly abandoned by Korzhakov and Soskovets. They also left open the matter concerning the order of March 18 (to postpone the Election) until the election results were tallied.

It turned out that a second round of voting had to be held as none of the candidates had received the requisite more than 50% of the votes. Nevertheless, the results were hopeful for Yeltsin. On June 16, Yeltsin received 35.28% of the votes, and Zyuganov—32.03%. The third candidate—General Alexander Lebed—received 14.52%. A second round, which included only Yeltsin and Zyuganov, was set for July 3, 1996.

After the first round, Yeltsin's campaign tactics were clear: creating a political block of Yeltsin and Lebed against Zyuganov. Lebed agreed to this alliance and called on his voters to support Yeltsin. On June 18, the general received for his efforts the powerful posts of Secretary of the Security Council of Russia 'with special powers' and of National Security Advisor to President Yeltsin.

The math was simple. It became obvious that Yeltsin could get a second term through winning the election and not by its cancellation. Korzhakov, Barsukov, and Soskovets now had very little time to seize the initiative. On June 19, 1996, the day after Lebed was sworn in, they made their final desperate attempt to sabotage the situation and provoke Yeltsin to show force and call off the elections and a state of emergency. On the evening of June 19, Korzhakov (from the SBP) and Barsukov (from the FSB) sent officers to arrest members of Yeltsin's campaign staff who were leaving the White House with a cardboard box full of papers. They were Yevstafyev, Lisovsky and Boris Lavrov, an employee of the National Reserve Bank, which was headed by a member of the Pitovranov-Bobkov group, Alexander Lebedev, and who was involved along with his bank in financing the presidential campaign.[264]

The cardboard box contained $538,000. The detainees were brought back to the White House, placed in specially equipped rooms 306 and 310, and subjected to questioning, during which Lavrov said he brought the money to the White House from the Department of Foreign Loans in the Ministry of Finance.

Korzhakov had another card to play. A few days earlier, on the evening of June 19, Korzhakov's SBP broke into the office of the Deputy Minister of Finance German Kuznetsov, a former partner of Birshtein in his Kyrgyzstan project exporting gold to Switzerland, and secretly unlocked his safe. The safe contained $1.5 million (but no one knew about this 'catch' of Korzhakov's yet, except the SBP insiders).

Berezovsky, Gusinsky, and other members of Yeltsin's campaign staff who were located during those hours at 40 Novokuznetskaya Street building (Chubais was in contact with them), interpreted this as the beginning of yet another coup. The arrest of Yevstafyev, Lisovsky, and Lavrov could be only the beginning, and Korzhakov-Barsukov-Soskovets could try to arrest Yeltsin's entire campaign staff, justifying their actions with trumped-up evidence of 'embezzlement' from the President's own campaign funds. But the cash in question was actually intended for various payments related to the campaign. Korzhakov certainly knew that. This was another demonstration of power, a 'Nose in the Snow' type provocation.

On June 20, Yeltsin listened to the explanations of all the participants of the dramatic events of June 19 and 20 and took Chubais's side. The Korzhakov-Barsukov-Soskovets plot had failed. On that same day, June 20, Yeltsin reshuffled his team and Korzhakov troika was terminated: all three conspirators were let go. Chubais was appointed as his new Chief of Staff. Bobkov had won and vanquished the Korzhakov team. This was the troika's 'Nose in the Snow' moment. In the second round, Yeltsin, thanks to Lebed's support, received 53.82% of the votes; Zyuganov—40.31%.

By now, the war in Chechnya was practically over. But someone stubbornly tried to sabotage the signing of a formal peace through further acts of terror. On July 11, trolleybus No 12 was blown up at Pushkin Square. Six people were wounded. The next day, a No 48 trolleybus exploded on Mira Avenue. Twenty-eight people received injuries of varying severity. Rumors began to spread quickly in Moscow about a 'Chechen trail' of the attacks, and Moscow's Mayor Luzhkov announced from the site of the latest trolleybus blast that he would evict the entire Chechen *diaspora* from Moscow. It was a very strange announcement. No terrorists had been apprehended, or proof of Chechen involvement put forward. In fact, the Chechens, who had just won a decisive victory over Russia, could not have been interested in the least in resuming fighting and sabotaging a peace agreement that was beneficial to Chechnya and ready to be signed.

Luzhkov could clearly only have received the information about a 'Chechen trail' to the attacks from the AROs in his circle: Stepashin and Savostyanov, or from his old friend Bobkov—who had him in mind as a potential Yeltsin alternative. Another thing was curious. The second wave of terror, just like the first, did not lead to anti-Chechen panic in Russia. On August 31, the Minister of State Security Lebed and the new President of Chechnya Aslan Maskhadov (the previous one, Dzhokhar Dudayev, had been killed with a rocket attack by Russian Security forces on April 21, 1996) signed the Khasavyurt Accord. The Chekist warmongers lost, and the terror attacks stopped (that is, until the FSB began a new 'terrorist' operation against Russians to ignite another war with Chechnya before the Presidential Election in 2000).

Having ensured Yeltsin's victory in the presidential elections, supported Chubais in the clash with Korzhakov, ensured an ambiguous peace accord for Russia with the Chechen Republic, and ended a bloody war, Lebed was no longer needed by Yeltsin.

On December 17, the ungrateful Yeltsin dismissed Lebed on suspicion of planning a coup (an investigation later revealed these charges to be baseless).

From the Lubyanka's perspective, another round in the fight for power in Russia was lost—considering the dismissal of two Kremlin leaders, Korzhakov and Barsukov, and the return of democrat Chubais to the Kremlin. But looking at the situation holistically, it was far from hopeless for the FSB. The Intelligence Services had managed to capture extremely high positions everywhere at the Kremlin and a formal takeover of power in Russia was now within arm's reach.

Having lost another fight, for the third time (1991, 1993, 1996), the Communist Party gave up. The Lubyanka had no competition left. But the roles were redistributed. Korzhakov, ousted by Yeltsin, became an ARO and received a new 'post'—chief Duma critic of the President. Meanwhile, the former SBP Director, as before, remained untouchable. He could utter any insult about the President and his circle, including the President's family, and even about all future Presidents, mixing facts with fiction, and nobody, including Yeltsin and his power brokers, would dare object to Korzhakov, let alone try to silence him. In 1997, Korzhakov became a Duma delegate and stayed there until 2011. For reasons beyond ordinary understanding, Korzhakov received a lifetime pardon.

From the outside, it may seem like Korzhakov's unprecedented level of criticism should have been directed not just at Yeltsin and his circle of 'democrats,' but against Bobkov and *Most* as well since he was the rival of Korzhakov's SBP from 1991 to 1996. But, in fact, Korzhakov and Bobkov were partners in a shared cause—the battle for the victory of the Cheka. There could never have been any personal hatred or dislike between them. They both wholeheartedly served the Lubyanka and the Motherland to the extent of their knowledge, abilities, and talents. 'I made peace with Army General Filipp Bobkov,' Korzhakov recalled in 2010. 'We hugged and exchanged phone numbers.'[265] Clearly, they had each other's phone numbers well before that.

In the summer of 1996, everyone thought that democracy prevailed in Russia. But Yeltsin's electoral victory raised a lot of questions, and even the most fervent supporters of Yeltsin agreed that he won the 1996 Presidential Election unfairly. In the Presidential race, everyone played along and helped Yeltsin. Not surprisingly, the finish line that Yeltsin was the first to cross on July 3, 1996, became the start line for the corruption, unscrupulousness, and cynicism of Russian 'democracy' that followed, the most prominent representative of which was Berezovsky. The Russian oligarchs, receiving from a grateful Yeltsin a big cake called 'Russia' as a gift for organizing his victory in the 1996 Election, planned to cut it into pieces and consume whatever they could over the next four years. That is—divide the country into spheres of influence, expand businesses, consolidate power, and become the single source of this power by absorbing or buying out all potential opponents—first and foremost, the Intelligence Services.

Publicly, this amalgamation took place in the second half of 1996—smoothly and bloodlessly. People who were involved in the process and possessed information could not honestly tell who worked for whom: the Lubyanka for business, or business for the Lubyanka; Gusinsky for Bobkov, or Bobkov for Gusinsky... The oligarchs thought that by 1996, they were able to re-recruit, buy off, and make fervent allies and colleagues out of all former Cheka officers. It is impossible to know what these 're-recruited' individuals thought, as their assignments, as well as their status as Active Reserve officers, continued to be treated as a state secret.

Korzhakov's rivals in the battle for power from the State Security side, Pitovranov and Bobkov, remained untouchable. The former, as always, remained in the shadows. The latter wielded power through organizations now associated with 'oligarch' Gusinsky, who hastily proceeded to establish a mass media holding to ensure the rise to power of the Pitovranov-Bobkov's 'appointee'—whomever he might be—in the 2000 Election. In January 1997, Gusinsky stepped down as the President of *Most*-Bank and General Director of the *Most* Group Holding, becoming the head of the Media Division of *Most* Group Holding which included all of the company's media assets.

Now the foothold for the takeover of the Kremlin by Pitovranov and Bobkov was secure. They had money through the financial institutions of *Most* Bank; they had a pool of Active Reserve officers serving at the *Most* SS; they had the mass media organizations built by Gusinsky; they had a potential civilian leader, Luzhkov, and two candidates for the presidency from the Lubyanka: Primakov and Stepashin. Their victory was assured. The 2000 Presidential Elections were steadily approaching. It had become merely a matter of time and logistics.

However, having successfully rebuilt their empire to fight for the Presidency in the coming electoral campaign, Pitovranov, Bobkov and Gusinsky missed the emergence in the political arena of a nondescript, relatively young officer of the KGB/FSB, always with unkempt hair and a jacket that was out of proportion to his figure. That man was Vladimir Putin. His name meant absolutely nothing to the majority of Russian citizens at the time.

4: The Lubyanka Seizes the Kremlin (April, 2000)

The Chekists as an organization learned one important lesson from its victories and defeats in 1991, 1993, and 1996. Power in Russia must not be seized via a coup, putsch, or by declaring a state of emergency and cancelling elections. Russia is a strange country in which illegitimate power is best seized through lawful elections. They only needed to swindle one office from the electorate—the Presidency.

If you fail, try again. The 2000 plan was virtually identical to the scheme originally hatched by Korzhakov, Barsukov and Soskovets. One masterful change was thought up by Bobkov and Pitovranov—one person would fill all three roles: the FSB director resigned to become an Active Reserve Officer to become Prime Minister; the ARO Prime Minister to become Acting President; and the ARO Acting President to be elected as President of the Russian Federation.

This sophisticated improvement was successfully implemented in 2000, when the three-card deck was placed before Yeltsin with the names of (former SVR Director) Primakov, (former FSK Director) Stepashin, and (former FSB Director) Putin. It was not the only play. In his pocket, Bobkov had a back-up card for the third choice—Moscow Mayor Luzhkov.

In another way, the 2000 Presidential Election was also a repeat of Chekist moves. It was again staged to take place against the backdrop of a (provoked) Chechen War to provide for a possible contingency in case unforeseen circumstances created the need to declare a state of emergency and cancel the elections (based Korzhakov's 1996 scheme) or Yeltsin resigning or dying before the next date of the official elections. One could never be certain…

As usual, during key moments of Soviet and Russian history, as if it were necessary to throw dust in the air to cover up this or that track, the Intelligence Services were to be reformed, restructured and renamed. It could only be a purely cosmetic exercise.

On the one hand, the situation behind the scenes was more complex than it ever was in Soviet times. There was the Lubyanka, filled with Cheka officers and their mini satellite offices around the Russian Federation. Invisibly, there was also still the enormous army of undercover AROs deposited in all walks of life in Russia, who held down two jobs—the one everyone else could see and the Chekist one they could never leave, reporting back covertly to the Lubyanka as required. But there was now, in addition, the Firm's privatized control center held by Pitovranov and Bobkov, financed through the *Most* group who had vanquished Korzhakov. Without the Party to control it, the Lubyanka itself had become the tip of the iceberg of a parallel state that was really in all but complete control of the federation except its armed forces.

New times called for a new approach. In 1989, the 5th Directorate of the KGB (fighting dissidents and other enemies of the Soviet regime) became the more positive sounding Directorate for the Defense of the Constitutional Order—Directorate Z(*ashchishchat*, defend). Alexander Karbainov was instrumental in bringing about this repackaging, along with General Ivanov, the Deputy Head of the 5th Directorate, and a member of the Pitovranov Firm, while Bobkov was still the First Deputy. Nothing changed in the engine room in other words.

In 1990, Karbainov, already a Major General, took command of the KGB Press Office to put Cheka optics on a more professional footing. He replaced its previous Director Strunin, who had a serious alcohol problem. Under Karbainov, the office was renamed the Center for Public Relations (CPR) and became an effective propaganda mouthpiece of Russia's Intelligence Services. Colonel Maslennikov, Bobkov's friend, was Karbainov's First Deputy and his deputy was Colonel Alexei Kondaurov. The CPR had regional branches, including the Regional KGB office for Moscow and the Moscow Region.

The CPR promptly started selling the Lubyanka to the Russian public. Alexander Mikhailov, a Security officer with a degree in journalism, led the Moscow group (his father was a Head of Military History at the KGB institute where future intelligence officers studied). Viktor Olegov was Mikhailov's Deputy, and Sergei Bogdanov, the son of Moscow's Chief of Police Petr Bogdanov, was one of his employees. Mikhailov and his Deputy began using television news as cover for the activities of the Moscow KGB during regular broadcasts.

Just to show how important its public profile was to the new Cheka, General Karbainov, the founder of the CPR, managed to obtain special organizational privileges for the new PR department. It included being assigned the offices of all former KGB directors, not least Andropov's office. On Karbainov's suggestion, it was called the 'memorial office'—presumably because the KGB Chief was the first one from Lubyanka to make it to the Kremlin top. Karbainov himself had the sunlit office previously occupied by the head of Andropov's Secretariat, General Vladimir Kryuchkov.

The Lubyanka took its PR department very seriously. Karbainov had to leave the CPR after a scandal involving his administrative assistant. Following Karbainov, his First Deputy Maslennikov also left CPR (to work for Bobkov at *Most*). Following these departures, Alexei Kondaurov first became First Deputy, and then the Head of the CPR. Kondaurov was an excellent employee loyal to his superiors, but he was neither a leader nor a good presenter. The head of the Cheka CPR needed to be a lot more than merely not addicted to drink.[266]

With time, the institution of Active Reserve Officers (ARO) was also modernized—slightly. The Lubyanka does not typically make its internal documents accessible, but we do know that the Active Reserve was renamed 'APS'—the Apparatus for Seconded Personnel. There is a corresponding reference in the 1998 'Law Regarding the FSB', signed by Yeltsin:

> For the purposes of completing missions to ensure the security of the Russian Federation, military personnel of Federal Security Service can be seconded to state departments, enterprises, institutions, and organizations, with approval of their superiors according to the protocol established by the President of the Russian Federation, while remaining in military service.

In other words, just like in the good old Soviet times, Cheka officers continued to infiltrate all sectors of a potentially 'hostile country'. Only now the 'enemy' was the population of the Russian Federation instead of the Soviet Union.

The FSB had the right to deploy its personnel in all organizations at its discretion, and those organizations had to accept and support said personnel, in accordance with the new 'capitalist' market standards, as opposed to modest old Soviet standards. And because the Intelligence Services reworked all standards and rules for the Active Reserve/APS officers without scrutiny, unilaterally, and without the right of any state or public organization to influence, interfere with it, challenge, discuss, or oppose the process, a mafia-style system of control over the public and private Sectors was created that completely contradicted the country's economic efficiency or the laws of business, extorting money everywhere to 'feed' FSB personnel.

FSB personnel working in Russian organizations, institutions and businesses could now essentially be either 'seconded' or 'embedded.' In 1995, under a new version of the law 'On Intelligence Activities', it was forbidden to reveal the names of embedded FSB officers, punishable as disclosure of state secrets. As a matter of internal Cheka procedure, the embedded officer was only known to a limited circle inside the FSB. Appointments of seconded officers were usually approved with the leadership of non-Cheka organizations. Officers were sent to state companies or companies with partial state ownership, to various legislative or executive bodies, major political parties, law enforcement agencies, or to private companies, usually major businesses in which the FSB had an interest.

Vladimir Putin's career was no exception to this arrangement. He began his service in the KGB as a junior operative of the 5th Department of the KGB Office for the Leningrad Region (1st Section). In other words, he served at the same 5th Directorate that Bobkov led, but in Leningrad instead of Moscow. In 1984, having reached the rank of Major, he was sent to the Higher School of the KGB in Moscow where he studied under alias 'Platov' and specialized in German-speaking countries (Austria, Switzerland, West Germany and East Germany). Upon graduation in mid-1985, Putin was recruited to the KGB office in the GDR where he worked undercover as the Director of the Dresden House of Soviet-German Friendship.

Putin returned to his native Leningrad in 1990 as a Senior Aide to the Department

Head and a member of the Party (KGB Representative Office in East Germany). 'When we came back from Germany in 1990, I was still with the KGB, but started thinking more and more about a backup plan,' Putin recalled, as he addressed journalists. He meant that he had 'started thinking' about transferring to the Active Reserve. This happened in the Spring of 1990. As his official role, he became an aide to the Provost of the International Affairs at the Leningrad State University (LSU). This post was traditionally reserved for the 5th Directorate officer who monitored foreign and graduate students at LSU.

Former Major General of the KGB, Oleg Kalugin, who previously led Directorate K(*ontrrazvedka*, foreign counterintelligence) at the PGU, and then became First Deputy Head of the Regional KGB Office for the Leningrad Region, said that Putin was also the KGB's resident agent at LSU. If that was the case, all the agents at the University would have been his subordinates. Putin's direct supervisor at LSU was another KGB officer and the Dean of International Affairs Yuri Molchanov, the future Vice-Governor of St Petersburg for Investments.

But Putin soon got a new job working for Anatoly Sobchak, a popular professor at the university. Sobchak said in his last published interview that he remembered Putin as 'a good student' and thus he invited him to come work for him after the two met randomly in a university hallway. However, Sobchak was clearly not telling the truth. Putin was sent by the KGB leadership to work for Sobchak since they considered Sobchak a promising democratic politician and were trying to get someone from the Cheka close to him for keeping tabs on him, as they had done with Yeltsin.

Sobchak was not naïve. He tried to do his political work but they would not let him. He tried to find an intermediary for cooperating with the KGB to get the Cheka to loosen the leash around his neck just a little. He contacted Kalugin: 'Dear Oleg, I feel lonely. I need someone to connect with the KGB who controls the city.' Sobchak asked Kalugin to recommend someone. Kalugin replied that there was no such person. That is when Putin materialized by Sobchak's side. Putin was also not the person Sobchak was hoping to get, but he had no choice. The KGB leaders were delighted to hear that Sobchak had decided to hire Putin.

Putin recalled in 2000 arriving to report this opportunity to work for Sobchak:

I came to my superiors and said: 'Anatoly Sobchak wants me to leave the University and come to work for him. If that is not possible, I'm prepared to quit.' They answered: 'No, why do that? Go ahead and work, no issues there.'

As we know, Putin did not 'quit' the KGB and went to work for Sobchak as an Active Reserve officer.

On June 12, 1991, Sobchak was elected Mayor of Leningrad in the midst of *glasnost* and *perestroika*. Upon a referendum decision in September 1991, the city would be renamed to its original name: St Petersburg. Putin later claimed to have played a major role in persuading the city's deputies to create St Petersburg's mayoral office.

I played a special role in Sobchak becoming the first popularly elected Mayor of the city. I convinced many deputies to introduce the Office of Mayor to St. Petersburg, just like in Moscow. Those same deputies could have removed Sobchak from the Lensovet [Leningrad Municipal Council of Deputies] at any second…. I managed to convince some of the deputies that it would be beneficial for the city. Besides, I was able to mobilize leaders at the City District level who supported that view. While they technically could not vote on the matter, they could influence their deputies. In the end, the Lensovet decided in favor of the Office of Mayor by a single vote in a narrow victory.

A one-vote margin sounds impressive. But in 1991, most deputies had never heard of Putin and he had no authority. The idea to introduce the Office of Mayor came from a Commission chaired by Mikhail Gorny, and not from Putin. Putin could only have been 'convincing deputies' as a KGB officer, using the power of the organization backing him and relying on the KGB's network of numerous agents embedded in the Lensovet.

On June 28, 1991, like many government institutions, Sobchak established a public relations department. It was called the Committee for External Communications (CEC). And he put his KGB shadow—Putin—in charge of it. From that moment on, Putin's authority as Sobchak's assistant began to increase. Putin was now the Director of an office with overseas reach that was rapidly growing in importance.

In August 1991, Putin played a role in the difficult negotiations led by Sobchak with the leadership of the Leningrad KGB to achieve (and achieving) local KGB neutrality in the confrontation between the City's democratic forces and those sympathetic to the SCSE coup organized by the Lubyanka. During these talks, they agreed on guarantees for the KGB in case the democrats won. After August 21, Anatoly Kurkov, Leningrad's main KGB operative and an SCSE supporter—'a very decent fellow', according to Putin—was not only spared prosecution but continued to hold the office of KGB Director for the Leningrad Region until the end of November 1991 when he became an ARO and was appointed to a job in the banking sector. It is clear what else was part of the deal Sobchak had closed with Putin. To replace Kurkov, Sobchak appointed Putin's colleague and friend, KGB General Viktor Cherkesov, despite the protests of former dissidents about Cherkesov's record of prosecution of democrats.

Obviously, Putin risked nothing by standing behind Sobchak during the August coup. Even if the putschists had won, he was merely there as Sobchak's minder to keep the Lubyanka's finger in all pies. All of his decisions to get publicly involved were first approved by his KGB bosses. Only after the SCSE failed did Putin leave the Party, submit his KGB resignation to change into the KGB's Active Reserve. The optics paid off. At the end of 1991, Sobchak appointed Putin, the Chair of the CEC, to become his Deputy. With all his contacts from his Cheka network, he proved invaluable to Sobchak. On March 16, 1994, as part of yet another reorganization, Sobchak established the Municipal City Government in Saint Petersburg and became its Chair. Putin was confirmed as the Government's Deputy Chair, Vice-Mayor for International and Foreign Economic Relations, and Chair of the CEC. Later that same year, Putin's title was modified again: First Deputy Mayor of Saint Petersburg and Chair of the CEC of the Government of Saint Petersburg.

In March 1996, Putin joined the St Petersburg staff of a group called the Movement for Public Support of the President which consisted of the organizations supporting Yeltsin's re-election campaign. While leading the Regional Campaign Office for Yeltsin, Putin simultaneously worked on Sobchak's campaign for Governor (the new mayoral title) of St Petersburg. Here there was a snag caused by the Bobkov-Korzhakov feud. In public, Korzhakov spoke out against Sobchak's re-election and began to thwart the St Peterburg elections since they interfered with his plan to postpone the elections and seize power in Russia through the Korzhakov-Barsukov-Soskovets triumvirate.

The monitoring of Sobchak by Korzhakov's team began at the latest in May 1995. It was handled by the Internal Affairs Department at the SBP (Counteracting Economic Crimes desk, 2nd Division, Anti-Corruption). Soon both the Lubyanka and the Kremlin doubled down on St Petersburg. In December 1995, the unprecedented joint order 'Regarding the Creation of the Inter-Agency Operational Investigative Group to Explore Instances of Bribery by Officials in the Office of the Mayor of St Petersburg' was issued by two Ministers—Director of the Security Service of Russia (as the former KGB and future FSB was called at the time) Barsukov, and Minister of Internal Affairs Anatoly Kulikov, with support from the country's General Prosecutor, Yuri Skuratov. One of the investigative angles was looking into the circumstances surrounding the purchase by Sobchak of a luxury apartment in the center of Saint Petersburg.

The political harassment was obvious. The group of St Petersburg investigators was led by Leonid Proshkin, the General Prosecutor's Deputy Head of the Investigative Department, who was one of the most famous Russian investigators who handled important state corruption cases. In the course of a year, the team of investigators gathered a case file with several dozen volumes of evidence.

Sobchak tried to defend himself. On May 20, 1996, the Saint Petersburg branch of *Nash Dom Rossiya* (our home is Russia, or NDR), one of Russia's parties at the time, sent an open letter to the President, the General Prosecutor and the Prime Minister in defense of Sobchak, expressing 'strong protest against the harassment and slander launched by the General Prosecutor.' Who was one of the people signing the letter? The Chair of the NDR branch in Saint Petersburg—Vladimir Putin.

The mud slung by Korzhakov's agents stuck and Sobchak lost the election to Vladimir Yakovlev, who became Governor on June 2, 1996. It was pointless to leave Putin wrapped around Sobchak after his defeat. A new ARO role had to be found for him and in June 1996, Putin went to Moscow to work as Deputy Manager of Presidential Affairs.

After Sobchak's election defeat, the 'apartment investigation' did not go away. In December 1996, a new investigator from the General Prosecutor's Office, Nikolai Mikheyev, took charge of the investigation and soon arrested three people. In the summer of 1997, Valentina Lyubina, the Head of the Planning and Economics Department of the Supply Department at the Saint Petersburg Mayor's Office; Larisa Kharchenko, a former aide to Mayor Sobchak on Housing issues; and Viktor Kruchinin, the Ex-Mayor's Chief of Staff, were arrested in connection with the case. By the autumn, relying on the testimony of the arrested and other materials, the prosecution was ready to press charges against Sobchak himself, as well as against the members of his inner circle, with arrest warrants planned.

By that time, Putin had already moved out of harm's way and was in Moscow. Nevertheless, he covered for Sobchak, realizing that he was indirectly protecting himself, as the 'luxury apartment' investigation had also uncovered Putin's own abuses of office while working for Sobchak. An investigation memo 'Regarding Certain Aspects of Working with the Investigative Team of the Ministry of Internal Affairs in Saint Petersburg' contained the following reference to Putin:

> Information has been received containing signs of a crime—abuse of official position—in relation to Putin, one of the top officials in the President's administration and a member of [Anatoly] Chubais's team. Putin's current position creates a substantial impediment to the investigation and allows A. Sobchak to feel relatively safe.

Putin did all he could to block Sobchak's investigation and struck back. The Prosecutor General of St Petersburg now began several criminal cases in relation to the city police officers involved in the Sobchak investigation. A few of the police officers, including those holding leadership positions, were arrested.

Both investigations continued apace. Sobchak's wife Lyudmila began visiting Putin in Moscow. They always spoke in private, and thus the subject matter of their conversations remains unknown. But it was Narusova who informed Putin that the Board of the Russia's General Prosecutor's Office, after a long debate, had reached a decision to arrest Sobchak. And Sobchak's arrest threatened Putin's position in Yeltsin's administration.

On October 3, 1997, Sobchak was finally summoned for questioning by the St Petersburg Prosecutor General. It was expected that he would be charged and arrested at this meeting. Neither the democrats, for whom Sobchak was a symbol, nor Putin, who was potentially next in line to be prosecuted, could afford to allow this to happen. On Putin's request, a special SWAT team from the Regional Department for Combating Organized Crime (RUBOP) moved Sobchak directly from the Prosecutor's Office to the hospital, where Yuri Shevchenko, Chief Physician of the

Military Medical Academy, a close Sobchak family friend and a good friend of Putin's, said that Sobchak suffered a massive heart attack, a diagnosis that was deemed highly suspicious at the time.

Realizing that Sobchak had been swept out of reach, St Petersburg investigator Mikheyev contacted top Ministry of Health officials and agreed with them to have Sobchak examined by a board of medical experts. It was an examination that would never take place. Three days before the group of Moscow cardiologists were to arrive in Saint Petersburg, the FSB intervened in a move overseen by Putin. On November 7, 1997, RUBOP officers Dmitry Shakhanov and Dmitry Milin, led by Alexander Grigoryev, FSB St Petersburg's First Deputy, transported Sobchak from the hospital to Paris on a private jet operated by Finnish Airline Jetflite. It had been chartered undercover by cellist Mstislav Rostropovich (monitored in Soviet times by Bobkov's colleague Balev). The ambulance drove right onto the runway at Pulkovo Airport. Anatoly Sobchak and his wife Lyudmila got out, boarded the plane, and took off.

Putin's new position in Moscow was clearly a promotion. As Deputy Director of the Office of the Presidential Affairs (OPA), Putin oversaw real estate worth roughly $600 billion. After the collapse of the USSR, on Yeltsin's order, Russia's overseas property was also within the purview of OPA and consisted of 2,559 properties with a total area of 2,000,000 square meters in 120 countries and a net worth of $2.667 billion. It was a plum position, even more so if one belonged to a mafia that rewarded graft.

A portion of the Russian overseas property was located in the former Soviet Republics. Some of these properties handed over to the former Soviet Republics and Eastern European countries free of charge.

For an enterprising mafioso, this created all kinds of opportunities, as property could be transferred for an agreed-upon amount or for free. With this approach, the contract price of the sold assets differed from their real selling price. Obviously, the difference ended up in the pockets of those involved in the transactions and could amount to tens of millions. Filipp Turover, a former Soviet citizen living in Switzerland and consultant to a major Swiss bank, recalls both Yeltsin and Putin's involvement in this area:

Volodya [Vladimir] Putin is a special and long story. I crossed paths with him... for eight months in my work in the Office of Presidential Affairs in 1996-1997. Putin looked after the Soviet property overseas. Let me explain. Besides the debts of the former Soviet Union, Russia inherited multi-billion-dollar properties overseas, including some that belonged to the Communist Party. In 1995-1996, various organizations tried to claim ownership of it—e.g., the MFA, Minmorflot [Ministry of the Maritime Fleet], and many others. But at the end of 1996, Yeltsin issued an order transferring all overseas property of the USSR and of the Communist Party not to the Ministry of State Property, but to the Office of Presidential Affairs, for some reason. And that's where Mr Putin got his paws on it. Obviously, he was acting on orders from above. When he started the process of the so-called 'classification' of overseas property in 1997, that is when all sorts of the various corporate organizations and shell companies were created. A major portion of the most expensive real estate and other foreign assets were registered to these entities. Thus, the State itself received a highly reduced share of the overseas property.[267]

The OPA was formally led by Pavel Borodin. Until 1993, he was the Chair of the Yakutsk Municipal Council. In that role, he impressed Yeltsin, who visited Yakutia in December 1990, and in November 1993, Borodin became the first Director of the new office—OPA. But Borodin never got along with his Deputy Putin. From Borodin's perspective, Putin, as the resident Active Reserve officer, was a Cheka operative sent to monitor him and gain access to all OPA's information on its assets. OPA's size was comparable in scale only to Gazprom. The suspicious Borodin did not even let Putin access OPA's main office on Nikitsky Lane. The Chekist 'invader' was given an office at the less prestigious location on Varvarka Street.

On March 25, 1997, Putin was moved on and given the title Deputy Director of the President's Administration and Head of the Main Control Department (MCD). His immediate superior in the President's Administration was Yumashev, the long-time Cheka agent who replaced Chubais as Yeltsin's Chief of Staff. Despite Korzhakov's removal, the Lubyanka's grip around the alcoholic Yeltsin's neck was tightening. More and more KGB/FSB generals and AROs populated the Kremlin. During that same year, 1997, thanks to the efforts of Deputy Director of the President's Administration Savostyanov (the Chekist who shut out the Party from its Kremlin offices) made Lieutenant General Viktor Kondratov, an FSB officer Yeltsin's Governor ('Authorized Representative') of the Primorsky Region. Moreover, after leaving office in 1999, Kondratov returned to serve in the FSB's Headquarters in Moscow.

Meanwhile, Putin moved from his OPA office on Varvarka Street to a luxurious office on *Staraya Ploschad'* (old square) that had once belonged to Politburo member Arvids Pelše, the Chair of the Party Control Committee. Discussing his plans in the new position, Putin announced internal audits over various state organizations, monopolies, the military, and the military-industrial complex. He wanted to uncover abuses and report them to the Office of the General Prosecutor. Combating the misappropriation of federal funds was designated as another direction of inquiry.

Putin painstakingly collected information about governors to whom Yeltsin gave absolute freedom of action. Reports on the situation in the regions began to arrive in the Kremlin and Lubyanka from the bowels of the MCD. The MCD's Regional audits intensified and became more frequent. Some governors suggested that Putin was using this strategy to collect compromising information about them, which was not hard—misappropriation of federal funds was a collective sport among top civil servants.

In May 1998, Yeltsin's Administration ordered another reorganization of staff. On May 25, Putin became the First Deputy Head of the President's Administration, an enormous promotion. On June 1, FSB Lieutenant General Nikolai Patrushev, a St Petersburg native and Putin friend, whom he had brought over to Moscow, moved into the seat Putin vacated and became the new MCD Director. Naturally, it was Putin who had recommended Patrushev for the MCD job. Once it had claimed an office, the mafia did not let it slip out of its control.

On June 4, during the first press conference in his new post, Putin described how exposing misappropriation was one of his achievements as Head of the MCD. In particular, he discussed financial abuses uncovered in Russian Arms company *Rosvooruzheniye*. In reality, the audit happened in the wake of Korzhakov defeat by Bobkov. Korzhakov's man, Yevgeny Ananyev, was in charge of that company, having replaced Korzhakov's previous protégé, Alexander Kotyolkin, former head of Directorate V. Putin decided he wanted to have his own man lead this third (after oil & gas) juiciest 'slice' of the Russian economy. He had Ananyev fired and appointed his fellow intelligence officer Andrey Belyaninov to lead *Rosvooruzheniye*. As Belyaninov's First Deputy, Putin appointed another KGB friend, Sergei Chemezov, with whom he had served in Dresden.[268]

The Communists, now reduced to one among many parties and infiltrated like all the others by Cheka AROs and KGB officers, did hope to play one more card in the summer of 1998. This last twitch of the Communist corpse went almost entirely unnoticed, but interestingly ex-Cheka Chief Korzhakov was one of the co-conspirators.

The man on which the Communists pinned their last hopes was General Lev Rokhlin. Rokhlin gained fame during the Chechen War Korzhakov had provoked to create the (failed) State of Emergency and call off the elections. It was not the first war in his military career. He had also commanded troops in Afghanistan and the Caucasus. The young general commanded a motorized rifle division, which was merged in January 1990 with the KGB Transcaucasian Border Troops. By extension, Rokhlin and the officers in his division joined the KGB from that moment. After the collapse of the USSR and 'dissolution' of the KGB, Rokhlin became the commander of the 8th Guards Corps stationed in Volgograd on the Caucasus border with Kazakhstan. He also became the Chief of the city's KGB garrison. From December 1, 1994, to February 1995, Rokhlin led the efforts to subjugate Chechnya, which included the worst bombing of a city since Dresden in World War II. The 8th suffered the least number of losses, but General Rokhlin was given a Hero of Russia medal (which he refused) for his combat success.

In December 1995, Rokhlin began his career as a politician when he was elected as a Deputy of the Duma. In September 1997, he founded the Movement to Support the Army, the Defense Industry, and Military Science. Its leaders included senior members of the Cheka and the Army, in particular, General Kryuchkov, former

Head of the KGB, Andropov's righthand man and SCSE putschist, General Igor Rodionov, a former Minister of Defense, and General Vladislav Achalov, a former Airforce Commander. Rokhlin was elected Chair of the Duma's Defense Committee, from January 1996 to May 1998, but was removed from that post due to his sharp opposition to President Yeltsin.

A month later, in June 1998, Rokhlin visited the (now) KGB's 8th Guard Corps in Volgograd, where he enlisted support from for overthrowing the Yeltsin Administration with military support. A few days before the coup's D-Day, he was killed at his dacha in mysterious circumstances on the night of July 2, 1998, that have never been fully explained. The rebellion never took place. The 8th Guard Corps was promptly reformed, and a significant portion of its officers were discharged from military service.

Korzhakov, the former Director of Yeltsin's SBP, admitted in 2016 that he was one of the supporters of the rebellion. It was Korzhakov, Duma Deputy of the Tula Region, who placed an order with a Tula factory to manufacture 200 heavy-duty trailers for transport of the 8th Guard Corps and its tanks from Volgograd to Moscow. He reckoned it would be easy given that Yeltsin was an absentee President:

> There were various individuals plotting with us. There were some who had been with Khasbulatov [in 1993]. They had completely different goals: bring back the USSR and Communism. I was against it. I didn't need the USSR back. I'd had enough […] My job was to help Rokhlin so his troops could be transported from their deployment location, from Volgograd, to the Kremlin. To cover that distance, we needed trailers to attach to tanks and armored transports. As the Deputy from Tula, this task fell to me. I ordered trailers for 240 thousand dollars. They are still sitting there—all rusted because the buyer never showed up. No one was there to show up. They are still waiting for me at the Skuratov Plant in Tula. Using his plans, I ordered enough to bring Rokhlin's entire corps here to Moscow from Volgograd. I was in on the plot. I am not shy to admit it. When Chubais was in power as [Yeltsin] viceroy, taking the Kremlin would have been easy. Piece of cake! One corps would have been more than enough. And nobody would have remained loyal to Yeltsin after 1993 and 1996.

Who, then, ordered Rokhlin's premature death? The recollections of a man from President Yeltsin's inner circle on this matter are highly interesting. Mikhail Poltoranin, a former deputy Prime Minister and Minister of Information and Media, said on November 10, 2010, in a presentation in Moscow of his book *Vlast' v Trotilovom Ekvivalente: Nasledie Tsaria Borisa* (TNT: the chronicles of Tsar Boris), that he believed Rokhlin's assassination was organized by Putin and that the head of the FSB, Nikolai Kovalyov, was relieved from his job:

> I could not come out and say that Putin organized Rokhlin's assassination. I would

be immediately taken to court and asked for evidence. And, you see, I have no direct evidence. However, all the reliably established facts and circumstances surrounding this murder demonstrate that this is far from being just my 'guess' or 'assumption.' The decision to carry out the murder, I know for certain, was made at a dacha by a close circle of four people—Yeltsin, Voloshin, Yumashev and Dyachenko. At first, they wanted to assign it to Savostyanov, Director of the Moscow FSB, but then settled on the Chekist 'with the cold fish eyes,' who was capable of anything. And it is hardly a coincidence that, practically right after Rokhlin's murder, the Head of the FSB in those days [Nikolai] Kovalyov was woken up in the middle of the night and quickly, within 20 minutes, was forced to transfer his authority by order of the President to Vladimir Putin.

Kovalyov served as FSB Director from July 9, 1996, to July 25, 1998. So, Poltoranin compresses the timeline slightly when he states that Kovalyov was 'woken up in the middle of the night' and forced to resign. It happened some three weeks after the assassination, on July 25. He also claimed that it was Yeltsin who gave Putin the order for the murder.

Putin was not the only one in the ascendant at that time, it seemed. Savostyanov was another one considered for the job of the old-school Kremlin (assuming Yeltsin had given the order) elimination of Rokhlin. Savostyanov led the FSB Office for the Moscow Region until December 2, 1994, and remained close in subsequent years to Luzhkov, Bobkov, and the *Most* group, where he worked as ARO until the summer of 1996. In June 1996, he was involved in the conflict that ended with the resignations of Korzhakov, Barsukov, and Soskovets. He, too, was moved across to the Kremlin. From August 1996 to December 1998, Savostyanov was Yeltsin's Deputy Director for Personnel and oversaw the assignment of military ranks and official appointments. In February 2000, he even entered himself as a candidate for the Russian Presidency, running against Putin, but he soon withdrew his candidacy.

And so, on July 25, 1998, Putin was appointed as a Director of the FSB to replace Kovalyov, who had until then been considered an ally of Luzhkov and thus had ties to the Pitovranov-Bobkov group. Putin's first order of business was to fill the FSB Board his friends and fellow St Petersburg cronies: Generals Viktor Cherkesov, Sergei Ivanov and Alexander Grigoryev. In October 1998, Putin also made his friend Patrushev his Deputy at the FSB. And Putin brought to Moscow other colleagues from the Leningrad KGB: Vladimir Pronichev, who came to lead the Anti-Department to Combat Terrorism, and Viktor Ivanov, who was appointed Head of the Department of Interior Security (domestic counterintelligence) of the FSB. Putin's private secretary and trusted advisor at the FSB became Igor Sechin, who was promoted to colonel in less than six months (As FSB Director, Putin himself was also promoted to the rank of colonel).

Then Pitovranov died at the age of 84 on November 30, 1999, leaving Bobkov with the reigns. He just lived long enough to see the Lubyanka, coming within an inch of assuming power on September 10, 1998, when Yevgeny Primakov, the former SVR (foreign intelligence) Director, was appointed to lead Yeltsin's Government. On September 11, Primakov's candidacy was approved by the State Duma. 315 deputies out of 450 voted for him, including the Communist Party opposition faction, which had twice rejected the candidacy of Viktor Chernomyrdin, who had never been a Cheka officer. Yeltsin's days were truly numbered at this point. Primakov was supposed to wait patiently for Yeltsin's early resignation and become the Acting President of Russia. That was the final stage of the operation to seize power in the country. State Security just had to wait for the 2000 Presidential Election.

Primakov never made it. Using support from a parliamentary majority and the sensational revelations of General Prosecutor Skuratov about Yeltsin and his family, Primakov gradually gained a stronger hold on power. Communists in the State Duma tried to turn the tide of anti-American sentiments against Yeltsin over the crisis in Yugoslavia and hatched plans to impeach him. Under Primakov as Prime Minister, former Party functionaries were receiving key appointments and State power was gradually transferred into the hands of the old pro-Communist forces and seeping away from Yeltsin at the Kremlin. It was his final stronghold, but, lacking executive power, it could do very little. At the same time, Primakov, who was taking the lead in this development, skillfully created the impression that he was the wall holding back another attempted Communist revanche. The political situation started to resemble March 1996, and Primakov heavily favored the old Korzhakov scheme of declaring a State of Emergency and canceling the elections over war in Chechnya. The fact that the second Chechen War had not yet been provoked was a detail that did not stand in the way of this logic.

Thus the Lubyanka's campaign to start a new war began in March 1999. That is when two important appointments took place. On March 19, Yeltsin's Chief of Staff Yumashev was replaced by Alexander Voloshin, who was brought into the Kremlin by Boris Berezovsky. And on March 29, Putin's portfolio was expanded when the Lubyanka's Chief was also appointed Secretary of the Security Council of Russia.

In January 2000, Putin's friend General Sergei Stepashin, former Director of the FSK and organizer of the First Chechen War, shed light on these appointments: 'The decision to invade Chechnya was made back in March 1999'; the operation was 'planned' for 'August-September'; 'it would have happened whether or not the explosions in Moscow took place [the September 1999 terror attacks on Moscow apartment blocks].' 'I prepared for active intervention. We planned to come from the north of the Terek River in August-September' of 1999. Putin, 'the Director of the FSB at the time, had this information.' Stepashin was once again tasked with planning the second Chechen War. That is precisely why, on May 12, 1999, Primakov, who was at the zenith of his power and popularity, was removed as Prime Minister and replaced with Stepashin, who was supposed to do the heavy lifting for Lubyanka with his new partner, FSB Director Putin.

Since the Lubyanka was behind these reappointments, it was no surprise that the volley of changes—Primakov's removal, Stepashin's new appointment, and Putin's promotion—did not trigger objections among the 'leftist' opposition in the Duma. It controlled this faction as well. The supposed might of the Communists in the Duma collapsed like a house of cards. The provocative conversations about impeaching President Yeltsin suddenly stopped. The zealous General Prosecutor Skuratov retired. Having rid himself of Prime Minister Primakov—the former director of the SVR—Yeltsin picked the next card from his Cheka deck of cards to be first his Prime Minister and then successor—Stepashin, former Director of the FSK. Under Bobkov's blueprint, in the event of Stepashin succeeding Yeltsin, Luzhkov would lead the Government.[269]

Nothing was left to chance. At the Kremlin, Sergei Zverev was tasked with handling the public relations that would sell the Stepashin-Luzhkov scenario to the Russia people. He was appointed Yeltsin's Deputy Chief of Staff on the same day Stepashin was elevated to the Yeltsin Administration as its Prime Minister—May 12, 1999. By that time, Zverev had at least two important posts on his curriculum vitae that were needed for participation in 'Operation Successor.' In 1996, he was the President of Bobkov's *Most* group and in 1998—Deputy Chair of the Board of Directors of Gazprom, another Lubyanka stronghold.

From the moment Stepashin was appointed Prime Minister by Yeltsin, everyone in his daughter Dyachenko's oligarch circle—Voloshin, Yumashev, Abramovich, and Berezovsky—rose up as one to remove Stepashin from the Kremlin, in order to avoid having a situation where two Chekists occupied the two highest offices in the land. Undermining the authority of the two men in the eyes of Yeltsin would achieve the required result. From the Special Services' angle, the undermining of Stepashin's authority in Yeltsin's eyes was arranged through the provoked invasion of Dagestan by Chechen separatist Shamil Basayev and his fighters (Basayev had been Stepashin's undoing before, in 1995). The undermining of the Mayor of Moscow Luzhkov's authority would be achieved through the terrorist attacks staged in the Russian capital.

The Zverev team struck back on July 2, 1999—that is, a month or so after the appointments of Stepashin and Zverev. Alexander Zhilin at *Moskovskaya Pravda* got hold of a file called 'Storm in Moscow', dated June 29, 1999.[270] Zhilin thought that Zverev had arranged the 'leak'. He published its contents in the paper on July 22, 1999. It described a plan 'to discredit' Moscow Mayor Luzhkov by launching major terror attacks against Moscow in general, and him in particular. The article predicted so accurately what was going to happen in a little over a month that, had it been published after the September 1999 Moscow apartment explosions, everyone would have dismissed it as a forgery.

Next, on August 3, 1999, Moscow newspaper *Versiya* (version) published an article called 'Conspiracy' about a secret meeting between the Kremlin's Voloshin and Chechen leader Basayev in Nice, France, on July 3 and 4, 1999—organized by GRU Colonel Surikov. The central theme of the extensive news piece, the first in a series of articles about the preparation of Basayev's Chechen troops for invading Dagestan, was that the invasion of Dagestan by Basayev's Chechens was carried out with the Kremlin's approval communicated to the leader through Voloshin.

This incredible allegation seemed impossible to believe, but after the *Versiya* publication, almost-surreal things started happening in the Kremlin. On the day of the publication, August 3, Zverev was removed from his post (becoming the shortest-running Deputy Chief of Staff ever); on August 7, Basayev did, in fact, invade Dagestan with a group of Chechen militants; next, on August 9, Stepashin was summarily removed as Prime Minister (becoming the shortest-running Prime Minister of Russia ever) and replaced with Putin; and on August 24, Colonel Surikov gave a lengthy interview to *Versiya*, in which he confirmed that he really did organize the meeting of Voloshin and Basayev in Nice.

Several days later, events started happening that the 'Storm in Moscow' file had predicted. On August 31, 1999, there was a terror attack at the shopping center Okhotny Ryad on Manege Square. One person was killed and 40 were injured. The Government immediately proposed investigating the 'Chechen theory,' though it was hard to believe the Chechens would attack a building complex whose CEO was a famous Chechen businessman—Umar Dzhabrailov. According to law enforcement spokespeople, 'someone with a last name Ryzhenkov… posing as an FSB General' was later arrested for preparing and carrying out the attack.

In August 1999, something else happened that would appear to be of no historical significance. On August 2, 1999, Vladimir Putin's father, Vladimir Putin, died in Saint Petersburg. Putin's mother—Maria Putina-Shelomova had died earlier, on July 6, 1998. At least, this is the official version. But in 2015, in an autobiographical sketch in *Ruspioner* (Russian pioneer), mysteriously, Putin himself said something different about these simple facts. He wrote that his mother 'lived until 1999,' but his father 'died at the end of 1998.'[271] In 2017, giving an interview to American film director Oliver, Putin said that his 'father died literally two months before I was appointed Prime Minister.'[272] But Putin was appointed Acting Prime Minister a week after the official date of his father's death and became Prime Minister on August 16, two weeks after that.

It is difficult to imagine Putin had forgotten when exactly his parents might have died. In any case, with the 'death' of Putin's 'Leningrad parents', his past, a very important chapter in his life, became a closed book burying the answers to many questions the media—then still free—might have. It is as if in 1998-1999 preparatory work was being done to clear Putin's path to the Kremlin by creating an uncomplicated national biography that would be 'suitable' for public consumption and not stand in the way of becoming the next Russian President. There was, of course, the Georgian woman by the name of Vera Putina, the spitting image of Putin, who claimed that she was his real mother.

Further signs that Putin's rise to power was planned are the cascade of appointments. In Korzhakov's plan it was crucial that Soskovets served as Deputy Prime

Minister. Under Russian law, only from that office could Yeltsin appoint him Acting Prime Minister by decree, and from thereon he was the only one government official who could then be appointed Acting President by decree. It was the only way to sideline interference from the Duma. After Korzhakov's demise and Soskevets's removal, the post of Deputy Prime minister was abolished. But on August 9, 1999, it was resurrected for Putin. This appointment came first, then, Yeltsin removed Stepashin from office, and appointed Putin as Acting Prime Minister. Patrushev, Putin's friend, took over the office Putin vacated and became the new Director of the FSB.

In a televised address by Yeltsin on August 9, he named Putin as his successor, giving him a ringing endorsement as the man who would bring back 'Great Russia':

> I have now decided on the person who, in my view, is capable of consolidating society. Relying on the widest political forces, he will ensure the continuation of reforms in Russia. He can unite around him those who in the new XXI century must renovate Great Russia. That person is Secretary of the Security Council of Russia and FSB Director Vladimir Putin… He has my confidence. But I want everyone who will go to the polls to cast their vote in July 2000 to be also confident in him. I think he has sufficient time to prove himself.

Putin announced in a televised addressed the same day that he—the man who had never held an elected office—would be running for President in 2000.

Again the Duma showed no sign of rebellion—the die had been cast and it was going to be a contest between the Putin-Yeltsin team and the Primakov-Luzhkov team, first in the Duma elections in December, next the presidential elections in 2000. On August 16, 1999, the 450 deputies of the Duma duly confirmed Putin as Prime Minister (233 voted 'yes', 84 'no', and 17 abstained). 52 Communist deputies were opposed; 32 deputies (including Duma President Seleznev) voted to confirm; the rest abstained (e.g., Gennadiy Zyuganov did not vote). It was the largest party with 157 seats, dwarfing the 42 other blocs. Some delegates from the 'left' faction of *Narodovlastiye* (people's power) also voted against. From the *Yabloko* (apple) faction, which had supported Stepashin, 18 deputies voted in favor of the confirmation, while 8 were against. Other factions voted to confirm practically unanimously.

Following Primakov's and Stepashin's resignations, the Lubyanka had two fronts gunning for the Kremlin: the Primakov-Luzhkov front with PR cover from Gusinsky-Zverev's media clout of *Most* group; and the Putin-Yeltsin 'family' front with PR cover from TV Channel One, controlled by Berezovsky. To the Lubyanka it made absolutely no difference who won the fight. The Cheka would take power no matter what.

It was now up to the Russian voter to decide which way the die would be cast. The Duma elections were a litmus test, which of their contenders for the president's office was more worthy of it and would claim the office with greatest electoral clout to win the presidential 'July elections' of 2000 (the fact that they ended up being the

'March elections' tells its own story).

The two sides began ferociously battling for deputy seats in the Duma. Primakov quickly joined the *Otechestvo-Vsya Rossiya* (fatherland—all Russia, OVR) party, which Luzhkov had created in the hope of his promotion from Moscow Mayor to Prime Minister. This party had been put together from the *Otechestvo* party established by Luzhkov in January 1999, and the *Vsya Rossiya* party established in April 1999. The unification of these two parties suddenly posed a serious threat to the succession planned by the Yeltsin 'family' in the Kremlin. Like Yeltsin, Putin did not have a party. He urgently needed one to defeat the Primakov-Luzhkov tandem. To the oligarchs, the calculation was simple. It was the choice between two Chekists, or just the one Chekist in power—Putin seemed the less dangerous option (and in a way, he was: having just one was to delay the speed with which the Russian Federation, its population, businesses, government, art, sports were brought under full Lubyanka's control through invisible layers of ARO-APS, its new acronym, with Chekists seconded everywhere it mattered—as in Soviet times but without the nuisance of the Party.)

Berezovsky took on that difficult task, and in record time, with money from Sibneft Oil Company (owned by Abramovich), he created the *Yedinstvo* (unity) party. Berezovsky called *Yedinstvo* the 'Governors' Party' and it was his baby. He had made a deal with all the Governors of the federation's regions that, in exchange for supporting Putin—first in the Duma elections and then in the presidential elections—Putin would, after winning, let the governors keep the autonomy from Moscow they had been given under Yeltsin. The Kremlin would not undermine and reclaim their decentralized power relationship with the center.

Television journalist Sergei Dorenko became the main 'weapon' of Berezovsky and Channel One's PR campaign on behalf of Putin. Berezovsky sincerely believed that he 'created' Dorenko. However, unbeknownst to him, Dorenko had long ago been recruited as an agent of the 5th Directorate of the KGB. In his new role, he merely picked sides in the Cheka battle between Putin and Primakov—on Putin's side.

Dorenko was born in 1959 and his father was a military pilot who finished his military service as a Major General. Naturally, he raised Dorenko in the spirit of patriotism, which influenced his fate to a certain degree. In the mid-to-late 1970s, Dorenko enrolled at the People's Friendship University (PFU) in Moscow. The University was established in 1960 to provide cultural support to countries liberated from colonial dependence. The PFU's primary task was training highly qualified professionals to aid countries in Asia, Africa, and Latin America. At least that was the official story behind its establishment. In fact, PFU's main goal was spreading Soviet economic and political influence in third-world countries. Specialists trained at PFU ended up with senior government positions in their home countries. Many were recruited as agents of Soviet intelligence while at PFU and continued to operate as agents in the interests of the USSR when they returned home. The most promising students were recruited by the PGU's Department of Undercover Intelligence and became regular personnel employees involved in Soviet espionage.

Lieutenant Colonel Vyacheslav Kiktev was the head of the 5 Directorate department (3rd, 2nd Section) that oversaw the PFU. His officers recruited, student Dorenko, the future star of Russian TV, as their agent. Besides monitoring foreign and Soviet students at PFU, Dorenko also worked with foreign delegations arriving in the USSR from developing countries. This activity both earned extra money and was a chance to hone his intelligence skills for the Lubyanka. Because of his promising qualities, Dorenko was sent overseas after graduating from the PFU in 1982. His overseas assignment was in the Firm's stomping ground Angola. He worked as an interpreter in several Soviet bodies, including the prestigious Office of the State Committee of Soviet Ministers of the USSR for Foreign Economic Relations. It was that body that facilitated arms sales to foreign countries through its Main Engineering Department. A year after Dorenko's return, KGB agent Igor Sechin (Putin's future private secretary and advisor) was sent to Angola. He and Dorenko had the same KGB handler during their stints in that country.

On his return from Angola to Moscow in 1984, despite having no education in journalism at all, Dorenko was posted to a job at Central Television (Ostankino) as the editor of the Service for External Relations. No wonder, because Central Television in those days fell under the same 5th Directorate colonel who previously oversaw PFU where Dorenko had studied. As often, in the Cheka the same people crossed each other on different paths. At the time, Komelkov headed the 14th Department monitoring Ostankino. Later, he was fired for renting out Ostankino to businesses, opening a restaurant frequented by the underworld, only to be elevated by Korzhakov in 1995 to once again head the 5 Directorate's TV section in order to curb Bobkov's influence (since Komelkov hated his former fellow officers who had fired him).

The propaganda campaign surrounding the Duma Elections of 1999 and the Presidential Elections of 2000 pitted Gusinsky's organizations—primarily, the NTV channel owned by *Most* group—against Dorenko/Berezovsky. NTV supported the Primakov party and sharply criticized the pro-Kremlin Governors' party. Both sides were bluffing. Yeltsin Chief of Staff Voloshin publicly threatened Gusinsky and Malashenko that he would destroy Gusinsky's empire if his side won and put Gusinsky in prison. Gusinsky, a longtime Bobkov agent, knew better than to explain to Voloshin that he was merely a proxy and followed orders of the Firm and Bobkov. When Putin became president, Gusinsky was imprisoned as a prelude to forcing him to hand over his share in Most for $773 million.[273]

While the two Cheka sides squared up, the preparations for the State of Emergency carried on as before. Stepashin did not have time to repeat the provocation for another Chechen war before his resignation. The completion of this part of the process fell on the shoulders of Putin and Patrushev. In that sense, the 1999 Duma and 2000 presidential elections were business as usual: terrorism and war as a pretext for declaring a State of Emergency and cancelling the elections in case the need for such measures arose.

It is noteworthy that Basayev's invasion of Dagestan in August 1999 was not announced or used by the Russian leadership as the reason for launching military actions in the Chechen Republic. And that is not at all because the invasion wasn't a good reason for beginning a war. The invasion of Dagestan itself was not enough on its own to declare a State of Emergency throughout the Federation and cancel the elections. 'Chechen' terrorism was needed. But the underwhelming failed 'terrorism' of the 1994-6 Chechen War meant that the bar needed to be set higher.

On September 4, 1999, in the Dagestani city of Buynaksk, a parked car full of explosives blew up near an apartment building on a military base. 64 people died—soldiers and their family members. That same day, a mined car ZIL-130 was discovered in Buynaksk containing 2.706 kilograms of explosives. The car was parked in the area of a residential neighborhood and a military hospital. The explosion was prevented due to the vigilance of local citizens. In other words, the second terrorist act in Buynaksk was not prevented by Russia's enormous army of Intelligence Services, but by ordinary civilians.

The reason was simple. The terror attack in Buynaksk on September 4 was prepared and carried out by the GRU under the command of Colonel General Valentin Korabelnikov. The operation was led by the Head of the 14th Directorate of the GRU, Lieutenant General Nikolai Kostechko. A group of twelve GRU officers who were sent to Dagestan on a business trip carried out the attack. This came to light during the testimony of GRU Senior Lieutenant Alexei Galkin, who was taken prisoner by the Chechens in November 1999.[274]

The terrorist attacks in Moscow, Volgodonsk and Ryazan followed several days after the apartment bombing in Buynaksk. In the early morning hours of September 9, an apartment building exploded on Gur'yanova Street in Moscow. In the early morning hours of September 13, a residential building exploded on Kashirski Highway. On September 16, another bomb went off in a residential building in Volgodonsk. On the evening of September 22, local residents and local police prevented the bombing of another apartment building in Ryazan. After more than 20 years, even the FSB's version of the story makes clear that not a single Chechen was involved in these terrorist attacks. Not one. Not, even according to the FSB.

On this part of the attack on Kremlin power, the Primakov and Bobkov factions acted in complete agreement. In March-April 1999, under Primakov (with Stepashin as deputy), the Kremlin's preparations for the September terror attacks on Russian targets began. The execution of the plan was entrusted to the FSB and GRU. In Buynaksk, the apartment building of military servicemen was blown up by the GRU. If the FSB had run this operation, it would have led to an inter-departmental conflict between the FSB and the Ministry of Defense. However, in Moscow, Volgodonsk, and Ryazan, it was the FSB that took charge of the attacks.

From August, the chain of command changed to Putin (Kremlin)/Patrushev

(FSB). FSB General German Ugryumov (head of the Counterterrorism department) had operational control. Agents were: Abdulgafur (according to some sources also known as Max Lazovsky, who was behind the terrorist attacks of the First Chechen War) and Abubakar—the FSB operatives directly responsible for the implementation of the attacks. Tatyana Koroleva, Achemez Gochyayev, Alexander Karmishin—the individuals who registered the entity that owned the warehouses where the sacks of hexogen disguised as sugar were delivered; Adam Dekkushev, Yusuf Krymshamkhalov, and Timur Batchayev—the individuals recruited by 'Chechen separatists' (in reality by the FSB) who transported the explosives disguised as sacks of sugar to the buildings' basements but thought they were acting on orders from 'Chechen bosses' and that the delivery location for the bombs was just transit storage and 'federal buildings' were the actual targets. And, finally, FSB operatives Vladimir Romanovich and Ramazan Dyshenkov, the individuals who carried out the bombings of the buildings in Moscow, as well as the FSB officers, arrested but not named, who tried to blow up the apartment building in Ryazan on the night of September 22, 1999. Of the three people involved in the Ryazan operation (two men and one woman) the men were detained. The female 'terrorist' (Chekist officer) managed to get away.

On September 23, the two FSB officers were arrested in Ryazan. On the same day, the Head of the Moscow FSB Alexander Tsarenko announced that the Moscow bombings were organized by Chechens and that the offenders had already been arrested. Both arrested individuals were of Ingush descent, whom Tsarenko misnamed as 'Chechens', were subsequently released later as they had nothing to do with the attacks. All that didn't matter. On cue, on the same day, the Russian Air Force carried out rocket and bombing strikes on the airport in Grozny, an oil refinery and residential neighborhoods in the northern outskirts of the Chechen capital.

Responding to journalists, Putin said on September 23: 'As for the strike on the airport in Grozny, I cannot comment. I know there is a general mindset that criminals will be pursued no matter where they are. I am not fully aware, but if they were at the airport, then that is where we are going to strike. I cannot really add to what has already been said.' In other words, not yet having been made aware of the failure in Ryazan, the Russian Government had already begun military action against the Chechen Republic in retaliation to the attack in Ryazan. It was as if Putin had special powers to divine the future.

On September 24, while giving a speech in Kazakhstan's capital of Astana, Putin said that the air strikes were 'exclusively hitting military bases and would continue wherever the terrorists are found....' Famously, he added 'If we find them in the toilet, we'll soak them there.' Yet, on that same day, Patrushev reported that there had been no terrorist attempt to bomb Ryazan. The FSB was merely conducting a 'training' exercise there. It was an extraordinary moment. A war had been declared in response of an innocent 'training' exercise on Russian territory by the Russian Intelligence Services—surely unprecedented?

On October 1, Russian armored vehicles crossed the border of Chechnya (one of the Russian Federation's republics) and advanced for 5 kilometers into the Republic. The largest terrorist attacks in Russian history took the lives of approximately 300 people and became the false flag for launching an invasion with the Chechen Republic, leading to the deaths of many thousands and crippling the fates of millions of people. Yeltsin removed Primakov, on account of 'flirting' with the Duma. He then removed Stepashin on account of 'flirting' with Luzhkov. At the same time, he did nothing about Putin and Patrushev's failures in connection with the 'terrorist' attacks and the false Ryazan episode. Yet they kept their posts because by that time Yeltsin had been cornered and was solely interested in immunity and the undisturbed future of his family.

On December 19, 1999, in the 3rd Congress of the State Duma, Putin-Berezovsky's 'Governors' party received 23.32% of the votes, placing them second after the Communists (24.29%). The Primakov-Luzhkov's party received no more than 13.33%, a complete failure of their side. They had been expected to capture 40% against Putin/Berezovsky party 14%. The winner in the Cheka stakes was clear and Primakov withdrew from the Presidential race, clearing the path for Putin to stand as the only plausible Chekist.[275] His only serious rival now was the Communist Zyuganov, whom Yeltsin had seen off in 1996. In all but the final formalities, the Lubyanka had won the Kremlin. On December 20, the 'Day of the Chekist,' Putin restored a memorial plaque in honor of former KGB Chair Andropov on the wall of the Lubyanka.[276]

On the evening of December 20, while briefing the Cheka leadership, Putin reported: 'I would like to report that the group of FSB personnel sent to work [as AROs/APSs] in the government is successfully handling its first stage of assignments.' The *Moskovskiy Komsomolets* newspaper also quoted these words of Putin's at the time: 'The criminal group was successfully penetrated.' On December 31, 1999, President Yeltsin gave his New Year's Eve address and announced his resignation as President and his appointment of Putin as his successor until early Presidential Elections were held (now set for March 26, 2000). In consideration, Putin issued in early January 2000 full immunity to Yeltsin and relevant family members.

On January 13, 2000, during his official trip to Saint Petersburg, Putin publicly confirmed his intention to run for the post of the President of Russia. On February 15, 2000, he formally registered as a candidate. The day before, on February 14, 2000, Anatoly Sobchak was appointed as adviser to Putin and head of the political consulting group The Council of Democratic Parties and Movements of Saint Petersburg. After fleeing from prosecution in Leningrad, Sobchak had returned to Russia on July 12, 1999, safeguarded by Putin, then still FSB Director and Secretary of the Security Council. It was not a lucky moment in Sobchak's life. On the night of February 19, 2000, he suddenly died prematurely during a campaign trip to the city of Svetlogorsk in Kaliningrad Region.

Sobchak's untimely death gave rise to many rumors, many fueled by subsequent events. The results of his autopsy were classified and other exceptional measures were taken to conceal information regarding his death. Theories inevitably surfaced that he had been poisoned.[277] Of course, nothing was ever officially confirmed. An alarming fact surrounding Sobchak's premature death was the presence of the Soviet intelligence agent, Shabtai Kalmanovich, and businessman and former GRU officer, Andrey Burlakov, in Svetlogorsk at the time of his death. Kalmanovich once said in an interview, Sobchak 'died in his arms'.

The presence of the two Intelligence officers at Sobchak's death proved to be unlucky too for the Chekists themselves. A few years later, on November 2, 2009, Kalmanovich's Mercedes was pierced by fire from two submachine guns in the center of Moscow, in broad daylight. Having been hit with eighteen bullets, Kalmanovich had little chance of surviving the vicious attack and died at the scene. His driver Pyotr Tumanov was seriously injured. $1.5 million was found in the car, which the assassins had left where it was. Two more years passed and then Andrey Burlakov also died at the hands of a hired killer. Neither the assassins, nor their clients, were ever identified or found, let alone prosecuted.

There were other premature deaths, apart from Sobchak's. The famous Russian journalist Artyom Borovik died on March 9, 2000, when the chartered plane taking him to Georgia to meet Putin's putative mother, Vera Putina, a resident of the Georgian town of Metekhi, crashed shortly after take-off. Russian investigators soon established that the catastrophe occurred because of a very unfortunate combination of a gross pilot error and an oversight at the airport by flight engineers. Any suggestion of foul play was rejected out of hand by Russian prosecutors.

On March 26, Putin realized the dream of all Cheka leaders: Dzerzhinsky, Beria, Andropov and Kryuchkov. The Lubyanka had once again captured the Kremlin. He was duly elected, having received, according to official data, 39,740,434 votes (52.94%). In fact, Putin received roughly 48-49% of the votes. The other votes were assigned to him so he could defeat his opponent Zyuganov in the first round. Now he just had to consolidate power in the country by relying on the Active Reserve/APS personnel of many thousands. On May 13, Putin signed an order establishing seven Federal Districts and outlining the powers of the President in those Districts. He began imposing his 'power hierarchy' based on strict, military-style obedience.

The order establishing seven Federal Districts became a classic mold for reclaiming all State authority by Moscow. Between the elected President and the elected Governors, Putin created a layer of officials appointed by him. On May 18, he announced who they were. In the Central District, which included Moscow, FSB General Viktor Cherkesov was named the Representative of the President. In the Northwest District, which included Saint Petersburg, it was FSB General Georgy Poltavchenko. Three of the other five Representatives were also KGB/FSB officers.

The next most important law proposed by Putin was the federal law 'Regarding the Procedure for the Formation of the Federation Council.' This law replaced the Federation Council of elected governors with the representatives he had just appointed. The elected governors were *de facto* stripped of their authority in the Regions and of the influence at the center. In less than two months, the power in the country belonged to Putin and his appointees. Despite the Constitutional requirement of a two-thirds majority Duma vote, these measures were not even tabled for discussion.

Everything that happened in Russia after the creation of the seven Federal Districts became a consequence of what had already been set in motion. The Lubyanka began to rule the country without outside control, following their own (mafia) rules, norms, standards, and habits.

Russian sociological researchers have conducted numerous studies to determine the level of involvement by the Intelligence Services in the country's civil life after 2000. According to the Moscow Center for Post-Industrial Society Studies, 15% of working men in Russia were involved in various enforcement agencies. Famous Russian sociologist Olga Kryshtanovskaya estimated that the percentage of the Cheka operatives and people directly involved with the Intelligence Services governing the country has only grown. In the final years of the USSR and of Mikhail Gorbachev, roughly 3% of the country's top state officials were Chekists; in the Yeltsin years, it was over 30%; after Yeltsin's resignation, it went from 43-50% at the beginning to 70-80% in a matter of years.

The list of the FSB and Active Reserve (ARO)/APS Officers appointed to various state offices at various levels is limitless. The principal difference between appointments made before and after Putin became President is that these appointments were without any shame or attempt to hide from the public the official's involvement, past or present, with an Intelligence body or with the KGB/FSB. Starting in May 2000, there was pride in a Cheka connection (including the KGB/FSB) and it became useful to have one.

As when Andropov became Soviet leader in 1982, the assumption of power in the Federal and Regional government was absurdly simple. All that needed to be done was appoint new heads at all levels where there were vacancies. Given the enormous depth and hierarchy of AR/APS officers in all walks of life since the 1950s, it was not difficult to make suitable appointments at a rapid pace to any level of government. The Kremlin officer in charge of its execution was FSB General Ivanov, responsible for human resources management in Putin's administration. He was the one who, with the President's knowledge and approval placed FSB agents in all vacant positions. By 2001, almost all key ministerial posts were held by the FSB.

The appointment of FSB Lieutenant General Zdanovich (who moved to the Active Reserve) as Deputy General Director of the Russian National State Television and Radio Company on June 3, 2002, was symbolic. It was a direct signal if not challenge to the still free Russian media. In protest against this appointment, Alexander Abramenko, the Editor-in-Chief of the news program *Vesti* (lead), resigned. In response to whether the had remained in the Active Reserve, Zdanovich merely responded with the brazenness that had become possible: 'As we all know, there are no [ex-Chekists]. But I would not want to get into the details. My colleagues will certainly be helping me solve the tasks set before me. Out of solidarity.'

But there were also colleagues who would not be 'helped'. The Pitovranov/Bobkov Firm had lost the Cheka stakes. He knew what was coming—revenge. In tandem with senior FSB officers being appointed to key leadership positions in the Federation by General Ivanov, companies were being created to which Active Reserve officers on the wrong side fled to safety to carry on with their jobs out of harm's way. Specifically, in the first half of 2000—foreseeing the inevitable arrest of Gusinsky and the collapse of the *Most* media empire that had fought against Putin—Bobkov created a new organization. It was called The Institute of Strategic Assessment and Analysis (ISAA) and the main analytical team that was employed by the once-mighty *Most* SS decanted smoothly into this organization, located at 40/14 Solzhenitsyn Street (formerly, Communist Street).

As always, Bobkov preferred to remain in the shadows. ISAA was a private company with no public information about its shareholders or employees other than that its Institute 'had operated since 1995'. This predecessor was none other than *Most* SS. Bobkov's former KGB head in Azerbaijan General Vagif Guseinov, was now Director and Editor-in-Chief of the ISAA magazine *Vestnik Analitiki* (analytics courier). Clearly, Bobkov was able to insulate his team at ISAA. Azerbaijan sought Guseinov's extradition since 1996 for the massacre and pogroms but Russia continued to decline to do so.

ISAA also embraced Putin's former Head of the 5th Directorate, Lieutenant General Ivanov (not to be mistaken with Putin's Leningrad friend), and others from the same directorate: Vladimir Maslennikov, Valery Shiryaev, an Active Reserve officer who later became Deputy Director at *Novaya Gazeta*. Sergei Chaplinsky, a former officer of the 8th Department (monitoring Zionist nationalists) of the 5th Directorate, an aide to another Head of the 5th Directorate General Abramov, and 5th Directorate's Komsomol Organization Secretary, also ended up at ISAA. His successor in both the Komsomol organization and at the 5th Directorate, Alexander Svechnikov, also found his way to ISAA as a Chief Scientific Consultant.

Bobkov's use as the last Cheka mastermind had come to an end, however, as the Firm had successfully ferried the Lubyanka across the finish line from Beria's assassination. Although revolutions usually devour their own children, after the Cheka capture of the Kremlin, the obedient and low-profile Bobkov and his new institute were put to good use by the Kremlin for this and that. From the man who controlled writers, he became one himself towards the end of his life. Together with Ivanov, Chaplinsky and Svechnikov, he co-authored *Modern Global Capitalism* in 2003. A year earlier, Svechnikov had co-authored a book with Bobkov titled *Global Capitalism: Ruminations on the Subject*. Bobkov still had more to say in public and wrote his memoirs with Svyatoslav Rybas, a KGB recruit from his second year at the Gorky Literary Institute.[278] Bobkov died in 2019 at the age of 93. In 2022, the contribution of the Firm was honored with a stamp of the legendary General Pitovranov whose intellect, invention of the 5th Directorate, subjugation of Russia's culture in all its forms, had been the Cheka's driver of success—down its former recruit, President Colonel Putin. Tellingly, it was, though, at 40 Rubles one of Russia's cheapest.

The State Duma and its political parties, all of which had been founded with the involvement of Chekists, now became a stronghold of former KGB/FSB officers. Where the Duma had previously been out of bounds for a Lubyanka *rezidentura*, now that the Kremlin was won, it was no different from any other Russian organization. It needed to be infiltrated for the collection of data and in order to manage it. As a result, an unconstitutional Intelligence Services body comprising of officers and their agents was formed in Russia's supreme legislative body.

Otari Arshba was a typical example of the new wind that was blowing through the White House's corridors of power. After graduating from the Higher School of the KGB in 1978, he was recruited by the Department in the 5th Directorate that supervised the Ministry of Higher and Special Education (including the MSU, PFU, KMO universities) and that was led by Colonel Vladimir Golovin. In 1998, Arshba transferred to the Active Reserve (APS) and led various companies. In 2003 and 2007, Arshba was elected as a Deputy in the Duma. He became Chair of the Committee for Procedure, which ensured that his fellow former 5th Directorate officers Valery Vorobyov (Head of the Secretariat of the Duma's Chair) and Yuri Bezverkhov (a Duma leader)—successfully guided the Duma's activities in the right direction for the FSB. Everything seemed to have become straightforward. And it was for Arshba.

But it was not entirely the case for Duma leader Vorobyov. Effectively—though behind the scenes—the Cheka had now taken over the role of the Party and the army of thousands of Chekists around the country were the Kremlin's real constituency. As between Primakov-Bobkov and Putin-Patrushev, there were differences of opinion and these started to matter more, forcing the Duma's army of Active Reserve officers to come up with creative approaches. While Bezverkhov's activities were wholly aimed at supporting Putin, the situation was quite different for Vorobyov. His former boss, Valery Vorotnikov, a general, was a deputy in the Communist faction. Meanwhile Bobkov was also still hovering in the background. Vorobyov had to show due deference to all his former chiefs at the KGB.

Vorobyov's dilemma made clear the difference with Soviet times. Publicly, the Party only ever allowed one dogma because only the (voting) members Politburo could make changes to the Party line. The Party broached no discussion in its lower reaches or the USSR and staying on top of dissension was the pre-eminent role of the Cheka since the 1950s. Now that the Lubyanka had won the Kremlin, the absence of ideology started to show. Putin had no party or program of his own other than the Andropov/Pitovranov plan of preserving the Kremlin system of power over the country without bloodbaths. Their plan merely called for monitoring ideas in Russia and managing them to ensure they did not get out of hand (5th-Directorate style). But what does 'out of hand' mean without a native ideology other than the preservation of central power in aspic. The Slavophilism cultivated by the KGB in the 1950s in order to replace Stalinist ideology was ultimately not something to believe in, more a way of switching on or off this or that current of Russian nationalism? Some other useful ideology might brew up as well.

After 2000, politics became a bottomless pit. There were early signs. At the end of 1996, Russian Nationalists, together with the Special Security officers, held an event in Moscow to celebrate the second anniversary of the organization uniting 'Vympel' Special Forces—the Firm's combat veterans. On behalf of the Duma, Vorobyov was the keynote speaker while the writer, Vladimir Soloukhin, gave a speech on behalf of the Nationalists. The latter said, among other things: 'You should not look calmly at what is happening. You see our Russia surrounded from all sides by its ravenous "brethren" who are ready to tear fighting for a bigger piece of the pie. You see the 'fifth column' indulging them without conscience or fear. So … don't let them do it…! Don't let your Motherland perish!'[279] Svyatoslav Rybas and Alexander Prokhanov, both writers and 5th Directorate agents covered this event alongside Vorobyov.

In the Duma, one of Vorobyov's righthand men was Yuri Sharandin. He was another long-time 5th Directorate agent (2nd Section of the 11th Department). Born in 1952, Sharandin was recruited in the late 1970s when he worked in the Propaganda Directorate of the Soviet Committee for Sport and was its head of protocol. In the late 1980s, Sergei Kugushev, a former Andropov economist, formed *Russkii Kapital* (Russian capital). Sharandin became one of its Chekist shareholders and soon became the Editor-in-Chief at the newspaper *Solidarnost'* (solidarity) published by the Federation of Professional Unions in Moscow. After a conflict with Federation Chair Mikhail Shmakov, he was forced to leave the newspaper.

Sharandin landed on his feet and became first the Deputy Head of Putin's powerful Office for Domestic Policy (ODP)—a watered-down version of the Politburo—and then deputy director of the Federation Council's Secretariat and head of its legal department. It was the ODP that oversaw practically all the domestic political life in Russia from the Kremlin. Its tasks included preparing briefing materials on the socio-political situation in the country for the President. Its employees also facilitated interactions between the president and other governmental bodies, including those in the regions. Since it was a mini-Politburo, ODP personnel had a major impact on the results of the State Duma elections.

One of the tasks was managed or 'systemic' nationalism. The ODP's office of male 'patriots' was 'decorated' by Natalya Narochnitskaya. She herself was a skilled Cheka agent from the time that she worked at the UN mission in New York from 1982-1989. She had a PhD in history and Narochnitskaya's views were both anti-Western and anti-American. She was elected to the Duma in 2003 as part of the newly invented nationalist *Rodina* (motherland) block which towed such views. It was the first successful example of the Kremlin and Lubyanka creating a managed 'systemic' nationalism.

Several political movements of the nationalist and leftist (then) leanings formed the basis of *Rodina*. Dmitry Rogozin and Sergei Glazyev became the leaders of the party. In the 2003 elections, Homeland managed to mop up the protest vote among the electorate. But by the time the elections were over, the party had split into several factions. And in 2005-2006, when Rogozin and his Chekist 'patriot' comrades decided to strike out on their own, without fully coordinating their program with Putin's all powerful ODP, *Rodina* was excluded from the elections for the Moscow Duma. Rogozin was forced to leave the party and was temporarily dispatched to Brussels on a diplomatic assignment, to teach him a lesson and to intimidate NATO.

The Party of the Soviet Union may have been despotic, but its ideology had a compelling logic. This was another change. After 2000, the pendulum swung past logic to loyalty. In the Duma, deputy Alexey Podberezkin, the former Pitovranov-Bobkov 5th Directorate academic at RAU and *Most* SS, supported the Communist Zyuganov. In 2000, he even ran against Putin for the Russian Presidency, receiving only 0.13% of the votes. All this 'opposition' work might have cost him his career, one might have thought. Nothing could be further from the truth. From 2001, Podberezkin became an advisor to Sergei Stepashin, Russia's 2-month Prime Minister in 1999. Stepashin was exiled the Federation's Accounting Chamber as Chair was and First Deputy to Sergei Shakhray, Director of the State Institute of System Analysis of the Accounting Chamber of Russia.

Podberezkin's academic work revered patriotism, at the heart of which lay a profound belief in Russian nationalism. In this regard, we should a the 'scientific report' prepared by Podberezkin, together with Valery Vorotnikov from the 5th Directorate and Vladimir Rubanov from the KGB's Analytics Department. In his role as First Deputy Director of the Institute of System Analysis, Podberezkin was directly responsible for the report. The report was called *Global Processes: Tendencies of Development in Russia and Worldwide before 2020*. Under the section 'The New Type of Bio-Security and Bio-Defense of the Fatherland' these 'scientists' called for a 'Satan-predictor' in connection to the USA and NATO:

> To prevent a new round of Cold War, a global peace movement that is unique in world history is required consisting of all righteous peoples and forces on the planet under the banner of the Universal God-Power Predictor.... Realistically considering the current essentially planetary expansion of the Global Satan Predictor and his social agents, we cannot rule out the possibility that the path to the future Planetary Alliance lies through the forced creation of a Pan-Eurasian Defense Alliance as the geopolitical alternative to the current expansion of the USA and NATO.

Podberezkin drew the Kremlin's attention like a laser beam. Is it any surprise that, after delivering this report, Podberezkin became the recipient of the Andropov Prize in 2003 for his substantial contribution to Russia's defense capability?

5: The Russian-Orthodox Church of Spies

On July 8, 2000, Vladimir delivered his first address to the Federal Assembly (the Duma and the Federation Council, the senate). The word 'democracy' was absent. In subsequent addresses to the Assembly he only ever included the term once. In December 2000, Putin insisted that new state symbols would be created by the Duma. It became a hodgepodge of the past. The state flag still remained red, white and blue; the tricolour adopted under Yeltsin. The state seal, however, became the two-headed eagle of pre-revolutionary Russia. At the same time, the Soviet-era red banner became the official banner of the Russian Army, and the old Soviet anthem was adopted as the Russian state anthem—with slightly altered words avoiding references to the Soviet Union. There was something 'Russian' for everyone.

Putin's concept of a 'Russian World' was more widely derived entirely from the rhetoric of Alexei Podberezkin, one of the authors of the election program of the (Communist) National Patriotic Union which became part of the *Rodina* bloc in 2003. 'National dignity', 'national sovereignty,' 'a unified spirit of command,' 'the will of the state,' 'orientation toward a multipolar world,' 'the restoration of geopolitical authority'—it was from Podberezkin's Communist manifesto that Putin lifted phrases that he was to use frequently.

In his 2005 address to the Federal Assembly, Putin reminded his audience that the collapse of the USSR had been a 'catastrophe'—while ignoring that something called 'the Party' had ever existed: 'First of all, we must admit that the collapse of the Soviet Union was the greatest geopolitical catastrophe of the century. And, for the Russian people, it was a real tragedy. Tens of millions of our fellow citizens and compatriots found themselves outside Russian territory.' He announced a concept of a new empire—one in which all territories densely populated by ethnic Russians become a part of the Russian Federation and, more broadly, all 'compatriots' scattered all over the world are united into a virtual *Russkiy Mir*, a 'Russian World.'

In this new 'Russian World' an important role was allotted to a long-standing Russian institution, the Russian Orthodox Church—originally considered undesirable in Soviet times as a Marxist measure of the people's suppression. Even before the start of *perestroika* and the collapse of the USSR, the Cheka had started 'cross-breeding' the nationalists with the Church. The tradition of using the Church in the service of Soviet tyranny was not new. Even in Soviet times the Orthodox Church hierarchy was infiltrated by Intelligence officers, Active Reserve officers, and agents, perhaps even more than other organizations given the fact that it had a longstanding ideology that bound the Russian people.

Stalin himself created the Council on Russian Orthodox Church Affairs. Moreover, it was he who came up with its name. The task of this agency was to serve as a liaison between church and state at the height of World War II and was founded in September, 1943, shortly before Stalin's meeting with Roosevelt and Churchill in Tehran. By Stalin's calculation the Church as an institution could be revived and utilized by the Soviet state both in the USSR and, particularly, beyond its borders. Stalin's handpicked chief of the Council was NKVD colonel Georgy Karpov. A year later, similar Councils on religious affairs were created for other faiths. They, too, were headed by Lubyanka (NKVD) officers.

Karpov's *curriculum vitae* was well-tailored to the tasks Stalin assigned to him. Born in 1898, Karpov had worked for the Cheka his entire adult life. A major at the start of the Great Patriotic War (World War II), he was a major general by 1945. Then came March 1955 and the general was fired from the KGB for being a Beria supporter. His 'case-file' established that 'while working at the Leningrad Directorate and at the Pskov Regional NKVD, Comrade Karpov violated socialist legal norms, conducted mass arrests of innocent citizens, used sadistic methods of questioning during investigations, and falsified the transcripts of interrogations.' In particular, Alexander Tammi, who was arrested in Leningrad in 1937, recalled that 'Karpov at first pummeled him with a stool and then choked him with a leather belt which he slowly tightened.'

Accusations of sadism notwithstanding, Karpov remained Chair of Stalin's religious council (September 1943-February 1960) for the Russian-Orthodox church. It was only after he was expelled from the Party for his Stalin-era crimes in January 1960 that he was replaced in this post by another KGB general, Vladimir Kuroyedov. From the moment the KGB 5th Directorate was created under Andropov, the Deputy Chair of the Council of Religious Affairs was always an officer of the 4th Department, the department that monitored the leadership of all religious denominations in the Soviet Union. It was an important post and in the KGB hierarchy, it required the rank of a general.

Any clergy needed to be registered with the Council in order to undertake their pastoral tasks. The Council itself controlled the governing bodies of all religious organizations, including the Synod of the Russian Orthodox Church. Until the collapse of the USSR—the deputy chairs of religious organizations were held by undercover KGB Active Reserve officers who worked under the 4th Department. Sometimes, things got comical: in 1983, 'Sayan,' a leading Buddhist cleric, agent received a KGB certificate of merit 'for many years of cooperation and active assistance with the Intelligence Services.' After the fall of the USSR, the large number of agents recruited among the leadership of the Russian Orthodox Church became clear. The previous patriarch—the Russian-Orthodox equivalent of the Catholic pope in Rome—Alexy II (1990-2008), was for decades a Soviet agent with codename

'Drozdov'. Similarly, the current Patriarch, Kirill (2009-), was a Cheka agent with codename 'Mikhailov'.[280]

In an interview with the Ukrainian online publication *Weekly.ua* in 2012, Patriarch Filaret—also known by the secular name Mikhail Denisenko—said that 'all bishops, without exception, had ties to the KGB. Without exception. In Soviet times, no one could become a bishop if the KGB did not give its approval. Therefore, it would be a lie if I said that I had no ties to the KGB; I did, like all the others.' Many clerics abroad were among the recruits the KGB ranked most highly:

'Svyatoslav'—Metropolitan Nicodemus (Boris Rotov); in 1970, he was made temporary head of the Patriarchates of *North and South America*; then, headed the Department of External Church Relations (DECR) of the Russian Orthodox Church;

'Chrysostom'—the Archbishop of *Vilnius*;

'Reader'—the Primate of the *Latvian* Orthodox Church,

'Petrov'—Pyotr Kuzmich Raina, the Exarch of the Moscow Patriarch with the Patriarch of *Alexandria and all of Africa*;

'Voronov'—Arkady Tyshchuk, cleric of the St. Nicholas Russian Orthodox Cathedral in *New York* (1977-1982);

'Fyodor'—Ivan Borcha, priest of rural parishes of the Ukrainian and Rumanian communities of the *Canadian provinces of Alberta and Saskatchewan* (early 1970s);

'Patriot'—Viktor Petlyuchenko, cleric of the Russian Orthodox parish of Edmonton, *Alberta, Canada*;

'Icarus'—Igor Zuzemel, bishop of the Russian Orthodox Church, Metropolitan of *Vienna and Austria*;

'Esaulenko'—Iosif Pustoutov, who served in Russian Orthodox churches in the *Netherlands*, West Germany, *Italy and France*. In 1976, became the primate of the Moscow Patriarchate at the headquarters of the Christian Peace Conference in *Prague*

Reports by the 4th Department (religion) were delivered monthly to the heads of the 5th Directorate and placed in salad-green folders marked 'Secret' or 'Top secret.'[281] Among political scheming and straightforward propaganda, the Orthodox agents did not shy away from more repulsive interventions: '1980… Hailo has been convicted under Article 190, Part 1 of the RSFSR Criminal Code and sent to a psychiatric hospital for compulsory treatment'. An operation such as this was hardly an exception to the rule. In 1982 another report read, 'At present in the entire country … 229 church members and sectarians are serving their sentences (up from 220 in 1981). Another 18 individuals are in internal exile (down from 24 in 1981). KGB agencies have over 2500 operative cases monitoring hostile elements from this category of citizen (up from 2,225 in 1981). The most significant results are as follows: the Russian Orthodox Church and the Georgian and Armenian churches remain staunchly loyal due to the work of top agents. ... During the year 1982, a total of 1,809 meetings have been held and 704 reports have been received. Thirteen safe-houses and two top-secret safehouses are used for meetings with agents. Signed: Deputy Chief of 4th Department, Colonel Romanov'.

To maintain cover at all times, the KGB gave codenames not only to its agents but to those who were 'targets of operative surveillance, monitoring or development.' The man behind the codename 'Ascetic' was the world-famous physicist and dissident Andrei Sakharov; his wife Elena Bonner was 'Fox'; the writer Alexander Solzhenitsyn, 'Spider.' 'Pharmacist' was Alexander Ogorodnikov, a religious dissident whom the KGB considered an adversary. *Perestroika* and *glasnost* notwithstanding, the KGB's attacks on him through religious agents made his life a misery with pin-point preci-sion: 'August 1988. As part of the case "Pharmacist" case, measures have been con-ducted to further compromise the target in the eyes of like-minded people and Western contacts.... Via agents and by other means, "Pharmacist"'s' wife has been persuaded to file for divorce.... Signed: Chief of 4th Department, Colonel Timoshevsky.'

Even before the creation of the 5th Directorate under Pitovranov in the 1950s, the Russian-Orthodox Church was the second most important spy-nest after the Lubyanka, permeated with Chekist AROs from top to bottom. To Stalin, religion was of interest for a number of important reasons. At stake was not only control over the minds of believers, and over believers themselves within Russia, but the opportunity to use religion as a launch pad for contacts with churches abroad and with branches of the Russian Orthodox Church Abroad, as well as with Russian and Soviet émigrés who often had close ties through the Russian-Orthodox Church.

Alexander Kazem-Bek was a prominent example of a Soviet double-agent, a white-Russian émigré who was both a spy and a church insider. He was born in 1902 into an old aristocratic family. His father, Lev Kazem-Bek (1876-1952), had graduat-ed from the Page Corps, a military academy for sons of the nobility, where he had shared a school desk with Count Alexei Ignatyev, the future general in the Tsar's Army who would go on to serve the Bolsheviks and became a well-known Soviet intelligence officer and *agent-provocateur*.

In August 1917, in the wake of the Russian Revolution, the Kazem-Beks left for Kazan, then in March 1918, they retreated to Kislovodsk, where 'all Petrograd' had gathered to escape the violence. In 1920, the Kazem-Beks fled from Novorossiysk on the Black Sea to Thessaloniki, Greece, and from there to Yugoslavia. In September 1920, 18-year-old Alexander Kazem-Bek began to study languages at the University of Belgrade, finding a role as an interpreter for the Committee on the Affairs of Russian Refugees in Belgrade. Then, from Yugoslavia, the Kazem-Beks moved on to France and, from 1925 to 1929, they lived in Monte-Carlo.

Life as an exile from revolutionary Russia left its mark. By the early 1930s, Kazem-Bek had become a prominent Russian Fascist, a follower of Italian Fascism and German Nazism. He was well-known in Fascist circles. The Italian special services' file on Alexander Kazem-Bek mentioned that he was 'the only one of the white-Russian émigrés to have had a personal audience with Mussolini, meeting him in May 1934.' Kazem-Bek also maintained a friendly relationship with Achille Starace, the Secretary of the Italian Fascists, participated in the congress of Russian émigré fascist parties in Berlin, and headed the fascist publication *Nashe znamya* (our banner) printed in Vezin, Belgium, where he lived at the time. He had radically anti-Soviet views and urged white émigrés to join a war against the Soviet Union.

Then, oddly enough, Kazem-Bek's attitude toward the USSR changed 180 degrees. By 1937, he was a Stalin supporter and welcomed Stalin's repression as a method of exterminating international communists. At the heart of this remarkable change of mind, stood his childhood friend Count Alexei Ignatiev, then in charge of Cheka *rezidenturas* in Europe.[282] His Damascene conversion saved his life. After the start of World War II, in 1940, Kazem-Bek was arrested and sent to a camp where he was held until 1942. He managed to move to the US with his family—though not all of them. His father, Lev Kazem-Bek, returned to the USSR in 1947, only to be arrested, accused of espionage, and exiled to Kazakhstan, where he starved to death. In America, Alexander Kazem-Bek resumed a distinguished role that complemented his aristocratic background and taught Russian at Yale University and, for a while, headed the Department of Russian Language and Literature at Connecticut College in New London.

The reacquaintance with Ignatyev in 1937, had evidently turned Kazem-Bek into an agent for Soviet intelligence. Belatedly, in 1956, during Eisenhower's Presidency but after McCarthyism had ended, the FBI took a belated interested in him, and Kazem-Bek fled hastily to the USSR, leaving his wife and two children in the United States. This was not an impromptu decision and he had first obtained permission from his Cheka handlers: in 1957, he was granted Soviet citizenship.

Having returned, Kazem-Bek wrote a 'letter of penance' about his wretched fate for *Pravda* and a series of articles about 'soulless America' for leading Soviet publication *LG*. He also got a new job within the Department of External Church Relations (DECR), the Russian Orthodox global outreach department. Officially, Kazem-Bek was a translator/interpreter. But he was also the *de facto* 'right hand' and assistant to Metropolitan Nikodim (Rotov), KGB agent 'Svyatoslav', who handled relations with churches abroad. In *Anatomy of a Betrayal: A CIA 'Supermole' within the KGB* (2005), KGB agent Alexander Sokolov reported that he was the one who got Kazem-Bek the job with the DECR.

Kazem-Bek was fêted in Soviet Russia. In his (Russian) memoir, *The Last Twenty Years: Memoirs of a Chief of Political Counterintelligence*, Bobkov described numerous meetings and conversations with Kazem-Bek. In Soviet times, he had had unlimited credit at the elite Moscow restaurant Prague. He and his new family (he married Silva Tsvetayeva, an 18-year-old) received an apartment in a prestigious building on Frunze Embankment which otherwise only housed top bureaucrats of the Ministry of Defense. The wife he had left in the US to support two children by herself knew nothing of his second marriage and sent him from the US anything he asked for without receiving financial support from him. When his bigamy was uncovered, Kazem-Bek's wife in America sent a letter to the Patriarch of the Russian-Orthodox Church, Alexy II, asking if it was true that her husband now had a second wife. On January 15, 1967, the Patriarch replied vaguely, 'With regard to Kazem-Bek, I cannot tell you anything since I am not familiar with the intimate aspects of his life. I am very fond of him. He is a wonderful, refined person, and I see him quite often. He helps us a great deal with our relations with various foreign delegations.... Alexy.'

The KGB saw the letter from Kazem-Bek's American wife as a plot by the CIA. In order to counteract it, a priest and DECR staffer named Boris Kudinkin—also a KGB agent—was sent to have a meeting with her.

Vera Reshchikova, who worked with Kudinkin at the DECR, later recalled that he was involved in creating *kompromat* by starting affairs: 'That man was thoroughly vile.... He was a spy. He would lure women [to his apartment], and [KGB] agents would hide in the next room and take their pictures. One of his victims, a Czech woman, complained to her country's consulate. Yet in spite of the scandal, he continued to work at the DECR.'[283] His education skills were very useful to the KGB. He seduced a secretary at the Embassy of the Netherlands in Moscow. The middle-aged woman was captivated by his 'Slavic charm,' after which she lapsed into a depression and was recalled. A year later, while working in one of the capitals in the Middle East, she was contacted by Soviet intelligence.

On Kazem-Bek's return, the Lubyanka's esteem for him was nothing less than impressive. They would expunge records that would condemn other Soviet citizens for life. It was Kazem-Bek's brother-in-law, Mikhail Chavchavadze, who had (re-)introduced him to Ignatyev in 1937. He was also an émigré in France. But in 1947, like Kazem-Bek's father, he fatefully returned to the USSR with his young family. He, too, was deported to Kazakhstan after he was arrested on charges of espionage, convicted in 1949, and sentenced to 25 years in the camps. Upon Kazem-Bek's return, in 1956, however, he was released from exile and moved to Alma-Ata in Kazakhstan.

There was a price, of course. Zurab Chavchavadze, Mikhail Chavchavadze's son and Alexander Kazem-Bek's nephew was born in German-occupied Paris in 1943, brought back to the USSR by his parents in 1947, and part of the Kazem-Beks/Chavchavadzes' deportation to Kazakhstan as son of 'an enemy of the people.' Despite this indelible stain, in 1969, 26-year-old Zurab Chavchavadze graduated from Tbilisi State University, Georgia, with a degree in West European philology as his career took off on the back of his recruitment as a KGB agent. In 1967-1971, he worked as a senior scholar at a research institute in Tbilisi, then taught at Tbilisi University until 1989. In 1990, he became one of the organizers of the Russian Nobles' Assembly (the Union of Descendants of the Russian Nobility) and not by accident.

Thanks to Stalin, the Russian Orthodox Church, with its deep penetration of spies and global network, was fully integrated and a prized Lubyanka asset. Counterintelligence, the church abroad, émigrés, Russians abroad, Russians living abroad, a 'Russian World'…, all of it was tied up into a web the Lubyanka continued spinning for decades after Stalin. When Slavophilism was infiltrated, curated, managed and developed by Pitovranov's 5th Directorate experimentation with a merger between Russian Orthodoxy and nationalism soon followed—since both fell under Pitovranov's Directorate.

Already back in 1978, at Pitovranov's suggestion, Andropov had ordered the creation of a special unit within the PGU (foreign intelligence) which worked exclusively on émigrés from the Soviet Union. It was called Department 19, headed by Colonel Yuri Mitkavicius from the late 1980s. This department's mission was to cultivate reliable agents among Soviet/white-Russian émigrés, especially second- and third-generation immigrants who had become integrated into the establishment of the countries where they lived.

The same department was involved in a long-term project to terminate the 'anti-Kremlin' Russian Orthodox Church Abroad (ROCA). Seen from the Moscow Patriarchate, ROCA was a breakaway group that had split the Russian-Orthodox world after 1917. Absorbing ROCA would restore the patriarch's complete authority. Seen from the outside, this operation was intended to look like ROCA's 'voluntary' unification with the Moscow Patriarchy (in turn, entirely controlled by the Lubyanka). Among those of particular interest was Archfather Alexander Kiselev, a prominent figure in ROCA, born in the Tver province in 1909. After the 1917 Revolution, his family emigrated to then-independent Estonia, since his father was born in Tartu (Yuriev), Estonia. It was there that Kiselev became active in one of the most significant organizations of Russian-Orthodox church life in the first half of the 20th century, the Christian Student Movement (RSKhD), which had a branch in the Baltics.

In 1933, Alexander Kiselev graduated from the Riga Seminary, Latvia, and planned to continue his education in theology at the St Sergius Institute in Paris, France. However, somehow he was able to skip these stages. Just a short while later, in August 1933, he was ordained as a priest and went on to serve in several parishes: first in Narva, then at the St. Nicholas Church in Tallin (both in Estonia). It was a fortunate coincidence that a fellow RSKhD member served as a deacon, Alexei Ridiger the future Patriarch of Moscow Alexy II (Cheka agent 'Drozdov'). They made a deep connection. At the funeral mass for Father Alexander on October 4, 2001, Alexy II tearfully recalled those distant years and the image of the 'good shepherd' which Kiselev exemplified for him in his own youth.

In 1940, when the Red Army occupied the Baltics, Father Alexander left for Germany (his wife's part-German blood helped). After June 1941, he began to organize Russian-Orthodox parish life for dozens of thousands of Soviet citizens who found themselves on German territory in wartime—both prisoners of war and people taken to the German Reich as laborers. It was then that Father Alexander met former Soviet Army commander, General Andrei Vlasov, who had defected to the

Nazis. Father Alexander regarded Vlasov's Russian Liberation Army (RLA) as a legitimate continuation of the Russian people's struggle against Communism during the civil war and the Soviet peasant uprisings. He became the chaplain at the RLA headquarters and General Vlasov's spiritual guide. He spent the final months of the war with the Committee's army units in Münsingen and retreated with these Russian units deep into Bavaria. Father Alexander later told Vlasov's story in extensive detail in his memoir, *The Portrait of General Vlasov: Memoirs of a War Priest* (in Russian but published in the US, 1976).

After the war, Father Alexander was dispatched to resettle in New York, where he created the St Seraphim Foundation and publishing house which specialized in religious philosophy. From 1978, he published a magazine whose contributors included prominent émigré writers, scholars, and clerics. He was co-founder and chaplain of the largest Russian émigré organization in the US, the Congress of Russian Americans. His impeccable anti-Communism manifested itself in a deep desire to cleanse Russia of its terrible 'disease' and bring the people back on 'a path of penance and service to Christ'.

Then came 1990, the height of *perestroika* and *glasnost* and the penultimate year of the USSR's existence. A new Patriarch of the Russian Orthodox Church was 'elected' in Moscow and who was chosen but KGB agent Drozdov, Alexei Ridiger, Father Alexander's long-time friend. One revealing indication of the real power behind the Patriarchate was KGB Major General Valery Lebedev, advisor on economic and other issues to patriarch. All appointments to key religious posts required the KGB general's approval. Under Putin, this Cheka practice continued without interruption—Lebedev continued in the same role with Alexy II's successor, Patriarch Kirill in 2009. Nor was the general a neutral Chekist bystander. In 1991, Lebedev was one of the participants in the failed August coup, prosecuted and later amnestied like all the others. It had no impact whatsoever on his career. After the coup, Lebedev—who sometimes styled himself a 'theology professor'—became the head of the Russian Orthodox Television Foundation and chaired the Board of the Directors of the Moscow Patriarchate's cable TV and radio station—the misnamed 'Free' People's Television.

With Patriarch Alexy II in the saddle, Archfather Alexander Kiselev now had a reason to visit his native country—which he did despite the years of bile. What was truly even more perplexing was that a staunch anti-Communist, the spiritual shepherd of the traitorous Soviet-then-Nazi-then-Dissident General Vlasov of an anti-Soviet army, received a visa for travel to the country against which he had waged war his entire life. The religious might have glossed over this life of treason, but it was not up to Patriarchate to decide who could visit them from abroad (as little, one might add, as whom to elect as patriarch other than the 5th Directorate's 4th Department choice).

Needless to say, it was only the KGB that could greenlight Father Alexander's trip to the USSR. To the 5th Directorate, the long-term objective was the fusion of

ROCA under the Moscow Patriarchate. When the KGB developed contacts with anti-Soviet centers abroad, with the ROCA and with prominent émigré figures, it was conducting a complex, multistep operations, seeing several moves ahead like a chess player. Patriarch 'Drozdov' followed his handlers' instructions and worked on his old friend Father Alexander—who had influence in ROCA—in order to convince him of the need for the unification of the Russian Orthodox Church and ROCA, despite its implacable hostility.

The ground had been carefully laid in the 1980s, when Father Alexander's home in New York was the location of secret meetings between ROCA hierarchs and those of the Moscow Patriarchate. It was there that Father Alexander had his first unofficial meeting with his friend and future patriarch contender Ridiger. Many years later, Ridiger, now Alexy II, described their first reunion since Estonia as entirely spontaneously, initiated by Father Alexander:

I had known Father Alexander since the days of my youth, when, as a boy, I assisted him at church services. ... At the end of the war, he left Estonia. Neither I nor my parents heard anything about him. And then one day, when I was on a work trip in the U.S., already in the rank of bishop, I suddenly got a phone call from Father Alexander at my hotel and got an invitation to visit his church. Our reunion was very moving.

In 1998, Father Alexander kept up the initiative and gifted an *iconostasis* (a church partition with icons) formerly located in an émigré church in New York to the Church of the Holy Martyr Tatiana.[284]

An important new move followed in August 1991 during the 'First World Congress of Compatriots', a coming together of expat Russians of all hues to visit Moscow for two weeks. The fact that it straddled the attempted coup, an event also organized by the Lubyanka—made little difference to the Lubyanka's long game. One of its prominent participants was the new head of the Russian Orthodox Church, Patriarch Alexy II. International events, and particularly subsequent 'congresses of compatriots,' held in Moscow with enviable regularity, were an excellent opportunity for KGB/FSB Intelligence purposes. Those who were invited to participate were studied long before the actual event. The congress participants list represented a recruitment 'wishlist' that was the culmination of selection, development and recruitment of participants who were of interest to the FSB. Sooner or later, it would bear fruit.

During the first congress of compatriots in Moscow—as the coup took place elsewhere in the city—Patriarch Alexy II immediately put it to good use. He received Gleb Rahr, a prominent Russian émigré and long-time (anti-Kremlin) Radio Liberty staffer who was involved with the ROCA. Rahr delivered to ROCA the reunification offer of freshly-minted patriarch in which he offered its Synod of Bishops terms that would allow ROCA to retain full autonomy. ROCA's leader Metropolitan Vitaly promptly declined despite circumstances that to most looked like a gust of new air blowing from Gorbachev's Russia—but ostensibly not to the Metropolitan.[285]

In November 1991, the young Patriarch made an official visit to the US. At his invitation, his old friend Father Alexander took part in a joint prayer service at the St Nicholas Cathedral in New York, the chief cathedral of Russian Orthodox parishes in the US. Metropolitan Vitaly, however, still categorically opposed a joint prayer service by representatives of two Churches that held diametrically opposed views of the system that existed in the USSR. The Metropolitan in fact repeatedly reproached Archfather Alexander's stance, saying, 'You're with us, but you're not one of us.'

The Metropolitan's intransigence called for a different tactic to neutralize ROCA. For one, in 1991, Alexander returned to Russia as a ROCA outpost. He settled in the Donskoy Monastery in Moscow (under whose roof he died on October 3, 2001). Next, in January 1992, the Synod of ROCA Bishops dispatched Barnabas (Prokoviev), the Bishop of Cannes and the vicar of the West European bishopric, to Russia for the purpose of organizing a Synodal Priory of ROCA in Moscow. He opened it in a building of the Convent of Mary and Martha which belonged to a medical clinic. By a remarkable coincidence, it also housed the headquarters of the radical, fascist, nationalist, anti-Semitic *Pamyat* (the People's Patriotic Front led by Dmitri Vasielev and his bodyguard Alexander Barkashov under the control of the 5th Directorate).

Also in 1992, the St Andrew the Holy and All-Praised First-Called Apostle charitable foundation was created. Its website stated that it 'carries out projects aimed at developing positive attitudes in society toward Russia's traditional and unifying pillars: state, church and army' and that the foundation 'advocates the awakening in the human soul of spiritual principles solidly linked to the people's history and culture.' The 'transfer of Russian Orthodox holy relics within the boundaries of the Russian Orthodox Church' was declared to be one of the principal directions of the Foundation's work. Two other lofty associations were registered at the same time: The *Andreyevsky Flag* (St Andrew's flag) publishing house, specializing in 'Russian Orthodox, military, maritime and historical literature,' and a second foundation, an interregional public fund called the Center for National Glory.

All three were registered at 35 Bolshaya Ordynka Street (a large building of 594sqm) in Moscow. Before the revolution, the adjacent number 34 had been a Russian Orthodox women's monastery, the Convent of Mary and Martha. This convent was briefly revived after 1991 and populated with a community of about 100 Russian-Orthodox nuns in order to lull the suspicion of the ROCA's Metropolitan and Bishops. Both premises had been requisitioned at General Bobkov's request with help from Moscow Mayor Gavriil Popov and his successor Luzhkov.

On March 19, 1992, the convent hosted a press conference during which Archfather Alexei Averyanov—acting on behalf of ROCA Bishop Barnabas and with a mention of Metropolitan Vitaly—announced an alliance with *Pamyat*. The latter was, according to Archfather Averyanov, 'creating rapid response squads to protect ROCA churches from being taken over.'

In fact, there were no such plans, nor were there any ROCA churches. It was, however, a well-panned provocation designed to undermine ROCA. At the same press conference, *Pamyat* leader Vasiliev threatened to form a 'triple ring blockade' around Moscow that summer in order to overthrow the government. Two months later, on May 19, Bishop Barnabas even participated in a *Pamyat* demonstration on the Garden Ring Road in Moscow. The bishop also frequently accompanied Vasiliev on trips around Russia.

Needless to say, ROCA's proximity to, and alliance with, extremist *Pamyat* did irreparable damage. ROCA was now divided between supporters and opponents of Metropolitan Vitaly, and he was soon forced out of the post he had occupied for years. The Convent of Mary and Martha, having served its purpose, was disbanded once the Lubyanka had successfully pushed Vitaly out of office.

This disposable use was standard in 20th-century Lubyanka operations. But between 1991-1999, Communism lost all remaining currency as Russia's ideology, leaving only the Russian Orthodox Church standing as Lubyanka's puppet. Under Putin there was on this point a major shift in strategy. During the 20th century, charitable foundations were merely created as part of single-purpose Intelligence operations of one kind or another. Back in 1985, for example, the singer Iosif Kobzon was invited to serve as vice president for 'humanitarian issues' at the 21st Century Association. This was really a front created by the brothers Anzor and Otari Kvantrishvili with help from the KGB. Otari (codename 'Otarik') was both one of the godfathers of Russian organized crime and an agent of the KGB Directorate for Moscow and the Moscow Region (2nd Service). In 1986, another initiative was 'The Lyre and the Shield'—also headed by the singer—which had a more permanent if still prosaic purpose: assistance to employees of Soviet Internal Affairs agencies. Similarly, the KGB also created the National Athletes Foundation, headed by agent Tarpishchev, and the Unity Social Foundation for the Promotion of Peace and Cooperation in the Caucasus, headed by SVR agent Pyotr Suslov. They were all exceptions, however.

All that was to change in 2000 under Putin as Russia's president. Foundations and charities became essential working tools of the Lubyanka bureaucracy in creating a virtual 'Russian World'. After the capture of the Kremlin in 2000, the Russian Orthodox Church was ready made to replace the Communist ideology (whose Politburo was deflated and had been a thorn in the Cheka's side for too long). The expansion of Russian religion to Russians abroad instead allowed the creation of an extremely powerful 'fifth column' beyond the borders of the Russian Federation— and a key instrument of projecting Russian foreign policy in a new direction. It, of course, all remained smoke and mirrors. If it didn't work, the operation would be terminated. In that respect everything remained the same as it always had during Putin's formative KGB years at the 5th Directorate in Dresden.

6: The *Russkiy Mir*

On October 11 and 12, the 2001 World Congress of Compatriots took place in Moscow, in the Columns Hall of the House of Soviets. Delegates from 47 countries and prominent Russian politicians participated. In his welcoming speech, Putin launched the term 'Russian World' and outlined the directions for further development of relations between Russia and those abroad, calling for new paths toward the consolidation of the Russian diaspora and the strengthening of its ties to Russia.

Success soon followed. On May 17, 2007, at a reception at the Kremlin to celebrate the signing of the Act of Canonical Communion (reunification) of ROCA with the Russian Orthodox Church, Putin summed up the first results of the long-term operation aimed at the destruction of ROCA. 'The restoration of the unity of the Russian Orthodox Church is important not only to the Church; it is also an important spiritual stimulus toward the consolidation of the entire Russian World,' Putin said in his speech. Hearing these words, Archfather Mikhail Ardov of the Russian Orthodox Autonomous Church exclaimed: 'This is the final victory of the KGB over the Russian Church Abroad. But at the same time, it is an extremely foolish decision.… The [Moscow] Patriarchate is always in the pocket of whoever sits in the Kremlin.'[286]

What better example of this new tangled religious web than the career shift of KGB agent and *Pamyat* leader Barkashov. Twice, in 1996 and 1999, he tried to translate his militant base to the Duma as deputy of the nationalist bloc *Spas* (salvation), and in 2000, he backed Putin in the elections. Trying to catch the new mood in 2005, however, he became a monk taking the name Mikhail. In 2006, he used the Moscow region branch of the paramilitary *Russkoye Natsionalnoye Yedinstvo* (which had assisted with the 1993 putsch until Bobkov ordered them to escape) as a basis for the new project: the Barkashov Movement. Its ideology had a strong religious component. Barkashov himself, as 'Father Mikhail', became the movement's spiritual guide.

The convent building on Bolshaya Ordynka Street that in 1992 had played a brief role in the removal of ROCA Metropolitan Vitaly also indicated the new direction. It was taken over, raider-style, by the Russian Railroads Shareholder Association. Despite its unwieldy name, it was a corporation chaired by yet another high-level Chekist, Vladimir Yakunin. Just like Gazprom, Russian Railroads was a state within a state. It had 1.3 million employees, a media empire of its own, a budget of 1.3 trillion rubles, and an armed security force of 30,000. In 2006, in tandem with taking over the building, Yakunin became the head of the Foundation of St. Andrew the Holy and All-Praised First-Called Apostle on Bolshaya Ordynka Street and took it over completely, becoming one of the most powerful Russian-Orthodox Chekists.

In 2004, Yakunin had started to organize annual congresses of Russian conservatives—church figures and politicians—at the Russian-Orthodox monastery on the island of Rhodes, Greece. Alexander Dugin, the Lubyanka-agent Fascist, one-time *Pamyat* member, participated in nearly every one of them. 'We work on the same assembly belt,' Yakunin said of Dugin in one of his interviews. In his 2006, *The Russian School of Geopolitics* (in Russian), Yakunin quoted the Russian fascist Dugin no fewer than eight times. He was also the editor of two Dugin anthologies published by one of Yakunin's media ventures.

On March 5, 2013, Yakunin, as Chair of the board of trustees of the St Andrew Foundation and of its association Center for National Glory, registered the *Istoki* (fountainhead) Endowment. Sergei Sheblygin was appointed its director. The fund quickly became one of the five largest endowments in Russia. On July 23, 2013, Yakunin and his wife Natalia also endowed a Foundation of St. Andrew in Geneva. Its stated purpose was support for the study and preservation of Russian national legacy as well as the promotion of peaceful coexistence of peoples and religions. Natalia became the president of the Fund, Yakunin its vice president.

The administration of the Swiss organization also included Yakunin's former colleague in his work as Cheka agent, a regular Lubyanka officer Mikhail Yakushev. From 2004, Yakushev was listed as first vice president of the Foundation of St Andrew and the Center for National Glory. Born in 1959, Yakushev graduated from MSU and then enrolled in the KGB's School No 101. In 1988, Yakushev was dispatched to work abroad under diplomatic cover, as a staff member in the Soviet embassy in Tunisia. From 1994 to 1999, he served as First Secretary of the Russian embassy in Israel, then as an advisor at the Russian Foreign Ministry. From May 2002 to April 2003, Yakushev headed the staff of the Foreign Affairs Committee of the Federation Council.

In an interview to the website *Pravoslavie i Mir* (orthodoxy and the world) on April 23, 2013, Yakushev had the following to say about his work in Israel: 'I dealt with issues of Russian properties. We were able … to get the Ministry of Foreign Affairs to re-register Soviet real estate holdings as Russian ones, because the disintegration of the Soviet Union was another blow. Above all, there were Ukraine's claims to some of those church properties. The Israelis spent a long time thinking about how to handle this…. It also helped that Yasir Arafat spoke out categorically in support of the Moscow Patriarchate.'

Russian real estate abroad was a top priority for the Russian Federation as they were the stepping stones to foreign influence. When the USSR fell apart in 1991, the share of each successor state was determined in accordance with a 1983 treaty, the international Convention on Succession of States in Respect of State Property, Archives and Debts signed in Vienna. Shares were calculated according to each republic's share of imports and exports and of gross national income, as well as each republic's population between 1986-1990. Russia's share came to 61.34 percent, Ukraine's to 16.37 percent, Belarus's to 4.13 percent, Uzbekistan's to 3.27 percent, Kazakhstan's to 3.86 percent, Georgia's to 1.62 percent and so on, with Estonia last at 0.62 percent.

After reviewing this arithmetic, however, Russia proposed a so-called 'zero version' in which Russia undertook the entire burden of the USSR's foreign debt in exchange for its assets. All the former Soviet republics accepted the offer, except for two: Georgia and Ukraine. They wanted Moscow to give them their share of former Soviet assets to which they were legally entitled under the Treaty. They never got anything. Despite their relatively modest fraction of foreign assets, their intransigence was noted by the Kremlin (and by their former colleague states). Instead of sharing Soviet property, Russia went to war against them: against Georgia in 2008, against Ukraine in 2014 under the virtual banner of a 'Russian World'.

It was a new watershed moment. Until 2008, Putin could have been faulted mainly for his desire to usurp power in Russia on behalf of the Cheka. But as long as he did not cross the borders of the Russian Federation, the US and Europe did not see Putin as an existential threat in the same sense that Lenin, Stalin, Khrushchev, or Brezhnev had with their theory of world revolution and the promise to introduce the Party 'socialism' all over the world. Putin seemed to be the most progressive, the most predictable, and even the most pro-American Russian leader that foreign governments had ever had to work with. With the exception of Gorbachev and Yeltsin (early in his tenure as President), Putin was seen as a man with whom you could do business.

It was against this apparently sunny backdrop that, in August 2008, Russian troops invaded Georgia. Only a few months earlier, in April 2008, Putin had declared at a NATO summit that Ukraine was a 'failed' state and that certain Ukrainian territories should be transferred to Russia. At the time, everyone in attendance, including U.S. President George W. Bush, took Putin's remarks as a joke. But he was not joking.

The history of the August 2008 Russian-Georgian war is tangled and complicated. The Russian mass media mobilized into a disinformation war and did everything they could to shout down the world press. Among the noise, Western politicians, journalists and citizens, who had a hard time even finding Georgia on the map—let alone Abkhazia or South Ossetia—could not make sense of this genuinely complex conflict between several nations in the Caucasus who alternated between peaceful coexistence and hostilities.

Once it became clear before the end of August that the Russian army had no plans to go on to Tbilisi, the capital, and seize all of Georgia, Western powers breathed a sigh of relief and put their geographical maps back where they came from. Gradually, the Russian-Georgian conflict receded into the past and was forgotten about. Abkhazia and South Ossetia, which remained occupied by Russian troops, held Kremlin-controlled referendums and proclaimed 'independence', which was recognized by no major country apart from occupier Russia. Georgia broke off diplomatic relations with Russia in protest.

Unlike Georgia, Ukraine was easy to find on the map. It was a large country comparable to France in land mass and population. But as little as the 2008 invasion of Georgia, the spring 2014 invasion of Ukraine was anything but spontaneous. Rather, it was the continuation of Putin's 'Russian World' strategy by other means that had started much earlier, if not at the beginning of Putin's term in 2000.

The Soviet invasion of Afghanistan began with the failed poisoning of Amin. The Russian invasion of Ukraine began with the failed poisoning during the presidential elections in Ukraine of leading candidate, Viktor Yushchenko. In September 2004, Russian Intelligence attempted to remove Yushchenko, who was running against Kremlin favorite Viktor Yanukovych. On September 5, 2004, at the height of the presidential race, Yushchenko met with friends, ate and drank and conducted negotiations with no sign of trouble. On September 6, he felt ill; on September 10, he was hospitalized at the Rudolfinerhaus clinic in Austria, where he was diagnosed with acute pancreatitis with complications caused by poisoning with toxins. The time of poisoning: approximately five days prior to hospitalization.

Traces of chemicals that are usually not contained in food were found in Yushchenko's body. In particular, a group of American doctors found highly toxic dioxin in his blood. In the end, the Kremlin failed as Yushchenko defeated Yanukovych despite not being able to speak for most of the campaign.

On September 21 2004, the Ukrainian General Prosecutor opened a criminal investigation into the poisoning. An examination of evidence in late May of 2006 once again confirmed the presence of dioxin in Yushchenko's system. The tests were conducted by a commission made up of Ukrainian, American, German and Japanese experts. They confirmed the previous findings of Dutch, German, British and Belgian labs that Yushchenko's body contained dioxin.

On September 7, 2009, Ukrainian President Yushchenko declared that the investigation into his poisoning in 2004 was over: 'The investigation has been completed, the prosecutor's office interviewed about a thousand witnesses. I myself went down to the General Prosecutor several times to give my testimony. A number of deputies, among them opposition leader Viktor Yanukovych, did not testify.'

According to Yushchenko, the people behind his poisoning were in Moscow for four years: 'I appealed to the President of Russia three times to allow them to be interrogated by Ukrainian investigators. The investigators are prepared to conduct the interrogations at our embassy in Moscow. The suspects are a former Deputy Chair of the SBU [the State Security of Ukraine], a cook, and a member of the service personnel. All those people are now in Moscow.'

On September 10 and September 11, 2007, Yushchenko once again stated that the Russian government was refusing to turn over key suspects and provide the samples needed to solve the case. He also said that the rare poison used in the attempt on his life was produced only in three countries in the world: the US, Great Britain, and Russia. The US and Great Britain had provided samples of their stocks long ago.

The development of a detailed program that would justify the expansion of the Russian Federation's border and rely on the concept of the 'Russian World' was entrusted to a new think tank that had once been a part of SVR. In the spring of 2009, shortly after the Russian invasion of Georgia, it was split off from the Lubyanka and reorganized as an autonomous body, the Russian Institute for Strategic Research (RISR)—created in a way like Bobkov's *Most* SS in the 1990s, though RISR was run directly by the Kremlin rather than privately. RISR's founder and main client was the administration of the Russian President. Formerly a top-secret SVR institute, RISR was located on the northern outskirts of Moscow under the protection of special troops. It employed more than 200 staff who were previously at the SVR.

The man appointed to the post of RISR director, Leonid Reshetnikov, was an SVR Lieutenant General who had previously headed the SVR's Information and Analysis Directorate, and prior to that had been the SVR's point man for the Balkans (Bulgaria, former Yugoslavia, Greece).

Reshetnikov was born in 1947 in the family of a military man stationed in Potsdam. In 1970, he graduated from Kharkov State University with a degree in history, then studied in graduate school at the University of Sofia (1971-1974). In 1974-1976, he worked at the Institute of the Economy of the World Socialist System at the USSR Academy of Sciences. From April 1976 until April 2009, he served in foreign intelligence. In April 2009, he became an Active Reserve officer (APS); on April 29, 2009, he was appointed as director of RISR by Putin.

The chief expert at Reshetnikov's RISR institute was Alexander Sytin, a historian who left the Institute because of differences. He became a critic of Kremlin foreign policy, and specifically of the background to the Russian government's decision to invade Ukraine in 2014. In his opinion, problem arose after Reshetnikov 'got churched'—smitten with the idea of a virtual Russia the size of the White Russian Empire rather than Soviet Russia—with local populations overwhelming hoping to be part once again of White Russia.[287]

Only on January 4, 2017, was Reshetnikov removed from the post of RISR director on Putin's orders. The Institute's newly appointed director was Mikhail Fradkov, former Prime Minister of Russia (2004-2007) and former SVR director for even longer (2007-2016). Even so, Reshetnikov remained a part of the expert council at the Russian Foreign Ministry, the expert council at the Security Council of Russia, and the Public Council at the Russian Defense Ministry. He also became Chair of the supervisory board of Tsargrad TV, founded by a different Russian-Orthodox oligarch, Konstantin Malofeyev.

Malofeyev was directly involved in the Russian leadership's foreign-policy operations via various informal bodies through the Lubyanka. For many years, he was a parishioner—as if there were no other churches in Moscow—at a church with a Putin connection, the Holy Martyr Tatiana at Moscow State University (MSU). On January 22, 1995, this church had been returned to the Russian Orthodox Patriarchate and Vladimir Vigilyansky served as its head priest (protopriest) since 2012. In 2005,

Vigilyansky, who was already a priest by then, headed the Press Service of the Moscow Patriarchate. He reorganized as the Press Service of the Patriarch of Moscow and All the Russias in 2009.

But it was not this that made Malofeyev flock to him. In 1995, Vigilansky worked in the Patriarchate's publishing department, headed by Pitirim, Metropolitan of Volokolamsk and Yuriev. Pitirim's codename was 'Abbot' in the 5th Directorate KGB (4th Department) and he only hired staffers at the department based on recommendations from his Cheka handlers. Vigilansky became a deacon to everyone's surprise in the year the church was handed back. At the same time another one of 'Abbot's agent was Tikhon Shevkunov, later Father Tikhon, who became part of President Putin's close circle and the jewel in the 'Abbot's crown. When Father Tikhon served as vicar of the Sretensky Monastery in Moscow, Vigilyansky served as a deacon. The 'Abbot's team moved up together. Vigilansky took over as Martyr Tatiana's proto-priest from Maksim Kozlov, who also worked at the 'Abbot's publishing department. In 2012 Kozlov moved up to protopriest of the prestigious Church of the Reverend Seraphim of Sarov on the Kranopresnensky Embankment.

Rather than a religious devotee, Vigilyansky was always more a dyed-in-the-wool KGB agent. In the 1970s, as a student at the Gorky Literary Institute, he drew the attention of 5th Directorate Major Vladimir Gusev (1st Section of the 9th Department) who kept tabs on target 'Spider' (Aleksandr Solzhenitsyn). Gusev thought that student friends of Vigilyansky were circulating his 'target's works in *samizdat* after 'Spider's exile in 1974. Gusev's Chief, Lieutenant Colonel Vyacheslav Shironin instructed him to recruit Vigilyansky whose career thereafter advanced with leaps and bounds. With Gusev's approval, Vigilyansky began to work as a freelancer for 'Abbot's publishing department, where he worked until 1986. In 1988, he was hired—despite 'lack' of Party membership—by *Ogonyok*, where KGB agent Yumashev, who was to become both Yeltsin and Putin's Chief of Staff, also worked since 1987. Vigilyansky even became a member of *Ogonyok* editorial board with the approval of the Secretariat of the Party CC. Before his turn as a cleric, Vigilyansky was a member of the USSR Writers' Union was sent to US for a series of lectures in the fall, presumably on a spying mission.

The realm of the Russian spiritual world had as many surprising coincidences as that of the secular. From Malofeyev's adolescence, his religious role model was the nephew of Kazem-Bek, 'White-Russian monarchist' Zurab Chavchavadze—both loyal Chekist agents. In January 2007, Malofeyev became the founder and Chair of the St. Basil the Great Orthodox Fund. Chavchavadze became the Fund's general director and the head of the St. Basil the Great Russian Orthodox gymnasium, launched with Malofeyev's money. Chavchavadze, in turn, was one of the ideologues of the informal group of 'Russian Orthodox Chekists' and one of the principal propagandists of the 'Russian world.'

In early 2014, shortly before the seizure of Crimea, they worked together on an FSB religious operation. This concerned the 'gifts of the Magi'—the most precious holy relics of the Orthodox-Christian world. They had never before left Mount Athos in Greece but were now taken on a tour thought up, organized, and financed, by Malofeyev's fund. They first toured Russia and thereafter went on a visit of Ukraine. Over 400,000 people in Ukraine (population 50 million) came to pay homage to the gifts.

Like the first World Congress of Compatriots in 1991, the event happened to coincide with civil war provoked by the FSB. But on this occasion, not in Moscow but in Ukraine. Malofeyev's 'gifts of the Magi' happened to arrive during the prolonged political crisis known as *Euromaidan*. On February 20, 2014, more blood was spilled in Kiev, three weeks after the Gifts' show closed. The next day, the president of Ukraine, Viktor Yanukovych (whom the FSB had finally hoisted into the presidency after he had failed to win against his mute opponent Yuschenko in 2004), fled from Kiev to Russia.

In reality, the purpose of bringing the holy relics had little to do with any religious sentiments of Malofeyev's. Their Ukrainian worshippers were meant to create facts on the ground that could be used to justify Russia's foreign policy decisions. The crowds who came to worship the 'gifts' numbered some 280,000 people in Kiev, 50,000 in Simferopol, 100,000 in Sevastopol. Later, Malofeyev even pretended that the 100,000 Sevastopol pilgrims had prayed for Crimea's return to Russia. He also claimed that, on account of the Gifts, 'everyone' was now talking about the possibility of Crimea's unification with Russia, including Sergei Aksyonov, a member of the Supreme Council of the Autonomous Republic of Crimea—Crimea's highest body of state authority—and the Council's Chair, Vladimir Konstantinov.

Operation 'Russian Spring', the annexation of Ukraine by Russia, began precisely then, in February 2014. It was conducted by Russian Special Forces and was intended to destabilize the situation in Ukraine in order to prepare for the subsequent takeover of parts if not the whole of the country. The operation involved three principal elements: Russian regular agents and agents of influence; local pro-Russian 'separatists' and 'volunteers'; and regulars from special commando and diversionary units of the GRU and the FSB—the same kind of 'Vympelers' that, back in Soviet days, were dispatched to Africa or Latin America for the purpose of fomenting mutiny and civil war. Except that now, they could get by speaking their own native Russian rather than Portuguese or Spanish, which greatly simplified the infiltrators' work and made it much harder for Ukraine's law enforcement agencies to combat them.

The immediate goal of the 'Russian Spring' was to unleash an information war, to provoke ethnic, religious, and interregional conflict, and to create conditions that would allow Russian troops to enter Ukraine and occupy first a part of the country and then all of its territory. The political and geopolitical endgame was to eliminate Ukraine as an independent state and incorporate it into the Russian Federation, which would simultaneously gain direct access to the border of Moldova and annex Transnistria, the part of Moldova closest to Ukraine.

In the Russian documentary, *Crimea: Road to the Motherland*, shown by Moscow TV in April 2015, Putin gave his version:

> It was the early morning hours of February 23; we finished around 7am, and I dismissed everyone and went to bed at seven. And I won't deny it—when we were parting, before everyone left, I told all my colleagues—there were four of them—that the situation in Ukraine was unfolding in such a way that we are forced to start working on returning Crimea to Russia … but I immediately stressed that we would only do it if we are absolutely convinced that it's what the people want for themselves, the ones living in Crimea. It turned out that approximately 75 percent of the general population there wanted to join Russia. You understand, it was an internal poll, outside the context of possible unification.

Putin did not quite explain what he meant by 'an internal poll'. It turned out that this was no more than the footfall generated by Malofeyev's 'Gifts of the Magi' visit. The Russian Orthodox Chekists had attached to the glowing virtual reports generated by Reshetnikov's RISR institute a few (flimsy) facts ahead of the real operation 'Russian Spring'.

During the war with Ukraine, the Kremlin finessed their methods of creating a virtual reality through TV and the new Internet media. If one were to view only Russian media and Russian websites, Eastern Ukraine was Russian territory temporarily that had been occupied by the enemy. Russian artists, writers and journalists, just like Russian soldiers, were now ready to kill the 'Ukrainian occupiers' with words, images and fake news reports. Writer Alexander Prokhanov waxed eloquent in his personal show *Replika* (my line) about how the Ukrainians were on the verge of 'cutting open the bellies of pregnant Russian women.' Channel One of Russian television, available virtually everywhere in Russia and the main source of news for much of its population, aired reports about Ukrainians crucifying Russian children.

All of this was broadcast in Russian to Russia and Ukraine 24 hours a day, seven days a week by the special news channel Rossiya-24. Simultaneously, state-owned Russian channel Russia Today (rebranded as 'RT' so that the word 'Russia' would not leap out at foreigners) started broadcasting all over the world in foreign languages. Soviet propaganda, which had been the Communist Party's main ideological weapon, gave way to the Lubyanka's propaganda.

In the spring of 2014, on the back of high gas prices (the invasion of Georgia occurred on a massive spike, preceded by one two years prior), Putin believed that Russia was strong and Europe and the US unlikely in a position to resist Moscow's transgression. Germany addicted to Russian gas, England to Russian capital. France wanted to sell war ships Mistral; Switzerland, to continue keeping Russian oligarchs' money in its banks. America was tied up in Bush wars against Islamic extremism, while Barack Obama was perceived by Putin as a pacifist, having been given the Nobel Peace Prize before he even started, wasn't ready to take on Russia.

The Kremlin counted on a repeat of 2008 when Russia invaded Georgia and the

West ignored the Kremlin's first military act since the Soviet invasion of Afghanistan in 1979. Given the extraordinarily swift success of Crimea's bloodless occupation, RISR's and others' forecasts appeared correct. There was no military response, except in Eastern Ukraine where the invasion did not go too smoothly and became the grave of the Kremlin's expectation that the whole of Ukraine would fall into its lap as its 'friends' in Kiev rolled over. Overall, however, the Kremlin was pleased and thought it had created a *carte blanche* to claim former Russian territories by moving in troops.

Speaking at the Aspen Security Forum on July 24, 2014 US Chair of the Joint Chiefs of Staff, General Martin Dempsey, compared Putin to Stalin and Russia's actions to the Soviet invasion of Poland in September 1939 because 'he's got a play-book that has worked for him now two or three times':

> You've got a Russian government that has made the conscious decision to use its military force inside of another sovereign nation to achieve its objectives—first time, I think, probably, since 1939 or so that that's been the case... They clearly are on a path to assert themselves differently, not just in Eastern Europe, but in Europe in the main and toward the United States. ... Putin, the man himself ... considers [this] to be an effort to redress grievances that were burdened upon Russia after the fall of the Soviet Union, and also to appeal to ethnic Russian enclaves across Eastern Europe. ... And he's very aggressive about it, and he's got a playbook that has worked for him now two or three times. And he will continue... Joseph Stalin used similar rhetoric and justifications when he invaded Poland in September 1939. 'The Soviet Government cannot regard with indifference the fact that the kindred Ukrainian and White Russian people, who live on Polish territory and who are at the mercy of fate, are now left defenseless. In these circumstances, the Soviet government has directed the high command of the Red Army to order the troops to cross the frontier and to take under their protection the lives and property of the population of Western Ukraine and Western White Russia.'[288]

Next, Russia wanted 'to take under their protection the lives and property of the population of Western Ukraine and Western White Russia'. Dempsey took this quote from the Soviet Foreign Minister's declaration to the Polish Ambassador in Moscow, dated September 17, 1939.

In 1939, Stalin was deliberately preparing to provoke a world war in 1939 as a battle of strength that would see Communism expand—which it did: the Iron Curtain cast Moscow's control far beyond what Catherine the Great had ever dared to dream about. In 2014, Putin, too, prepared for squaring off with the armies of those who had taken away Stalin's prize. Military training exercises were conducted in all Russian districts near the border, from the Kuril Islands to the Kaliningrad region, from the Black Sea to the Baltic Sea. Technical, bilateral military agreements were unilaterally annulled by the Russian Federation. Thus, on May 5, 2014, amidst the din of clashes in Eastern Ukraine, the Moscow broke the terms of its agreement with Lithuania to strengthen trust and security of mutual borders. This agreement required Russia to share information with Lithuania about its military presence in the Kaliningrad region and allow military inspections of the troops jointly with the Lithuanian side.

Occupied Crimea was rapidly turned into a powerful military beachhead. Top-level Russian officials, including Putin, began to state that Russia had a nuclear arsenal it was prepared to use. Russian regular forces amassed on the Ukrainian border. Russian troops in the Moldovan breakaway region Transnistria received reinforcements. Joint Russian-Belarussian military exercises were conducted in Belarus. Russian strategic bombers increasingly violated NATO airspace while Russian fighter planes chased after NATO ones. Russian naval ships, especially submarines, ventured into Scandinavian waters. Army reservists were called up more often under a new law. Spending on arms and propaganda was increased. The Russian Central Bank start buying up gold; gas was no longer delivered on credit. Kremlin-adjacent structures such as Lukoil began to ditch foreign shares.

Soon after the Russian occupation of Crimea, German chancellor Angela Merkel remarked that the President of Russia was 'living in another world'. She did not mean to say that Putin was insane. She meant that Putin thinks in long-outdated concepts, from the 19th century and the first half of the 20th century, when all statesmen thought in terms of seizing land to combine those who spoke a common language. The problem was that Putin had revived this way of thinking in the new 21st century when he launched of the 'Russian World' in July 8, 2000, at Russia's Federal Assembly. Running up against the world's refusal to recognize Russia's right to occupy neighboring states, the Russian leadership improved its tactics. Putin realized that, before attempting another assault in Europe, it was necessary to undermine Western democracies from within by destroying the European Union and NATO.

7: Russia's Fifth International

Karl Marx was involved in the creation of the First International (1864-76). Friedrich Engels was involved in the creation of the Second (1889-1916). Vladimir Lenin created the Third International (Comintern, 1919-43). Lev Trotsky created the Fourth International (1938-?). Vladimir Putin, deploying the same methods as his predecessors, spearheaded a Fifth International, though one without a public announcement. His International was a quasi-return to the Soviet Communist International (Comintern) policies of 1920s and 1930s, when Communists formed tactical alliances with the Nazis against the Democratic movements in Europe. Unlike the first four Internationals, this was the International of Right-Wing Neo-Fascist forces using fragments of the Communist world that collapsed in 1991 in their struggle against Democracies—that is, the International connecting two extremist wings, the Right and the Left in a fight against capitalism.

Right-wing forces saw an ally in Putin as the president of a nationalist and Christian Russia standing against the European Union, globalization and Islam fundamentalists. The left saw him as the heir of the former Soviet Union, president of a country with a Soviet past, the Soviet anthem, Lenin's tomb, and the Red Flag of the Soviet/Russian Army, ready to stand up to western democracies and NATO. Everyone saw what they wanted to see in him, because Putin used the very same recruitment method on everyone. This was the Lubyanka's primary skill—that of Pitovranov's 5th Directorate—recruiting agents, foreigners in particular.

Putin was especially interested in right-wing parties because, once they received a relative majority in the European parliament, they could vote to have their countries leave the EU, thereby fracturing and destroying it. His main window into Western European politics was Silvio Berlusconi, the multi-term Prime Minister of Italy, billionaire, media magnate, and real estate owner like Putin himself. When nearly all traditional European leaders, such as Merkel, turned away from Berlusconi because of numerous scandals and corruption accusations, Putin came to his aid, easily establishing an informal, friendly relationship with the Italian leader as he saw no moral issues.[289]

Berlusconi came to stay at Putin's dacha; Putin's daughters, and Putin himself, vacationed at Berlusconi's villa in Sardinia... And after 2014, when Russia occupied Crimea and Europe turned its back on Putin, Berlusconi visited Crimea with Putin in 2015 and spoke out in support of the Russian annexation of Crimea and endorsed plans for further expansion by the accession of Ukraine.[290]

In 2013, Matteo Salvini, a young Italian right-wing politician and member of the nationalist party Lega Nord, claimed victory in his party's election and became the party Chair. At the 2013 party convention where the new Chair was elected, two Russian politicians were among the invited guests sitting in the front row, ready to congratulate Salvini on his expected victory: Viktor Zubarev, a member of the Duma, and Alexei Komov, a business partner and associate in Italy of Konstantin Malofeev.

One of Salvini's earliest acts as Lega Nord's Chair was to establish the Russia-Lombardy Cultural Association, designed to promote business ties with Russia and led by Lega Nord spokesman and businessman Gianluca Savoini, who maintained long-running business and political ties to Malofeev and Komov. Komov was elected as the honorable president of the association and hosted shows on Malofeev's TV channel Tsargrad, occasionally taking interviews with Europe's right-wing, pro-Kremlin politicians. One of the association's events in 2015 invited Dugin (whose structure was financed by Malofeev) to a symposium held in Milan.

Starting in 2013, Salvini himself, usually accompanied by Savoini, began flying to Moscow with surprising regularity.[291] He made no effort to hide his trips, publishing photos about them on the Internet.[292] In fact, his connection with Putin and the Russian leadership bought Salvini resounding success in Italy.

In right-wing European circles, it became a public secret that Putin financially supported European right-wing political parties pushing for their countries to leave the EU and NATO. In particular, after meeting and negotiating with Putin, the head of the French National Front, Marine Le Pen, actually received financial assistance in the form of a bank loan.

In the case of the Lega Nord and Salvini, financial assistance came via the tried and tested Soviet scheme that can make any organization, party, or person rich by selling them mineral resources below market prices. The difference between the market price and the purchase price finds its way as a subsidy into the pockets of the organizations or individuals the Kremlin is interested in supporting.

Partners and businesses created by Lega Nord businessman and activist Savoini in time for this transaction received a certain amount of Russian gas. The gas made it to Italy via a broker (for example, one in Hungary) selling Russian gas that he, in turn, purchased from a Russian company that in turn was established for this project and controlled by or directly owned by the FSB. To complete the transaction, the broker received a license from Gazprom for the right to sell an additional, let's say, 300 million cubic meters of gas with the obligation to sell the gas below the market price to specific structures in Italy. The operation was repeated the following year, but this time with a sale volume of 1.6 billion cubic meters of gas to meet Lega Nord's growing financial needs.

On October 10, 2014, Salvini flew to Moscow with a Lega Nord delegation to discuss options with the Russian leaders for removing sanctions levied after the occupation of Crimea. The delegation, which included right-wing members of the

European Parliament, met with the Head of the Duma Committee on Foreign Affairs, Alexei Pushkov, and Chair of the Duma, Sergei Naryshkin, a career intelligence officer and also the future head of the SVR (foreign intelligence, previously the KGB 1st Directorate).

Salvini and the Lega Nord members visited Crimea on October 13, 2014 and met with the Prime Minister of the Russian puppet government, Sergei Aksyonov. Four days later, Salvini huddled with Putin at the Asia-Europe Meeting (ASEM) held in Milan. In a subsequent interview, Salvini said that sanctions 'are destroying the Italian economy'.[293]

On December 8, 2014, Salvini returned to Moscow and once again met with Pushkov. It was during this trip that Salvini began insisting, later often repeating, that the Italian economy had lost five billion euros because of sanctions levied against Russia, using this argument as a political slogan in his speeches. In December 2014, the Lega Nord next launched a campaign to create the 'Friends of Putin' parliamentary group in Italy. On May 18, 2016, the local assembly of the Province of Venetia, controlled by the Lega Nord, passed a resolution to cancel sanctions and move to recognize Russia's sovereignty over Crimea.

This was only the beginning. Salvini began publicly criticizing NATO for military maneuvers in Latvia, which Italian troops participated in, asserting this was an act of war against Russia. Finally, in an interview on October 16, 2016, Salvini stated that Italy must consider the question of its NATO membership[294]. In other words, that Italy leave NATO. This all took place against the backdrop of preparations for a referendum to reform the country's governance initiated by Prime Minister Matteo Renzi's government.

Russian TV channel RT participated aggressively in the campaign to discredit Renzi's government and destabilize the political situation in Italy. It reported nonstop that the country was on the edge of crisis, resorting to outright lies. In particular, in October 2016, when a mass demonstration was held in Rome to defend the referendum and support Renzi's government, RT reported that the demonstrations were being held by opponents of the referendum and the government. This sensational lie went viral on social media and traveled quickly across the country as if it was true. A majority voted against, and Renzi and his allies lost the referendum on December 4, 2016.

On March 6, 2017, Salvini met with Russian Foreign Minister Sergei Lavrov in Moscow. On March 7, the Lega Nord signed an agreement with Putin's Duma party—*Yedínaya Rossíya* (united Russia, founded in 2001)—on security issues, protecting traditional values, and Russian-Italian economic interests, including removing sanctions. Since new elections were supposed to take place in Italy because of the failed referendum and Renzi's resignation, the agreement amounted to cooperation between the Lega and Russian leadership in the run-up to the Italian elections. The Kremlin had scored a major success by inserting recognition of its occupation of Crimea as a political platform into one of EU's largest member states.

The Lega's election tactics deployed remarkably sophisticated tools for a splinter party. Luca Morisi, who managed Salvini's Facebook presence, had by this time (after three and a half years of hard work) increased Salvini's 'likes' from 518 thousand to almost three million, making him the most-followed European politician on Facebook. The Lega Nord also utilized the services of the British company Cambridge Analytica, which Steve Bannon, the American conservative activist, publicist, and orator, a dedicated and committed supporter of radical nationalism and equally enthusiastic opponent of globalization, was directly involved in creating and operating. Bannon himself was no stranger either. He spent March 4, 2018, the day of Italy's parliamentary elections, in Rome at Salvini's side.

In the end, against all expectations, the Lega achieved a very strong election result: it won a third of the votes, receiving the right to form a conservative coalition government under Prime Minister Giuseppe Conte. Conte urged the cancellation sanctions imposed on Russia in his very first speech in parliament. The next day, April 27, the Italian government addressed the Council of Europe with a proposal to resume issuing loans to Russian businesses through the European Bank for Reconstruction and Development. In the new Conte government, Salvini held the influential post of Minister of Internal Affairs.

On October 17 and 18, 2018, during another visit to Moscow, Salvini and Savoini discussed new sales of Russian minerals, but this time it was for Russian oil, as part of the Russian leadership's program to give financial aid to the Lega Nord and capture positions in Europe to advance its attack on the EU and NATO.[295]

Who else was doing Russia's bidding in disrupting consensus among NATO and EU countries refusing to recognize Crimea and the two satellite occupations in Eastern Ukraine regions Luhansk and Donbas by Russian troops?

The promoter of Putin's policy at the international level was none other than Steve Bannon. Back in 2014, at a conference at the Vatican, Bannon, a Catholic, expressed support for Putin on a whole range of issues: 'Putin supports traditional institutions and tries to do it from a nationalist position,' Bannon said.[296] He added that the Judeo-Christian West should look at Russia as the standard of the ideals of nationalism and state sovereignty.[297] Not surprisingly, after these statements in support of Putin, Russian Fascist and FSB agent Alexander Dugin began to wonder whether Bannon might not be a fellow traveler in ideological terms.[298]

In May and September 2018, Bannon traveled to Prague twice with the idea of making the city his base of operations in uniting right-wing European forces. In fact, the political platform of anyone visited by Bannon would strengthen the Kremlin's hand. Among Europe's leaders, Bannon considered his main allies to be Putin, British euro skeptic and Brexit supporter Nigel Farage, Le Pen, Orbán, Zeman, and Salvini. The *Guardian* newspaper in wrote a succinct summary:

Steve Bannon is on a mission. [He] has visited Europe twice in the past four months, touring several capitals. He has been spreading the gospel of the 'national populist revolt', and he sees Europe as fertile ground for his global crusade. Maybe there is some truth in that. Italy's current politics are a gift to him. But he has also been applauded by audiences in Prague, Budapest and France…. His trips across the Atlantic are part of an ideological struggle between 'nationalists' and 'globalists', a battle that he is seeking both to frame and to escalate…. What's clear is that Bannon has been busy nurturing relationships with some of the most disruptive forces in Europe…. In 2014 Bannon chose a Vatican palace as the venue to set out his worldview, before an audience composed of ultra-conservative Catholic groups. In Budapest he was recently introduced on stage as 'a great thinker'. In Italy he hailed the new far-right populist coalition as a 'historic alliance'. In Prague he called the postwar liberal order a 'fetish'. Earlier this year, in northern France, he attended a gathering around Marine Le Pen, where he electrified the crowd with these words: 'Let them call you racist, xenophobes, nativists, homophobes, misogynists—wear it as a badge of honor!'[299]

In the Czech Republic, it so happened that Bannon's like-minded soul, Putin, had already captured the key person. It was accomplished through the same tactics as those in Russia in 2000, where one merely needed to capture one office to gain control of the entire country—that of the leader of the state. In the case of the Czech Republic, it was the President.

In the late 1960s, when Andropov became KGB Chief, the Democratic movement to end the One Party system was gaining momentum in Czechoslovakia, culminating in the Prague Spring and the invasion of Czechoslovakia by troops of Warsaw Pact member countries on Moscow's orders. Afterwards, the Soviet intelligence network operating from the diplomatic mission in Prague began expanding rapidly. The total number of Soviet diplomats and Intelligence agents reached approximately 120-140 persons (versus approximately 40 people working in the US Embassy). According to 2016 data, 51 diplomats and 86 administrative and technical staff worked at the Russian Embassy in Prague and at the Russian Consulates in Karlovy Vary and Brno. The Czech Republic itself has 20 diplomats and 45 non-diplomatic employees in Russia. The Security Information Service (BIS), the Czech national intelligence agency claimed that a significant number of these Russian diplomats were engaged in intelligence and surveillance activities, and that any Russian diplomatic representative should be treated as suspicious.

This was hardly the whole picture. From 1993, the number of Russians granted citizenship in the Czech Republic amounted to approximately 4,764. As of 2017, according to official figures, another 38,223 Russian citizens lived in the Czech Republic. Given the deep penetration of the Cheka in particularly the lives of expats, the pool of potential Lubyanka recruits amounted in fact to more than 40,000 Russians. To improve recruitment, the FSB/SVR created the Coordinating Council of the Russian Compatriots in the Czech Republic, in order to promote the goals of Russian foreign policy and intelligence abroad.

Between 2003 and 2013, Václav Klaus was the Czech Republic's President. Born in 1941 in Soviet Czechoslovakia, he was also an important politician when the country hadn't peacefully deunified itself from Slovakia (1989-92). He was Minister of Finance during these years. From 1998 through 2002, Klaus was the Chair of the House of Representatives. In 2013, Miloš Zeman, the former Prime Minister (1998-2002) succeeded Klaus as the President. In other words, together, Klaus and Zeman were in power in the Czech Republic from 1998 in an arc parallel to Putin's.

Apart from this political arc, there was a practical, financial link between the Russian and the Czech sides: national debt. As the successor state of former Warsaw Pact country Czechoslovakia, the Czech Republic had refinanced the old Soviet debt. Effectively, the Czech Republic was, together with Slovakia, an investor in the construction of Russian Federation oil and gas pipelines and refineries. When Putin became the President of Russia in 2000, the Czech Republic's share of that debt was $3.6-3.7 billion.

The Kremlin was no fan of Václav Havel, President of the Czech Republic from 1993-2003, and was in no rush to continuing repaying the debt from his accession. The repayment schedule was not followed, refinancing blocked, etc. When negotiations reached an impasse, the Czech Minister of Industry and Trade, Vladimír Dlouhý, travelled to the Kremlin to deliver the message that Prague was turning over the Russian debt matter to the Paris Creditors Club of major creditor countries.

In 1998, Ivo Svoboda, the Czech Minister of Finance, put forward new intermediaries for the debt negotiations with Russia: two Austrian-Israeli businessmen of Russian descent who were part of a firm with an interesting reputation: Shlomo Alon and his son Barak Alon. Their firm BCL Trading was in 1996-1999 linked to Czech Komerční Banka loss of CZK 8 billion, an illegal arms trader and the Oilgate scandal.

In addition to the Alons and Ivo Svoboda, another person gave a helping hand with the Russian debt 'problem'. His name was František Mrázek, both a controversial Czech businessman and the head of Czech organized crime who was assassinated in 2006. In 1999, Mrázek was a member of a Czech delegation that discussed the details of Russia's debt repayment at the Hotel Bellevue in Prague. The negotiations were also attended by future president Michal Kraus, Miroslav Šlouf, a Social Democrat Party deputy and adviser to future president Zeman, and by Russia's Minister of Finance, Mikhail Kasyanov. Together with his good friend, Shlomo Alon, Mrázek then arranged the first meeting of Russian and Czech politicians in Moscow with Yevgeny Primakov, then Yeltsin's Prime Minister (September 1998 to May 1999). Nothing came of it.

Things changed dramatically after the capture of the Kremlin and the launch of the 'Russian World'. On June 1, 2001, Czech Prime Minister Zeman and Russian Finance Minister Kasyanov met again in St Petersburg. They agreed on an unusual plan to sell the Czech Republic's Government debt to a private entity named Falkon Capital—a suggestion made by the Russian side.

Falkon Capital was established in Prague on November 28, 1995—with an initial capital of CZK 2.5 million (less than $70,000)—by a group of individuals from the former Soviet Union. Its founders included Panteleimon (Paat, Paato) Mamaladze and several other individuals. Around the same time, two weeks before the company was set up, on November 10, 1995, as sister company with a similar name—Falkon GmbH—was registered in Switzerland with a far more substantial initial capital of CHF 2 million by Mamaladze. In 2001, a BIS officer said in an interview, 'The KGB got him planted and in the early 1990s, he was one of the organizers of the arrival of the first Russian gangs,' recalled one BIS employee.[300] Mamaladze was a GRU officer who had moved to Soviet Czechoslovakia late 1980s.

Publicly, the Czech Government announced that Falkon Capital won a tender for the sale of the debt. However, no documents were ever released regarding the tender itself or the names of the other businesses that participated. The proposed terms were likewise kept secret. On October 9, 2001, Kasyanov travelled to Prague to sign the debt settlement. On October 11, 2001, the agreement and four accompanying protocols were executed by Zeman.

The secrecy raised questions and caused puzzlement in the Czech Republic, particularly since Russia had blatantly refused to make its debt payments from 1993. Zeman announced that the confidentiality was requested by the Russian side but that any Parliamentary Deputy with the requisite security clearance could have access to the documents. Falkon Capital also insisted on not disclosing the terms of the agreement, arguing that they were protecting a 'trade secret' from their competitors.

Yet the Czech public interest had a point. The deal with Falkon Capital looked curious. By paying $400 million to the Czech Treasury, a Prague-based Falkon received the Czech Republic's right to collect $3 billion from the Russian State, and the Russian State was to render its payment to Falkon through Unified Energy System of Russia (UES), the Russian Energy company headed by one-time Yeltsin minister (1992-1998), Anatoly Chubais. On September 13, 2001, Chubais petitioned the Minister of Finance of Russia, Alexei Kudrin, to compensate UES for the $1.35 billion UES paid to Falkon Capital. On those terms, Falkon Capital's expected profit from the deal was $900 million, while Chubais's UES was to receive $50 million for services rendered.

Finally, on October 9, 2001, during a Czech visit by Mikhail Kasyanov, Prime Minister of Russia, Zeman's officials agreed to transfer another tranche of Russian debt, $3.6 billion, to Falkon Capital at a discount of 78%, totaling $2.5 billion. The Czech Republic would receive $500 million in kind and cash over 19 years, and Russia would pay UES RUB 40 billion (or approximately $1.35 billion). The difference of $800 million was presumably pocketed by Falkon Capital and UES, as they had now become the parties to the debt.

As the deal involving Falkon Capital was inter-governmental, it could not have been concluded without the approval from the Czech Government—and specifically, Zeman who was then the Prime Minister. One lobbyist for the deal in the Czech Ministry of Finance was Zdeněk Rachač. He had been advisor to Václav Klaus as

Minister of Finance, and Klaus was Chair of the House of Deputies (1998-2002). Russia had just settled all Soviet debt with the Paris Club without any discounts, and the Czech deal was the first one with a former Warsaw Pact country.

As President Klaus, too, proved pro-Putin. He refused to condemn Russia's 2008 war against Georgia and liberally copied other Putin talking points, comparing the EU to the USSR and calling global warming 'a religion, not a science'. Russian oil company Lukoil, whose owner Chubais was a friend of Klaus's, underwrote the Russian-language publication of his anti-global warming book. Klaus also personally received the Pushkin Medal from Putin.

In 2014, Klaus supported the Russian invasion into Ukraine, penning an article that he sent to his friend Anatoly Chubais, the man who had been so instrumental in liquidating the Czech Republic's Russian debt. Chubais tweeted enthusiastically: 'My old comrade, Václav Klaus—the former Czech President—sent me a link to his article about Ukraine; Probably not everyone will agree with him; but you cannot accuse him of being superficial or biased. I read it. The article is very interesting. Read it!'

In Klaus's 'unbiased' article, he claimed other things, that 'contemporary Ukraine is the sad legacy of Stalin's mixing of peoples and borders', which 'completely lacks the historical tradition of its own statehood'. He called *Euromaidan* the 'Kyiv *putsch*' and predicted Ukraine's break-up. In January 2015, soon after the annexation of Crimea and Russia's invasion of Eastern Ukraine, Klaus announced that Ukraine ought to repeat 'the good experience of the division of Czechoslovakia' into Czech Republic and Slovakia, that Russia is not fighting in Ukraine, that Ukraine has not managed to become a 'state', and that Crimea has always been a part of Russia. 'It is quite clear that the Crimea was not part of Ukraine, and you know it. The Crimea has always belonged to Russia,' Klaus stated. After this article riddled with conclusions based on gross historical errors, Klaus was expelled from Washington's Cato Institute.[301]

Zeman's 'dividend' from being part of the team that solved the Soviet debt crisis (1993-2001) came after Klaus's last term. Thanks to the Kremlin's financial and political support of its many cronies, he became the President of the Czech Republic in 2013. A grateful Zeman followed in Klaus's footsteps and said during a meeting with Putin in Sochi in 2017 that 'Ukraine does not remember its own history', called the annexation of Crimea by Russia a '*fait accompli*' and a 'restoration of historical justice,' while admonishing Ukraine to think about 'financial compensation or compensation in the form of oil and gas supplies', a mysterious piece of advice.

In line with the key Kremlin objective, Zeman also demanded the cessation of the sanctions by the EU against Russia implemented after the invasion of Ukraine. Sanctions against Russia needed to end since Czech businesspeople wanted to establish economic ties with their Eastern neighbor and promote their interests in the region. 'I spoke with [Foreign Minister] Lavrov, and he assured me that there were no Russian soldiers there [in the Ukraine]. There is no proof of the Russian presence in

Donbass,' Zeman parroted to journalists.[302]

However, perhaps nothing showed Zeman's level of support for Moscow as much as his view of the origin of the deadly *Novichok* poison that was used in the UK against former Russian GRU officer Sergei Skripal and his daughter Julia. On May 4, 2018, in an interview with Czech TV Channel Barrandov, Zeman said that *Novichok* nerve agent had been produced in a small quantity and tested in the Czech Republic, after which it was destroyed. Zeman claimed to have obtained this information from a Czech military counterintelligence report. He noted that, according to the report, the Military Research Institute in Brno had produced a nervous-paralytic substance called A230 that was the same as *Novichok*.[303] Remarkably, BIS (ordinary) counterintelligence said that A230 was not the same as the Novichok used in Britain. Even so, Zeman said that he preferred the *view* of military counterintelligence. In the interview, Zeman stated: 'There is the conclusion that Novichok was produced and tested here, though in a small quantity, and then it was destroyed. We know when and we know where it was… It is hypocritical to pretend that this was not so.'[304]

Putin's policy vis-à-vis former members of the Warsaw Pact was architected by Vladimir Yakunin, the 'Russian-Orthodox Chekist' and oligarch since 2005 of behemoth Russian Railroads. Apart from funding Russian-Orthodox strongholds, he also founded the Dialogue of Civilization Research Institute think tank in Berlin, Germany (with representative offices in Vienna and Moscow). Not unlike the 1950s 5th Directorate *rezidenturas*, it became the pivot for relationships with EU politicians and public activists. The Institute had a five-year budget of EUR 25 million and it organized the 'Rhodes Forum', an annual conference on the Greek island of Rhodes.[305]

Yakunin only invited either 'his own insider politicians', or those that he intended to make 'his own', to the Rhodes Forum. Not surprisingly, President Klaus, who was also a member of the supervisory board of the Rhodes Forum, and later, President Zeman, were on the permanent guest list. For each Forum speech, Zeman would receive a handsome fee, paid through Yakunin's foundation.

In 2003 Zeman retired to a Czech village in the countryside, after losing the elections against Klaus in 2003 and remaining in voluntary exile until Klaus's last term in 2012. During this time Yakunin continued to pay his undivided attention the retired politician with invitations. Since 2003, Yakunin has been inviting him to the Dialogue of Civilizations Forum, and Yakunin's organizations have been covering his various expenses.

The 2016 Forum,[306] which was the first one formally held by Yakunin's Institute, gathered around 300 participants, including Zeman (this was his 9th visit, and he was the only head of state at the Forum), Klaus, then-Prime Minister of Slovakia Robert Fico and Prime Minister of Hungary Victor Orbán. The organizers covered the travel expenses of the Czech President, his wife and four employees. During the conference, Zeman repeated his call for lifting sanctions against Russia and compared to the situation in Ukraine as 'a simple case of flu.'[307]

On 8 January 2018, Czech journalist Robert Břešťan wrote in a new publication called *Hlídací pes* (watchdog): 'There is a connection between the Kremlin and Zeman, and the Russians had a hand in financing the current President's large-scale election campaign.' On the same day, Pavel Šafr asked on the portal *Forum 24*: 'Where does President Miloš Zeman get money for election billboards across the country for which other candidates have no money?' Šafr noted that the campaign was officially being funded by 'a club of Zeman's friends' backed by Czech businessmen linked to the Russians. Šafr also wrote that during Zeman's first term as President, he fundamentally changed the Czech Republic because of his characteristically autocratic style of Government, and that the once liberal-democratic Czech Republic had begun to resemble the centralized Russian system.[308]

Zeman won the Presidential election in January 2018 during the second round and with a small margin. On August 21, 2018, as the Czech Republic marked the 50th anniversary of the crushing of the 'Prague Spring' in 1968 by the Warsaw Pact troops, there was an outpouring of sympathy and remembrances from many places. There was one notable exception, the Prague Castle, the official residence of the Czech President. Even though 1960s Communism couldn't be further removed from Putin's 2010s 'Russian World', Zeman understood the sensitive historical issue. Only if the Kremlin says jump you jump. He did not deliver a speech or attend any commemorative events on that day.[309] During an earlier meeting with Putin, Zeman remarked that the Czech Republic needs Russia more than it needs the EU. He did not rule out a possibility of holding a referendum for the Czech Republic to leave the EU and NATO.[310]

This was the precise tactical goal that was envisioned by Putin. However, its realization required installing as a President yet another ally in the largest and most influential NATO member country. Indeed, it required installing as a President of the United States an old friend of Steve Bannon—Donald Trump.

8: Icebreaker Donald Trump

Stalin called Hitler the icebreaker of the revolution. He understood that Europe would be easier to conquer after a grueling battle of Democratic countries against Nazi Germany. Accordingly, at the heart of Soviet politics in the 1920s and 1930s was the secret support of Hitler and German 'militarists,' who railed against the 'humiliation' of articles of the Treaty of Versailles—even though Versailles was less harsh than the Treaty of Brest-Litovsk agreed to by Lenin (for tactical reasons, to rip up at the right time)—for arming Germany, and for the collapse of the Weimar Republic. It is why under Stalin, Comintern (the Third International) was tasked with funding and organizing joint Nazi-communist protests and riots. What else explains the chances of Hitler's Beer Hall Putsch, organized by the Nazis, and the Communist Uprising, organized by the German Communists, falling on the very same day: November 8, 1923?

The Soviet-German agreement of August 1939 and the signing of the Molotov-Ribbentrop secret pact to divide Europe was not a random product of an unexpected meeting. It was the result of many years of well-thought-out, calculated, long-standing provocation, the kind the Kremlin was expert in: start a revolution in Europe and attack her at the crest of a new world war, as Lenin once planned to do at the crest of the World War of 1914-1918 (then, evidently, not yet thought of as 'First', except by some at the Kremlin top). Stalin realized half of his plan: the Soviet Union captured part of Europe, which became known as Eastern Europe.

The Kremlin-Lubyanka decided to find another icebreaker,[311] whose task was simple: divide America. Unlike the Marxist revolutionary splits of the past century into poor and rich or workers and peasants, Americans were naturally split into Republicans and Democrats who viciously opposed each other on their domestic agendas, but worked together in a non-Partisan manner on foreign policy. What if that cozy cooperation on international matters were disrupted and replaced by the same bipartisan extremism? By helping Democrats and Republicans bash their heads together, the Kremlin would remove the US from global politics and leave Europe one-on-one with FSB- Russia.

Europe's unity itself was easily fractured given divergent national interests in Russia's natural resources and capital, and the Democratic structure of the EU that preserved national vetoes on many issues. The capitulation of the main Western democracies before a piecemeal, staggered return of the countries Moscow conquered under Stalin was a given in this scenario. Unlike the US, the EU had flaccid rules on foreign funding of political parties from abroad, and even laxer enforcement—even self-congratulatory Britain was as wide open as the Eurasian steppes had been to the Golden Horde. At low cost, Putin's Fifth International created multiple FSB flash-points made up of political parties, groups, and organizations standing for national-ism, isolationism, the dissolution of the EU, closed borders, terminating emigration, banning abortions, and infringing on the rights of groups with non-traditional orien-tations.

Recruiting potential agents is no easy task, especially when it comes to finding foreign agents, even for the Lubyanka with its excellence gained over almost a century. Oleg Kalugin dedicated many years of his professional life to this task. He was a KGB General, a former head of KGB Directorate K (*ontrazvietka*, counterintelligence) of the 1st Directorate (SVR from 1991), both stripped of and restored in rank by Gorbachev in 1990 and 1991, respectively before and after his role in supporting Yeltsin during the August putsch. He was born in 1934 in Leningrad, a Fulbright scholar at Columbia University with Aleksandr Yakovlev, the future Politburo member and Gorbachev supporter, and emigrated to the US in 1995 as an outspoken critic of the KGB.[312]

In 2019, Kalugin gave an extensive interview to Ukrainian news site *Gordonua.com* about Donald Trump. Not surprisingly, after this interview, SVR Director (2016-) Sergei Naryshkin paid special attention to Kalugin, who had by now lived in the US for many years, calling the former top general a 'traitor' on Russian state channel *RIA Novostia* (RIA news).[313] Kalugin said that the KGB first spotted Trump as a mark after he married Ivana Zelnickova, a Canadian ski instructor born in Czechoslovakia and the couple started inhabiting the gossip pages and before Trump traveled to the Soviet Union in 1987.

At the time, Kalugin himself was 'recruiting informants, my targets included Americans who at the time did not have much by way of an access but could get it in time' in Leningrad. 'Trump, when he was still in Russia and long before he became a politician, he behaved in a way that, let's just say, KGB took notice…. I do not recall whether he was married or not at the time, but he behaved rather freely…. There were some documents. As you know, there was a time when I had complete access to all the documents of that certain organization. I mean, that was before the collapse of the Soviet Union…. At that time, all foreign visitors—especially those who expressed spe-cific interest in Russian everyday life—e.g., girls and the like—they were always noted and observed, as they say, with great interest…. The majority, especially those from the United States and Europe, they were always monitored', the general said.[314]

Any atypical foreigner who traveled to the USSR, or Russia today, including the young Donald Trump, fell under the sights of the Soviet-Russian special services. In particular, 'when he was in Moscow, he met there with Soviet 'female comrades'… the predominant majority of those 'random' women who worked (that is, slept) with for-eigners, were controlled by the KGB. There were certainly more spontaneous rela-tionships… But sooner or later, they all became informants. They were either pun-ished for prostitution or had to work as informants… to earn something extra. Plus, there would be a guarantee that they would not be arrested for prostitution.

Foreign citizens who could represent KGB interests were monitored from the moment they contacted the consular offices of Soviet embassies or consulates general. For that very reason, vice consuls, and often consuls themselves, were foreign intelligence personnel. Requests for entry visas to the Soviet Union from consular departments always went to two addresses—the Ministry of Foreign Affairs, and the KGB Central Node Operational Search System, which transferred visa applications to the appropriate departments. An application for someone wanting to enter as a tourist went to the 7th Department of the VGU (2nd Directorate, internal affairs). Applications through the Ministry of Culture or trade unions, however, went to the specialists at the 1st Department of the 5th Directorate. Only if the Lubyanka agreed would a visa be granted.

Trump was intensely studied by Russian intelligence during his visits to the USSR/Russia.[315] Such surveillance was not necessarily mounted only with the prospect of subsequent recruitment. It was important for the Lubyanka to build a psychological portrait, to figure out a mark's political orientation, their attitude towards their country and to Russia. And only after gathering and analyzing the necessary operational materials (a whole complex of measures: outdoor surveillance, auditory and video monitoring of places of stay or even 'honey traps'), would a 'case file' be transferred to recruitment and facilitate recruitment conditions (blackmail or voluntarily).

Leaving aside the question of whether Trump was recruited as an agent during those early years, the year 2000 was as important for Trump as it was for Putin. In 1987, the year of Trump first visit to Russia, the *New York Times* had first mooted a presidential bid. In 1999, while Putin was groomed to take over from Yeltsin, Trump started his first run as a Reform Party candidate against George W. Bush and Al Gore. Although his campaign failed after a couple of primaries, he still made his mark as a candidate, receiving 7% of the vote in some polls against the two main candidates. Significantly, George Bush took the presidency even though Gore had more votes through the arbitrage of the Electoral College, an atavism of the US electoral system—leading to Bush winning Florida acrimoniously through 984 'hanging chads' that carried him across the finish line, despite Gore's majority of over 500,000 votes nationwide.

Even though Gore conceded defeat after the Supreme Court ruled on Florida, the *fracas* did not go unnoticed in the Kremlin. Inadvertently, the Founding Fathers had handed them a magnificent tool to throw US politics in disarray. The Kremlin understood that the Republicans, who benefited from the antiquated body, would never give up the advantage the Electoral College created when it came to dominating the national agenda from the White House-down. The Kremlin also understood that moving small bodies of voters in targeted states could yield extraordinary presidential results— both in primaries and the actual election—results that would be impossible to achieve if a foreign body had to change the minds of many 100s of thousands of American voters across the enormous geographical and cultural range of the US. It had found its adversaries Achilles heel and the perfect means to influence who occupied the White House, and therefore the control room of US foreign policy. Against this backdrop, the candidature of the ambitious opportunistic money-obsessed playboy Donald Trump, who only dated porno stars and married fashion models, who first registered as a Republican and then as an independent, stood out like a sore thumb. The Lubyanka pulled up its 'case-file' with *kompromat* (according to Kalugin) and saw that her was fertile 'working material'.[316]

2000 was also a pivotal year for two unknown Russian businessmen: Dmitri Rybolovlev and Seyfeddin Rustamov. Rybolovlev was born on November 22, 1966, in Perm. After the collapse of the Soviet Union, he, along with many others, became an entrepreneur. Also, just as many others, he discovered this was complicated. This was not just because in order to do so, many business people had to deal with criminals and the Chekist mafia (if they weren't the same people). The officials in the Prosecutor's Office (which survived unchanged in the new Russian Federation) considered any successful business person in those murky times *prima facie* criminals and initiated criminal proceedings against them. This was not entirely unreasonable. It was genuinely challenging to determine who was or was not a criminal.

Rybolovlev and several of his friends, were charged in Federal Case No 4902 and accused of staging and carrying out a homicide involving their business competitor, the head of Neftehimik enterprise, Yevgeny Panteleimonov. Journalists from *Novaya Gazeta* (new gazette, the publication supported and protected by Gorbachev) insisted on calling them the 'gang'. Rybolovlev was arrested in May 1996 and was held in pre-trial detention in Perm for 11 months. While being investigated, he refused to testify or give any evidence, citing the right against self-incrimination in Article 51 of the Russian Federation Constitution. He was acquitted in 1997. He was very fortunate according to the *Novaya Gazeta*. Although the primary defendant, he was the only one of them acquitted of all charges: 'others in the same proceeding received considerable sentences for various crimes.'[317] Rybolovlev stated that in prison (or from prison?) he was 'saved' by another business partner, Seyfeddin Rustamov. How exactly he 'saved' Rybolovlev is not known.

Rustamov was imprisoned but Rybolovlev was freed. It is not surprising, therefore, that Rustamov's biography contains a few gaps. He was born on June 17, 1962, in Azerbaijan. From at least 1993, according to the records of the criminal case, Rustamov worked in what *Novya Gazeta* called Rybolovlev's 'gang'. He specialized in auctions of Soviet state property, in particular in neutralizing potential competition:

In 1994, during privatization and auctioneering of various enterprises in the Perm Region, D. Rybolovlev [acquitted] conspired with O. Lomakin, V. Nelyubin, V. Chernyavsky, S. Rustamov and S. Makarov, with the purpose of purchasing the ownership interests in mainly chemical and petrochemical enterprises located in the Perm Region—e.g., limited companies Uralkalii, Neftekhimik and Metafrax—at prices barely exceeding start-up costs, as well as purchasing shares on secondary securities markets, while preventing competitors from making similar purchases by exerting their influence in various criminal organizations.[318]

Thereafter, Rustamov disappeared, which would make sense if he was incarcerated. However, from 2000, his life followed the straight and narrow. According to his official biography (provided on several different websites), he was 'actively involved in trading in chemical and petrochemical industry, making investments in energy funds and oil and natural gas extraction industry projects, as well as making investments in commercial and residential real estate.' Not only that, he quickly became a millionaire.

In 2014, Rustamov was a 'beneficial owner of a chemical company Metafrax' located in the same Perm Region where Rybolovlev's business interests were concentrated. Rustamov managed MetaHolding, a majority owner of Metafrax. By 2017, Rustamov consolidated 92.37% of the shares in the company, transformed it into a group holding structure with production entities in Russia (Perm and Moscow) and in Austria. It was extraordinarily successful and became the largest producer of methanol, formaldehyde and synthetic resins in Russia and Europe. During that period, annual revenue of the Metafrax Group exceeded RUB 40 million, and its distribution network covered over 50 countries worldwide. As a quirk, Rustamov and his family (his wife, Marina, and their three children) lived in the United States from 2000, 'in a luxurious villa in Virginia' according to 2017 press reports.[319] So, Rustamov, after a turbulent conviction, settled down comfortably in a Washington, D.C. suburb.

Rybolovlev, who was acquitted and did not receive a 15-year prison sentence for the premature death of his competitor (the second defendant in the criminal case— Oleg Lomakin—did), became involved in Perm regional politics and in 2000 sponsored Mayor Yuri Trutnev in the governor elections in the Perm Region, the location of Rybolovlev's main business interests.

Meanwhile Donald Trump first came to Moscow in July of 1987. In his memoirs, he described that journey as 'an extraordinary experience' and mentioned that he stayed in the 'Lenin suite' at the National Hotel.[320] At the time, Trump was in negotiations with the Soviet Foreign Tourism Committee about the construction of a luxury hotel in the center of Moscow. Moscow media even reported that Trump agreed to refurbish the Soviet-era Hotel Moscow.

Although, the project never materialized, in December, 1996, Moscow City officials continued discussions with Trump regarding the reconstruction and renovation of the two hotels—Hotel Moscow and Hotel Russia. The project had an estimated cost of around $300 million. Russian media reported in 1998 that Trump was willing to invest about $200 million into the reconstruction of Hotel Moscow in exchange for a 65% stake in the project. However, as was the case previously, parties failed to reach an agreement.

In addition, around the same time, Trump considered building a skyscraper in Moscow but the project never took off as Moscow Deputy Mayor Vladimir Resin did not approve a construction permit, stating, 'we will not build any skyscrapers in a historic part of the city as we have no right to turn a historic area into Manhattan', presumably a reference to the Trump proposal of a 51-58-floor building on Novy Arbat Street at the center of Moscow.

Moscow negotiations were renewed in the Putin-era in 2004 but instead of new a construction and renovation, Trump was now interested in franchising, which involved exclusively just monetizing his name. The co-owner of MosCityGroup, Pavel Fuks, was very keen on Trump's brand at the time. 'I had an idea to use Trump's name for one of the towers that was under construction in Moscow-City –that is, '*Imperia* (empire) Tower'. However, no agreement was reached,' Fuks said in an interview for the Russian newspaper *Kommersant*.[321] Trump was not willing to invest his own money but wanted to receive a 20-25% stake in the project for the use of his Trump brand. As an overall investment in the *Imperia* Tower project was estimated to come in approximately $1.2 billion, Fuks would have to pay Trump $240-300 million as a fee, which he thought too steep.

The Trumps needed money at the time. In 2004, Trump filed for bankruptcy of the Trump Hotels and Casino Resorts, which affected three casinos in Atlantic City and one in Indiana. While bankruptcy allowed Trump to get from underneath a $1.8 billion debt burden, traditional lenders shied away from lending him money.[322]

Then, from no later than 2005, Felix Sater, a Russian-born US-citizen became Trump's 'agent' in Russia. Sater was a man of questionable reputation, with convictions for a first-degree assault—stabbing someone with the stem of a wine glass—and for fraud in the US, with alleged Russian mafia connection, and with childhood and business connection to Trump's personal lawyer, Michael Cohen. Sater's name was mentioned alongside Cohen's, as well as in the context of the Trump Organization's projects—which explains why he would become one of the main persons of interest in the Mueller investigation.

In 2005, Felix Sater was pursuing an ambitious plan in Moscow to build a Trump Tower on the site of an old pencil factory along the Moscow River that would offer hotel rooms, condominiums and commercial office space. Letters of intent had been signed and square footage was being analyzed. 'There was an opportunity to explore building Trump Towers internationally,' said Mr. Sater, who worked for a New York-based development company that was partnering with Trump on a variety of deals during that decade. 'And Russia was one of the countries' where Trump Towers could be built.

In 2006, Sater traveled to Moscow again with two of Trump's children, Donald Jr and Ivanka, who stayed in the Hotel National for several days to meet potential partners for real estate development. 'Let's do a deal here,' Sater said during that trip which created the first Putin link to the Trumps. He wrote later that during the 2006 visit to Moscow, he 'arranged for Ivanka to sit in Putin's private chair at his desk and office in the Kremlin'.[323]

It was through Sater that Trump also met Tevfik Arif, formerly a Soviet Government official from Kazakhstan and the founder of a development company named Bayrock Group, in which Sater was among the stakeholders. Bayrock Group was also interested in deals in Russia. As described by Sater himself, 'We looked at some very, very large properties in Russia', I think of a large Vegas high-rise'.

In April of 2007, trademark 'Trump' was registered in Russia for the services industry, as well as for commercial, residential and hospitality real estate industries. As before, Trump was not planning to erect any buildings but was instead looking to open franchises in Russia, something that did not appeal to his potential Russian business partners at the time.[324]

Then came 2008, the year of the invasion of Georgia. For Trump, as for everyone, it was the year marked by the financial crisis in the US and when its real estate market tanked. On this occasion, the Trumps' 'empire' was on the brink of bankruptcy. But suddenly, in May 2008, some 'crazy Russian' decided to rescue Trump from his sixth bankruptcy and pay $95 million for a villa that on some valuations was now worth very little. The villa was located at 515 North County Road, Palm Beach, Florida. The total building area amounted to 62,000 square feet, while the total lot size—to 6.26 acres.[325] Trump had purchased the property for approximately $41.4 million in 2004. He may or may not have made some capital repairs since then and listed it for sale in 2006 but was unable to sell it. By 2008, given the downfall of real estate prices, it was impossible to sell. The villa was uninhabited and mold overtook it. Yet, all of a sudden, Trump lucked out.

The 'crazy Russian' was Rybolovlev. According to Rybolovlev's ex-wife, Elena Chuprakova, on April 1-2, 2006, Rybolovlev, Elena, and their Russian-American friends Rustamov (who 'saved' him from prison in 1996-1997) and his wife Marina Kotova, found themselves near the Florida villa one day and saw it from the outside, accessing the lot from the beach. Two years later (during which time no one had expressed any interest in the villa, except Florida mold), on May 3-6, 2008, the Rybolovlev family found themselves in Florida again and, this time, decided to buy the villa at the nadir of Florida's real estate market by paying more twice the price it had fetched during the height of the market. Like the mold, their passion for the beach-front property had multiplied.

This is the 'official' version of the events as recounted in court by Elena Rybolovlev. Other parts of the chain of events related to the purchase of the villa are marked by a measure of uncertainty. According to the numerous sources, including information provided by Elena, the purchase of the villa by the Rybolovlev family was at break-neck speed, defied logic and surrounded by mystery. Remarkably, Elena Rybolovleva said that she was dead against the purchase (and that Dmitri Rybolovlev had little interest in his wife's opinion). On May 5, 2008, Rybolovlev told his wife about the purchase. Already, on May 9, 2008, the purchase was executed with the couple's County Road Property LLC as their ownership entity. On May 12, 2008, a trust, with Elena and Anna (the Rybolovlevs' daughter) as the beneficiaries, paid the purchase price of $95 million. It seemed little wonder that Elena was displeased that her opinion did not matter.

Rybolovlev's reason for the purchase remained unclear. Neither Rybolovlev himself nor his wife saw the villa before or after the 2008 purchase and seemed to have purchased it blindly. They did not spend a single day in the villa. It was impossible to resell at a profit any time soon given the logic-defying purchase price. In March 2016, Rybolovlev obtained a demolition permit, and removed the villa for an additional $234,000, subdivided the lot into three sub-lots and listed them for sale. By that time, the former owner of the property had become the President of the United States.

The media got interested. Rybolovlev's explanations were confusing. He said, for example, that he purchased the villa in order to ensure that his family had a home in Florida for years to come; he said suggested that he made this purchase as an investment and that he was hoping to resell the villa later at a profit; another motive was that he planned to demolish the villa from day one and to build a palace in its stead; finally, he also said that he had to demolish the building since it was completely covered in mold—inevitable when not turning on air conditioning in an uninhabited building in humid Florida. With all these questions remaining, it was clear that Rybolovlev threw a lifeline to Trump as he faced bankruptcy?

Rybolovlev previous brush with elections was in 2000 when he supported the governor elections in Perm of Mayor Trutnev. After Rybolovlev left Russia in 2000, it was Trutnev who represented and protected Rybolovlev's interests with the government in Moscow. At the same time, Rybolovlev became an advocate for Trutnev's interests outside of Russia, in as much as it was possible given his limitations—he did not speak any language other than Russian.

Trutnev's career meanwhile continued its upward trajectory. From 2004-12, he was Putin's Minister of Natural Resources and Ecology, a very lucrative post in the natural-resources-rich Russian Federation. When a major accident occurred in one of the mines of Uralkalii in October 2006, Rybovlev and Trutnev were in contact again. It was Trutnev as minister who headed up the government commission investigating the accident. The commission determined that a combination of technological and geological factors was the cause of the accident and Rybolovlev's company got away with a fine, *Novaya Gazeta* reported in 2016.[326]

Around the time Rybolovlev completed the purchase of Trump's villa in Florida on May 12, 2008, Trump had business dealings with Lev Levayev. Levayev's father, a Hasidic Jew, had been able to emigrate from the USSR to Israel with his fortune intact to start a diamond business which had dealing with 5th Directorate agent Arkadi Gaydamak who handled Pitovranov's Angola interests. Lev was a co-owner of AFI Development and visited the US on numerous occasions to discuss deals with Trump. The subject matter of these projects was never made public, but, according to Natalia Ivanova, AFI Development's press agent, no agreement was reached between the parties with respect to any joint projects in Russia.

Then, on December 24, 2020, light was cast on the curious transaction by a former Trump associate who had been sent to prison. In a lengthy interview with MSNBC, Trump's former attorney Michael Cohen explained that Trump understood the $95 million paid by Rybolovlev in 2008 for the Florida villa to be Putin's money, that the order to purchase the property was given by Putin himself, along with instruction to other Russian oligarchs to invest in Trump.

Indeed, on June 4, 2008, Donald Trump's son, Donald Jr, participated in the Real Estate in Russia conference organized in Moscow by Adam Smith Conferences, a company with a base in London linked to Russians, as a keynote speaker. He described plans for elite residential real estate and hotel construction in Moscow, St Petersburg and Sochi, and added that the US mortgage crisis had forced many investors to look for projects elsewhere and that was the reason why he had visited Russia six times during the previous eighteen months. Donald Jr also stated that the Trump Organization was not considering any real estate development projects in the US at the moment, but instead it focused on strengthening its brand in the 'global market,' which included real estate development projects in Panama, Seoul, Honolulu, Istanbul, Dominical Republic, Dubai and Russia. 'When we announced our intent to enter the Panamanian market, local real estate prices immediately increased by 25%,' said Donald Jr 'Compared to a stagnation in the U.S. real estate market, a recent 50% increase in Russia of a price per square meter was a revelation for me,' he added.

And while at the beginning, before his first trip in 2007-2008, Donald Trump, according to one of his own tweets, had 'ZERO investments in Russia,' the situation changed significantly by the last trip during that same period, when Donald Trump Jr pointed out at another event, Manhattan Real Estate Conference, that 'Russians make up a pretty disproportionate cross-section of a lot of our assets... We see a lot of money pouring in from Russia.'[327] He added that he preferred Moscow 'over all cities in the world'.[328] The timing for these franchise deals that were suddenly coming out of the woodwork, Trump did not have to invest a single dollar in Russia. On the other hand, Russian investors began making substantial investments by buying up Trump licensing deals for the Russian real estate market.

In 2009, Trump changed his voter registration from Democrat to Republican. He considered running for President as a Republican in the primaries for the 2012 election against Obama. In May 2011, when Mitt Romney and Newt Gingrich declared, he decided not to run but boasted: 'I maintain a strong conviction that if I were to run, I would be able to win the primary and, ultimately, the general election.'[329] Few thought the maverick showman stood any chance. In 2012, Trump re-registered as a Republican and publicly endorsed Mitt Romney.

Meanwhile Trump was becoming an 'insider' in Russia and a great fan of the Russian government's ease with real estate deals. In the winter of 2008, he sent all his children to Moscow. On one particular Moscow group picture[330] (from left to right): Elena Baronoff (before emigrating to the US, her name was spelled Baronova), a real estate broker for Trump in Florida, Ivanka Trump, Michael Dezer, CEO of Dezer Development, Trump's developer in Florida, Mikhail Babel, Donald Jr and Eric Trump (Jared Kushner, who married Ivanka Trump on October 25, 2009, was not yet a part of the Trumps.) In freezing Moscow, Ivanka Trump and Elena Baronoff received as chinchilla fur coats, the most expensive fur on the market. About the projects discussed little is known except that the discussions were orchestrated by Mikhail Babel.

Babel was born in 1962. In 1984, he graduated from the V.V. Kuibyshev Moscow Construction Engineering Institute as a construction engineer, and for the next 30 years, he worked in construction in Moscow, Moscow suburbs and other Russian regions. In 1994, Babel registered NBM-*Stroyservice*, a construction company, which he used in 2006 as holding company for establishing NBM, through which he became the exclusive project developer for Soviet-era spy Shabtai Kalmanovich. In that capacity, Leningrad Mayor Sobchak—the man to whom Putin was attached for years as an FSB ARO—had died in his arms 1999. Also in that capacity, Kalmanovich died prematurely in November 2009 in his Mercedes, which was left with bullet holes and $1.5 million.

Babel joined *Glavmosstroy* company as its Vice-President in 2003, which was an integral part of the *Glavstroy* Group in turn owned by Basic Element, the industrial group owned by Oleg Deripaska, one of Russia's richest oligarchs closest to Putin. It seemed that this partnership of Babel also collaborated with Russian Intelligence. According to Iskander Muhamudov, one of Deripaska's business partner, Deripaska was an FSB agent from the late 1990s, after agreeing to work for the FSB in writing. This agreement was obtained by coercion from the Russian government through the FSB by threatening to take away his business. Iskander Muhamudov himself had given similar written consent. Deripaska would later become the Kremlin/FSB contact to Paul Manafort, a future Trump's Presidential Campaign manager. It was in the context of Deripaska's *Glavmosstroy* that Babel invited to Trumps, Dezer, and Baronoff, who accompanied Dezer on all his trips.[331]

Baronoff's curriculum vitae also featured the Russian government. In 1989, she emigrated from the USSR, finding herself in Iowa and subsequently relocating to, and settling in, Florida, where she first became a travel agent and eventually a real estate broker. By 2004, she was listed as a Vice President of Customer Relations at Trump Grande, one of the subsidiaries in the Trump Organization's corporate group. She was featured alongside Trump and his daughter Ivanka on *The Women's City* magazine cover, with the article branding her as 'Donald Trump's Russian Hand' in 2004.[332] At the same time, without going into any details, she noted in her biography that she was 'serving as a cultural attaché at diplomatic branches of the Russian government.' Cultural-attaché positions in Russian Embassies around the world are traditionally a cover for KGB/FSB 5th Directorate officers. Baronoff's sketchy autobiographical details led some to assume that she was a Soviet intelligence officer and a Soviet/Russian spy in the United States.[333]

Baronoff's mention of 'international business' include her active and long-term involvement in the political life of the small but elite Sicilian town Taormina—a picturesque town featured in many movies, most recently in 2022 the location of a popular Netflix series. As early as 2010, Dino Papale, an influential local politician, became an acquaintance and then a political supporter of Trump,[334] who himself spent three days visiting Papale in 2013.[335] Baronoff organized numerous events through Papale in Taormina. These events were aimed at establishing friendly relations between Russia and Southern Italy. Many of the events were attended by official representatives of Russia, including the General Council of Russia in Sicily, Vladimir Korotkov, and the Russian Minister of Foreign Relations, Sergei Lavrov, who came to Taormina, according to Papale, to meet with him.[336]

In 2008, Baronoff became the International Ambassador of the City of Sunny Isles Beach—the city in Florida where Trump was selling residences developed by Dezer to the Russian clients through Baronoff. Indeed, 2008 proved extraordinarily successful for Trump. After many visits to Moscow, the Trump Organization's scheme to sell properties to clients from Russia proved highly lucrative at the right time. Russians bought real estate in Trump's buildings for a total exceeding $100 million it was reported in 2017.[337]

Neither the Trump Organization members nor Baronoff's firm asked any questions about the sources of the buyers' money. Any Russian official or government officer, regardless of the source of his/her wealth, was welcome. All that they had to do was wire the funds to the seller, whether from a personal, corporate, offshore, Russian or non-Russian account, whether it was an account in their own name or in the name of someone else. US-based attorney would be involved, whereby a payment from the buyer would be first transferred to an attorney, who, in turn, would transfer the funds on behalf of his/her client to the seller: either an entity at the Trump Organization or an intermediary selling the property. In the case of intermediaries, there were cases of senior executives of corporations or banks used corporate funds to purchase properties for themselves, without the knowledge or approval of the Board of Directors or shareholders.[338]

Five skyscrapers that were built by Trump/Dezer in Miami and ownership by Russians made up more than 50% according to one of the brokers in Sunny Isles Beach and Hollywood, both cities near Miami, Florida, there were about 30,000 of 'Russians'.[339]

Naturally, Dezer needed capital from the Trump Organization to start construction. This funding was provided by the banks. It is useful to describe here the history of a relationship between Trump and/or Trump Organization and the Deutsche Bank, headquartered in Frankfurt, Germany.

From 1998, Deutsche Bank extended $2.5 billion in loans to Trump's companies, including $125 million that were advanced on a New York skyscraper. In 2005, Deutsche Bank lent Trump $640 million for the construction of a high-rise building in Chicago. Due to mortgage and financial crises of 2008, Trump underpaid Deutsche Bank about $40 million, arguing that the crisis created *force majeure*. Deutsche Bank sued for the shortage and Trump counterclaimed, seeking a compensation for a $3 billion loss. While the court did not accept Trump's counterclaim, it ordered Deutsche Bank to restructure Trump's debt. The term of the borrowing was extended and finally settled on new conditions. After that, Trump was *persona non-grata* with Deutsche

Bank's corporate team. Similarly, Citibank, JP Morgan Chase and Morgan Stanley no longer wished to do business with Trump on account of his bankruptcies. Goldman Sachs executives also 'have enough sanity to keep away from any deals related to Trump.'[340]

At the private banking division of Deutsche Bank, however, Trump remained a valued client. During 2012-2015, this division financed $170 million of Trump's Washington hotel construction, as well as $125 million of his projects in Miami. There were unconfirmed rumors that the loans extended to Trump by Deutsche Bank had in fact been taken on by *Vnesheconombank*, a Kremlin-owned bank. There was a meeting between Trump's son-in-law, Jared Kushner, and Sergei Gorkov, an FSB officer (a 1994 alumn of the FSB Academy) and the Chair of *Vnesheconombank* in Washington in December of 2016, soon after Trump was elected as US President of the US. It may have had the financial situation of Trump Organization, including the old and new borrowings, on the agenda. Jared Kushner was also heading Trump's presidential transition team.

Having decided not to stand in 2012, in 2013 Trump decided to hold the Miss Universe Pageant in Russia, an event agreed to with the Russian government. It provided another opportunity for the Kremlin to fund Trump, on the one hand, and, on the other hand, to gather (compromising) information on Trump. For the budding US presidential candidate, it was a calculated political and financial move, which was by no means random or reckless after the $95 million he thought he had received from Putin for his worthless Florida villa. Trump was trying to build bridges to a new and important strategic business ally. The Miss Universe Pageant was one of these bridges.

A final decision regarding this matter was made in mid-June of 2013 in Las Vegas during Trump's meeting with Aras Agalarov and his family. It included Agalarov's son, Emin, the future moderator of the Pageant. Aras Agalarov, a Russian billionaire, like all Russian oligarchs, was naturally under the Kremlin's cosh.[341] Trump certainly assumed so. From the Trump side, the meeting was attended by Rob Goldston, a musical producer involved in the Moscow Pageant.

The day after the Vegas meeting, Trump tried to set up his first meeting with Putin. On June 18, 2013, the would-be President wrote in Twitter: 'Do you think Putin will be going to the Miss Universe Pageant in November in Moscow—and if so, will he become my best friend?'[342] Intended for Putin's eyes and ears, it was an invitation to meet with Trump and discuss business deals. Aras Agalarov recalled that Trump was fixated on meeting Putin in November, and Agalarov, of course, promised to do his best. In October, Trump asked Agalarov to consider this once more, and Agalarov (apparently) called Putin's Press-Secretary, Dmitri Peskov, and again attempted to set up the November Trump-Putin meeting.[343]

On October 29, 2013, Putin personally presented the Order of Honor to Agalarov. Was it related to the meeting with Trump and financing of the 'Miss Universe' pageant, which partially ended up in Trump's pocket as profit? Trump also seems to have got what he wanted—a private business meeting with Putin. In 2013, Trump told late-night host David Letterman that Putin was a 'tough guy' and that he had 'met him once'.[344]

What was discussed remained unclear. But, Trump did publicize that he had written to Putin, inviting him to attend the Miss Universe Pageant and hinting that this could be a good opportunity to see many beautiful girls. However, Putin never attended the Pageant. Instead, he sent him a gift and a letter. Putin himself had no intention of compromising the very useful Donald Trump by having a picture of the two of them circulating the internet.

On November 9-10, 2013, Agalarov and Trump held the Miss Universe Pageant at the Crocus City Hall just outside of Moscow and owned by Agalarov. Trump was paid $12.2 million out of the total budget of $20 million for participating in the Pageant. He felt he was personally indebted to Putin:

When I went to Russia with the Miss Universe pageant, [Putin] contacted me and was so nice. I mean, the Russian people were so fantastic to us[345].... I do have a relationship [with Putin] and I can tell you that he's very interested in what we're doing here today. He's probably very interested in what you and I are saying today and I'm sure he's going to be seeing it in some form. But I do have a relationship with him, and I think it's very interesting to see what's happened. I mean, look, he's done a very brilliant job in terms of what he represents and who he's representing. If you look at what he's done with Syria, if you look at so many of the different things, he has really eaten our president's lunch, let's not kid ourselves.[346]

Trump also said during his Presidential Campaign in June of 2016 about Putin: 'He said one nice thing about me. He said I'm a genius.'[347]

Trump's Russian business went from strength to strength. On November 11, 2013, Trump and his business partners from the Trump SoHo Development, Alex Sapir and Rotem Rosen, met with oligarch Agalarov to discuss potential real estate projects. Among them were plans to build a hotel in Moscow. This was now Trump's third attempt to break into the Russian real estate market, with his first two franchising attempts dating to 2004 and 2007-2008. In those years, Russian investors saw no commercial point in getting into bed with Trump, but in the year before Russia's first invasion into Ukraine, all of a sudden oligarchs couldn't get enough of Donald Sr. 'The Russian market is attracted to me. I have a great relationship with many Russians, and almost all of the oligarchs were in the room,'—stated Trump in an interview to *Real Estate Weekly* on November 12, 2013, upon returning from Russia.[348] This particular get-together was organized by Herman Gref who had served in the various key roles in the Russian government, including that of a CEO of *Sberbank* of Russia.

No wonder that, on the same day, Trump thanked the Agalarov family through Twitter: 'I had a great weekend with you and your family. You have done a FANTASTIC job. TRUMP-TOWER MOSCOW is next. EMIN was WOW!' 'Mr. Trump, thank you for bringing the Miss Universe to us we had an awesome time TRUMP tower Moscow—let's make it happen,'—replied Emin Agalarov to the future US President who spent two nights at the hotel outside Moscow. 'I called it my weekend in Moscow,' Trump reminisced in September of 2015. 'I spent some time with the top-level people—oligarchs, military personnel, top government officials. I cannot go into too much detail, but I will tell you that I met with some very important people and was treated extraordinarily.'

'It' (Trump Tower Moscow) did not happen. What did happen was something completely different. In June, 2015, Trump officially declared he was running for President and began working on his election campaign. 'Our boy can become president of the USA and we can engineer it,' Sater wrote in a November 2015 email. 'I will get all of Putin's team to buy in on this, I will manage this process'.[349] The Kremlin, seemed to have been well ahead of cultivating Trump, without Sater knowing it.

By January of 2016, Trump was leading in the polls for the Republican nomination. At that same time, January of 2016, at the request of Felix Sater, Michael Cohen contacted President Putin directly (through an email to his press-secretary, Dmitry Peskov). Despite the primaries, Trump hadn't forgotten about Trump Tower Moscow. Sater wanted to contact Putin because, according to Trump, the planned massive real estate development in Moscow would require the Kremlin's approval. Cohen wrote:

> Over the past few months, I have been working with a company based in Russia regarding the development of a Trump Tower-Moscow project in Moscow City. Without getting into lengthy specifics, the communication between our two sides has stalled. As this project is too important, I am hereby requesting your assistance. I respectfully request someone, preferably you, contact me so that I might discuss the specifics as well as arranging meetings with the appropriate individuals. I thank you in advance for your assistance and look forward to hearing from you soon.[350]

According to the *Washington Post*, 'Cohen told congressional investigators that the deal was a licensing project, in which Trump would have been paid for the use of his name by a Moscow-based developer called IC Expert Investment. Cohen said that he discussed the deal three times with Trump and that Trump signed a letter of intent with the company on Oct. 28, 2015. He said the Trump Company began to solicit designs from architects and discuss financing. However, the project was abandoned 'for business reasons' when government permission was not secured.'[351] It seems that Putin knew better than pay Trump publicly in the middle of his Election bid.

In his interview for MSNBC on December 24, 2020, Michael Cohen stated that he thought the whole election project for Trump was nothing more than the business project of promoting the 'Trump' brand. In other words, Trump was not counting on winning the 2016 Presidential Election. This opinion was not shared in Russia. In March-April of 2016 by one of the leaders of the City Development in Moscow said, 'We have invested in Trump so much money that he cannot lose.' To Trump's great surprise, he really did win.

It was the Lubyanka most successful operation since the FSB's Putin came to power in Russia in 2000, and the Klaus-Zeman tandem in the Czech Republic in 2003 and 2013. However, giving the complexity and of ferrying Trump into the White House, a man who before and during the Presidential race used his own Putin-linked money, it was a tribute to the unmatched audacity and skillfulness of, in particular, Andropov's former 5th Directorate to plan its sophisticated provocation and blunt dis-simulations over the long term. Indeed, the Kremlin would harvest ample fruit of its labor and reconstruct the world during Trump's four years in office.

During his four governing years Trump inflicted infinitely more harm on the US, US democracy and US economy than Bin Laden. Bin Laden, through his terrorist acts, united the US public behind a not very popular President, George W. Bush. Trump managed to polarize the US into Democratic and Republican camps even further and proceeded to skillfully provoke African-Americans by increasing racial tension. Through leveraging the power of the presidential office with simple political black-mail, threats and bribery, he shifted the base of the Republican Party towards his own personal interests. While the Kremlin did not succeed reshaping the world as much as it might have expected—NATO is still standing—it is worth remembering that what robbed Trump from being reelected was not his politics as such, but his laconic response to COVID and the disquiet it caused among the demographic he shared with the virus—the older voter.

Trump's final piece of destabilization was also his most disruptive—the organized uprisings of a small Fascist crowd occupying the Capitol at another stage Constitutional instrument previously considered ceremonial only—confirmation of the majority of votes in the Electoral College to Joe Biden on 6 January 2000. It was in many ways a carbon copy of the August 1992 putsch in Moscow, and a first in the history of the United States. By that time Trump had installed staunch loyalists at key department including, at the Justice Department, as US Attorney General someone who was loyal to him personally as in a 'banana republic'. And that resulted in more damage to two centuries of pre-2016 US consensus, than Trump's unrealized promis-es to the Kremlin to lift the sanctions, recognize the annexation of the Crimea and dis-solve the NATO.

The events that unfolded in Washington, DC on January 6, 2021, were a 'final accord' of the Trump presidency. The Icebreaker accomplished his mission: his sup-porters seized the enemy's capital without any significant losses that would have made it seem like civil war, accompanied by the enthusiastic voices of the Trump-minded crowds, in plain daylight, while the whole world was watching. At the same time, US Congressmen and Senators, having been abandoned by the guards and surrounded by the rebels, were taken hostage. In the Kremlin, champagne corks must have popped. This was an attempt to overthrow the US Government undertaken under the leader-ship of Trump who lost the Presidential election but was not willing to leave the White House. It is good to remember that the only reason why it failed is because the hostages managed to escape through Capitol underground tunnels, just in time.

9: War on Foreign Territory

Donald Trump was not the only man activated in Operation Icebreaker, and not the only one on whom money—and a substantial amount of money at that—was spent. What's money when it comes to reconquering a lost 'Russian World'? That's worth any amount of money, especially if you have a plan, the experience, and the hunger to do so. As in Russia from the moment the Lubyanka seized the Kremlin, manipulating the US from outside its borders required more than financing Donald Trump and trusting his gift for gathering a Twitter audience of 90 million followers. Social media handed the Kremlin the keys to the US's front door. Unlike the traditional media, algorithms made no difference between lies or the truth and piped both to its billions of customers dependent merely on the amount of money views or clicks generated in advertising revenue. Between them, the Kremlin and the Lubyanka shared almost two centuries of manufacturing lies. Channeling this skill was the next step.

That Michael Flynn joined Trump's staff was no accident. He had been a Kremlin and Lubyanka target for the post of National Security Advisor for a considerable time. His speech at the Republican National Convention on July 20, 2016, when Flynn led the crowd chanting 'Lock her up!' in reference to Hillary Clinton, was the final stretch of Flynn's preparation for a new role and post in the Trump White House as an *agent provocateur*. If Trump was the captain of the Icebreaker, Flynn was its purser. Was there a better way to split America than to tell your voters to lock up your rival?

Among other things, Flynn claimed to know a few things about Clinton in his July 20 speech: 'If I, a guy who knows this business, if I did a tenth, a tenth of what she did, I would be in jail today.'[352] The clip of these words, with credit 'Lt-General Michael Flynn' soon spread like wildfire via Trump's Twitter account and other social media.

What didn't spread anywhere, however, is that, whatever Flynn meant with 'did' in his sentence, he himself had been handed a lot of Russian money, much like the man of the moment at the Conference—candidate Donald Trump.

Between 2015-2016, Flynn received some $600,000 from Russia, but only some $70,000 was paid directly from Russian bank accounts. Most of it seemed to originate from a Turkish businessman Alptekin who transferred $530,000, to Flynn in 2016. What the payment was for became clear only in 2017. On the face of it was a payment for lobbying for Turkish interest in the United States because Flynn registered himself as a lobbyist for 'Turkey'—after the considerable payments to him became known to US law enforcement agencies and information about payments was leaked to the media. Questions were asked. On March 7, 2017, Flynn filed with the Department of Justice's National Security Division disclosure under the Foreign Agent Registration Act (FARA) that his Flynn Intel Group Inc was paid $530,000 by a small Dutch company, Inovo BV, owned by Turkish citizen Kamil Alptekin.

Flynn's contract with Inovo BV itself was signed on August 9, 2016, according to one source, or on 9 September 2016, according to another, but, in any case, after Flynn's Convention speech. The three months of work were paid in tranches and the last transfer of $145,000 was received by Flynn on November 14, 2016, after Trump won the election.

Having finished his 'work' for Alptekin, Flynn sent Alptekin a final report further to the contract with Inovo BV, and indicated that November 16, 2016, was his last day of work. The next day, November 17, 2016, he was appointed as the National Security Advisor-Elect by President-Elect Trump.

This contractual paper trail was submitted to the Senate only in 2017 after the Justice Department showed an interest in Flynn's interactions with Inovo BV. In 2017, however, it showed that only $5,000 received by Flynn Intel Group Inc for its 'Turkish' services'.[353] On March 10, 2017, the *New York Times* drew the reasonable inference: 'that presumably indicates that [Flynn] did not define most of the services he would provide Mr Alptekin as lobbying under [FARA]'.[354]

What was the $525,000 in that case payment for? 'I disagree with the filing'—said Alptekin on the telephone from Istanbul in reply to the reporter's question about the extent of Flynn's FARA work for Turkey. 'It would be different if I was working for the government of Turkey, but I am not taking directions from anyone in the [Turkish] government.'[355]

In other words, Turkey had nothing to do with the Inovo BV money according to Alptekin in conversation, who spoke to Isaac Arnsdorf of Politico's. Alptekin clarified in so many words that 'he hired Flynn with his own money and did not coordinate any lobbying for the Turkish government'.[356]

Indeed, it appeared that Alptekin had never worked for the Turkish government. Furthermore, his modest Dutch company Inovo BV only had losses to show for in its financial reports.[357] It was difficult to see how it could pay $530,000 to Flynn unless it had received this money from elsewhere first. For whom was Alptekin working, and why did he have to make an urgent payment ahead of the US Presidential elections of 2016?

Much like Trump's financial interests in Russia until 2008, Flynn Intel Group Inc had not flourished from its foundation in 2014. In April, 2014, General Michael T. Flynn lost his job after two years as Obama's head of the Defense Intelligence Agency. In October 2014 he started his own consulting firm, but everything about it was opaque—including its business address:

The business was opaque, making little public, not even an address. When a reporter went looking for it last fall, he tracked it down to an Alexandria, Va, office building operating out of the nondescript headquarters of another firm, called the White Canvas Group. In the interview in October, Mr. Flynn offered only a vague description of the firm. He said he had clients in Japan and the Middle East and that he worked on cyber training, aviation operations and energy business.[358]

Then, from August, 2015, Flynn's company started enjoying $11,250 per month. In August 2015, the first $11,250 was received from a Russian charter cargo airline Volga-Dnepr Airlines. In September 2015, it was followed by a payment of $11,250 from Kaspersky Government Security Solutions Inc, a US subsidiary of Kaspersky Lab—a Russian-based cybersecurity firm generally assumed to be affiliated with the FSB. The same payment pattern continued with monthly payments of $11,250 in October 2015, November 2015, December 2015 (a total of $33,750 for three months). Officially, Flynn received this money for traveling to Moscow for a few days in December 2015.

The $33,750 was a fee for an interview for Russian propaganda TV channel Russia Today (RT). During his stay in Moscow, he took part in a celebration of RT's 10th anniversary. It was a star-studded evening. At the ceremony he was seated at the same table as Vladimir Putin. Since he was the new National Security Advisor and Putin an FSB colonel and leader of Russia, the 2015 dinner drew worldwide media attention when Flynn was about to begin his job in 2017.[359]

In 2015, Trump's presidential campaign was in full swing and it raised the question why a former US intelligence general attended a jubilee hosted by RT a Russian TV channel that in the course of a decade had devoted itself to a torrent of anti-American propaganda. RT had just run an extremely aggressive anti-Ukraine campaign a year after Russia's 2014 invasion and occupation of Eastern Ukraine and Crimea—now annexed to the Russian Federation in Moscow's eyes, but not recognized by others.

Perhaps $11,250 in October and December by RT was as nothing compared to a similar fee from FSB affiliate Kaspersky in September. RT's fee was paid in January, 2016, by Leading Authorities (LA), the organizer of Flynn's Moscow appearance. Two sets of business-class tickets to Moscow were also provided for free to Flynn and his son with LA's compliments, as well as their stay in Metropole Hotel and other little things, like guided tours and theater tickets—valued at another $10,500.

Initially, in 2017 the media focused on the Russian payments mounting to $56,250, or even $67,500, including the extras, of Flynn's flailing business. It was then 'discovered' that Flynn was acting as a foreign agent for the Turkish government who had paid $530,000 for his lobbying work. The 'Russian trail' in Flynn's biography was quickly forgotten while everyone now focused on Turkey. It was then that the $5000 rabbit was pulled out of the hat, and the bulk of the money was apparently not connected to political work in the US—not according to the parties involved at any rate.

It is worth to pause here for a moment. There is little doubt as to the view from the Kremlin-Lubyanka has of people like Flynn. An American officer who is paid with Russian money is seen as an intelligence mule, however the officer in question may see themselves: as a successful businessman, or a media star, or an advisor, or an academic. The money seals the deal, the target is now on the payroll and can via the Chekist officers handling his file be induced to undertake further tasks by finding the right carrot.

A foreign 'intelligence mule' can be paid small amounts, like lecture fees or interview fees of, say, some $45,000, from Russian bank accounts. But, evidently, a major problem arises when the carrot runs to paying hundreds of thousands to the likely National Security Advisor for the President of the United States. It starts to attract FARA interest from US law enforcement. How do you shield the nature of such a large transaction from flagging the Kremlin connection you would like to conceal?

A further look at the first Russian transfer of $11,250 by Volga-Dnepr Airlines to Flynn's business would provide an answer to this complex question. In 1990, the Russian Ulyanovsk Aviation Industrial Complex (now Aviastar-SP or just Aviastar) founded Volga-Dnepr Airlines operating cargo aircrafts AN-124, called 'Ruslan' in the USSR. The same company had a subsidiary registered in the USA as Volga Dnepr Unique AirCargo, held through the Volga-Dnepr Group. It was this company that paid Flynn his first $11,250 for participation in a Washington conference on Logistics and National Security in the Middle East and Africa in 2015.

In 2004, Roland 'Roel' Pieper, a Dutch citizen, and Daniil Kazhdan, a Russian, had founded the European Technology and Investment Research Center (ETIRC) with several entities around Europe. Pieper was the president of all the ETIRCs outside of Russia ('ETIRC Europe'). Meanwhile, in Russia, Kazhdan founded *ETIRK Rus* with himself as sole owner and the president of the company.[360] It appeared that Kazhdan was more widely known under an alias, 'Daniel Bolotin', a name frequently mentioned by the Russian and foreign media as an entrepreneur and an inventor. Their cooperation was even more complex, however. In 2004, Kazhdan registered yet another company, *ETIRK Aviation Rus*. As before, he was the company's sole owner. Simultaneously, Pieper and Kazhdan together incorporated ETIRC Aviation, in Luxembourg. The companies' titles suggested that both of them intended to engage in aircraft construction. In 2005, *ETIRK Holding Rus* (owner, Daniil Kazhdan) and Daniil Kazhdan as a private person incorporated another company, *STK Razvitie (Development)*. This was a company with a lot of existing business. Its customers included major Russian names such as Gazprom, Transneft, Bank of Moscow, Alfa Bank, Rostelecom, Russian Railways, Mosenergo, Rosneft and many other Russian blue chip businesses.[361] It was easier to list Russian companies that were *not* clients of the enterprising Kazhdan-Bolotin.

After the incorporation of a flurry of eponymous holding companies, ETIRC announced its intention to launch the production of Eclipse-500 airplanes in Ulyanovsk at the Aviastar airplane factory (the same one that was a subsidiary of the Volga-Dnieper company which later made the first payment of $11,250 to Flynn). It was at this point that they were joined by Alptekin from Turkey. On May 9, 2006, Turkish newspaper *Big Para Hurriyet* in Turkey reported that ETIRC was part owned by Turkish businessman Ekim Alptekin.[362] In 2017 Alptekin confirmed this information, and that he was a partner in ETIRC since 2006 and had procured a share in Eclipse Aviation.[363] He was of course also the person who would pay $5000 to Flynn in 2016 for 'Turkish' FARA work and $525,000 in the same year for 'non-FARA' work.

After Alptekin joined Pieper and Kazhdan's ETIRC, wondrous things started to happen with their Eclipse-500 jet project at ex-Soviet Aviastar in Ulyanovsk. In December 2007, Russian *Sviaz* (connection) Bank lent $150 million to ETRIC Aviation, Pieper-Kazhdan's company, held by investment group ETIRC now co-owned by Alptekin. With its $150 million sails billowing, the new Eclipse-500 enterprise organized the first stone laid in a February 2008 ceremony in Ulyanovsk. Distinguished businessman Vern Raburn, appointed as ETIRC Aviation president, took part, as well as guest of honor Sergey Stepashin. The former director of the FSK (KGB-FSB), former Prime Minister of Russia, former FSB candidate in Yeltsin's succession, now Director of the Accounts Chamber of the Russian Federation, promised to take the project personally 'under his wings.' He was as good as his word, in June 2008, an interdepartmental tender committee, with Stepashin's support, sanctioned the creation in Ulyanovsk of a special new economic zone in which Volga-Dnepr Airlines, Aviastar and ETIRC Aviation were keen to participate.[364]

Unfortunately 'engine failure' followed after this auspicious start. At any rate, the Alptekin-Kazhdan-Pieper subsidiary went bankrupt after but a short existence, taking the $150 million loan down with it. It now turned out that *Sviaz* Bank had never demanded a collateral, despite the fact that two experienced bankers were in charge: Andrey Kazmin and Alla Aleshkina. Until 2007, the two had run Russia's largest state-owned bank, *Sberbank*. It seemed an extraordinary oversight that they were unaware that in return for the loan the Alptekin-Pieper-Kazhdan's trio had offered no security in case what happened might happen—particularly given the fact that Stepashin, one of Russia's most senior Chekist regulators, had said he was looking over their shoulder. Even more miraculous for all concerned was the fact that no one was penalized for the unsecured loan when the bank itself collapsed in 2008 and the paper trail of the loan came to an abrupt end.[365]

Traditionally, it is a fact that the Russian aircraft industry is riddled with classified information and Chekists. There is also the fact that whatever chunk Alptekin received of the $150 million under his arrangement with his 'business' partners was now legitimately parked outside Russia in foreign bank accounts. It was also of course the case that, since the 1970s, the Lubyanka had been executing Andropov's

'Operation Net' by creating a mass of foreign companies—in complexity much like the numerous ETIRCs that started popping up 2004—to handle payments to foreign agents beyond scrutiny of foreign states. In the long Cheka tradition of laundering many tens of millions of dollars abroad as a discreet foreign cash reserve, the Kremlin-Lubyanka controlled many such accounts. Once abroad such money could be used, for example, to pay General Flynn for 'advice' unrelated to Russia through a company with a Netherlands bank account.

If this was one odd thing about Flynn's activities, there was another one. In December 2015, Jill Stein, the US Green Party presidential hopeful also found herself at Putin and Flynn's table celebrating 10 years of RT TV's tilted news.[366] Stein had come to Moscow to secure the Kremlin's support for her own presidential campaign. Surely Flynn, a former head of US military intelligence must have found the table seating disconcerting. Unusual enough to wonder why a Russian FSB president who only months earlier had intentionally broken 68 years of peace in Europe, deploying military assets beyond Russian Federation borders, and had invited him and a left-wing US politician to Moscow to celebrate a source of English-language misinformation in the US? In his job for the US intelligence, he must have seen how sudden foreign payments created pawns controlled by a foreign power?

Flynn didn't even have to go back very far to uncover suspicious events relating to RT TV's unsavory type of English-language newscasting in the US. On November 5, 2015, the 57-year-old Mikhail Lesin, a well-known media tycoon, Putin's former Media Minister, former head of Gazprom Media, and creator of the Russia Today TV itself, died prematurely at the Dupont Circle Hotel in Washington, DC. The question of exactly what happened to Lesin, and who benefitted from his premature death, remained without an official answer. In late October 2016, the FBI closed the investigation and Lesin's death was classified as an 'accident'. It was reported that Lesin suffered from 'acute' intoxication that night.

Confusingly 'acute' intoxication itself was not the cause of death. Despite the 'acuteness', like Lazarus, Lesin apparently managed to stand up again only to fall several times. Not only that, cumulatively these falls of the intoxicated man apparently gathered force to such an extent that the 'accidentally' self-inflicted injuries caused the 57-year-old to die alone in his hotel room. In particular, the chief federal prosecutor said—listing the dizzying array of what the incapacitated man had been capable of doing to himself—Lesin was killed by 'blunt force injuries to his head, with contributing causes being blunt force injuries of the neck, torso, upper extremities, and lower extremities'.

On July 28, 2017, BuzzFeed published new investigative material regarding the circumstances of Lesin's death.[367] Based on the comments of two FBI agents and a US intelligence officer, the authors suggested that Lesin was assassinated in Washington on the eve of his meeting with the US Department of Justice (DoJ) officials. Allegedly, the cause of his death was a baseball bat with which he had been beaten to death.

BuzzFeed also quoted the medical examiner's office statement that the death was, in fact, caused by one thing only: 'blunt force injuries of the head'. Besides these injuries, Lesin also 'had fractured ribs' and lesions. 'What I can tell you is that there isn't a single person inside the Bureau who believes this guy got drunk, fell down, and died. Everyone thinks he was whacked and that Putin or the Kremlin were behind it'—said one of the BuzzFeed sources.

What information could Lesin provide to US law enforcement officials in 2015 ahead of the 2016 elections? What information was so sensitive that he needed to be eliminated?

One needs to look no further than Jill Stein, the US Green Party candidate and Flynn's fellow traveler in December 2015 to see what the plan was. RT was never an informational channel. It was designed and created by the Kremlin as a propaganda tool to be used for 24/7 ideological indoctrination and for interference in elections, and not just in the US. Russia Today acted as a liaison between the Kremlin and Russian agents. Stein did not receive cash, like Flynn did, but RT was the only TV station in the U.S. that covered her Presidential Campaign and invited her to the studio starting from day one. RT even became a debate platform for the primaries of The Green Party that resulted in Stein's victory. The value of these PR efforts in real numbers

Stein, in turn, received her share of electoral votes during the Presidential Election 2016; incidentally, those were roughly the votes that deprived Clinton of presidency. For example, in Michigan, Stein earned 51,000 votes, while Trump was only 11,000 votes ahead of Clinton. Similarly, in Wisconsin, Trump received 23,000 votes more than Clinton, while Stein got 31,000 votes; and in Pennsylvania, Trump's advantage amounted to 44,000 votes, while 50,000 votes went to Stein.[368] It is obvious that without Russia Today's PR support, Stein would probably not have been able to steal the victory from Clinton. During the 2020 elections, in which there was no friendly Russian channel to aid Stein, the Green Party and Stein were unable to repeat their 2016 success.

Lesin, however, knew so much more than met the eye. He was the mastermind who created Russia Today, a TV network that would broadcast its content in foreign languages—primarily in English—in more than a hundred countries around the world in 2005. He got Putin to agree to finance the network from the federal budget. And if, in 2005-2006, the network was getting a modest $30 million in financing a year, during later years—e.g., 2008-2009—the grant amounted to approximately $100 million per year. And in special years, when the Kremlin-Lubyanka had something planned, RT's budget soared proportionately. In 2014, the year of the Russian invasion into Ukraine, the channel's budget was more than quadrupled to $445 million to provide propaganda support to Russian troops fighting in and occupying Ukraine. In 2015, its grant was approximately $236 million (or $320 million, according to another source); and, in 2016, it was approximately $210 million (or $250 million). By comparison, the annual budget of the entire BBC, funded by the British government, is

$375 million. RT TV's precise figures are shrouded in great secrecy. RT only ever published one official statement and it was a report consisting of 3 lines.

In Russia, (authorized) embezzlement from the government is an attractive business that yields the highest return for its entrepreneurs. The greater the budget, the greater the opportunities to generate a profit. Lesin, the former Media Minister (1999-2004), advisor to Putin (2004-2009), Russia Today's founder (2005) and general manager of Gazprom Media (2013-2015), was not a poor man. He was a frequent traveler to the US; he was very fond of his yacht and of fishing; he also owned mansions in Los Angeles, California, and his flamboyant personal life was played out in the public eye. Photos of Victoria Rakhimbayeva, his last romantic interest, an ex-model and ex-flight attendant, frequently appeared in popular magazines and on Internet sites. On September 25, 2015, just a few weeks before his death, their daughter Tamara was born.

The wealth Lesin amassed over the years was unlikely to have come from savings he made from his government salary. After his death, his two Los Angeles properties were put up for sale for $51 million.[369] The Lubyanka must have had a considerable 'case file' on him and have known intimately how Putin's former advisor had amassed his fortune. But, since he was a fellow member of the Kremlin mafia, there were no objections on that front from 'higher authorities' (Putin). Regular Russian law enforcement never paid any attention to the deals that inflated Lesin's fortune beyond his salary.

In 2014, however, US storm clouds started appearing in Lesin's charmed life. After Russia occupied Crimea and invaded Eastern Ukraine, Russian companies and individuals came under scrutiny and were subjected to US sanctions. On July 29, 2014, 5 months after Russia's first Ukraine invasion, Lesin found himself in a precarious position. Roger Wicker, US Senator from Mississippi, asked the DoJ to investigate the origin of the $28 million that Lesin, whom he characterized as Putin's propaganda chief, had used in 2009 to purchase a mansion in Los Angeles, California.[370] Lesin responded that the real estate in question was owned by his children. This begged the question and US officials did not stand down, especially after they secured the cooperation of Lesin's friend and junior business partner, Alexei Yazlovsky, who was also a head of RT's US channel.

A Soviet émigré, Yazlovsky knew Lesin well from their college years. They both attended the prestigious Moscow Institute of Civil Engineering (MISI) where Lesin graduated in 1984. They both joined MISI's team on *Klub Vesolykh i Nakhodchivykh* (KVN)[371]—a famous televised game-show challenge between Russian universities—of which Lesin was team captain. In 1990, the year before the collapse of the USSR, the friends registered their first business, a production company called MA after their first names' initials (Mikhail and Alexei). But in 1991, Yazlovsky emigrated to the United States while Lesin soon started his stellar career under Yeltsin and Putin and became the Kremlin head of PR and Media Minister (1999-2004), an important role given the fact that, whomever was picked as Yeltsin's successor, had to be shoehorned as Acting President into winning the 2000 presidential elections.

In June of 2005, after Lesin's plans were announced to launch a new global 24-hour-a-day English-speaking news channel, Russia Today, Yazlovsky, who became US citizen in 2002, incorporated two companies in the US: RTTV America Inc and RTTV Studios Inc with himself as a president of both. It made Yazlovsky the owner of the trademark 'Russia Today' and its logo, which were only transferred in 2010. There were about 45 people on RTTV America Inc.'s staff. On paper, the company produced TV and video content for Russia Today.

In truth, Yazlovsky acted as the owner of the US branch of RT, known as 'RT America'. The two businesses shared the same address on their US tax returns and RTTV America's offices in four U.S. cities—Washington, D.C., New York, Miami and Los Angeles—were in the same offices as the local bureaus of 'RT America'. On their tax returns, including W-2 forms, US employees of RT America declared that they were employed by Yazlovsky's company, RTTV America. Additionally, Yazlovsky controlled the Voice of Russia radio station, which, in 2013, on Putin's orders, was closed, reorganized and incorporated, into RT America. All of the US RT activities were headed up by Lesin, however.

It was through Russia Today that Lesin made his fortune, or some of it. Via numerous 'dead souls' registered as RT employees and via fake or massively inflated contracts, Russia Today was running a multi-million-dollar money laundering scheme through fake employment records and phony contracts. For the most part, this was business as usual. But in this case, money was being siphoned off on US territory and in dollars. Some of this money went to Lesin, some to Yazlovsky, who was also able to put together an attractive property portfolio consisting of a house bought for $1.873 million in Potomac, Maryland (a suburb of Washington, DC), as well as an apartment in New York City, and a summer home in Naples, Florida.

Rather than Russia Today's propaganda activities in the US, it was Yazlovsky's bad fortune that set the ball rolling. By pure accident, American prosecutors got on his trail. In 2007, DoJ officials suspected UBS AG, one of Switzerland's two biggest banks, of facilitating dubious financial operations. As a result, Swiss regulatory officials started an investigation into the financial activities of three Israeli banks: Napoalim, Leumi and Mizrahi-Tefahot.[372] It discovered massive irregularities and the fine of bank Leumi alone ultimately amounted in 2015 to $400 million, paid into US Treasury.[373]

In comparison, Yazlovsky's money-laundering at RTTV America was hardly sensational and part of the rank-and-file cases uncovered as part of the larger investigation against the three banks and UBS. His 2013 court papers mentioned 'large' amounts. There was $2.6 million transferred by Yazlovsky's 'Russian client' to an account at a Luxembourg branch of one of the three Israeli banks; $2.83 million transferred by Yazlovsky's 'Russian client' to an RTTV Studios account in the US. In addition, there was $7.65 million that Yazlovsky attempted to hide from the IRS through a different scheme. The DoJ was not particularly interested and on July 1,

2013, Yazlovsky pleaded guilty to tax fraud and admitted that he intentionally misinformed the IRS and concealed $2.6 million in 2008.

A month and a half after Russia's invasion of Ukraine regions Crimea and Donbas and Luhansk, Alana Goodman of a local publication, *Washington Free Beacon*, published an article on Yazlovsky's trial April 1, 2014.[374] It seemed entirely insignificant as it was the only US publication that paid any attention to this footnote to the larger banking story. However, it caused complete panic at the offices of RT TV. On April 8, 2014, seven days later, RT TV's Editor-In-Chief Margarita Simonyan distanced herself in Moscow newspaper *Kommersant* from Yazlovsky and his US company RTTV America as one of 'hundreds' of private counterparts. It was an intentional falsehood as RTTV America employed RT TV's US staff.

> Alexei Yazlovsky, owner of RTTV America, has been charged with tax fraud by U.S. authorities. Investigation considers him to be an actual owner of American branch of Russian state TV channel RT (Russia Today). The company itself stated that Mr Yazlovsky was one of the channel's counterparts, but not a branch owner by any means. RT's Editor-In-Chief, Margarita Simonyan, declared that Mr. Yazlovsky was a counterpart, one of the hundreds RT dealt with: 'RTTV America is a commercial legal entity, it independently reports to the IRS. RT has no authority and no ability to monitor or verify their business practices and integrity in tax matters.' According to Simonyan, the investigation itself was a 'routine investigation,' which Western media had inflated up to a level of a 'wild scandal.' Ms. Simonyan was sure that 'no one would ever care about this kind of news' if Yazlovsky were not linked to RT. According to her, RT was going to terminate its contract with RTTV America due to reputational losses RT suffered. 'We vigorously disagree with an assumption that American authorities' tax claims to our counterpart have anything to do with Russia Today.'

If this was panic at RT HQ in Moscow, behind the scenes, the Kremlin-Lubyanka was taking note, too. On March 9, 2015, the United States District Court for the Central District of California sentenced Yazlovsky to a year of supervised release, a $60,000 fine and 640 hours of community service.[375] It was difficult to imagine a lighter sentence. It raised suspicion inside the Kremlin-Lubyanka that Yazlovsky had gotten off so easily because he had told the Americans absolutely everything. It started to suspect that among other things, US investigators now had information on RT's money laundering activities in general and Lesin in particular. This suspicion was confirmed by Senator Wicker's request to the DoJ that they should investigate Lesin for money laundering.

Although, RT Russia and its US subsidiary walked away scot-free from the Yazlovsky debacle, and—more to the point in 2014—from Ukraine sanctions and penalties imposed by the US on Russian involved in the occupation, there was trouble in Lesin's 'case-file'. Lesin was gradually stepping back from the management of RT

TV. This was partly due to health issues after a serious spinal injury in 2012 from a skiing accident from which he never fully recovered. From the middle of 2014, he started dating Victoria Rakhimbayeva and his visits to the US became more frequent.[376]

None of this would perhaps have unduly worried his case handler at the Lubyanka if, in December 2014, he had not told RT TV's Editor-in-Chief Simonyan that he wanted to give up working and just travel with his pregnant girlfriend Victoria. In 2015, just as the Kremlin-Lubyanka operation Icebreaker was gathering pace in which RT America had a star role, Lesin suggested that Simonyan should leave Russia for the US and get into the US movie business in Los Angeles:

—You should think about your future, you know. I am worried about you. How long can you be the Editor-In-Chief for Russia Today? You'd better move to Los Angeles. You will write scripts, Tigran [Keosayan—film director, Margarita Simonyan's husband] will shoot films; I will be your producer.

—You know very well, Mikhail, I will never leave.

—Eh, you are an adult now and still you arc a silly girl

In Soviet times, such advice would be seen as an invitation to 'become a defector'. In the midst of the election campaign in the US, it was certainly a betrayal of Putin and of the Kremlin's cause. With Senator Wicker accusing him publicly of money laundering, and his friend Yazlovsky getting off so lightly, Lesin would have had a compelling reason to talk in secret to the DoJ. For Putin—whom Russia's Constitution licenses as the only Russian to kill single enemies abroad—letting a potential defector loose on DC was certainly dangerous.[377] The last time DuPont Circle Hotel surveillance cameras recorded Lesin alive was when he entered the hotel at 10:48 am on November 4, 2015.

The last thing, given the massive investment in Jill Stein, RT America, Micheal Flynn and others, the Kremlin-Lubyanka needed was Lesin giving inside information to the Americans. He was a Kremlin insider, profiled by a US senator as Putin's spin doctor, familiar with all of Russia Today's inner workings, projects and plans as one of its founders and top directors. He was also a corrupt alcoholic who owned laundered expensive real estate in the US with US dependents. With only a little pressure, he could divulge a wealth of detailed information that could potentially fatally harm the Kremlin-Lubyanka's multilayered plan to influence the 2016 US elections and reveal that RT was a set piece in a precision provocation of the strength of US Democracy.

Through RT America Putin could attack Hillary Clinton from both sides. From the 'Left', the Kremlin used Jill Stein. As early as September 2015, as the Green Party's candidate for the President, Stein attended an RT even in New York and shook hands and had a friendly chat with Kremlin heavyweight Foreign Minister Sergey Lavrov, who 'accidentally' happened to step by. In October-November 2015,

RT stepped and got talking to Flynn who had already received $11,250 as a bribe from FSB companies: Volga-Dnepr Aviation and Kaspersky Lab, apart from other payments received that gave Flynn's company a first wind. The payments certainly fell on fertile ground when he called for Clinton's imprisonment and, judging by his Ukraine stance from 2023, was in favor of revoking US sanctions against Russian interests and recognizing the invasion of Crimea as legitimate (as well as moving the US towards Christian nationalism).

Like Jill Stein, Julian Assange and Wikileaks proved the extraordinary media power RT had built up to move the needle in the key states in the US. Another RT accomplishment was how they, too, were deployed as Kremlin mules to deliver Trump to the White House doorsteps. On July 27, 2016, Trump addressed Putin with a request to make 30,000 of missing Clinton's e-mails public. 'I will tell you this— Russia, if you're listening; I hope you're able to find the 30,000 emails that are missing,' he said.[378] These emails had been hacked from Clinton's office by Russian intelligence and filtered to Wikileaks two weeks earlier by the GRU on July 14, 2016. They were dumped on the same day the 2005 'bragging' tape between Trump and Billy Bush was made public.[379]

On November 5, 2016, the eve of Election Day, RT delivered its final body blow. It broadcast Assange's interview regarding Clinton's e-mails, in which he assured US voters falsely that Russia had nothing to do with their publication.[380] Assange's interview was aired by RT on television and on the Internet and was watched by millions of American voters. YouTube videos with Assange that were 'uploaded by RT' got a surprising 2,420,000 hits. American voters were not the only ones transfixed by Assange. A press photo of Putin, Flynn and Stein sharing their Russia Today table in Moscow in December, 2015, that became well-known around the world in 2017 has all three watching a TV screen closely. It turned out that Russia Today was broadcasting Assange's welcome speech before the gathering celebrating the channel's 10-year jubilee. Despite Flynn's connection to both Assange and Putin, the FBI established that contact between Wikileaks and the Trump campaign was made via Donald Jr.

Pitovranov's 5th Directorate Protocol and the US

When the KGB's 5th Directorate was formed by Andropov in the 1960s to control Soviet culture, its reach beyond the Iron Curtain was limited by the mere fact that few Russians were permitted to leave the USSR. In the thirty years to the Soviet collapse, however, the 5th Directorate established indirect ways of directing culture through a vast web of agents that as often as not reported on Soviet citizens as well as on fellow agents as a double bind. It was an infinitely more sophisticated system of control than Stalin's thuggish vast GULAG imprisonment of intellectuals considered to be on the wrong track. The rebranding as Directorate Z(*ashchita konstitutsionnogo stroya*, protection of Constitutional order) made little difference and, as part of the FSB, it has gained another three decades of experience in perfecting its skills in a new setting.

Over the second thirty years, the potential reach of the Directorate expanded beyond even Andropov and Pitovranov's wildest dreams. When the former Soviet borders were opened in 1991, hundreds of thousands of former Soviet citizens moved to the US (and to Europe). This Russian avalanche of mainly the well-educated appeared to be a release from the yoke of the Party, which it of course was. But, inevitably, the wave of emigrants included a disproportionate number of 5th Directorate agents and 'intelligence mules', some of whom rose to prominent positions in American society—positions that allowed them to influence the minds of the country's present and future political elites, form public opinion and teach their host countries' student publication. The successful embedding of such Russians, who eventually received US citizenship, was an entirely new phenomenon. As Communism was a spent force, no one particularly cared as Russia no longer had an ideological agenda. All that was left was national interests, the staple of any Intelligence Service around the world.

Putin's Presidency changed all that from 2000 when the Kremlin and the Lubyanka merged into one under him and the full scope of the 5th Directorate's abilities was once again activated. The mafia state of the Russian Federation was programmed with the idea of the 'Russian World'. It changed everything. The FSB's cultural web now extended widely across the world and even deep into the US ready to be activated. To be sure, this was not an ideological Fifth Column trying to tip another country into One Party Communist rule. It was instead a global network of leashes in support of the Kremlin-Lubyanka's ambitious plans.

The well-honed Directorate Z playbook consisted of pouring oil on water whenever the Kremlin-Lubyanka launched a provocation. A number of simple yet effective arguments were amplified to create a counterweight to Russian provocation. These arguments were not unreasonable in themselves, but the billions channeled to Chekists inside and outside Russia through its mafia system were available for lubrication:

A few examples: *enemies of Russia* (in 2006, Polonium 210 was used to blacken Putin, Russia wouldn't be so stupid); agreeing with Russia's false flag (in 2008, Georgia started a civil war, Russia was forced to invade to 'protect' 'Russians'); *what can you do?* (in 2014, Crimea 'always' belonged to Russia, Ukrainian Russians want to join Russia, it's better to save lives by finding a compromise with Russia); *probably the other guy* (in 2014, in the absence of proof Malaysian Airlines Flight 17 was probably shot down by Ukrainians); *confusion* (in 2018, the Novichok used to poison Sergei Skripal and his daughter was available in other countries, too); *lack of proof* (in 2020, we don't exactly know what happened when Russian nationalist Alexei Navalny was poisoned); *fear* (in 2022, opposing what Russia wants has become too risky).

As was the case with the KGB in Soviet times, not all operations succeeded. In some situations, botched Russian intelligence operations caused the Kremlin-Lubyanka to direct their agents to engage with damage control and depending on the scale of the operation—such as Trump's election—it was permissible to 'burn' agents, that is, to get them involved in work that could get them identified and exposed as foreign agents.

On July 15, 2018, 29-year-old Russian citizen Maria Butina was arrested in Washington, DC, in connection with illegal activities on behalf of Russia. The FBI had many questions about her presence in the US and suspected that she was a Russian spy. Butina accompanied Alexander Torshin, then the Deputy Governor of Russia's Central Bank and also Butina's Russian handler,[381] on his tour of the United States in pre-election year 2015. Torshin was a high-level Russian official and member of Putin's Party, who was doubtless considered by the Kremlin-Lubyanka as 'one of their own'.[382] He graduated from the All-Union Correspondence Law School, where KGB officers usually studied in the Soviet era to get a formal higher education. Torshin was also a link to Russian crime syndicates.

Butina's first US appearance came courtesy of Anton Fedyashin, an associate history professor at American University (AU) in Washington, DC. She was a Russian exchange student whom Feydashin featured on the AU website on April 6, 2017, gushing that the US should 'focus on similarities that unite us more than on the differences' including a photograph of the two of them at the Eisenhower Institute, Gettysburg:[383]

The picturesque town of Gettysburg, Pennsylvania, has a distinguished place in the American tradition of overcoming profound divisions. On the weekend of February 11-12, 2017, it witnessed a remarkable dialog between two distant worlds—the American and the post-Soviet.... The meeting of young minds aimed at breaking through the seemingly impenetrable wall of stereotypes that has sprung up between Russia and America over the past few years.... SIS [The School of International Service] MA student Maria Butina put it this way: 'Our trip was like a time machine that took us through the present, the future and the past of U.S./Russia/Ukraine/Belarus/Azerbaijan relations. We had a great time learning about each other—students from all of these countries (and two American universities!) that represented different generations and cultures. It helped us to focus on similarities that unite us more than on the differences that divide us.'[384]

Plugs like these build up an agent's career in the country of residence. Butina named Fedyashin as another of her handlers in the US during FBI interrogations after her arrest. The FBI found no cause to arrest Fedyashin on account of her accusation and he continued as a professor at AU after Butina's arrest. Even so, it is of interest to discuss him in greater detail to illustrate how far Russian money and soft-power reaches into academia in the 21st century.

Fedyashin was a historian specializing in Russian history at the American University in Washington, DC. He has the typical educational trajectory of someone who ends up with a history professorship at a prestigious academic institution, a BA at a top 50 US college, a Harvard MA and a Georgetown PhD.[385]

What was less common is that he was born in the USSR and emigrated as a child with his father, Andrey Fedyashin. His father was a graduate of the MSIIR and a staff reporter at TASS—first in London and later in Washington, where he moved with Anton in the mid-1980s—both 5th Directorate strongholds. MSIIR only accepted children of the top Soviet *nomenklatura*. Jobs abroad—TASS reporter in 'capitalist countries,' especially in the US and UK—were bestowed only upon the most trusted Soviet journalists, typically Party members and KGB operatives to minimize the risk of humiliating defection. In fact, Andrey Fedyashin was sent on these plum assignments with his son. The Soviet government must have placed inordinate trust in Andrey as it was standard USSR practice that children were left in Russia as a small reminder of the cost of loyalty.

Anton Fedyashin's grandfather, Andrey's father Georgy, doubtless was one of the reasons why Andrey belonged to Russia's golden youth. Georgy was a General at the elite 1st Directorate of the KGB (today's SVR) that focused on foreign intelligence. Just like his son Andrey, Georgy worked abroad—except, he was outed as a Soviet spy and sent back to the motherland where he was employed by official Press Agency *Novosti* (RIA) from 1965. At RIA, he was both a deputy chief editor for the section of Western Europe and simultaneously, as KGB general, the agency's ARO handler for the Lubyanka.[386] RIA was practically an ARO subdivision of the KGB where KGB, GRU and SVR recalled and resigned officers were employed. Remarkably, Georgy soon left RIA to once again work at the Lubyanka.

Anton Fedyashin had his own *niche* in Washington—namely, he served as director of the 'Carmel' Institute after benefactor Susan Carmel, the Institute of the Russian History and Culture (IEHC), also known as the Initiative for Russian Culture (IRC). In the words of a 2017 report, it was a cultural outpost of the Russian embassy in that it 'sponsors screenings of Soviet classics and modern Russian films at the Embassy of the Russian Federation in Washington, D.C., and hosts big social events: galas, parties, dinners and evenings geared toward networking. Susan is also the main financier of the American-Russian Cultural Cooperation Foundation (ARCCF), which also sponsors large and varied networking events, concerts, exhibitions and commemorative meetings that almost invariably happen with the support of the Russian Embassy....' It noted that Fedyashin took students on trips to the US to hear from Putin apologists and received ample Russian praise for his US-Russia *rapprochement* advocacy (not very popular before the Trump presidency).[387]

Russian diplomats who wooed American students was a phenomenon that well preceded this 2017 report. In October 2013, the FBI accused Russian diplomat Yury Zaytsev of recruiting Americans as potential intelligence assets. Zaytsev was head of the Washington-based Russian Cultural Centre, which itself was part of *Rossotrudnichestvo*, a federal agency established by the Russian Ministry of Foreign Affairs.[388] According to the FBI, Zaytsev was 'a Russian Foreign Intelligence officer and a professional spy, acting as the Director of the Russian Cultural Center (RCC) in Washington, DC,… only so that he can maintain a residence here in the United States.' In fact, Zaytsev's mission seemed to involve a standard task of the 5th Directorate, as the FBI found he was tasked with: 'sending young professionals from the United States to Russia as part of a cultural program wherein participants are evaluated and/or assessed for Russian counterintelligence purposes.'[389]

Zaytsev's two-year Russian youth program was a series of short educational trips to the Russian Federation organized like an old Soviet joke: free cheese in a mouse-trap. 'Rossotrudnichestvo paid for meals, travel, lodging, and every other expense associ-ated with the trip, down to the visa fee. During the St. Petersburg leg of a June 2012 trip, participants stayed at the Sokos Hotel Palace Bridge, a luxury hotel that has hosted delegations for the G8 and G20 summits. Participants on that trip met with the governors of Moscow and St. Petersburg and with Aleksander Torshin, a high-ranking member of Vladimir Putin's United Russia party. Since 2011, Rossotrudnichestvo has organized six trips.'[390]

Defending himself, Zaytsev said that the program carefully selected only future civic leaders to take on these 5-star propaganda trips: 'The first group of 50 people departed for Russia in December 2011 and spent two weeks in Moscow and St. Petersburg, completely at the expense of the Russian Federation. In 2012, we were able to send two groups of 25 people, but, this time, one of the groups was able to visit not only Moscow but also Kazan. On August 6, there was one more delegation that had the chance to visit Moscow and Kaluga.' 'The average age of our candidates is 25-35 years…. It is interesting that most of them have nothing to do with Russia: They often work as assistants to mayors, senators, in the administration of cities and states…. Participants were chosen based on applications', he said. Who was going to be useful was carefully logged as 'After the trip, the center asked them to share their impressions of Russia'.

In addition to these trips for 'young professionals,' Zaytsev's RCC sent 'laureates' of different contests to Russia. One of them was apparently a group at the American University. 'A while ago, we organized an essay contest on the following topic: 400 years of the Romanov family. Nine laureates and one professor from the American University came to St. Petersburg in August to see for themselves the places of the czar's family,' said Zaytsev.[391] In 2014, diplomat Zaytsev was asked to leave the US. The new director of the RCC, Oleg Zhiganov, was deported from the US for the same reason at the end of March 2018.

Zhiganov was the one who handled Maria Butina. The exact number and fre-quency of their meetings is not clear, but several occurred at the RCC and in the Russian Embassy in Washington where Zhiganov served as First Secretary. At least one of the meetings in January 2018 took place in a French bistro and where they were photographed by the FBI agents. There was no risk for Zhiganov given his diplomatic status, but Butina visited the US on a regular Russian passport. She was arrested and accused of being 'as a covert Kremlin agent under the direction of a top Russian government official and central banker.' The 'central banker', Alexander

Torshin, was to whom Zaytsev sent American visitors for recruitment purposes while he was in charge of the RCC.

Butina, who was held at a pretrial detention facility on account of not being a diplomat turned out to be a link between several Russian supporters: her handler Torshin, who employed her at high-level meetings as an interpreter, requiring a high level of Russian clearance in any event; Zaytsev, who had sent her to Russia to recruit American students; Zhiganov, the new RCC head; and Fedyashin, with whom Butina enrolled as a graduate student in his master's degree program at the School of International Services (SIS) and who featured the Russian spy on his web page.[392]

After Butina's arrest, material gradually started disappeared from Fedyashin's April 6, 2017 online article, 'East and West Meet in Gettysburg.' First, Fedyashin's text about Butina herself vanished. Then, the quote from Butina in the text was replaced with a comment from another Russian female student; in between, the entire paragraph went missing. The photo showing Fedyashin and Butina together, originally published with the article, disappeared from internet search engines.[393] The publication of April 6, 2017, also disappeared from Fedyashin's detailed 20-page curriculum vitae, which covered his professional activities up until December 2017.[394] His curriculum vitae did mention that in March of 2015, 2016 and 2017, Fedyashin was a visiting lecturer at the MSIIR—the institute from which his father Andrey graduated.[395]

Torshin, Butina's Kremlin-handler in the US, had a cultural role apart from his other offices in the Russian government. He was introduced to US politics in 2010 by Edward Lozansky, yet another Kremlin supporter in Washington, DC,[396] president of the World Russian Forum, and 'the main Russian lobbyist in US,' as he was called by the Russian media.[397] The first meeting between Lozansky and Torshin featured in the press dated back to Moscow, November 6, 2009, noted on the website of the Russian Federation Council (of which Torshin was a member at the time).[398]

It was to commemorate the 'meeting on the Elbe' in 1945 between the US Army and Red Army, and celebrate US-Russian postwar friendship. Five years later, on April 25, 2015—after the military invasion of Ukraine by Russia—Anton Fedyashin received a statue gifted to the Carmel Institute during the same celebration. In Russia, press bureau TASS reported Fedyashin's words, 'It's a great gift in that it symbolizes the friendship between the people of two countries and serves as a reminder of the period when they were allies'. It also reported that, 'One of the loudest rounds of applause followed the performance by Anton Fedyashin and James Simington, head of the Russian-American Cultural Cooperation Fund, of the song with music written by Jimmy McHugh and lyrics by Harold Adamson titled 'Comin' in on a Wing and a Prayer' that became popular in the Soviet Union…. Fedyashin and Simington performed it in both languages'.[399]

Not that Fedyashin's activity in the United States did not raise suspicions or provoke criticism. However, it is absolutely clear that all of this criticism went unnoticed and had no consequences for Fedyashin, even after Butina's arrest. Even so, it is salutary to look at Fedyashin's writings as a potential X-ray of the golden youth among America's new and growing Russian demographic from 1991.[400]

There seemed to be very little daylight between what the Kremlin might say and his opinion as a scholar. In 2009, after the Russian invasion of Georgia, Fedyashin, based in Washington, DC, mentioned 'internationally-approved' Russian peacekeepers no one else was aware of. Not only that, he proposed supporting the Kremlin rather than Georgia or Ukraine to gain 'a more cooperative Russian ally':

> [Georgian President] Mr Saakashvili was also a Washington favorite for NATO membership. But his luck ran out when he recklessly attacked a breakaway region with internationally-approved Russian peacekeepers in it.
>
> .... As long as Mr. Yushchenko tried to square Ukraine's geopolitical circle by 'bringing the country into the West' via NATO–instead of via a functional and solvent economy–the gas problem persisted. Russia is willing to cooperate with a Ukraine integrated into European political and economic structures, but not with a government disdainful of its benefactor's geopolitical interests. By suspending its unequivocal support for Ukrainian (and Georgian) membership in NATO, the Obama administration will gain a more cooperative Russian ally.[401]

Though he saw 'approved' peacekeepers in Georgia no one else saw, during the initial stage of the Russian occupation of Crimea, at the end of February 2014, Fedyashin did not see the Russian presence everyone else saw and chastized Obama for criticizing Putin:

> 'I don't think anyone knows exactly what is going on,' said Anton Fedyashin, a Russia expert who directs the Initiative for Russian Culture at American University in Washington. '[The White House] are sending a signal without knowing what the hell is going on.'[402]

Even when the occupation of Crimea and the war in the Eastern Ukraine became a reality after two months, Fedyashin saw no Russian presence in Ukraine. On Russia Direct (founded in 2013 by *Rossiyskaya Gazeta*, a Russian government newspaper), he argued that 'Russia's absorption of Crimea' was merely an internal Ukraine problem caused by its 'deep ethno-linguistic divisions and socio-economic implosion'. As to Russia's 'phantom' presence, he both saw none and yet posited in the same breath that 'every' nation was active in Ukraine: 'Indeed, intelligence agencies from all over the world are operating in Ukraine—the Russians have no doubt activated their sources of information, so has MI6, and the CIA's John Brennan has visited Kiev— but the phantom Russian units have become a convenient excuse for ignoring Ukraine's problems.'

It was, therefore, wrong to punish Russia with sanctions, because 'antagonizing Russia diplomatically and hurting it economically will slow down (and may even prevent) Ukrainian economic recovery.'[403] In June, 2014, in DC newspaper *Washingtonian*, he further developed the argument that there was really nothing more than met the eye—that is, there were no Russian troops, special forces or *agents provocateurs*—in Ukraine: 'The Ukraine situation is a geopolitical dispute largely between ancient neighbors…. which goes back 1,000 years.'[404]

When GRU officer Sergei Skripal and his daughter Yulia were poisoned with *Novichok*, a 1970s Soviet military-grade poison, in Salisbury, UK, Fedyashin wrote a piece for Eurasian Strategies, a well-staffed 'consultancy' presided over by the Chair of the MSIIR. He accused British Prime Minister Theresa May of 'crafting' a James Bond theory to face off domestic issues: 'The media coverage of the Skripal case, the alleged chemical attack in Syria, and the military response to it play into London's hands geopolitically by making Britain internationally relevant at a time when its divorce from the EU demonstrates the exact opposite.' At the same time, he seemed to condone Russia's 'breaking international norms'—if for the sake of argument—because Western actions 'triggered unravelling of the world order that the West itself established on the ruins of World War II'. Apart from the pot calling the kettle black—a favorite Kremlin argument—the UK found facts that were too 'elaborate', not how the poisons 'usually' work, and anyway, the two victims recovered: 'A happy ending indeed'.[405] Three months later, an innocent Salisbury bystander died when she happened to find the vial of poison and a policeman was severely injured.

One of the subjects that the 5th Directorate covered with great interest from the 1960s was literature. Political views, as well as psychological patterns, weaknesses and proclivities, can be determined far more easily through the discussion of fiction, given the emotional dynamics of stories, than through non-fiction and facts. It is an excellent litmus test for screening opponents or potential agents or influencers and creating case files on potential 'targets'.

It just so happened that, apart from teaching American University students, for example, 'Russia in World Politics' (2022), 'The Soviet Union' (2023), Fedyashin specialized in Cold War thrillers, and a course, 'The Cold War and the Spy Novel' (2010-), an idea of his from the 1990s. Though his family's KGB background might have sown the seed of this interest, Fedyashin claimed in 2014 to the *Washingtonian* that it was 'a juvenile obsession with James Bond movies'.[406] Talking about the course in 2019, he wrote, 'Could it be that the moral and ethical compartmentalization between the tools of the Cold War and the freedoms they aimed to protect may have been illusory? The Cold War's global espionage conflict corrupted even the most open societies by forcing them to compromise the civil liberties they championed. Fought with propaganda and fear, the Cold War empowered state-sponsored fictions to influence reality on an unprecedented scale.'[407]

Though not a Russian spy, Fedyashin's take on Bond was provocative: 'the Bond movies were really about international crime, not the KGB', one interviewer summarized.[408] In the same interview, Fedyashin argued that Bond thought Communism was better at capitalism, 'In *From Russia with Love*, published in 1957, Bond complains about the Soviets being better armed, better supplied and better funded than he and his service are.' It certainly must have felt like that to Fedyashin as growing up as part of the USSR's golden youth. 'My students often ask, "Why would anyone ever believe in Communism?",' Fedyashin said, a question he no doubt put to his grandfather and father. In his course he put it that, 'The overt racism of *Live and Let Die* reflects the general treatment of African Americans and other non-Caucasian ethnic groups in the United States at that time. When one remembers the difference between that and Communist propaganda's racial and ethnic inclusion, one understands why Communism so often appealed to Third World societies going through decolonization.'[409]

One can see that FSB agents Zaytsev, Zhiganov, Butina and Torshin would be very keen to discuss with Dr Fedyashin which of his students should come to their events and on luxury trips they organized to Russia. If creating case files and recruiting was on their minds, Fedyashin's academic information was pivotal in selecting those with a susceptible mindset and potential for future development. Certainly, the American University exchange students subsidized from Russia, Ukraine, Belarus, and Azerbaijan seemed hand-picked for Fedyashin. Meeting Susan Eisenhower, the granddaughter of General Ike Eisenhower, one Ukraine student ignored the crisis engulfing her home country to observe 'nicely' in April, 2017: 'The future is ours and our generation is very ambitious to change the relations between Russia and the US in a positive direction and I think we can do it.'[410] Mystifyingly, she seemed to equate Ukraine with Russia.

Butina's second booster in the United States was Dimitri Simes, Director of the Center for the National Interest (CNI) and publisher of the eponymous journal the *National Interest*. It was he who organized a meeting between Maria Butina, then-U.S. Federal Reserve Vice Chair Stanley Fischer, and then-Treasury Department Undersecretary for International Affairs Nathan Sheets on April 7, 2015 via The Center for the National Interest. In addition, Simes published Butina in his journal, *The National Interest*.[411] Unlike Fedyashin, who emigrated to the US in the tenth grade, Simes emigrated as a precocious 26-year-old.

In 1967 in Moscow, while a part-time student at the History Department of the MSU, Dimitri Simes started working at Institute of Global Economics and International Relations (IMEMO) when its Chekist deputy head was future SVR chief and potential Yeltsin successor, Yevgeny Primakov. This in itself was a rather extraordinary achievement of the 20-year-old. It was there that he became active in party life and quickly rose as a deputy secretary of the Institute's Komsomol (Party youth) Committee and a press agent for international affairs of the Moscow City Committee of the Party. His academic achievements were no less stellar. He received his degree in 1969. In 1971, he became a junior research fellow concentrating on 'socio-political problems in the United States.' By the spring of 1972, in a little more than a year no less, his PhD thesis was complete, approved, and runner up for a prize.[412]

This immaculate background typical of a 5th Directorate recruit notwithstanding, Simes resigned from his position at KGB spy-nest IMEMO on July 3, 1972. Ostensibly, he wanted to emigrate to the 'hostile' state of Israel, with which the Soviet Union had no diplomatic relations because of the aggressive policies of 'Israeli warmongers'. Primakov, evidently saw no problems, and signed off on the resignation, and Simes left the Institute.

Applying for emigration to Israel entailed a complicated procedure in the 1970s and would have resulted in unpleasant treatment, including being expelled from Komsomol. In the case of Simes, whose status within the organization was fairly senior, this procedure would have required authorization at a high level—Moscow City Committee or even at the Central Committee of Komsomol. Mysteriously, there were no records of Simes having been expelled and the details remained unclear.

However, what was clear is that an event occurred on September 5, 1972, that was to influence the life and destiny of Simes: the Israeli Olympic team members were taken hostage at the Olympic Games in Munich by Palestinian terrorists. Since it was known (at least in the USSR) that the terrorists had flown in from Lebanon, Soviet Jewish activists seeking to immigrate to Israel organized a protest in front of the Lebanese Embassy in Moscow.

On September 6, 1972, at approximately 6pm, about 25-30 people gathered in front of the Lebanese Embassy in Moscow. They were surrounded by approximately 100 members of police and several police buses were parked nearby. The activists were told that the demonstration was forbidden and to disperse. When they refused to do so and unfolded banners they had brought with them, all were immediately apprehended, put into the buses and taken to the Alcoholic Detox Center at the *Rechnoy vokzal* (river station) subway stop. Men were put into one room, and women—into another. Each room had beds.

It turned out that Simes was among the arrested. In November 1972, Simes was again arrested and detained for two weeks for participating in a protest in front of the Central Telegraph building in Moscow. By the end of the year, the Komsomol protester received a permission to relocate to Israel. In January 1973, fêted as a martyr, dissident and a political prisoner, Simes arrived in Rome by way of Vienna, sidestepping his Israeli destination (as did all other Soviet immigrants who decided not to go to Israel, after all).

What Simes told (or did not tell) US officials at the US Embassy in Rome in 1973 when applying for the US visa, is not known. It seems unlikely that his Komsomol leadership activities ranked high, or that that his departure was sanctioned by KGB officer Primakov. Simes had to wait in Rome for three months before receiving a visa to enter the US. He arrived in the US around March or April of 1973 and settled in its capital, Washington DC.

Simes went back to politics, swopping the Komsomol for top US politics. He contacted Richard Perle, a conservative Republican who served at the time as a staffer for Senator Henry M. Jackson (the co-sponsor of the famous Jackson-Vanik amendment); with Brent Scowcroft, the future National Security advisor for Presidents Gerald Ford and George Bush, Sr; and with James Schlesinger, who served as both the Director of Central Intelligence and as a US Secretary of Defense. With the support of his influential friends, Simes became a senior associate at the Carnegie Endowment for International Peace.

Nevertheless, not everything went smoothly. When he applied for his US citizenship, Simes was approached by the FBI. The FBI official with whom he met pulled up a file and said:

> This folder contains written statements of people alleging that you are a KGB agent. Here they are. But these are all just statements with no proof. Therefore, we do feel that we cannot oppose your citizenship application on the basis of these statements. However, I am telling you this so that you understand that these statements exist and that we will be watching you closely.

Simes nonetheless became a US citizen, and his activities ceased to be monitored for one reason or another. Sometime later, Simes went to work for former President Richard Nixon, whom he met in the mid-1980s, and became one of his close associates and an informal advisor on matters related to the USSR/Russia. In particular, Simes accompanied Nixon during his trips to Russia, including his last trip to Moscow in 1994. On January 20, 1994, a few months before Nixon died (April 18), the Nixon Center for Peace and Freedom was established under the auspices of the Nixon Fund, with Simes as its president as 'a leading US expert on the issues of political challenges in modern Russia'.

'Simes-the-Expert' became like Fedyashin, a typical former Soviet national who advocated that rather than fighting the 'Evil Empire' instead we should focus on the usefulness of dialogue, preferably on Kremlin's terms. The *National Interest*, a magazine founded in 1985, became the platform for these views and the Center of National Interest (CNI) headed by him became the center of pro-Kremlin propaganda at the heart of Washington, DC. It received the ringing endorsement of Nixon stalwart, Henry Kissinger, who was honorary chair of the institute.

Clearly, the 1980s were the time of the 5th Directorate's *glasnost* and *perestroika* and great transition in Moscow. Russia in 1991-1992 (the collapse of the USSR) was drastically different from the USSR of 1984-1985 (when the magazine was first published) and from the Russia of 1995-1996 (Yeltsin's second term), and then of 1999-2000 (Putin's first term). And so on. The only constant there was Simes. 'We are frequently accused here in Washington of taking a pro-Russia stance.... As they say— life is hard but we are prepared to live with it,'—he said in an interview.[413] In that sense, Fedyashin fit into an existing tradition.

Vladimir Popov, co-author of this book and a former GRU colonel, confirms that from the first days of the Cheka, agents and officers—even *agents provocateurs*—were forbidden to criticize the country's leader. Even the most shameless NKVD provocateur must not disparage Stalin in order to flush out dissidents. Similarly, no Chekist is licensed to question or speak negatively of Putin's decisions.

Certainly, *The National Interest* from its inception in 1985 did not criticize Russian foreign policy, the Kremlin or, indeed, Putin. The entire body of publications, interviews and commentary emanating from the magazine promote the same thing: there has to be an agreement with Russia because otherwise, US will suffer. The political stories are interspersed with publications featuring the latest developments of Russian military equipment—invariably found to be superior to its US equivalent. Russia's capability of being able to destroy US in 30 minutes is repeated ad infinitum. In November 2014, for example: 'Russia is self-evidently the only country that could destroy America as we know it in 30 minutes with strategic nuclear weapons. Russia also has ten-to-one superiority in tactical nuclear weapons in Europe.'[414] Or, just after Trump's election, 'First and foremost, Russia remains the only nation that can erase the United States from the map in thirty minutes.'[415] A variation on the theme is that Putin must not be cornered, lest he becomes erratic and decides to destroy the US for lack of a better solution. Published in Russian, his latest book appeared in the year before the US elections—*Putin and the West: Do Not Tell Russia How to Live Her Life!* (2015)—when he also met the subject of his exhortation in the Kremlin.[416]

In 2006, Simes, too, had an opinion about the dramatic nuclear poisoning of Putin's former FSB subordinate Colonel Alexander Litvinenko in a botched operation in London by FSB agents Lugovoy and Kovtun. At that time, Putin was still a welcome guest anywhere in the world. Yet, two weeks after Litvinenko's death, on December 6, 2006, Simes published a blog on his *National Interest* page, 'Litvinenko: Kremlin Conspiracy or Blofeld Set-Up?', going through all the theories memo-style.[417]

On past performance, it was hardly surprising that the only theories that got a look in were ones that deflected from the Kremlin-Lubyanka. But what was unusual was that the article appeared a day later in a flawless Russian translation on Memorial, a body formed in 1989 by the (then) Soviet Ministry of Justice. Given the Soviet law-enforcement origin of this dusty website—Memorial celebrated the freeing of political prisoners in 1989—Simes's words can only have been reproduced there with the express imprimatur of FSB Department Z (Pitovranov's former 5th Directorate). What was unusual was to see that the concise list of media optics by consummate DC media insider Simes replicated so quicky and made public around the world in Russian. Stealing a march well before Feydashin, Simes framed his piece with 'James Bond' tropes to ridicule the idea of the Kremlin-Lubyanka's involvement:

> ... the leader of a major nuclear power is dangerously devoid of basic common sense and any instinct for self-preservation—defies our previous experience with Putin.
> ... Killing a fairly insignificant political opponent in a key European capital with a highly traceable material would demonstrate an appalling lack of judgment

… Litvinenko was quite close to at least some Chechen rebels

… Litvinenko—a recent convert to Islam

… any involvement he could have had with Islamic extremist organizations that might be interested in polonium-210 for dirty bombs or other uses.

… Litvinenko's poisoning comes straight from the James Bond movie You Only Live Twice.

… [Oligarch Boris] Berezovsky would be the mastermind of an effort to set Britain and the West against Putin.

… anyone familiar with Berezovsky's activities in Russia would have to entertain the possibility that he would have the combination of imagination, resources and utter ruthlessness

… A Russian academic in England recently claimed that Litvinenko was thinking about making money by blackmailing Russian businessmen.

… Suspicions that groups of current and former FSB officers are responsible for killing Litvinenko fit right into this theory

…. not in the West's interest is to allow Putin's political enemies at home and abroad to bring both him and the West into a confrontation based on a set-up.[418]

Simes has not written anything else about Litvinenko since, despite the wealth of additional information that emerged and despite writing 'The Putin government, assuming it has nothing to hide, should cooperate with the British'. And if Simes has written nothing else in his life, just this article would have been enough to draw an unequivocal conclusion about its author. A large section of blog, at any rate, seemed no longer accessible from the *National Interest* website.[419]

Simes's involvement in the 2018 Butina affair might have gone unnoticed, but Simes also turned out to be a participant in the far more important Russian operation Icebreaker: the election of Donald Trump as president of the United States.

On April 27, 2016, at the Mayflower Hotel in Washington, DC, Simes's Center for the National Interest hosted an event with leading Republican presidential candidate Donald Trump. It was at this event that Trump first laid out his foreign policy program, with input from Simes. Two months prior to this, Simes had met personally with Putin and other Russian leaders in Moscow.[420] Before the start of Trump's speech, Simes introduced Trump to the Russian Ambassador in Washington, Sergey Kislyak. It was at the same event that Kislyak first met future Attorney General Jeff Sessions and Trump's closest aides: Paul Manafort, Carter Paige, Michael Flynn and Jared Kushner.

Even in 2016, it was an odd choice. In the previous decade, Simes and his organization had become known for towing a slavish pro-Putin agenda. As a result of his defense of Russia's 2008 military invasion in Georgia, his long-standing connection to the Nixon family was severed: Politico reported in 2011, 'the Center and—particularly—its longtime president, Dimitri Simes, had become nothing less than an embarrassment to the Nixon family name. Simes, an imposing eminence of Russia policy, was—in their view—offering apologies for Russian autocrat Vladimir Putin and even attacking their party's presidential candidate, John McCain, for his denunciations of Russia's invasion of Georgia.'[421]

Already in 2014, Alana Goodman uncovered in a little-known piece in *Washington Free Beacon* that Republican unease began in 2000, Putin's first year in office: ironically, when he was shredding General Bobkov's rival media empire at Gusinsky's *Most* Group. 'Simes mounted a vigorous defense of the Kremlin.... His comments prompted an angry letter from the late US Ambassador to Russia Robert Strauss. "Dear Dimitri: You ought to be ashamed of yourself," wrote Strauss in a letter on Apr. 20, 2001.... "Irresponsible statements attributed to you... do a disservice to the new administration, the directors of The Nixon Center and many distinguished members of the American press. As for me personally, if you understood this country and its people a bit better, you would know the kind of personal references you make can only diminish The Nixon Center,' Strauss added.", she revealed.[422]

Trump, for whom the spigot of Russian money that had finally opened in 2008 had saved him from bankruptcy, and to whom Putin himself had unlocked further access to the vast financial dominion wielded by the Kremlin. Putin had made so much money, and there was more to be made. Putin was a knight in white armor. That was precisely why no one but Trump accepted Simes's invitation for advice on Russian interests.

Finally, the US Congress became interested in Simes's activities. In particular, the House Permanent Select Committee on Intelligence was interested whether Simes played a central role in drafting the Russian portions of Trump's foreign policy speech at the Mayflower Hotel, with Kushner, Flynn, Sessions, Simes and Ambassador Kislyak in attendance.[423]

Kushner took it upon himself to address the matter on July 26, 2017. In his testimony to the Congressional Committee, he made an interesting slip of the tongue, confusing the Committee members by claiming that not only Trump's speech but the CNI meeting itself were exclusively his (and not Simes's) idea—Simes being no more than the gopher:[424]

> The first that I can recall was at the Mayflower Hotel in Washington, DC, in April 2016. This was when then candidate Trump was delivering a major foreign policy speech. Doing the event and speech had been my idea, and I oversaw its execution. I arrived at the hotel early to make sure all logistics were in order. After that, I stopped into the reception to thank the host of the event, Dimitri Simes, the publisher of the bi-monthly foreign policy magazine, the *National Interest*, who had done a great job putting everything together.

However, he corrected this later. He evidently 'misspoke' and none other than 'Simes and his group had created the guest list and extended the invitations for the event.' Kushner also attempted to testify that he was, in fact, not in any form or shape involved in organizing and planning of the Mayflower meeting:

> I had no ongoing relationship with the Ambassador before the election, and had limited knowledge about him then. In fact, on November 9, the day after the election, I could not even remember the name of the Russian Ambassador. When the campaign received an email purporting to be an official note of congratulations from President Putin, I was asked how we could verify it was real. To do so I thought the best way would be to ask the only contact I recalled meeting from the Russian government, which was the Ambassador I had met months earlier, so I sent an email asking Mr Simes, 'What is the name of the Russian ambassador?'[425]

Kushner was apparently so unfocused on the event that he couldn't even remember the ambassador's name. Fortunately, he did remember Simes's name and emailed him, otherwise he might have had to use Google to find this hard-to-get information.

In fact, Kushner's testimony at the time did not tell the whole story. He had met Simes a month and a half prior, on March 14, 2016, at a lunch organized by the CNI, at Manhattan's Time Warner Center in honor of DC *éminence grise* Kissinger, *Bloomberg* reported:

> The main attraction of the March 14th event was Henry Kissinger, the Center's [CNI] honorary Chair, who gave a talk that included analyzing US-Russia relations for a small group of attendees,—writes Bloomberg. Kushner meeting Simes at the lunch turned out to be a solid match. In the weeks following they discussed the possibility of an event hosted by the center to give Trump a chance to lay out a cohesive foreign policy speech. Simes's organization, more pro-Russian than most in Washington, had invited other presidential candidates but none accepted.[426]

Due to the ongoing scandal and investigation, Kislyak was recalled to Russia on 11 July, 2017, after Trump's victory. For Simes, however, the event he organized at the Mayflower was the peak of his career as a Washington policy analyst and Kremlin collaborator.

Small wonder Simes received a great deal of attention in the Mueller Report ('Investigation into Russian Interference in the 2016 Presidential Election'). He was mentioned 49 times, and his testimony ranked eighth in number of citations. Simes, a journalist with a long and refined insight into the US media and security establishment, was open as to what his Mayflower advice included. In a CNN interview on April 24, 2019,[427] he said that he advised Kushner not to expose his connections to Russia and to handle these matters with great caution, something that was specially noted in the Mueller Report:

> Simes raised the issue of Russian contacts with Kushner, advised that it was bad optics for the campaign to develop hidden Russian contacts and told Kushner

both that the campaign should not highlight Russia as an issue and should handle any contacts with Russians with care.

It proved to be life-saving advice. The Mueller Report concluded that Russia 'interfered in the 2016 presidential election in sweeping and systematic fashion' violating US law, but absolved the Trump team. Simes's was such effective advice that Sessions even forgot to mention meeting Ambassador Kislyak in his application for security clearance. Simes knew exactly what was required. In March 2, 2017, CNI formally covered the same issue and said 'Mr Simes noted that Mr Sessions, then a senator from Alabama, was there, but he did not notice whether he and the ambassador spoke at that time'.[428] Flynn was to fall on his sword within weeks for failing to remember discussions with Kislyak.

How much disassociation was on his mind, Simes proved in a truly devastating argument (devastating to himself, that is). In the heat of the Mueller interrogation and the CNN interview, he was apparently not quite aware that this comment showed Simes to be a Russian agent: 'And more broadly [I suggested that], they should be extremely careful about any contacts with Russia during the campaign. I myself was not even a single time in Russia since Trump became a candidate and until 2017 when he already was president.'[429] In other words, Simes, a pivot in Putin's Icebreaker plan, denied himself trips to Russia after being introduced to Trump at the Mayflower meeting in order not to cause suspicion that he was being directed by the Kremlin-Lubyanka.

When did the Kremlin first insert its Operation Icebreaker into Simes's CNI to begin signaling to the Trump camp, and its pro-Putin candidate? It looked as if that moment came on June 12, 2015. On that day Russian agent Butina published a 'manifesto' in the pages of Simes's journal that was evidently not an accidental contribution by an innocent Russian graduate student studying at American University with Carmel Institute professor Fedyashin. It was a political appeal to Trump and the Republican Party to start a dialogue with Kremlin—four days before Trump's formal announcement of his Presidential candidacy.

It may take the election of a Republican to the White House in 2016 to improve relations between the Russian Federation and the United States. As improbable as it may sound, the Russian bear shares more interests with the Republican elephant than the Democratic donkey.… Perhaps a Republican president would look for ways to move past the increasing confrontation that has characterized the U.S.-Russia relationship in the past few years.… Perhaps only a Republican can repair relations between the U.S. and Russia today. How could a Republican president help in building that relationship? First, shared economic interests can lead to political resolutions.…

A second point of shared interest revolves around the global oil market. As long as America maintains its ban on selling its oil reserves to foreign markets,

American oil companies seeking international markets will need international sources of oil. Russia has them. Huge proven reserves in the Arctic and huge proven reserves of oil shale within the Russian mainland. But Russian oil companies lack the technology to exploit these reserves. And the current economic sanctions have frozen cooperative agreements like that between Russian Rosneft and American ExxonMobil like an Arctic drilling rig…. Finally, many Russians have taken note of recent Pew Research Center data that shows that the American Republican Party derives much of its support from social conservatives, businessmen and those that support an aggressive approach to the war against Islamic terrorism. … At the very least, it would appear that modern Russia has more to talk about with American Republicans than American Democrats. …My plea is simply to not surrender to what many view as inevitable conflict between these two great nations, no matter the consequences…. Global maps may be redrawn, global economies will ebb and flow, but chaos need not reign. A time may be coming when Russia and America can move from turmoil to calm.

Fatefully, Butina signed signed the article as 'The Founding Chair, The Right to Bear Arms [*Pravo na oruzhiye*], a Russian version of the NRA.'[430] According to Butina, the American 'Republican Elephant' (Trump) simply had to back down in order to save his own skin and cede ground to the 'Russian Bear' (Putin). The 'Bear' trope from then on appeared regularly in the pages of the *National Interest*. As a leading Russian expert, Simes must have known that no such association exists in Russia. The FBI experts certainly knew it and tracked how the Russian national began to worm her way into the US National Rifle Association (NRA) and Republican Party.

Georgi Kunadze, a former Deputy Minister of Foreign Relations of Russia (1991-3) and a research fellow at the IMEMO (where Simes worked during the Soviet times) certainly picked up on it. 'The first version of the article was an "instruction" of sorts to the new US President Trump, and the current version—the second one—concludes that he was not able to follow that "instruction".' He used this term in an article in Russian called, 'On the Usefulness of Useful Fools', a euphemism for a different term.

It is noteworthy that the former director of the NSA and CIA Michael Hayden referred to Trump by the same phrase: 'Trump is Russia's useful fool', though the term may have had a different meaning. 'We have really never seen anything like this. Former acting CIA director Michael Morell says that Putin has cleverly recruited Trump as an unwitting agent of the Russian Federation. I'd prefer another term drawn from the arcana of the Soviet era: *polezni durak*. That's the useful fool, some naïf, manipulated by Moscow, secretly held in contempt.'[431]

On Election Day, November 8, 2016, Simes no longer had to stay away from Russia and commented on Russian TV on the US elections. He stated falsehoods that evening that would have shocked his DC colleagues to the core in 2016 but would have caused shoulder shrugs from 2020:

Dimitri Simes, the political scientist and the President of The Center for the National Interest, is with us live, narrating how the Presidential Election voting is taking place in different States in the US…. 'I personally heard how the Clinton Campaign representative was describing the strategy of working with agitators'— Simes observes. 'Each agitator receives $300 per vote that is cast for the right candidate—in this case, Hillary Clinton.' In addition, Democratic Party organized transportation for the voters from the predominantly African-American and Latino neighborhoods. It is expected that they would be loyal to Hillary Clinton.[432]

Simes claim that he 'personally heard' US voters were given '$300 per vote' by the Clinton camp was the type of falsehood that became common during the 2020 US Presidential Election.

Simes gave another interview on that day—to the Russian newspaper *Izvestiya*, in Soviet times the official government paper, in which he told one 'little-known' story about the President, hinting that his trip to Moscow was paid for by the unknown interests. Simes emphasized that he did not have any evidence to support that claim.

He was not talking about Trump's trip to Moscow in 2013, for which, as is well known, he received $12.2 million through Russian billionaire Aras Agalarov regarding the 'Miss Universe' pageant. Instead, Simes told *Izvestiya* about a trip to Moscow 50 years ago, in 1968, by Bill, the husband of Hillary Rodham Clinton, Trump's opponent:

> Clinton and her entourage had a multitude of contacts in Russia at different levels. There is one little-known story. In December 1968, a few months after the Soviets invaded Czechoslovakia, a young anti-war activist Bill Clinton arrived in Moscow. He came to take part in the international forum of pacifists. While the majority of the guests of the forum stayed at hotels like 'Tourist,' Clinton stayed at 'National' for some reason. It was unusual back then. Only people for whom meetings at a certain level were planned could stay at such hotels, and not young students, especially since someone supposedly paid for his accommodation…. This topic was raised by Bush Sr.'s team during the Presidential Campaign of 1992, but there was no corroborating evidence.[433]

It was an extraordinary piece of KGB archive information Simes, a member of the American political elite, was releasing. Simes was of course good friends with all Putin's Ministers of Foreign Affairs. Igor Ivanov (1998-2004) was his colleague at IMEMO when headed by Primakov. When Igor Ivanov was succeeded by Lavrov started to meet regularly. Simes had official meetings with Lavrov in 2006, 2008, 2011 and 2016. It was no coincidence that the ministry's website featured such items as:

Yesterday, the Ministry of Foreign Affairs had a visit from the director and president of the Nixon Center, a major American think tank, Mr Dmitri Simes. Foreign Minister Lavrov had a lengthy conversation with Mr Simes in which the two discussed vital and urgent Russian problems.

This was not the only exceptional insight Simes had access to. After the infamous meeting in Helsinki between Trump and Putin on July 16, 2018, during the two-hour private conversation between the two presidents without staff, the Kremlin claimed, that as part of this conversation, Putin sought Trump's support for holding a referendum in the two Russian-occupied Ukrainian territories in the Lugansk and Donetsk—akin to the referendum held in Crimea, as Putin noted inadvertently. No further details regarding this provocative idea were released by the Kremlin, and, soon, the White House made clear that a Crimea-style referendum in these Donbas regions would not be supported.

Astonishingly, however, on July 20, four days later, on a US TV news program, Simes explained that the referendum under discussion had not been one regarding secession of Eastern Ukrainian regions but a referendum regarding Ukraine's entire autonomy.[434] This despite the fact that no such thing was ever hinted at by Putin, Lavrov, let alone the White House, or the US State Department. Simes must have obtained these additional details through channels open only to him.

In August 2018, the interest Simes attracted—among others, from the Mueller and congressional investigations looking into Russia's interference in the 2016 presidential election—became too much for him. He left for Russia, where he joined Russian television's Channel One as a host of *Bol'shaya Igra* (big game), a program created for Simes by Duma deputy Vyacheslav Nikonov. It launched on August 28.

Simes and Nikonov had known each other for years. Nikonov traveled frequently to the United States; whenever he came to Washington, he would go to see Simes before anyone else. Simes would always visit Nikonov on his trips to Moscow. Vyachelav Nikonov was a grandson of Vyacheslav Molotov, named after his grandfather. Nikonov's father, Alexei Nikonov (1917-1992), had worked for the NKVD and served as secretary of the KGB Party organization. Later, after becoming ARO officer, he was a professor at MSIIR and an editor at the Central Committee journal, *Kommunist*.

Vyacheslav Nikonov, who was admitted to the history program at MSU in 1973, confidently followed in his grandfather's and father's footsteps. After graduating from Moscow State University in 1978, he became a Party section chief. In 1991, he became an aide to KGB Chair Vadim Bakatin. In 1993 Nikonov became a deputy in the State Duma and a member of the presidium of the General Council of Putin's United Russia party. In 2007, President Putin appointed Nikonov executive director of the Russian World Fund; in 2011, he became the Fund's Chair of the board. The Russian World Fund, which has chapters in about 100 countries around the world, has been one of the main propagandas and recruitment instruments abroad for the Russian government and for state security.

The fact that it was for Nikonov that Simes went to work on television is both revealing and symptomatic. The Russian leadership (which has now merged with Russian state security) was demonstrating that it did not leave its fellow travelers in the lurch when they were forced to return to their native country or are exposed in the course of operations. All those who returned to Russia after carrying out their assignments received lucrative positions that allowed them to earn large amounts of money in Russia. This was true of Lugovoy, of Chapman, and of Butina, who was freed from the American jail after a five-month stay in detention plus time served and was sent back to Russia in October of 2018. And it was also true of Simes when he was forced to ask for a well-paid job in Moscow—which, of course, was done at once. Simes began a new 'big game'—this time on Russian rather than American soil.

It was a visible reminder for Chekists abroad that, in the Russian Federation, official 'case-files' are long and the Kremlin faithful when they remained close. After several nerve-racking weeks, realizing that even after the midterm elections no one in America was planning to arrest—especially with Trump firmly wedged in the White House—Simes gradually returned to the United States once again, even to give interviews once in a while, while reserving his right to the lucrative and comfortable safe haven on Channel One, with his colleague Nikonov. In the West, the Intelligence Services were comparatively understaffed and scrutiny public and short-lived.

The strength of the 5th Directorate lay in the subtle art of persuasion. The biggest testament to its scheming in the US may be with Americans such as Robert Merry, a regular author and one time at Simes's *National Interest*. On December 24, 2016, Robert Merry, published an article in the magazine called 'Stop Poking the Bear.'[435] On August 19, 2017, Merry published in the same periodical another article on the same topic, having changed only one word in the title: 'Stop Poking the Russian Bear.'[436] Merry's article was an accurate carbon copy of the Russian World as the Kremlin-Lubyanka would like it to be seen from the outside.

The gravest crisis facing America and the West is also the most unnecessary: the ominous deterioration in relations with Russia. Far from the danger posed during the Cold War, Russia nonetheless remains positioned upon the crucial Eurasian heartland, a strategic bastion that cannot be ignored. It has always been, and remains, a potential threat to Europe, and that must always be borne in mind. And yet the most provocative actions in this relationship in recent years have come from Europe, NATO and America—against Russia. NATO, a military alliance, has expanded right up to the Russian border. It has deployed components of a missile-defense shield in Poland and Romania. NATO has flirted with allowing both Georgia and Ukraine, both traditionally part of Russia's sphere of influence, into the Western alliance. US officials undermined the democratically elected leader of Ukraine, whose government tilted toward Russia, and have taken actions bent on pulling Ukraine from Russia's orbit. When Russia responded by securing Crimea, with its crucial harbor, and providing military support to rebels in eastern

Ukraine who don't want to be pulled Westward, the United States and Europe imposed debilitating economic sanctions.

All this has Russian officials seething. Although Western opinion has demonized President Vladimir Putin as an aggressive, land-hungry autocrat, he is but one official. The Kremlin is replete with elites who believe their country now is so beleaguered by these Western encroachments that they want an aggressive pushback strategy, even if it means war.

It could mean war. That would be a disaster for America and the West. For America, it would pull attention and resources away from much more serious strategic threats, most notably the rise of ISIS in the Middle East and the rise of China in Asia. For Europe, it likely would threaten the eastern nations liberated in 1989 after some forty-five years of Soviet domination.

But, of all the 2016 presidential candidates, only Donald Trump embraced a policy prescription designed to reverse the West's provocative eastward expansion, reduce tensions and test Russia's true intentions.

Trump should start with Ukraine, a land of crucial strategic significance to Russia, but of paltry strategic consequence to America. It is a tragically split country, with Western-oriented Ukrainians in the western regions and ethnic Russians in the eastern reaches. Russia has dealt with this delicate situation for decades; let it continue. Also, Russia's annexation of Crimea should never be allowed to sour relations between that country and the West, as Crimea had been part of Russia for centuries until artificially severed by Soviet leader Nikita Khrushchev. Besides, some 1.5 of its 2.3 million people are ethnic Russians. Let it go; withdraw the sanctions.

Second, the president should assure Russia that the West has no designs on Ukraine, Georgia, Moldova or Belarus—or, for that matter, any other nations identified with the Orthodox Christian tradition. No NATO designs....

So, give diplomacy a chance. End the Western provocations. Give the Russians some breathing room in their own neighborhood. And then, we can find out just how expansionist and threatening they really are. If it turns out that they want to be threatening even in the face of these conciliatory actions, then Western power, under American leadership, certainly is sufficient to handle the situation.[437]

The US was but one of the countries where the Lubyanka deployed its formidable power of carefully planned provocation.

Conclusion

Starting in December 1917, when the VChK was created, a battle for power began between the Communist Party and the VChK-OGPU-GPU-NKVD-MGB-KGB. This book argued that this twentieth-century battle remained invisible to anyone but the small group of Chekists and Party leaders at the top of the Lubyanka and the Kremlin. From the perspective of the Party, the early leaders who controlled the VChK-KGB tried to usurp Kremlin power for decades, sometimes succeeding in destroying the Party cadres. The Party leadership, in turn, won victories over the VChK-KGB and shot or eliminated the top State Security leadership, while simultaneously restructuring the agency itself, renaming it and making it less dangerous to the Party—or so it seemed during each reorganization.

With the formation of the KGB in the 1950s, the Party thought it had tamed the Lubyanka and the Lenin-Stalin cycle of violence around the Soviet Union as a whole. Shorn of their utopian zeal, however, the Party became an increasingly troubled administrator of the sprawling USSR, with the Politburo as its increasingly geriatric dictator. In November of 1982, after the death of Leonid Brezhnev, KGB Chair Andropov became the General Secretary of the CC and the Head of State. Thus, in 1982, for the first time since December 1917, the State Security finally achieved its cherished historical objective: absolute control over the State by Chekist technocrats.

It did not last long. Andropov died in 1984, and the Communist Party took the initiative once again. After a series of deaths among Kremlin elders vying for power, in March 1985, Mikhail Gorbachev came to power proclaiming '*glasnost* and *perestroika*.' It is incorrect, however, to suggest that *glasnost* and *perestroika* were the initiative of Mikhail Gorbachev alone. The decision was made collectively by the Politburo and at the cradle of its initial gestation stood one man, KGB General Yevgeny Pitovranov, head of the 4th Directorate, a man who saved his own life from Stalin's axe by writing such a compelling letter from jail that Stalin thereafter treated him with the utmost respect. He and Andropov formed a special group beyond the view of the Kremlin that was to hollow out the Politburo's hold over the Party through a carefully planned campaign of provocation.

In August, 1991, the KGB, under the leadership of General of the Army and Politburo Member and former Andropov KGB right-hand man Vladimir Kryuchkov, attempted a violent takeover of power. It was a coup directed not at overthrowing *perestroika*, but at overthrowing the Communist Party. And it succeeded in that. By the end of 1991, the CPSU and Gorbachev lost power, and the Soviet Union he led collapsed. New players entered the scene: in Moscow—President Yeltsin and his KGB bodyguard Korzhakov, in Leningrad—Sobchak and his assistant KGB Major Putin... The democratic revolution in Russia was just getting started, but the Chekist chess pieces were already arranged on the board. Alongside every democratic figure with a chance of gaining power in the Kremlin stood a KGB officer to control them.

In December of 1994, Yeltsin played right into the hand of the power ministries by allowing them to pull Russia into the First Chechen War provoked by the Lubyanka. He had very little room for maneuver as the same Lubyanka was provoking the largest party in the Duma—the Communists baying for his blood. Because of this, by March 1996, when Yeltsin prepared for the second Presidential Election to win his second and final term, he was both hampered by the fact he was not the head of a party of his own been and by the fact that he was so compromised in the eyes of the electorate. It seemed that he had no chance of beating the leader of the Communist Party of Russia Gennady Zyuganov in an election that wasn't 'managed' and he allowed the Lubyanka to create a false State of Emergency and extend his term by deceit—a coup in effect—which he only called off at the last moment. Thanks to the efforts of the 'oligarchs,' who were in turn controlled by Russia's Chekists via Generals Pitovranov and Bobkov, Yeltsin won the election for a second term. It remained unclear whether Yeltsin's Kremlin, in desperately trying to beat Zyuganov, engaged the Lubyanka in vote-counting fraud.

The Lubyanka, as an agency, learned a very important lesson from the 1991 coup against Gorbachev, the two against Yeltsin, and 1996 Presidential campaign: 'Democratic' Russia was no different from 'Soviet' Russia. It is a country whose central power can only be seized by capturing one post through the correct protocol—the Presidency. On May 7, 2000, the former director of the FSB under the letter of federal electoral law became the President of Russia. And that is how the story of the VChK/FSB's struggle for power in the USSR/Russia ended with the victory of the Chekists.

Yeltsin's 'democratic period' lasted less than nine years, from August 22, 1991, to December 31, 1999. It was a slice of democracy inherited by the Russian people from the failed August coup, dressed up as a State of Emergency Committee, but transparently an act of insubordination. In those nine years, Russia became a market economy with shareholder companies, open borders and a free press, the Soviet states finally faded away, and new sovereign states were created from the former Soviet Republics. A major domestic achievement of Yeltsin was the decentralization of the Russian government and rejection of the rigid centralized system that made Moscow the country's single decision center, far away from everyone.

Attempts to create a system of fair central and local elections fell victim to Russia's culture of corruption and the sabotage of the Lubyanka, which dispatched thousands of its own employees and agents around the country as candidates. In the end, Yeltsin was not able to create a robust democratic electoral system in Russia that was secure against Chekist usurpation. Moreover, he made the same mistake as before and allowed the FSB to pull Russia into a new Chechen War in 1999, organized according to the same false-flag scenario and objectives as the last one.

After all these years of corruption, the economy of Russia was left at the mercy of market prices for mineral resources. Neither the Soviet Politburo, nor 'Yeltsin-the-Reformer', nor 'Putin-the-Corrupt-Marketeer' were able to change this constant of Moscow rule.

Not wanting to, or unable to, compete with the West as a thriving economy, Putin proved more than competitive in launching the military and related campaigns. In particular, the military actions against Georgia in 2008 and Ukraine in 2014 were accompanied by anti-Georgian and anti-Ukrainian propaganda campaigns at a scale and intensity not previously seen, igniting nationalist sentiments among Russian citizens.

As a result of these incessant campaigns—in which television broadcasting, the press, and the Internet under the Intelligence Services' control played the most active role—a large part, if not the majority, of ordinary Russians went from being neutral or apolitical to militant-fascist. Western Democracies, like in Soviet times, were once again the mortal enemies of Russia. In contrast, Right-Wing nationalist forces inside the country and beyond its borders became the allies and partisans of the Kremlin and Lubyanka. Public, and, if necessary, clandestine support by the Russian leadership and the Lubyanka enhanced the influence of Right-Wing and Neo-Fascist movements in Russia and abroad—in Europe and in the US in particular.

Additionally, another powerful weapon was added to the arsenal of war: interfering in elections. Aided by the enormous potential created by social media's bias towards provocation to engage its audience and the diaspora of Russians who had emigrated from 1991, this turned out to be a far more effective and efficient way of weakening the enemy. Install your man in the top office, just as in Russia in 2000 and you use democracy against itself.

The specific strategic objectives of the Kremlin were also determined: starting wars in former Soviet Republics that did not join NATO yet in order to create an open military conflict and, by doing so, prevent the expansion of the North Atlantic alliance, which traditionally has not accepted countries with unresolved territorial disputes into its ranks; the weakening and dissolution of NATO; the collapse of the EU, by strengthening Right-Wing nationalist parties in Europe that are calling to leave the EU; expanding the territory of Russia by acquiring land from its neighbors. From 2000, Russia grew *de facto* by 268,128 sq. km with a population of 16,357 million (Transnistria, Abkhazia, South Ossetia, Crimea, and the Donetsk and Lugansk 'People's Republics,' seized from continental Ukraine).

Putin's latest, super-expensive export was nuclear blackmail of Europe and the United States, which the Russian President occasionally broadcast to a dumbfounded world in interviews, documentaries and cartoons. In 2018 documentary

Miroporyadok (world order), made at Putin's personal request, Putin himself said only true thing: '50 years ago, the streets of Leningrad taught me one rule: if a fight is unavoidable, make sure you throw the first punch.'

In the same film, in response to the director's question whether there will be a World War III, Putin answered: 'there will be, and we are going to win it'.

This was not the first but the second documentary about global thermonuclear war. The first one appeared after the Annexation of Crimea in March of 2014. In it, the Russian President said that Russia was ready to use a thermonuclear weapon if a military confrontation broke out over Crimea.

In *Miroporyadok,* Putin gave another ultimatum: to the countries who interfere with Russia's 'New World order,' it will not stop at using nuclear weapons. Considering the President's phrase about 'throwing the first punch,' Putin made his intentions regarding the 'Russian World' clear.

Carrying out such a plan is only possible in a country with a government system approaching an Italian-style fascist dictatorship, where a junta consisting of Intelligence Services officers hold the real power, regardless of Parliament or the government, like in Russia today. After two decades, the Cheka controlled the highest state, political, managerial, economic, and commercial posts in the country. FSB officers either serve in the senior leadership positions at major businesses or serve as the deputies of those who do, controlling the business in the interests of the Kremlin-Lubyanka.

The merging of state and big business is another classic element of a Fascist regime, when business is interested in having a strong State, government orders, and protection from foreign competition, and the state is interested in controlling business by putting pressure on shareholders and managers, or even dissolving businesses and arresting businessmen themselves, if that seems expedient 'in the interests of the State.' There is no independent business in Russia. Big business relies on the State in the form of the FSB and senior government officials; middle business relies on other officials and law enforcement personnel; small business relies on local authorities (depending on who the authority is in each specific case), numerous Active Reserve officers, and agents deployed in businesses. None of any longer bears resemblance to Yeltsin's free market economy.

The idea that your country is besieged by the enemy and that the rest of humanity lives exclusively to do as much harm as possible to your country and people was very beneficial for domestic consumption in Russia. However, it is not clear why the entire world would be preoccupied with the maniacal idea of hurting Russia. It is especially confounding why, alongside this trend, millions of representatives of the 'great Russian people' are emigrating from Russia to different cities around the world, and those remaining strive to acquire second citizenship or permanent residency in one of these countries they 'resent'.

But it remains a fact that most Russians (even those who very recently voluntarily left their homeland) suffer at heart because the rest of the world does not love them; or it does, but not selflessly; or it is polite, but not sincere; or it respects them, but does not fear them (that is, it does not respect them enough). This majority, according to surveys, are ready to surrender (or have already surrendered) freedom in exchange for stability; they do not need a free press and fair elections, and they are in favor of conquering neighboring countries—particularly if ethnic Russians live there, or if those countries once belonged (fully or partially) to ancient *Rus'* (a Slavic empire that started in Ukraine), the Russian Empire, or the Soviet Union.

The Russian leadership led by Putin was convinced that it was acting in the interests of Russia and the 'Russian World'—communities of Russian-speaking people scattered across the globe. And since there has been no free, equal, and anonymous vote within the 'Russian World' to approve or disapprove of Putin's policies, it was impossible to determine to what extent the 'Russian World' supported the aggressive and perhaps suicidal policy of the Russian leadership and whether this 'Russian World' even existed outside of Kremlin public relations department that controlled Russia Today, or RT TV as it was rebranded around the world.

The Kremlin's 'Russian World' did not promise people peace, kindness, prosperity and the rule of law. She brought war accompanied by destruction, depravity, and death that come with it as its natural byproduct. Eastern Ukraine, ruined and depopulated by the Russian army, as well as the bombed-out Lugansk and Donetsk, offered the best illustration of Putin's 'Russian World'—a war zone where Ukrainians are ordered to fight fellow Ukrainians under Russian commanders. This project was the sole reason why the Lubyanka seized the Russian Presidency on behalf of Russia's Chekists rather than its population. That was why the Lubyanka absorbed power across the entire country and stocked up resources—to throw all of it at restoring the 'Russian World' or 'Empire', intended to be as feared as the USSR once was when the Lubyanka did its bidding across Soviet borders. It did not really matter what they called 'their country' at this point.

History tells us that one can only deal with Fascism from a position of strength because neither the people who have gained power nor those brainwashed by them are able to independently leave the war path on which they find themselves. None of them fully realize the extent of danger and disaster that would result from traveling down the path of war—first and foremost, for themse, as well as for others.

Nonetheless, there remain a few encouraging lessons from history, too. An ideology based on the hatred and dominion of one population over another is doomed in the modern world. The sooner Russia realized that being 'Russia the Great' is a meaningless state for an ordinary country with its own ordinary people, the lower the price paid for waking her up from its Cheka-induced stupor. Saving Russia, and the rest of the world, from the Kremlin-Lubyanka's threat of a thermonuclear war, which Putin threatened more and more often, required just one stroke of the pen dissolving and abolishing the Lubyanka and terminating its Active Reserve program and prohibit its reformation under new names and acronyms. It may be better not to wait until 2036, the last year of Putin's term as President in case there was no one left to sign at that point.

[1] After the collapse of the USSR in December of 1991, former Russian Soviet Federative Socialist Republic (RSFSR) was renamed and became the Russian Federation or Russia. Both new names were approved as official names of the new state.

[2] The 'interdisrictites,' or *Mezhrayontsy*.

[3] The All-Russian Central Executive Committee.

[4] On April 28, 1918, the German occupation authorities arrested the Ukrainian government and made Hetman Pavel Skoropadsky, who supported a pro-Germany course, Ukraine's new ruler.

[5] People's Commissar of Foreign Affairs.

[6] Lev Karahan, the deputy People's Commissar of Foreign Affairs.

[7] *Germany and the Revolution in Russia, 1915-1918: Documents from the Archives of the German Foreign Ministry* by Z. A. B. Zeman. Oxford University Press. London. 1958.

[8] *Sed'moi ekstrennyi s'ezd RKP(b)*. P. 63.

[9] An ancillary conspiracy was the attempted assassination of the German consul in Petrograd. Long before July 6, two operatives, 'Mikhail' (M.A. Bogdanov) and 'Baron' (E.N. Malm) had been dispatched to Petrograd to carry out this terrorist act. However, since the assassination of the consul failed, we know very little about the details of this operation.

[10] *Krasnaya Kniga VChK (VChK Red Book)*. Vol. I. 2nd Ed. Moscow. 1989. p264.

[11] *Ibid.* p197.

[12] The German embassy had already forgotten about the matter. The Danish consulate was waiting for Robert Mirbach's release from the VChK. But two weeks passed, and Robert Mirbach was not released. Consequently, on June 26, Haxthausen, the consul general of Denmark, sent the VChK an official request to 'release from arrest the Austrian prisoner of war Count Mirbach on the condition of the consulate's guarantee that the said Count Mirbach will present himself before the Extraordinary Commission [VChK] as soon as he is requested to do so until the investigation [of the Landström case] is concluded.' Haxthausen's request, however, was denied.

[13] 'I, the undersigned, German citizen, prisoner of war and officer of the Austrian army Robert Mirbach, pledge voluntarily and of my own free will' to convey to the VChK 'secret information about Germany and the German embassy in Russia.' Ibid. P. 200.

[14] There was no signed text of the 'pledge' in German; at least, no one ever saw such a text, nor was it ever submitted into evidence. It's entirely possible that Robert Mirbach never even saw, let alone signed it.

[15] The first edition of the *VChK Red Book* was published in 1920 but was quickly taken out of circulation and became a bibliographic rarity.

[16] Even the German Ministry of Foreign Affairs now knew about the Chekists' commotion around the German embassy and the case invented by them.

[17] Dzerzhinsky took no interest in any of this, except for the names of the German embassy's informers.

[18] The Germans agreed to meet with Dzerzhinsky at the Metropol Hotel and brought one of their informers, who confirmed to Dzerzhinsky that as far as he knew the assassination was being planned for July 5 or 6 and that VChK agents were involved in the operation.

[19] The People's Commissariat of Foreign Affairs

[20] The authorization read: 'The All-Russian Extraordinary Commission authorizes its member Yakov Blumkin and Revolutionary Tribunal representative Nikolai Andreyev to enter negotiations with the German ambassador to the Russian Republic concerning a matter that has a direct relation to the ambassador. Chair of the All-Russian Extraordinary Commission: F. Dzerzhinsky. Secretary: Ksenofontov.' *Ibid.* p195. Riezler and the embassy interpreter, Lieutenant Leonhart Müller, came out to talk to the VChK agents; for them, the visit from Blumkin and Andreyev was a continuation of Riezler's conversation with Karahan that morning. All four proceeded to the reception hall and took their seats around a large marble table.

[21] Blumkin informed the ambassador that he had come to discuss the case of Robert Mirbach who was involved in a 'case of espionage.' For confirmation, Blumkin presented documents of some kind. Mirbach replied that he 'had nothing in common with this officer' and that 'this matter was completely foreign to him.' Blumkin responded that in ten days this matter would be taken up by the Revolutionary Tribunal. Andreyev, who had not taken part in the conversation up to this time, asked whether the German diplomats would like to know what kinds of measures will be taken by the tribunal in the Robert Mirbach case. The same question was repeated by Blumkin. Evidently, this was a cue. Mirbach, suspecting nothing, replied in the affirmative. With the words 'I will now show you,'

[22] Blumkin also fired at Müller and Riezler (but missed). They were so stunned that they remained seated in their deep armchairs (they were unarmed). Blumkin continued shooting at Riezler and Müller but kept missing.

[23] After that, Blumkin, who had injured his leg jumping from the window and was wounded (also in the leg) by an embassy guard who opened fire on the terrorists as they ran, no longer had any direct involvement in the events. Andreyev, who killed the German ambassador, had disappeared somewhat earlier. For some reason, it was Blumkin, not Andreyev, who got all the credit for the Mirbach assassination.

[24] Ksenofontov had also signed it.

[25] A little after 3pm, Karl von Bothmer, an embassy official, and Müller, the interpreter, took the embassy's car and drove to the People's Commissariat of Foreign Affairs, at the Metropol Hotel.

[26] Georgy Chicherin, the first People's Commissar for Foreign Affairs.

[27] Trotsky did not join them since he did not want to play the hypocrite. Chicherin and called Trotsky at the ministry of defence.

[28] Except by the Chekists themselves and the editors of *VChK Red Book*, which was quickly recalled. The authorization issued to Blumkin and Andreyev and bearing the signatures of Dzerzhinsky and Ksenofontov has been published by historians on many occasions, always with the disclaimer that Dzerzhinsky's and Ksenofontov's signatures were 'forgeries.' Those signatures certainly didn't look 'forged,' even though Dzerzhinsky did testify that his signature had been 'copied by Blumkin.' But what else could Dzerzhinsky say, given that he was denying any complicity in the operation carried out by Chekists on July 6?

[29] On a possible breakdown of the peace treaty.

[30] *Izvestiya VTsIK* (newspaper). July 8, 1918. No. 141.

[31] V.I. Ginch and Benderskaya.

[32] On August 26, 1918, Sverdlov sent a letter to the Vologda party committee signed with a new title: 'CC Chair Yakov Sverdlov.' *Izvestiya TsK KPSS*. 1989. No. 5. P. 155.

[33] Ya. Peters. *Vospominaniya o rabote VChK v pervyi god revolutsii.—Byloe* (journal) [Paris], No. 2. 1933. P. 110.

[34] *Vystrel v serdtse revolutsii.* Edited by N. D. Kostin. Moscow. 2nd Ed. 1989. Chapter 1. P. 1. Here and in a few other instances, texts and quotations are taken from Web editions that do not indicate the exact numbers of the corresponding pages in paper format.

[35] Lenin's pronouncement was cited and quoted on January 21, 1929, at a formal assembly commemorating the fifth anniversary of Lenin's death, when Anatoly Lunacharsky—a famous Bolshevik and the People's Commissar of Education—delivered a tedious speech with the mawkish title, 'Radiant Precious Genius.' Lunacharsky expatiated on the fact that, for Lenin, the internal enemy within the party was more dangerous than the external one and quoted Lenin.

[36] A. V. Lunacharsky. *Siyauchshii dorogoi genii. (Radiant Precious Genius).* Speech delivered on January 21, 1929, at a formal assembly commemorating the fifth anniversary of Lenin's death. Transcript. – Dialog (journal). Moscow. 1995. No. 3. P. 66.

[37] Leonid Kannegisser.

[38] Grigory Semenov and Lidiya Konopleva.

[39] Semenov (also known as Semenov-Vasiliev) and Konopleva,

[40] They said during the trial of the SR Party that they had tried to kill Lenin at the direction of the Central Committee of the SR Party. It is quite clear that they were not SR hitmen as Soviet prosecutors publicly charged during the trial.

[41] Before the Revolution, they would have been considered classic provocateurs. In the modern world, they would be called intelligence agents operating in the enemy's camp, classic 'illegals.'

[42] GPU/OGPU/NKVD.

[43] Transcript of the trial – *Istochnik* (journal). Moscow, 1993. No. 2. P. 72.

[44] Pavel Mal'kov.

[45] P. Mal'kov. *Zapiski komendanta Kremlya.* p146.

[46] *Fanni Kaplan. Ili Kto strelyal v Lenina?* Collected documents. Ed. by Professor A. Litvin. Kazan. 1995. P. 118.

[47] *Fanni Kaplan. Ili Kto strelyal v Lenina?* P. 122.

[48] *Istochnik.* 1993. No. 2. P. 80-81; *Fanni Kaplan. Ili Kto strelyal v Lenina?* P. 153-156, 171-177.

[49] *Fanni Kaplan. Ili Kto strelyal v Lenina?* P. 131.

[50] Kaplan had another significant defect as an assassin: she was half-blind and very hard of hearing.

[51]

[52] *Istochnik.* 1993. No. 2. P. 80.

[53] P. Mal'kov. Zapiski komendanta Kremlya p146.

[54] *Istochnik.* 1993. No. 2. P. 160.

[55] Ibid. P. 73.

[56] Avel Enukidze, Leonid Serebryakov, and Nikolai Krestinsky.

[57] Nikolai Bukharin, Ivan Smirnov and Matvei Shkiryatov.

[58] *Fanni Kaplan. Ili Kto strelyal v Lenina?* P. 19.

[59] Ibid. P. 32-33; *Istochnik.* 1993. No. 2. P. 72.

[60] Volodarsky, Uritsky, Trotsky, Zinoviev.

[61] In particular, Alexander Kolchak and Anton Denikin.

[62] Thus, the organizers of the attack on Lenin in August 1918 were rehabilitated in the USSR not even as part of the general wave of rehabilitations in 1956, when victims of Stalinist terror were being rehabilitated en masse, but by individual resolutions of the military tribunal in 1960 and 1961.

[63] Among other top Soviet leaders. At some point, no later than January 1937, the GPU began collecting compromising information for the trial of Bukharin.

[64] *Materials of the February/March plenary session of the CC of the Communist Party, 1937.—Voprosy istorii* (journal). Moscow. 1992. No. 2—3. C. 27-28.

[65] *Bol'shaya Sovetskaya Entsiklopediya.* 1st Ed. Moscow. Vol. 36. 1938. The entry, "Lenin and Leninism." P. 374.

[66] *Istochnik.* 1993. No. 2. P. 86-87.

[67] Why ???

[68] *Vystrel v serdtse revolutsii.* P. 148.

[69] V. D. Bonch-Bruevich. *Tri pokusheniia na Lenina.* Moscow. 1930. P. 81.

[70] P. Mal'kov. Zapiski komendanta Kremlya p154.

[71] Alexei Rykov.

[72] Chair of the Executive Committee and Secretary of the CC, Chair of the Politburo and Chair of the CC.

[73] V. D. Bonch-Bruevich. *Tri pokusheniia na Lenina.* P. 102.

[74] Reynbot.

[75] Varlam Avanesov.

[76] People's Commissar for Military and Naval Affairs.

[77] The government of Max von Baden, with the participation of the leader of the right wing of Germany's Social-Democrats, Philipp Scheidemann, came to power.

[78] With Karl Liebknecht.

[79] Drawing its membership from the ranks of the Spartacist movement and the radical left wing of the German Social Democratic Party

[80] Wife of the future Commissar of Internal Affairs Yagoda (Sverdlov's second cousin).

[81] V. Bonch-Bruevich. *Lenin v Petrograde i Moskve.* Moscow. 1982. P. 55-56.

[82] Grigory Zinoviev.

[83] People's Commissar of Internal Affairs.

[84] Leonid Serebryakov in a letter to Alexander Vinokurov, People's Commissar of Social Welfare

[85] Yet the identities of the three who are to constitute the Directory are not entirely clear. The Executive Committee has withdrawn Rykov's candidacy. It is true that Kamenev is fighting hard for him, but we well understand that he needs Rykov only as a screen, a loyal minion. As for Stalin, he has flatly refused to work with Kamenev.... I have already drawn attention to this, but all our colleagues are completely consumed by their own squabbles and rivalry, and they pay no attention to my words, with the sole exception of Stalin—who, it seems, is the only person to see things as they really are. The letter was published in in *Rul'* on August 2, 1922 in back-translation from English.

[86] As we will demonstrate below, Trotsky was being inexact: Stalin's remarks at the Politburo were made on March 17, 1923, not in February of that year.

[87] 'But what can one do if it is suggested by the situation, by the facts, and particularly by the personality of Stalin? Lenin warned us urgently in 1921: 'This cook will prepare only spicy dishes.' It turned out that the dishes were not just spicy, but poisoned, and not just figuratively, but literally... In front of

me, I saw Kamenev, silent and pale… and Zinoviev, at a loss, as always during critical moments. Did they know about Lenin's request before the meeting? Or had Stalin sprung unexpected news on his allies in the triumvirate as well? 'I told him all that,' Stalin objected, not without disappointment, 'but he just waves it off. The old man is in pain. He says he wants to have poison near him … he will resort to it if he becomes convinced that his situation is hopeless.' 'All the same, it is out of the question,' I insisted, this time, I believe, with Zinoviev supporting me. 'He can fall prey to a temporary impression and take an irreversible step.' 'The old man is in pain,' Stalin kept repeating, looking absently past us and still not taking either one side or the other….' L. Trotsky. *Portrety revolutsionerov.* Moscow. 1991. P. 65-79.

88 'Stalin acted as he would have if Lenin had already been dead. But the patient thwarted his expectations…. It was at this moment that Stalin must have decided for himself that he had to take immediate action. He was surrounded by collaborators whose fate was completely tied up with his own. The pharmacist Genrikh Yagoda was near at hand.' Trotsky indicated only one date in his article—February 1923—which was wrong. L. Trotsky. *Portrety revolutsionerov.* Moscow. 1991. P. 65-79.

89 Abdurakhman Avtorkhanov, *Novyi Zhurnal (The New Review).* New York. 1983. Book 152. P. 240-259.

90 Ibid. P. 251.

91 *Istochnik.* 1993. No. 2. P. 70.

92 Rykov, Kamenev, and Alexander Tsyurupa.

93 The Transcaucasian Regional Committee was their counterpart.

94 Lidiya Fotieva.

95 Doctors Vasily Kramer and Alexei Kozhevnikov.

96 V.I. Lenin. *The Complete Collected Works.* Vol. 45. P. 710.

97 *Pravda.* February 26, 1988, No. 57.

98 Yegor Yakovlev. *Poslednii intsident. Konspect dramy Vladimira Il'icha.—Moskovskie Novosti [Moscow News]* (newspaper). January 22, 1989, No. 4. P. 8-9.

99 *The Trotsky Papers,* 1917-1922. Vol. 2. The Hague. 1971. P. 760-762.

100 Maria Ulyanova.

101 Ibid. No. 12. P. 198.

102 On the history of the final Lenin papers. From the archives of the writer Alexander Bek who spoke to Lenin's personal secretaries in 1967. *Moskovskie Novosti,* April 23, 1989. No. 17, p. 8-9. [Infra: A. Bek's Archive.]

103 V.I. Lenin. *The Complete Collected Works.* Vol. 45. P. 591-592.

104 Stalin, Kamenev, and Bukharin (the three, it is important to note, were acting in concert against Lenin).

105 Ibid. P. 710.

106 Fotieva. *Vospominaniya o Lenine.* April, 1938. A.I. Marshak's publication.—*Sputnik* (journal), April 1990. No. 4. P. 50.

107 Ibid.

108 N. Krupskaya. *O Lenine.* Collection of articles and speeches. 5th ed. Moscow. 1983. P. 84-85.

109 Maria Volodicheva.

110 Fotieva.

111 And its Organizational Bureau. It was signed by Politburo and Organizational Bureau members Andreyev, Bukharin, Dzerzhinsky, Kalinin, Kamenev, Kuibyshev, Molotov, Rykov, Stalin, Tomsky, and Trotsky.

112 Maria Ulyanova.

113 'The fact that Lenin made such a request of Stalin is open to serious doubt: by this time, Lenin regarded Stalin without any trust, and it is not clear how he could have turned to him, of all people, with such an intimate request. This fact acquires particular significance considering another story.' B. Nikolaevsky. *Tainye stranitsy istorii.* Moscow. 1995. P. 228-229.

114 *Ot pervogo litsa. Pazgovory s Vladimirom Putinym (Conversations with Vladimir Putin).* Moscow. 2000. C. 7

115 Fotieva.

116 V. I. Lenin. *The Complete Collected Works.* Vol. 45. P. 485-486, 607.

117 Volodicheva

118 V. I. Lenin. *The Complete Collected Works.* Vol. 54. P. 329.

119 Volodicheva

120 *Arkhiv Trotskogo. Kommunisticheskaya oppozitsiya v SSSR, 1923-1927.* Documents and materials from the Trotsky archives in four volumes. Compiled and edited by Yu. Felshtinsky. Vol. 1. 1923-1926. Moscow. 1990. P. 35.

121 V. I. Lenin. *The Complete Collected Works.* Vol. 54. P. 329-330.

122 Ibid. Vol. 54. P. 330.

123 Ibid. Vol. 45. P. 486.

124 Volodicheva.

125 'I was advised by my comrades, in particular [Lenin's secretary] Maria Ignatievna Glasseur. [...] She said that it was absolutely necessary to go in and show this letter to Kamenev, because Stalin might write something that could aggrevate Lenin. Kamenev read it and returned it to me saying that the letter could be handed over.'

126 Volodicheva.

127 Maria Ulyanova.

128 A. Bek's Archive.

129 I. Stalin. *The Collected Works* (in Russian). Vol. 16. 1946-1952. Moscow. 1997. P. 252.

130 *Arkhiv Trotskogo.* Vol. 1. P. 89.

131 L. Trotsky. *Portrety revolutsionerov.* P. 77.

132 N. Valentinov-Volsky. *Nasledniki Lenina.* Moscow. 1991. P. 214.

133 Yves Delbars. *The Real Stalin.* George Allen & Unwin Ltd. London. 1951. P. 124—130.

134 Arrested on the night of December 1, 1934, in connection with the murder of Sergei Kirov

135 Elizabeth Lermolo. *Face of a Victim.* Harper & Brothers Publishers, New York. 1955. P. 132-137.

136 L. Trotsky. *Portrety revolutsionerov.* P. 77-78.

137 Maria Ulyanova.

138 Fotieva.

139 Paul Lafargue, Karl Marx's son-in-law, committed suicide with his wife in 1911 by swallowing cyanide. Lafargue was seventy.

140 Stylistically too, the note smacks of forgery. Lenin could not have 'dictated' the phrase: 'Do not forget to take all measures to acquire and… deliver.' Only Stalin could have dictated that. Nor could Lenin have said that he was intending to do away with himself 'as a humane measure and in emulation of Lafargue.' That phrase also, in its entirety, could have come from Stalin. On December 22, a day before he started to work on his 'Last Testament,' Lenin would hardly have been thinking

about how best to emulate Lafargue in suicide

141 L. Shatunovskaya. *Zhizn' v Kremle*. New York. 1982. P. 227-230.

142 He candidly told me of his conviction that Stalin had actively and deliberately accelerated Lenin's death, since no matter how sick Lenin was, if he lived the road to absolute dictatorship was closed to Stalin

143 Ibid. P. 232-235.

144 Stalin had four meetings with writers in 1932. They were hosted by Gorky at his home, in the former Ryabushinsky mansion. These meetings were not recorded by a stenographer, but the literary critic Korneli Zelinsky attended one of them. (*Voprosy literatury* [journal]. 1989. No. 2. P. 154, 169).

145 K. Zelinsky. *A Meeting at M. Gorky (diary entry)*. Published by A. Zelinsky. *Voprosy literatury*. May 1991. P. 144-170.

146 The book *Unknown Lenin: From the Secret Archive*, edited by American historian Richard Pipes (Yale University Press, 1996, p. 77), has a photo of Dzerzhinsky walking at the head of the Politburo members who served as Lenin's pallbearers. Dzerzhinsky himself was not a Politburo member.

147 Stalin, Zinoviev, Kamenev, Bukharin, Vyacheslav Molotov, Yan Rudzutak, Dzerzhinsky.

148 While Lenin's devoted comrades-in-arms stood freezing at the funeral.

149 Until February 1922, he was the Chair of the VChK. From March 1, 1922 onward, the Chair of the GPU at the NKVD of the RSFSR.

150 The People's Commissar of Internal Affairs etc.

151 Even after the birth of the USSR the all-union NKVD was not created until 1934.

152 Stalin became the head of state via the Secretariat of the Party's Central Committee.

153 Ignatii (Ludvig) Reiss was a Soviet intelligence officer who defected in Europe in the summer of 1937. He was murdered by Soviet intelligence in Switzerland, near Lausanne, on September 4, 1937.

154 N. Valentinov-Volsky. *Nasledniki Lenina*. P. 214, 216-217.

155 The 'Mikhail Tukhachevsky plot'.

156 *I.V. Stalin's speech at the People's Commissariat of Defense.* — *Istochnik*. 1994. No. 3. P. 72—88.

157 In full support of Ordzhonikidze and Stalin.

158 *Istochnik*. 1996. № 4. C. P. 103.

159 21.

160 On July 20, 1920, Menzhinsky became the head of the Special Department of the VChK from which a separate Foreign Department was split off in December 1920. The Special Department also became the basis for the VChK's Secret Operative Directorate, which included the Information Department, the Secret Department, the Operative Department, and the Foreign Department. In July 1927, a year after Dzerzhinsky's death, Yagoda replaced Menzhinsky as Secret Operative Unit chief.

161 On July 20, 1920, Menzhinsky became the head of the 'Special Department' of the VChK from which a separate Foreign Department was split off in December 1920. The 'Special Department' in turn became the basis for the VChK's Secret Operative Directorate, which included the Information Department, the Secret Department, the Operative Department, and the Foreign Department. In July 1927, a year after Dzerzhinsky's death, Yagoda replaced Menzhinsky as

Secret Operative Unit chief.

162 Unlike Dzerzhinsky, Yagoda, Yezhov, or Beria.

163 People's Commissar of Internal Affairs.

164 On the other hand, nearly all high-level commanding officers in the Red Army were victims of violent elimination during those years.

165 People's Commissar of Internal Affairs.

166 People's Commissar of Communications

167

168 People's Commissar of Internal Affairs.

169 Lenin's younger sister Maria I. Ulyanova had died somewhat earlier, on June 12, 1937—the day of the execution of the Red Army's military leaders, including Tukhachevsky, who had been accused of a conspiracy against the Soviet regime.

170 the People's Commissar of Internal Affairs.

171 By then, the people's commissariats had been changed to ministries.

172 After Kirov's murder.

173 The MGB was formally called "The MBG of the USSR." In order to facilitate reading, we will use the abbreviated "MGB" except when quoting or referencing official documents.

174 Shcherbakov had been a candidate member of the Politburo of the Communist Party CC since 1939, First Secretary of the Moscow City Party Committee since 1941, head of the Chief Political Directorate of the Red Army and simultaneously head of Soviet news agency since 1942; he had also headed the CC's International Information Department in 1943-1945.

175 He held multiple posts at the time, including the People's Commissar of Internal Affairs, the Minister of Defense and the Head of the Council of People's Commissars.

176 It is in the context of all these events, as if rewinding the tape back several years, that one should consider the removal, arrest and execution of Colonel General Viktor Abakumov, the Minister for State Security of the Soviet Union:
From a report by the CC of the Communist Party
Regarding the Troubled Conditions in the Ministry of State Security of the Soviet Union
11 July 1951
On July 2, 1951, the CC received a statement from Comrade Ryumin, Senior Special Matters Investigator at the Ministry of the Intelligence Services, in which he described the dire situation within the Ministry with respect to investigations of major national criminal offenders and placed the responsibility for these omissions on Comrade Abakumov, the Minister of Intelligence Services.
Upon receiving Comrade Ryumin's statement, the CC created the Politburo Commission consisting of Comrades Malenkov, Beria, Shkiryatov and Ignat'ev, and tasked them with confirming the information provided by Comrade Ryumin. As part of its investigation, said commission questioned Comrade Leonov, Head of the Major Crimes Unit of the Investigation Department—Ministry of State Security, and his deputies, Comrades Likhachev and Komarov; Comrade Shubnyakov, Head of the Second Chief Directorate, and his deputy Comrade Tangyiyev; Comrade Putinzev, Assistant to the Head of the Major Crimes Unit of the Investigation Department; Comrades Ogoltsov and Pitovranov, Deputy Ministers of State Security; and, of course, heard from Comrade Abakumov himself.
The investigation confirmed the facts stated in Comrade Ryumin's statement, and therefore the CC removed Comrade Abakumov from his post with immediate effect and appointed

his First Deputy Comrade Ogoltsov as a temporary Minister of the Intelligence Services. This occurred on July 4, 1951.

Based on the investigation, the Politburo Commission established the following facts.

1 In November of 1950, Dr Etinger, a Jewish nationalist who held strong anti-Soviet views, was arrested. Upon being questioned by Comrade Ryumin, Senior Special Matters Investigator at the Ministry of State Security, and without any undue pressure, Dr Etinger admitted that he treated Colonel General Alexander Shcherbakov with criminal intent, and employed all practical means available, to cut short his patient's life. The CC believes that this admission by Dr Etinger merits serious attention. Without doubt, a criminal conspiracy exists among some medical doctors, with the ultimate goal of inflicting serious harm to the physical health and well-being of the leaders of the Communist Party and the Soviet Government in the course of medical treatment. Let us not forget the crimes committed by Drs Pletnyov and Levin who carried out the orders from foreign intelligence by poisoning Valerian Kuibyshev and Maxim Gorky. These villains confessed to their crimes in open court, and Levin was executed while Pletnyov got a 25-year prison sentence.

However, the Minister of the Intelligence Service Comrade Abakumov, having obtained Dr Etinger's testimony about his terrorist activities, characterized said testimony as 'far-fetched' in the presence of Investigator Ryumin, Deputy Head of the Major Crimes Unit of the Investigation Department Likhachev and Dr Etinger himself. Comrade Abakumov also stated at the time that the case does not warrant any further attention, led Ministry of Internal Affairs into a maze and closed the case. Despite all this, Comrade Abakumov disregarded the advice of Ministry's physicians and placed Dr Etinger, who was seriously ill, in knowingly dangerous conditions—that is, a damp and cold prison cell—which led to Etinger's death in prison on March 2, 1951.

Accordingly, by closing the Etinger case, Comrade Abakumov prevented the CC from exposing a clearly existing criminal conspiracy perpetrated by a group of medical doctors who carried out subversive terroristic activities working on behalf of foreign intelligence against the leaders of the Communist Party and the Soviet Government. It must be noted herewith that Comrade Abakumov did not deem it important to inform the CC of Dr Etinger's confession and thusly concealed this important matter from Party and Government leaders.

In view of the foregoing, the CC hereby directs as follows: 1. That Comrade Abakumov be removed from the post of the Minister of the Intelligence Services as an individual who committed a crime against the Communist Party and the Soviet Union; that he be expelled from the ranks of the Communist Party of the Soviet Union; and that his case be referred to court. 2. That Comrades Leonov and Likhachev be removed from their posts as the Head of the Major Crimes Unit of the Investigation Department—Ministry of State Security and Deputy Head of the Major Crimes Unit of the Investigation Department, respectively, due to them acting as Comrade Abakumov's accomplices in the plot to deceive the Communist Party; and that these individuals be likewise expelled from the Communist Party ranks. 3. That Comrades Ogoltsov and Pitovranov, First Deputy Minister of State Security and Deputy Minister of the Intelligence Services, respectively, be issued a severe reprimand for their lack of Party spirit and urgency in reporting to the Communist Party leadership the unfortunate situation that has arisen at the Ministry of State Security. 4. That the Ministry of State Security resume its investigation of the terrorist activity by Dr Etinger.

177 Also, Deputy Minister of the CPSU Central Control Committee Shkiryatov; and finally, Head of the Department of the Communist Party Governing Board (and the one who was to replace Abakumov as the new Minister of the Intelligence Service) Ignat'ev

178 Also Ignat'ev.

179 The formal name of the "KGB" is the "KGB of the USSR" or the "State Security Commission". When referenced herein, we will use the term "KGB" except when citing to official documents.

180 Belonging to the Chief Directorate of the Guard of the Ministry of the Intelligence Services. Yegorov, born in 1926, retired in 1961 as a guard officer of KGB Chair Alexander Shelepin.

181 In early November 1936, taking advantage of the civil war in Spain, Soviet intelligence stole nearly three quarters of the Spanish government's gold reserve—about 600 tons, in gold bars and coins—and transported it to the USSR. This gold was not returned even after the deaths of Stalin and Franco. Officially, the theft was disguised as a request by the Spanish republican government to take the gold to the USSR for safekeeping during the civil war.

182 Two and a half months after Pasternak's death—August 16, 1960—Ivinskaya was arrested again. On September 5, 1960 her daughter, Irina Yemel'anova, born in 1938, was also arrested. She was released in October 1964.

183 By order of the Presidium of the Supreme Soviet of the USSR.

184 In 1973, Andropov became the second State Security leader after Beria who was also the Politburo member.

185 The formal name of the PGU was the PGU of the KGB of the USSR. For more comfortable reading, when not discussing quotations or formal documents, we will use the abbreviated "PGU."

186 The formal name of the VGU was the VGU of the KGB of the USSR. For more comfortable reading, when not discussing quotations or formal documents, we will use the abbreviated "VGU."

187 Department V of Directorate S.

188 Lyalin's defection led to the deportation on September 25, 1971 of 105 Soviet diplomats from Great Britain. Lyalin worked in the 5th Department of the PGU, which handled methods for terror attacks and sabotage in enemy territory. Formally, he was considered an employee of the USSR's trade office in London. Oleg Kalugin writes in his memoirs that Andropov gave the order to kill Lyalin, but the KGB could never find him, as Lyalin had changed his name and appearance. However, on February 12, 1995, at the age of 57, Lyalin died.

189 Sakharovsky passed away in 1975.

190 However, different directors described its functions differently. Department V was named for the last name of its first director—Colonel Vladimir Viktorov. The office was renamed and became the 8th Department in 1976 as punishment for the non-return of its officer Lyalin from England in August 1971. Kiselev's predecessor in 1965-1966 was B.S. Ivanov.

191 A. Kiselev. Stalinsky favorit s Lubyanki. 2003. P. 115

192 V.N. Stepankov, A.V. Kiselev, E.P. Sharapov. *Chekisty Stalina.* SPB. 2006. P. 440.

193 A. Kiselev. *Stalinsky favorit s Lubyanki.* P. 138.

194 In 1991, Khlystov took the post of Minister of Trade in the first Russian government.

195 A. Prokhanov. *Taina perestroiki. – Zavtra,* No. 26, June 30, 2010

196 O. Grinevsky. *Perelom. Ot Brezhneva k Gorbachevu.* Moscow. 2004. P. 135.

197 The formal name of the 5th Directorate is the 5th Directorate of the KGB of the USSR. For more comfortable reading, when not discussing quotations or formal documents, we will use the abbreviated "5th Directorate."

198 *Vlast'*(magazine). No. 16. April 26, 2004

199 *Chekisty Stalina.* P. 442.

200 On September 10, 1981, by KGB order No. 00170, a different KGB 4th Directorate was created at the Administrative Base T of the Second Chief Directorate of the KGB; its task was counterintelligence for the purpose of safeguarding transportation and communications.

201 'On changes in the structure of the State Security Committee (KGB) under the Council of Ministers of the USSR and its local agencies and on reductions in their staffing'.

202 When the 5th Directorate of the KGB was created by the July 17, 1967 resolution of the Politburo of the CC, Bobkov became its First Deputy Chief; on May 23, 1969, after Kadashev's resignation, he was appointed Chief of the 5th Directorate. In 1983, Bobkov also became deputy Chair of the KGB.

203 Interview with Yegor Yakovlev. — *Fakty I kommentarii,* March 23, 2000.

204 V. Syrokomsky, "The Patriarch's Enigma," *Znamya* magazine, No. 4, 2001.

205 V. Syrokomsky, "The Enigma of the Patriarch."

206 The Soviet composer Rodion Shchedrin also worked closely with Pitovranov as one of his agents. They were introduced to each other by another long-time Soviet State Security agent: Vasily Katanyan, married since 1937 to Lilya Brik, whose previous lovers included the legendary Chekist Yakov Agranov (executed in 1938). Brik—like her last husband, Katanyan—was part of State Security's network of agents. The couple hosted a literary salon where writers, artists and other cultural workers would gather. It was at their place that Shchedrin met his future wife, the ballerina Maya Plisetskaya.

207 Stanislav Kunyayev, "Treason is the Sale of Inspiration." — *Nash Sovremennik* magazine, 2005, No. 7.

208 *Kto yest' kto* [Who Is Who] magazine, 2008, No. 6.

209 Vladimir Voinovich, "Case Number 34840," — Vladimir Voinovich, *The Plan,* Moscow: Eksmo, 2003.

210 In 1983-1990, Kochemasov worked in East Germany a second time, in the post of extraordinary and plenipotentiary ambassador. In the Party hierarchy, Kochemasov was a candidate member of the CC from 1963 to 1983 and a member of the CC from 1983 to 1990.

211 Ilya Glazunov, *Russia Crucified.*

212 Interview with I. Glazunov, in *Fakty* (newspaper), Moscow, December 16, 2010.

213 The KGB Plays Chess.

214 See https://www.apn.ru/publications/article19573.htm.

215 Transcript of conversation between V. Ganichev and V. Bondarenko, *Zavtra* ("Tomorrow") newspaper, June 4, 2002.

216 Of the 2nd Section of the 1st Department of the 5th Directorate.

217 L. Mlechin. Sluzhba vneshnei razvedki. Moscow. 2004.

218 Invading Afghanistan required a reason, so Ivanov and Pitovranov created one: 'Our Intelligence officers suspected Amin of having ties to American intelligence. Perhaps the fact that he once studied in the US caught their attention,' remembers Boris Ponomarev, Secretary of the CC for International Affairs.

219 Publ. of Yana Kovalskaya – Bul'var Gordona (newspaper, Kiev). No. 54. December 22, 2009.

220 Of the 8th Department of Directorate S of the PGU.

221 Publ. of Yana Kovalskaya – Bul'var Gordona. No. 54. December 22, 2009.

222 A. Kiselev. Stalinskii favorit s Lubyanki. St. Petersburg. 2003. P. 153.

223 KGB special purpose unit.

224 Yu. Drozdov. Zapiski nachal'nika nelegal'noi razvedki. Moscow. 1999. C. 136.

225 Voenno-promyshlennyi kur'er (journal, Moscow). April 1, 2009.

226 A. Kiselev. Stalinskii favorit s Lubyanki. P. 154.

227 A. Kiselev. Stalinskii favorit s Lubyanki. St. Petersburg. 2003. P. 153.

228 Ibid. P. 156.

229 Alexei Chikishev. Spetsnaz v Afganistane. Moscow. 2004.

230 A. Kiselev. Britanskie perekrestki. P. 255.

231 I'm Iranian by nationality. But I grew up and studied here in the [Soviet] Union. My father moved to the USSR in 1953, my mother and I came a bit later. In 1961, our family moved to West Germany, but… I came back and continued my studies in the town of Ivanov. I finished school and went to university. Now I'm a businessman; I do business in the Soviet Union as well.

232 A. Bovin, "Five Years Among Jews and Diplomats," published in Russian by Zakharov Publishing House, 2002.

233 Vedomosti (newspaper), November 18, 2009, No. 218.

234 Le Journal Du Dimanche, November 16, 2009.

235 Sergey Kugushev, Maksim Kalashnikov. Tretii Proekt: Pogruzheniye. 2007.

236 On May 3, 1993, Podberezkin and Zhukov said the following about their business to Kommersant: 'RAU-Corporation was registered in April 1992…. It has roughly 400 employees which include two Academics and more than a hundred Master and PhDs. Its main areas of activity are economic and political consulting, as well as the publishing business.' Valery Vdovenko was a unique employee of RAU-Corporation. He claimed that his father Zakharii was the assistant to one of the Deputy Chairs of the KGB for several years. Valery himself was recruited in 1978 to the operational technical branch of the KGB. He later served in the PGU, and in 1990 he was directed through the CC of the CPSU and the KGB to work (as an Active Reserve officer) for the RAU-Corporation and for Podberezkin, Rogozin, and Zhukov.

237 Interview with O. Shenin by Alexander Golovenko — www.Pravda.ru (October 8, 2001).

238 Quote from V. Legostayev "SCSE Celluloid" — newspaper Zavtra, 2002, No 33-35.

239 In September 1999, a CIA officer investigating the matter, Richard L. Palmer, testified before the U.S. House Committee on Banking and Financial Services: 'Plans for the looting of then Soviet State were first discussed in 1984 by specific sectors of the Soviet Politburo, the top officials of the Communist government…. Their primary goal was to ensure their financial and political status in the future, by taking control of the vast funds and resources of the Party and converting them into per-

sonal assets that could not be tracked or confiscated by future governments.

By late 1986, the informal planning committee had been given the services of two KGB First Chief Directorate (foreign espionage) officers who were experienced in moving funds overseas both for the Party Central Committee, but also for other operational purposes. No written records existed of their meetings or proceedings, except for one copy to the Chair of the KGB and one copy to the Central Committee official responsible for the Administrative Organs of the Politburo…. This 'planning group' determined that while the local KGB residencies via the diplomatic pouch system and simply smuggling suitcases of money over borders could be used initially, this temporary system could not be used in the long term due to the frequency and amounts of the funds that would need to be transferred, as well as the need to reduce the number of knowledgeable persons to an absolute minimum. Further, the existing system utilized the Soviet bureaucracy which required too many written records. Further, it was also decided that the overt ties to the KGB and other official agencies had to be minimized….

As the 1980s drew to a close, it became clear that General Secretary Mikhail Gorbachev was rapidly losing control of his attempts to make incremental adjustments to the government and economy while retaining the preeminent position of the Communist Party. At this point, the elite economic group began to put into effect contingency plans to move assets to safety abroad. Soviet state enterprises transferred assets to subsidiary enterprises newly established in foreign countries from Cyprus to the Caribbean. Subsidiary enterprises included export-import offices, banks and trading companies established to market Soviet products. Some had no obvious ties to the Soviet government, but were instead formed by individuals who had obtained 'loans' from the associated banks. The result was that most of the ostensibly private cooperatives formed in the Soviet Union in the late 1980s and hailed as success stories of 'perestroika' (restructuring) were formed with state funds and were fronts or covers for state interests.

Trading companies established to market an assortment of state resources took on a larger role. These firms obtained products from petroleum to cotton and diamonds at the state-subsidized price and sold them abroad at market prices for hard currency. The profits were enormous and were not sent back to Moscow, but were placed in all the world's tax havens such as from Switzerland to Hong Kong and from Cyprus to the Cayman Islands. There, the profits could be 'laundered' by being put to use in forming a new generation of companies in which the Soviet Party and state origins were even harder to discern. Some of the money did come back to the USSR, sometimes in joint ventures with Soviet entities, but was represented as Western direct investment. This practice gained momentum in the period from 1989 through the dissolution of the Soviet Union in December 1991. Statement of Richard L. Palmer, President of Cachet International, Inc. On the Infiltration of the Western Financial System by Elements of Russian Organized Crime Before the House Committee on Banking and Financial Services.' September 21, 1991—https://archivesfinancialservices.house.gov/banking/92199pal.shtml.

240 V. Smirnov, A. Katz. *Velikoye Vorovstvo: Kommunisty i Oligarkhi*. – "Naslediye Otechestva" Research and Information Agency. *See* www.nasledie.ru.

241 Publ. by Vladimir Mezentsev—*Zhurnalist* magazine. 1993. No. 11

242 *Apparat TsK KPSS: The Steal of the Millennium—Duel* (newspaper), No. 11 /206/, March 13, 2001

243 Interview with Viktor Beloseltsev—Fontanka.ru. November 21, 2017

244 The Analytics Department was recreated in 1990 from its predecessor, the Operational Analysis and Information Office of the KGB. Leonov later was sent as Active Reserve officer to serve as professor at MSIIR and became State Duma delegate from the Motherland political block.

245 In 1980, Yanayev became Deputy Chair of the Union of Soviet Societies for Friendship and Cultural Relations with Foreign Countries. In 1986, he got another promotion and became Secretary for International Affairs of All-Union Central Council of Trade Unions. In 1989, he became Deputy Chair, and in 1990, the Chair of that organization.

246 Yevgeny Savostyanov. *This Is How We Live – In a Chasing Dog Projectory*, 2015.

247 Roy Medvedev – Sovietsky Soyuz. Posledniye gody zhizni. Konets sovetskoy imperii. Moscow. 2015. P. 163-180, 126.

248 https://www.dailyherald.com/article/20160819/news/3081999 41

249 "The Invisible Man" Article. No author indicated. http://www.compromat.ru/page_9954.htm

250 Interview with V. Korotich, the former Editor-in-Chief of *Ogoniok*, published February 6, 2013 https://daily.afisha.ru/archive/gorod/archive/pundits-korotich/

251 https://meduza.io/feature/2019/03/11/oni-dolzhny-mne-po-zhizni

252 Interview with A. Korzhakov — *Nasha Versiya*, November 17, 2008.

253 *Ibid.*

254 Interview with F. Bobkov "I Guarantee to Speak Only the Truth at All Times" *[Ya garantiruyu, chto govoryu vsegda tol'ko pravdu]*—*Top Secret* newspaper [Gazeta *Sovershenno Sekretno*] 1998. No. 1.

255 Dunayev was the minister of internal affairs of the RSFSR prior to the dissolution of the USSR. Starting April 18, 1992, he held the post of First Deputy Minister of Internal Affairs of Russia.

256 B.N. Yeltsin. *President's Notes [Zapiski Prezidenta]*, p.333. Moscow, *Ogonyok* Publishing House, 1994.

257 The Secret Designer of Most– www.kompromat.ru; March 14, 2001.

258 https://www.mk.ru/politics/article/2010/01/21/416001-esche-odno-slovo-o-gaydare.html

259 *Express-gazeta*, April 12, 2002

260 Trofimov remained the Head of the FSB for Moscow and Moscow Region until February of 1997. On April 10, 2005, he and his wife were shot dead with a firearm near their home in Moscow. The crime was never solved.

261 A. Korzhakov's interview "I Know Them All" with journalist Maksim Solopov – *Mediazone*, September 5, 2016. https://zona.media/article/2016/05/09/korzhakov

262 It is no accident that on September 23, 1999, in Ryazan, an event, which we will describe later, involved another group of three people—"two men and a woman"—who turned out to be terrorists (and FSB officers).

263 https://www.svoboda.org/a/31003447.html

264 Joining the ARO in 1992, Lebedev became the Head of the National Reserve Bank in 1995. In his own words, he made his fortune trading Russia's foreign obligations. In 2003, Bobkov tried to replace Luzhkov with Lebedev as Mayor of Moscow (aged and corrupted by big money, fame, and his

spouse's business, Luzhkov had become difficult for Bobkov to control). The attempt ended in failure: Lebedev received only 12.65% of the votes in the Mayoral Election for Moscow in 2003. The standoff between Luzhkov and Lebedev continued for some time. It ended with one of them being fired and the other encountering problems with law enforcement. On September 28, 2010, Luzhkov was removed from his post by the order of Russian President Dmitry Medvedev. On November 2, 2010, a search was conducted at the National Reserve Bank; the persecution of Lebedev and his business empire had begun.

265 From an interview with A. Korzhakov on Radio "Svoboda," January 26, 2010

266 He was well looked after, however. After reaching the rank of a General, he resigned to the Active Reserve and went to work for Bank Menatep due to the connections through his old friend, Colonel Alexander Yevdokimov, with whom he served in the 5th Directorate (7th Department) and who now led one of the departments at that bank. A bit later, after the formation of the Yukos conglomerate, Kondaurov was assigned as an Active Reserve officer to work for the former Komsomol leader and future Russian oligarch and political prisoner, Mikhail Khodorkovsky. At Yukos, Kondaurov became head of the Information and Analytics Department. As for CPR of the FSB (the Lubyanka's 1995 incarnation), Alexander Mikhailov and Alexander Zdanovich were transferred there and soon advanced to leadership positions.

267 Oleg Lurie. Turover's List — http://www.compromat.ru/page_9275.htm

268 In 2004, Chemezov replaced Belyaninov and became Director of Rosvooruzheniye, which was restructured and forti-fied, and was now called Russian Arms Exports or Rosoboroneksport.

269 We can find confirmation of the fact that Yeltsin consid-ered Luzhkov to be a candidate for the office of the Prime Minister's or even the presidency in the recollections of Yeltsin's daughter, Tatyana Dyachenko: 'What would have hap-pened to the country if in the Fall of 1998, Yuri Luzhkov was elected Prime Minister, as he was 99.9% certain to become President in the Summer of 2000? I was always convinced that nothing good would have ensued.'

270 Reliable sources report the following. One of the analytical groups working in the President's Administration developed a plan to discredit Luzhkov by organizing events intended to provoke and destabilize the socio-psychological situation in Moscow. Amongst themselves, the analysts referred to this plan as 'Storm in Moscow.' According to sources, the city will be shaken. Major acts of terror or attempts thereof are planned with respect to a range of State institutions: buildings of the FSB, MVD, Federation Council, Moscow Municipal Court, Moscow Arbitration Court, and other buildings. Kidnappings of public figures and ordinary citizens by 'Chechen fighters' are also envisioned. A separate chapter describes 'criminally force-ful' actions against commercial organizations and businessmen supporting Luzhkov. The order has been given to find and process additional 'operational' material on Kobzon, Gusinsky and Most group, as well as… other persons.

271 http://ruspioner.ru/cool/m/single/4655.

272 https://tass.ru/obschestvo/4341490

273 After Putin's Election win and inauguration, on May 11, 2000, personnel from the Prosecutor's Office, the FSB, and the Federal Service for Tax Policy of the Russian Federation con-ducted searches in the central offices of Gusinsky's Media Division of Most Group Holding in relation to a criminal case brought by the government against the holding company. On June 13, 2000, Gusinsky was detained on charges of large-scale fraud; he was placed into Butyrskaya Prison. On June 16, he was released on his own recognizance. On July 20, Gusinsky signed a contract (the so-called "Protocol No. 6") to sell Media Division of Most Group Holding to Gazprom for $773 million. The document was initialed by Press Minister Mikhail Lesin. Following this development, on July 26, the case against Gusinsky was closed and he left Russia.

274 After escaping, Galkin did not claim in a 2002 interview with Novaya Gazeta that the testimony he gave to the Chechen rebels was given under torture and did not reflect reality.

275 Leaving public political life, Primakov, the former SVR director, former Prime Minister, former Russian Presidential candidate, and among the top five most influential and popular public figures in the country, was offered in December 2001 the post previously held by the deceased Pitovranov and took over the Chamber of Trade and Industry, as if to emphasize the importance of Pitovranov's role in the state.

276 The plaque was quietly removed under the cover of the night in the days of the August Coup of 1991 by Chekists themselves, fearing it would be smashed after opponents of the SCSE doused it with paint.

277 https://www.svoboda.org/a/31003447.html

278 By Senior Lieutenant Yuri Balas, an officer of the 1st Section of the 2nd Department of the 5th Directorate.

279 *Nash Sovremennik* magazine. 1997, No. 7.

280 According to the KGB's own records, its 'top agents' among Church hierarchy included: 'Mikhailov'—Vladimir Gundyayev, Patriarch of Moscow and of all the Russias, Metropolitan of Smolensk and Kaliningrad; 'Abbot'—Pitirim, Metropolitan of Volokolamsk and Yuriev (Konstantin Nechaev); 'Adamant'—Metropolitan Juvenalius (Poyarkov); 'Antonov'—Filaret, Metropolitan of Kiev (Denisenko); 'Pavel'—Methodius, Metropolitan of Voronezh; 'Ostrovsky'—Filaret, Metropolitan of Minsk; 'Svyatoslav'—Metropolitan Nicodemus (Boris Rotov); in 1970, he was made temporary head of the Patriarchates of North and South America; then, headed the Department of External Church Relations (DECR) of the Russian Orthodox Church; 'Topaz'—Clement, Archbishop of Kaluga; 'Chrysostom'—the Archbishop of Vilnius; 'Reader'—the Primate of the Latvian Orthodox Church, Kudryashov; 'Kuznetzov'—Borovoi Vitaly, honorary abbot of the Moscow Temple of the Spoken Resurrection at the Uspensky Gorge; 'Anatoly'—Ivan Mirolyubov, staffer of the DECR; 'Iverieli'—Georgian Catholicos Eli; 'Petrov'—Pyotr Kuzmich Raina, the Exarch of the Moscow Patriarch with the Patriarch of Alexandria and all Africa; 'Voronov'—Arkady Tyshchuk, cleric of the St. Nicholas Russian Orthodox Cathedral in New York (1977-1982); 'Fyodor'—Ivan Borcha, priest of rural parishes of the Ukrainian and Rumanian communities of the Canadian provinces of Alberta and Saskatchewan (early 1970s); 'Patriot'—Viktor Petlyuchenko, cleric of the Russian Orthodox parish of Edmonton, Alberta, Canada; 'Icarus'—Igor Zuzemel, bishop of the Russian Orthodox Church, Metropolitan of Vienna and Austria; 'Esaulenko'—Iosif Pustoutov, who served in Russian Orthodox churches in the Netherlands, West Germany, Italy and France. In 1976, became the primate of the Moscow Patriarchate at the headquarters of the Christian Peace Conference in Prague; 'Vladimir'—Nikolai Cherpitsky, personal secretary to the Metropolitan Nicodemus; 'Simonov'—Archbishop Cyprian (Zernov), abbot of the Church of All the Grieving on Big Ordynka Street in Moscow.

281 1967: Agents 'Svyatoslav,' 'Voronov,' 'Antonov' and others

condemned the aggressive actions of the USA in Vietnam and of Israel in the Middle East at meetings of the Executive Committee and the CC of the World Council of Churches in September on this year on the island Crete. The delegation of the Russian Orthodox Church voted against the resolutions on Vietnam and the Middle East proposed by representatives of Western churches and demanded a discussion of the condition of Black Americans; August 1969. Our agents were able to advance the agent 'Kuznetzov' to a leadership post in the World Council of Churches; 1983. From September 28 to October 3 of this year in Moscow, a meeting of representatives of the religious press was held in Moscow at the offices of the publishing department of the Moscow Patriarchate, with 12 foreigners participating.... Via the agents 'Abbot' and 'Grigory,' the foreigners were subjected to politically beneficial influence. Signed: Chief of 4th Department, Colonel Romanov; 1987. The agent 'Potemkin' participated in the meeting of the CC of the World Council of Churches in West Germany. He obtained information on the situation in the organization's headquarters and on upcoming personnel changes in the leadership of its sections.... Comrades Shirokopoyas V.N. and Spiridonovam were dispatched to the GDR to secure counterintelligence measures for the Committee meeting, for the continuation of the work of the Christian Peace Conference, and for operative missions conducted jointly with friends (PRB [Bulgaria], PRV [Vietnam], GDR, Cuba, CSSR [Czechoslovakia]). Twelve State Security agents also made the trip. In the course of this mission, attempts at provocations and attacks against the churches of socialist countries were neutralized, undesirable personnel changes were prevented, and politically beneficial final documents were adopted. ... Signed: Chief of 4th Department, Colonel Timoshevsky; 1988. For the first time, the agent 'Adamant,' one of the hierarchs of the Russian Orthodox Church, participated in the general UNESCO session as part of the Soviet delegation.... The personal and work-related files of five agents from territorial agencies recommended for advancement to the leadership of the Russian Orthodox Church have been reviewed. Signed: Chief of 4th Department, Colonel Timoshevsky; August 1988. As part of the operational case 'Pharmacist,' measures have been conducted to further compromise the target in the eyes of like-minded people and Western contacts.... Via agents and by other means, 'Pharmacist's' wife has been persuaded to file for divorce.... Signed: Chief of 4th Department, Colonel Timoshevsky; 1989. An agent, codenamed 'Rake,' has been installed at target unit publishing department of the Moscow Patriarchate.... The latest issue of the magazine Slovo [Word], published under the oversight of our agents, has been printed and is circulated in clerical and church-adjacent circles. Signed: Chief of 4th Department, Colonel Timoshevsky.

282 In 1937, journalists took note of Alexander Kazem-Bek's meeting with Ignatyev at Café Royal in Paris; it caused a huge scandal in Russian émigré circles, already terrorized by the abductions and murders organized by Soviet intelligence in Europe in those years.

283 Mireille Massip, "Truth, the Daughter of Time. Alexander Kazem-Bek, Russian Émigré (1902-1977)." Trans. from French. Zvezda magazine, 2000, No. 10.

284 The same one where KGB agent Father Vladimir (Vigilyansky) served since 1996.

285 The offer was declined by ROCA Metropolitan Vitaly (Ustinov).

286 The Wall Street Journal ran the following commentary on Putin's statement on May 25, 2007: 'Not only are there theological and moral issues at stake, but there is also the suspicion among some that Mr Putin is building new networks of influ-

ence by using the church to reach out to Russian émigré communities all over the world.'

287 Back when he was still working in the Balkans, he 'got churched.' This step, generally understandable for an aging man in poor health, took almost clinical forms in his case. For Leonid Reshetnikov, formerly a general in the First Chief Directorate of the KGB and a Communist, it was expressed via extreme fascination with the White movement, the White Russian Orthodox idea, and the spiritual and territorial revival of the [Russian] Empire. ...
By the start of Putin's third presidential term, the Institute had a fully formed Orthodox-Imperial dominant bloc of Reshetnikov, Tamara Guzenkova, and Mikhail Smolin. ...
During the 'trade war' between Russia and Ukraine on the eve of the Vilnius summit, the presidential administration was receiving memos and reviews which asserted that the Ukrainian people has been invariably loyal to Russia from the time of the Pereyaslav Council, that 'insignificant Western influences' have been marginal and are provoked by a small cluster of fascist sympathizers from Western Ukraine—the territories that were part the Austro-Hungarian empire and have a sociocultural code different from the majority. On the other hand, these documents said, the overwhelming majority of Ukrainians cherish the memory of our common history and the Great Patriotic war and dream of the revival of a common state—the Empire or the USSR. Everything that attested to the opposite in one way or another was ascribed to the activities of NGOs financed by the U.S. State Department, Brussels, Warsaw and Vilnius. The memos written or edited by Guzenkova called for maximum pressure on Yanukovych via energy and trade blackmail in order to persuade him not to sign the Vilnius preliminaries and to ensure the Eurasian integration of Ukraine. It's hard to say with any certainty whether those memos formed the Kremlin's position toward Ukraine or simply strengthened it, reinforcing prior decisions. What is evident, however, is that the content of RISR materials accords almost completely with the actual steps made by the leadership of the Russian Federation in the foreign policy arena. Of course, the Institute's leaders not only failed to predict the Maidan, but strenuously convinced both themselves and their clients/addressees that such a scenario was fundamentally impossible. ... Russian analysts have two universal and unfailing, albeit mutually discordant explanations: fascist conspiracies and State Department/CIA/globalist backroom conspiracy. ... At the same time, the presidential administration was receiving memos asserting that the people of Crimea want to join the Russian Federation, that they fear Ukrainization, bans on the Russian language, and the displacement of Russian Orthodoxy by the uniate faith. ... Dozens of memos talked about the need to form a combat-ready pro-Russian underground in Ukraine, to send in commando units, to prepare for a charge to the south toward Mariupol/Nikolayev/Odessa, and to create a Great Novorossiya which would include Transnistria and would, like Crimea, unify with Russia. However, not a word was written about Ukraine's possible resistance, about the mobilization of the army and volunteer detachments, about possible sanctions and their consequences. The reaction of the USA and European NATO countries was not even discussed. ... When 'Project Novorossiya' increasingly revealed itself to be unfeasible and unmanageable while the Kremlin was signaling that it wasn't ready to get involved in a full-scale war with Ukraine and execute a charge via Mariupol to Transnistria... it became obvious that the Institute's experts bore some blame for the adoption (or reinforcement) of decisions that led Russia to a serious economic and international crisis. ... Under RISR's influence, the presidential administration—and therefore, the President himself—was being persuaded that: The states in post-Soviet space are not fully legitimate entities under interna-

tional law. The very fact of their appearance on the world's political map and their subsequent existence is little more than the result of the Russian catastrophes of 1917 and 1991, instigated by Russia's enemies and especially the USA. Their sovereignty is a temporary phenomenon that does not deserve to be taken seriously, a kind of historical error that needs to be corrected within the framework of the Empire's revival; The West is weak, cowardly and greedy and will swallow the annexation of Crimea and the war in Donbass for the sake of oil and gas, just like it swallowed Russia's military action in Abkhazia and South Ossetia in 2008; The public mood in Eastern Ukraine, including Kharkov and Mariupol, favors reunification with Russia; … It's possible to create a strong pro-Russian movement by creating alternative expert and public opinion and relying on the special services of Ukraine and now Belarus as well (since, in any case, it's next in line for the Russia integrators); such a movement can not only influence public opinion but change these countries policies and leadership in the direction Russia needs; Ukraine is a quasi-state and the Ukrainians are a quasi-people with no historical or political role of their own. Russians are the only true state-building people in post-Soviet space; therefore, the only form of political existence in that state is a Russian Empire.

288 https://www.defense.gov/Explore/News/Article/Article/6029 42/dempsey-russian-attacks-change-europes-security-landscape/; https://www.thedailybeast.com/us-military-chief-compares-putins-ukraine-move-to-stalins-invasion-of-poland

289 https://www.washingtonpost.com/news/worldviews/wp/2015 /07/24/silvio-berlusconi-and-vladimir-putin-the-political-bromance-that-endured/; https://www.telegraph.co.uk/news/worldnews/europe/italy/81 66090/WikiLeaks-to-highlight-Putin-and-Berluscons-special-relationship.html.

290 https://www.ft.com/content/2d2a9afe-6829-11e5-97d0-1456a776a4f5.

291 https://bylinetimes.com/2019/09/04/putins-funding-of-italys-far-right-the-pivotal-role-of-aleksandr-dugin/; https://mainichi.jp/english/articles/20181106/p2a/00m/0na/005000c.

292 https://www.buzzfeednews.com/article/albertonardelli/flight-records-gianluca-savoini.

293 http://www.lombardiarussia.org/index.php/component/content/article/57-categoria-home-/392-lsanzioni-allarussia-fanno-interessi-solo-delle-lobbyr-intervista-a-matteo-salvini-e-gianluca-savoini

294 https://www.youtube.com/watch?v=2nJZb6OREm4

295 https://www.buzzfeednews.com/article/albertonardelli/matteo-salvini-russia-inquiry; https://www.buzzfeednews.com/article/albertonardelli/salvini-russia-oil-deal-secret-recording

296 https://www.theguardian.com/news/2017/oct/27/the-war-against-pope-francis

297 https://www.newsweek.com/steve-bannon-donald-trump-jared-kushner-vladimir-putin-russia-fbi-mafia-584962 and https://www.vanityfair.com/news/2018/07/sinister-history-behind-the-rights-putin-mania-steve-bannon-china

298 https://assets.donaldjtrump.com/Pro-Life_Coalition.pdf

299 Steve Bannon is on a far-right mission to radicalise Europe | Steve Bannon | The Guardian

300 https://kostlanova.blog.idnes.cz/blog.aspx?c=469324. Citing information from the Czech Police Department's organized crime unit, the journalist Yan Kovalik (*Respekt*) also reported that Mamaladze was a GRU agent and that another co-founder of Falkon was under investigation by a special unit of the Czech Police Department (*The Moscow Times*, January 25, 2001).

301 https://www.politico.eu/article/the-monarchs-of-prague-castle/

302 http://uacrisis.org/38646-chech

303 On January 26, 2018, Jakub Janda, the director of the Prague-based think tank European Values, concluded in that regard as follows: 'Czech President Miloš Zeman has become the most influential Kremlin ally in Central Europe. He holds ceremonial powers as head of state, but his position also allows him to support Russian President Vladimir Putin extensively. In foreign policy, Zeman has often stood contrary to the Czech government, which generally defends the positions of the EU and NATO. Like many Kremlin proxies, Zeman often reiterates Kremlin messages, including denying the presence of organized Russian troops in Ukraine, arguing that Crimea is Russian, and demanding that the West lift the sanctions it imposed on Russia. He is portrayed by Russian propaganda as an independent, strong anti-American leader who adores Putin. If size of countries is taken into account, Zeman, the president of a country with 10 million people, is the second most quoted European leader in the Russian information space, right after German Chancellor Angela Merkel…. Zeman systematically aids Kremlin goals inside the Czech Republic. Local extremists and conspirators are fed pro-Kremlin disinformation, which they gladly reproduce, as they share the same enemy as Moscow: media and the political mainstream. The disinformation community is usually fringe and irrelevant, unless they find strong political figures who deliver legitimacy. As the Czech Security Information Service (BIS) points out, Russia's goal is to create the perception that 'everyone is lying' to 'weaken the society's will for resistance.' Zeman has spent years legitimizing disinformation outlets by giving them dozens of interviews in which he attacks mainstream politics.' https://observer.com/2018/01/how-czech-president-milos-zeman-became-vladimir-putins-man/

304 www.china.org.cn/world/Off_the_Wire/2018-05/04/content_51121608.htm

305 https://intpolicydigest.org/2018/08/24/how-russian-oligarchs-exert-political-influence-in-the-west/ It was there in 2003 that a Czech businessman Zdeněk Zbytek introduced Zeman to Yakunin. Zbytek, an army colonel in the Soviet times and a commander of the armored division, became famous for his suggestion that the pro-Soviet Czech Government use tanks to suppress the student demonstrations, which evolved into the Velvet (or Gentle) Revolution in 1989.

306 US journalist and writer Anne Applebaum summarized the 2015 Rhodes Forum in her article 'Russia's New Kind of Friends', which was published on October 16, 2015. This article was not so much about the Forum per se, but about Putin's steps towards creating the Fifth International. 'The forum … continued, as in the past, to gather people willing to endorse Russian views of the world. There was Václav Klaus, the former Czech president, who called Putin's Syrian adventure a 'logical step.' There was John Laughland, political director of a Russian-backed think tank, the Institute for Democracy and Cooperation, who argued that the CIA, as part of a US plot to subjugate Europe, conceived the European Union. In addition, dozens of others, from all around the world… Klaus, who is not an idiot, does not hide his financial links to Moscow. The forum does not hide its links to Russia, either. Instead, they

both seek openly to legitimize the anti-NATO, anti-European, anti-Western views of the Russian elite … Andrej Babiš, the Czech finance minister [now Prime Minister], and Miloš Zeman, the Czech president—once a regular at the forum—frequently echo or repeat Russian slogans, as occasionally does the [then] Slovak Prime Minister, Robert Fico. In August and early September of 2014, all three argued against Western sanctions on Russia, using similar language. Zeman called them 'ineffective,' Babiš called them 'nonsense' and Fico called them 'pointless.' Later, they shifted their rhetoric, and began to point to the refugee crisis and radical Islam as the 'real' threats to Europe. 'The refugee crisis threatens the Czech Republic more than Russia,' said Babiš in September. 'Islamist terrorism is a greater threat to Europe than Russia,' said Zeman in May. Like Hungarian Prime Minister Viktor Orbán, all of these men have domestic political reasons for offering verbal support to Putin: They want to ride the anti-European Union, 'anti-establishment' wave that has washed across all of Europe, and to capitalize on economic discontent. Since the EU began, politicians have long found it useful to blame 'Brussels' for problems that they cannot fix. However, there may be other motives, too. Zeman's close adviser ran the office of Lukoil, the Russian oil company. Babiš, who is also one of the Czech Republic's richest men, owns companies that consume a good deal of Russian gas. However, I should not unfairly single out Central Europeans, for there are many other Europeans who support Russian foreign policy with similarly mixed motives. Former Italian Prime Minister Silvio Berlusconi maintains both a political and a financial relationship with Putin. So does Gerhard Schroeder, the former chancellor of Germany. These men are not idiots either—but neither is they secret agents, spies or traitors. At the same time, they are working steadily, in their own ways, to undermine Western security and support the spread of Russian authoritarianism in Eastern Europe as well as the Middle East. So, what do we call them? We need a new vocabulary for a new era. https://www.washingtonpost.com/opinions/neither-agents-of-influence-nor-useful-idiots/2015/10/16/73fdc478-7423-11e5-8248-98e0f5a2e830_story.html?noredirect=on&utm_term=.a551e1e5c1ab

307 https://observer.com/2018/01/how-czech-president-milos-zeman-became-vladimir-putins-man/

308 https://news.rambler.ru/other/38862880-smi-chehii-milosh-zeman-sluzhitel-rossiyskoy-propagandy/?updated

309 https://www.respekt.cz/politika/zeman-dal-svym-mlcenim-prednost-loajalite-k-ruskemu-vedeni

310 http://uacrisis.org/38646-chech

311 https://www.theguardian.com/world/2021/jul/15/kremlin-papers-appear-to-show-putins-plot-to-put-trump-in-white-house

312 General Kalugin survived many dark days of the KGB's existence, and even to quietly emigrate to the U.S., a sign of obvious wisdom.

313 Russian publication: Нарышкин назвал экс-генерала КГБ Калугина предателем Родины - РИА Новости, 03.11.2020 (ria.ru)_["Naryshkin names ex-KGB General Kalugin a Traitor"]

314 'The KGB was the largest organization world-wide by the number of people, by the financing it received, and by other measurements. And, by the way, by the number of foreign agents. I can quote one specific figure—until 1962, I think, the Soviet intelligence had several hundred Americans in the States who were working for them. They mainly worked for the Soviets out of the ideological convictions…. Trump is a businessman who is rather successful as the scale of his operations shows…' 'must have left some mark…. I know that since the

time when I still worked for the KGB…. since I was the Head of the Department of Foreign Counter-Intelligence Services…. Yes, I remember. It was a long time ago and he was noted even back then…. It does not mean that he could have been recruited. But KGB for sure had a dossier on him…. It could be that nothing would happen, at least during that period. But at some later point of history or life, someone could have 'remembered' about it. KGB generally had a pretty good 'memory….' And, by the way, you know, he is rather friendly towards Putin, and I think it makes sense…. I think it is partly because of that—what I am talking about…. I read archive materials. By the way, it was already in Leningrad, when I was working as the First Deputy of the Head of the Leningrad KGB and had unlimited informational access, including access to different historical documents. And it was in Leningrad, since it was as important of a capital as Moscow, that I happened to read a lot of rather interesting materials, including those pertaining to the United States, and to the Great Britain, of course…. They could have been random…' 'The fact that the current President is friendly towards the Russian leader, is one of the indicators, in my opinion, that makes one think: 'Why are they so friendly?' …By the way, when I was recruiting informants, my targets included Americans who at the time did not have much by way of an access but could get it in time…. I think that any reasonable person who is concerned with his career and personal life would not want this kind of publications wherever it was and whenever it was…. I think that this is one of the reasons for his friendly predisposition towards some of the Russian leaders…. There may be something else too. But this is one of the serious reasons…. It is obvious that he is trying to find some common ground with Putin. That much is clear… I have one theory, which I already mentioned: when he was in Moscow back in the day, he could have left a 'mark', and naturally, someone made use of it. Since his friendliness towards the current Russian government is somewhat unusual, I would say, for an American President. Somewhat unusual, indeed, and too heartily warm…. I know for sure that there was compromising material. But I do not know whether it was used…. His friendliness towards the current Russian government raises questions, of course… We could guess that this is connected to his presence in Moscow a long time ago. I personally think that this is connected to his Moscow experience….' 'the fact that he left a trace in the KGB documents at that earlier time—this is certain. I do not have any doubts about that…. It was a known fact that hundreds, if not thousands, of Americans used the services of Russian girls, street walkers. And, of course, Soviet and Russian intelligence who were familiar with this situation, could use these girls in a specific way to make them earn money as they normally would…'
https://gordonua.com/publications/kalugin-na-trampa-kgb-imel-materialy-tochno-na-kakom-to-etape-mogli-vspomnit-ob-etom-kgb-vsegda-otlichalsya-horoshey-pamyatyu-1231157.html

315 https://www.theguardian.com/world/2021/jul/15/kremlin-papers-appear-to-show-putins-plot-to-put-trump-in-white-house

316 It is worth noting that the compromising materials are a very standard and frequently used instrument for recruiting or eliminating persons of interest to the Russian State Security. We generally become aware of these stories only when there is revenge or reprisal at play. We are not notified about the successful use of compromising materials when it results in recruitment. Here are a few examples of the materials that were made public by the State Security: a compromising video depicting Yury Skuratov, Prosecutor General of Russia, in 1999 when he was attempting to force the resignation of Yeltsin on the charges of corruption but ended up resigning himself amid the scandal

https://www.youtube.com/watch?v=9fuZ0QB4RG0; compromising documents concerning Yevgeny Kiselyov, a journalist from the TV channel (NTV) that stood in opposition to Putin in 2001 http://www.compromat.ru/page_11360.htm; a compromising video depicting Mikhail Kasyanov, one of the leaders of the Russian opposition and former Prime Minister of Russia, in 2016 https://www.youtube.com/watch?v=jS3AXeg3yho. Finally, of course, there are several tapes involving honey-traps, such as Ekaterina Gerasimova (nicknamed "Katya Mumu"). But all this concerns only those who needed to be punished and not those who were recruited successfully. We will never see the recordings of the latter category.

317 https://www.novayagazeta.ru/articles/2016/10/05/70066-rybolovlev-sbrosivshiy-cheshuyu

318 https://www.novayagazeta.ru/articles/2016/10/05/70066-rybolovlev-sbrosivshiy-cheshuyu

319 https://haqqin.az/news/113183

320 https://www.politico.com/magazine/story/2017/11/19/trump-first-moscow-trip-215842. Notably, many years later, in 2013, Trump would stay in the "Obama suite" at the Ritz-Carlton Hotel.

321 https://www.kommersant.ru/doc/901088

322 https://www.washingtonpost.com/opinions/trump-loves-vladimir-putin-could-his-tax-returns-explain-why/2016/09/12/fe797fb0-7923-11e6-beac-57a4a412e93a_story.html?utm_term=.c4af6ea2d22f

323 https://www.nytimes.com/2017/01/16/us/politics/donald-trump-russia-business.html

324 In November of 2007, Trump arrived in Moscow as a guest of the Moscow Millionaire Fair that opened on November 22, 2007, at the Crocus Expo Center. He was promoting Trump Vodka, which cost $40-50 per bottle ("Donald Trump Is Selling His Name" – Kommersant, June 4, 2008, №95).

325 http://www.palmbeachdailynews.com/business/real-estate/trump-former-estate-the-story-behind-the-million-mansion-tear-down/5qgtlikl46SX7KXGdtDPUI/; http://www.tampabay.com/news/politics/why-did-russian-oligarch-pay-so-much-for-mansion-owned-by-trump/2316032).

326 https://www.novayagazeta.ru/articles/2016/10/16/70202-vyshli-dengi-iz-provala

327 http://www.businessinsider.com/donald-trump-jr-said-money-pouring-in-from-russia-2018-2

328 https://www.washingtonpost.com/news/fact-checker/wp/2016/07/27/trumps-claim-that-i-have-nothing-to-do-with-russia/?utm_term=.3ec78d41d237

329 https://www.washingtonpost.com/blogs/the-fix/post/donald-trump-wont-run-for-president-in-2012/2011/05/16/AF14G14G_blog.html?utm_term=.ed22e29 dd1bf. Everyone was making fun of Trump in 2011. In 2016, this was no longer a laughing matter.

330 https://gordonua.com/publications/pole-chudes-v-strane-durakov-tramp-v-pogone-za-russkimi-dengami-rassledovanie-istorika-felshtinskogo-230326.html

331 Babel presently resides in Chicago. In Russia, he is wanted on the various financial criminal charges. To avoid arrest, he first fled to Israel and then managed to relocate to the U.S..

332 https://www.propublica.org/article/the-international-man-of-mystery-linked-to-flynns-lobbying-deal

333 http://ania.com/2017/05/19/exclusive-female-ex-russian-spy-appointed-trump-organization-launder-money/.

334 https://www.nytimes.com/2017/05/25/world/europe/taormina-sicily-group-of-7-summit-donald-trump.html

335 Papale even hinted that Trump met some "Russians" who frequently used Taormina for the various confidential gatherings. https://www.nytimes.com/2017/05/25/world/europe/taormina-sicily-group-of-7-summit-donald-trump.html; http://www.lasicilia.it/news/messina/41608/io-siciliano-fra-i-30-vip-alla-festa-per-il-trionfo-del-mio-amico-donald.html

336 http://www.ceur.it/System/12811/RASSEGNA%20DIA-LOGHI%203%5E%20ed.%20File%20unico%20al%2003.07.20 12.pdf; http://www.taorminafilmfest.it/news.asp?lang=2&an=55&idp= 136&id=326

337 https://www.nytimes.com/2017/05/25/world/europe/taormina-sicily-group-of-7-summit-donald-trump.html?mcubz=0

338 Baronoff was diagnosed with cancer (leukemia) in 2014. She died in 2015. Some sources say that Trump visited Baronoff in the hospital and even paid for her funeral. Other sources say that this was not true. In any event, Baronov's son, Georgy Baronov, replaced her as a real estate broker in the Trump's "organization" in Florida.

339 In the sixth skyscraper, following the same business plan, South American transplants were the main buyers.

340 https://www.wsj.com/articles/when-donald-trump-needs-a-loan-he-chooses-deutsche-bank-1458379806

341 https://www.cnn.com/2017/07/12/politics/video-trump-relationships-russian-associates/index.html

342 https://twitter.com/realdonaldtrump/status/347191326112112 640?lang=en

343 https://www.motherjones.com/politics/2018/05/new-documents-trump-pushed-hard-for-a-meeting-with-putin-in-2013/.

344 Donald Trump on David Letterman 17 October, 2013 Full Interview - Bing video; http://www.chicagotribune.com/news/nationworld/politics/ct-trump-putin-invitiation-miss-universe-20180309-story.html

345 http://www.cnn.com/interactive/2017/03/politics/trump-putin-russia-timeline/

346 https://www.nbcnews.com/news/us-news/trump-putin-tried-meet-moscow-three-years-ago-source-n619006

347 http://www.newsweek.com/heres-all-times-trump-has-praised-putin-708859

348 http://rew-online.com/2013/11/12/hotel-trio-aims-to-bring-manhattan-to-moscow/

349 https://www.nytimes.com/2017/08/28/us/politics/trump-tower-putin-felix-sater.html

350 Washington Post, August 28, 2017.

351 https://www.washingtonpost.com/politics/top-trump-organization-executive-reached-out-to-putin-aide-for-help-on-business-deal/2017/08/28/095aebac-8c16-11e7-84c0-02cc069f2c37_story.html?utm_term=.8423d1ffef23

352 https://www.theguardian.com/us-news/video/2017/feb/14/michael-flynn-rnc-speech-video; https://www.washingtonpost.com/news/the-

fix/wp/2017/02/14/michael-flynns-speech-at-the-republican-national-convention-predicted-his-demise/?utm_term=.fcf33740e2f8

353 https://soprweb.senate.gov/index.cfm?event=getFilingDetails&filingID=C68C8A30-5542-4D75-9B95-43D036BD34B5&filingTypeID=81

354 https://www.nytimes.com/2017/03/10/us/politics/michael-flynn-turkey.html?_r=0

355 http://www.nydailynews.com/news/politics/michael-flynn-registers-foreign-agent-earned-530k-lobbying-article-1.2993217

356 http://www.politico.com/story/2017/04/25/michael-flynn-turkey-russia-237550

357 http://www.huffingtonpost.com/david-l-phillips/lt-gen-michael-t-flynn-gu_b_13013248.html

358 https://www.nytimes.com/2017/03/10/us/politics/michael-flynn-turkey.html?_r=0

359 http://www.motherjones.com/politics/2017/05/flynn-putin-dinner-payment-security-clearance-photo; https://www.nbcnews.com/news/us-news/russians-paid-mike-flynn-45k-moscow-speech-documents-show-n734506.

360 Kazhdan's ETIRK Holding Rus still exists in Russia, but somehow it has a different tax number. The original company filed for bankruptcy in 2013.

361 http://www.stcd.ru/clients

362 http://bigpara.hurriyet.com.tr/haberler/genel-haberler/taksi-jetler-turkiye-de-satilacak_ID562881/)(http://bit.ly/2qh3CTz

363 Alptekin discussed this with the American journalist Isaac Arnsdorf, author of the article, "Flynn's Turkish lobbying linked to Russia," *Politico*, April 25, 2017.

364 *Vedomosti*, June 4, 2008.

365 *Vedomosti*, July 8, 2010 and December 27, 2010.

366 http://www.nationalobserver.com/2017/01/14/opinion/trumps-ill-begotten-victory-intel-dossier-says-putin-helped-sanders-stein

367 https://www.buzzfeed.com/jasonleopold/putins-media-czar-was-murdered-just-before-meeting-feds?utm_term=.wwLb82989#.gowO0LW0W

368 http://www.politico.com/magazine/story/2017/06/20/jill-stein-green-party-no-regrets-2016-215281

369 http://www.runyweb.com/articles/business/real-estate/two-mansions-linked-to-former-putin-aide-mikhail-lesin-lists-for-51m.html

370 https://www.rferl.org/a/lesin-wicker-real-estate/25477122.html

371 *KVN* – an improvisational game show, during which the teams from different universities competed among themselves and which was (and continues to be) quite popular in Russia/USSR.

372 http://www.reuters.com/article/usa-tax-idUSL1E8HFEJJ20120615

373 http://www.financialbuzz.com/us-clients-accuse-hapaolim-bankers-of-helping-them-to-avoid-taxes-232542

374 http://freebeacon.com/national-security/russia-today-president-facing-prison-for-tax-fraud/

375 http://freebeacon.com/culture/rt-america-boss-out-on-supervised-release-following-tax-fraud-conviction/

376 In 2013, he was there twice (from May 29 to June 6 and from August 28 to September 7). In 2014, there were four visits: January 8-12, March 2-9, July 10-20, December 15-25.

377 Possible consequences of that loose end were unpredictable; he was a risk factor. His testimony and even his off-the-record drunken conversations could pose a threat to already compromised activities of RT and wreck the 'Trump for President' operation. It is possible that the Kremlin had no real reasons to be afraid of Lesin's revelations but paranoia, traditional for Russian State Security, took its toll. One man's life (it was not the first time, and it would not be the last one, as we discovered) was considered a reasonable price to ensure success of the most complicated and brilliant Russian undercover operation. Lesin who had health and alcohol addiction issues, was an easy target for those who were responsible for eliminating possible leaks—the leaks that eventually allowed American society and politicians to start to put together the pieces of a puzzle to get an unpleasant picture that they called 'Russian interference' in the U.S. Elections and 'collusion with Russia.'

378 https://www.nytimes.com/2016/07/28/us/politics/donald-trump-russia-clinton-emails.html; https://www.nytimes.com/2016/07/28/us/politics/trump-conference-highlights.html

379 https://www.nbcnews.com/politics/donald-trump/trump-campaign-planned-wikileaks-dump-tried-acquire-clinton-emails-mueller-n996081.

380 https://www.youtube.com/watch?v=_sbT3_9dJY4

381 https://splinternews.com/accused-russian-agent-maria-butina-met-with-treasury-f-1827786726

382 http://zampolit.com/dossier/torshin-aleksandr-porfire-vich/

383 https://english.gordonua.com/news/exclusiveenglish/my-name-is-fedyashin-anton-fedyashin-who-is-anton-fedyashin-and-what-was-he-teaching-maria-butina-investigation-by-yuri-felshtinsky-342703.html

384 It is worth noting that later, after Butina's arrest, Fedyashin removed that article from the website and replaced it with a different one, also written by him, with the same title and the same date, but with a different text that made no mention of Butina. (https://www.american.edu/cas/carmel/news/gettysburg-dialog.cfm) That text had previously accompanied the photos published here: (https://www.flickr.com/photos/eisenhowerinstitute/sets/72157680608916755/). Thus, Fedyashin did not even have to bother to write a new text—he just used an older one of his own. (https://www.american.edu/cas/carmel/news/gettysburg-dialog.cfm).

385 https://www.american.edu/uploads/docs/FedyashinCV2017.pdf

386 http://flibusta.site/b/420209/read 20/257

387 http://www.4freerussia.org/kislyaks-spider-web-of-networks-of-oligarchs-and-putins-apologists-in-the-u-s/

388 Also known as the Federal Agency for the Commonwealth of Independent States, Compatriots Living Abroad and International Humanitarian Cooperation. https://www.thetimes.co.uk/article/russian-diplomat-tried-to-recruit-us-spies-says-fbi-8qvgrdn8ml7

389 https://www.motherjones.com/politics/2013/10/fbi-

investigating-yury-zaytsev-russian-diplomat-spy/

390 https://www.motherjones.com/politics/2013/10/fbi-investigating-yury-zaytsev-russian-diplomat-spy/

391 https://www.rbth.com/international/2013/10/26/fbi_accuses_russian_culture_center_of_espionage_31197.html

392 Fedyashin and Butina can be seen in numerous photos with their students (https://english.gordonua.com/news/exclusiveenglish/my-name-is-fedyashin-anton-fedyashin-who-is-anton-fedyashin-and-what-was-he-teaching-maria-butina-investigation-by-yuri-felshtinsky-342703.html).

393 The missing photo, copied from Fedyashin's article before it vanished, remains only in this article. Butina is indicated with an arrow; Fedyashin is second left. (https://english.gordonua.com/news/exclusiveenglish/my-name-is-fedyashin-anton-fedyashin-who-is-anton-fedyashin-and-what-was-he-teaching-maria-butina-investigation-by-yuri-felshtinsky-342703.html). Next to it, the same photo, before its disappearance, copied by someone on Twitter. (https://mobile.twitter.com/ShtSpkldMpptFrt/status/1019020195589967877).

394 https://www.american.edu/uploads/docs/FedyashinCV2017.pdf.

395 https://www.american.edu/uploads/docs/FedyashinCV2017.pdf

396 https://thesternfacts.com/a-gop-kremlin-insider-connected-alexander-torshin-to-congressmen-then-he-joined-the-nra-df959b5834e

397 https://www.kp.ru/daily/26726.5/3752833/

398 At the meeting of the First Deputy Chair of the Council of Federation Alexander Torshin and the President of the World Russian Forum Edward Lozansky, the possibility of holding a joint Russian-American event in the framework of celebrating the 65th anniversary of the Victory in the Great Patriotic War and World War II was discussed. In particular, E. Lozansky said that for 28 years in the United States in honor of Victory Day a 'meeting on the Elbe' for the veterans participating in this historic event has been held. He proposed in the anniversary 2010 to hold a similar meeting in Washington, on April 25, with the participation of Russian officials…. In turn, Alexander Torshin supported this idea and promised to discuss the possibility of participation of the Russian side in this project.

399 https://tass.ru/obschestvo/1970053

400 At the same time, Fedyashin could not find anything positive to say about the Russian opposition and Alexey Navalny during the challenging times when Navalny was running for Moscow City Mayor in September 2013 against the Kremlin candidate Sergey Sobyanin: Anton Fedyashin is a professor of Russian history at American University in Washington, DC, but he's a native Muscovite who spent the summer in Moscow watching the campaign develop. He says the campaign has been a learning experience for both sides, teaching Navalny's supporters that it's one thing to protest the existing system. 'But it's another thing to actually appeal to mass audiences, to do the pavement pounding, which the liberals have never had to do.' And in fact, Navalny lost that election to Sergei Sobyanin, apparently because he spent little time in contact with 'mass audiences' of voters. https://www.npr.org/2013/09/05/219177444/campaign-for-moscow-mayor-could-change-the-citys-politics

401 https://larussophobe.wordpress.com/2009/02/20/reada-long-with-professor-anton-fedyashin-russophile-liar/

402 https://www.heraldonline.com/latest-news/article11548283.html

403 http://www.russia-direct.org/opinion/espionage-fiction-cold-war-and-ukraine

404 https://www.washingtonian.com/2014/06/17/decoding-the-cold-war/

405 http://eurasian-strategies.com/media/insights/theresa-mays-james-bond-moment-from-salisbury-to-syria

406 https://www.washingtonian.com/2014/06/17/decoding-the-cold-war/

407 https://www.phikappaphi.org/docs/default-source/phi-kappa-phi-forum-documents/online-extras-spring-2019/cracking-open-the-cold-war-spy-novel.pdf?sfvrsn=7a99f4e0_2

408 http://www.washdiplomat.com/index.php?option=com_content&view=article&id=9517:moscow-piques-student-interest-as-geopolitical-relevance-rises&catid=1506:august-2013&Itemid=535

409 http://www.washdiplomat.com/index.php?option=com_content&view=article&id=9517:moscow-piques-student-interest-as-geopolitical-relevance-rises&catid=1506:august-2013&Itemid=535

410 Anton Fedyashin, April 7, 2017, https://www.american.edu/cas/carmel/news/gettysburg-dialog.cfm.

411 https://nationalinterest.org/feature/the-bear-the-elephant-13098?page=0%2C1

412 During his four years at the Institute, Comrade Simes D.K. established himself as an employee who expresses initiative, follows directions and thinks creatively, and who is deeply interested in the problems of political struggle of the working class in the developed capitalist countries. He carried out all of the curriculum, as well as specific, assignments, in a timely manner, at a high scientifically-theoretical level. In recognition of his flawless performance, Comrade Simes D.K. received a bonus on three occasions. His article titled 'Working Class in the Political Life of United States' received second prize at the competition of works authored by non-degreed junior research fellows. In addition, Comrade Simes D.K. published eight scientific articles addressing anti-monopolistic struggles in the United States, totaling about 80 pages. Comrade Simes's articles, which discuss socio-political problems in the United States, are published regularly in such periodicals as Komsomolskaya Pravda, Literaturnaya Gazeta, and others. Comrade Simes D.K. combines his workplace productivity with extensive public service in that he serves as a deputy secretary of the Komsomol Organization of the Institute, a Chair of the bureau of international department of Moscow City Committee of the Komsomol. He lectures frequently at the request of the Moscow City Committee of the Communist Party of the Soviet Union.

413 http://www.pseudology.org/information/SimesDK.htm

414 https://nationalinterest.org/print/feature/dealing-putin-11694

415 https://regnum.ru/news/2219164.html

416 https://hillreporter.com/former-nra-president-linked-to-infamous-Mayflower-hotel-meeting-4168

417 https://web.archive.org/web/20090211084937/http://www.nationalinterest.org/BlogSE.aspx?id=13150.

418 http://old.memo.ru/hr/hotpoints/caucas1/msg/2006/12/m83806.htm

419 https://nationalinterest.org/commentary/the-litvinenko-matter-kremlin-conspiracy-or-blofeld-set-up-1322.

420 https://www.bbc.com/russian/news-44916396

421 https://www.politico.com/story/2011/04/divorce-for-nixon-center-foundation-053384

422 https://freebeacon.com/politics/rand-pauls-russian-connection/

423 On March 13, 2018, the Democrat Minority leader on the House Permanent Select Committee on Intelligence, investigating Russia's interference in the 2016 US Presidential Election, made the following request regarding Simes: 'Mr Simes serves as President and CEO of the Center for the National Interest, which hosted President Trump's April 27, 2016 foreign policy speech at the Mayflower Hotel. The Committee is investigating matters related to the speech and communications that may have occurred at the event, and the Committee has reason to believe that Mr. Simes played a central role in drafting portions of the speech related to Russia. The Committee should also obtain relevant personal correspondence between Mr Simes and Trump campaign officials and any individuals with direct or assumed links to the Russian government.' https://democrats-intelligence.house.gov/uploadedfiles/final_-_minority_status_of_the_russia_investigation_with_appendices.pdf

424 https://www.dailykos.com/stories/2018/7/31/1784866/-Why-is-a-Think-Tank-with-Ties-to-Russia-treated-as-a-pro-US-non-partisan-entity

425 http://www.newsweek.com/kushner-constructs-careful-defense-his-annotated-testimony-642344; https://www.politico.com/story/2017/07/24/full-text-jared-kushner-prepared-statement-to-the-senate-240871

426 https://www.bloomberg.com/news/articles/2018-08-13/kushner-s-ties-to-russia-linked-group-began-with-kissinger-lunch

427 https://www.cnn.com/videos/tv/2019/04/24/amanpour-simes-mueller-interview.cnn?fbclid=IwAR37dfxzOBwDCrKlX0EfRLj70VYFnwLK2POQnIqtuvXC4hTfWfm7Ujxc3qk

428 https://www.nytimes.com/2017/03/02/world/europe/sergey-kislyak-russian-ambassador.html

429 http://www.cnn.com/TRANSCRIPTS/1904/24/ampr.01.html

430 https://nationalinterest.org/feature/the-bear-the-elephant-13098?page=0%2C1

431 https://www.washingtonpost.com/opinions/former-cia-chief-trump-is-russias-useful-fool/2016/11/03/cda42ffe-a1d5-11e6-8d63-3e0a660f1f04_story.html?utm_term=.b06744e63180

432 https://tsargrad.tv/news/dmitrij-sajms-agitatory-poluchajut-po-300-za-kazhdyj-golos-v-polzu-klinton_33706

433 https://news.rambler.ru/politics/35215632-sayms-rasskazal-o-maloizvestnom-vizite-klinton-v-moskvu/

434 https://www.youtube.com/watch?v=HCH6S4NdHFE&t=6s

435 https://nationalinterest.org/feature/stop-poking-the-bear-18838

436 https://nationalinterest.org/feature/stop-poking-the-russian-bear-21956

437 Analyzing an article by 'useful fool' Robert Merry, Kunadze wrote on his Facebook page: 'In my opinion, all these simplistic conclusions of Robert Merry are highly biased and cannot withstand any serious criticism. Popular Russian TV rhetoric of impending war looks like a bluff by the slightly insane. It is unclear why Robert Merry would want to repeat this rhetoric. In any event, the respective gigantic nuclear arsenal of both Russia and U.S. makes any serious warfare between them practically impossible. Even a localized military conflict that has a potential to expand is not quite realistic. Russia cannot handle both balancing on the edge of the war and an accompanying arms race. This is what strained USSR, which far exceeded Russia in terms of its military and economic potential, while boasting a defective but holistic ideology, a multitude of obedient satellites at its disposal, and, importantly, which depended on the rest of the world to a much lesser degree. Georgia really did not initiate a war with Russia. It just somewhat recklessly tried to carry out a limited military operation aimed at restoring the constitutional order on its own territory. Due to a mysterious chain of events, Russia turned out to be quite ready for the Georgian operation and responded with an extensive intervention. As for an idiotic thesis regarding the revolution in Ukraine that was 'organized' by the West—it does not even merit any commentary since all of the relevant events are very recent and seem to make sense to everyone except Robert Merry. As for estimating the distance between Russia and the closest NATO countries, it does not prove anything except for author's paranoia of an unknown origin. In the first version of the article, its author counted Moldavia as part of Russia's sphere of influence, whereas in the second version, he substituted it for Serbia. He must have conflated the two. In general, the 'sphere of influence' concept itself is an archaic one and cannot be taken seriously. In addition, it is unclear why liberating the former countries with 'people's democracy' regimes from the Soviet rule is necessary and useful, while liberating of post-Soviet countries from the Russian rule is not….The fact of near-total antipathy towards Putin in the West is real. But how else can it be if all of Russia's policy is officially associated with his name. This policy is completely unacceptable for the West, hence the negative attitude towards the person who initiates it. As for author's ruminations about Russians as the nation that is besieged by the Americans and their allies, it brings to memory Henry Kissinger's expression: 'There is nothing more offensive than Russia on the defensive.' President Trump, due to his certain, to put it mildly, character traits, manages to discredit everything that he touches. That includes his 'Russian initiatives' that are described by Robert Merry with such admiration. As a whole, his article is noteworthy if only for the surprising unity in the views of the independent American author and of the numerous advocates of the official Russian propaganda. One cannot help but recall the term 'useful fool'—but who knows, maybe Robert Merry is sincere in his thinking…. I used the term 'useful fool' only because I do not have any evidence of Robert Merry being paid by the Russians to act in their interest. Nevertheless, I am inclined to consider him a pure mercenary and an ordinary participant in the so-called 'active operations.' The former deputy Minister of Foreign Affairs of Russia must have omitted the words 'of the Russian State Security' when referring to the 'active operations' due to the diplomatic concerns.

Milton Keynes UK
Ingram Content Group UK Ltd.
UKHW042050291123
433486UK00001B/1